PARENTS AS PART
IN EDUCATIO

The School and Home Working Together

THIRD EDITION

Eugenia Hepworth Berger
Metropolitan State College

Merrill, an imprint of
Macmillan Publishing Company
New York

Collier Macmillan Canada, Inc.
Toronto

Maxwell Macmillan International Publishing Group
New York   Oxford   Singapore   Sydney

Cover Photo: Myrleen Ferguson
Editor: Linda A. Sullivan
Production Editor: Gloria Schneider Jasperse
Art Coordinator: Vincent A. Smith
Text Designer: Debra A. Fargo
Cover Designer: Russ Maselli

This book was set in Garamond.

Macmillan Publishing Company
866 Third Avenue, New York, NY 10022

Collier Macmillan Canada, Inc.

Library of Congress Catalog Card Number: 90–62581

Photo Credits: All photos copyrighted by individuals or companies listed. Peggy Lore, Catherine Smith, Paul Freeburn, Debra Berger McClave, Elena Machina Berger, John Berger, or Eugenia Hepworth Berger, pp. 2, 4, 7, 9, 13, 14, 17, 18, 21, 23, 50, 53, 56, 58, 59, 65, 66, 67, 69, 70, 73, 86, 87, 89, 92, 93, 94, 101, 102, 105, 107, 109, 117, 120, 136, 139, 140, 153, 157, 158, 160, 168, 174, 179, 185, 186, 189, 201, 211, 237, 248, 256, 259, 269, 274, 279, 285, 289, 301, 387, 393, 395, 397, 398, 411; The National Gallery of Art, pp. 34, 35, 37, 38, 40, 42, 43, 44, 45, 46, 47, 49; The Metropolitan Museum of Art, (all rights reserved) pp. 32, 34, 48, 51, 55, 57.

Printing: 1 2 3 4 5 6 7 8 9
Year: 1 2 3 4

To my extended family
my parents, Gladys and Richard Hepworth
and
Anna and Henry Berger
my sisters, Cora, Marian, and Jo
my aunt, Cora
my cousins, Ethelynn and Marion
my children, Dick, Debra, and John
and my husband, Glen

It was through my participation
in an extended family
that I became aware of the importance
of support, nurturance, and love.

PREFACE

Since publication of the second edition of *Parents as Partners in Education,* there has been a continuing emphasis on the importance of families' and parents' involvement in children's education. Although financial support from federal and most state governments has been reduced, political leaders recognize the importance of families' commitment to and interest in their children. Research analyzing schools and home emphasizes the need for increased parent involvement. Federal reports continue to stress that parental involvement in a child's education makes a great difference in that child's success.

Research emphasizes the necessity of collaboration between school and home. However, the placement of responsibility for this collaboration is still in question. Should the parents be singled out as uninterested or should the schools be criticized for not using innovative or old fashioned methods to encourage parents to participate? Both sides must share the responsibility for parent involvement. This book, however, is designed to reach professionals working in the field of education. Therefore, its emphasis is on the role of the school.

During the last decade many schools have included parents in policy decisions. The 1990s will provide an opportunity for schools and homes to strengthen this partnership. Longitudinal studies demonstrate that early education has been successful in supporting families with education and resources.

The link between education and financial security for parents became more apparent as inflation and limited employment opportunities for the undereducated resulted in greater differences between the middle or upper-middle class and the poor. Although a partnership between parents and schools is no panacea for the ills of society, it is a critical part of the solution to providing for all our nations' population. Schools and parents must work together to help children become productive and mentally healthy adults.

As a parent educator and sociologist, I observed the increase in programs for children and families during the 1960s and 1970s. I supported programs such as Head Start, Follow Through, and Home Start, as they recognized the need for parent involvement and initiated parent advisory councils. I watched the changes in political climate during the late 1970s and 1980s with great interest, but I was unable to predict the outcome of the policies that were put into effect. I wondered if the reduction of federal support for programs that helped poor families would mean the end of worthwhile and meaningful endeavors. Instead, the research from those earlier programs and the continued work by many compassionate and dedicated individuals have resulted in a renewed commitment to early childhood education, parent education, family life, and teenage education. Whether the recognized need will be given financial support is yet to be seen. The knowledge base, which is still growing, needs to be disseminated among the various disciplines working with and for families and children. Next, it must be shared with the families and children along with the support necessary to allow them to become enablers.

Parents, viewed as the primary caregivers and teachers of children, are partners with professionals whether or not they are accepted as such. Their interaction with their children makes them a part of the system. The school and home are intertwined. It rests, therefore, on the shoulders of the schools to develop or to strengthen a positive relationship with parents in order to ensure the continuity and developmental environment that children so desperately need. This book was written with the hope that it might help bring about a collaboration between home and school.

Many persons are involved in producing a book. I thank all those who willingly allowed me to use their works. They were cooperative and gracious, and their encouragement helped me to continue. Professional friends, John Porreca, Judy Popp, Cynthia Franklin, and my colleagues at Metropolitan State College counseled and shared with me. I am indebted to my MSC students who have been wonderful in their suggestions, discussions, and responses to my class presentations.

The Metropolitan Museum of Art and The National Gallery of Art allowed me to use prints from their collection. Peggy Lore, Catherine Smith, and Paul Freeburn allowed me to use family photographs. Other photographs were taken by Debra Berger McClave, Elena Machina Berger, John Berger, or me. Even the best photographer could not get such winning smiles without charming subjects. Most of the children photographed attended the Metropolitan State College Child Developement Center or the Auraria Child Care Center. I appreciate the cooperation and help of the staff at both centers as well as the care Walter Hazelbaker took in processing the prints. My friend, Martha Piper Aune, a fellow educator, gave me invaluable support through suggestions, criticisms, and editing for the first edition.

My family was an essential ingredient in the entire project, each time around: first, my three children, Dick, Debra, and John, who were responsible for my entrance into the field of parent education; second, my husband, Glen, whose confidence in my ability to write and revise this book supported me throughout the endeavor; and last, my parents, who were my first educators, and who set an unexcelled example of supportive child rearing.

Finally, I want to thank the following individuals for their comments and suggestions during the development of this text: Nancy Benz, South Plains College; Gary E. Cook, University of Toledo; Jeffrey Schilit, Florida Atlantic University; Richard F. Purnell, The University of Rhode Island; and Randall R. Wallace, Central Washington University.

Eugenia Hepworth Berger

CONTENTS

1

Parent Involvement—
Essential for a Child's Development

If we want to educate a person in virtue we must polish him at a tender age. And if someone is to advance toward wisdom he must be opened up for it in the first years of his life when his industriousness is burning, his mind is malleable, and his memory is strong. (Comenius, *The Great Didactic*)

P arents are children's first nurturers, socializers, and educators. It is almost impossible to overemphasize the significance of parenthood. Society would not survive if a culture stops either procreating or rearing its young. Infants cannot survive without being nurtured by someone who feeds them and gives them care. The manner in which infants are nurtured varies within each subculture as well as across cultures. The well-being of the child is affected by both quality of care and the resiliency of the child. One child may thrive, while another may deteriorate, in environments that seem identical. The child, the caregiver, and the environment intertwine in the childrearing process, making every child's experiences unique. The essential bond between child and caregiver emphasizes the significance of the parents' role. Although other roles such as breadwinner, food-gatherer, or food-producer are necessary, they can be fulfilled in a variety of ways, depending upon the culture. In childrearing, however, certain obliga-

tions and responsibilities transcend all groups of people. Every child must be fed, touched, and involved in communication, either verbal or nonverbal, to continue to grow and develop. Childrearing, whether by natural parents or alternative caregivers, requires a nurturing environment. Perhaps the ease with which most men and women become parents diminishes the realization that parenthood is an essential responsibility. It has been assumed that parenthood is a natural condition and that becoming a parent or caregiver transforms the new mother or father into a nurturing parent. As a result, society has not demanded that parents have the prerequisite knowledge that would ensure competence in one of the most important occupations—childrearing. Some basic understanding of child development on which to base parenting skills, allowing for individualization and cultural diversity, should be expected.

The ability to nurture does not automatically blossom when one gives birth to a child. It involves many diverse variables, ranging from parent-child attachment, previous modeling experiences, and environmental conditions that allow and encourage a positive parent-child relationship. The parent also needs a support system of family, friends, and/or professionals.

Many new parents have not had the good fortune to learn from a role model or they may

Parents nurture their children's growth and development.

be faced with a difficult situation that makes the rearing of children an overpowering burden rather than a joy. The parents of the 12.5 million poor children in the United States have a very difficult time providing a productive environment. Those in poverty cross ethnic lines: 47% are white, 34% are black, 16% are Hispanic, and 3% are distributed among other groups (U.S. Department of Education, 1987, p. 4). Minority children have the highest risk of living in poverty; four out of ten black and Hispanic children are part of poor families (p. 5). These parents need economic stability and a support system. With the birth of a child, the need for a strong family system, a supportive environment, and parenting skills is even greater.

CONTINUITY AND DISCONTINUITY

Throughout childhood, many caregivers—teachers, child care workers, doctors, administrators—are involved with the child and family. Ideally, they can provide a stable environment where each of the society's institutions contributes to the child's growth in an integrated and continuous

approach. (*Continuity* is defined as a coherent whole or an uninterrupted succession of development. *Discontinuity* means a lack of continuity or logical sequence. It refers to changes or disruptions in the child's development.)

From a population that finds strength in its diversity, it is impossible to produce a curriculum that assures perfect continuity for all, but it is possible to work toward support systems that foster the child's continuous development. To provide continuity today, the professional must look beyond the individual to the social system in which the child lives.

Change is pervasive in parents' lives. High mobility, a decrease in extended families, an increase in poverty, and the devastating impact of drugs are some concerns of today's parents. Parents, schools, child care programs, recreation centers, and public agencies must work together to ensure continuity of provisions, discipline, and nurturing.

Parents can more easily adapt to new conditions, and children can handle change better if they can depend on a stable environment. Families, child care programs, and schools are the first line of defense in the provision of stability for children. Those who work with children need to know what kinds of provisions, discipline, and nurturing the child is receiving from each of the other providers—family, schools, recreation facilities, churches, care-providers, and public agencies. Only then can they attempt to offer the continuity that children need.

Research has revealed that parents who provide active support of their children contribute more to their child's success in school than those who provide passive support. The least effective parents—in terms of the child's ability to succeed—are those who are nonsupportive. Parents must actively help their children as well as encourage them to achieve (Watson, Brown, & Swick, 1983). Parent behaviors that support the child's cognitive development include active teaching of specific skills, provision of a variety of activities and experiences, opportunities for the child to explore and try out skills, conversations and play with the child, response to verbal and nonverbal signals, nurturance, avoidance of interference with learning (Rutter, 1985), high expectations for achievement, knowledge about the child's development, and authoritative rather than authoritarian control (Hess & Holloway, 1984). If the parents and other child care givers provide a supportive environment to the children, their entry into formal schooling will be more continuous and more successful.

A study of parent involvement in four federal programs—Follow Through, Title I, Title VII Bilingual, and the Emergency School Aid Act—found that parent involvement helps and allows for more continuity.

- Children whose parents help them at home do better in school. Those whose parents participate in school activities are better behaved and more diligent in their efforts to learn.
- Teachers and principals who know parents by virtue of their participation in school activities treat those parents with greater respect. They also show more positive attitudes toward the children of involved parents.
- Administrators find out about parents' concerns and are thus in a position to respond to their needs.
- Parental involvement allows parents to influence and make a contribution to what may be one of their most time-consuming and absorbing tasks—the education of their children (Lyons, Robbins, & Smith, 1983, p. xix).

Two concerns need to be addressed. The first is the school's responsibility to have a school environment that enables the child to succeed—with enough continuity that the children do not feel that they are entering foreign territory. This concern is important for young children and young adults alike. The second concern is the pushing of first grade curriculum into the kindergarten and early childhood program. These two issues are interrelated. If schools provide a positive environment with a developmentally appropriate curriculum, they will enable the child to succeed. An environment that is patterned after an ideal home environment will have the elements that are needed for

a child to learn (Silvern, 1988). If the curriculum is not developmentally appropriate, the environment changes into a hostile arena where the children cannot accomplish their tasks. As a result of the concern that inappropriate curriculum is being pushed down to kindergarten and early childhood programs, several professional organizations have endorsed positions on what is appropriate (see Bredekamp, 1987). This concern must be addressed to ensure continuity for young children.

Is all continuity beneficial? Silvern (1988) points out that continuity in and of itself is not always positive. If a child comes from an ideal home environment, the educational climate at the school would benefit from incorporating the positive aspects mentioned earlier. If the child comes from a culturally diverse home, the child will feel more comfortable if the school acknowledges the cultural diversity and enriches the curriculum by incorporating aspects of the culture into the school setting. This will help the child make the transition from home into the school. However, discontinuity is clearly appropriate if a child comes from a sterile or abusive home. Rather than continue an oppressive situation, the school must provide school lunches and/or breakfasts and a nurturing environment.

Silvern points out that in early childhood settings, time, space, and language can be home-like in their approach, allowing children, within guidelines, to feel secure. The home provides space that is "characterized by dimensions of warmth, closeness, sharing, security, and support" (1988, p. 150). School space is often individual and insecure. The home is flexible in time, but school schedules are usually rigidly constrained. Language at school is formalized, whereas the home encourages a shared understanding of language meanings. Therefore, early childhood programs and schools can furnish "continuities that allow children to make sense of the world and discontinuities that afford children important experiences that they do not obtain at home" (Silvern, 1988, p. 149).

Socioeconomic status is not the primary causal factor in school success or lack of it; it is

Greater continuity is possible when schools continue the home's warmth and caring.

parental interest and support of the child. Watson, Brown, and Swick examined environmental influences of neighborhood support, home support, income, and educational level of the home in an attempt to determine their individual and collective effects on children as they entered school. They found a significant relationship between the support that a parent is given by the environment and the support that the parent gives the child. Couple this relationship with one that shows that the support given to the child at home makes a difference to the child's achievement in first grade. "Regardless of the income and/or educational level of the home, the [supported and supportive] home was effective in helping the child achieve" (Watson, Brown, & Swick, 1983, p. 178).

Formal institutions such as schools and child care socialize children with "inputs . . . loosely characterized as opportunities, demands, and rewards." Inputs from the child's more personal home environment include "attitudes, effort, and conception of self. . . . The environment that

most affects them is, for nearly all children, the social environment of the household" (Coleman, 1987, p. 35).

Continuity is much easier to define than it is to accomplish. Various behaviors and characteristics can be observed among children in groups. They may be happy, resilient, and alert or depressed and lethargic; tall or short; self-actualized or dependent on direction; secure and outgoing, or reticent and shy. Children encounter a wide variety of teachers—creative or structured; open or closed; authoritarian, laissez-faire, or authoritative; self-actualized or discouraged—and each of these may vary day by day. Families are just as varied—disorganized or stable, extended or nuclear, enriching or restrictive, verbal or nonverbal, nurturing or punishing—with many of the characteristics changing with conditions. All of these variables shape children's development. The aim for families and schools is not to attain perfection but to adapt to each other in a close, productive working unit. This is an enormous challenge to families, schools, and communities and is an issue that will need continued investigation.

EVIDENCE IN SUPPORT OF HOME-SCHOOL COLLABORATION

The urgent public outcry to improve students' academic success and reduce the drop-out rate brought forth a strong response from many professional and governmental organizations. The link between home and school and parent involvement is recognized as very important (Anastasiow, 1988; Anderson, Hiebert, Scott, & Wilkinson, 1985; Bloom, 1986; California Task Force on School Readiness, 1988; Clark, 1983; Coleman, 1987; Comer, 1988; Epstein, 1986; Gotts, 1989; Henderson, 1987; Herman & Yen, 1980; Hess & Holloway, 1984; Kagan & Zigler, 1987; Levenstein, 1988; Lipsky & Gartner, 1989; Macchiarola, 1989; National Association of State Boards of Education [NASBE], 1988; National Commission on Excellence in Education, 1983; Rutter, 1985; Silvern, 1988; Umansky, 1983; U.S.

Department of Education, 1986; Walberg, 1984; Wasik, 1983; Watson, Brown, & Swick, 1983).

Numerous studies have reached the same conclusion: "Most schools can greatly improve school learning in their students if they can involve the parents in support of their children's school learning" (Bloom, 1986, p. 6). The National Commission on Excellence in Education, in their report *A Nation at Risk: The Imperative for Educational Reform,* told parents:

... you bear a responsibility to participate actively in your child's education. You should encourage more diligent study and discourage satisfaction with mediocrity and the attitude that says "let it slide"; monitor your child's study habits; encourage your child to take more demanding rather than less demanding courses; nurture your child's curiosity, creativity, and confidence; and be an active participant in the work of the schools (1983, p. 35).

The New Parents as Teachers program (Meyerhoff & White, 1986) has shown great success. Reaching parents even before the birth of a child can ease the transition to parenthood and offer the support that new parents need. Often the knowledge, support, and techniques provided can divert an otherwise difficult childhood into a positive one.

New Parents as Teachers was developed in Missouri. Begun as a research-service project in 1982, it served families whose mother was in the third trimester of pregnancy by offering group sessions, private home visits, and a resource center for the parents from before birth until the child was age 3. The average private contact with families was once a month for about an hour. Parents were given booklets that described appropriate expectations for and interaction activities with their infants. At the resource center, located in a school, more learning materials and child care services were available. In addition, comprehensive educational screening services were offered to monitor each child's social, language, and intellectual progress. If any special assistance was required, the parents were referred to specialists.

The program worked! An independent research study showed strong success in intel-

lectual and linguistic development. The children, who represented all social and economic levels as well as varying family styles, scored well above average. It was expanded to all counties in the state and soon 34,000 families were being served (Meyerhoff & White, 1986; U.S. Department of Education, 1987; White, 1985).

HOPE, Home-Oriented Preschool Education, a program that was created in 1966 by the Appalachia Educational Laboratory, completed a detailed five-phase follow-up study in 1989. HOPE was "highly successful in preventing early school failure, with all its ill effects" (Gotts, 1989, p. 10). The research analyzed two groups: children who had received home visits along with television instruction (HOPE) and those who had television instruction only (control).

The results were striking. Of the control children, 22% were retained at least once; HOPE children had about 10% held back. Only 12% of HOPE participants did not graduate from high school (typically, these schools had 28% dropout rates). The dropout rate for the control group was twice as high as for the HOPE group. This home-based program enhanced parent effectiveness and "empowered and trained parents in essential skill areas" (Gotts, 1989, p. 14). Gotts found that the effective parent practices were found in the control group parents as well as the HOPE parents. HOPE parents "just became better! HOPE promoted parent actualization more than it did parent change" (p. 14).

Powell (1989), in an extensive monograph for the National Association for the Education of Young Children, analyzes research on families and early childhood programs, including attended Head Start and other funded programs. Issues examined include continuity, relationships between parents and programs, parent education, and needed research. Powell pointed out many inadequacies in much of the research, and neglected to include either New Parents as Teachers or the HOPE programs. Nevertheless, he concludes that "research findings justify recommendations for strengthening relations between families and early childhood programs that serve ethnic minority children and/or children whose parents have limited education" (p. 51). He notes that "the theoretical grounds are significantly stronger than the empirical foundation of rationales for establishing and maintaining cooperative relations between families and early childhood programs" (p. 51).

Relying on theory and their experience, teachers are calling for more parental involvement. In a survey returned by more than 21,000 elementary and secondary teachers, the Carnegie Foundation for the Advancement of Teaching found that 90% of the teachers felt that they receive little parent support, and that the lack of support contributed to students' poor performances. According to the survey, teachers would like parents to attend parent-teacher conferences, supervise homework, stress the importance of education to their children, read to children often, take their children to cultural facilities and museums, visit the classroom, and volunteer for school activities (Carnegie Foundation for the Advancement of Teaching, 1988).

In The Metropolitan Life Survey of the American Teacher 1987, a randomly selected sample of 1,002 teachers and 2,011 parents were questioned. Both groups recognized the need for involvement of home and school: 75% of the teachers wanted parents involved inside the school and 74% of the parents wanted to be more involved.

Parents who had the most contact with the schools were those with elementary school children, with some college background, and in upper-income brackets. Core city parents, single parents who worked outside the home, and parents of secondary students wanted to have more active consultation in the schools. Teachers in central-city schools also wanted more involvement by parents. Although groups acknowledged the need for more collaboration, these parents felt they did not receive enough attention from the school.

As children progressed from elementary schools through upper grades, contact with school diminished. With this decrease there was an increase in dissatisfaction about the amount of contact with the schools. Six out of 10 parents desired a newsletter to keep them informed about school and a hotline to help their children with homework. Low-income and minority parents were especially in favor of these contacts. Yet less than half of the teachers saw this as helpful. These surveys illustrate that a large majority of parents want more involvement and that teachers recognize the value and necessity of parent involvement. The challenge ahead is the ability to implement the desired changes.

One school system that reached out to parents succeeded in such a turnaround of parent participation that the program has now extended to more than 50 schools. Comer (1988) and the Yale University Child Study Center started working with two schools in the New Haven, Connecticut school system in 1968. Initially, Comer found a misalignment between home and school. This was overcome by involving parents in the restructuring of the school. Parents were involved on three levels: (1) as aides in the classroom, (2) as members of governance and management teams, and (3) as general participants in school activities. Parents' distrust of the school needed to be overcome, and this could only happen when they were involved in meaningful cooperation with each other.

Students were viewed as having unmet needs rather than as being behavior problems or bad children. The children were served by a mental health team that attempted to understand children's anxiety and conduct. A Discovery Room encouraged children to regain an interest in learning and a Crisis Room provided positive alternatives to children who had behavior problems. The greatest turnaround in intellectual development occurred when social skills were incorporated into the program. Parents were able to join in as partners and the school became a force for increased self-esteem and desire for learning.

Becoming a Nation of Readers: What Parents Can Do emphasized the importance of parents in the reading process. "Learning to read begins at home. Just as your children naturally learned to talk by following your example they may naturally learn a great deal about reading before they ever

Reading begins early. Children benefit when families read and encourage their children to enjoy books.

set foot inside a school building" (Binkley, 1988, p. 1). This booklet, developed for parents by the Commission on Reading, states "a parent is a child's first tutor in unraveling the fascinating puzzle of written language" (p. 1). Parents of preschool children are urged to read to them, discuss stories and experiences, and "with a light touch" help them learn letters and words. For school-aged children, parents should support homework, obtain children's books, be involved in school programs, support reading, and limit TV (Anderson et al., 1985, p. 117).

One of the groups that advocates most strongly for education of their children are the parents of exceptional students. Strong parent involvement enabled passage of Public Law 94–142 (The Handicapped Children Act of 1975). Since that time, parents have continued to be involved with the education of their exceptional children. Public Law 99–457 includes education for very young children, and provisions for an Individualized Family Service Plan (IFSP), similar to the Individualized Education Program (IEP) of Public Law 94–142.

Evidence that public and private schools can successfully adapt to the needs of school-aged children and families is reported by the U.S. Department of Education (1986, 1987). Schools that successfully educated children from low-income homes used many approaches. The schools in New Haven, Connecticut, described earlier in this chapter, enlisted parents, helped students and parents bond with the school, and instilled pride in their accomplishments.

In George Washington Preparatory High School in Los Angeles, parents and students signed contracts. Students agreed to follow school rules, dress according to code, and finish school assignments. Parents agreed to attend workshops where they learned how to support their child's work in school. In addition, there was a parent advisory group and parents monitored school attendance (U.S. Department of Education, 1987).

There is a growing recognition across the nation that schools must respond to student needs and, though they must respond with or without parent involvement, parent collaboration makes for more continuity and improves the opportunity for success.

This book focuses on the roles of parents and schools in the continuing development of children. Research indicates that the home has an enormous impact on the developing child and that a partnership between home and schools is supportive of the developing child. Although all of the evidence is not yet gathered, the concept is supported by enough data to encourage educators to include parents as partners in the educational process. This dictates that parents be active participants—real partners—in the process. It also requires that teachers know what children do at home and which special interests and talents they have. It requires that they teach with a knowledge of what went before and what is to follow, but without the limitations of discrete levels and curriculum restrictions. It focuses on a common effort by the school, home, and community to provide for the student's growth through integrated successive learning experiences that allow for variation in

skills, cognitive development, creative abilities, and physical development.

PARENT PROGRAMS

From infancy to young adulthood, varying needs require different types of programs. Brief descriptions of programs related to age levels are discussed to provide the reader with an overview of current parent involvement. Following these descriptions are the rationale for parent involvement and the research that supports it.

Infancy

If continuity is to be achieved, the teamwork of parents, schools, and the community begins before the child is born. Prenatal and postnatal care of the mother and subsequent early stimulation and initial bonding of the infant require the cooperative effort of medical care systems and families. The need for parent education during the child's infancy may be critical if the new family does not have an extended family that is knowledgeable about child development and child care. Even with a support system within the extended family, new knowledge in the field of infant development enables adults to enrich traditional childrearing practices. Infant program information in this book includes the following:

1. Parent education (infant-toddler programs, Chapter 7; reaching the parent of the young child, Chapter 8; and New Parents as Teachers project, Chapters 1 and 8)
2. Home visits (Chapter 8)
3. Comprehensive health education (Chapter 7)

Preschool

A second period calling for effective parent education and involvement is when the child is toddler through preschool age. During these years, parent education and preschool programs meet the educational needs of and lend emotional and social support to the family of a young child. Center-based programs often include

Parents of infants need programs that help them recognize the stages of development and emphasize the importance of human contact and relationships.

home visits. Typical preschool programs for parents include:

1. Parent education and preschool experiences for children (see Chapters 6 and 7 for information on parent education and preschool programs)
2. Head Start (Chapter 7)
3. Home visitations (Chapter 8)

Primary and Intermediate Grades

While the child is in elementary school, a wide variety of activities is available. Parents are involved as tutors, teaching assistants, policymakers, and partners with the school. The following programs represent opportunities for parent involvement:

1. School participation (Chapters 4 and 7)
2. Policy board (Chapters 8 and 11)
3. Partnership in educational planning (see Chapter 4 for closer school-home partnership; Chapter 9 gives details for developing an IEP)
4. PTA/PTO (Chapter 4)

Secondary Schools

Historically parents have participated less in school activities during their child's junior-senior high years than they did during the elementary school years. In this period of tre-

mendous social change, however, child development specialists and parents recognize that parent involvement may be more necessary than previously believed. Increasing numbers of teenage pregnancies mandate more child and family education. Peer pressure and easy availability encourage students to use drugs and alcohol. Many students have difficulty obtaining satisfying jobs. These pressures and problems are rooted in discontinuity in development. Lack of self-direction in and opportunity for the meaningful use of spare time set adolescents adrift. A unified effort by school, home, and community could develop appropriate programs both during and after school for young adults. Needed programs include:

1. Support groups (Chapter 4)
2. Curriculum in school (Chapter 7)
3. Education and support for young parents (Chapter 7)

Exceptional Children

Discussions of exceptional children, communication, and program ideas are included in the following:

1. School response (Chapter 4)
2. Communication (Chapter 5)
3. Working with parents of exceptional children (Chapter 9)

A full circle of support services has been developed, beginning with the expectant family and continuing to the time when that infant becomes a new parent. Special programs have emerged in many areas of the country that speak to the infant, preschool, elementary, and secondary levels. These programs will be discussed in detail in later chapters.

THEORIES CONCERNING INTELLECTUAL DEVELOPMENT

One of the first theorists to raise questions concerning the development of intelligence in children was J. McVicker Hunt. In his book *Intelligence and Experience* (1961), he challenges the assumptions of fixed intelligence and predetermined development. The belief in fixed intelligence had far-reaching implications for education and childrearing. If IQ were fixed, intellectual growth could not be affected. The role of parents, therefore, had been to allow intellectual growth to unfold naturally toward its predetermined capacity. Hunt (1961) cites that, during the decades between 1915 and 1935, parents were even warned against playing with their infant, lest overstimulation interfere with the child's growth. Hunt's belief that IQ is not fixed led to a change in perception of the parental role from one of passive observation to one of facilitation.

Hunt's book focuses on the outcome the title implies—the effect of experience on the development of intelligence. In it he thoroughly reviews studies and research concerning the development of intelligence in children. He devotes a large portion of his book to the works of Jean Piaget, a genetic epistemologist who wrote a prodigious number of books and articles on knowledge and cognitive development. Piaget emphasizes that development involves the interaction of the child with the environment. Piaget's book *To Understand Is to Invent* (1976) succinctly illustrates his basic concept of the importance of activity on the part of the learner—the need to act or operate upon the environment in the process of developing knowledge. It is through this process of interaction with the environment that the child develops intelligence. Piaget sees this as an adaptive process that includes *assimilation* of experiences and data into the child's understanding of the world; *accommodation,* by which the child's thought processes are adjusted to fit the new information into the schemes or models already constructed; and finally *equilibrium* that results from the adaptive process. This model of acquiring new knowledge was important to the cognitive theorists and had an impact on the educator's curriculum development because it emphasized the importance of experience to the developing child. A child without a rich environment was at a disadvantage.

Another aspect of Piagetian theory that reinforces his description of the developmental process of learning is his analysis of the developmental stages of the child's thought. Children, in the process of acquiring intellect, form concepts differently than adults. They relate to experience at their own levels of understanding. Hunt (1961) described these three major stages—sensorimotor, preconceptual, and formal—in this way:*

The first period of intellectual development, the sensorimotor, lasts from birth till the child is roughly between 18 months and 2 years old. The reflexive sensorimotor schemata are generalized, coordinated with each other, and differentiated to become the elementary operations of intelligence which begin to be internalized and which correspond to the problem-solving abilities of sub-human animals. During this period, the child creates through his continual adaptive accommodations and assimilations, in six stages, such operations as "intentions," "means-end" differentiations, and the interest in novelty (Piaget, 1936). On the side of constructing reality, the child also develops the beginnings of interiorized schemata, if not actual concepts, for such elements as the permanence of the object, space, casuality, and time (Piaget, 1937).

The second period of concrete operations in intellectual development, beginning when the child

*From Hunt, J. M. *Intelligence and experience.* New York, 1961, pp. 113–115. Copyright © 1961, John Wiley & Sons, Inc. Reprinted by permission of John Wiley & Sons, Inc.

is about 18 months or 2 years old, lasts till he is 11 or 12 years old. It contains, first, a preconceptual phase during which symbols are constructed. This lasts to about 4 years of age, and during it the child's activity is dominated by symbolic play, which imitates and represents what he has seen others do, and by the learning of language. The accommodations forced by the variation in the models imitated along with the assimilations resulting from repetitions of the play-activities gradually create a store of central processes which symbolize the actions imitated (Piaget, 1945). As the images are established, the child acquires verbal signs for those which correspond to the collective system of signs comprising language. At this point the child comes under dual interaction with the environment, i.e., with the world of things and the world of people. The child's action-images greatly extend the scope of his mental operation beyond the range of immediate action and momentary perception, and they also speed up his mental activity, for the sensorimotor action is limited by the concrete sequence of perceptions and actions. This period contains, second, an intuitive phase. This is a phase of transition that lasts till the child is 7 or 8 year old. In the course of his manipulations and social communications, he is extending, differentiating, and combining his action-images and simultaneously correcting his intuitive impressions of reality (space, causality, and time). It contains, third, the phase of concrete operations. As the child interacts repeatedly with things and people, his central processes become more and more autonomous. Piaget (1945, 1947) speaks of his thought becoming "decentred" from perception and action. With greater autonomy of central processes come both differentiations and coordinations, or groups, of the action-images into systems which permit classifying, ordering in series, numbering. . . . The acquisition of these "concrete operations," . . . bring a distinctive change in the child's concrete conceptions of quantity, space, causality, and time.

The third period of formal operations starts at about 11 and 12 years when the child begins to group or systematize his concrete operations (classifications, serial ordering, correspondences, etc.) and thereby also to consider all possible combinations in each case.

Piaget's theories clearly indicate that intellectual development is a *process* that commences in infancy and continues throughout childhood.

The early years are important even though the development of intelligence in the young child differs from that of an older child. Hunt's book kindled interest in Piaget and in the importance of experience for young children during a time when their prime caregivers or teachers are the parents. Hunt (1961) stated:

It is no longer unreasonable to consider that it might be feasible to discover ways to govern the encounters that children have with their environments, especially during the early years of their development, to achieve a substantially faster rate of intellectual development and a substantially higher adult level of intellectual capacity. (p. 363)

The time was ripe for consideration of intervention and parent involvement. Equal educational opportunity was a high priority. The nation had been aroused by the USSR's launching of Sputnik in 1957. Many people wondered if children were learning as well as they should. There was concern that the United States was falling behind Russia in scientific discovery. It was hoped that an emphasis on early childhood education would help overcome learning and reading deficiencies. These considerations supported arguments for early intervention in education.

Benjamin Bloom's book *Stability and Change in Human Characteristics* added fuel to the fire and had great impact on establishing the importance of early childhood education. If early childhood is a prime time for children's learning and development, their caregivers have the opportunity to be their primary teachers. Bloom (1964) described the importance of the home:

It would seem to us that the home environment is very significant not only because of the large amount of educational growth which has already taken place before the child enters the first grade, but also because of the influence of the home during the elementary school period. (p. 110)

Bloom investigated many aspects of human development, including general intelligence, general achievement, specific aptitudes, reading comprehension, vocabulary, sociometric status, aggression, and dependence, as well as such physical aspects as height, weight, and strength. His statements about intellectual development in the very young attracted national attention. He and his colleagues analyzed many classic research studies. Based on information from Bayley's correlation data and/or Thorndike's absolute scale, Bloom (1964) made the following astounding observations on general intelligence:

It is possible to say, that in terms of intelligence measured at age 17, at least 20% is developed by age 1, 50% by age 4, 80% by about age 8 and 92% by age 13. Put in terms of intelligence measured by age 17, from conception to age 4, the individual develops 50% of his mature intelligence, from ages 4 to 8 he develops another 30%, and from ages 8 to 17 the remaining 20%. (p. 68)

With this in mind, he questioned the concept of absolute constant IQ and suggested that intelligence was a developmental trait similar to other characteristics such as height or strength. His figures suggest that the early years, particularly between the ages of 1 and 5, are very important in the development of intelligence. Again, he pointed out the impact of environment on the child's development.

In addition to general intelligence, Bloom (1964) also related general achievement or learning to age. Again, the early years are of the utmost importance. Between birth and age 6, 33 percent of the child's achievement at age 18 can be accounted for. Another 17 percent of growth, which takes place between the ages of 6 and 9, results in 50 percent of general achievement accomplished by age 9. Although the achievement pattern is not as extreme as with intelligence, both place the early years as a "crucial" time for children. Bloom suggested that the remaining 9 years of schooling are affected by what the child has gained by the end of third grade. His findings indicated that early extreme deprivation has a greater effect on children than deprivation in later years. During the first 4 years of life, environmental deficiency can stunt the development of intelligence approximately 2.5 IQ points per year. During the years from 8 to 17,

extreme environmental deprivation can depress average IQ growth by only 0.04 points a year.

Bloom did not discount the importance of heredity in the development of intelligence; rather, he and his colleagues focused on change and stability in human characteristics and in so doing, recognized that some of the variations in IQ must be attributed to environment. Because parents have great control over their child's environment in the early years, they are an integral part of the educational system.

Although Bloom recognized the importance of learning in the early years, he did not support the teaching of reading, writing, and simple arithmetic in nursery or kindergarten. Schools build on the foundations that children learn at home. The critical years should go toward important goals such as learning to learn rather than on skills that are developed better at a later time. "That it is good for children to learn to read at ages 6 and 7 does not mean that it is better to learn these skills at a younger age" (Bloom, 1981, p. 69).

Elkind also warned against pressured learning for early childhood. He described the scores of intelligence tests at age 4 as being able to predict with an accuracy of 50% what the child's score will be at 17. It does not mean that the child has half of all the skills that the child will attain by age 17. Nor does it mean "that this calls for formal, teacher-directed learning. . . . We serve [children] best by providing an environment rich in materials to observe, explore, manipulate, talk, write, and think about" (Elkind, 1987, p. 10).

STUDIES ON HUMAN ATTACHMENT

One of the areas of research of paramount importance to parents is that of human attachment. Since the 1930s there has been increasing research on bonding and attachment. Those in the field recognize attachment as an essential ingredient for a healthy personality. Attachment is defined as a form of behavior that has its "own internal motivation distinct from feeding and

Bloom suggested that in terms of intelligence, this child, aged four, has developed about 50% of his intelligence (as measured at age 17).

sex, and of no less importance for survival" (Bowlby, 1988, p. 27). Attachment behavior is the behavior that the person exhibits in order to obtain and maintain close proximity to the attachment figure, generally the mother, but also the father and, in their absence, someone the child knows. It is strongest when the child is sick, tired, or frightened. Human attachment is crucial throughout the life cycle.

During the 1930s, questions about the importance of human attachment in the young child were raised. Harold Skeels, a member of the Iowa group of child researchers, studied the effect of environment on the development of children during a period when most researchers were studying maturation or behaviorism (e.g., Gesell and Watson). One of Skeels' studies, a natural history investigation, had startling findings (1966). Skeels placed 13 infants and tod-

dlers from an orphanage in an institution for the mentally retarded. Each subject fit the following criteria: (1) under 3 years of age, (2) ineligible for placement for legal reasons, (3) not acutely ill, and (4) mentally retarded. The 13 children, 10 girls and 3 boys, ranged in age from 7.1 to 35.9 months and had IQs from 36 to 89, with a mean IQ score of 64.3. Each child in the control group of 12, also chosen from children in the orphanage, fit these criteria: (1) had taken an IQ test when less than 2 years of age, (2) was still in the orphanage at age 4, (3) was in the control group of the orphanage preschool study, and (4) had not attended preschool. These children had IQs of 50 to 103, with a mean IQ of 86.7 points, and were 12 to 22 months old. The children placed in the wards for the feebleminded were showered with attention by the attendants and supervisors. They were cared for, played with,

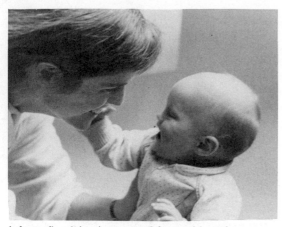

Infants flourish when cared for and loved.

loved, and allowed to go along on excursions. Almost every child developed an attachment to one person who was particularly interested in the child and the child's achievements. The control group of children in the orphanage, however, received traditional care with no special treatment. When retested, after varying periods from 6 to 52 months, the children in the mental institution had gained 27.5 IQ points, but the ones left in the orphanage had lost an average of 26.2 IQ points.

Although the research could be criticized because variables were not controlled (there were more girls than boys placed in the wards) and changes in IQ can partially be explained by statistical regression, the results were so dramatic and unexpected that the impact of early environment had to be considered. Skeels (1966) followed up the subjects of this research and almost 20 years later found evidence to reinforce the initial findings. Of the 13 children who had been transferred to the mental institution, 11 had been adopted and reared as normal children. Twelve of the experimental group had become self-supporting adults, who achieved a median educational level of 12 years of schooling. Of the 12 who had been left in the orphanage, 4 were still in institutions; 1 was a gardener's assistant; 3 were employed as dishwashers; 1 was a floater; 1 was a part-time worker in a cafeteria, and 1 had died. Only 1 had achieved an educa-

tional level similar to that of the experimental group, and he had received different treatment from the others. He had been transferred from the orphanage to a school for the deaf, where he received special attention from his teacher. The children who had been placed in the mental institution and later adopted received personal love and developed human attachments; they had achieved a typical life-style, while those left in the orphanage had only a marginal existence. Evidence strongly supports the importance of a nurturing early environment and also indicates that poor initial environment can be reversed by enriched personal interaction (Skeels, 1966).

René Spitz, a physician, also became involved in the observation of infants during the 1930s. In his book *The First Year of Life,* published in 1965, he described his research and observations of the psychology of infants. He studied babies in seven situations, which included private families, foster homes, an obstetrics ward, an Indian village, a well-baby clinic, a nursery, and a foundling home. Both the nursery and foundling home were long-term institutions that guaranteed constancy of environment and dramatically illustrated the necessity of human attachment and interaction. Both institutions provided similar physical care of children, but they differed in their nurturing and interpersonal relationships. Both provided hygienic conditions, well-prepared food, and medical care. The foundling home had regular daily visits by a medical staff, while the nursery called a doctor when needed. The nursery was connected to a penal institution where delinquent girls, pregnant on admission, were sent to serve their sentences. Babies born to them were cared for in the nursery until the end of their first year. The mothers were primarily delinquent, psychopathic, feebleminded, or socially maladjusted minors. In contrast, some of the children in the foundling home came from well-adjusted mothers who were unable to support their children; others were children of unwed mothers whose children were admitted on the condition that they come to the home and nurse their own and one other child during the first 3 months.

Spitz filmed a representative group of the children he studied in both institutions. In the nursery, he studied 203 children, and in the foundling home, 91. The major difference in the care of the two sets of children was the amount of nurturing and social interaction. The nursery, which housed 40 to 60 children at a time, allowed the mothers or mother-substitutes to feed, nurse, and care for their babies. The infants had at least one toy; they were able to see outside their cribs and to watch the activities of other children and mothers caring for their babies. These babies thrived. In the foundling home, however, the babies were screened from outside activity by blankets hung over the sides and ends of their cribs, thus isolating them from any visual stimulation. They had no toys to play with, and the caretakers were busy tending to other duties rather than mothering the children. During the first 3 months, while the babies were breast fed, they appeared normal. After separation, they soon went through progressive deterioration. Of the 91 foundling home children, 34 died by the end of the second year. Spitz (1965) continued to follow up 21 of the children who remained in the foundling home until they were 4 years of age. He found that 20 could not dress themselves; 6 were not toilet trained; 6 could not talk; 5 had a vocabulary of two words; 8 had vocabularies of three to five words; and only 1 was able to speak in sentences. Spitz attributed the cause of the deterioration of the infants to lack of mothering. The children in the nursery had mothering, while those in the foundling home did not:

Absence of mothering equals emotional starvation . . . this leads to progressive deterioration engulfing the child's whole person. Such deterioration is manifested first in an arrest of the child's psychological development; then psychological dysfunctions set in, paralleled by somatic changes. In the next stage this leads to increased infection liability and eventually, when the emotional deprivation continues into the second year of life, to a spectacularly increased rate of mortality. (p. 281)

In 1951 John Bowlby reviewed the literature on studies of deprivation and its effect on personality development. He then made a systematic review for the World Health Organization in which he described those works that supported theories on the negative aspects of maternal deprivation. In his monograph Bowlby (1966) stated:

It is submitted that the evidence is now such that it leaves no room for doubt regarding the general proposition that the prolonged deprivation of the young child of maternal care may have grave and far-reaching effects on his character and so on the whole of his future life. (p. 46)

Bowlby (1966) emphasized that the greatest effect on personality development is during the child's early years. The earliest critical period was believed to be during the first 5 or 6 months while mother-figure and infant are forming an attachment. The second vital phase was seen as lasting until near the child's third birthday, during which time the mother-figure needs to be virtually an ever-present companion. During a third phase, the child is able to maintain his attachment even though the nurturing parent is absent. During the fourth to fifth year, this tolerable absence might extend from a few days to a few weeks; during the seventh to eighth years, the separation could be lengthened to a year or more. Deprivation in the third phase does not have the same destructive effect on the child as it does in the period from infancy through the third year.

Rutter's *Maternal Deprivation Reassessed* (1981) and Bower's *Development in Infancy* (1982) questioned whether the term *maternal deprivation* was too restrictive to cover a wide range of abuses and variables. In was suggested that maternal deprivation was too limited a concept—that human attachment and multiple attachment should be considered and that warmth as well as love be regarded as vital elements in relationships. Rutter suggested that the bond with the mother was not different in quality or kind than other bondings. In addition, individual difference among children resulted in some children being more vulnerable to "mother deprivation" than were other children.

Thus, questions regarding the irreversibility of deprivation were raised. Would sound childrearing reverse early deprivation? It appeared that good childrearing practices and a good environment would help the child, but early deprivation continued to be a problem and deprived infants often remained detached. In research by Tizard and Hodges (1978) children raised in an institution were studied to see if the lack of personal attachment had lasting affects. The children who were adopted did form bonds as late as 4 or 6 years of age, but they exhibited the same attentional and social problems in school as those who remained in the institution.

In reviewing the research, "It appears that although attachments can still develop for the first time after infancy, nevertheless fully normal social development may be dependent on early bonding" (Rutter, 1981, p. 190). Rutter broadened his work to include many aspects of the environment that affect the child. He found that poor parent attachment did not harm intellectual development in the same way that it harmed psychosocial development if the child was reared with opportunity for learning experiences and stimulation. Did multiple risks compound the ability of a child to survive, not only intellectually, but also socially and emotionally? Rutter's evidence established that disturbed family relationships were a key variable in resulting conduct disorders and delinquency in children. Adequate parent relationships in infancy, though seemingly essential, cannot necessarily protect the child from multiple risk factors that may arise later in life. One of these factors is the schools that the child attends. Good schools make a difference in the mental and intellectual health of a child. Rutter concluded that risks, loss, and discordant families all have an effect on children, but "it may be that the first few years do have a special importance for bond formation and social development" (p. 217).

Research concerning parent-child relationships and the attachment of infant and parents continued in the United States and abroad during the 1970s and 1980s. The importance of early attachment became clear even though there were differences in interpretation and in the areas of research emphasis. Klaus and Kennell (1982) focused on the bonding relationship between the newborn and the parents. Their emphasis was on the sensitive period immediately after birth and their work took into consideration the environment of the institution in which the child was born. There was concern for mothers to have sensitive caregiving during and following birth and the opportunity for parents to be able to attach to their baby immediately. It was pointed out that parents, who need help in adjusting to the role of a new parent, could be encouraged to interact with their infants by using eye-to-eye contact, touching their baby, talking (high pitched) to their child, and developing entrainment of movement to the rhythm of baby and parent. Brazelton also emphasized the attachment between parent and child and noted the tremendous effect the mother and child have on one another. All three physicians stressed eye-to-eye contact of the mother with the newborn. "Eye-to-eye contact serves the purpose of giving a real identity or personification to the baby, as well as getting a rewarding feedback for the mother" (Brazelton in Klaus & Kennell, 1982, p. 74).

Parents of premature infants were of particular concern to Klaus and Kennell. They made it possible for these parents to touch and provide tactile comfort to their infants. These seemingly simple changes allowed the opportunity for attachment and offered support to parents who had special problems in attaching to their premature infants (Klaus & Kennell, 1982).

Klaus and Kennell have been criticized for emphasizing that the opportunity for bonding and attachment was essential immediately following birth. The crucial nature of immediate bonding and the long-lasting effects of this bond were questioned. As we have seen, others, including Rutter (1981), viewed the attachment period as extending from between the first few weeks of life up until 2 years of age.

Ainsworth (1973) has written that parent-child attachment is necessary for the development of a healthy personality but that attachment may occur beyond the early "sensitive period." Bowlby (1982) described attachment in a family setting. Most babies around the age of 3 months show more attention and are more responsive to

Klaus and Kennell emphasized early parent-child attachment.

their mother or primary caregiver by smiling at, vocalizing to, and visually following the adult. It is not until around 6 months that infants become concerned about being near their caregiver. This attachment continues and strengthens in intensity from 6 to 9 months, although when the child is ill, fatigued, hungry, or alarmed, the intensity increases. During the same period the infant demonstrates attachment to others as well, primarily the father, siblings, and caregivers. Attachment to others does not reduce the attachment to the mother or primary caregiver. At 9 months most children try to follow primary caregivers when they leave the room, greet them on return, and crawl to be near them. This behavior continues throughout the second year of an infant's life and on into the third. When children reach around 2 years 9 months to 3 years of age, they are better able to accept a parent's temporary absence (Bowlby, 1982).

Bowlby (1982) also cited research that illustrates the need for concern about young children who must go to the hospital for an extended length of time or those who must have institutional care. His research revealed that when children, 15 to 30 months, were placed in residential nurseries or hospitals, in places away from the mother-figure and other familiar persons and in an unfamiliar environment, they commonly go through three stages: (1) protest, (2) despair, and (3) detachment. The phases do not start and stop abruptly but may have days or weeks of transition or shifts back and forth. The first phase, protest, may last from a few hours to a week or more. The child reacts to the environment and may cry, display distress and anger, and seem to be looking for the missing parent. The second phase is a period of despair when the child withdraws, makes no demands, and appears to be in a state of mourning. The final stage is the detachment period which appears to be adjustment and recovery, but is actually a withdrawal from the parent and an absence of attachment behavior that is normal for the child's age. The child becomes more sociable, accepts food and toys from the nurses, but withdraws from the former attachment figures. If separation continues the child may stop attaching to anyone and appear to care for no one—the child will become detached.

Brazelton and Yogman (1986), in their extensive studies of infants, analyzed the process of early attachment and wrote specifically about the interaction between infant and parent, even covering the effects of experiences in utero. The child appears to be born with predictable responses including the ability to develop a reciprocal relationship with the caregiver. Four stages vital to the parent-infant attachment process, which lasts from birth to 4 or 5 months, were described. In the first stage the infant achieves homeostatic control and is able to control stimuli by shutting out or reaching for stimuli. During the second stage the infant is able to use and attend to social cues. In the third stage, usually at 3 and 4 months, the reciprocal process between parent and child shows the infant's ability to "take in and respond to information" as well as withdraw. During the fourth stage the infant develops a sense of autonomy and initiates and responds to cues. If the parent recognizes and encourages the infant's desire to

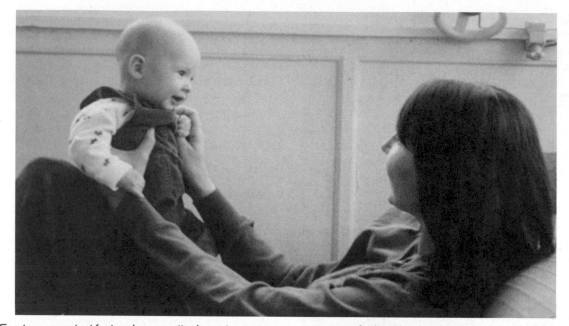

Eye-to-eye contact fosters human attachment, a necessary component for healthy development of young children.

have control over the environment, the infant develops a sense that leads to a feeling of competence. This model is based on feedback and reciprocal interaction and allows for individual differences.

As early as the 1973 *Review of Child Development Research,* Ainsworth called for "a new kind of child development counselor," who would help promote infant-mother figure attachment as a necessary prerequisite for healthy social development in the young. After surveying theory and research on attachment, Ainsworth drew 11 inferences concerning attachment. She noted that no system for development of attachment matches the quality of a family-type environment although attachments may be formed with more than one parent figure. A prolonged separation of parent and child is stressful for a child, with the period from 6 months to 3 years being the most tenuous. Parents who foster attachment cannot spoil the child; instead, it is very desirable to be responsive and sensitive to the "infant's signals." A good infant-mother attachment tends to result in a more secure child.

Two groups of parents are of particular concern. Some parents have never had models

in parenting and may have been reared in abusive homes. They need help in learning how to care for children. The other group is the parents who are busy and away from home for extended periods. The importance of early bonding and attachment development is such that these parents should be aware of the consequences of not devoting time to their young children.

Parents who are at risk for abusing children can be helped. Bowlby (1988) described a Home Start program in Leicester, England, in which volunteers went to the home and helped parents with their roles as parents. The C. Henry Kempe Center in Denver has also worked with parents who were likely to become child abusers and with parents who had already abused their children. Modeling of good child care and support for parents during periods of stress helps parents develop more appropriate childrearing skills.

Parents who lack the time or interest to care for their infants might read and respond to *High Risk: Children Without a Conscience* (Magid & McKelvey, 1988). It contains convincing arguments about the necessity for giving young children time, interaction, and commitment. The text is very strong in its pronouncements, and so parent educators may want to use it as a starting point for discussion. The authors focus on psychopathy and unattached children and warn alarmingly about the sensitive period of attachment. "If, at any step, things go wrong, lasting and severe psychopathology may result. . . . The results of such trauma are not pretty, and they last a lifetime" (Cline, 1979, as cited in Magid & McKelvey, 1988, p. 73). Some parents may need help in organizing their lives so that they can devote the necessary time to their children or can arrange for high quality assistance with childrearing responsibilities.

These implications for childrearing also challenge all parent educators. New parents should be encouraged to become actively involved with and responsive to their infants. To achieve these goals, child development and family life courses that include information on attachment and bonding should be offered in all high school curricula. Continuing or adult education classes should offer childrearing classes for parents who are no longer in school. Innumerable channels exist for disseminating information to a wide audience through health services, schools, television, or social agencies.

EDUCATIONAL INTERVENTION PROGRAMS

The social climate of the nation during the 1960s mandated a concerted effort to provide equality of opportunity, as reflected in the Civil Rights Act of 1964. One result was a comprehensive national survey of 645,000 students in 4000 schools. These findings were revealed in *Equality of Educational Opportunity* by James S. Coleman et al. in 1966. Although the main thrust of the report was to investigate the effects of de facto and de jure segregation on educational achievement, the report had implications for educators who might institute early intervention. The researchers found that school curricula and expenditures on facilities and materials did not affect school achievement, but the quality of

teachers did. The students who achieved felt that they had some control over their own destiny. "Minority pupils, except for Orientals, have far less conviction than whites that they can affect their own environment and futures" (Coleman, et al., 1966, p. 23). The most important single factor shown to affect achievement was family background. Important variables included the home's effective support of education, number of children in the family, and parents' educational levels.

Other reports shattered the idea that intelligence was fixed and that the home environment had nothing to do with a child's intellectual success (Skeels, 1966; Spitz, 1965; Hunt, 1961). These reports, along with the national mood of the mid-1960s supporting equal rights and opportunity, propelled the country to respond to the needs of the poor and disadvantaged. One of the most effective responses was to provide educational intervention for the children of the poor.

These experimental programs emphasized the value of an enriched environment for the child and were designed to show the impact that the environment has on the intellectual development of young children. Very high hopes for the changing of intelligence existed. Could a very short program change children's lives? Whereas the research on attachment was based primarily on ethological studies and psychoanalytic examination of the influences on the child's emotional growth, educational intervention programs initially focused on cognitive development of children. It was thought that intervention in the lives of economically disadvantaged young children would help them become equal. Because the environment was recognized as important, these new programs were designed to include the parents.

The proposed projects would have a two-pronged approach. The child would benefit from an enriched early education program, and the parents would be included as an integral part of the programs as aides, advisory council members, or paraprofessional members of the team. In the summer of 1965, as part of the War on Poverty, the first Head Start centers were opened. Head Start was a comprehensive program of health, nutrition, and education as well as a career ladder for economically disadvantaged families. Rather than wait for results of the long-range effects of early intervention, numerous Head Start programs, funded by the federal government and developed at the local level, sprang up over the nation.

Researchers in the 1960s demonstrated startling gains in IQ in children enrolled in Head Start and other programs (Caldwell, 1968; Deutsch & Deutsch, 1968; Gray & Klaus, 1965; Weikart & Lambie, 1968). Those looking for sustained intellectual gains, however, were disappointed with the results of one of the first studies, the so-called Westinghouse Report/Ohio State University Study (Westinghouse Learning Corporation and Ohio State University, 1969), that indicated no sustained intellectual development (see Lazar et al., 1982; Consortium for Longitudinal Studies, 1983).

From the beginning, early childhood researchers criticized the Westinghouse Report (Campbell & Backer, 1970; White, 1970). Other studies that followed, based on federally funded programs and analyzed by other early childhood researchers, had optimistic findings. It was not until the Consortium for Longitudinal Studies was formed in 1975, however, that researchers united to determine if indeed there were gains from educational intervention. These gains were not to be determined solely by improvement in IQ scores; reduction in special education placements and drop-out rates, health improvement, and families' ability to cope were also indicators of success.

Studies conducted in the 1970s consistently demonstrated the importance of an enriched early home environment to the child's school success (Hanson, 1975; Shipman et al., 1976; White et al., 1973). Shipman and her colleagues (1976) studied black, low socioeconomic status children. The mother's educational aspirations and expectations were higher for children in high reading groups than for those in low reading groups. A higher level of parental education was also associated with academic success of children:

Thus, a higher level of parental education is associated with greater academic knowledge, increased awareness of public affairs and popular culture, more informed perceptions of school, and continued seeking of new knowledge as in reading books and magazines (cf. Hyman, Wright, and Reed, 1975), all of which may have impact on the child's knowledge and motivation for learning. (p. 34)

Powell's more recent review of the research on the effects of families is less definitive (1989). He noted studies and programs that had positive results but also suggested that additional and more controlled research is needed to determine the real effects of parent-school partnerships. His monograph looked at the "effects of continuity and discontinuity on children" and the "effect of efforts to strengthen connections between family and early childhood program" (p. iii).

The goals for many of the programs developed in the 1960s included (1) the expectation that the child would become more competent, (2) the parents would grow and develop their own feelings of self worth and skills, (3) parents would become more knowledgeable consumers, and (4) parents would be resources in the children's programs. Powell found little research on whether children benefited if the child care setting was similar to the home setting. For example, the Kamehameha Early Education Program (KEEP) research found student performance improved when the school became more compatible with the children's culture. However, this does not reveal effects for children from middle-class, dominant-culture families. Powell suggested that this was one of many areas that need further investigation.

Powell's monograph focuses on early childhood programs. He discussed many programs in such detail that it would be impossible to summarize his recommendations here. It is suggested that the reader go to this source for an in-depth look at the research in families and early childhood programs. In addition to the effects on families, the Consortium for Longitudinal Studies set out to determine the effect that experimental early intervention programs of the 1960s had on the children in their programs.

The task was challenging. All the researchers, both those connected to Head Start programs and those who worked on individual early childhood projects, had assessment designs in their projects. However, each program was developed independently of the others, so the task of analyzing the data was tremendous. The programs differed according to the children's ages, the curriculum involved, the duration of the program, and the amount of parent involvement. The Consortium selected a total of 11 research groups for analysis. Principal investigators included Beller, Deutsch and Deutsch, Gordon and Jester, Gray, Karnes, Levenstein, Miller, Palmer, Weikart, Woolman, and Zigler. Each researcher agreed to send raw data to an independent analytic group in Ithaca, New York, to be recorded and analyzed. Although the programs differed, they were all well-designed and monitored, so there was an excellent data base.

The Consortium's findings were positive; early childhood intervention affected five areas (Consortium for Longitudinal Studies, 1983):

1. Ability in early to middle childhood
   a. Improved scores on Stanford-Binet Intelligence Test
   b. Improved scores on achievement tests
2. Greater school competency in the middle to adolescent years
   a. Special education placement reduced
   b. Less grade retention
3. Improved attitude toward achievement in adolescence
   a. Pride in activity
   b. Mother/child occupational aspiration
   c. Self-evaluation of school performance
4. Educational attainment
   a. High school completion related to competence at grade 9
   b. High school completion/educational expectations
5. Occupational attainment
   a. Employment/school competence
   b. Occupational aspiration

The data imply that five characteristics are important for successful intervention programs (Royce, Darlington, & Murray, 1983, p. 442). Three of the items relate to parent involvement.

1. Begin intervention as early as possible.
2. Provide services to the parents as well as to the child.
3. Provide frequent home visits.
4. Involve parents in the instruction of the child.
5. Have as few children per teacher as possible.

In a discussion of the Consortium's findings, Lazar summarized two important points. First, a good preschool program pays off in two ways: benefits for children's development and financial savings as a result of less special education placement. Secondly, "closer contact between home and school and greater involvement of parents in the education of their children are probably more important" than generally realized by administrators (Lazar, 1983, p. 464).

The research findings have been substantiated (see Gray, Ramsey, & Klaus, 1982; Levenstein, 1988; Lazar et al., 1982; Spodek, 1982; Consortium for Longitudinal Studies, 1983).

More data followed the Consortium report. A follow-up study on Weikart's Perry Preschool

Early childhood education programs allow children to learn through play with other children and to grow in self-esteem.

Program vividly illustrated the impact that early educational intervention can have on children's lives (Berrueta-Clement et al., 1984). The Perry Preschool Program continued to follow the children to age 19, four years beyond the report published by the Consortium. Berrueta-Clement et al. compared children who had attended the Perry Preschool with children who did not. The researchers found that former Perry Preschool students grew up with more positive school success, placed a higher value on school, had higher aspirations for college, had fewer absences, and spent fewer of their school years in special education than the children in the control group. But though Weikart's program had a strong parent involvement component, the contributions of parents to the program's success were not analyzed because the researchers were unable to separate parent involvement from the preschool effect. In fact, however, the influence of caregivers, whether teachers or parents, cannot be separated from the well-being of the child and the success of a program.

The Frank Porter Graham Child Development Center (University of North Carolina at Chapel Hill) has reviewed more than 180 research reports concerning the understanding and prevention of hampered development. Among the major projects that the center directed were the Carolina Abecedarian Project and Project CARE. The Carolina Abecedarian Project found that educational intervention of home/school teachers was effective. The home/school teacher filled the following roles: curriculum developer, teacher of parents on use of activities, tutor of children, provider of supplemental classroom materials, advocator for child and family, and provider of summer experiences and activities (Ramey, 1985, pp. 4–5). Another longitudinal study, Project CARE, taught problem-solving techniques to parents as one of their intervention approaches. The program aimed to help parents act more responsively to their children, to view the problem, and to be able to work on it (Wasik, 1983).

Elementary schools joined in researching parent involvement. A study of 250 California elementary schools found parent involvement related to both parent satisfaction and student achievement (Herman & Yen, 1980). The "curriculum of the home" that includes parent/child discussions about everyday occurrences, monitoring and viewing television together, encouragement and discussion of reading, and emotional support and interest in the child's world led to greater academic achievement. In 29 controlled studies 91 percent of the children in the program benefitted when the learning environment at home improved. The home environment affected the outcome twice as much as socioeconomic status (Walberg, 1984).

BENEFITS FOR CHILDREN AND PARENTS

School/home collaboration helps many families in their interaction and support of children. This knowledge prompted the Association for Childhood Education International to promote the linkage among home, school, and community:

We believe that teachers and parents need to establish a stronger bond with one another.... Closer contact between parents and teachers will give each a more complete picture of the child's abilities and improve consistency in working toward desired goals. Most important, perhaps, the child will identify both the school and the home as places to learn, and parents and teachers as sources of learning. (Umansky, p. 263, 264)

The U.S. Department of Education's book *What Works* emphasized the "curriculum of the home." It states:

Parents can do many things at home to help their children succeed in school.... They do this through their daily conversations, household routines, attention to school matters, and affectionate concern for their children's progress.

Conversation is important. Children learn to read, reason, and understand things better when their parents:

• read, talk, and listen to them,
• tell them stories, play games, share hobbies, and
• discuss the news, TV programs, and special events.

In order to enrich the "curriculum of the home," some parents:

- provide books, supplies, and a special place for studying,
- observe routine for meals, bedtime, and homework, and
- monitor the amount of time spent watching TV and doing after-school jobs.

Parents stay aware of their children's lives at school when they:

- discuss school events,
- help children meet deadlines, and
- talk with their children about school problems and successes.

Research on both gifted and disadvantaged children shows that home efforts can greatly improve student achievement. For example, when parents of disad-

vantaged children take the steps listed above, their children can do as well at school as the children of more affluent families. (U.S. Department of Education, 1986, p. 7)

One of the most promising directions of parent partnership with schools involves the ability to read. *What Works* reports that

the best way for parents to help their children become better readers is to read to them—even when they are very young. Children benefit most from reading aloud when they discuss stories, learn to identify letters and words, and talk about the meaning of words. (U.S. Department of Education, 1986, p. 9)

The report stresses that there are many ways parents can encourage reading, but reading to

Parents who talk with, read with, and listen to their children help their children learn.

children and relating stories to everyday events are most significant. Just talking together and having conversations while reading is as important as the reading itself. When parents don't discuss the story or ask questions that require thinking, the children do not achieve as well in reading as children of parents who do involve the child.

Other studies concerned with reading ability support the importance of parents reading to and with their children. Investigations of the importance of parent encouragement of and interest in their children's reading have found that the children who achieve well in reading have parents who actively guide and help their children develop reading ability. Their homes contain available reading material and parents use encouragement rather than punishment. Parents also assist their children in setting realistic goals, elicit questions about their reading, and spend time with their children (Beecher, 1985).

Meier (1978) reported on benefits of parent participation for both parents and children. Parents who participated in an early education program gained a sensitivity to their child's emotional, social, intellectual development and needs; greater acceptance of their children; the ability to respect individual differences; a greater enjoyment of their children; an ability to sense and reduce their children's distress; more affection; use of more elaborate language patterns; more communication through reasoning and encouragement rather than through authority; development of parental educational goals; and effective use of community agencies. Children were (1) more aware and responsive, (2) equipped with better skills for problem solving, (3) able to vocalize in early years and develop more complex language skills in second and third years, (4) more successful in both short-term and long-term intellectual development, and (5) stronger socially and emotionally with improved attachment to parents; there was also increased and richer interaction with the mother and, later, others.

ISSUES DISCUSSED IN THIS TEXT

A more comprehensive discussion of the issues with suggestions for improving school-home collaboration is found in the following ten chapters. Chapter 2, Historical Overview of Family Life and Parent Involvement, contains a summary of the history and trends of education as it relates to parents. Parent involvement is not new; parents have always been prime educators of their children but, through the years, the emphasis of parents as partners in education has changed. Since the 1960s increased concern for school and home cooperation has resulted in parent participation in schools and home visitation programs. The chapter describes the growth of parent education programs and notes the changes in childrearing practices throughout the past 60 decades. In closing it outlines the issues that face the nation today.

Chapter 3, The Family and Community, describes families in the United States today. Demographic changes in the nation since the 1950s place many families at high risk. These include high mobility, increased number of women working outside the home, out-of-wedlock teenage mothers, high divorce rates, and poverty. The chapter discusses how schools can respond to the high rate of change and stress in society. Note is made of diversity including a discussion of Black American, Spanish surnamed, Native Americans, and recent Asian-American immigrants from Vietnam, Cambodia, and Thailand.

The special activities that schools need to offer parents are included in Chapter 4, Effective Home-School-Community Relationships. One-way communication, in the form of newsletters and notes, is illustrated. Techniques are suggested for utilizing parents and other community members as volunteers. Tips for parent-teacher conferences, acknowledged as one of the most effective means of communication between parent and teacher, are discussed in detail.

Chapter 5, Communication and Parent Programs, focuses on communication among parent, child, and schools. Open responses, listening skills, and ways to encourage good communication help parent, teacher, and child communicate more effectively. Techniques of good parenting (as illustrated by programs such as Systematic Teaching of Effective Parenting, Parent Effectiveness Training, and Active Parenting) are included.

Leadership training and types of meetings are the themes of Chapter 6. The chapter gives tips on leading meetings and on the types of meetings that can be used for parent education.

Many schools are already accomplished in their ability to collaborate with parents. Chapter 7, School-Based Programs, describes many of these successful schools and includes the special characteristics that make them effective.

Working with the family as well as the individual child has been shown to be most effective. In Chapter 8, home-based programs are seen as ways to educate and support all members of the family. The chapter describes new approaches to home-based education as well as reviews the research done by Home Start.

Chapter 9, Working with Parents of Exceptional Children, was written by Jo Spidel. She is an educator who holds an advanced degree in special education, with the main emphasis on learning disabilities. The chapter includes mainstreaming, the development of the Individual-ized Education Program, and the unique needs of handicapped children and families.

One can read the daily newspaper and find in detail the problems of child abuse in the United States. Teachers and child care workers need to be able to recognize child abuse and to relate to the parents of the abused child. Chapter 10, The Abused Child, includes data on abuse and recommends procedures for dealing with this problem.

Chapter 11, Rights, Responsibilities, and Advocacy, concerns student rights and responsibilities. Advocating for good child care is used as an illustration of the responsibility of advocating for change that is needed to help children and families.

The book closes with Appendix E that provides lists of books, pamphlets, films, organizations, and references that can be used to develop a parent education program.

Consider the suggestions and curricula in the following chapters as a guide to working with parents, be they parents who need an opportunity to use their talents or those who need support. Join in the exploration of parents as partners in the educational process. Expand and adapt the ideas presented in this book, and develop an individual way of effectively working with parents.

SUMMARY

Parenthood is an essential role in society. The support given by parents, interrelated with other agencies—particularly the school—should be integrated and continuous. Parent programs that respond to parent needs range from infancy, preschool, and primary and intermediate grades to secondary and young adult programs.

The renewed interest in parent involvement, which manifested itself with concern over the child's intellectual development, was reinforced by the writings of Hunt, Bloom, and Coleman. The time was ripe for consideration of intervention and parent involvement. Concurrently, the concern for equal opportunities resulted in the initiation of Head Start, Follow Through, and Chapter I programs.

Studies on human attachment (Skeels, Spitz, Bowlby, Ainsworth, and others) emphasized the significance of a parent figure, nurturing and warm. Many intervention programs included parent involvement as an integral part of the process.

Research on the intervention results of Head Start, home visitation, and parent involvement programs showed that parents were an important component in a child's development. Researchers emphasized the value of an enriched environment for the child and the importance of parents as part of that environment. Positive changes in parent behavior not only resulted in improved conditions for the child during the program but also continued after its completion. In addition, parenting skills helped subsequent children in the family.

In studies involving children at all levels, from infancy through high school, parent involvement made a difference. Reading specialists stressed the importance of parents reading to and with their children, encouraging, eliciting questions, and setting realistic goals for their child's learning.

SUGGESTIONS FOR CLASS ACTIVITIES AND DISCUSSIONS

1. Survey a preschool, elementary school, or junior high or high school in your area and find out how each involves parents.
2. Invite a social worker to discuss the problems involved in foster home and institutional placements.
3. Discuss Bloom's findings. What is the difference between intellectual potential and achievement?
4. Give Piagetian-type tests to children age 3 months to 9 years. Focus on the way the child thinks and the changes in ability.
5. Discuss the importance of Hunt's book *Intelligence and Experience.* How has it helped change the belief in fixed IQ?
6. Visit an infant center or nursery. Observe children actively involved in their environment. Are some more actively involved in their environment than others?
7. Visit a Head Start center. How are parents involved in the program?
8. Keep a log of brief encounters where you observe parents and children, infancy through young adulthood. Which kinds of interactions did you find at the grocery store, in the park, at the zoo, in the department store, or at home? Which interactions were most positive?
9. Can you defend the importance of parents as teachers of their own children and parents as partners with the school?
10. Look into the research on attachment. How are both parents important to the infant?
11. Which research points to involving parents in the education of their children?
12. Investigate types of parent responses that facilitate their child's intellectual and emotional growth. Discuss them.
13. Explain why educators work with the whole child (emotional, social, physical, and intellectual) rather than separating intellectual and other domains.
14. Discuss the ways parents who participated in early education programs gained from the experience.
15. Visit a parent cooperative. Talk with some parents about their responsibilities for the preschool program. Interview the director and discuss the roles parents play in the total program.

BIBLIOGRAPHY

Ainsworth, M. D. The development of infant-mother attachments. In B. M. Caldwell & H. N. Ricciuti (Eds.), *Review of child development research.* Chicago: University of Chicago Press, 1973.

Anastasiow, N. Should parenting education be mandatory? *Topics in Early Childhood Special Education,* Spring 1988, pp. 60–72.

Anderson, R. C., Hiebert, E. H., Scott, J. A., & Wilkinson, I. A. G. *Becoming a nation of readers: The report of the Commission on Reading.* Champaign, Il.: Center for the Study of Reading, 1985.

Beecher, R. M. Parent involvement and reading achievement: A review of research and implications for practice. *Childhood Education, 62,* September 1985, pp. 44–49.

Berrueta-Clement, J. R., Schweinhart, L. J., Barnett, W. S., Epstein, A. S., & Weikart, D. P. *Changed lives: The effects of the Perry Preschool Program on youths through age 19* (Monograph of the High-/Scope Educational Research Foundation, No. 8), Ypsilanti, Mich.: The High/Scope Press, 1984.

Binkley, M. R. *Becoming a nation of readers: What parents can do.* Lexington, Mass.: D. C. Heath, 1988.

Bloom, B. S. *Stability and change in human characteristics.* New York: Wiley & Sons, 1964.

————. *All our children learning.* New York: McGraw-Hill, 1981.

————. The home environment and school learning. In Study Group of National Assessment of Student Achievement, *The nation's report card.* Washington D.C.: U.S. Department of Education, 1986. (ERIC Document Reproduction Service No. ED 279 663)

Bower, T. G. R. *Development in infancy* (2nd ed.). San Francisco: W. H. Freeman, 1982.

Bowlby, J. *Maternal care and mental health.* New York: Schocken Books, 1966.

————. *Attachment.* New York: Basic Books, 1982.

————. *A secure base.* New York: Basic Books, 1988.

Brazelton, T. B. *Working and caring.* Reading, Mass.: Addison-Wesley, 1987.

Brazelton, T. B., & Yogman, M. W. *Affective development in infancy.* Norwood, N.J.: Ablex Publishing, 1986.

Bredekamp, S. (Ed.) *Developmentally appropriate practice in early childhood programs serving children from birth through 8,* Expanded edition. Washington, D.C.: National Association for the Education of Young Children, 1987.

Caldwell, B. The fourth dimension in early childhood education. In R. Hess & R. Bear (Eds.), *Early education: Current theory, research, and action.* Chicago: Aldine Publishing, 1968.

California Task Force on School Readiness. *Here they come: Ready or not.* Sacramento: California Department of Education, 1988.

Campbell, D. T., & Backer, A. How regression artifacts in quasi-experimental evaluations can mistakenly make compensatory education look harmful. In J. Hellmuth (Ed.), *Disadvantaged child. (Vol. 3): Compensatory education: A national debate.* New York: Brunner/Mazel, 1970.

Carnegie Foundation for the Advancement of Teaching. *The conditions of teaching.* Princeton, N.J.: Author, 1988.

Clark, R. M. *Family life and school achievement.* Chicago: University of Chicago Press, 1983.

Coleman, J. S. Families and schools. *Educational Researcher, 16,* 1987, pp. 32–38.

Coleman, J., Campbell, E. Q., Hobson, C. J., McPartland, J., Mood, A. M., Weinfeld, F. D., & York, R. L. *Equality of educational opportunity.* Washington, D.C.: U.S. Government Printing Office, 1966.

Comer, J. P. Educating poor minority children. *Scientific American,* November 1988, pp. 42–48.

Consortium for Longitudinal Studies. *As the twig is bent.* Hillsdale, N.J.: Lawrence Erlbaum Associates, 1983.

Deutsch, C. P., & Deutsch, M. Brief reflections on theory of early childhood enrichment programs. In R. Hess & R. Bear (Eds.), *Early education: Current theory, research, and action.* Chicago: Aldine Publishing, 1968.

Elkind, D. The child yesterday, today, and tomorrow. *Young Children,* May 1987, pp. 6–12.

————. Early childhood education on its own terms. In S. L. Kagan & E. F. Zigler (Eds.), *Early schooling.* New Haven: Yale University Press, 1987, pp. 98–115.

Epstein, J. L. Parents' reactions to teacher practices of parental involvement. *Elementary School Journal,* 1986, pp. 227–293.

Gotts, E. E. *Hope revisited: Preschool to graduation, reflections on parenting and school-family relations.* Occasional Paper 28. Charleston, W. Va.: Appalachia Educational Laboratory, 1989.

Gray, S. W., & Klaus, R. A. An experimental preschool program for culturally deprived children. *Child Development, 36* (4), 1965, pp. 887–898.

Gray, S. W., Ramsey, B. K., & Klaus, R. A. *From 3 to 20: The Early Training Project.* Baltimore: University Park Press, 1982.

Hanson, R. A. Consistency and stability of home environmental measures related to IQ. *Child Development, 46,* 1975, pp. 470–480.

Harris, L. & Associates. *The American teacher, 1987. Strengthening links between home and school. The Metropolitan Life Survey.* Washington, D.C.: U.S. Department of Education, 1987. (ERIC Document Reproduction Service No. ED 289 841)

Henderson, A. *The evidence continues to grow.* Columbia, Md.: National Committee for Citizens in Education, 1987.

Herman, J. L., and Yen, J. P. *Some effects of parent involvement in schools.* Paper presented at the American Educational Research Association Meeting in Boston, April 1980.

Hess, R. D., & Holloway, S. D. Family and school as educational institutions. In R. D. Parke, R. N. Emde, H. P. McAdoo, & G. P. Sackett (Eds.), *Review of child development research: Vol. 7. The family.* Chicago: University of Chicago Press, 1984.

Hunt, J. M. *Intelligence and experience.* New York: John Wiley & Sons, Inc., 1961.

Hyman, H. H., Wright, C. R., & Reed, J. S. *The enduring effect of education.* Chicago: University of Chicago Press, 1975.

Kagan S. L., & Zigler, E. F. *Early schooling.* New Haven: Yale University Press, 1987.

Karnes, M. C., Teska, I. A., Hodgins, A. S., & Badger, E. D. Educational intervention at home by mothers of disadvantaged infants. *Child Development, 41,* 1970, pp. 925–935.

Klaus, M. H., & Kennell, J. S. *Parent-infant bonding.* St. Louis: C. V. Mosby Co., 1982.

Lazar, I. Discussion and implications of the findings. In Consortium of Longitudinal Studies, *As the twig is bent.* Hillsdale, N.J.: Lawrence Erlbaum Associates, 1983.

Lazar, I., Darlington, R., Murray, H., Royce, J., and Snipper, A. *Lasting effects of early education: A report from the Consortium for Longitudinal Studies.* Monographs of the Society for Research in Child Development, *47,* 1982.

Levenstein, P. *Messages from home: The Mother-Child Program.* Columbus: Ohio State University Press, 1988.

Lipsky, D. K., & Gartner, A. Overcoming school failure: A vision for the future. In F. J. Macchiarola & A. Gartner (Eds.), *Caring for America's children, 37,* 2. New York: The Academy of Political Science, 1989.

Lyons, P., Robbins, A., & Smith, A. *Involving parents in schools: A handbook for participation.* Ypsilanti, Mich.: The High/Scope Press, 1983.

Macchiarola, F. J. Schools that serve children. In F. J. Macchiarola & A. Gartner, (Eds.), *Caring for America's children, 37,* 2. New York: The Academy of Political Science, 1989, pp. 170–181.

Macchiarola F. J., & Gartner, A. (Eds.), *Caring for America's children, 37,* 2. New York: The Academy of Political Science, 1989.

Magid, K., & McKelvey C. A. *High risk: Children without a conscience.* New York: Bantam Books, 1988.

Meier, J. H. Introduction. In B. Brown (Ed.), *Found: Long-term gains from early intervention.* Boulder, Colo.: Westview Press, 1978.

Meyerhoff, M. K., & White, B. L. New parents as teachers. *Educational Leadership,* November 1986, pp. 42–46.

National Association of State Boards of Education. *Right from the Start.* Alexandria, Va.: Author, 1988.

National Commission on Excellence in Education. *A nation at risk: The imperative for educational reform.* Washington, D.C.: U.S. Department of Education, 1983.

Piaget, J. *To understand is to invent.* New York: Penguin Books, 1976.

Powell, D. R. *Families and early childhood programs.* Washington, D.C.: National Association for the Education of Young Children, 1989.

Ramey, C. T. *Does early intervention make a difference?* Paper presented at the National Early Childhood Conference on Children with Special Needs, Denver, Colo., October 1985.

Royce, J. M., Darlington, R. B., & Murray, H. W. Pooled analysis: Findings across studies. In Consortium for Longitudinal Studies, *As the twig is bent.* Hillsdale, N.J.: Lawrence Erlbaum Associates, 1983.

Rutter, M. *Maternal deprivation reassessed.* Harmondsworth, England: Penguin Books, 1981.

———. Family and school influences on cognitive development. *Journal of Child Psychology and Psychiatry, 26,* 1985, pp. 683–704.

Schaefer, E. S. Parents as educators: Evidence from cross-sectional, longitudinal, and intervention research. *Young Children.* April 1972, pp. 227–239.

———. Parent-professional interaction: Research, parental, professional, and policy perspectives. In R. Haskins (Ed.), *Parent education and public policy.* Norwood, N.J.: Ablex, 1983.

Schorr, L. B., & Schorr, D. *Within our reach: Breaking the cycle of disadvantage.* New York: Doubleday, 1988.

Shipman, V. C., Boroson, M., Bidgeman, B., Gart, J., and Mikovsky, M. *Disadvantaged children and their first school experiences.* Princeton, N.J.: Educational Testing Service, 1976.

Sigel, I. E. Early childhood education: Developmental enhancement or developmental acceleration? In S. L. Kagan & E. F. Zigler (Eds.), *Early Schooling.* New Haven: Yale University Press, 1987.

Silvern, S. B. Continuity/discontinuity between home and early childhood education environments. *The Elementary School Journal, 89* (2), 1988, pp. 147–159.

Skeels, H. Adult status of children with contrasting early life experiences: A follow-up study. In *Monographs of the Society for Research in Child Development, Vol. 31.* Chicago: University of Chicago Press, 1966.

Spitz, R. A. *The first year of life.* New York: International Universities Press, 1965.

Spodek, B. (Ed.). *Handbook of research on early childhood education.* New York: Free Press/Macmillan, 1982.

Tizard, J., & Hodges, J. The effect of early institutional rearing on the development of eight-year-old children. *Journal of Child Psychology and Psychiatry, 19,* 1978, pp. 99–118.

Umansky, W. On families and the re-valuing of childhood. *Childhood Education, 59* (4), March/April 1983, pp. 259–266.

U.S. Department of Education. *What works: Research about teaching and learning.* Washington, D.C.: U.S. Government Printing Office, 1986.

_____ . *What works: Schools that work: Educating disadvantaged children.* Washington, D.C.: U.S. Government Printing Office, 1987.

Walberg, H. F. Families as partners in educational productivity. *Phi Delta Kappan, 65* (40), February 1984, pp. 397–400.

Wasik, B. H. *Teaching parent problem-solving skills: A behavioral-ecological perspective.* Paper presented at the American Psychological Association Meeting, Anaheim, Calif., August 1983.

Watson, T., Brown, M., & Swick, K. J. The relationship of parents' support to children's school achievement. *Child Welfare, 72* (2), March/April 1983, pp. 175–180.

Weikart, D. R., & Lambie, D. A. "Preschool intervention through a home teaching program." In J. Hellmuth (Ed.), *Disadvantaged child. Vol 2: Head Start and early intervention.* New York: Brunner/Mazel, 1968.

Westinghouse Learning Corporation and The Ohio State University. *The impact of Head Start: An evaluation of the effects of Head Start on children's cognitive and affective development.* Springfield, Va.: Clearinghouse for Federal Scientific and Technical Information, 1969.

White, B. The Center for Parent Education newsletter. Newton, Mass.: Center for Parent Education, October 1985.

White, B. L., Kaban, B. T., Attanucci, J., & Shapiro, B. B. *Experience and environment: Major influences on the development of the young child. Vol. 1.* Englewood Cliffs, N.J.: Prentice-Hall, 1973.

White, S. H. The National Impact Study of Head Start. In J. Hellmuth (Ed.), *Disadvantaged child. Vol. 3: Compensatory education: A national debate.* New York: Brunner/Mazel, 1970.

Yarrow, L. J., Rubenstein, J. L., & Pederson, F. A. *Infant and environment.* New York: Wiley & Sons, 1975.

Yogman, M. W., & Brazelton, T. B. *In support of families.* Cambridge: Harvard University Press, 1986.

2

Historical Overview of Family Life and Parent Involvement

How long have you been aware of or concerned about parent involvement in education? The eruption of parent education and parent involvement programs in recent decades tended to erase the historic roots of the parent education movement. Schools and government agencies stressed the importance of teachers working with parents as if a new strategy were emerging.

Actually, a traditional concept was being re-emphasized. The many new programs that resulted were rich in design and control and produced additional knowledge about the whys and hows of programs involving parents. There have been periods in the past, however, when parents *were* the natural advocates of their children and partners in the educational process.

It is meaningful to compare the emergence of educational programs to the economic conditions and social thought of the corresponding historic periods, for there is a relationship between societal developments and the childrearing practices and educational theories of the times. Note the impact of the Russian Sputnik on the emphasis on cognitive development during the 1960s. Or go back into history and relate the needs of the poverty-stricken children in Switzerland in the 1700s to the educational beliefs and practices of Pestalozzi. The history of parent education and involvement can be pictured as the constant ebb and flow of the ocean's tide. Some eras portray a calm; others are characterized by tumult. As rapid changes, social problems, poverty, and political unrest produce turbulence for families, their need for stabilizing forces increases. So in the 1960s with the call for a "War on Poverty" and the achievement of a "Great Society," there emerged a focus on the family as one institution that could affect the lives of millions of disadvantaged children. The call was strong and resulted in renewed interest in programs in child care centers, home-based education, and combined home-school intervention projects. The emphasis on individualism and families in the 1980s and 1990s has called for increased parent involvement. Concentrating on the fabric of recent programs, we tend to overlook the threads of the past.

PART 1
Early History

PREHISTORIC PARENT EDUCATION

Since the beginning of civilization, family groups and parents have been involved with the rearing of their young. Before the development of written records, which is believed to have occurred between 6000 and 5000 B.C., early humans had developed a primitive culture. To ensure survival they had to develop means to obtain food and water for sustenance and provide protection from harsh weather and predators. Picture a primitive family group with children modeling their parents' actions. Children accompanied their parents on food forays and learned to obtain their food supply, whether through hunting, fishing, producing crops, or gathering wild foods. Parents also taught them rules and regulations for participating as members of both the family group and of a larger society. A study of contemporary primitive groups in Brazil substantiates the fact that nonliterate people use the oral tradition to pass on accumulation of time-tested wisdom and practices.

Primitive education aims to transmit unchanged from the adults to the young, the beliefs, practices and attitudes that have stood the test of time and proved successful in the environment in which one's ancestors lived. (Frost, 1966, p. 8)

Primitive societies did not develop schools; the prime educators were the family and community. "The pressures of the group plus the need to survive and to be accepted are powerful incentives to learning" (Frost, 1966, p. 9). Children were valued for both their contribution to survival and for their implied continuance of society. They were the future—they would carry on the traditions of the culture as well as provide the basic needs of the group.

An important education agency in every culture is the family. Here [are] to be found both formal and informal education. Parents teach their children by merely living with them in the family group. They are examples which children follow instinctively. They also teach directly by telling and showing, by praising when the children conform and punishing when they fail to measure up to the standards set by the family group. The family is first in time, and in many ways the most important teaching agency in any society. (Frost, 1966, p. 12)

For thousands of years the society's important customs, rules, values, and laws were learned and internalized by children so that they could function within their cultural groups. This process of socialization is prevalent in all groups, primitive or highly developed. Without it, children do not develop into functioning human beings as defined by the culture in which they live.

There continue to be cases in highly developed societies where children have not been socialized. Isolated children who have been forced into closets and neglected exhibit characteristics that are not recognized as human. They may speak in croaking noises, waddle instead of walk, exhibit intense fear, and react in a manner atypical of a socialized child. Informal learning and socialization are necessary ingredients in human development. Emile Durkheim declared: "Education consists of a methodical socialization of the young generation" (as cited in Brembeck, 1966, p. 12). During prehistoric times, just as today, the first teachers—the socializers—were parents and families.

FORMAL EDUCATION IN EARLY SOCIETIES

Our knowledge of education in cultures of ancient civilizations with written records is more extensive. In the valleys of the Tigris-Euphrates and the Nile Rivers, where the ancient civilizations of Sumeria, Babylonia, Assyria, and Egypt flourished, formal learning joined forces with informal learning. Concern for formal education emerged when there was a need to "preserve order in communities of mankind and to main-

Egyptian boys were educated in the home during the Old Kingdom. During the Middle Kingdom, schools developed outside the home. Portrait panel from mummy of a Jewish boy, probably from the Fayum. Encaustic on wood panel, second century A.D. (The Metropolitan Museum of Art. Gift of Edward S. Harkness, 1917–18.[18.9.1])

tain a stable society and a viable state . . . and to help man become more fully and completely himself, more attuned to God, the possessor of greater personal fullness of being" (Braun & Edwards, 1972, p. 4). During the Old Kingdom in Egypt, 5510 to 3787 B.C., children were educated in their homes. During the Middle Kingdom, 3787 to 1580 B.C., there were indications that school outside the home developed (Frost, 1966). Artwork depicts Egyptians as placing their children in high esteem. Adults show affection for their children by holding them on their laps and embracing them. Children were also viewed as children, running, playing with balls, and jumping at leapfrog and hopscotch (Bell & Harper, 1980). As in Sumeria, both boys and girls were important to the family and were given opportunities to learn (Chambliss, 1982). Formal systems of education also existed in ancient India, China, and Persia, as well as in the pre-Columbian New World, particularly in the Indian cultures of the Mayas, Aztecs, and Incas. The system that had greatest carry-over and effect on Western thought, however, was the educational system of ancient Greece (Braun & Edwards, 1972).

PARENT INVOLVEMENT IN EDUCATION AND FAMILY LIFE IN GREECE

The Athenian state produced philosophy and social thought that is still studied in schools. As far back as the sixth century B.C. regulations governed schools: parents were responsible for teaching their sons to read, write, and swim; schools were to be in session for a certain number of hours; a public supervisor was to be appointed; and free tuition was provided for sons of men killed in battle. Schools were nonetheless private, and parents had the right to choose the pedagogue or school they desired for their children.

Greeks viewed children as children but also as a link to the future, the conveyors of culture and civilization, as well as valued members of a family. They focused on close supervision rather than physical punishment as the way to guide children (Bell & Harper, 1980).

Real concern over education blossomed during the golden age of Greece. Plato (427 to 347 B.C.) questioned theories of childrearing in his dialogues in the *Republic.*

Do you not known, then, that the beginning in every task is the chief thing, especially for any creature that is young and tender? For it is then that it is best molded and takes the impression that one wishes to stamp upon it.

Quite so.

Shall we, then, thus lightly suffer our children to listen to any chance stories fashioned by any chance teachers. . . .

By no manner of means will we allow it.

We must begin, then, it seems by censorship over our storymakers and what they do well we must pass and what not, reject. And the stories on the accepted list we will induce nurses and mothers to tell to the children and so shape their souls by these stories far rather than their bodies by their hands. But most of the stories they now tell we must reject. (as cited in Hamilton & Cairns, 1971, p. 624)

Plato even felt that the games children played should be controlled. He believed so strongly that a child could be molded to fit the needs of society that he wrote in his *Laws:*

To form the character of the child over three and up to six years old there will be need of games. . . . For when the programme of games is prescribed and secures that the same children always play the same games and delight in the same toys in the same way and under the same conditions, it allows the real and serious laws also to remain undisturbed. (as cited in Bell & Harper, 1980, p. 15)

In the *Republic,* "an exercise in philosophic imagination" (Becker & Barnes, 1961, p. 180), Plato designed an ideal city-state in which genetics and procreation would be controlled by the state to produce children who, when grown, would be capable of administering affairs of state (Chambliss, 1982). Parent education was not for the benefit of the family or its individual members; it was designed to strengthen the communal state.

Although Aristotle (384 to 323 B.C. disagreed with Plato's thoughts about the desirability of a communal ideal state, he, too, felt education was too important to leave to the financial ability of the parents. Aristotle did not place the privilege or the burden on the parents. In providing education by the state, he attempted to control the socialization and education of children to fit the needs of the state (Chambliss, 1982; Frost, 1966).

PARENT INVOLVEMENT AND FAMILY LIFE IN ROME

During approximately the same period, family life in Rome was flourishing, and parents were actively involved with their children's education. The high priority placed on children resulted in concern for their development, with the parents being their first educators. Polybius (204 to 122 B.C.) and Cicero (106 to 43 B.C.) both wrote of the importance of the family in the development of good citizens. Cicero declared:

For since the reproductive instinct is by Nature's gift the common possession of all living creatures, the first bond of union is that between husband and wife; the next, that between parents and children, then we find one home, with everything in common. And this is the foundation of civil government, the nursery, as it were, of the state. (as cited in Chambliss, 1982, p. 226)

Cicero believed, as Aristotle had, that man was a social and political creature and that human virtues are developed through social participation.

In Rome, as in Sparta, the mother was the first teacher of her children, but she had a greater role in academic education than the Spartan mother and taught the children to read. The father soon encouraged his sons to learn business acumen and citizenship. The mother taught her daughters the obligations, responsi-

Families were important to Romans, and fathers placed high priorities on their sons' education. Francesco Sassetti and His Son Teodoro. Fifteenth century portrait by Domenico Ghirlandaio (Domenico di Tommaso Curradi di Doffo Bigordi). (The Metropolitan Museum of Art. The Jules Bache Collection, 1949, [49.7.7])

bilities, and skills necessary to be a homemaker (Frost, 1966).

It should be noted that from the era of primitive cultures, through Greco-Roman days, to modern times, laws and customs illustrate that infanticide, abandonment to exposure, and sale of children were common practices. (Read de-Mause, 1974, pp. 25–33.) Children had few rights. Roman fathers held power of determination over their children, even to the extent of deciding upon life or death. In primitive societies, when the population became too large for the limited food supply, infanticide or exposure was used to reduce the population (Bossard & Boll, 1966). The need for survival became a guide for practices of infanticide. "Sometimes it was under the direction of the state, as in ancient

Sparta, or among the Romans, whose Twelve Tables forbade the rearing of deformed children, or at the discretion of the parents, as among the Athenians" (Bossard & Boll, 1966, p. 491). In most societies where infanticide or similar practices occurred, once the decision to keep children was made, they were raised as were other children within the culture.

Concern for eradication of child desertion, infanticide, and the selling of children began to grow around the first century A.D. Rewards were offered to those who reared an orphan. Refuge and asylum for abandoned children were offered by the church, which further testified to

Christians believed that all lives were sacred in the eyes of God. This reduced the practice of infanticide and abandonment of young children. Madonna and Child, Fifteenth century. Fra Filippo Lippi. (National Gallery of Art, Washington, D.C. Samuel H. Kress Collection.)

the emergence of concern for children (Bossard & Boll, 1966). Finally, in 374 A.D. an imperial edict prohibited the exposing and consequent death of infants (Bell & Harper, 1980).

Education and family life during the golden civilizations of Greece and Rome and in early Christian times had become important. A subsequent decline in the importance of the family occurred during the Middle Ages, and the concern for parent involvement did not emerge again until many centuries later.

EUROPEAN CHILDREN DURING THE MIDDLE AGES

As the Roman Empire declined, turmoil, famines, and warfare made family life very difficult if not impossible. The major concern of all was for survival. Adults and children were not given different treatment (Bell & Harper, 1980).

A feudal system emerged, which provided a protective though restrictive social order for the people. During the Middle Ages, approximately 400 to 1400 A.D., children were very low among society's priorities. "The prevailing image of the child was that of chattel, or piece of property consistent with the ideology of serfdom" (Elkind, 1987, p. 6). Children of serfs and peasants learned what they could from their parents and peers. There was no system of education and, due to the lack of privacy, very little family life. Living conditions did not provide the poor with an opportunity for privacy or time with their families. Thus, learning was accomplished by working with parents in fulfilling the menial tasks required to subsist on the feudal estates (Aries, 1965; Frost,

Peasant children worked the fields with their parents. Landscape with Peasants. Louis Le Nain, c. 1640. (National Gallery of Art, Washington, D.C. Samuel H. Kress Collection.)

1966). As children worked and participated in everyday life, they were socialized into the way of life—the values, customs, and means of existence for the poor.

On the other hand, children of noblemen were reared and taught in their homes until the age of 7. Life in a medieval castle, built for defense rather than for family life, was difficult for children. The children of nobles were precursors of the emerging middle- and upper-class families of the seventeenth and eighteenth centuries. They inherited property and were educated for their future duties. They, too, were socialized into the values and social graces of their families, but beyond that they were also taught reading, ciphering, and the art of penmanship. Because the men were often away on missions and women were left to run the estates, both sexes were taught the practical needs of caring for the household and land. After the age of 7, boys were sent to apprentice in another family. Boys from the upper classes learned skills and duties befitting a nobleman and the art of chivalry, while commoners were apprenticed to learn a craft, trade, or agriculture. The custom of education by apprenticeship existed for many centuries.

EARLY PARENT EDUCATION BOOKS

The invention of the printing press around 1450 made books available to a much larger segment of the population. Only the wealthy, however, were able to purchase them for personal use.

Savonarola (1452–1498), a physician and teacher, gave advice on teaching children to talk:

Around the age of 2, when the infant begins to talk and to have some knowledge, one should skillfully and alluringly encourage the child to utter different words, while saying "My little-baby" and calling him by name; and at that time you should have a certain thing that he likes and say, "I will give you this if you repeat what I say," and then similarly vary from one word to another. In this, women are usually quite experienced. (as cited in Demaitre, 1977, p. 476)

The change in children's lives between the fourteenth century, when children were still tied to apprenticeship systems, and the seventeenth century, when the family was organized around children, is illustrated by the change in etiquette books. Those published in the 1500s were restricted to etiquette, while *La civilitie nouvelle,* written in 1671, included children as part of the family system. One of the very early parent education books contained directives for parents to use as they taught children their letters. It even included the proper way to discipline and control children (Aries, 1962). For the first time in history, authors were speaking directly to parents.

CHILDREN OF THE REFORMATION

Beginning with the twelfth century and continuing through to the seventeenth century, an awareness of childhood began to evolve, as depicted in the art of the time. European societies, emerging from a time of suffering and hardship, along with the influence of the Protestant Reformation and the Catholic Counter-Reformation viewed the child as one in whom evil must be suppressed and the soul nourished. (Bell & Harper, 1980) Throughout the Middle Ages, the Catholic church was a primary influence on people's behavior. When Martin Luther (1483–1540) introduced his Ninety-five Theses, he opened the floodgate for religious change. The most important aspect of the Protestant Reformation was the concept of a priesthood of believers, where people were expected to learn to read and study the Bible for themselves and thereby find their own salvation. Luther believed that people should be able to read the Bible in their own language. He brought his beliefs to the people and wrote the Sermon on the Duty of Sending Children to School, in which he pointed out to parents that they should educate their children. He recommended that children learn their catechisms, and he encouraged the use of Aesop Fables for the teaching of morals.

Noble children, dressed as young adults, were reared to run estates by other noble families rather than their own parents. Edward VI as a Child. Hans Holbein, the Younger, sixteenth century. (National Gallery of Art, Washington, D.C. Andrew Mellon Collection.)

As the church grew in medieval times, children began to be viewed as pure and innocent, representative of the Virgin Mary and infant Jesus, on the one hand and depraved and evil because of original sin on the other (Bell & Harper, 1980).

The Catholic Counter-Reformation saw the founding of the Jesuit Order, which made much progress in religious education. These advancements in education permeated educational practices both in Europe and the United States. The religious tenor of the times also influenced social thought and, consequently, childrearing practices for centuries.

THE BEGINNINGS OF MODERN PARENT EDUCATORS AND CHILD DEVELOPMENT THEORISTS

The modern parent educator began to emerge during the seventeenth century, but the general population was not affected until the nineteenth century. New ideas about education and the importance of the home in the education of children were developed by social thinkers such as Comenius, Locke, Rousseau, Pestalozzi, and Froebel, all of whom rejected the concepts of original sin and depraved children.

Paintings depict society's view of the young. Poussin's painting is one of the earliest to show infants as plump babies rather than small adults. The Assumption of the Virgin. Nicolas Poussin, 1626. (National Gallery of Art, Washington, D.C. Ailsa Mellon Bruce Fund.)

John Amos Comenius (1592–1670)

Comenius, born in Moravia in 1592, was a member and bishop of the Moravian Brethren. A religious man, he believed in the basic goodness of each child as opposed to the concept of original sin. This idea is reflected in his writing about education methodology; his thinking was more advanced than that of others who lived during the same period. In *Didactica Magna,* a large treatise on education, he discussed the importance of the infant's education, stressing that children, when young, can be easily bent and shaped. In the *School of Infancy,* written in 1628, he emphasized that education began at home and described in detail the manner in which young children should be educated. Comenius also wrote textbooks for children. *Orbis Pictus* (The World in Pictures) is considered to be the first picture book for children (Morrison, 1984). Although a prolific writer, he was unable to change the direction of education during his lifetime.

John Locke (1632–1704)

John Locke, an Englishman who was educated at Christ Church College, Oxford, had far-reaching and innovative ideas concerning government and education. Probably, he is best known for the concept that the newborn's mind is a *tabula rasa,* or blank slate, at birth. All ideas develop from experience; none are innate. It is incumbent upon family and teacher to provide optimum environment and valuable experiences for the thriving of the child's mind.

Locke, who lived during the period when hardening of the child was in vogue, was a staunch supporter of the concept. If children were exposed to cold baths and other methods of hardening, they were supposed to be more resilient to diseases and ailments. A strong body would house a quick and able mind.

Although Locke recognized the home as the optimum environment for children, he suggested, as Commissioner of the London Board of Trade, that orphans and children of the poor be taken from homes at 3 years of age and placed in working schools until they were 14, at which time they would be apprenticed to learn a trade (Frost, 1966). Although the plan might seem harsh, indigent families of the late 1600s did not have the means or family system to provide an adequate environment for growing children. Locke devised the plan so mothers could help secure an income and children would receive a basic education of religion, vocational training, and discipline.

Jean Jacques Rousseau (1712–1778)

Rousseau was another giant in the development of changing European social thought. As thoughts of greater freedom for humans evolved, stirrings of freedom for children also emerged. As a political analyst, Rousseau wrote *Social Contracts* in 1762, in which he described government through consent and contract with its subjects. This desire for freedom extended into his writings concerning children. Although Rousseau allowed his five children to be placed in foundling homes soon after birth, he wrote charming books about child development. In *Emile,* written in 1762, he charged, "Tender and provident mothers . . . cultivate, water the young plant ere it die; it will one day bear fruit delicious to your taste. Set up a fence betimes round your child's soul, others may mark its circuit, but you must build the barrier" (as cited in Archer, 1964, p. 56). In *Julie* and *La Nouvelle Heloise,* he expressed concern that children be allowed freedom: "Nature means children to be children before they become men" (as cited in Archer, p. 28). Rousseau's writings resounded with the child's need to grow free and untainted by society.

Johann Heinrick Pestalozzi (1747–1827)

Johann Heinrick Pestalozzi was a Swiss educator and a sensitive social activist influenced by the writings of Rousseau. After his father died when he was only 5, he was reared by his mother and nurse in a sheltered restrictive environment. His greatest joy came during his visits to his grand-father, Andrew Pestalozzi, pastor at Hoenigg near Zurich. Here he accompanied his grandfather on pastoral calls and saw the mean and hungry depths of abject poverty starkly contrasted with the accumulated luxuries of wealth. These impressions and his later work at the university fermented into a zeal for righting the wrongs inflicted on the poor.

He read Rousseau's *Emile* and was so impressed that he used it as a guide for the education of his own child. Pestalozzi believed in the natural goodness of children and struggled for many years teaching and caring for poor children in his home.

Pestalozzi based his teaching on use of concrete objects, group instruction, cooperation among students, and self-activity of the child. To teach mathematics, he used beans and pebbles as counters and divided cakes and apples to demonstrate fractions. The child's day also included recreation, games, and nutritious snacks and meals (Gutek, 1968). Pestalozzi is remembered primarily for his writings; in his first successful book, *How Gertrude Teaches Her Children,* he declared: "Dear Gessner, how happy shall I be in my grace, if I have contributed something towards making these springs known. How happy shall I be in my grave, if I can unite Nature and the Art in popular education, as closely as they are now separated" (Pestalozzi, 1915, p. 29). His statement rings of the free and natural education of children as professed by Rousseau.

Pestalozzi wanted to help the poor and give their children an opportunity for education. The Cottage Dooryard. Adriaen van Ostade, 1673. (National Gallery of Art, Washington, D.C. Widener Collection.)

The first modern theorist to stress the parents' vital roles in the education of their children, Pestalozzi can be hailed as the "Father of Parent Education." He stridently emphasized the importance of the home. "As the mother is the first to nourish her child's body, so should she, by God's order be the first to nourish his mind" (Pestalozzi, 1951, p. 26). He saw the effects of the environment on the young charges he taught and noted the significance of parents in this way: "For children, the teachings of their parents will always be the core, and as for the schoolmaster, we can give thanks to God if he is able to put a decent shell around the core" (Pestalozzi, 1951, p. 26).

Friedrich Wilhelm Froebel (1782–1852)

The "Father of Kindergarten," Friedrich Froebel, was born in 1782, 35 years after Pestalozzi. Although Froebel is most noted for his development of a curriculum for the kindergarten, he also recognized the importance of the mother in the development of the child. He saw the mother as the first educator of the child and wrote a book for mothers to use with their children at home. The book, *Mother Play and Nursery Songs with Finger Plays,* included verses, pictures, songs, and finger plays still used today, such as "pat-a-cake, pat-a-cake." Froebel's plan for education grew around a concept of unity. He organized his curriculum to follow the natural unfolding of the child with the mother assisting in the development. The child and mother enjoyed the language and interaction. Visualize the small child and mother playing the following game:

> *Count your baby's rosy fingers.*
> *Name them for him, one by one.*
> *Teach him how to use them deftly.*
> *Ere the dimples all are gone;*
> *So, still gaining skill with service,*
> *All he does will be well done.*

> (Blow & Eliot, 1910, p. 147)

The mother was involved in teaching her child, guided by Froebel's curriculum.

The development of his kindergarten had significant impact on the current philosophy of education. Instead of a prescribed curriculum designed by the adult to teach the child to read, write, and be moral, the curriculum was developed from the needs of the child. The concept of child development and teaching to the individual levels of each child was a radical departure from lockstep education.

CHILDREN IN THE SEVENTEENTH AND EIGHTEENTH CENTURIES

Ambivalent feelings about children and their place in the social system were reflected during the seventeenth and eighteenth centuries. Montaigne reflected this attitude in the following statement:

Our jealousy in seeing children appear and enjoy life when we are about to part with it makes us more grudging and strict with them. We resent it when they step on our heels as if to urge us to be gone. And if we are afraid because, to tell the truth, it is in the order of things that they can exist and live only at the expense of our existence and our life, then we should not get mixed up in the business of being fathers. (as cited in Hunt, 1970, Preface)

Childrearing during this era was analyzed by Hunt (1970) in *Parents and Children in History.* The use of a wet nurse to nourish and provide milk for the child was a necessary and common occurrence during this period. Another characteristic of the period was the swaddling of young infants, which seems to have been done primarily to provide warmth, because buildings were damp and drafty. The infants were bound from head to toe in a cloth band (maillot) approximately 2 inches wide with their arms at the sides and legs extended. Later, between the first and fourth month, the arms were released, and the child could use them. Usually at around 8 or 9 months, the infant was unswaddled. Babies were unwrapped when it was necessary to clean them. Although it may seem that swaddling might have retarded growth and development, this does not

Froebel recognized the importance of the mother's interaction and play with her children. Madame Stumpf and Her Daughter. Jean-Baptiste-Camille Corot, 1872. (National Gallery of Art, Washington, D.C. Ailsa Mellon Bruce Collection.)

appear to be the case. After they were unswaddled, babies were soon encouraged to walk. Louis XIII was running by 19 months of age and playing the violin and drum at approximately 1 ½ years (Hunt, 1970).

Strict discipline and physical punishments were the mode of child guidance. Children could be physically punished for crying, lying, and being obstinate or headstrong. Louis' father wrote to Madame de Montglat, who was caring for Louis, and requested punishment:

I have a complaint to make; you do not send word that you have whipped my son. I wish and command you to whip him every time that he is obstinate or misbehaves, knowing well for myself that there is nothing in the world which will be better for him than that. (Hunt, 1970, p. 135)

Belief in physical punishment was stronger in France and England during the late 1700s than it was in Italy and other European countries.

The eighteenth century was one of tremendous upheaval, filled with social change and

Van Dyck's painting illustrates the manner in which children were dressed and treated as adults. Filippo Cattaneo, Son of Marchesa Elena Grimaldi. Sir Anthony van Dyck, seventeenth century. (National Gallery of Art, Washington, D.C. Widener Collection.)

poor and poverty-stricken, who lacked the means to have much semblance of family life.

The disinterest of the wealthy in their children encouraged the continuation of placing babies to be fed and reared by a wet nurse. In France and England mothers placed their children with countrywomen to be cared for until they were 2 or 3 years of age. Or, if very wealthy, they hired nurses to come into their homes.

The use of wet nurses was not condoned by authorities in England and France. The French physician, Guillemeau, in *De La Norriture et Government des Enfans,* stated "there is no difference between a woman who refuses to nurse her own children and one that kills her child as soon as she has conceived" (as cited in Lorence, 1974, p. 3). William Cadogan criticized the practice when he wrote in 1748, "I am quite at a loss to account for the general practice of sending infants out of Doors to be suckled or dry-nursed by another woman.... The ancient Custom of exposing them to wild Beasts or drowning them would certainly be much quicker and humane ways of despatching them" (as cited in Lorence, 1974, pp. 3, 4).

These writings and those of Comenius, Rousseau, Pestalozzi, and Froebel illustrate a new spirit of humanism and a recognition of children as human beings with some rights. Sometimes these rights were subjugated to the belief that children must be totally obedient to their parents in order to grow properly. These parents represent the second category, those who wanted to guide, direct, and mold their children in very specific patterns.

Susanna Wesley, mother of John Wesley, the founder of the Methodist religious movement in England, could never be criticized for overindulgence. Regarding her child-rearing beliefs, she wrote:

I insist upon conquering the will of children betimes, because this is the only strong and rational foundation of a religious education, without which both precept and example will be ineffectual. But when this is thoroughly done, then a child is capable of being governed by the reason and piety of its parents, till its own understanding comes to matu-

restlessness. In France this political and social unrest resulted in the French Revolution. In England growth in industry created a demand for labor. Toward the latter half of the eighteenth century and during a major portion of the nineteenth century, the Industrial Revolution created an atmosphere of poverty and misuse of children as laborers.

Families tended to fit into three categories: the wealthy, who allowed others to rear their offspring and who exhibited indifference to children; the emerging middle class, who wanted to guide, direct, and mold their children in very specific patterns (Lorence, 1974); and the rity, and the principles of religion have taken root in the mind. (as cited in Moore, 1974, p. 33)

Children of poor families were often sent to workhouses and foundling homes, and these were hardly nurturing environments for the young. As soon as the child was old enough to work, apprenticeships were found, and, most often, the child was misused as a source of cheap labor.

Despite the strict discipline imposed on the young of all classes, there was a degree of light and free times for some children in England. There were many recreational diversions. The theater was immensely popular and occasionally upper-class children accompanied parents, but, more often, children attended puppet shows. They also played organized games, including many that are still popular today such as blind-man's bluff, hide-and-seek, teeter-totter, cricket, hockey, and football (Bossard & Boll, 1966). Rhymes and fairy tales prevailed. Mother Goose tales, published in 1697, gave parents a collection of rhymes and stories to read to their children. Many of the favorite nursery rhymes

read to children today originated during this period, including, among others, "To Market, To Market"; "Little Boy Blue"; "Baa, Baa, Black Sheep"; "Jack and Jill"; "Who Killed Cock Robin?"; "Tom, Tom, the Piper's Son"; and "The House That Jack Built." Many of the rhymes were political statements of the times but were used then, as today, as favorite poems for children.

Such were the diverse methods of childrearing in Europe at the time of the settling and colonization of the future United States. Depending on their station in life in the old country, settlers had varied childrearing practices, but there was some homogeneity within the colonies. More consistency developed as colonists faced common conditions in a new frontier.

THE FAMILY IN COLONIAL NORTH AMERICA

Colonists settled three major areas: New England, the middle colonies, and the southern colonies. In the new country, the concept of the

Life was not all work and no play. Children and adults found pleasure in games and outdoor activities as depicted in this ice skating scene. A Scene on the Ice. Hendrick Avercamp, 1625. (National Gallery of Art, Washington, D.C. Ailsa Mellon Bruce Fund.)

family had unique importance. Children were valued in the frontier because cutting homesites from raw land, constructing houses and outbuildings, tilling the soil, and harvesting the crops required great physical efforts. Eager hands were needed to survive.

The religious zeal of the New England Puritans permeated family life and influenced childrearing practices as it defined the duties of parents and children, husbands and wives, and masters and servants. Benjamin Wadsworth, in a 1712 essay entitled *The Well Ordered Family: Or Relative Duties,* gave directives on proper marital relationships. Husbands and wives were to be supportive of and loving toward one another. "Though they owe duty to one another, yet to God's Law that declares and prescribes what that duty is; when therefore they fail in duty, they not only wrong each other, but they provoke God by breaking his Law" (1972, p. 41).

Wadsworth further advised parents on their relationships with their children. He also out-

Cards were another popular pastime in the Eighteenth Century. The House of Cards. Jean Baptiste Simeon, c. 1735. (National Gallery of Art, Washington, D.C. Androw W. Mellon Collection.)

Visualize a young man passing the time of day by blowing soap bubbles. Soap Bubbles. **Charles Amedee Philippe vanLoo, 1764. (National Gallery of Art, Washington, D.C. Gift of Mrs. Robert W. Schuette.)**

lined the duties of the children to their parents. Both mothers and fathers should love their children as Abraham had loved Isaac. Mothers were expected to nurse their children. Parents were required to provide religious instructions, pray for their children, and see that they were well "settled in the World." Although parents were to care for their children, they were not to be overindulgent. Children were to be brought up with diligence and to have respect for the law.

Children were not "to laugh or jear at natural defects in any, as deafness, blindness, lameness, or any deformity in any person but teach them rather to admire God's mercy; that they themselves don't labour under such inconveniences." Children were to love, fear, revere, and honor their parents. They were to be obedient and faithful, for "when children are stubborn and disobedient to Parents, they're under awful symptoms of terrible ruine (sic)."*

---

*Quotations from Wadsworth are from Rothman & Rothman, 1972, pp. 55, 58, 87, and 97.

Wadsworth's essay was followed in 1775 by Eleazar Moody's *The School of Good Manners.* In the preface, his theme was supported by a quote from Proverbs 22:6—"Train up a Child in the Way he should go, and when he is Old he will not depart from it." The complete title, *The School of Good Manners: Composed for the Help of Parents in Teaching Children how to Behave During Their Minority,* explains the purpose of the essay. Indeed, this was a parent education book for the colonies. Chapter 2 contained 163 rules for children, which included those governing behavior at the meeting house, at home, at school, or in the company of others. Following are a few of the rules:

Be not hasty to run out of the Meeting-house when the Worship is ended, as if thou wer't weary of being there.

Never sit in the presence of thy Parents without bidding, tho' no stranger be present.

Approach near thy Parents at no time without a Bow.

Dispute not, nor delay to Obey thy parents Commands.

There were many rules of behavior to be followed in company. Children were not to sing, hum, cough, or sneeze. They were not to gnaw their nails, lean upon the chair, spit on the fire, cross their legs, or play with their fingers. As if these requirements were not enough, the child was to speak clearly and not drawl or stumble. Perhaps it was easier for them to be seen and not heard! Parents were not without ample guidance in the rearing of their children.

New England schools reinforced stern discipline and instruction in good manners, as well as providing religious teachings. Breaking the will of obstinate young pupils was handled through corporal punishment. The birch rod, the flapper (a 6-inch-wide leather strap with a hole in the center), ferules (flat pieces of wood used to smart the palms of students' hands), and the cat-o'-nine-tails were used in schools to enforce discipline (Bossard & Boll, 1966).

The essays of Cotton Mather, Benjamin Wadsworth, and Eleazar Moody, all published in Boston, reflected the lifestyle in New England.

Families were important to the new settlers in the United States. Children were expected to act with respect and to follow specific rules of conduct. The Copley Family. John Singleton Copley, 1776–1777. (National Gallery of Art, Washington, D.C. Andrew W. Mellon Fund.)

Childhood in the northern colonies implied adherence to a strict and complicated code. The families in the middle colonies were a more heterogeneous group ranging from the Dutch in New York to the Quakers in Pennsylvania. Those who settled in the south, though as concerned about their children, were more gentle and solicitous in their guidance.

The families in all three regions were patriarchal, and the father's word was an ultimatum for children. Colonial laws supported parental authority. An early New York law exemplified the extreme to which demands for respect of parental authority could be carried.

If any Child or Children, above sixteen years of age, and of Sufficient understanding, shall smite their Natural Father or Mother, unless provoked and forct for their selfe preservation from Death or Mayming, at the complaint of said Father or Mother, and not otherwise, they being sufficient witness thereof, that Child or those Children so offending shall be put to Death. (as cited in Bossard & Boll, 1966, p. 504)

The early settlers had brought a diversified and rich cultural heritage from Europe. They were still influenced by European social thought, but they were developing their own individual life-styles and educational systems. Through the colonial years, the "family carried the greatest burden. . . . The family continued to be an important center of training even after colonial society developed" (Middlekauff, 1969, p. 281).

The voyage to the Americas was difficult and the mortality rate was high. Many children arrived parentless in their new land. The Steerage. Alfred Stieglitz, 1907. (Metropolitan Museum of Art. Collection of Alfred Stieglitz, 1933. [33.43.420−469])

EARLY EDUCATION IN THE SPANISH SOUTHWEST

While family life on the eastern seaboard of North America was developing, Spain was extending its settlement of Mexico and the American Southwest. Spain's initial reason for exploring north of the Rio Grande was to seek wealth.

Later, settlements were established to claim the land for Spain and spread the Catholic faith.

Life in these settlements developed quite differently from the structures of the eastern colonies of the northern Europeans. Some of the Spaniards had been given land for their military service; others obtained their land by "squatters' rights." Spanish colonists included continentals (those born in Spain), Spaniards born in the New World, mestizos (offspring of Spanish and Indian marriages), Indians, and slaves. Each of the first three classes looked down on the classes below it. Wealthy Spaniards, who received land grants from the viceroys, seldom mixed with the mestizos or Indians, except to employ them as overseers for their haciendas. The major educational force was the family, with religious guidance coming from Catholic missionaries. Families resulting from intermarriage, however, tended to mix religious customs. The parents of the Indian child, as well as the parents of the mestizo and the Spanish child, served as the major educators of their children. Parents and the extended family were responsible for what was largely the informal education of their children into the customs and work ethic of the area.

The Spanish brought their value of strict supervision of their daughters to the Southwest. A Girl and Her Duenna. Bartolome Esteban Murillo, ca. 1670. (National Gallery of Art, Washington, D.C. Widener Collection.)

The Jesuit and Franciscan priests, who wanted to convert all people to Catholicism and teach Spanish to the Indians, were not encouraged by the viceroys from Spain to establish schools, so no formal system of education was developed during the early days in the Southwest. Children did not need to learn to read the scriptures because priests cared for their religious needs.

DEVELOPMENT OF THE FAMILY CONCEPT

Concurrent with thoughts of the child as a unique individual was the development of the family into a more cohesive and private unit. In eighteenth century Europe, however, this evolution was limited to families of means. In the early nineteenth century, the greatest proportion of families, those who were poor, lived as they had in medieval days, with children separated from their parents. Living conditions were crowded, and there was little privacy. Children were either apprenticed at a young age or remained with their parents and labored from dawn to dusk to earn their keep. Between the eighteenth and twentieth centuries, the European concept of family did not change, but the ability to have a family life extended to those who were not wealthy (Aries, 1962).

In this respect, the pattern in the colonies differed from that in Europe. Families were able to become cohesive social entities in early colonial life. They were able to establish homes and work together to provide food for the table. The Puritans took their roles as parents especially seriously and, in their zeal, developed strong family patterns and rigid goals and guidelines.

The land of opportunity did not exist, however, for persons brought to the New World as slaves. Family life was not allowed to develop; mothers and children were separated from fathers by the whim of their owners. It was not until after the Civil War that former slaves were free to redefine their family roles and structures. This early loss of human rights had a complex and

The family was strong and developed as a basic social unit in the United States.

continuing effect on the economic and social history of the black family in the United States.

CHILDREARING IN THE 1800s IN THE UNITED STATES

The colonies were now the United States. The first hard years of recovering from a war for independence, of building a new nation, and fighting the War of 1812 were over. Instead of looking to Europe or relying solely on the religious guides of the clergy, families began to read from steadily increasing publications in the United States.

Robert Sunley analyzed this period by drawing from original works concerning childrearing in nineteenth century magazines, journals, re-

ports, children's books, medical books, and religious texts. Some of the earliest included *Advice to Mothers on the Management of Infants and Young Children,* written by W. M. Ireland in 1820, and *Hints for Improvement of Early Education and Nursery Discipline* by Louise Hoare, published in 1829. *Mother's Magazine* published "To Mothers of Young Families" and "Hints for Maternal Education" in 1834 and "Domestic Education" in 1838 (Sunley, 1955). *Parents' Magazine* (not related to the current publication) was published from 1840 until 1850. Childrearing advice consistently emphasized the significance of the mother's role in the care and upbringing of the child. Fathers were, for the most part, ignored in the childrearing literature.

Mothers were encouraged to breastfeed their children. Babies were to be weaned between 8 and 12 months of age, and mothers were not to extend the period by many months. Loose, light clothing was recommended, but heavy overlayers seemed to be prevalent, and swaddling was customary in some areas. Cradles were used, although mothers were not to rush to the side of the cradle if the baby cried. Immediate response to a baby's crying was thought to encourage more crying.

Early toilet training was recommended as a means of "establishing habits of cleanliness and delicacy." Standards for personal neatness and cleanliness were high, and children were expected to wash often (Sunley, 1955, p. 157).

Articles advised strict moral training, reflecting the Calvinist doctrine of infant depravity, which required strict guidance reminiscent of earlier days. Children were not to be spoiled, and parents were to expect total and immediate obedience. "It was considered fatal to let the child win out" (Sunley, 1955, p. 160). Breaking children's wills freed them of what was believed by many to be children's basically evil natures. European influence was thereby evident and reflected a strong cultural carryover.

Mothers were intent on their responsibilities of childrearing. Brim (1965) cited parent group meetings as early as 1815 in Portland,

Even after emancipation, black Americans had a difficult life and worked long hours while they attempted to keep their families together and cared for. *Cabbages.* Thomas Pollock Anshutz, 1879. (The Metropolitan Museum of Art. Morris K. Jesup Fund, 1940. [40.40])

Maine. Mother study groups were formed before 1820 in other parts of the country as well. Called Maternal Associations, these parent groups generally consisted of middle-class members of Protestant-Calvinist religious groups (Brim, 1965). They were interested in proper moral training and discussed methods of childrearing that included discipline and breaking the child's will. Sunley pointed out that there were two

other theories of childrearing besides the religious moral emphasis discussed earlier. One was the idea of "hardening" the child, which probably stemmed from Locke and Rousseau. "Children should become strong, vigorous, unspoiled men like those in early days of the country" (Sunley, 1955, p. 161).

A third theory had a more modern ring of nurturing. Sunley cited the theory as having "its roots in English and European movements." Children were treated in a gentle and persuasive manner with "understanding and justice" and with "consistency and firmness" underlying the nurturing (Sunley, 1955). This guidance was thought to enable children to reach their potential.

It seems that the third theory reflected thoughts of Pestalozzi and Froebel. Their influence was felt in the United States through the interest of professional educators and new prominent German immigrants. In 1856 Mrs. Carl Schurz founded the first kindergarten in the United States in Watertown, Wisconsin (Weber,

During the nineteenth century, three theories of childrearing prevailed: strict childrearing as reflected in the Puritan ethic, hardening of the child as suggested by Locke, and looking at children as flowers that needed to be nurtured. Miss Juliana Willoughby. George Romney, 1781–83. (National Gallery of Art, Washington, D.C. Andrew W. Mellon Collection.)

1969). This school, based on Froebelian theory, was in marked contrast to the authoritarian and rigid traditional schools of the period.

Economic upheavals made the young country ripe for change. "The Industrial Revolution was one of the most severe social crises which had thus far taken place in the history of human society" (Becker & Barnes, 1961, p. 598). There was great misery and suffering among the poor, and those concerned with human lives either sought to improve or ignore the paralyzing conditions. Those who wanted to remedy the dire plight of the poor came from a school of philosophic thought represented by Owen, Robertson, and Mill, English social scientists who advocated improvement of the human condition. The other attitude was exemplified by Herbert Spencer, who felt that government interference and social reforms would not help the poor but would produce greater social ills (Becker & Barnes, 1961).

On the other hand, education for parenthood was essential for direct and indirect self-preservation and was considered more significant than preparation for citizenship (Spencer, 1900). Although parenthood was considered of great importance to Spencer, government intervention to improve the quality of family life was not. Although not the originator of Social Darwinism, his thought echoed the belief in the survival of the fittest and was reflected for years in the lack of government programs for the poor. The use of private philanthropic programs to ease the burdens of the poor was acceptable to Spencer, because those who were giving received satisfaction from their contributions and were doing a social "good."

In the 1860s, the country was torn apart by the Civil War. During the war and Reconstruction, change came about for women. Women began to take over farmwork and to carry out all the obligations generally reserved for their husbands. Women also filled the void left by men who resigned from teaching (Calhoun, Vol. 2, 1960), and their prior experience with children brought forth a more nurturant environment in the educational system.

After the Civil War, women did not return to the same subservient positions they had held previously. Calhoun described the change:

The whole movement signifies an extension of woman's economic independence of man, and the breaking down of that barrier of inequality that had so long served to keep woman in a subordinate place in the household. While the Civil War did not start the movement, it did greatly stimulate, and . . . helped to unsettle the foundation of "mediaeval" family which was now passing out and through a transition of storm and stress yielding to the new family of equality and comradeship. (Vol. 2, pp. 361 and 362)

The change in woman's role in the family and the new feeling of equality encouraged later formation of women's clubs and the resultant emphasis within those organizations on parent education.

The Civil War tore the nation apart. Women were called upon to teach in the schools to take the place of teachers who left to fight the war.

Change was coming to education as well as to family life. During this same period, the mid-1800s, the kindergarten movement was gaining strength. Henry Barnard, Secretary of the Connecticut Board of Education and later United States Commissioner of Education, became enthused by Froebelian materials at the International Exhibit of Education Systems in London in 1854. Information was disseminated by Barnard in the *American Journal of Education* and a volume, *Kindergarten and Child Culture Papers,* edited by him. He became recognized as the father of the kindergarten movement in the United States.

Elizabeth Peabody, a sister-in-law of Horace Mann, was also a staunch supporter of the kindergarten movement and helped to spread the "good word" about the kindergarten methods of Froebel. Most importantly, Elizabeth Peabody crusaded to introduce the kindergarten throughout the land and spread her beliefs about the natural goodness of children. Throughout her life, she was an apostle of Froebelian kindergarten. She believed that the system had come to him through revelation (Weber, 1969). Since she and Henry Barnard had great stature in educational circles, they were able to make a substantial impact on educational thought.

Froebel's *Mother Play and Nursery Songs* was translated into English. This gave parents an opportunity to use Froebelian activities in their homes. In 1870 there were only four books on kindergarten, but by the end of the decade five more books had been translated, four more written, many articles printed and distributed, and two journals, *The Kindergarten Messenger* and *The New Education,* were flourishing (Vandewalker, 1971).

Peabody and Barnard firmly established Froebelian kindergarten in the United States. Pestalozzi and Froebel's belief that parents are integral components of education influenced the educational roles of parents. A climate for change, the possibility of perfectibility of man, and reverence for motherhood prevailed. Thus, the time was ripe for the parent education movement to begin.

PART 2
More Recent History of Parent Education and Child Development

Parent education and childrearing practices reflect the times in which they occur. The first parent education programs held in Maine in 1815 reflected the concern of the time—breaking the will of the child. Children in the United States were still viewed as willful and depraved, needing to have their sinfulness banished. The free kindergarten programs of the 1890s reflected the perceived need that immigrant and poor children had to learn the ways of the establishment, particularly in regard to health habits and cleanliness. Many of the parent education programs established in the 1920s were the consequence of tuberculosis and the need to spread health information.

The theories that were taught during parent education sessions reflected the beliefs of the time. As you read the rest of this chapter, reflect on the changes in childrearing practices. Note the impact that G. Stanley Hall, Freud, Watson, Skinner, Erikson, Spock, and Piaget made. As their theories became known, childrearing practices changed. Relate that to today as the process of sharing information continues. The remainder of this chapter is divided into decades that reflect the changing parenting skills and childrearing practices.

1880 TO 1890

Toward the close of the nineteenth century there was a growing belief in the perfectibility of man and society. Education was viewed as an avenue to achieve that end. Thus, kindergarten was believed to be an excellent instrument to reach children while they were still young enough to be guided in their moral development. Settlement houses were established in the 1880s and 1890s for the urban immigrant groups who arrived in the new land, destitute and without

sufficient means to earn a livelihood. The kindergarten was used by the settlement houses as a means of alleviating the suffering of young children. Educators were also able to reach parents with information about childrearing and Froebelian curriculum. Industry, neatness, reverence, self-respect, and cooperation were seen as results of the properly directed Froebelian kindergarten, and these moral beliefs were linked to both individual and societal advancement" (Weber, 1969, p. 39).

The Women's Christian Temperance Union (WCTU) also supported the kindergarten movement and education of parents by establishing WCTU kindergartens in at least 20 cities (Weber, 1969). Free Kindergarten Associations were formed throughout the United States. By 1897, there were more than 400 of these Associations actively involved in the education of young children and parents. The WCTU developed a course using Froebel's belief in unity with a sequential curriculum for use with mothers of young children. Settlement houses and Free Kindergarten Associations worked with the lower socioeconomic groups and new immigrants. The concern and interest shown the poor and the philanthropic commitment to alleviate suffering reflected the awakening of renewed social conscience. The kindergarten movement and parent education were strengthened by the development of humanism and the belief in the child's innate goodness (Weber, 1969).

By the 1880s, this growing emphasis on childrearing and education emerged from two additional sources. Associations organized by women in the late 1800s were the first source and included The Child Study Association of America (CSAA), formed in 1888 by a group of interested New York City mothers; The American Association of University Women, founded in 1882 by college graduates; The National Con-

An upswing in the infuence and activities of women began in the 1880s. Many of the groups were interested in child development and children's learning. They recognized the importance of parent involvement as shown in this painting. Jungle Tales. James J. Shannon. (The Metropolitan Museum of Art. Arthur Hoppock Hearn Fund, 1913. [13.143.1])

gress of Parents and Teachers, the PTA, organized by women who gathered from across the nation at a meeting in 1897; and The National Association of Colored Women established in 1897.

The associations founded in the 1880s made a lasting impact on parent education in the United States. Throughout its history, the CSAA emphasized child study and parent education; it was the earliest and largest organization solely committed to the study of children. Its earliest programs were studies by authorities of the time, that is, Spencer, Rousseau, Froebel, and Montessori (Brim, 1965). The organization engaged in a wide variety of activities and services—all related to children and parents. These included child study groups, lectures and conferences, consultation services, lending libraries, publications on subjects of interest to parents, a monthly magazine, and leadership training (Brim, 1965; Fisher, 1933; National Society for the Study of Education, 1929; Schlossman, 1976).

The second group, The American Association of University Women (AAUW), has implemented a diverse educational program, including the study of children and parent education. The third,

PTA, has been concerned with parent-school relationships since its inception. The National Association of Colored Women focused on civic service, social service, and education with committees on home and the child, mothers, and legislation. Another group, the General Federation of Women's Clubs, formed in 1889, ushered in an even greater interest in women's roles as leaders. These organizations, with the exception of the Child Study Association, are still actively involved in the field of education in the 1990s.

When G. Stanley Hall, a charismatic psychologist at Clark University, was elected president of Clark in 1889, he founded a child study center. Children had not been the center of scientific research prior to that time. Hall wanted to determine what was in children's minds. Using a questionnaire method of research, he first used associates and assistants at the university to gather data. As his research progressed, he extended the use of questionnaires to teachers throughout the country and then to thousands of parents. To answer the questions, parents needed to observe their child's speech and behavior. This natural observation was a learning experience for the observer as well as a device for collecting data. Although many of the completed questionnaires contained questionable answers, Hall and his associates (Patty Smith Hill and Anna Bryan studied under him) compiled some very provocative recommendations. "Above all, he counseled parents, be indulgent with young children; treat them as young animals, who simply have to behave as they do. Childhood was an easygoing, cavorting stage which youngsters must pass though peaceably if they were eventually to become mature, self-controlled adults" (Schlossman, 1976, p. 443). Even though his child study movement was short lived and was replaced by the research of Thorndike, Cattell, and Watson in the 1900s, he remains important to parent education for his

institutionalization of child study and his influence on the founding of the PTA.

From this period forward, the development of effective childrearing practices and parent education was not the effort of just a few interested individuals. Child study had been made a part of a college program by Hall, and strong organizations, founded and sustained by dedicated, interested men and women, are actively involved in parent education today.

1890 TO 1900

The 1890s were centered around the family, with defined roles for mother, father, and children. The father's duty was to financially support the

Most American families in the late nineteenth century lived in small rural communities or on farms such as the one pictured here.

family while the mother controlled the home. Women's clubs were flourishing. Well-to-do mothers were able to join one of the many clubs available to them. Those who were on a lower socioeconomic level were served by settlement houses and the Free Kindergarten Association.

Stendler (1950)—who analyzed the first year of every decade from 1890 until 1950 from articles in three popular magazines, *Good Housekeeping, Ladies' Home Journal,* and *Woman's Home Companion*—found an immense amount of interest in childrearing in the 1890s and early 1900s. The home environment was recognized as very important in the formation of character. Mothers were idolized as the epitome of purity and goodness, and children were thought to model after the mother in their character development. It was important then that the mother be the right kind of person. The father was earning the family fortune, and the mother was looked up to as knowledgeable and

capable of rearing children. If these magazines reflected the interests of their readers, the subjects of physical development and character formation were overwhelming in their appeal, for 73% of the articles were written on these two subjects in 1890 and 50% in 1900. It was very important to provide a good home environment for the rearing of children, as reflected by 61% of the articles in 1890 and 53% in 1900. To achieve this environment, young children were given tender loving care, and infants were fed on demand. Character was best formed through provision of a good home with love and affection between mother and child, although 15% of the articles said that divine aid was also a help.

This style of childrearing reflects G. Stanley Hall's belief in the goodness of the child. Hall's study on children indicated that the young child should not be overdirected but allowed to grow easily and naturally. Hall thought that children should be kept out of school until they were 7 or

Country schools educated many of the youth in the primarily rural nineteenth-century United States. This famous painting depicts young men playing crack the whip during a recess. Crack the Whip. Winslow Homer, (The Metropolitan Museum of Art. Gift of Christian A. Zabriskie, 1950. [50.41])

8 and allowed freedom to explore or be given a kindergarten experience in an unstructured environment (Schlossman, 1976).

Hall's influence at the turn of the century was strongly felt due to espousal of his theories by the PTA. The organization was active in political affairs and worked toward passing child labor laws, pure food and drug acts, and housing legislation (Schlossman, 1976). The PTA was always concerned about child study, and study groups were formed in connection with the public schools. Publications about children and education were issued, and there was a strong focus on interaction and cooperation between parents and teachers. Parent education and in-

The period between 1890 and 1910 witnessed an explosion of popular interest in children as evidenced by the great number of magazine articles on child development. G. Stanley Hall, who felt children should be kept out of school until they were 7 or 8, represented the growing academic interest in children.

volvement became an institutionalized part of the school through action of the PTA.

1900 TO 1910

Two additional organizations related to parent education were created during the first decade of this century. In 1908 the American Home Economics Association was formed. Primarily an organization of teachers of home economics in colleges, public schools, and after 1914, extension programs, the organization emphasized home management related to homemaking and parenthood such as food preparation and nutrition. Their mission was to share their expertise with students and families. Members did this through county extension classes for homemakers, parent groups, conferences, public school and college classes, and publications. Emphasis gradually included child development and family enrichment (Brim, 1965; National Society for the Study of Education, 1929). In 1909, the second organization, the National Committee on Mental Hygiene, was formed. Because there was concern with improving mental hygiene, the emphasis on mental health increased during succeeding decades. In 1950 this group merged with others to form the National Association of Mental Health.

This period saw change emerging in education as well as in childrearing. John Dewey, along with Hall, emphasized the need for change in childhood education. Dewey, William Kilpatrick, Francis Parker, and Patty Smith Hill drew away from traditional structured educational practices toward a curriculum that included problem solving, learning by doing, purposeful activity, and social aspects of education.

While educators in the United States were moving toward a child-oriented, problem-solving curriculum, Maria Montessori was establishing another educational form in Italy. Concern for poverty-stricken children caused Montessori, an Italian physician, to establish Casa dei Bambini, a children's home in a tenement section of Rome. In 1907, she designed a specific program, structured so that children learn by

Families were important in the late 1800s and early 1900s. Mothers were revered. The extended family supported and helped one another.

doing. By teaching children precisely how to use equipment, she was able to help children overcome their impoverished environment. Her methodology—more structured than that of American theorists—did not find wide acceptance in the United States until the 1960s.

There were also poverty-stricken children in the United States. Forced to work under horrendous conditions at a very young age, children who were undernourished, neglected, or abused prompted a rising social concern. As a result, the first White House Conference on Care of Dependent Children was called in 1909. The Children's Bureau was created in 1912 as a consequence of the conference, a first step in government concern for children.

1910 TO 1920

Soon after the first White House Conference on Care of Dependent Children in 1909, the gov-ernment began disseminating information on child care. The first *Infant Care,* a popular parent education book on child care for infants, was published in 1914 by the federal government agency that is now the U.S. Department of Health and Human Services. The Smith-Lever Act of 1914 provided 2000 County Home Demonstration agents. This county extension program included education in homemaking, improved nutrition, and child care. Later, the Smith-Hughes Act of 1917 established "home-making" as a vocation and included a provision for education in child care and nutrition through extension classes, demonstrations, and institutions under the auspices of the Office of Education. The next year, the United States Public Health Service began programs for parents on children's health (Brim, 1965). Government entered the field of parent education through creation of the Children's Bureau, provision for county demonstration agents, and concern for children's health.

Colleges and universities also entered the field by establishing research and teaching centers devoted to the study of children. The State University of Iowa instituted a child study center in 1911. In 1917, the Iowa Assembly appropriated funding for the establishment of the Iowa Child Welfare Research Station at the State University of Iowa. Its purpose was the "investigation of the best scientific methods of conserving and developing the normal child, the dissemination of the information acquired by such investigation, and the training of students for work in such fields" (as cited in National Society for the Study of Education, 1929, p. 286). Thus, preschool laboratories for psychologic studies and an infant laboratory for study of nutrition were established. The first concerted effort to distribute findings to parents did not occur until the 1920s, when programs in parent education were offered throughout the state. The Yale Psycho-Clinic and The Merrill-Palmer School of Homemaking were also pioneers in the study of children and made valuable contributions to the understanding of children and to the development of parent education (National Society for the Study of Education, 1929).

Twelve faculty wives at the University of Chicago—with guidance from the university—established the first parent cooperative in the United States in 1916. The women wanted quality child care for their children, parent education, and time to work for the Red Cross during the war (Taylor, 1981). This cooperative, the only one established in that decade, followed the tradition of English nursery schools established in 1911 by Margaret McMillan. McMillan originally designed an open air school for the poor in England. She emphasized health, education, play, and parent education, rather than mere child watching. The concept of the nursery school was welcomed by middle-class American families, as illustrated by the first parent cooperative in Chicago. Thus, parent cooperatives and the growth of nursery schools in the United States strengthened and promoted parent education.

Although authorities during the 1890s and early 1900s had emphasized love and affection in the formation of character, a new trend suggested that discipline through punishment was necessary to assure character development. Parents were advised to use more discipline in the establishment of character in their children. Discipline (reward or punishment) was discussed in 14% of the surveyed magazine articles in 1900 and jumped to 34% in both 1910 and 1920. Providing a good home influence, which had commanded the attention of 53% of magazine articles in 1900, was the focus of only 30% in 1910 and dropped to 12% in 1920 (Stendler, 1950). The increased attention to strict childrearing was illustrated by the first issue of *Infant Care*. Autoerotic activities, such as thumbsucking and masturbation, were thought to be extremely dangerous. It was felt that if such activities were not brought under control, they could permanently damage the child. "While he was in bed, he was to be bound down hand and foot so that he could not suck his thumb, touch his genitals, or rub his thighs together" (as cited in Wolfenstein, 1953, p. 121). During the day, thumb-sucking was handled by covering the hand with cotton mittens or making the hand inaccessible to the child (Wolfenstein, 1953).

A drastic change in attitude was reflected by scheduling the infant's activities rather than responding to the baby's needs. In 1890, the infant's life was loosely scheduled. By 1900, 22% of the articles recommended tight scheduling for infants, and by 1910, 77% of the articles called for rigid scheduling of infants (Stendler, 1950). While breastfeeding was still highly recommended, a supplemental bottle could be given at 5 months, and the child was supposed to be completely weaned by the end of the first year (Wolfenstein, 1953). Mothers were told to expect obedience, to ignore temper tantrums, and to restrict physical handling of their children. These severe attitudes continued into the 1920s when all magazine articles on the topic recommended strict scheduling of infants (Stendler, 1950).

Throughout these periods there were exceptions to every trend (Brim, 1965). Although strict scheduling began around 1910 and continued through the 1920s and early 1930s, a book published in 1894, Holt's *The Care and Feeding of Children,* recommended "strict, routinized care of the child" (Brim, 1965, p. 169). Watson's *Psychological Care of Infant and Child* stated, "There is a sensible way of treating children. . . . Let your behavior always be objective and kindly firm. Never hug and kiss them, never let them sit in your lap. If you must, kiss them once on the forehead when they say goodnight. Shake hands with them in the morning" (as cited in Vincent, 1951, p. 206). Published in 1928, Watson's book appeared "when Freudian theory was well in its ascendancy" (Brim, 1965, p. 169). Between 1910 and 1920 the Child Study Association of America was emphasizing "love, support, and intelligent permissiveness in child care, based on the work of Freud, G. Stanley Hall, and other leaders in the clinical movement" (Brim, 1965, pp. 169–170). Vincent (1951) also noted that overlaps in theories occurred with reference to "tight scheduling" as late as 1948, and preference for self-regulation appeared as early as 1930. Even though the period of 1890 to 1910 stressed love and freedom, the period of 1910 to 1930 emphasized strict scheduling and discipline and self-regulation appeared in the late 1930s and 1940s, other theories were interwoven with these during the same periods.

1920 TO 1930

Early childhood as an important period for character formation was stressed in the 1920s. This belief was on the other end of the pendulum from Hall's belief in allowing the child to grow free and unrestricted. Behaviorists warned that parents should "do it right early or else" (Schlossman, 1976, p. 462).

During the 1920s many teenagers and young adults were viewed as reckless, overindulged, and spoiled (Schlossman, 1976). To reverse this scandalous situation, children were to be trained early to be responsible, well-behaved individuals. Watsonian behaviorism was beginning to be felt. This childrearing theory was mixed in the

1920s with the learning-by-doing theories of Dewey, a small portion of Freudian psychology, and Gesell's belief in natural maturation and growth. Although each theorist had a different approach, all recognized the importance of early experiences and the influence of the environment on the child's development.

The 1923 edition of *Infant Care,* issued by the Children's Bureau, admonished parents that "toilet training may begin as early as the end of the first month. . . . The first essential in bowel training is absolute regularity" (as cited in Vincent, 1951, p. 205). Although breastfeeding was recommended for 6 to 9 months, once weaning was commenced it was to be accomplished in 2 weeks. If the parents insisted on substitution to "artificial food," "the child will finally yield" (as cited in Wolfenstein, 1953, p. 125).

An explosion of parent programs accompanied the prosperity of the 1920s. The era reflected a swing from parent education offered by settlement houses for immigrants and free kindergartens for the underprivileged to the involvement of many middle-class parents in study groups for their own enlightenment and enjoyment. Yu studied the growth of parent education and reported that the decade of the 1920s brought forth 26 significant parent education organizations (as cited in Brim, 1965).

Abagail Eliot, who had worked with the McMillan sisters in London, started the Ruggles Street Nursery in Boston in 1922. Eliot was especially interested in working with parents as well as their children. The nursery school movement emphasized the family as partners in education (Osborn, 1980).

Parent cooperatives emerged at the following five locations in the 1920s: (1) Cambridge, Massachusetts, (2) the University of California at Los Angeles, (3) Schenectady, New York, (4) Smith College, and (5) the AAUW at Berkeley, California. The last, called Children's Community, has continued to flourish over the years and is the oldest continuous parent cooperative program in the United States (Taylor, 1981).

The parent cooperative movement, which developed rapidly in California but grew more slowly elsewhere until after World War II (Osborn, 1980), was a way for parents to obtain quality education for children. To participate, parents must share responsibilities—an excellent example of parent involvement.

Organizational membership growth also illustrated increased interest in parent education. PTA membership expansion depicted, in terms of sheer numbers, the growth in interest in parent programs. The organization grew from 60,000 in 1915 to 190,000 in 1920, to 875,000 in 1925, to nearly 1,500,000 in 1930 (Schlossman, 1976). AAUW membership rose to 35,000 in the 1920s, and each issue of its journal contained a column on parent education. Concurrently, the CSAA, recognized as the educational leader in parent education during the 1920s, grew from 56 parent groups in 1926 to 135 in 1927 (National Society for the Study of Education, 1929).

In 1922 Benjamin Gruenberg published *Outlines of Child Study: A Manual for Parents and Teachers.* This text on childrearing was used as a study guide for many parent groups. Succinct discussions on issues of child development were included in each chapter; for example, speech development, early years, habitual and emotional aspects of development, heredity, obedience, freedom and discipline, mental tests, adolescence, and emotional and intellectual development. Following each discussion was an outline and references for further reading (Gruenberg, 1927). Parents, along with a professional or lay leader, could read and discuss the issues. A need for trained leaders resulted in CSAA sponsorship of the first university course in parent education held at Columbia University in 1920.

Across the country many school systems implemented parent education and preschool programs. The Emily Griffith Opportunity School (Denver public school system) initially funded a parent education and preschool program in 1926. The early emphasis was on health education for families and expanded to childrearing theories and other parent skills as interests and needs changed.

The mushrooming of new parent organizations resulted in the CSAA's initiation of the National Council of Parent Education as a clearinghouse for parent education activities. The National Council was formed in October 1925. Representatives of 13 organizations attended and expressed concern that greater coordination was needed. Seventy organizations joined together in a concerted effort to coordinate various parent education efforts throughout the nation. The Council had a significant influence during its existence (1925 to 1938) on the expansion of parent programs through federal agencies, conference leadership, and advisement to parent education groups (Brim, 1965; Fisher, 1933; Gruenberg, 1940).

The tremendous strides in parent education that occurred in the 1920s could not have happened without financial support. Federal programs initiated from 1900 to 1920 continued to be funded through state and federal appropriations. The emergence of parent education in the schools was largely supported by local tax money and tuition or fees paid by the participants. Two private foundations, however, enabled many unique and innovative programs to progress. The Laura Spelman Rockefeller Memorial and the Spelman Fund contributed to private and public associations for the development of research and programs in parent education. Both funds were devoted to child study and parent education, and, as a result, many unique opportunities for research and implementation were offered associations and institutions. They contributed to child development study and parent education training programs, research centers for child study, and self-study programs by associations, such as the Home Economics Association and the National Congress of Parents and Teachers (Brim, 1965; Fisher, 1933; Gruenberg, 1940).

Colleges and universities received money from the Memorial and Spelman Fund for research, teaching, and dissemination of findings from their child study centers. Prominent during the 1920s were state universities in California, Minnesota, and Iowa; private universities (Yale and Columbia); and private institutions such as the Merrill-Palmer Motherhood and Homemaking School and the Washington Child Research

Center. In Canada, programs were established at McGill University and the University of Toronto. The goals of the universities and other institutions varied, but primarily they focused on three purposes: (1) research on the development of children, (2) training of professionals for services for and research on children, and (3) dissemination of information and education of parents (National Society for the Study of Education, 1929).

Most educational institutions established nurseries to be used in connection with their research and training. These nurseries involved parents and their children in an interactive process with the institution. With the exception of the parent cooperative established at the University of Chicago in 1916, the nursery school movement did not become a major part of the early childhood scene until the 1920s. Three were in operation in 1920, 25 in 1924, and 89 by 1928 (Goodykoontz, Davis, & Gabbard, 1947). Early childhood educators during this period saw the nursery school as a descendant of the English nursery. In England, however, the nursery fulfilled a need for the poor, while in the United States, the early nurseries were connected with universities and involved middle-class parents (Schlossman, 1976).

Concern for the mentally retarded emerged during the 1920s with separation and custodial care seeming to be the answer. "In regard to all mentally deficient children, it may be said that while we cannot improve their mentality we have reached the point where, by recognition of their capabilities and limitations, we can so place them in our social scheme that they may lead happy and useful lives" (Gruenberg, 1927, p. 230). This thinking has gradually changed over the years to the position of mainstreaming for the handicapped since the 1970s, and increased parent involvement and advocacy by parents of exceptional children.

The impact of early childhood concerns and parent education was so great during the 1920s that the *Twenty-Eighth Year Book* of the National Society for the Study of Education was devoted to preschool and parent education. This issue described the programs and listed conferences and agencies engaged in parent education during the 1920s. Refer to the *Twenty-Eighth Year Book* for a comprehensive report on the 1920s.

As the 1920s drew to a close, middle-class parents were active in parent groups, optimistic about the future, and concerned about health, nutrition, and shaping their children's actions. The financial crash of 1929 brought a tremendous change in the lifestyle of many families and set the stage for the 1930s.

1930 TO 1940

The 1930s ushered in the depression era with a necessary response to the needy and a broadening of concern for the family and family relationships as well as for the individual child (Fisher, 1933; Gruenberg, 1940).

The decade began with a White House Conference on Child Health and Protection in November 1930. Attended by more than 4000 specialists, the conference produced the following statement on parent education:

In view of the responsibilities and obligations being laid upon the family as the primary agency for child health and protection, as revealed by the recommendations of the various sub-committees of the White House Conference, this Committee strongly recommends that various educational associations and organizations and the educational departments of the different states be requested to study the possibilities for organizing parent education as part of the system of public instruction and that the professional groups and organizations concerned with children to be asked to study their opportunities and obligations for parent education. (as cited in the Pennsylvania Department of Public Instruction, 1935, pp. 9 and 10)

The 1930s reflected varying viewpoints on childrearing, ranging from strict scheduling to self-regulation. Fewer articles were written in the early 1930s than in the early 1920s, and when published, they emphasized physical development, nutrition, and character formation. Character formation began to take on broader meanings. Whereas it had meant moral development earlier in the 1900s, articles in magazines now included personality development (Stendler, 1950). Thumbsucking was still considered dangerous, but parents were admonished to divert the child's attention, rather than use restraints. "It is a natural habit . . . it should not excite parents unduly" (as cited in Wolfenstein, 1953, p. 123).

Parent education continued at a high level of participation during the first half of the decade. For example, Bulletin 86, *Parent Education* by the Pennsylvania Department of Public Instruction reported that parents were being reached through study groups, with more than 700,000 parents involved in group participation. Parents in the U.S. were also receiving information through the mass media: radio series, lectures, magazines, and distribution of more than 8 million copies of *Infant Care*. The following statement from the Bulletin emphasized the importance of parent education:

More and more it is being recognized that educators have a responsibility for providing professional leadership and for furthering the coordination of parent education activities in their communities. The job of the school is only half done when it has educated the children of the nation. Since it has been demonstrated beyond doubt that the home environment and the role played by understanding parents are paramount in the determination of what the child is to become, it follows that helping the parent to feel more adequate for his task is fully as important from the point of view of public education and the welfare of society as is the education of the children themselves. Moreover, an educated parenthood facilitates the task of the schools and insures the success of its educational program with the child. (Pennsylvania Department of Public Instruction, 1935, p. 12)

This high priority on parent education in the early 1930s extended across the United States. Parent education courses were offered in at least 25 states in 1932 (Brim, 1965). Aims and objectives published by the Pennsylvania Department of Public Instruction (1935) reflected the following high ideals:

1. To aid parents to interpret the findings of specialists in regard to various aspects of child and family life.

2. To give parents an opportunity to modify or change their attitudes toward their children and their behavior.
3. To serve as a device for personal adjustment.
4. To give an opportunity to consider civic problems affecting family living, and the relation of these problems to social and economic life in the community.
5. To provide a forum in which parents may verbalize their conceptions of the mores and attempt to adapt them to present conditions and trends.
6. To help develop a better understanding of the functions and purposes of education of various types and needs for these services. (p. 15)

These aims and objectives illustrate the trend toward environmental considerations and inclusion of the family as a part of parent education. Social and economic conditions were having an impact on family life and, consequently, the children within the family. The depression and a need to support families by offering information on budget, clothing, health, physical care, and diet precipitated parent education for the poor. Rehabilitation projects of the 1930s (Works Progress Administration) offered a forum for parents who were not active in women's clubs or parent-teachers associations to learn about home management practices. Established in October 1933, the Federal Emergency Relief Administration (FERA) authorized work-relief wages for unemployed teachers and others to organize and direct nursery schools; approximately 75,000 children were enrolled during 1934 and 1935 (Goodykoontz et al., 1947). It was the intention of FERA that the nursery programs be taken over by the schools when funds from the federal government were terminated. "It is my desire that . . . schools shall be so administered in the states as to build toward a permanent and integral part of the regularly established public school program" (Goodykoontz et al., 1947, pp. 60 and 61). Few, however, were taken over by the schools.

Parent education continued during the 1930s, and additional programs were available for the needy. Skeels (1966) and the Iowa group commenced their study of the effect of the environment on child development (see Chapter 1). Toward the end of the decade there was reduced emphasis on child development research in most areas and withdrawal of foundation support. The National Council of Parent Education had coordinated parent education programs and published a professional journal, *Parent Education,* from 1934 to 1938, but the support of the Spelman Fund was terminated in 1938, and this organization and the publications were disbanded.

In the early 1930s mothers were strongly influenced by scientific opinions from psychologists. The scientific method of discovering truths gave immense credibility to Watsonian psychology and behaviorism as opposed to the sentimentality of earlier childrearing practices. During this same period, the Freudian view of infantile fixation and the need for expression of repressed emotion by the child began to influence beliefs about children. This set the stage for the concern about emotional development prevalent in the 1940s.

1940 TO 1950

The parents of the 1920s and early 1930s who followed the specific rules of the behaviorists changed in the 1940s to persons who recognized

that no one answer could work for all situations (Brim, 1965). The emotionally healthy child was the goal for professionals and parents. Stendler (1950) pointed out that in 1940, 33% of the surveyed magazine articles on infant discipline favored behaviorism, while 66% endorsed self-regulation. "The swing from the 'be-tough-with-them, feed-on-schedule, let them cry-it-out' doctrines of the twenties and thirties was almost complete" (Brim, 1965, pp. 130, 131). Self-regulation allowed the development of trust and autonomy in the young child.

Vincent (1951) suggested that the decade between 1935 and 1945 could be called "baby's decade" with the mother "secondary to the infant care 'experts' and the baby's demands" (p. 205). By the early 1940s, mothers were told that children should be fed when hungry, and bowel and bladder training should not begin too early. Babies were to be trained in a gentle manner after they developed physical control. The latest version of *Infant Care* depicted the child as interested in the world around him and viewed exploring as natural. "Babies want to handle and investigate everything they see and reach. When a baby discovers his genital organs he will play with them. . . . A wise mother will not be con-

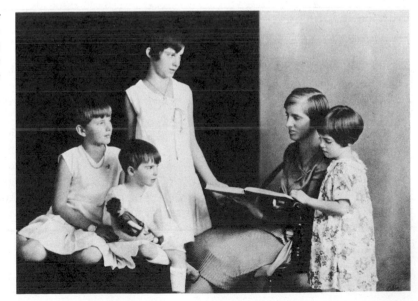

This mother, reading to her children, illustrates the emphasis on parent education that expanded in the 1920s and continued through the 1930s.

cerned about this" (as cited in Wolfenstein, 1953, p. 122).

Wolfenstein described the change in attitude toward the basic nature of humans as follows:

One of the most striking changes in American thinking about children from the nineteenth and early twentieth centuries to the more recent past and the present is the radical change in the conception of the child's nature. From the nineteenth-century belief in "infant depravity" and the early twentieth-century fear of the baby's "fierce" impulses, which, if not vigilantly curbed, could easily grow beyond control and lead to ruin, we have come to consider the child's nature as totally harmless and beneficient. (Mead & Wolfenstein, 1963, p. 146)

Shifts in beliefs about children were reflected in the childrearing practices of the period.

In 1946 Benjamin Spock, now a national best-selling author and parent educator, pub-

lished *The Common Sense Book of Baby and Child Care.* He believed the rules and regulations imposed on parents during the 1920s and 1930s caused undue pressure, and advised parents to enjoy their children and the role of parent. Spock pointed out the following in the 1957 edition of his book:

When I was writing the first edition, between 1943 and 1946, the attitude of a majority of people toward infant feeding, toilet training, and general child management was still fairly strict and inflexible. However, the need for greater understanding of children and for flexibility in their care had been made clear by educators, psychoanalysts, and pediatricians, and I was trying to encourage this. Since then a great change in attitude has occurred, and nowadays there seems to be more chance of a conscientious parent's getting into trouble with permissiveness than with strictness. So I have tried to give a more balanced view. (pp. 1–2)

Spock's book answered questions on feeding, sleeping, clothing, toilet training, management, and illnesses; he had an answer for almost all of the questions a new parent would have. No wonder it was a best seller. It is an example of widespread parent education through the media, and because it was used by many parents as their educational guide, it continued to have great influence on child rearing through the 1950s and beyond as children raised by Spock's methods became parents.

The 1940s, although consumed by the outbreak of World War II, saw no reduction in offerings for parent education. Parent groups continued in public schools, and county extension programs prospered. At least three states, Mississippi, South Carolina, and Georgia, expanded their state-supported programs. While services continued and emergency-relief nursery schools for workers involved in the war effort expanded, research and training in child development declined (Brim, 1965).

Both the depression and World War II brought federal support for children's services at a younger age. The Federal Emergency Relief

Having delayed becoming parents during the Depression and World War II, couples quickly made up for lost time and the Baby Boom began.

Administration regulated the child care funds originally, followed by the Works Progress Administration, and, during World War II, the Federal Works Agency (Goodykoontz et al., 1947). The need for support for families during the depression emanated from the necessity for parents to work to support their families. During World War II women needed child care services so they could join the war effort.

Parent education found added direction in the 1940s through the mental health movement. In 1946 the National Mental Health Act was passed. States were authorized to establish mental health programs and related parent education (Goodykoontz et al., 1947). The need to understand oneself and one's children was recognized as necessary for healthy parent-child interaction.

The decade ended quietly. The war was over, and the establishment of families, delayed by the war, was in full swing.

1950 TO 1960

The 1950s were years of relative calm, with emphasis on children and family life. Schools were feeling the increase in numbers of children and were rapidly expanding to meet the needs. Many young adults had postponed marriages and the starting of families during the war. With its completion, however, the "baby boom" began. The PTA had more than 9 million members and thousands of study groups among its 30,000 local chapters. Study groups used material on childrearing and special concerns of parents published by the PTA. Parents were involved with the schools as room parents and fundraisers for special projects. The view, "Send your child to school, we will do the teaching; your responsibility as a parent is to be supportive of the teachers and schools" prevailed as the basic philosophy between school and parents. The formal learning of reading, writing, and arithmetic started when the child entered first grade, the same as it had for many decades.

In a survey by the National Education Association, 32% of adult education classes were on family life (Brim, 1965). Parent education and preschool programs, part of adult education in many school districts, continued as a vital source of childrearing information. Pamphlets from the Child Study Association, Public Affairs Committee, Science Research Associates, and Parent Education Project of Chicago, plus books by authorities such as Arnold Gesell, Erik Erikson, B. F. Skinner, Benjamin Spock, Lawrence Frank, and Sidonie Gruenberg, were used as curriculum guides. During the 1950s James L. Hymes wrote his first book on home-school relations.

Orville Brim, sponsored by the Russell Sage Foundation and the Child Study Association,

In the 1950s, many families included the mother as a homemaker, father as the breadwinner, and two to three children.

examined the issues involved in parent education in his book *Education for Child Rearing*. His analysis of the effects of parent education continues to be relevant to the study of parent education today.

Your Child from 6 to 12, published by the U.S. Department of Health, Education and Welfare in 1949, illustrated the attitude that prevailed in the 1950s and subsequent years. The preface of the booklet reflected the change from the absolutism of the 1920s and 1930s: "There are many more things that we don't know than we know about children. . . . Every child is unique in temperament, intelligence, and physical make-up" (U.S. Department of Health, Education and Welfare, 1949, p. 39).

In the early 1950s thumbsucking was viewed as a natural rather than a negative occurrence. A baby "may try to get pleasure out of his thumb or fingers. Sucking is a poor substitute for being held, or talked to, or fed; but it is better than nothing" (as cited in Wolfenstein, 1953, p. 124).

Concern for mental health gave parents double messages; it was difficult to combine firm guidance and advice on emotional health. One such view on emotional health stated, "Any action that causes children to feel guilty . . . should be avoided. It is often better to say nothing whatever to the children, for fear of saying too much, or the wrong thing. Instead, divert their minds, give them new interests" (U.S. Department of Health, Education and Welfare, 1949, p. 38).

Erikson popularized the eight stages of personality development in *Childhood and Society*, first published in 1950. His neo-Freudian theories emphasized social and emotional development based on interdisciplinary theories from biology, psychology, and sociology. His theory outlines eight stages of growth from infancy to old age, beginning with development of trust and ending with achievement of ego integrity. Erikson and the childrearing practices of the 1950s reflected the belief that social and emotional health were of utmost importance to the child.

In a content analysis of *Ladies' Home Journal, Good Housekeeping,* and *Redbook,* 1950 to 1970, Bigner (1985) found articles primarily concerned with parent-child relations, socialization, and developmental stages. Spanking was condoned by some in the early 1950s, but by the end of the decade it was consistently discouraged and described as an inefficient and barbaric method that does no more than show the youngster that parents can hit. Most articles encouraged self-regulation by the child. Parents were told it was important that children feel loved and wanted. Parents were advised to hold, love, and enjoy their children and rely on their own good judgment for childrearing decisions.

Parents were encouraged to provide a home life that was supportive of individual differences and allowed each child to grow into a well-adjusted adult. Development was a natural process, and maturation could not be pushed. Gesell's work on development in psychomotor and physical areas supported theories that children proceed through innate developmental stages. As a consequence, parents were encouraged to provide a well-balanced nutritional diet and an environment that allowed children to grow and learn at their own rate.

To carry this idea a step further, the Parent Education Project of the University of Chicago, with financial aid from the Fund for Adult Education, developed a study curriculum, *Parenthood in a Free Nation*. The curriculum was concerned with rearing children to become "mature, responsible citizens of a free nation" and was based on six characteristics: "(1) feelings of security and adequacy, (2) understanding of self and others, (3) democratic values and goals, (4) problem-solving attitudes and methods, (5) self-discipline, responsibility, and freedom, and (6) constructive attitudes toward change" (Kawin, 1969, p. v.). The series of books discussed basic concepts for parents; early, middle, and later childhood; and adolescence. It also included a manual for group leaders and participants.

The Department of Health, Education and Welfare (HEW), established in 1953 with the

In the late 1940s and 1950s, children were fed on demand, loved, and cherished.

Social Security Administration, Office of Education, and Public Health Service under its jurisdiction, continued a diversified approach to parent education. The Office of Education was involved with parent education through state and local school systems and through the Home Economics Branch, whose specialists served as consultants and teachers at the state and local levels (Brim, 1965). The Children's Bureau, part of the Social Security Administration, had three sections related to parent education: the Research Division, Health Services, and Nursing. The Research Division was responsible for the publication of *Infant Care*. More than 60 million copies had been distributed to parents by 1955. The Division of Health Services, working through state social services and maternal and child health programs, supported parent education through training of nurses for leadership in parent education (Brim, 1965). Within the Public Health Service the National Institute of Mental Health continued education and developed research studies to evaluate the effects of parent education. Federal concern for and involvement in child rearing were reflected in the establish-

ment of HEW and the subsequent development of more programs.

Toward the end of the 1950s the nation's calm was disturbed. Russia's success in placing Sputnik into space caused a ripple effect across the United States. Why had the Russians achieved a feat not yet accomplished by the United States? Americans looked for an answer.

1960 TO 1970

The 1960s was a decade of sweeping changes in parent involvement, social and civil rights, and family characteristics. The family had been gradually changing since the early part of the century when the family was viewed with great sentimentality, mothers were revered, and the family was a sacred institution that few dared to question. By the 1960s it was common for all institutions—family, education, religion, economics, and government—to be criticized and questioned. Great changes in the American family took place from 1890 until 1960 as the country changed from a basically rural nation to an urban nation. The majority of families, which had been self-sufficient rural families with authoritarian parents, became dependent on others for income. As a mobile society evolved, one person in five moved each year for better jobs and better education. Children were no longer economic assets who helped their parents with the family farm or business; instead, they became financial liabilities, costing $20,000 to raise from infancy to 18 years of age (Hill, 1960). The many women who had continued working after World War II were joined in the 1960s by many more who returned to the labor force to supplement their husband's income or to increase their own economic freedom. For many women, who were single parents or were a supporting member of a two-parent family, working was an economic necessity.

The 1960s began a period of concern for intellectual and cognitive development in the young, but little change was evident between the 1950s and 1960s concerning social and emotional childrearing practices. Acceptance of the child was still emphasized. "Your pleasure in him as an infant and child will be the most precious gift you can give. Through your enjoy-ment of him as an infant and child, he becomes an adult who can give enjoyment to others and experience joy himself" (U.S. Department of Health, Education and Welfare, 1963, p. 1).

The importance of the father's relationship with his children was stressed, and although his obligations to his children were not the same as the mother's, early interaction with his newborn baby was recognized as very beneficial. "Fathers who feel comfortable giving physical attention to their babies at the start are lucky" (U.S. Department of Health, Education and Welfare, 1962, p. 29).

Parents had many child care books or booklets from which to choose. Publications from the Child Study Association and Science Research Associates and public affairs pamphlets covered many of the problems parents faced. Benjamin Spock continued to publish books on child care, and in them he advised firm, consistent guidance of the child. "A child needs to feel that his mother and father, however agreeable, have their own rights, know how to be firm, won't let him be unreasonable or rude. He likes them better that way. It trains him from the beginning to get along reasonably with other people" (Spock, 1957, p. 326).

The extended family gave strength to the African-American family.

Spock's efforts were aided by psychologist Haim Ginott, who offered parents a method for talking about feelings and guiding the child in a manner that avoided placing guilt and helped the child understand the parents' feelings, thus disciplining the child in a positive manner.

Professionals working with children and parents were greatly influenced by Piaget's theories of cognitive development. His ideas, clearly discussed by Hunt in his book *Intelligence and Experience* (see Chapter 1 of this book), emphasized active involvement of the child with the environment. Parents became much more concerned about their child's intellectual development and were no longer satisfied that development would unfold naturally.

When the Golden Anniversary White House Conference on Children and Youth convened, it delved into the concerns of the family and social change, development and education, and problems and prospects for remediation (Ginsberg, 1960). This conference was followed by a White House Conference on Mental Retardation in 1963. The time was ripe to meet the needs of all people—not just the dominant social class. The depression of the 1930s and World War II of the 1940s had kept the country occupied with emergencies. The affluent 1950s, impaired by the Korean War and the Cold War with Russia, gave cause for reflection. The 1960s brought forth many questions. Was the United States able to provide advantages for all its people? Was democracy and the free enterprise system capable of providing the best life for the most people? Could the United States surpass the Russians in the space challenge? These were the difficult questions, concerning millions of people, that faced the nation.

Although prosperity was available for most of the United States and the standard of living had steadily improved to the highest in the world, minorities, the handicapped, and the economically disadvantaged were still underemployed, poverty stricken, and ignored. The United States government had high hopes for a Great Society where poverty could be eliminated for all citizens. In the War on Poverty programs, children of the poor, who were undernourished, in poor health, without proper housing, and lacking educational opportunities, were chosen as a major target to realize hope for the future. The works of behavioral scientists and educators presented overpowering evidence that early environment has a profound effect on a child's development (Bloom, 1964; Hunt, 1961; Skeels, 1966). If children could be given equal environmental opportunities, the cycle of poverty could be broken. The stage was set for the birth of Head Start. As research indicated that parent involvement and family background were positively correlated with academic success, the inclusion of parents in their child's education program was entrenched from the beginning of the Head Start program.

In 1965 the Office of Economic Opportunity began an 8-week summer program for disadvantaged preschool children. In the fall the trial program was enlarged to encompass many Head Start programs, funded by federal money but administered by local agencies. Its name described its aims. Children who were disadvantaged would be given an opportunity to have a head start on school. The objectives included a comprehensive approach to child development centering on (1) strengthening and improving the child's physical health, social and emotional development, self-concept, mental processes, and cognitive development; (2) strengthening family relationships; and (3) encouraging self-help and self-determination by the family through career development and parent education.

To accomplish these objectives the specialists who planned the programs included a comprehensive approach with six major components: education, social services, health services, career development, administration, and parent education. A center-based program for children 4 to 5 years of age with outreach for parents through parent education, participation by parents on advisory boards, and career opportunities within Head Start made this an innovative and developmentally strong program for parents. The expectation of changing the cycle of poverty for all Americans with just one program for young children was unrealistic, but many success stories of parents and their families who were helped by Head Start can be related, and research supports the educational benefits. Head Start's influence was also felt in the public schools where parent components were mandated in many federally funded programs.

Shortly after the formation of Head Start, the Office of Education, Department of Health, Education and Welfare undertook direction for the Elementary and Secondary Education Act (ESEA) of 1965. Suddenly, twice the amount of federal money poured into schools that applied for and received grants. Public schooling, although still controlled by local boards of education, began to be influenced by federal spending. The federal money, funded through state agencies, was used to help eliminate the educational disadvantages of children in the public schools. Some of the Title (now entitled Chapter) projects under ESEA included:

1. Title I, which assists local school districts in improving the education of educationally deprived children. From its inception parents were involved in the program.
2. Title IV-C (formerly Title III), which promoted the innovative programs that enrich educational opportunities. Many of these projects included home visitation programs for preschool children, identification of handicapped children prior to school entry, and working with these parents for the benefit of their children.

Concern about continuity of educational success after Head Start resulted in the implementation of the Follow Through program as part of the 1967 Economic Opportunity Act. Designed to carry benefits of Head Start and similar preschool programs into the public school system, parent participation was a major component of the program, and as with the Head Start program, parent advisory councils were mandated.

Although not directly connected with parent education, the Civil Rights Act of 1965 had great influence on the role of minorities and women

during subsequent decades and, through this, had an impact on the family. Affirmative action, requiring minorities and women to be treated equally in housing, education, and employment, resulted in psychological as well as empirical changes in conditions for these populations. Although the increase in equality was not accomplished as the Civil Rights Act demanded, heightened awareness on the part of minorities and women had profound effects on their understanding of themselves, their relationships within the family unit, and their concern for equal opportunities.

Throughout most of this decade the Vietnam War affected family relationships, values, and social change. The war diminished the opportunity for success of the Great Society by funneling money and energy away from domestic programs. It also had immense impact on family unity because many families were torn apart over diverse values concerning drug use, participation in the war, and moral responsibilities. The parent of the adolescent cried for direction and guidance when confronted with overwhelming value changes in their children. Television, peer group influence, lack of consistent social and moral guidance, and involvement in the Vietnam War thrust parents into an arena for which they were not prepared by previous modeling of their parents or by education.

The decade closed with greater emphasis on parent involvement and education for low socioeconomic families than in any other era. Services for the disadvantaged were the concern of Montessori's work in Rome, Pestalozzi's school in Switzerland, Froebel's kindergarten, and, around the turn of the century in the United States, the settlement houses and Free Kindergarten Association's programs. Parent involvement of the 1960s, although reminiscent of these earlier programs, overshadowed them in scope, size, and participation. Backed by federal money rather than philanthropists, the War on Poverty attacked many areas. Whereas early programs were structured to inculcate immigrants and the poor into the values and customs of the dominant culture, the 1960s attempted to recognize the importance and viability of diverse cultural backgrounds and draw from the strengths of diversity with parents as active advocates for their children and themselves. Blacks, Chicanos, Puerto Ricans, underprivileged whites, and others of low socioeconomic background had the opportunity to express their needs and desires, and the Head Start program reflected each community.

1970 TO 1980

The enormous number of programs implemented in the sixties came of age in the 1970s. Development occurred in both private and public sectors with churches, local agencies, public schools, and clubs, as well as state and federal agencies, showing concern for families caught in the stream of social change. The country was still confronted with the Vietnam War at the beginning of the decade. With its end in 1973, one of the major disruptive forces on family unity was resolved.

The decade could be described as the era of advocacy. Groups were no longer willing to sit and wait for someone to do something for them; they had learned in the 1960s that the way to help is through self-help and self-determination. Parents of handicapped children, individually and through organizations such as the Association for Retarded Children, the Council for Exceptional Children, and the Association for Children with Learning Disabilities, advocated equal rights for the special child and won (see Chapter 9). Advocate groups for children sprang up across the land with training sessions on political power and means to implement change and protection for children. Child abuse and neglect were recognized as debilitating and destructive forces against children, and the concerns of the 1960s became a mandate to report all suspected cases of child abuse and neglect (Chapter 10).

The public schools were not immune. Parents began to question programs and their par-

The importance of fathers and grandparents was emphasized in the 1970s and 1980s. The opportunity for grandfather, father, and child to enjoy time together supports the child's development of self.

ticipation with schools and teachers. Forced integration and required busing were issues confronting schools and parents. Without family cooperation the schools were powerless to find an appropriate solution. In some cities parents who were not supportive of the schools were destructive to the integration process. Parents and schools had to work together in a partnership to have the educational system work, and many parents were interested in participating although not necessarily in a constructive way.

Over the years parent involvement in school decision making had diminished. Families in earlier centuries had the prime responsibility for education of their children. When formal education joined with informal education, parents still had decision making rights in regard to their child's schooling. In colonial days the church and family were the major institutions for the socialization of children. During the eighteenth and nineteenth centuries the community school increased in importance, but parents were still involved in decision making. Schools were small. Many country schools were dispersed across the nation, and schoolteachers were hired by the local school board, lived in the community, and were responsible to the local school district. Between 1890 and 1920 there was a shift from community to urban schools (Butts & Cremin, 1953; Goodson & Hess, 1975). The dramatic change from a rural society to an urban society resulted in a change in the control of schools. The process transferred control of schools from the community to professionals. Consolidation of rural schools into a larger, centrally located school improved equipment, facilities, and diversity of staff, but it took away parent influence. From the 1920s until the 1970s the steady flow from rural to urban areas increased the separation of school and families. Minorities and the poor were most alienated from the educational process. In the 1960s, with the recognition that the powerless must be instruments of their own change, parents were included on advisory councils, in career development programs, and in education of children. Parents had become involved in the educational process again.

In 1972, 16 Home Start programs serving 1200 families were launched. Eleven Child and Family Resource Programs serving 900 families were started in July 1973. "These programs, all built around a Head Start program, promote continuity of service by including all children in the participating family from prenatal stage through age 8, and broaden the program focus from the age-eligible child, to the entire family" (U.S. Department of Health, Education and Welfare, 1974, p. iii).

Concern about the link between Head Start and the public school resulted in funding for developmental continuity. Two types of program designs were investigated. One was based on a cooperative model with both Head Start and the schools working out a continuous educational program for the child. The other caused change within the existing school system and included programs for children 3 years and up as part of the school system as well as a curriculum struc-

tured for ages preschool through age 8. Both programs involved parents throughout preschool and school years.

Head Start and Follow Through continued to flourish with increasing emphasis on parent participation. The involvement of parents in the Follow Through program had an effect on public schools. Schools could model parent participation and use the same ideas in other school programs. The concept of partnership rather than intervention reflected the belief that it is only through parents, school, and agencies working together that lasting change in education is possible.

Children in the 1970s, according to the experts, continued to need love, consistent guidance, and an enriched and responsive environment. Concern over parent-child separation, particularly in a required hospital stay, was evident in advice given to parents. They were told to stay with the child if hospitalization were necessary. Bonding and the importance of early child-parent interaction was reflected in the research of Spitz, Bowlby, Ainsworth, Brazelton, and Klaus and Kennell.

Sexist referrals in texts, which implied innate differences between boys and girls or referred to children in masculine terms, became noticeable by their absence. Feminists joined civil rights activists and advocates of rights for the handicapped in elimination of stereotypes and inequality of opportunity. The 1970s moved forward, slipped backward, and consolidated gains for many who were not a part of the mainstream of life in the United States.

Mass media, affluence, the fast pace of life, employment of both parents, and unemployment or underemployment put a strain on family life. To complicate matters, children were maturing at a younger age. Communication among family members became more essential than ever because values and customs were changing so rapidly.

Concern over teenage pregnancies and the lack of parenting skills of young parents resulted in the development of curricula for young adults. *Exploring Childhood* (Education Development Center, 1977) was published in 1974, and *Education for Parenthood,* a compilation of curricula from youth organizations, was distributed in 1978.

Government publications ranged from the traditional *Infant Care* and *Your Child from One to Six* to curriculum materials for Head Start, Home Start, Follow Through, and two new series, *Family Day Care* and *Caring for Children.* Attention continued to focus on the total family rather than the individual child. The Office of Child Development became the Administration for Children, Youth and Families.

The decade closed with school, government, social agencies, and families concerned with educational programs and support systems for children and parents. Plans for the White House Conference for Families were underway. The diversity of underlying philosophies was exemplified in the concern for a definition of family composition. Differing opinions ranged from those who believed families were composed of two parents and children to those who believed any unit living together was a family. The times were difficult; inflation was causing great hardships. From among the many issues, one concern raised hope for the future—parents were vitally concerned about the future of the family.

1980 TO 1990

The 1980s commenced with the White House Conference on Families, held in July 1980 at three locations: Baltimore, Minneapolis, and Los Angeles. Interest was high. Families were important to the citizens, but divisive interests complicated the work. Despite this, the conference approved 20 recommendations to support families, including flexible work schedules, leave policies, job sharing, more part-time jobs, and more child care services.

The decade ended with little movement toward achievement of these recommendations. Few companies offered flexible work schedules and job sharing. Congress defeated the Family and Parental Leave Act in 1988. Child care was viewed by two presidents as a private or state concern, not a federal issue, although the child care tax credit was implemented. The ambivalence and reaction of the federal administration toward the well-being of families and children was exemplified by the cancellation of the White House Conference on Children and Youth, which had been scheduled for December 1981, and had been held every decade since President Theodore Roosevelt convened the first conference in 1909. The 1960s and the 1970s were times for expansion of civil rights and family programs; the 1980s were a time for retrenchment.

Of all the programs that were started in the late 1960s and 1970s, the most politically enduring was Head Start. It continued to receive funds throughout the 1980s, although it reached only 18% of those eligible. The state of Missouri led in providing programs for preschool children by offering New Parents as Teachers, a program for infants through 3 years, to all their school districts.

Families in this decade were under stress caused by financial pressure, lack of available time, high mobility, lack of an extended family in close proximity, drugs, abuse, violence on the streets and on television, health concerns, inadequate nutrition, and difficulty in obtaining or providing adequate child care. On the positive side of the 1980s, inflation steadied. Those who did not have housing, however, were caught in a crunch. Home buyers were faced with high down payments or extremely high monthly payments. Many could not afford any housing, and the number of homeless increased to become a national shame.

Poverty existed in all parts of the United States. Thirty-two-and-one-half million people were poor; 12.5 million were children. One child out of five lived in poverty. The ratios were even higher for two minority groups: Nearly one in two black children and one in three Hispanic children lived in poverty (Children's Defense Fund, 1989). Poverty was most evident in the core cities. Shelters and churches offered warmth to the homeless on cold winter nights and food lines were set up by many private and church groups to keep those in poverty from going hungry. In rural areas where poverty was not so evident, little hope was available. Many children attended school without their basic nutritional needs being met. School lunches were a necessity for them.

In sharp contrast to the poverty, the 1980s were characterized by greater affluence. High salaries were available for those in business, technology, and communication. Education was recognized as one way out of poverty. Dealing in drugs was another. Those children and families living in central cities with crime and drugs needed comprehensive support to enable them to realize a more promising destiny (Schorr & Schorr, 1988). Poverty, social programs, and education were intertwined in an effort to change the high risk of poverty.

Two concerns that contributed to high risk for children were the increased numbers of teenage pregnancies and unmarried mothers. Very young mothers are not prepared physically, educationally, or mentally to rear children, yet one in five infants was born to an unmarried mother in the 1980s (Hymes, 1986; 1987). In addition, the increase in single mothers due to divorce, death of a spouse, or preference also increased the risk of poverty.

In more than half of the two-parent families in the United States, both parents worked (O'Connell & Bloom, 1987). This gave families greater monetary ability. However, time became a precious commodity, and some families found it difficult to save time for themselves and their children. Articles on handling stress and programs for stress reduction continued to grow in popularity. Parent education programs such as STEP, PET, and Active Parenting were offered by schools, hospitals, and social agencies (see Chapter 5).

Young people were increasingly faced with unstructured free time and were thus more likely to capitulate to the influence of drugs and alcohol. Parents started to join forces with the schools to reduce the use of drugs and alcohol by the young. Before- and after-school programs were supported by parents and other citizens. Younger children obviously needed care, but programs that met the needs of the middle-school and high school student, although not so evident, were also needed. Most parents wanted nonacademic, enrichment, after-school programs for their children. A few after-school programs were started, but the majority of children had several hours on their own each afternoon.

On the positive side, recognition of the need for early attachment began to reach the public. Knowledge of the importance of the first 2 years of life was more fully recognized in terms of children's physical, social, and emotional needs. Families who had their infants in child care had to be increasingly sensitive to their children's needs for high quality care.

Many "babyboomers" began families of their own, and some chose to use birthing rooms in hospitals so that parents and infants could have time together when the infant was first born. Lamaze classes helped prepare the parents for the birth, and the La Leche League helped the mothers with nursing after birth. Baby boomers had waited to start having children and were eager recipients of the parent education offered by these and other groups.

AIDS frightened the entire society. A deadly disease that was only recognized in the 1980s, AIDS can infect children and parents through blood transfusions, unclean syringe needles, and sexual intercourse. Schools and early childhood programs had to develop criteria to help children with AIDS attend school and lead as normal a life as possible while they were healthy.

The need for more parent education for teenagers and all parents was recognized. The country was divided throughout the 1980s just as it had been during the White House Conference on Families. The far right decried public interference in rearing of children, but polls showed that family life education was favored by the vast majority of people. Abortion clinics were bombed as the "right to life" faction demonstrated its feelings against "right to choice". "Pro family" had different meanings for different people. In the presidential election of 1988, though, both candidates claimed a commitment to better child care and support for families.

Early childhood preschool programs and public school kindergartens continued to increase. The effects of early academic pressure on children was a major issue, but so were the falling scores on the SAT. Continuing concern about the mismatch between the five-year-old's development and typical kindergarten programs (Hymes, 1987) was voiced. The National Association for the Education of Young Children prepared a position statement that outlined the components of developmentally appropriate curriculums for young children. Interest in programs for four-year-olds increased in individual states, and states began to fund programs that met the needs of four-year-olds who were at risk. The federal government, in the form of P. L. 99–457, offered incentive grants to support programs for handicapped and developmentally delayed children from birth until 2.

Child care programs were troubled with a variety of concerns. There was alarm that they could not be financially solvent when the insurance industry classified children as high risk and raised the premiums by 250 to 350%.

A second issue was the lack of qualified staff. The Child Development Associate (CDA) program continued, moving from Bank Street College of Education to the Council on Early Childhood Professional Recognition, under the auspices of the National Association for the Education of Young Children. More than 31,000 persons were credentialed by the end of the 1980s. Colleges across the nation continued to offer 2-year associate and 4- or 5-year teacher certification programs. After obtaining credentials or a certificate, however, caregivers were paid such low salaries that many could not afford to work in the field if they were sole support for a family.

Citizens and governments of many countries exhibited concern about nuclear waste and the environment. Political and economic changes occurred in China and in Russia: China began to accept tourists and exchanged students and goods with the rest of the world, and Russia, under Gorbachev, began a restructuring of the nation. There was hope these changes could bring the dawning of a new period of peace and prosperity to the world.

Although some positive signs for change occurred, the social concerns of poverty, at-risk children, AIDS, undereducated youth, drug and alcohol abuse, stress on families, environmental pollution, and homelessness continued to plague the country into the 1990s.

SUMMARY

Parental involvement in the education of children has been present since prehistoric times. (Table 2–1 presents a brief overview of important ideas about children over the centuries.) The family provided the first informal education for the child through modeling, teaching, and praise or discipline. From the times of early Egyptian, Sumerian, Hebrew, Greek, and Roman days, parents were actively involved in the selection of teachers and the education of their children.

During the Middle Ages (400 AD to 1400 AD), at 7 years of age, children of nobility were sent to live in another noble's home, and others became apprentices in trades. Children were treated as miniature adults rather than children. It was not until the fifteenth to seventeenth centuries that the concept of family began to develop.

Strict discipline was imposed on all classes of children. This philosophy prevailed until the writings of Rousseau, Pestalozzi, and Froebel in the eighteenth and early nineteenth centuries brought a touch of humanism to the rearing of children.

Family life in the United States was able to flourish from the early days. Childrearing practices varied according to the location of the founders but were basically tied to the religious background of

TABLE 2–1
A brief outline of important people and events influencing ideas about children and childrearing

6000–5000 BC	Primitive cultures developed. Parents modeled behavior for children to learn.
5510–3787 BC	Egyptian children were educated in their homes in the Old Kingdom of Egypt.
3787–1580 BC	Schools outside the home developed in Egypt.
427–347 BC	Plato questioned theories of childrearing. He suggested that young children's environment should be controlled so that they would develop the right habits. Infanticide was practiced by Greeks, Romans, and others.
384–323 BC	Aristotle, the father of the scientific method, promoted childrearing and education by the state.
204–122 BC	Polybius marked the importance of the family in the development of good Roman citizens.
106–43 BC	Cicero emphasized the family in the development of the Roman citizen.
318 AD	Emperor Constantine declared infanticide a crime.
400–1400 AD	Roman Empire declined and the feudal system emerged. There was loss of family life. Wealthy children were apprenticed to nobles. Commoners were apprenticed to learn trades. Peasants worked in fields as common laborers.
1450 AD	The printing press was invented. Books were available but were reserved for the wealthy.
1483–1540	Martin Luther introduced the Ninety-five Theses and began the drive for all to learn to read the Bible. He also recommended Aesop Fables.
1500–1671	Etiquette books changed from strictly adult etiquette to include children.
1592–1670	Comenius, a Moravian educator, wrote books with progressive educational theories.
1632–1704	John Locke believed the newborn's mind was like a blank slate. Nothing was innate; everything must be learned.
1697	Mother Goose tales published.
17th & 18th Centuries	Wealthy European children were reared by wet nurses. Colonial American children followed Puritanical religious beliefs, were disciplined, and trained to be obedient and faithful. Children in the Southwestern United States were reared in extended close-knit Spanish-Indian Catholic families.
1703–1791	John Wesley, founder of Methodism, was reared quite strictly by his mother, who believed in breaking the child's will.
1712–1778	Rousseau, author of *Emile,* wrote that children need to grow free and untainted by society.
1747–1827	Pestalozzi, father of parent education, developed a curriculum based on concrete objects and group instruction, cooperation among students, and self-activity of the child. Among his work is *How Gertrude Teaches Her Children* (published in 1801).
1782–1852	Friedrich Froebel developed a curriculum for the young child based on the concept of unity. He is regarded as the father of kindergarten.
19th Century	American parents began to rely on American publications in addition to European ideas and the tenets of the church.
1815	Parent group meetings were held in Portland, Maine.
1854	Henry Barnard, United States Commissioner of Education, supported Froebelian concepts.

TABLE 2—1
continued

1856	The first American kindergarten was established in Watertown, Wisconsin, by Margaretha Shurz. (It was a German-speaking kindergarten.)
1860	Elizabeth Peabody established the first English-speaking kindergarten in America. Peabody, sister-in-law of Horace Mann, crusaded for kindergartens.
1860–1864	During the Civil War women were encouraged to replace men as teachers.
1870	The National Education Association was founded.
1870–1880	A great extension of the kindergarten movement and parent education occurred.
1871	First public kindergarten in North America was established in Ontario, Canada.
1873	Susan Blow directed the first American public kindergarten, opened by Dr. William Harris in St. Louis, Missouri.
1882	The American Association of University Women was established.
1884	The Department of Kindergarten Instruction of the National Education Association was formed. In the 1960s it became the Department of Elementary-Kindergarten-Nursery Education (EKNE). The group dissolved in the mid-1970s.
1888	The Child Study Association of America was founded.
1889	The General Federation of Women's Clubs was founded. G. Stanley Hall started the first child study center.
1890–1900	Settlement houses were established to aid the poor and new immigrants.
1892	The International Kindergarten Union was established (now the Association for Childhood Education International).
1895	Patty Smith Hill and Anna Bryan studied with G. Stanley Hall.
1896	The Laboratory School at the University of Chicago was started by John Dewey. The National Association of Colored Women was established.
1897	The Parent Teachers Association (PTA) was founded.
1898	*Kindergarten Magazine* was first published.
1905	Maria Montessori established Casa dei Bambini in Rome. Sigmund Freud wrote *Three Essays of the Theory of Sexuality.*
1909	The First White House Conference on Care of Dependent Children was held.
1911	Margaret McMillan designed an open air nursery for children of the poor in England. Gesell started Child Development Clinic at Yale University.
1912	The Children's Bureau was established.
1914	First *Infant Care* was published by the Children's Bureau.
1916	First parent-cooperative was established in Chicago.
1917	Smith-Hughes Act was passed. Homemaking became a vocation. Iowa Child Welfare Research Station was established.
1920s	Emergence of 26 parent education programs occurred.
1920	Child Welfare League of America was founded. Watson, a behaviorist, emphasized that children were to be strictly scheduled and were not to be coddled.
1922	Nursery school was established in Boston, Massachusetts, by Abigail Eliot. Benjamin Gruenberg wrote the *Child Study Manual.*

TABLE 2—1
continued

1925	National Council of Parent Education was established.
	National Committee on Nursery Schools (now the National Association for the Education of Young Children) was started by Patty Smith Hill.
1927	First black nursery school in United States was founded by Dorothy Howard in Washington, D.C.
1928	The nursery school movement expanded from 3 in 1920 to 89 in 1928.
1930	Depression hit the United States.
	White House Conference on Child Health and Protection recommended parent education as part of the public school system.
	The International Kindergarten Union became the Association for Childhood Education.
1932	Parent education courses were offered in 25 states.
1933	Federal emergency Relief Administration authorized work-relief wages for nursery school teachers.
1934	*Parent Education,* journal of National Council of Parent Education, published from 1934 until 1938.
1940s	A new emphasis on mental health for children emerged.
1940	The Lanham Act provided money for child care so that mothers could join the war effort. Most of the money went for child care centers.
1946	Benjamin Spock published *The Common Sense Book of Baby and Child Care.*
1949	*Your Children from 6 to 12* was published by the Children's Bureau.
1950	Erik Erikson wrote *Childhood and Society,* which included the eight stages of human personality growth.
	James Hymes wrote *Effective Home-School Relations.*
1952	Jean Piaget's work, *The Origins of Intelligence in Children,* was translated into English.
1957	Russia launched Sputnik. New emphasis was placed on the intellectual development of children.
	Parenthood in a Free Nation was published by Parent Education Project of the University of Chicago.
1960	Golden Anniversary White House Conference on Children and Youth was held.
	The Parent Cooperative Preschools International was founded.
1960	Day Care and Child Development Council of America was founded.
1962	J. McVicker Hunt wrote *Intelligence and Experience,* one of the first books to question the concept of fixed IQ.
1963	White House Conference on Mental Retardation was held.
1964	Economic Opportunity Act of 1964 began the War on Poverty.
1965	Civil Rights Act was passed.
	Head Start was established.
	Elementary and Secondary School Act was passed. Title I provided money for educationally deprived children.
1967	The Follow Through Program was initiated to provide continuity of service to former Head Start students in elementary school.

TABLE 2—1
continued

1970	White House Conference on Children and Youth was held.
1972	The National Home Start Program was initiated. It involved parents in the teaching of their children.
1975	The Education for All Handicapped Children Act, P.L. 94–142, was passed. It mandated free and appropriate education for handicapped children.
1980	The White House Conference on Families was held.
1987	P.L. 99–457, designed to serve handicapped and developmentally delayed children from birth until 2, was passed.

the family. The major exceptions were the black families, brought from Africa to serve as slaves, who were not allowed to have a normal family life.

Childrearing practices were reflected by the Puritan belief in breaking the will of the child and the need for perfect behavior. The parent education groups in the early 1800s were based on the need to rear children according to these religious principles.

The modern parent education movement began in the 1880s and 1890s. Prominent women founded the National Congress of Mothers (PTA), the Child Study Association, and the American Association of University Women. Each included childrearing as a part of its program. G. Stanley Hall created the first child study center in the United States at Clark University. In addition, philanthropic organizations included parent education in their settlement schools and Free Kindergarten Association programs.

The federal government became involved in family life with the first White House Conference on Care of Dependent Children in 1909. As a result, the Children's Bureau was established in 1912, and the first issue of *Infant Care* was published in 1914.

Colleges and universities showed their concern for research in child development by the establishment of research and child study centers.

The years during the 1920s were the most productive in terms of the establishment of parent education programs. Twenty-six parent education organizations were founded during the decade, and many parent education groups emerged across the nation. Change had also come in terms of childrearing practices. Although authorities in the 1890s and the early 1900s emphasized love and affection in the formation of character, the 1920s focused on strict scheduling and discipline.

During the 1940s parent education programs continued, bolstered by child care money for mothers working in the war effort.

The 1950s showed more concern for the mental health of the child. Freud's and Erikson's writings on social-emotional growth, plus Benjamin Spock's famous child care book, helped shift attitudes from the strict scheduling of the 1920s to the "on demand" feedings and concern for mental health of the 1950s.

In the late 1950s the USSR launched Sputnik. Suddenly, there was concern for intellectual development in the young. This forecast the emphasis toward the cognitive development in the 1960s and 1970s. The total child—emotional, social, intellectual, and physical—was the focus of many professionals, and although cognitive development was emphasized and Piaget's theories on cognitive development had great impact on education, this developmental theory complemented the belief in the need for physical, social, and emotional health. Head Start, Follow Through, and Title I programs looked toward the child's total needs. The family was brought into the development and ongoing commitments of federal programs.

In the 1960s and 1970s Americans were confronted with great social change. The 1980s began with the First White House Conference on Families, which was attended by men and women representing diverse philosophic beliefs about families.

Parent involvement was recognized as an important element in a child's success at school. Monetary support for family support programs, however, decreased in the 1980s. Head Start continues but serves about one-fifth of the eligible children. Societal problems include increased drug and alcohol abuse by school-aged children and poverty for one in five children. Families are faced with a shortage of time and increased stress in a turbulent world.

SUGGESTED CLASS ACTIVITIES AND DISCUSSIONS

1. Visit an art museum. Explore the artists' portrayals of children. See if you can find pictures in which children were depicted as miniature adults. Are there time periods when children were idealized? Are there time periods when children were painted realistically? Discuss.
2. Ask the librarian for books from art museums throughout the world. Examine these for trends in childrearing practices and beliefs.
3. Divide into groups. Each group chooses a prominent figure in parent education, for example, Pestalozzi, Froebel, Locke, or Rousseau. Investigate their lives, beliefs, and the impact they had on education. Obtain copies of their original works. When reporting back to class, pretend you are a product of the relevant time period and defend the educator's beliefs.
4. Find a library that has federal publications. Look through books published by the Children's Bureau. Examine the changes in beliefs in child development.
5. Get a copy of the *Twenty-Eighth Year Book, Parts I and II, Preschool and Parent Education* by the National Society for the Study of Education. Compare the programs on parent education in the 1920s to the programs in the 1980s.
6. The periods of 1890s, early twentieth century, 1930s, and 1960s were ones when there was concern about the poor. What were the differing causes of poverty? Why did the concern seem to lessen in intervening decades?
7. Why did nursery schools serve the poor in England? Why do they tend to serve middle-class parents in the United States? How did their origins differ?
8. Discuss federal intervention. Trace its history from the "hands off" approach of Spencer to the start of the Children's Bureau. How has federal involvement grown since 1910?
9. Who are the past and current leaders in early child education? Read materials by Lilian Katz, Alice Honig, Constance Kamii, James Hymes, Ira Gordon, David Weikart, Bettye Caldwell, Merle Karnes, and others. Obtain copies of *Childhood Education, Young Children,* and *Children Today.* Listen to the *Living History* tapes by James Hymes. Do you find a trend in the direction of early childhood education today that will be history tomorrow?
10. Examine your community. How many new types of programs have been started since Head Start was initiated in 1965?

BIBLIOGRAPHY

Archer, R. L. (Ed.). *Jean Jacques Rousseau. His educational theories selected from Emile, Julie and other writings.* Woodbury, N.Y.: Barron's Educational Series, 1964.

Aries, P. *Centuries of childhood.* New York: Vintage Books, 1962.

Becker, H., & Barnes, H. E. *Social thought from lore to science.* (Vols. I and II). New York: Dover Publications, 1961.

Bell, R. Q., & Harper, L. V. *Child effects on adults.* Lincoln: University of Nebraska Press, 1980.

Bigner, J. J. *Parent-child relations.* New York: Macmillan Publishing Co., 1985.

Bloom, B. *Stability and change in human characteristics.* New York: Wiley & Sons, 1964.

Blow, S. E., & Eliot, H. R. *The mottos and commentaries of Friedrich Froebel's mother play.* New York: D. Appleton, 1910.

Bossard, J. H. S., & Boll, E. S. *The sociology of child development.* New York: Harper & Row, 1966.

Braun, S. J., & Edwards, E. P. *History and theory of early childhood education.* Worthington, Ohio: Charles A. Jones Publishing, 1972.

Brembeck, C. S. *Social foundations of education.* New York: Wiley & Sons, 1966.

Brim, O. *Education for child rearing.* New York: Free Press, 1965.

Butts, R. F., & Cremin, L. A. *A history of education in American culture.* New York: Holt, Rinehart & Winston, 1953.

Calhoun, A. W. *A social history of the American family* (Vols. 1, 2, & 3). New York: Barnes & Noble, 1960.

Chambliss, R. *Social thought.* New York: Irvington Press, 1982.

Children's Defense Fund. *A vision for America's future.* Washington, D.C.: Author, 1989.

Demaitre, L. The idea of childhood and child care in medical writings of the Middle Ages. *Journal of Psychohistory, 4*(4), 1977, pp. 461–490.

deMause, L. (Ed.) *The history of childhood.* New York: Psychohistory Press, 1974.

––––––. *The untold story of child abuse.* New York: Harper & Row, 1988.

Education Development Center. *Exploring childhood.* Newton, Mass.: EDC School & Society Program, 1977.

Elkind, D. The child yesterday, today, and tomorrow. *Young Children,* May 1987, 6–12.

Erikson, E. *Childhood and society.* New York: W. W. Norton, 1986.

Fisher, M. Parent education. In *Encyclopedia of the social sciences* (Vol. 2). New York: Macmillan, 1933.

Frost, S. E., Jr. *Historical and philosophical foundations of Western education.* Columbus, Ohio: Merrill, 1966.

Ginsberg, E. (Ed.). *The nation's children* (Vols. I, II, & III). New York: Columbia University Press, 1960.

Godfrey, E. *English children in the olden time.* Darby, Pa.: Folcroft Library Editions, 1977. (Originally published, New York: E. P. Dutton, 1907.)

Goodson, B. D., & Hess, R. *Parents as teachers of young children: An evaluative review of some contemporary concepts and programs.* Stanford, Calif.: Stanford University Press, 1975.

Goodykoontz, B., Davis, M. D., & Gabbard, H. F. Recent history and present status in education for young children. In *National Society for the Study of Education, 46th yearbook, part II.* Chicago: National Society for the Study of Education, 1947.

Gruenberg, B. C. (Ed.). *Outlines of child study.* New York: Macmillan, 1927.

Gruenberg, S. Parent education: 1930–1940. In W. B. Grave (Ed.), *Annals of the American Academy of Political and Social Sciences.* Philadelphia: American Academy of Political and Social Sciences, 1940.

Gutek, G. L. *Pestalozzi and education.* New York: Random House, 1968.

Hamilton, E., & Cairns, H. (Eds.). *The collected dialogues of Plato.* Princeton, N.J.: Princeton University Press, 1971.

Hill, R. The American family today. In E. Ginsberg, *The nation's children.* New York: Columbia University Press, 1960.

Hunt, D. *Parents and children in history.* New York: Basic Books, 1970.

Hunt, J. *Intelligence and experience.* New York: Ronald Press, 1961.

Hymes, J. L. *Effective home-school relations.* New York: Prentice-Hall, 1953.

Hymes, J. L., Jr. *Early childhood education: The year in review; A look at 1986.* Carmel, Calif.: Hacienda Press, 1987.

––––––. *Early childhood education: The year in review; A look at 1987.* Carmel, Calif.: Hacienda Press, 1987.

Kawin, E. *Parenthood in a free nation. Early and middle childhood* (Vol. 2). Lafayette, Ind.: Purdue Research Foundation, 1969.

Lorence, B. W. Parents and children in eighteenth century Europe. *History of Childhood Quarterly: The Journal of Psychohistory,* 1974, *2*(1), pp. 1–30.

Mead, M., & Wolfenstein, M. *Childhood in contemporary cultures.* Chicago: University of Chicago Press, 1963.

Middlekauff, R. Education in colonial America. In J. A. Johnson, H. W. Collins, V. L. Dupuis, & J. H. Johansen (Eds.), *Foundations of American education: Readings.* Boston: Allyn & Bacon, 1969.

Moody, E. The school of good manners: Composed for the help of parents in teaching children how to behave during their minority. In D. J. Rothman & S. M. Rothman (Eds.), *The colonial American family.* New York: Arno Press, 1972.

Moore, R. L. Justification without joy: Psychohistorical reflections on John Wesley's childhood and conversion. *History of Childhood Quarterly: The Journal of Psychohistory,* 1974, (1), pp. 31–52.

Morrison, G. S. *Early childhood education today* (4th ed.). Columbus, Ohio: Merrill, 1988.

National Society for the Study of Education. *Twenty-Eighth Year Book. Preschool and Parent Education (Parts 1 and 2).* Bloomington, Ill.: Public School Publishing, 1929.

O'Connell, M., & Bloom, D. E. *Juggling jobs and babies: America's child care challenge.* #12. Washington, D.C.: Population Reference Bureau, 1987.

Osborn, D. K. *Early childhood education in historical perspective.* Athens, Ga.: Education Associates, 1980.

Pennsylvania Department of Public Instruction. *Parent education.* Bulletin 86. Harrisburg: Author, 1935.

Pestalozzi, F. J. *How Gertrude teaches her children.* London: Allen & Unwin, 1915.

———. *The education of man.* New York: Philosophical Library, 1951.

Rothman, D. J., & Rothman, S. M. *The colonial American family.* New York: Arno Press, 1972.

Schlossman, S. L. Before Home Start: Notes toward a history of parent education in America. 1897–1929. *Harvard Educational Review,* 1976, *46,* (3) pp. 436–467.

Schorr, L. B., & Schorr, D. *Within our reach: Breaking the cycle of disadvantage.* New York: Doubleday, 1988.

Skeels, H. Adult status of children with contrasting early life experiences: A follow-up study. In *Monographs of the Society for Research in Child Development* (Vol. 31). Chicago: University of Chicago Press, 1966.

Spencer, H. *Education: Intellectual, moral, and physical.* New York: Appleton, 1900.

Spock, B. *Baby and child care.* New York: Pocket Books, 1957.

Stendler, C. B. Sixty years of child training practices. *Journal of Pediatrics,* 1950, *36,* pp. 122–134.

Sunley, R. Early nineteenth-century American literature on child rearing. In M. Mead & M. Wolfenstein (Eds.), *Childhood in contemporary cultures.* Chicago: The University of Chicago Press, 1955, pp. 150–163.

Taylor, K. W. *Parent and children learn together: Parent cooperative nursery schools.* New York: Teachers College Press, 1981.

U.S. Department of Health, Education and Welfare. (Welfare Administration; Children's Bureau). *Your child from 6 to 12.* Washington, D.C.: U.S. Government Printing Office, 1949.

———. *Your child from one to six.* Washington, D.C.: U.S. Government Printing Office, 1962.

———. *Infant care.* Washington, D.C.: U.S. Government Printing Office, 1963.

———. *Home Start/child and family resource programs. Report of a joint conference—Home Start, child and family resource program.* Washington, D.C.: U.S. Government Printing Office, 1974.

Vandewalker, N. C, *The kindergarten in American education.* New York: Arno Press, 1971.

Vincent, C. E. Trends in infant care ideas. *Child Development,* September 1951, pp. 199–209.

Wadsworth, B. The well-ordered family: Or relative duties. In D. J. Rothman & S. M. Rothman (Eds.), *The colonial American family.* New York: Arno Press, 1972.

Weber, E. *The kindergarten.* New York: Teachers College Press, 1969.

Wolfenstein, M. Trends in infant care. *American Journal of Orthopsychiatry,* 1953, *23,* pp. 120–130.

3

The Family and Community

FAMILIES

Families in the United States and around the world are living with change, but the essence of the family remains stable, with members of the family sharing a certain amount of commitment and support for each other. "Changes in family forms will come and go as economic and political conditions change but . . . the sense of connectedness is the essence of family" (Howard, 1980, p. x).

The family is the most stable component of society. Countries have emerged and disintegrated, but the family remains, changed in form, but not in essential functions. If there is a bond among its members, with young children receiving necessary nurturing as well as shelter and food, then the family unit will survive. If the family is connected, reducing isolation and alienation, then the family and those within it will flourish. As it bends with the winds of time, its basic structure and functions are amazingly secure. As the provider for and socializer of children, the family has no match. A family may be a nuclear two-parent family, a single-parent family, or an extended family, but as long as it functions to give the nurture and support needed by its members, it is a viable, working unit.

If you walked down a street in the United States today and knocked on a door, would you be likely to find a mother, father, and child in the house? Children live with parents in only 4 out of every 10 households. The family that is *considered* typical, two parents and children, is not the average family in the United States. In 1984, only 11% of families fit the concept of a father as provider, mother as homemaker, and two children in the family (Washington & Oyemade, 1985, p. 13). Three-fourths of the households are inhabited by related families, however, and only one-fourth are inhabited by unrelated individuals.

The nation is made up of approximately 250 million people; some are young; some are senior citizens; some are middle aged; and any of these may be single, divorced, widowed, or married. Eighty-five percent are white; 12% are classified as black; 3% are American Indian, Alaskan Natives, Asian, or Pacific Islanders (persons of Hispanic origin may be of any race and are not differentiated in these figures). By 2000, the country is projected to have a population of more than 268 million persons with 83% white, 13% black, and 4% American Indian, Alaskan Natives, Asian, or Pacific Islanders. The 139 million-person work force will be composed of 84% whites (including 10% Hispanics), 12%

A family may be one-parent, two-parent, or extended. As long as it can provide connectedness and underlying support, it is a viable family.

blacks, and 4% American Indian, Alaskan Natives, Asians, and Pacific Islanders (calculated from Fullerton, 1987, pp. 24, 25).

FAMILY STRUCTURE

Parents who cooperate with teachers and child caregivers are a varied group. Some are two-parent families, others are never married single-parent families, divorced single parents, or single parents whose spouses died—all with one or more children. Most parents who divorce soon remarry, so blended or reconstituted families may be families with joint custody, children living with the father and stepmother, children living with the mother and stepfather, stepbrothers and stepsisters, half-brothers and half-sisters, and brothers and sisters.

Although family forms vary, they provide similar functions. It is expected that the roles within families provide for the needs of the children, and parents have rights and responsibilities. Swick (1986) described these roles as "(1) nurturing, (2) guiding, (3) problem solving, and (4) modeling" (p. 72). Cataldo (1987) described similar roles providing "care, nurturance, and protection," socialization, "monitoring the child's development as a learner," and supporting "each youngster's growth into a well-rounded, emotionally healthy person" (p. 28).

The first function of a family is to provide nurturance and to supply nutrition, protection, and shelter. Families provide interaction, love, and support. The family has a right to rear the child as they see fit as well as a responsibility to see that the child is cared for adequately.

Parents socialize their children to be able to act following the norms of the society in accordance with the parents' cultural beliefs. Cultures vary in the manner in which they socialize their children. Families in some cultures demand respect toward their elders; others socialize their children in a democratic style that depends on mutual respect. There are also variations within cultures that often result from how the parents were raised. In the rearing process, most children learn and internalize their parents' value system.

Parents also have the obligation to see that the child is educated both at home and at school. In some families education is not recognized as a function of the family, but learning or lack of learning is very much a part of any family system. Parents are the first educators of their children, so the child's ability to function well in school rests to a great extent on the home's nurturance and environment.

In addition to recognizing the many family forms, professionals find it helpful to view parenthood as divided into different stages. Sometimes families are in several stages simultaneously such as families with a large number of children whose births are spread over 20 or more years. The stages developed by Galinsky divide parenthood into six levels of development much like the child's stages of development. The first stage, the *image making* stage, takes place before the birth of a child. Images

Although family forms vary, they provide similar functions of guiding, nurturing, and caring for their children.

organized and effective, over-protective, rigid and controlling, hostile and authoritarian, neglecting, and anxious neurotic (Jensen & Kingston, 1986).

If these eight types of families are multiplied by the number of configurations of families (single, two-parent, and blended) and the individual personality differences of each child and parent, it becomes apparent that in order to work effectively with parents you must individualize your suggestions and responses.

Some commonalities stand out, however. Both men and women questioned in polls placed importance on the family and were willing to adapt and make sacrifices in order to keep the family together. Keep in mind that children often are viewed by parents as an extension of themselves. If parents are approached in a way that lets them know the teacher wants the child to succeed as much as the parents do, a true collaboration can take place.

Approximately 80% of American children live in two-parent homes, although more than half of them will live in a one-parent family at some point; 12 million children (20%) live in one-parent homes. Many one-parent families have strong permanent families based on the parent and child. The high rate of remarriage, however, illustrates the desire to continue the traditional family lifestyle of two parents with children. Happy families come in many forms.

Family Forms

The structure, stage of the family development, family size, and ages and sex of children make for families of many varieties. Families described here are representative of the many types of families. Add to the list with your own descriptions.

Single-Parent Family
Tina is a young, divorced mother with one son, Tommy, age 3. They live with Tina's parents. In addition to working part time at a department store, Tina takes 6 hours of classes at the local college. Each day she gets up in the morning, prepares breakfast for Tommy and herself, bun-

are formed and preparation is made for the birth. The second stage is the *nurturing* period during infancy, when attachment develops. In the third period, the *authority* stage, families help their child understand the norms of the society. During the fourth stage, from preschool to adolescence, parents offer *guidance* and children learn to interpret their social reality. The teens, *interdependent* years, are the fifth stage of family development. When the children are ready to go out into the world for themselves, parents enter their last stage. During each of these stages, parents provide the guidance necessary for that stage of development (Galinsky, 1987).

Ideally, families need to provide a support system that allows the child to grow into a healthy, responsible person. Parenting styles (some of which are more effective than others) can be identified as democratic, overindulgent,

TABLE 3–1

Eight parenting styles, the characteristics of the parents, and the possible traits of their children.

Types of Parents	Characteristics of Parents	Possible Traits of Children
Democratic	Warm and supportive; rules set by parents and children	Confident, independent, socially outgoing
Indulgent	Lack of definite standards and limits	Independent, manipulative, antisocial, aggressive
Organized, effective (authoritative)	Structured limits; high standards; confident, warm, supportive	High achievement; responsible
Overprotective	Intrusive focus on their children's behavior; high standards	Dependent; strong conscience
Rigid, controlling	Restrictive and hostile	Neurotic, socially withdrawn, shy, anxious, self-punishing
Hostile, authoritarian (dictator)	Restrictive, punitive, frustrated	Socially withdrawn, self-punishing
Neglecting	Lack of concern and warmth; hedonistic and neglectful; low parental control	Delinquent
Anxious, neurotic	World perceived as out to get them	Anxious, antisocial, aggressively punitive

Source: From *Parenting* by Larry Cyril Jensen and Merrill Kingston, copyright © 1986 by Holt, Rinehart and Winston, Inc., reprinted by permission of the publisher.

dles him into his coat during cold weather, hopes that her aging automobile will start, and begins her long day. First, she deposits Tommy with her sister who runs a family day care home. She feels fortunate to have a relative who enjoys children to care for Tommy. He has been worried ever since his father left, and the security of spending his days at Aunt Georgia's helps compensate for his loss.

Tina figures that with family help and her part-time college work she will be able to graduate in a little more than 2 years, just about the time Tommy will start to school. Her ex-husband, Ted, does not send support money consistently, and Tina knows that her parents can help her only so much. As she clerks in the department store, she dreams of the time when she will make enough to give Tommy the home and opportunities he needs.

Unwed Single Teenage Mother

As Sherrill thinks back, she can't remember when she didn't want a baby. "When I have a baby," she had thought, "I'll be treated like an adult by my mother and I'll also have a baby all my own who will love me." Already, though, Gerald, age 3 months, has gotten to be a real handful.

Sherrill just had her 15th birthday yesterday, and instead of being able to bum around with her friends, she had to take care of Gerald. "If only my mother hadn't had to work," Sherrill complained, "I would have had a couple of hours between feedings just to get out. I never dreamed a baby would be so demanding. What makes him cry so much?"

The school down the street offers a program for teen mothers and their infants. Sherrill is on the waiting list and plans to enroll at the end of summer. "I never thought I'd want to go back to school," she muses, "but they help out by caring for my baby while I'm in class and my mother says that I need to be able to make a living for Gerald. Maybe I'll just continue with AFDC (Aid to Families of Dependent Children). I really don't like school. If only Gerald would start being more fun."

Two-Parent Homeless Family

When Barbara married Jed, things really looked good. Young, handsome, and willing to work, Jed thought that his job at the plant would last forever. That was before the layoffs. Who would have expected them? Jed's father worked at the plant for 25 years before he retired. Now Jed and Barbara, along with little Jessie, age 2, and Bob, age 6 are moving west in hopes of finding work.

It's hard to live out of a car. Barbara worries about Bob because he is missing first grade. She and Jed put him in school whenever they are in a city for any length of time, but schools want his permanent address. It embarrasses Barbara to say that their family is homeless, so she finds out the name of a street near the school and pretends they live there. Bob doesn't like school anyway. He says the children make fun of him and the teacher gives him seatwork that he doesn't understand. Jed feels like he has failed as a father and provider for his family. If he could just find a good job. Minimum wage doesn't give him enough to pay for rent let alone buy clothing and food. Last month they spent time at a church-run mission for the homeless. Jed was glad that they were in a town far from home so that none of his old school friends recognized him and Barbara. Maybe a good factory job will turn up.

Two-Parent Family

"Joe, the alarm. It's your turn to get up and start breakfast." Maria turns over to get 10 more minutes of sleep before the drive to school. Each day Maria teaches 28 second graders in the adjoining school district. Joe teaches mathematics at the local middle school. It works exceedingly well for them. The children stay with a neighbor until time for them to walk to school. Joe and Maria share the dashing home early enough in the afternoon to supervise the children after school.

At times the stress of work and the demanding days get to Joe and Maria. Some days their schedules do not blend and they scurry to find someone to care for the children after school. Karen and Jaime occasionally have been "latchkey" children. Neither Joe nor Maria want their children to be left

on their own. They see too many children in their classrooms in similar situations who feel as if no one really cares. Joe tries to be a nurturing father who also helps with the home, but he relies on Maria to clean, shop, and cook.

Summers are the best time for the family. Joe works for a summer camp, but Maria is able to spend more time at home, enjoying the children and organizing for the coming year. Periodically she thinks about how much easier it would be for her to quit teaching and be a full-time homemaker, but then reality sets in: They could not make the house payments if they were not a two-income family. And a family needs a home.

GROWTH OF A NATION

The first United States census in 1790 reported a population of 3,939,326. By the 1940s, the coun-

Our nation is home for many people—young, mature, and of many different ethnic backgrounds.

try had grown to a bustling, heterogeneous land of 131,409,119 (Kaplan, Van Valey, & Associates 1980, p. 25). During this period, the nation changed from small and rural to large, industrial, and urban. From 1940 until 1990, approximately 117 million more inhabitants were added to the United States. In just 50 years, the population nearly doubled. Most of the increase was from the net increase of births over deaths rather than from immigration. Infant mortality was reduced and senior citizens were living longer. During the 1970s the birthrate declined to 13,027,000, but with the arrival of refugees and immigrants, and with the increased number of senior citizens, the population steadily increased.

In the 1980s, children of the baby-boom era—1947 to 1964—began having children. They had delayed marriage and childrearing, and their children are ready for school in the 1990s. Most of these mothers will continue working: "By 1995, two-thirds of all preschool children and four out of five schoolage children will have mothers in the work force" (Children's Defense Fund, 1988b, p. 175).

The number of families in the United States is on the increase. Of the 62.7 million families in 1985, 50.4 million (80%) were married couples, 10.1 million (16%) were headed by women, and 2.2 million (nearly 4%) were headed by men (U.S. Bureau of the Census, 1985).

Think about how information in this overview of American families affects children and schools:

- Marriage and a happy family life are important.
- Eighty percent of children live in two-parent—original or blended—families.
- Twenty percent of the children (more than 12 million) live in one-parent families.
- Fifty-four percent of women with children younger than 6 and 55% of all women work outside the home (O'Connell & Bloom, 1987).
- More than one million children are affected by divorce each year.
- One million teenagers become pregnant each year.
- Eighty percent of single-parent families headed by women were poor in 1985.

- One-third of the homeless are families with children.
- More than 1,200 American children died from abuse and neglect in 1986.
- Twenty-two percent of births in 1985 were to unmarried mothers (Children's Defense Fund, 1988b).
- The U.S. Department of Education reported an estimated 220,000 homeless schoolage children and 65,000 of these do not attend school regularly (1989). The National Coalition for the Homeless estimates 500,000 to 750,000 homeless children.
- Half of all recent first marriages end in divorce.
- Poverty is on the increase and many are "new poverty" situations (Thornton & Freedman, 1983).
- Eight-four percent of black mothers, 79% of Hispanic mothers, and 69% of white mothers who worked outside the home worked full time (Children's Defense Fund, 1988a).
- One in every six Americans moves annually.

Greater Amount of Education for Parents

Today, it is necessary for many workers to have more education because of the large number of technical jobs. These better-educated parents are generally comfortable in their dealings with the school. In 1940, only 36% of men and 40% of women (24 to 29 years old) had completed high school, and only 7% of the men and 5% of the women had completed college. By 1987, 85% of both men and women in the work force had completed high school, and one in four (ages 25 to 64) had completed 4 years of college (Howe, 1988).

Parents who have not had educational opportunities also are often very supportive of the schools and desire an education for their children, but some tend to feel uncomfortable with teachers and principals. Parents who have had to quit school or who had an unpleasant experience in their own schooling may fear the schools and find it difficult to become a partner with the professional. The school must reach out to these reticent parents.

Working Mothers

Today, mothers who work outside the home outnumber mothers who work solely in the home (Hayghe, 1988). In 1987 more than half of the children younger than 6 (10.5 million children) had mothers in the labor force. In addition, 15.7 million children aged 6 to 13 needed before- and after-school care. Fifty-six percent of all children had mothers in the work force. Sixty-two percent of single-parent mothers worked outside the home. More than a million children cared for themselves before and after school.

Working parents provide child care in a variety of ways. They count on friends and family to help out. Some use family day care homes; others use child care centers. Many depend on the children to fend for themselves. A few mothers are able to care for their children while they work. Generally these parents either work from their home or administer their own business. Table 3–2 contains details about each arrangement.

Today, women are not as likely to leave the labor force when they have children as they once were. This is illustrated by the increase of children younger than one from 24% in 1970 to 46.8% in 1984 (see Table 3–3). By 1984, employment rates of single divorced parents were nearly 68% for mothers with children ages 3 to 5 and 56% of those with children younger than 5

TABLE 3–2
Parents rely on the school for the greatest amount of child care. Their own homes or another's home are the next most common settings.

	Percent
In own home	17.8
In other's home	14.4
Day care facility	9.1
School	52.2
Child cares for self	1.8
Parent	4.7
Total	100.0

Source: Hayghe, H. V. Employers and child care: What roles do they play? *Monthly Labor Review,* September 1988, p. 38.

TABLE 3–3
Percent of mothers who work, grouped according to their children's ages.

Age of Youngest Child	March 1970	March 1984
1 year and younger	24.0%	46.8%
2 years	30.5	53.5
3 years	34.5	57.6
4 years	39.4	59.2
5 years	36.9	57.0

Source: Hayghe, H. V. Working mothers reach record number in 1984. *Monthly Labor Review,* December 1984, p. 31.

(Hayghe, 1984, p. 32). Mothers with one or two children were most likely to work outside the home; as family size increased, outside employment decreased.

EFFECTS OF CHILD CARE ON YOUNG CHILDREN

Is it harmful for children if parents work outside the home? Part of the answer rests on the quality of child care. The better the quality of child care (small groups, trained teachers, staff stability, and developmentally appropriate activities) the more likely that children's development will be fostered, according to research studies conducted in a variety of settings (see Phillips, 1987). Children from low-income homes had greater success in school and required placement in special education less often if they had a good preschool experience (Berrueta-Clement, Schweinhart, Barnett, Epstein, & Weikart, 1984).

White (1980) encouraged mothers to give optimum care for their children at home at least for the first three years, because early attachment is essential (see Chapter 1). However, parents who need to work or want to work can feel comfortable that their child will thrive *if* they select a good early childhood program and spend adequate quality time with their child. Parents should visit centers or homes until they find one that fits their needs and has a positive environment.

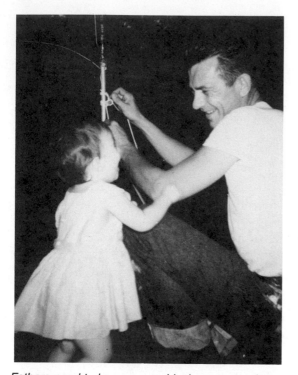

Fathers need to be warm and loving parents, interacting with their children in a nurturing manner.

GREATER INVOLVEMENT OF FATHERS WITH THEIR CHILDREN

Roles of fathers have changed and increased over the past two centuries. From the early Puritan times until industrialization, a "good" father provided his family with moral guidance. Fathers have long held the role of provider or breadwinner. Awareness of father as a sex-role model came about toward the end of World War II, but it was not until the 1970s that the role of nurturant father was emphasized (Lamb, 1987).

This new emphasis on father's role as nurturer involves him even from the child's infancy. Lamb (1976) found that fathers who took their roles seriously and showed warmth in their relationships with both daughters and sons promoted the children's development. Girls were affected most if their fathers were absent during adolescence; boys found the father's absence

more difficult at an earlier age. Fathers need to have extensive interaction with their children: "Masculinity of sons and femininity of daughters are greatest when fathers are nurturant and participate extensively in childrearing" (p. 23). The most influential fathers spent quality time with their children—children imitate behaviors of people about whom they feel positive more than those of whom they are afraid. Children did not see their father's involvement in childrearing as unmasculine. Warmth of the father-child relations also correlated with children's academic performances and the children's ability to feel good about themselves (Lamb, 1976).

Heightened interest in fatherhood goes hand in hand with the increasing number of women who work outside the home. More than ever, mothers need a cooperating husband to help with all the duties of homemaking. More importantly, many young fathers see the expression of love toward their children as a way of fulfilling their own lives with meaningful relationships. Some fathers are full time homemakers and care for the children while their wives work outside the home.

Despite these recent trends, however, mothers still carry the heaviest load of the homemaking tasks. This 'new' breed of father does not describe all fathers. The amount of paternal involvement relies on (1) motivation; (2) skills and self-confidence; (3) support, especially from the mother in the family; and (4) institutional practices. Work reduces the amount of time fathers can spend with their children. Even with the new emphasis on father nurturance, most mothers, even those who work outside the home, spend considerably more time with their children than do the fathers. In families where the mother stays home, fathers spend approximately 20 to 25% as much time with their children as do the mothers. In families where both parents are employed outside the home, the father spends approximately one-third as much time in child care responsibilities as does the mother. Fathers tend to be playmates with the children, rather than being responsible for children's care and rearing, or obtaining child

More fathers are interacting with their children while they are infants.

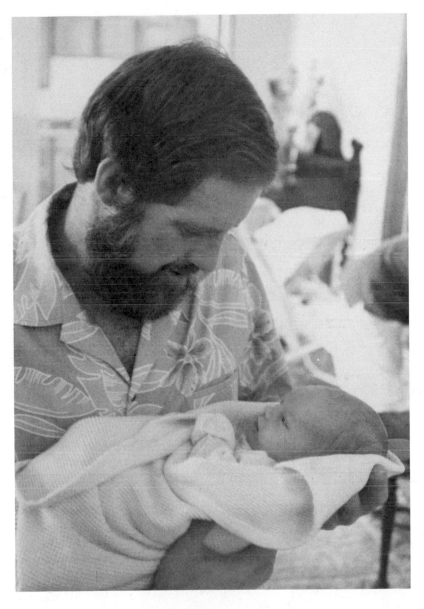

care for the children (Lamb, 1987). In fact, in studies of middle-aged bluecollar workers, men refused the responsibility of equal care for children (LeMasters & DeFrain, 1983).

Single parents, both men and women, often substitute a network of friends and kin in order to handle emergencies and everyday obligations. The extended network helps fulfill the demanding roles of nurturance and role model.

Swick and Manning offered ways in which fathers can participate in the family positively. Their suggestions included the father reinforcing the mother's efforts in child care; communicating with her about the children; playing, listening, and exploring with the children at all ages; and being involved in their education from the first preschool on through the upper grades (1983).

OUT-OF-WEDLOCK BIRTHS

The increase in out-of-wedlock births, especially for young teenagers, is alarming. Eighteen percent of all children are now born to unmarried mothers. The birth rate for unmarried women aged 15 to 19 increased steadily from 1940 through 1980 and then leveled off because of the decrease in the number of teenagers. These increasing birth rates outside of marriage do not mean there were more teenage mothers. Girls now do not marry as young as their counterparts in the 1950s, and teenagers are having infants without marrying the fathers. For many young mothers, marrying the fathers is not a viable option; many of these young men are unable to obtain employment that would bring the family out of poverty. Six of 10 infants born to teens are born to those living below the poverty level (Children's Defense Fund, 1988b).

Children are charming, but young teenagers are not ready—physically or emotionally—for the responsibilities of parenthood.

Two factors—the increase in births out of wedlock and the decrease or delayed births for married women—increased the percentage of births to unmarried mothers from 5% in 1970 to 18% in 1980 (Thornton & Freedman, 1983, pp. 20, 21). This startling figure points up the need for more family life education in the schools, especially for young mothers, and it also calls for an educational system that meets the needs of low-income families. Students need help in counseling and sex education, but they also need skills and self-esteem to give them hope for the future (Children's Defense Fund, 1988b). One in every five young females who has below-average educational skills and lives in a below-poverty-level home becomes a mother while still a teenager. No matter whether young people are white, black, or Hispanic, they are more apt to become pregnant if they are below average in academic skills. Higher infant mortality rates and greater risks to the child are just two of the problems associated with teenage pregnancies. Very young women are not prepared emotionally, economically, or physically to take on the challenge of childrearing.

SINGLE-PARENT FAMILIES

Single-parent families are not a new phenomenon. From the 1860s until the mid-1960s there was no increase in the number of single parents because the growing divorce rate was offset by the declining death rate. Young children in the last half of the 1800s and first half of the 1900s were raised in single-parent families most often because the mother was widowed. Single-parent mothers worked hard to raise their children by taking in boarders, doing laundry, and somehow managing (with help from their children) to rear the family.

By the 1960s, however, the divorce rate increased to such a degree that single-parent families increased because of divorce rather than death (Thornton & Freedman, 1983, p. 8). The divorce rate doubled from 1963 until 1979, but by the 1990s appears to have stabilized. Half of all recent first marriages will end in divorce. Although most divorced parents remarry, making it possible for 80% of the children to live in two-parent homes, children tend to feel ashamed of the divorce and feel rejected because of their parents' departures. Younger children seem to suffer the most at the time of the divorce, but in a 10-year follow up, older girls still harbored feelings of betrayal and rejection by men, making commitment to their own relationships difficult. If the quality of life after the divorce was good, children did well. If parents continued to fight over the children or burdened their children with too great a responsibility, "in short, if stress and deprivation continue after the divorce—then children are likely to suffer depression and interrupted development" (Wallerstein, 1985). On the other hand, divorce may improve the situation for the child if a successful re-established single family or a remarriage provides the child with a good quality of life.

What does this mean for a teacher? First, schools must accept the fact that single-parent families can supply the components necessary for a flourishing, functioning family. Teachers and administrators will also recognize that during the period of divorce, the family is in turmoil. Children will bring their distress with them to the classroom. The school can offer the child a stable and sensitive environment—one the child can count on—during that period. When parents and teachers communicate, they help children overcome the isolation and distress they feel. Although only one in every five children will probably be from a one-parent family at any given time, one in every two children will spend part of their childhood in a one-parent family.

Adapting for Single Parents

Single parents need to have their special needs accommodated. Unless they have established a strong network of friends or family, they may have difficulty meeting all the requests and obligations they have in their involvement with the school. What are some of their problems?

1. Convenient times for parent-teacher conferences. Single parents (and many two-parent families) need early morning, evening, or weekend times for their conferences. If you use a form such as the one suggested in Figure 4–7, you can find out when they are available. Single parents may also need child care while they attend a conference. This service is also nice for two-parent families so that both parents may attend.

2. Acknowledgment of and communication with noncustodial parents. If noncustodial parents receive report cards and other reports, they will be more interested in the child's work and better able to be involved with the child. Because most single parents are women, the noncustodial parent is generally the man. The percentage of men who pay child support is low. Schools can help sustain or even increase the father's interest by keeping him informed. Most fathers already have a keen interest in their child's schooling. They want to know what is happening without questioning the child. Honor their position; send them frequent reports unless the courts have specified that the noncustodial parent should not have contact or information about the child.

3. Awareness of parents' names. Always check the records to determine the names of the children and the parents, because they may not be the same. This applies equally to two-parent families, because half of them will have had a divorce. Calling the parents by their correct names is a simple gesture of courtesy.

4. Parent involvement. Find ways that single parents can be involved without putting great stress on the family. Early morning breakfasts allow working parents to attend meetings before work. Plan to have child care during the breakfast and provide breakfast for the children. Keep the number of parents at each breakfast small so you can talk with each parent individually. Find out how they would like to be involved, what their needs are, and if they have any ideas for their partnership with the school. Acknowledge their suggestions for improved home/school collaboration.

5. Communication among parents. Establish a newsletter that allows parents to communicate with other parents. Let the parents include what they want to say in the newsletter. Better yet, make it a parent-to-parent newsletter, so they can establish their own networks.

6. Care in communication. Take care when preparing invitations to programs. Perhaps you may wish to emphasize one group, but make sure the child and parent know that they do not need to have a father, mother, or grandparent to attend. For example, saying "Bring your grandparent or a grand friend to class next week" implies that the visitors, not their qualifications, are important. At the program make sure you have some get-acquainted activities so that no one feels left out or alone. Activities also encourage networking among parents, and may be the best opportunity for new single parents in the neighborhood to become acquainted with others. (See Chapter 4 for more school activities and Chapter 6 for ways to make group meetings work.)

BLENDED FAMILIES

"Schools are a powerful institution. Second only to the family, they are the most influential institution in the lives of children," (Crosbie-Burnett & Skyles, 1989, p. 63). School policies must recognize the unique concerns of the blended family to avoid detrimental effects on the growing number of stepchildren.

School personnel tend to view families as they have in the past. They look to the residential family—the family and children located within their school district—as the one family involved with the school and children. However, in 1987 almost 10 million children younger than 18 lived in remarried families (6 million of these

children born to one of the parents before remarriage and 3 million children born after remarriage). Of all children younger than 18 in married families in the United States in 1987, 21% were in remarried families, 19% were in stepfamilies and 13% were stepchildren (Glick, 1989). The difference in figures results from remarried families who do not have children before they remarry and so bring no children into the new marriage. Mothers have custody more often than fathers: 82% of the stepparents were stepfathers and 18 percent were stepmothers.

These figures illustrate the complex social organization of blended families. Some of the children may be offspring of the mother, some of the father, and the remaining may be born to the remarried couple. A child may be living in a home with a brother or sister, a stepbrother or stepsister whose biological parent is the mother or father in the home, and a half-sister or half-brother who is the child of the remarried couple. In addition, they may have visitation with their other biological parent and have the same types of configurations when they are living or visiting there. Families may have as many as 30 configurations (Manning & Wootten, 1987).

Stepfamily Cycle

When two persons marry and one or both of them have children from a previous relationship, the road to a secure, happy family is quite difficult. It can be accomplished, but the original thoughts of delight on the part of the children and acceptance of the new arrangement by the ex-spouses are complicated by the realities of the situation. One of the complicating circumstances occurs because both parents and children have come from single-parent status. During the single-parent stage, children and parent tend to become extremely close. The parent may have turned to the children for emotional support and decision making that had formerly been given by the spouse; "enmeshment seems to be a normal part of single-parent/child relationships" (Papernow, 1984, p. 356). The children of the newly married couple often see the remarriage as a double loss. First, they lost one of their parents through divorce. Now they are losing their special relationship with their custodial parent by having to share him or her with the new stepparent.

Thus begins the stepfamily marriage. The newly married couple fantasize that all the children will enjoy one another and both adults. The children, however, come into the remarriage generally hoping that their biological parents will get back together. Thus, fantasy is the first stage of the blended family cycle. The parents fantasize that the family will immediately become harmonious while the children fantasize that their biological parents will become happily married again—to go back to the old days whether they were good or not.

The cycle of the stepfamily as developed by Papernow (1984) starts with an early stage where they move from fantasy to recognizing their problems and needs, moves to a middle or restructuring stage, and then enters a final stage of solidifying the new family. The early stage includes (1) "Fantasy, (2) Assimilation: We're glad you're here but don't come in," and (3) Awareness: Getting clear." (pp. 357, 358). The middle restructuring stage includes (4) "Mobilization: Airing differences, and (5) Action: Going into business together" (p. 359). The final stage incudes (6) "Contact: Intimacy in step relationships, and (7) Resolution: Holding on and letting go" (pp. 360, 361).

The entire cycle affects the children. During the first stage, while the children are still feeling a loss, their participation in school often suffers. They may go through stages of grief similar to those experienced through divorce, death, or moving away from loved ones. Children may act out in class; they may be despondent, and they may not have interest in schoolwork. For school-age children the school is a known stable environment and can be a support for them, so staying in the same school with their friends can ease the transition.

During the early stage, stepparents become aware that they are not able to nurture children in the same way that biological parents do. Biological parents already have a strong bond with their children. Parents develop an awareness of these family pressures. Both partners recognize what they can handle and which attitudes need to be changed. In some cases the family is never able to restructure their lives, and many of these marriages do not succeed.

The restructuring period of stepfamily development allows for more openness in discussion of change. Parents and children continue to have strong biological ties, but the differences lead the way to action. The couple begins working together to find solutions. In the action phase, family boundaries are clarified and the couple attempts to work together to find solutions.

In the final stages, the roles of each stepparent have been more clearly defined. The stepparent has a specific role relationship with the stepchildren. Acceptance of the new family structure is evident.

Blended family stages are not rushed through within weeks. Papernow found that from 4 to 7 years were needed to complete the entire cycle, and some families were never able to develop their blended family into a strong stepfamily (Glick, 1989, p. 357).

Insights for Teachers

Crosbie-Burnett and Skyles (1989) suggest that four changes must occur in order for schools to accept the challenge of meeting the needs of stepfamilies. These are (1) focus on cooperative coparenting by the biological parents; (2) change thinking that there is a dichotomy between involved and uninvolved parents, but instead view the involvement as falling along a continuum; (3) view the stepparent as an additional parent, not a replacement; and (4) recognize that the extended family (nonresidential biological parents, residential or nonresidential stepparents, grandparents, or other relatives) has potential to support the child and the school. The exception to their suggestions is the noncustodial parent who does not have visitation or other legal rights.

Support for blended families may be provided by implementing the following practices (adapted from Crosbie-Burnett & Skyles, 1989; Manning & Wootten, 1987; and Visher & Visher, 1979).

1. Provide workshops for teachers to explain the varying configurations and the developmental stages of blended families. Review the possible effects on children according to age, sex, and needs.

2. Offer books, articles, and lists of resources about stepfamilies and single-parent families for parents and school personnel. Subscribe to the *Stepfamily Bulletin* from the Stepfamily Association of America (see Appendix E).

3. Eliminate the use of *broken home* and any other words that offend remarried or single families. Survey the parents to determine whether reconstituted, step, or blended are preferred terms. Children can devalue themselves if they hear terms that appear to be derogatory. Other children might conclude that some students are different and inferior.

4. Mail report cards, newsletters, and other informational items to both custodial and noncustodial parents.

5. Include noncustodial parents on field trips, in special programs, and in school activities.

6. Be aware of days when the student is likely to go on a visitation. Time messages accordingly.

7. Encourage children to make more than one Mother's Day or Father's Day card if they have more than one parent of the same sex.

8. Appoint parents from step- and single families to serve on advisory councils, Parent Teacher Associations, or other organizations.

9. Be sensitive to a child whose parent has just remarried. This is a period of stress for both the child and the family. Children may act out and need special handling during the transition.

10. Include stepfamily information and positive stories about children in stepfamilies or single families within the curriculum.

11. Provide peer support groups for stepchildren or single-parent children where they can meet, talk, and realize that they are not the only ones in a blended family.

"Schools are in a position to help support children during this life transition by giving them a safe place to express and explore their feelings, questions, and concerns about parental marriage," (Crosbie-Burnett & Skyles, 1989, p. 59).

POVERTY

Poverty is the greatest child killer in 1985, affluent America. More American children die each year from poverty than from traffic fatalities and suicide combined. Twice more children die from poverty than from cancer and heart disease combined. (Children's Defense Fund, 1985, p. 1).

Poverty is as prevalent now as it was when the War on Poverty began in 1966. When the War on Poverty began one in every five families—39.5 million people—lived in families who earned so little they fell below the poverty level. This was reduced in 1969 to 24.1 million. It remained fairly constant throughout the 1970s until 10 years later when 4.8 million more became impoverished. In 1986 32.4 million people lived below poverty level (Shapiro & Greenstein, 1988).

Poverty has been defined as "a physical and sociopsychological environment in which individuals have severely limited amounts of power, money, and social status" (Farran, Haskins, & Gallagher, 1980). To exist in the culture of poverty means to feel depressed, powerless to make change, and unable to control your own destiny. Alienation, anomie, isolation, and depression are common partners with poverty. Parents, who are depressed and unable to control their own world, pass that feeling on to their children.

One-fifth of children in the United States lived in poverty in 1987, a total of approximately 13 million poor children (Children's Defense

Fund, 1989, p. 40). Forty-three percent of black children; 37.4% of Hispanic children, and 15.6% of white children faced poverty. For children younger than 5, poverty is even more extreme. One-fourth of young children live in poverty (Hymes, 1988, p 19; Children's Defense Fund, 1989, p. 40). It is projected that unless trends are reversed, one in every three children will be poor by 2030 (Children's Defense Fund, 1989, p. 46).

According to Kenniston and the Carnegie Council on Children (1977), it is a myth that families are self-sufficient and able to solve their own problems. Nor does the United States provide equal opportunity for all. "One child out of four in America is 'being actively harmed by a stacked deck' created by the failings of our society" (p. 18).

Poverty is defined in the United States according to income of the person or family. In 1987, a family of four who made less than $11,629; a single person older than 65 whose income was $5,455; and a family of nine or more who earned less than $23,352—before taxes— were considered below poverty level. Of these, only one in nine were lifted out of poverty by state, federal, or local cash assistance.

Assistance varies according to states. In 1987, Alaska furnished Aid to Families with Dependent Children (AFDC) and food stamps for single parents at the 101.5% level; Mississippi funded AFDC and food stamps at 46% of the poverty level (Shapiro & Greenstein, 1988). In the United States those in poverty live surrounded by affluence. This creates an even more difficult situation than that which occurred during the depression when the majority of people were poor. Nevertheless, being hungry and cold hurts and kills no matter who or where you are.

The two groups that are hardest hit in the United States are black children and children of female-headed single families. Forty-two percent of black children and more than 50% of all children in single parent families headed by women lived in poverty in 1984. Blacks and Hispanics have a higher proportion of single-parent families than whites. More than 60% of single-parent Hispanic and black families and 36% of white single-parent families were below the poverty level. Two-parent families fared better; 20% black and Hispanic and 9% white fell under the poverty threshold (Hayghe, 1984, p. 33).

One of the greatest problems that half of all single mothers face is insufficient income. When working with these mothers, recognize not only their time constraints but also their financial bind, and avoid pressure in either area. You may be able to help some by providing information on social services. Find ways to involve them, for they need to know that they are wanted and are important.

If you teach in the inner city, you are likely to have many children who are in low socioeconomic levels in your classes. However, in 1983 only 14% of the poor people lived in inner-city ghettos; more—about 20%—lived in central cities outside the poverty areas. In 1983, 8.878 million—about one in four poor—lived in the suburbs of metropolitan areas. The rest, 13.516 million, lived in nonmetropolitan areas, rural areas, and small towns (O'Hare, 1985, pp. 15, 16). No matter where they work, teachers will find children from families having financial problems.

Contrary to popular opinion, only a portion of the impoverished (estimates in the 1980s range from .7% up to 10%) are poor for 8 or more years (O'Hare, 1985, p. 21). Most people who become poverty stricken move back out of poverty in 1 or 2 years.

Many younger adults are living at the poverty level. They found themselves competing in an overcrowded employment market at the same time there was a loss of jobs to automation, an increase in the female labor force, and increasing competition from foreign products. The greatest increase in unemployment has been males from 18 to 44 years of age. In the 1980s, nearly 20% were unemployed; for young black males the percentage was double (O'Hare, 1985, p. 14).

Families who have always been self-sufficient and who find themselves without employment have tremendous psychological adjustments as well as difficulty in providing shelter and food. For some, using social welfare is an acknowledgment of defeat. Before viewing a child as being neglected, find out the source of the problem.

Table 3–4 illustrates the number of poor according to race or cultural origin and family status. The black family has a particularly difficult time obtaining sufficient employment; nearly 40% of the blacks were below poverty level in 1983.

To counteract the stress of poverty on families, parents and children need at least

- a decent standard of living (jobs that pay enough to adequately rear children)
- more flexible working conditions so that children can be provided for,
- an integrated network of family services, and
- legal protection for children outside and inside families.

TABLE 3–4
Number of poor and poverty rate, by age, sex, race or cultural origin, and family status: 1959, 1978, 1983.

Characteristics	Number of Poor (in 1,000s)			Poverty Rate (percent)		
	1959	*1978*	*1983*	*1959*	*1978*	*1983*
Total	39,490	24,497	35,266	22.4	11.4	15.2
Age						
Under 18	17,208	9,931	13,807	26.9	15.9	22.2
18–64	16,801	11,333	17,748	17.4	8.7	12.4
65 and over	5,481	3,233	3,711	35.2	13.9	14.1
Race and Cultural Origin						
White	28,484	16,259	23,974	18.1	8.7	12.1
Black	9,927	7,625	9,885	55.1	30.6	35.7
Spanish origin[a]	—	2,607	4,249	—	21.6	28.4
Sex						
Males	—	10,017	15,182	—	9.6	13.5
Females	—	14,480	20,084	—	13.0	16.8
Family Status						
In families	34,562	19,062	28,434[b]	20.8	10.0	14.1
In male-headed families	27,548	9,793	15,940	18.2	5.9	9.3
In female-headed families	7,014	9,269	12,494	49.4	35.6	40.5
Unrelated individuals[c]	4,928	5,435	6,832	46.1	22.1	23.4

Sources: O'Hare, W. P. *Poverty in America: Trends and New Patterns.* Washington, D.C. Population Reference Bureau. June 1985, p. 17. O'Hare's study was adapted from Bureau of the Census, 1959 and 1978: "Characteristics of the Population Below the Poverty Level: 1978," Tables 1 and 11; 1983: "Characteristics of the Population Below the Poverty Level, 1983", Tables 1 and 11.
[a]Persons of Spanish origin may be of any race.
[b]The 1983 family data have been adjusted to include 630,000 persons living in "unrelated subfamilies" below the poverty line who are not included in these categories in the published Census Bureau report on poverty for 1983.
[c]Unrelated individuals are persons not living with persons related to themselves by blood or marriage.

WORKING WITH CULTURALLY DIVERSE GROUPS

When teachers work with children at school, they are not working with individuals, isolated and unaffected by their environments. Children do not live in a santitized capsule. Rather, they are a product of their own biology, influenced by others including parents, extended family, peers, teachers, and other caregivers. The family dwells in and is influenced by a larger community that includes the schools; service agencies; religious organizations; political, judicial, and economic systems; and the media.

Therapists have come to recognize that it is a mistake to send an emotionally disturbed child back into the same ecosystem in which the disturbance developed. Therapists must work with the family as well as the child. Therapists also need to understand the larger community in which the family lives. How does the larger community affect the family? Are there cultural norms that influence their communication skills? Is the family under stress? Is under- or unemployment a factor? Only when therapists arrive at an understanding of the concerns and culture are they able to guide the family and child toward healthier relationships. Working with children at school is similar. Teachers need to know their school neighborhood and the issues and problems that parents face in order to understand the children under their charge.

Our nation is culturally diverse. It includes many ethnic groups, varying socioeconomic levels, religious differences, as well as rural and urban influences. School personnel should be aware of and sensitive to these differences.

School personnel and parents may not understand the cultures that make up the school population. The term *culture* is most easily understood when viewed as a way of life. Other descriptive terms for culture are "blueprints for living" and "guidelines for life." Culture includes the way in which life is perceived. It is the knowing, perceiving, and understanding one brings to a situation. Culture may include artifacts such as housing, clothing, and utensils. It is easier to recognize that different artifacts stem from different life styles than it is to discern that individuals are perceiving information differently—viewing a situation or communication with varying interpretations.

Culture is both learned and internalized by the child. Children of any ethnic background learn the cultural patterns in which they are raised. They come to school with those perceptions. For example the concept that a child should be seen and not heard is common in various cultures. Such a child is usually well behaved, but does not offer to answer questions or is not comfortable talking in class. This cultural trait does not work to the child's advantage in a school when the student is called upon. Nor does it help the child develop extended language abilities. Teachers should be aware of this cultural pattern and make sure that the children have many opportunities to express themselves in an encouraging, safe environment. They must

Most children have great potential for academic success.

Understand children's cultural backgrounds and you will be able to help them reach their fullest potential.

be aware that the child has internalized the quiet behavior. It will be difficult for the student to change, but acceptance of the child's positive behavior plus encouragement and reinforcement of the desired behavior will help the child participate in the school's culture. High expectations based on knowledge and understanding of each child sets the stage for growth.

School personnel should get acquainted with the school neighborhoood prior to the starting of school. Take "block walks" with small groups in nice weather. A complete integrated study unit may also be developed on the neighborhood early in the school year.

Two challenges face the schools as they work with culturally diverse students. One is to understand the child's abilities and actions. The other is to eliminate ethnic discrimination. The more the school and home become involved with each other in a positive relationship, the greater are the opportunities for understanding the family and for reduction of discrimination.

Since the end of the Vietnam War, refugees from most of Indochina—Laotians, Hmongs, Cambodians, and Vietnamese have entered our schools. In addition many new arrivals have come from Mexico, Latin America, and South America. Immigration has continued from other countries as well, so you may find children in the schools speaking languages from Europe, Asia, Africa, and the Americas. Minorities are now one fourth of our entire population.

Because of the influx of new minority groups into the United States, teachers will have to increase their understanding of many cultures. This is not an easy task, but it requires an essential commitment. The first and most important thing to remember when working with culturally diverse groups is to avoid stereotyping. Although it is essential to understand their culture, it is also necessary to allow them to be individuals. Every group is composed of individuals, and those individuals may or may not fit the norm.

Successful work with minority parents involves three steps: (1) understand yourself, (2) understand other attitudes and value systems, (3) commit yourself to a bias-free curriculum. Insights and curriculum ideas are suggested in this chapter and in the resources listed in Appendix E.

Native American Families

"To every student in any culture, self respect is essential to success and good life" (Gilliland, 1988, p. 11). All individuals and cultural groups need to feel good about themselves. Carol Black Eagle (Crow Indian) said it well. "The greatest need among Native Americans today is having positive attitudes toward themselves" (p. 11).

American Indians, the native Americans, are indigenous to what is now the United States. The most prominent theory of their origin asserts that their ancestors crossed the Bering Strait into North America thousands of years ago. Although often portrayed as a homogeneous people, they are very diverse both culturally and physically. Their facial features, height, and hair texture vary; skin colors range from dark brown to very light (Banks, 1987, p. 140).

When the Europeans first came to the Americas, as many as 18 million Native Americans were living in North America (John, 1988, p. 325). Estimates of the number of spoken languages range from 300 (John, 1988) to 2,200 (Banks, 1987). Anthropologists have attempted to group the Indian nations who resided in what is now the United States. These groupings include the following areas: (1) Eastern Woodland, (2) Great Lakes Woodland, (3) Southeastern, (4) North Central Plains, (5) South Central Plains, (6) Southwest, (7) California, (8) Northwestern Plateau, and (9) Northwest Pacific Coast (Tiedt & Tiedt, 1989). Within each area numerous Indian tribes flourished. As Europeans settled the eastern portion of the United States, those natives indigenous to the East were forced and pushed westward. Most reservations are located in the midwest and western parts of the United States. The treatment of the American Indian is characterized by broken treaties, genocide, and persecution—a very oppressive chapter of American history.

Most descriptions of the European expansion into North American misrepresent the resistance of the Native American. This distortion of history influences the view other Americans hold about the Native Americans, as well as eroding the American Indians' own self-esteem. A study of different Indian nations, including the people indigenous to the area in which you live, will provide a more accurate and clearer picture of the history of the Native American. For example, the sophistication of the Cherokee nation (prior to the forced Trail of Tears journey from Georgia to Oklahoma and the Cherokee's subsequent ability to adapt to the Oklahoma territory) provides a different picture of the Native American than is generally portrayed in history books or the media.

American Indians have made important contributions to the United States and world cultures. One important contribution was representative government, which was practiced by the Iroquoi confederacy of Five Nations (Mohawks, Oneidas, Onondagas, Cayugas, Senecas, and later the Tuscaroras). Benjamin Franklin was one of the founders who studied this confederacy and learned about their representative government before the United States Constitution was written. The Indians who lived in North and South America were accomplished horticulturists. Corn, potatoes, peppers, tomatoes, peanuts, squash, maple sugar, and beans are some of the more common foods that were developed by the Indian. These foods are used extensively in the world today. Indians in the Southwest developed an elaborate irrigations system. These and other contributions of American Indians help show a more accurate picture of the Native American.

Insights for Teachers

Because the Native Americans come from diverse cultures, it is important that teachers who have these children in their classes learn as much as possible about the specific cultures and backgrounds of the children. "The acculturation of Native Americans should be looked upon as a continuum ranging from traditional orientation' to 'assimilated' " (Little Soldier, 1985, p. 186). Visit in the neighborhood, talk with parents in informal settings, attend a pow wow (unless it is a closed ceremony), and visit the parents in their homes after they feel comfortable having you there. "Visit with the people in the community at every opportunity" (Gilliland, 1988, p. 24).

As is the case in all ethnic groups, individual preferences and values exist. Use the background on culture as a guide to help you understand the individual child, not as a stereo-

typical absolute. Gilliland (1988) relates some cultural traits that may cause misunderstanding unless the teacher is aware. These are five of his suggestions of areas to understand:

1. Eye contact—To most Indians, looking down is a sign of respect (p. 25). In some Indian groups a person only looks another in the eye to show defiance (p. 26).

2. Time—Time has a different meaning to many Indians than it does to European-Americans. "They say 'time flies.' To the Mexican 'time walks.' However, the Indian tells, 'time is with us' " (p. 26). Patience is a highly valued characteristic.

3. The extended family is important to the American Indian child, so grandparents may be the ones to attend parent-teacher conferences. If the child is separated from the extended family by a move to the city or some other circumstance, the child may experience a loss of the sense of security.

4. The Native Americans respect nature, and spirituality remains an important part of the Indian culture. "Harmony with nature, and spirituality, are also necessary to good health" (p. 31).

5. The focus in the dominant U.S. society is on youth; in the American Indian tradition there is respect for age and the wisdom associated with the elderly.

In working with the parents of Native American children the teacher needs to show interest and acceptance. Teachers must expect to reach out to the parents and the extended family. Help them feel comfortable with you and the classroom. When they are at ease, invite them to share their specialties, perhaps crafts and folklore, with the class.

Curriculum in the schools needs to include an accurate history of the Native Americans in order to overcome the stereotypical misrepresentation of American Indians as savage hunters of the plains. The study of Indian nations that represent a variety of life styles and governmental forms can show the diversity and accomplishments of the American Indian prior to the coming of the Europeans.

Some strategies may be more effective than others in working with Native American children. Consider (1) group problem solving; (2) peer tutoring; (3) cooperative learning; (4) group pride, sharing, and replacing competition against others with self-competition; (5) culturally relevant materials; (6) parent volunteers; and (7) flexibility in timed events (Gilliland, 1988; Little Soldier, 1985). Observe the children and analyze their learning strengths and interests. Many Indian children learn best by modeling and observing (rather than just listening to instructions) before they proceed with the activity. As you learn about your students, adapt your class to the best ways of learning for the individual child and the class as a group.

The whole language reading approach is appropriate for Native American children. The majority of Indian students are holistic learners. They learn more easily if they see the whole picture first, then learn the details (Fox, 1988, p. 103). Whole language also encourages the use of creative writing, recording of children's own stories, use of folk stories related to the culture, production of newsletters and newspapers, and other original work of the children. Whole language approaches, used along with other traditional teaching methods, give an avenue for children of many cultures to be successful.

African-American Families

The strengths found in African-American families include strong kinship bonds, an achievement orientation, a strong work orientation with a desire for upward mobility, adaptability of family roles, and an emphasis on religion (Hale-Benson, 1986). The extended family, along with the adaptability of family roles, allows families to survive the hardships and trials that have been a part of their lives in the United States.

African-Americans have a marvelous heritage that includes a high development of music, art, literature, and an emphasis on religion. Blacks have a strong commitment to their

Give children opportunities to excel in creative expression.

churches, so children grow up in families where faith and religion are important aspects of their lives. Many black leaders have been ministers (for example, Martin Luther King, Jr. and Jesse Jackson). Music is an essential expression in their religion. Black musicians developed jazz. Although many blacks have a remarkable creative ability in music, this does not mean that all blacks are great musicians, nor do all blacks use the church as a focal point in their lives.

African-American people have been a part of the Americas since Diego el Negro sailed with Columbus in 1502. Blacks helped Coronado explore present-day Kansas in 1541, and helped establish St. Augustine, Florida in 1565 (Banks, 1987). As indentured servants, blacks landed on the eastern shores of the United States in 1619. Later, when they were brought over as slaves, their culture was eradicated as much as possible. Family life was discouraged and families were broken up if the master wanted to sell one member of the family and not the other. Children were most often left with their mother until they were old enough to be on their own. Most were not allowed to learn to read; schooling was usually forbidden. After the Civil War, times changed, but blacks were still not allowed to exist as first-class citizens. Not until 1965 and the passage of the Civil Rights Act was equality enforceable. Today, covert discrimination still exists.

Insights for Teachers

What should teachers know about black children? Each child, of any cultural group, is unique. Culture depends in great part upon the location and socioeconomic status of the family. The culture—black or white—in a lower-income neighborhood is much different from that in a middle-class and upper-class area. Middle- and upper-class blacks tend to accept the culture of middle- and upper-class society in the United States. If anything, these black parents require their children to be more perfect and behave better than corresponding parents in the white society.

Impoverished black families have different strengths and different problems. Black parents in ghettos face problems of poverty, powerlessness, alienation, and a negative environment. These children rarely see models of financial success as a result of education and hard work. A good standard of living is impossible if the parent is unemployed or only earning minimum wage. These children are raised in a culture of dropouts and school failure, as well as with the love of their extended family. In 1983 black urban youth were handicapped by a 70% unemployment rate in some metropolitan areas.

However, Clark (1983) suggests that family life style is a stronger indicator of a child's success in school than socioeconomic level. He found that children who were high achievers came from homes that supported and helped their children achieve, regardless of their income. The interpersonal communications within these families showed encouragement in their academics, nurturing interaction with frequent

dialogue, established rules and clear guidelines, and monitoring of their learning activities (p. 111).

Children who speak a black dialect of English at home will come to school knowing different language patterns than those who are surrounded by standard English. They will have to learn a second language—standard English—which is not always an easy task. "Speaking, listening, labeling, storytelling, chanting, imitating and reciting" (Hale-Benson, 1986 p. 161) are activities that should be encouraged in an early childhood classroom. There should be ample opportunity for all children to enjoy them.

Black families often have a strong network among family members and friends. Aunts, uncles, and grandparents help and support one another (Stevens, 1982). Most black parents are very interested in their children and their educational achievement.

Hale-Benson (1986) connects the roots of West Africa with the childrearing culture of African-Americans. "Black children may have distinctive learning and expressive styles that can be observed in their play behavior" (p. 5). A model early childhood classroom for all children includes (1) a supportive environment with frequent touching and lap sitting; (2) an emphasis on the development of self-concept through success experiences, compliments, and display of work; (3) opportunities for creative expression in music, dramatics, and visual arts; (4) involvement in arts and crafts with African-American and African art as part of the curriculum; (5) activities that involve physical movement, play, and dance with as much self direction as feasible; (6) exposure to artifacts, stories, and other aspects of African culture; (7) extracurricular activities that include bringing the community into the school and taking field trips; (8) celebration of holidays that include the holidays of many cultural groups (adapted from Hale-Benson, pp. 163, 164). The teacher must be aware of body language and be sensitive to its cues, model standard English, encourage the children to talk, emphasize group learning, incorporate music into the curriculum, and have a variety of learning activities (p. 165) that reach children with a variety of learning styles.

Until prejudice and discrimination are eliminated in the United States, most black children will receive mixed messages. At school, they need to receive one message: All children will succeed because they are first-class citizens.

Spanish-Surnamed Families

Although the Spanish-surnamed residents of the United States share some linguistic and cultural traits, each wave of immigrants from Spain, Cuba, Latin America, and Mexico has brought its own unique attributes. Varied social status and educational levels in their countries of origin, the isolation or hardships encountered on arrival, their desire to acculturate, and the length

Spanish-surnamed children may be from families who have been in the United States for years or who have just immigrated.

of their family's residence in the United States all contribute to a heterogeneous Hispanic-American population. Teachers must work to dispel any stereotypical ideas they may have about their Spanish-surnamed students.

Who are the many people who have contributed to the history of this varied group? The first group of Spanish-surnamed citizens in the United States was in North America before the Pilgrims arrived. Hardly immigrants, they had settled and lived with the Pueblo Indians long before the United States was interested in the territory. These Spanish Colonialists, given land grants by the Spanish Viceroys, continued their Spanish lifestyle in areas including Santa Fe, San Antonio, and San Diego. Missions, Spanish-style architecture, their methods of ranching, and irrigation systems show their contributions to the lifestyle of the Southwest. Many of these persons do not want to be called Mexican American or Chicano; their heritage is Spanish and the term, Spanish-American or Hispanic, better fits their culture and their heritage.

The Southwest United States was Spanish territory until 1821 when Mexico gained independence from Spain. Mexico held the Southwest until Texas was annexed by the United States in 1845. Arizona, New Mexico, Nevada, and parts of California and Colorado were acquired by the United States as the result of the Mexican American War. Thus, by 1848 many people whose ancestors had lived in traditionally Spanish-speaking areas since the 1600s suddenly became citizens of the United States.

The great influx of Mexican-Americans did not begin in the United States until around the time of the Mexican Revolution in 1910. Many of the first immigrants were upper-class Mexicans, refugees escaping for political reasons. Their assimilation into the United States society was relatively easy. A second influx of immigrants occurred in 1916 when Mexicans were hired to help maintain the railroad system across the United States. They were expected to work and return home, but many remained. They suffered bitter discrimination especially from those who felt that they were taking jobs from U.S. citizens. Nonetheless, the descendants of this group of Mexican-Americans are now assimilated into the society.

During World War II the United States needed help with its farm crops, so the bracero program was instituted. Mexicans were invited to work temporarily in the gardens of California and other states. In 1951, the Migratory Labor Agreement (Public Law 78) established a new bracero program (Banks, 1987).

After World War II many Spanish-surnamed people migrated to cities and northern states to work. Some came from Mexico, but many were United States citizens who moved up from New Mexico, Texas, and southern Colorado to work in cities and on ranches. These were the natives of the Southwest who were forced off their land when the mines closed and farms were automated. They were a rural people, trying to assimilate into an urban culture.

The use of braceros and migrant workers set a pattern for Mexican workers to come to the United States. Many began crossing the border illegally. In 1954, U.S. immigration authorities began deporting illegal Mexicans, but thousands of Mexican-Americans continued to pour across the borders (Banks, 1987). An amnesty bill passed by Congress and implemented in 1988 allowed illegal residents who could prove they had lived in the United States for five years to become citizens.

Illegal immigration continues today. The economies in Mexico and other Latin-American countries are poor. Many of these Latin-American nationals are grasping at an opportunity to provide for their families. The children of these new immigrants come to our schools with very little or no English. These children need special care and help to succeed in our educational system. This new group of Spanish-speaking Americans, coupled with the rural-to-urban movement of long-time citizens of Hispanic background, provide a challenge to the schools to provide both bilingual education and a strong program in language enrichment.

Insights for Teachers

Hispanic children are loved whether they achieve in school or not. Although this attitude can be positive, Spanish-surnamed parents need to be urged to acknowledge their children's efforts and encourage them in their school work.

Recently-arrived immigrants may be reluctant to get involved in the school—many fear being identified as illegal immigrants, even though schools are required to educate all children and are not responsible for determining who is legal and who is not. Many of these parents have not had a good experience in school themselves, and feel threatened by the school. See Chapters 4, 7, and 8 for ideas on ways to involve this challenging group of parents.

In a study that analyzed school success and failure among Mexican-American students, it was found that the Mexican-American students who were achievement oriented did not have a specific goal in mind, although they wanted to do well in school. Most, but not all, indicated that one reason for their success in school was their parents' interest and support. Male students felt that they received more support from home than did female students; some of the successful girls received their support from teachers and counselors rather than parents (Matute-Bianchi, 1986).

Spanish-surnamed children work best in a cooperative, rather than a competitive, atmosphere. Lack of extended language seems to be the biggest problem for the Mexican child. Opportunities for language expression need to be encouraged at all levels of education. Small group discussions, cooperative games that increase language skill, use of language on the computer, role playing, creative dramatics, puppetry, and general encouragement of language use are all essential for language development. Classrooms in which children are encouraged to talk with each other also encourage language development. If children are not allowed to talk in the lunchroom, the importance of language development is being ignored.

As is the case with all children, teachers working with Spanish-surnamed children must get to know the parents and work with them and their children to meet their needs.

Southeast Asians

The easiest mistake for teachers to make is to presume all Southeast Asians—from Vietnam, Laos (including the Hmong), Cambodia, and Thailand—share a common background. The first major group of refugees arrived from Vietnam in 1975 after the fall of the country to the North Vietnamese. This group included the wealthy and poor, highly educated scholars and professionals, as well as unskilled workers. Most were literate, but 18% had no education (Banks, 1987). The second wave of Indochinese refugees was more diverse and included Hmong, Laotians, and Kampucheans (Cambodians). They were more homogenous in their lack of education and their inability to speak English.

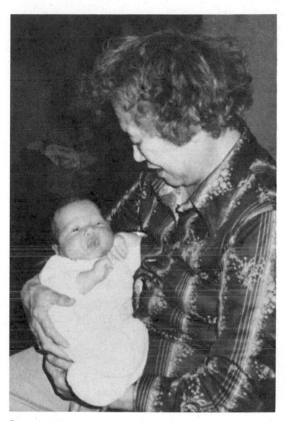

Grandmothers play an important role in the extended family.

Families of Asian descent have been assimilated in varying degrees into the dominant culture of the United States.

French Indochina, first proclaimed the Indochinese Union by the French in 1893, was made up of Vietnam, Cambodia, and Laos. Until that time, the countries were separate political entities; after the union they continued to differ from one another in language, history, and culture. The term *Indochinese* was given by the French and may be used to describe an area, but should not be used to designate individual countries. The countries of Laos, Cambodia, and Thailand were influenced by India; Vietnam and the Hmong (mountain people of Laos) were influenced by China. However, these countries do not view themselves as one area; they are separate countries. Throughout their long history, these countries were often enemies, controlled by one or the other as one empire thrived and was then destroyed. When working with children from this area of Asia, find out what country was the parent's homeland.

Language differences in these countries are illustrated in Figure 3–1. These children will have to use English as a second language (ESL) to communicate with each other the same as you do. Indochinese families also have different placement of names (see Figure 3–2) although many of the refugees have adapted their names

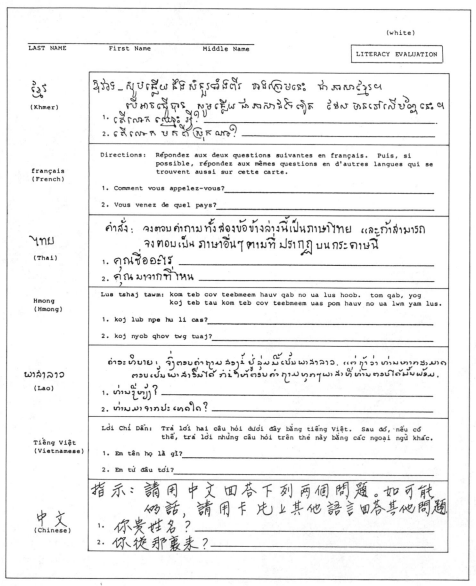

FIGURE 3–1

These examples illustrate the wide variety of written language of the Indochinese people. *Source:* Language and Orientation Resource Center. *Indochinese students in U.S. schools: A guide for administrators.* Washington, D.C.: Center for Applied Linguistics, 1981, pp. 60, 61.

to fit traditional name placement found in the United States, so schools may not find as much confusion in the 1990s as in the 1970s.

During the 2,000-year history of Indochina, its inhabitants were influenced by Chinese, Indian, Oceanic, and European cultures. The great variety of religious traditions are indicative of the many cultures in the region. Buddhism spread from India; Taoism and Confucianism originated in China. Christianity was introduced much later. An Indochinese person may believe in more than one religion because Eastern reli-

	Last name	Middle name	First name	Addressed as*
Vietnamese				
Nguyen Hy Vinh (M)	Nguyen	Hy	Vinh	Vinh Mr. Vinh
Hoang Thi Thanh (F) 1. Married (to Mr. Vinh)	Hoang	Thi	Thanh	Thanh Mrs. Thanh Mrs. Vinh
2. Unmarried				Thanh Miss Thanh
Cambodian				
Sok Sam Bo (M)	Sok	(none)	Sam Bo	Sam Bo Mr. Sam Bo
Rith Bopha (F) 1. Married (to Mr. Sam Bo)	Rith	(none)	Bopha	Bopha Mrs. Sam Bo
2. Unmarried				Bopha Miss Bopha
Lao				
Vixay Siharath (M)	Siharath	(none)	Vixay	Vixay Mr. Vixay

Douangkeo Malaythong (F)
  1. Married (to Mr. Vixay)
  2. Unmarried
	Malaythong
	Siharath
		(none)
		(none)
			Douangkeo
			Douangkeo
				Douangkeo
				Mrs. Douangkeo
				Douangkeo
				Miss Douangkeo

Hmong				
Chu Sao Thao (M)	Thao (clan name)	Chu	Sao	Chu Mr. Chu Sao
May Xee Vang (F)	Vang (clan name)	May	Xee	
1. Married (to Mr.Chu Thao)				May Xee Mrs. Chu Sao
2. Unmarried				May Xee Miss May Xee

*Adding *Mr., Mrs., Miss* makes the form of address more formal.

FIGURE 3–2

Name placement varies among the Indochinese ethnic groups. *Source:* Language and Orientation Resource Center. *Indochinese students in U.S. schools: A Guide for administrators.* Washington, D.C.: Center for Applied Linguistics, 1981, pp. 49, 50.

gions are based on philosophies of behavior more than deification of their leaders. In addition to the major religions, animism and ancestor worship are practiced in many rural areas. Polytheism is accepted. Most Eastern religions share an emphasis on the individual's search for peace and harmony, a reverence for ancestors, and a respect for the elderly.

Insights for Teachers

If children come from a culture where there was no formal education, they may have problems adjusting to school. The Hmong, for instance, did not have a written language until the 1960s. Children who are unable to write and read in their native language are sometimes called double illiterates, because they have no written language base upon which to draw. Teachers need to recognize these children's experiences and backgrounds and plan a curriculum to address their strengths and needs.

Most Asian-American families value education, and generally Vietnamese, Cambodian, and Laotian students work hard to obtain an education. Often parents or siblings will tutor young children or others before school. Their respect for education extends to teachers, so Indochinese parents do not question the teacher's decisions or expertise.

Southeast Asian children who were in school before coming to the United States were taught largely through lecture and memorization; active participation in the learning process may be new to them. Others may not have attended school at all.

Most Indochinese families form close-knit extended families. They often try to reunite when they arrive in the United States. They also work hard to save money, often sacrificing, in order to bring other members of their families to their new home. Many of the families suffered

extreme trauma in their escape to freedom. Use journals for older children and creative art for younger and older children to help them express feelings.

It is important for teachers to be sensitive to gestures and mannerisms that may have unintended meanings. For example, Southeast Asian students may not look steadily in the eyes of the teacher because such behavior is a sign of disrespect. A pat on the child's head may be meant kindly, but it is likely to offend. Children should not be called by a hand motion with fingers up since such mannerisms are reserved for animals. To call a child with your hand, place your palm and fingers down. Be sure not to criticize Indochinese children (or any others) in front of others; they need to be able to "save face." Indochinese pupils may come to school with small round bruises on the arm, but *coining* (pressure by coins) is used as a method to reduce illness or pain and is not a sign of abuse.

Parents and children may not let you know if they do not understand. They are more likely to agree and smile rather than to question. Indochinese children fit smoothly into a school system. They tend to compete for good grades, are well-behaved, and industrious. Teachers need to be concerned about the stress children are under in their desire to achieve. Teachers should give these students assignments that are realistic.

This chapter points out many of the diverse challenges that face teachers, parents, and schools. The changing world—accompanied by the birth and growth of a new generation and the arrival of newcomers from other lands—requires dedication to the task.

Children are like snowflakes.
At first they appear to be alike,
But on close examination they are all different.
Focus on their similarities,
But understand their differences.

SUMMARY

Families around the world are living with change, but the family, the most stable component of society, flourishes. Marriage and family life are important.

The population of the United States has increased dramatically in the last 50 years. Along with growth in numbers, the following trends are evident. More mothers are working outside the home. More people are completing high school and college. Out-of-wedlock births, especially to teenagers, have increased alarmingly. Eighteen percent of the children live with single-parent mothers. Fathers are getting more involved with their children.

Poverty in the United States has increased in the last decade. Almost one in every five children live in poverty. The greatest number are the children of single-parent mothers and children in black families.

Black families still face covert prejudice, although strides have been made to reduce overt discrimination. Spanish surnamed people, along with blacks, find it difficult to satisfactory occupations. Immigration of Southeast Asians—Vietnamese, Hmong, Laotians, and Cambodians—have challenged our schools. These immigrants have adjusted to the environment extremely well considering the great cultural shock and language differences.

Although it is important to understand cultural differences, teachers will encourage success in their students when they focus on the strengths of each child.

BIBLIOGRAPHY

Banks, J. A. *Teaching strategies for ethnic studies* (4th ed.). Boston: Allyn & Bacon, 1987.

Berrueta-Clement, J.; Schweinhart, L. J.; Barnett, W. S.; Epstein, A. S.; & Weikart, D. P. *Changed lives: The effects of the Perry Preschool Program on youths through age 19.* Ypsilanti, Mich.: The High/Scope Press, 1984.

Cataldo, C. Z. *Parent education for early childhood.* New York: Teachers College Press, 1987.

Cherlin, A. J. *Marriage, divorce, remarriage.* Cambridge, Mass.: Harvard University Press, 1981.

Children's Defense Fund. *A children's defense budget: An analysis of the President's FY 1986 budget and children.* Washington, D.C.: Author, 1985.

———. *Child care: The time is now.* Washington, D.C.: Author, 1988a.

———. *A children's defense budget: An analysis of our nation's investment in children FY 1989,* Washington, D.C.: Author, 1988b.

———. *A vision for America's future.* Washington, D.C.: Author, 1989.

Crosbie-Burnett, M., & Skyles, A. Stepchildren in schools and colleges: Recommendatons for educational policy changes. *Family Relations,* January 1989, pp. 59–64.

Elam, S. M. The twenty-first annual Gallup Poll of the public's attitudes toward the public school. *Phi Delta Kappan,* September 1989, pp. 41–54.

Fantini, M. D., & Cardenas, R. *Parenting in a multicultural society.* New York: Longman, 1980.

Farran, D. C., Haskins, R., & Gallagher, J. J. Poverty and mental retardation: A search for explanations. *New Directions for Exceptional Children, 1,* 1980, pp. 47–65.

Fox, S. J. A whole language approach to the communication skills. In H. Gilliland (Ed.), *Teaching the Native American.* Dubuque, Iowa: Kendall/Hunt Publishing Company, 1988.

Fullerton, H. N. Labor force projections: 1986 to 2000. *Monthly Labor Review,* September 1987, pp. 19–29.

Galinsky, E. *The six stages of parenthood.* Reading, Mass.: Addison-Wesley, 1987.

Gilliland, H. (Ed.). *Teaching the Native American.* Dubuque, Iowa: Kendall/Hunt Publishing Company, 1988.

Glick, P. C. Remarried families, stepfamilies, and stepchildren: A brief demographic profile. *Family Relations, 38* (1), January 1989, pp. 24–27.

Hale-Benson, J. E. *Black children: Their roots, culture, and learning styles.* Baltimore: The Johns Hopkins University Press, 1986.

Hayghe, H. V. Working mothers reach record number in 1984. *Monthly Labor Review,* December 1984, pp. 31–33.

———. Employers and child care: What roles do they play? *Monthly Labor Review,* September 1988, p. 38.

Howard, A. E. *The American family: Myth and reality.* Washington, D.C.: National Association for the Education of Young Children, 1980.

Howe, W. J. Education and demographics: How do they affect unemployment rate? *Monthly Labor Review,* January 1988, pp. 3–9.

Hymes, J. L., Jr. *Early childhood education: The year in review, a look at 1987.* Carmel, Calif.: Hacienda Press, 1988.

Jensen, L. C., & Kingston, M. *Parenting.* New York: Holt, Rinehart and Winston, 1986.

John, R. The Native American family. In C. H. Mindel, R. W. Habenstein, & R. Wright Jr. (Eds.). *Ethnic families in America* (3rd ed.). New York: Elsevier, 1988.

Kaplan, G. P., Van Valey, L., & Associates. *Census '80: Continuing the factfinder tradition.* U.S. Bureau of the Census, Washington, D.C.: U.S. Government Printing Office, 1980.

Kenniston, K., & The Carnegie Council on Children. *All our children.* New York: Harcourt Brace Jovanovich, 1977.

Lamb, M. E. *The role of the father in child development.* New York: A Wiley-Interscience Publication, 1976.

Lamb, M. E. (Ed.). *The father's role.* Hillsdale, N.J.: Lawrence Erlbaum Associates, Publishers, 1987.

Language and Orientation Resource Center. *Indochinese students in U.S. schools: A guide for administrators.* Washington, D.C.: Center for Applied Linguistics, 1981.

LeMasters, E. E., & DeFrain, J. *Parents in contemporary America: A sympathetic view* (4th ed.). Homewood, Ill.: Dorsey Press, 1983.

Little Soldier, L. To soar with the eagles: Enculturation and acculturation of Indian children. *Childhood Education,* January/February 1985, pp. 185–191.

Lowery, C. R., & Settle, S. A. Effects of divorce on children: Differential impact of custody and visitation patterns. *Family Relations,* October 1985, pp. 455–461.

Manning, D. T., & Wooten, M. D. What stepparents perceive schools should know about blended families. *The Clearing House, 60,* January 1987, pp. 230–235.

Matute-Bianchi, M. E. Ethnic identities and patterns of school success and failure among Mexican-descent and Japanese-American students in a California high school. An ethnographic analysis. *American Journal of Education,* November 1986, pp. 233–255.

O'Connell, J. C. Research in review: Children of working mothers: What the research tells us. *Young Children,* January 1983, pp. 62–70.

O'Connell, M., & Bloom, D. E. *Juggling jobs and babies: America's child care challenge.* #12. Washington, D.C.: Population Reference Bureau, Inc., 1987.

O'Hare, W. P. *Poverty in America: Trends and new patterns. Population Bulletin, 40*(3). Washington, D.C.: Population Reference Bureau, 1985.

Papernow, P. L. The stepfamily cycle: An experiential model of stepfamily development, *Family Relations,* July 1984, pp. 355–363.

Phillips, D. A. (Ed.). *Quality in child care: What does research tell us?* Washington, D.C.: National Association for the Education of Young Children, 1987.

Shapiro, I., & Greenstein, R. *Holes in the safety nets.* Washington, D.C.: Center on Budget and Policy Priorities, 1988.

Stevens, J. H., Jr. Support systems for black families. In J. D. Quisenberry, (Ed.), *Changing family lifestyles.* Wheaton, Md.: Association for Childhood Education International, 1982.

Swick, J. J. Parents as models in children's cultural development. *The Clearinghouse, 60,* October 1986, pp. 72–75.

Swick, K. J., & Manning, M. L. Father involvement in home and school settings. *Childhood Education,* November/December 1983, pp. 128–134.

Thornton, A., & Freedman, D. *The changing American family.* Population Bulletin, No. 38, 4. Washington, D.C.: Population Reference Bureau, 1983.

Tiedt, P. L., & Tiedt, I. M. *Multicultural teaching* (3rd ed.). Boston: Allyn & Bacon, 1989.

U.S. Bureau of the Census. *Current population reports. Population characteristics.* (Series P-20, No. 402), Washington, D.C.: U.S. Government Printing Office, 1985.

Visher, E. B., & Visher, J. S. *Stepfamilies: A guide to working with stepparents and stepchildren.* Secaucus, N.J.: The Citadel Press, 1979.

Wallerstein, J. Effect of divorce on children. *The Harvard Medical School Mental Health Letter,* 2(3), 1985.

Wallerstein, J. S., & Kelly, J. B. The effects of parental divorce: Experience of the child in later latency. In A. Skolnick & J. H. Skolnick (Eds.), *Family in transition.* Boston: Little, Brown, and Co., 1980.

Washington, V., & Oyemade, U. J. Changing family trends—Head Start must respond. *Young Children,* September 1985, pp. 12–20.

White, B. L. *A parent's guide to the first three years.* Englewood Cliffs, N.J.: Prentice-Hall, 1980.

Zill, N. *Basic facts about the use of child care and preschool services by families in the U.S.* Washington, D.C.: Child Trends, Inc., 1988.

4

Effective Home-School-Community Relationships

P arent-school cooperation brings the strengths of the home and the expertise of the school into a working partnership. Students who cannot read and write, the dropout rate, and low test scores are primary national concerns. Teachers call for more parental involvement; they cannot carry the responsibility for future generations alone (Harris, 1987). This crisis in education demands a societal response.

Home-school partnerships are an essential step forward. Recent research emphasizes increased opportunities for children's success when the home and school work together (U.S. Department of Education, 1986; 1987. More parent-school involvement is needed from birth through high school (Bloom, 1981; Brofenbrenner, 1976; Daresh, 1986; Epstein, 1986; Fehrmann, Keith, & Reimers, 1987; Meyerhoff & White, 1986). This chapter focuses on the goal of good school-home-community relationships with suggestions for procedures and methods to start the process.

Not everyone in the school will be comfortable with increased parent-school collaboration. Epstein (1986) pointed out two conflicting theories. One encourages homes and schools to work together because they share the same goals for the students. The other theory argues that schools can achieve their goals to educate most efficiently when school and home remain separate, that "professional status is in jeopardy if parents are involved in activities that are typically the teacher's responsibilities" (p. 227).

Of course, most teachers are also parents. Their role confusion was dramatically illustrated at a workshop involving parents, teachers, and administrators. The participants were asked to raise their hands if they were parents. Almost every person in the room raised a hand. Suddenly the teachers and administrators were in their parental rather than professional roles. Teachers described how different their feelings were when their roles were reversed from teachers to parents.

The emotional change between being a parent receiving services or being a professional responsible for the education of someone else's child was felt immediately. Prior to coming to the workshop, participants held varying views on parent involvement. Some believed in working with parents, some were already highly successful at parent involvement, and some wanted to keep parents at a respectable distance. As they experienced the change of roles, they recognized how their understanding of parents' feelings and concerns is a giant step toward creating effective home-school relationships.

As volunteers in the classroom, parents can support and help the teacher while they learn new activities to share with their children at home.

Picturing parents as a group separate from the school sets up an artificial barrier. Parents are no special breed. We are the parents of the current generation of young people. To understand ourselves as parents is to begin to understand others. What makes us effective participants in home-school-community relationships are those same qualities that make others productive members of the home-school-community team.

SCHOOL CLIMATE AND PARENTAL ATTITUDES

When you walk into a school, are you able to sense its spirit? Does it seem to invite you to visit? Does it make you feel unwelcome? Can you pinpoint the reasons for your feelings? Each school differs in its character (usually set by the administrators) and reflects the morale and attitudes of the personnel. Some say, "Come, enjoy with us this exciting business of education." Others say, "You are infringing on my territory. Schools are the professional's business. Send us your children. We will return them to you each evening, but in the meantime, let's each keep to our own responsibilities." In the first instance, there is joy in the educational spirit. In the second, fear or avoidance override all sense of joy.

Parents also bring their attitudes into the home-school relationship. One parent may feel excitement and anticipation about a forthcoming visit to the school, while another may be struck with dread over a required conference. Parents come from diverse backgrounds. If their past school experiences were pleasant and successful, they are likely to enjoy visiting schools again. If their experiences were filled with failure and disappointments, whether real or imagined, the thought of school is depressing; if they do approach the school, they do so with trepidation. When you recognize, understand, and respect parents' cultural/social background, you are more likely to bring those parents into the school.

Coupled with the parents' past experiences are present pressures. In some districts the burden of poverty will consume the parents. Parents concerned with mere subsistence have little energy left for self-fulfillment or for meeting their children's emotional and educational needs. Maslow's (1968) hierarchy of needs stresses that basic needs must be met before persons can climb to higher rungs of the ladder toward self-actualization. Parents contending with unemployment, inflation, and social change will need special understanding. "Humans of all ages get caught in a powerful web spun of two strong threads; the way they were treated in the past, and the way the present bears down on them" (Hymes, 1974, p. 16). The school must be a support system working cooperatively with the home rather than another agency viewing the parents as failures.

Add the parents' concerns for their children's welfare and you will recognize why school-home relationships can be either negative encounters or effective partnerships. Hymes (1974) eloquently described the parent-child-teacher relationship when he said that parents love their children, and if the teacher

feels this same love, then parents are your friends. Show your interest in a child and parents are on your side. Be casual, be off-handed, be cold toward the child and parents can never work closely with you. . . . To touch the child is to touch the parent. To praise the child is to praise the parent. To criticize the child is to hit at the parent. The two are two, but the two are one. (pp. 8, 9)

Debilitating experiences with schools, feelings of inadequacy, poor achievement by children, and pressures of the present can cause some parents to stay away from the school. On the other hand, some parents tend to dominate and to be compulsively involved with the schools. Between these two extremes are parents who need encouragement to come to school, parents who readily respond when invited, and parents who are comfortable about coming to school and enjoy some involvement in the educational process (see Figure 4–1). Each group requires a different response from the professional staff. The first group will need time to overcome past negative experiences and to appreciate that the school can be trusted to help their children. If the school has an inviting and responsive climate, the second, third, and fourth groups of parents will feel welcome. These three middle groups (which encompass the largest portion of parents) will soon become contributing resources to the school's activities. They can also form a supportive advocacy for future school plans.

Those in the fifth group can also become positive assets. Encourage them to take on responsibility, such as fundraising or organizing a social get together. Let them lead in this way. Offering a variety of tasks and different degrees of involvement assures parents that they may contribute according to their talents and avail-

able time and allows all of them to be comfortable about coming to school and enjoying involvement in the educational process.

THE CASE FOR IMPROVED RELATIONSHIPS

Schools have more contact with families than any other public agency. Almost every child from the age of 5 spends 9 months a year, 5 days a week, 5 or 6 hours a day, in school. If child care centers and preschools are included, the school-home-community relationship begins at an even earlier age. Locally controlled, schools can respond to the needs of the community. If schools and community join forces in a coordinated effort to support families and children, they can have an enormous impact. The school and home also have a natural opportunity to work together. With the community, they can achieve their goals for children.

In an extensive research project, Williams (1984) found both school personnel and parents concerned about the necessity of parent involvement in schools. A majority of school staff, administrators, and parents felt that parent involvement in education is both important and necessary. Williams' study included a sample of 950 teacher educators, 2,000 teachers, 1,500 principals, 4,800 parents, 2,500 school superintendents, 2,500 school board presidents, and 36 state department of education officials.

Parents were very interested in all aspects of their child's education. They differed with school administrators and teachers in their desire for more involvement in decision making. School staff want more educational involvement at home and support for the school program but little parental involvement in school decision making. Both groups agreed that training teachers to work with parents is important. The study recommended that parents be involved as real partners, beginning with the traditional roles and progressing until they function as partners in the educational process (Williams, 1984).

| Parents who avoid schools like the plague | Parents who need encouragement to come to school | Parents who readily respond when invited to school | Parents who are comfortable and enjoy involvement in school | Parents who enjoy power and are overly active |

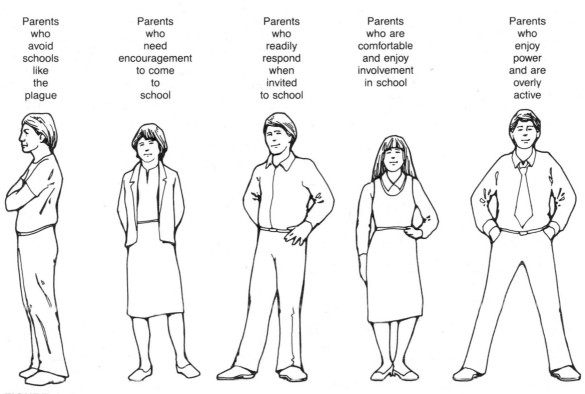

FIGURE 4–1
Parents respond to schools based upon past experience and the current situation.

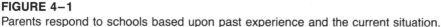

In another survey (Harris, 1987), 75% of the teachers wanted to have parents involved inside the school and 74% of the parents wanted to be involved. The group who felt it did not have enough contact were teachers working in inner-city schools, parents of secondary students, and single parents who work full time. "Home school links strongly affect teachers' job satisfaction, and job satisfaction strongly impacts on the likelihood of staying in or leaving the teaching profession" (Harris, 1987).

Epstein (1986) found that teachers who were leaders in parent involvement practices enabled all parents—regardless of the parent's educational level—to be involved. These teachers asked parents to conduct learning activities at home, such as read aloud, ask child about the school day, play games, visit classroom, go to library, and help children with homework.

Seefeldt (1985) called for parent involvement in which there is concern for the welfare of the parents along with the children. She recommended that schools be sensitive to the needs of families, offer real support for families, and provide true collaboration between home and school (p. 99). Parents' decision-making powers might include "decisions about the school's budget, selection of staff, and general operating procedures" (p. 102).

Parent-school-community partnership has been recognized in national programs such as Head Start and the Elementary and Secondary School Act, Chapter I, III, IV, or VIII. Follow Through and Right-to-Read programs, like Head Start, recommend that parents participate in policymaking. Parents became partners in program design when Public Law 94-142 required Individualized Educational Plans (IEP) for spe-

Parents working as partners with the teacher are more effective than parents as observers.

cial education students to be written by educators with parental input and approval.

Beginning in 1986, P.L. 99-457 provides incentive grants to states. States are encouraged to implement programs for early intervention of handicapped or at-risk infants and toddlers, birth through age 2. An interdisciplinary team, with parental participation, is required to develop an individualized family service plan (Heward & Orlansky, 1988).

Across the nation, school districts have started new alliances with parents and the community. Programs where parents have been active partners are successful. "I don't feel that I'm competing with the teacher any longer. For the first time I feel that I'm contributing to the education of my child," said one gratified parent (Benet, 1976, p. 31).

A Gallup Poll delved into the relationships among parents, community, and schools. It solicited recommendations for improving community relations and summarized responses to the survey. The recommendations are still valid more than a decade later.

1. Better communication. The local community cannot be expected to take a keen interest in the schools if people know little about them. The media should carry much more school news, especially news about the achievements of students and the schools, the means being taken to deal with school problems, and new developments in education. Media research has shown that there is far greater interest in schools and in education than most journalists think. At the same time, the schools should not rely solely on the major media. Newsletters are important to convey information that media cannot be expected to report.

2. More conferences. Many of those included in the survey recommend that more conferences about the progress and problems of students be held with parents—both father and mother. Special monthly parent meetings and workshops are also suggested as a way to bring teachers, administrators, and parents together. Survey respondents also recommend courses for parents and special lectures. PTA meetings, some suggest, could be more useful to parents if school problems and education developments were given more attention.

3. Invite volunteers. Some respondents suggest that, if more members of the community could serve in a volunteer capacity in the classrooms and elsewhere in the school, they would further better community understanding of the problems faced by the schools. In addition, their involvement in school operations would increase their own interest in educational improvement at the local level.

4. Plan special occasions. Interest in the schools and in education could be improved, some suggest, by inviting members of the community—both those who have children in the schools and those who do not—to attend meetings, lectures, and social events in the school buildings.... Only one person in three across the nation attended a lecture, meeting, or social occasion in a school building during the last year. In 1969, when the same question was asked, a slightly higher proportion said they had attended a lecture, meeting, or social occasion in a school building. (Gallup, 1979, p. 41)

Private schools, and virtually all colleges and universities, plan many occasions to bring their alumni back to their campuses in order to keep them interested in the school. The public schools could adopt the same policy to their advantage, inviting not only alumni to attend such events but members of the community who have attended schools in other areas.

HOME-SCHOOL CONTINUITY

Continuity between home and school is a necessary and important support system for families today. Look at the facts. One in five families has a single parent mother; one in two children has both parents working outside the home. This was not the case 30 years ago. More than half of schoolaged children now go home to empty homes or alternative child care. Families cannot afford to be caught in an adversarial position with the school. They need cooperation, support, and facilities that make it possible to supply their children with a stable environment.

Split sessions, classes finishing at 2:30 P.M., and a lack of after-school programs are indicators that our society has little concern for the family. Tradition controls the time school is held as well as how the school buildings are used.

The public is apparently in favor of having before- and after-school programs for latchkey children (Gallup, 1988). Seventy percent of those questioned in this more recent poll favored having programs, 23% opposed the idea, and 7% did not know. Forty-nine percent of those who favored programs, however, felt that they should be paid for by school taxes; 34% did not. Nearly half of the respondents felt that summer programs should also be offered. This community outreach to help families is a positive step toward achieving continuity and making it possible for parents to feel in control of their family's destiny.

The burden for providing continuity cannot be placed on individual teachers. Working with children for 6 hours a day, preparing class materials, grading papers, and comforting and supporting children is a full-time job. Other groups such as recreation programs, library services, special after-school teachers, and artists in residence should be enlisted to help extend the school day to accommodate parents' schedules. Parents who are not employed outside the home could volunteer or be paid to help with after-school and before-school programs. Enrichment activities, physical development, and social opportunities should be provided for children who have working parents and for others who wish to partake of the opportunities.

ROLES OF PARENTS

Within each school parents may assume a variety of roles (Figure 4–2). Most commonly parents observe what the school does with their children in the educational process. But parents may also assume other roles simultaneously.

The room parent, for example, who provides treats and creates parties is an accessory or temporary volunteer. Volunteers can provide needed services, but their involvement is geared only to a specific time and task.

Increasingly, parents are serving as more regularly scheduled resources to the schools. Some parents spend a morning or day each week working in the resource center, developing materials and sharing with other parents. You may find others making books with children's stories, or listening to children read and discussing ideas with them. Still others work as unpaid aides in the classroom.

Parents may also serve as policymakers. Local school boards have been composed of community leaders charged with education policymaking for many years. Early control of schools was accomplished by local community leaders who were generally the elite of the area. At least 50% of the Parent Advisory Councils in Head Start must be composed of parents served by the program. Chapter I recommends parent involvement, including input into the program. With this representative membership, policy

FIGURE 4–2
Possible roles for parents in schools.

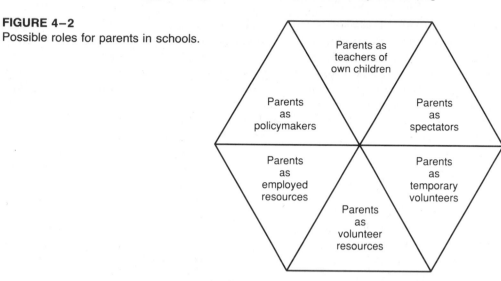

control has reached down to the grass roots of the constituency being served. The decisions of policymaking parents directly affect the schools their own children attend.

Clearly, parents are teachers of their own children. There is now emerging an increasing awareness of the link between informal and formal instruction. Parents can enhance the informal education of their children by knowledge of the formal education process, although they are encouraged to teach in an informal manner. Daily incidental teaching of language and problem solving, for example, encourages development of intelligence in the young child. As the parent lets the child select socks that match the color of the child's shirt, the child is learning color discrimination and matching. Setting the table and putting away the dishes involve classification of articles. Programs to help parents in their role as the child's early educator have been successful. Chapter I has encouraged parents to teach reading and reinforce the school's program. Parents who are aware of their roles in the educational development of their adolescent children promote the successful completion of their formal education. Parents are the one continuous force in the education of their children from birth to adulthood.

THE TEACHER'S ROLE IN PARENT INVOLVEMENT

The teacher is central to parental involvement in the educational process. Teacher roles include facilitator, teacher, counselor, communicator, program director, interpreter, resource developer, and friend. These roles are illustrated through the activities described later in the chapter, for example, parent-teacher conferences, volunteer programs, and program development.

THE ADMINISTRATOR'S ROLE IN PARENT INVOLVEMENT

School climate, the atmosphere in school, reflects the principal's leadership style. Four aspects of school-parent interaction are affected by this leadership. First, the *spirit* of the school and the enthusiasm of its staff reflect the administrator's role as morale builder. Supportive guidance, with freedom to develop plans based on individual school needs, allows the principal to function with productive autonomy. The principal builds staff morale by enabling staff to feel positive, enthusiastic, and secure in their work with children and parents.

A second leadership role, *program designer,* involves the implementation of the educational program. The principal needs to recognize the importance of home-school-community relationships in the success of the educational program and strive toward implementation of such a working relationship. If the principal allows teachers the autonomy to work with parents, using volunteers and aides in the development of individualized curricula, the school is on its way to an effective program of parent involvement.

The administrator's third role requires the development of an effective *principal-parent relationship.* The principal determines if the school atmosphere makes parents feel welcome. Besides influencing the general spirit and morale of the school, the principal is responsible for maintaining an open-door policy, scheduling open houses, providing and equipping resource areas for parents, arranging parent education meetings, developing parent workshops and in-service meetings, and supporting the PTA or PTO.

Finally, the principal serves as a *program coordinator.* Individual teachers may develop unique programs using the talents of parents, but the achievement of continuity requires the principal's coordination of parent-involvement programs.

A Word of Caution

A word of caution must be injected into this bright picture. If we depend upon improved home-school-community relationships to solve all educational and social problems, we are expecting too much. Improving home-school-community relationships is important, but we cannot expect such improvement to be the panacea for all educational ills.

TEACHERS' FEELINGS ABOUT PARENT INVOLVEMENT

The school needs personnel who accept parents, but sometimes teachers and administrators are unaware of how they feel toward parents. The questions in Figure 4–3 were developed to help teachers assess their attitudes toward parents. Kroth and Simpson (1977) used similar tools as teacher value clarification instruments. They suggest that you might want to add or delete statements and share the clarification instrument with a co-worker. Discussion with another person, evaluation of your apparent values by a close colleague, and comparisons of your real with your ideal values will help focus your attitudes about working with parents. There are no right or wrong answers; the purpose is to recognize your values and attitudes. If you want to explore your values in greater detail, refer to Raths (1978) or Simon, Howe, and Kirschenbaum (1985).

WAYS TO ENHANCE SCHOOL-HOME-COMMUNITY RELATIONSHIPS

Why does one school have superb relationships with parents and community while a nearby school does not? Most often the leadership of the administration and individual teachers makes the difference. Their leadership has made the schools responsive to the parents and the parents supportive of the school. Schools usually do not change overnight, but gradually the school, home, and community can become united in a joint effort.

Many of the techniques geared to improve home-school-community relationships are already in place. This chapter is a reminder to keep doing the positive activities that have helped in the past, to increase attention to making a partnership, and to change negative attitudes. It focuses on six areas: (1) one- and two-way communication techniques, (2) school atmosphere and acceptance of parents, (3) school activities and resources for parents, (4) contact early in the school year, (5) meeting the needs of the school area, and (6) volunteers. Changes in these six areas can turn a school around.

One-way and two-way communications can increase contact between family and school.

As a Teacher I . . .	How You See Yourself		How You Wish You Were	
	Yes	No	Yes	No
1. Feel that parents are more work than help.	☐	☐	☐	☐
2. Tense when parents enter my room.	☐	☐	☐	☐
3. Prefer to work alone.	☐	☐	☐	☐
4. Compare brothers and sisters from the same family.	☐	☐	☐	☐
5. Feel threatened by parents.	☐	☐	☐	☐
6. View parents as a great resource.	☐	☐	☐	☐
7. Believe that low-income children have parents who do not care.	☐	☐	☐	☐
8. Enjoy working with several outside persons in the classroom.	☐	☐	☐	☐
9. Have prejudiced feelings about certain groups.	☐	☐	☐	☐
10. Feel that parents let children watch too much television.	☐	☐	☐	☐
11. Feel parents are not interested in their children.	☐	☐	☐	☐
12. Work better with social distance between the parent and myself.	☐	☐	☐	☐
13. Believe parents who let their children come to school in inappropriate clothing are irresponsible.	☐	☐	☐	☐
14. Feel that a close working relationship with parents is necessary for optimal student growth.	☐	☐	☐	☐
15. Am pleased when all the parents are gone.	☐	☐	☐	☐
16. Anticipate parent conferences with pleasure.	☐	☐	☐	☐
17. Feel that parents have abdicated the parental role.	☐	☐	☐	☐
18. Enjoy working with parents.	☐	☐	☐	☐

FIGURE 4–3
Teachers can assess how they feel about collaboration with parents by answering these questions.

Communication ranges from the simplest note sent home by the teacher to a complicated news report in the media. Parents want to know what is happening at school and are interested in program development and curriculum decisions.

One-way communication informs parents about the school's plans and happenings. Two-way communication allows parents to feed into the school their knowledge, concerns, and desires and requires interaction between the participants. Both the school and parents gain. The steps to achieve effective communication among school, home, and community are easy to implement once the importance of effective communication is acknowledged. A number of strategies for establishing improved communication are described on the following pages. Choose the ones that fit your individual needs, and add others that work for you.

One-Way Communication

A newsletter may be used by the school as a message from the principal, or it may be sent home by each teacher. It is a simple form of one-way communication, and the format varies with the goals and objectives of each newsletter. Design ranges from a very simple notice to an elaborate and professional letter.

Simple Newsletters
The more newsletters you write, the easier it becomes. Not every newsletter contains all information, for it is an ongoing communication. The design may vary from a very simple newsletter printed by hand and copied, (Figure 4–4) to a letter printed on desktop publishing with the school computer. Items may include the children's activities in curriculum areas such as math contracts or contests, reading projects, group

	As a Teacher I . . .			As a Teacher I Believe That I Should . . .	
	Always	Some-times	Never	Essential	Not Important
1. Listen to what parents are saying.	☐	☐	☐	☐	☐
2. Encourage parents to drop in.	☐	☐	☐	☐	☐
3. Give parents an opportunity to contribute to my class.	☐	☐	☐	☐	☐
4. Have written handouts that enable parents to participate in the classroom.	☐	☐	☐	☐	☐
5. Send newsletters home to parents.	☐	☐	☐	☐	☐
6. Contact parents before school in the fall.	☐	☐	☐	☐	☐
7. Listen to parents 50% of the time during conferences.	☐	☐	☐	☐	☐
8. Contact parents when a child does well.	☐	☐	☐	☐	☐
9. Allow for differences among parents.					
10. Learn objectives parents have for their children.	☐	☐	☐	☐	☐
11. Learn about interests and special abilities of students.	☐	☐	☐	☐	☐
12. Visit students in their home.	☐	☐	☐	☐	☐
13. Show parents examples of the student's work.	☐	☐	☐	☐	☐
14. Enlist parent volunteers for my classroom.	☐	☐	☐	☐	☐
15. Accept differences among parents	☐	☐	☐	☐	☐
16. Encourage both mother and father to attend conferences.	☐	☐	☐	☐	☐
17. Make parents feel comfortable coming to school.	☐	☐	☐	☐	☐
18. Include parents in educational plans for their children.	☐	☐	☐	☐	☐
19. Try to be open and honest with parents.	☐	☐	☐	☐	☐
20. Send notes home with children.	☐	☐	☐	☐	☐
21. Include students along with parents during conferences.	☐	☐	☐	☐	☐
22. Let parents sit at their child's desk during back-to-school night.	☐	☐	☐	☐	☐
23. Keep both parents informed if parents are separated.	☐	☐	☐	☐	☐
24. Consider parents as partners in the educational process.	☐	☐	☐	☐	☐

FIGURE 4–3
continued

FIGURE 4–4

Newsletters can take many forms, ranging from this informal design to very sophisticated publications.

presentations in social studies, hands-on-work in science, practice in music skills, art experiences, field trips, care of classroom pets, contributions by resource persons, creative drama experiences, and accomplishments or remarks by individual children.

Newsletters may also be used at the secondary level with sections blocked for each course of study. Communication between home and secondary schools is essential.

Students who are old enough can be given the responsibility of writing the periodic newsletter. In this way, the newsletter serves two purposes: curriculum and communication. The students have a challenge to write neatly, spell correctly, and construct a readable newsletter. Younger children can make individual contributions.

Preschool. Parents love to hear about happenings in the preschool. Newsletters at this stage are your responsibility. Although children can contribute drawings and stories, you will need to publish the newsletter.

It is a good idea to collect newsletter ideas throughout the year. State home economic extension agencies will probably have some excellent ideas to contribute to your collection. See Appendix E for additional sources of newsletter material. There are also commercial newsletters that can be used with inserts from your own center that reflect your concerns and news. Subjects interesting to parents include nutrition, child development, communication, and activities for rainy days, as well as events specific to your center. As you collect interesting comments by the children or complete special projects, make a short notation for the newsletter. When time comes for publication, you will have more than enough news. If you include articles about individual children, be sure to include each child before the end of the term. It is more important to have a newsletter than to worry about its design. If typing isn't possible, write in your neatest script. A picture drawn by a child to accompany the news is an attractive addition.

Elementary. A newsletter is an excellent curriculum tool in elementary school. Although children in the first grade may not be able to produce their own newsletter, you will be surprised at how well young children can write and edit their news. Make the newsletter an ongoing project, with a center set up to handle the papers and equipment. Assign a group in each subject area to be responsible for the newsletter. Let them collect the news and determine the content and design of the letter. If you cut and paste, the children can be allowed to type their own

copy. Photocopy the master and print it by the most convenient method of duplication.

Middle and secondary. Although seldom used at this level, the newsletter is an excellent mechanism for secondary students to gain experience in writing, composition, and making layouts. You receive dual benefits; students learn through the process of doing, and a communication system between school and home is established.

A sophisticated newsletter may be the goal for upper-level students, but the importance of the newsletter as a communication tool should not be overlooked. If producing a sophisticated newsletter is too time-consuming, write the newsletter in a simple, informative style. The major objective is communication between the teacher and home. What is the class studying? What types of assignments are the students expected to do? Is there any problem solving being done in class? Which problems seem the most difficult? Are there any parents who would like to contribute to the subject being covered?

The newsletter is a short, practical form of newspaper. It is easily produced and is able to relate to a smaller and, therefore, more specific group of students. It can address current concerns and interests and can inform a select group of parents of the happenings that impact their children's lives.

Notes. When a child is doing well, send home an upslip to let the parents know. It is a good idea to buy small sheets of paper with a space large enough for a one- or two-line note. If you write too much, you may be forced by time limitation to postpone the incidental note, and the positive impact of timeliness is lost.

It has become popular to use happy faces, "glad-grams," or similar forms for teachers to periodically report something positive about each child. The concept behind each of these formats is the same—to communicate with the parent in a positive manner, thereby improving both parent-teacher relations and the child's self-concept. Make a concerted effort to send these notes in a spirit of spontaneous sincerity. A contrived, meaningless comment, sent because you are required to do so, will probably be received as it was sent. Preserving good relations requires that the message have meaning.

Newspapers

Most school districts have newspapers, yearbooks, and other school-sponsored publications. These, along with the district newsletter, are important school traditions and effectively disseminate information. Don't stop publishing them, but always remember that the newsletters that touch their children and, thereby, touch them are of greater importance to parents. Those parents most affected by yearbooks are those whose children are pictured in them. Parents most affected by newspapers are those who find articles in them concerning activities in which their children are involved.

Relying solely on newspapers and yearbooks for communicating with parents may promote complacency since some administrators and teachers assume that communication is complete because a newspaper comes out periodically and a yearbook is published when seniors graduate. Yearbooks have very little impact on school-home relationships. They arrive after the student's school career ends, they often picture a small segment of the school population, and they are generally the product of a small, select group of outstanding students. The majority of students may be omitted or ignored. The school newspaper cannot take the place of individual class newsletters. Parents are more interested in their particular children than in the school leaders and star athletes. Newspapers and yearbooks meet different needs and are both significant in their own way, but to establish a real working relationship between parents and schools, the school's publication must concern the parents' number one interest—their own children.

District Newsletter

Many school districts use newsletters to keep the community up to date on school events. Often produced by professional public relations firms, they may display excellent style and format and contain precise information, but they may also

lack the personal touch and tend to be viewed as a formal communiqué from the administration. District newsletters do have a place in building effective home-school-community relations, however, and, if supplemented by individual class reports (newsletters), the parent will receive both a formal and personal communication regarding their child's schooling.

Media

A formal and effective means of reaching parents is through the community newspaper, television, or radio. Television and radio often make public service announcements. Use them to inform the community about events at school.

Enlist the TV station as a partner in education. Some stations sponsor tutoring programs. Students are encouraged to call designated numbers (e.g., 000-HELP, 000-PASS or 000-AIDE) and talk to someone about homework. The station commits funds to hire tutors to answer questions children or parents might have about homework. It also works to have recognizable personalities take turns on the telephone. Watch the tutor service take off if parents and children know that local celebrities are willing to help.

Suggestion Box

The suggestion box brings suggestions from parents to school. Placed in the hallway, it encourages parents to share their concerns and their pleasures with the school anonymously. Although this is really a one-way communication system, it effectively tells parents, "We want your suggestions. Let us know what you feel," and encourages the parent to respond.

Handbooks

Handbooks sent to homes before the child enters school are greatly appreciated by parents. If sent while the child is a preschooler, the school's expectations for the child can be met early. If given to parents at an open house during the spring term, it can reinforce the directions given by the teacher at that time. Handbooks can help parents new in the area if they include information on community activities and associations available to families. A district handbook designed to introduce parents to the resources in the area, with special pages geared to each level of student, can be developed and used by all teachers in the district. Consider the following items in the compilation of your handbook:

- Procedures for registration
- Invitations to visit school
- Conferences and progress reports
- Special events
- Testing and evaluation programs
- Facilities at the school (e.g., cafeteria, clinic, library)
- Special programs offered by school (e.g., band, chorus, gymnastics)
- Summer programs
- Recreation programs
- Associations related to families and children
- Community center
- Special section related to child's grade level and academic program
- Child's assignment—teacher's name and short autobiography

The special section related to the child's grade level can be developed by classroom teachers at each level and inserted for children assigned to them. If a handbook does not give individualized, personal information, a note from the teacher mailed to the home during the summer will be appreciated by the family and will set the tone for a successful home-school relationship.

Two-Way Communication

Although one-way communication is important, two-way communication is essential, and it is possible only when school personnel meet the children and their parents. The school principals or center directors set the climate of acceptance within their institutions. Their perceptions of the role of the school in communicating with parents permeates the atmosphere, making parents feel welcome or unwanted.

Increased involvement is necessary for a true partnership. Telephone calls, home visits, visits to school, parent-teacher conferences, and

school activities encourage continued parental involvement. Visits to the classroom allow parents to become acquainted with their child's educational environment, the other children in the room, and the teacher. Conferences held periodically continue the dialogue on the educational progress of the child. Participation in school activities allows parents to become working members of the educational team.

Telephone Calls

Begin the dialogue with parents on a positive note. If it is impossible to visit, rely on a telephone call. An early telephone call produces many benefits from appreciative parents. Most parents wonder what is wrong when their child's teacher calls; this is quite an indictment of our communication system. Parents are generally contacted only when something is amiss. Change that tradition by setting aside a short period each day for making telephone calls to parents. Early in the year, calls can include information about who you are, why you are calling, and a short anecdote about the child. If each call takes 5 minutes and you have 30 children in your class, the calls will consume 2½ hours—a small amount of time for the results the calls bring. Divide the time into short segments of 20 to 30 minutes each evening. It saves time and is more considerate of the parent if you send a note home saying that you hope to call and asking for a convenient time. A sample letter is shown in Figure 4–5.

Home Visits

Some teachers make the effort to visit their students' homes early in the fall. This may be the only way to reach parents who have no telephone. It is also a rewarding experience for any teacher who can devote the time required. All parents are not receptive to home visits, however, and some are afraid that the teacher is judging the home rather than coming as a friendly advocate of their child. Take precautions to avoid making the family feel ill at ease. Always let the family know that you are coming. It is a good idea to write a note in which you request a time to visit, or you may give parents the option

Dear _____ ,

During the school year, I will be making periodic telephone calls to parents of my students. I am able to call on Tuesday evening from 7 PM to 9:30 PM or on Wednesday afternoon from 3:30 PM to 5 PM. Could you mark the time that would be most convenient for you?

Should you want to call me, you will find me available on Thursday evenings from 7 to 9 PM. Feel free to call my home at _____ if you have questions or would like to talk.

I am looking forward to visiting with you this year.

Best wishes,

_____

Telephone call preference

Tuesday: ☐ 7:00 to 8:00   Wednesday: ☐ 3:30 to 4:00
                  ☐ 8:00 to 9:30   ☐ 4:00 to 5:00

If none of these times is convenient, please let me know.

FIGURE 4–5
Asking parents when they are available for telephone calls and letting them know when they can call you encourages communication.

Visits to the Classroom

The traditional visit with parents invited for a specific event works very well in some school systems. In other schools, special events are complemented by an open invitation to parents to come and participate in ongoing educational programs.

Outside the room or just inside the door, hang a special bulletin board with messages for parents. It might display assignments for the week, plans for a party, good works children have done, requests for everyday items to complete an art project, requests for special volunteer time, or just about anything that would promote the welfare of the room. Parents can plan and develop the bulletin board with the teacher's guidance.

Once home visits become an accepted part of the parent involvement program, they become less threatening, and both parents and children look forward to them. Chapter 8 gives suggestions for making home visits successful.

Participation Visits

Directions for classroom participation are necessary if the experience is to be successful. Parents or other visitors feel more comfortable, teachers are more relaxed, and children benefit more if parents or visitors are given pointers for classroom visits. They can be in the form of a handout or a poster displayed prominently in the room, but a brief parent-teacher dialogue will make the welcome more personal and encourage specific participation.

The best welcome encourages the visitor to be active in the room's activities. Select activities that are easily described, require no advance training, and contribute rather than disrupt. You may want to give explicit directions on voice quality and noise control. If you do not want the parent to make any noise, request that a soft tone be used when talking with students in the room. Or you might want to ask the parent to work in one specific area of the room. Most visitors are happiest when they know what you want. If it bothers you that some parents tend to give answers to students rather than help the students work out their own problems, suggest the method of instruction you prefer. You might give them a tip sheet for working with students that describes your favorite practices. Keeping activities simple for the "drop-in" participant will keep problems to a minimum. If some parents prefer to sit and observe, don't force participation. As they become more comfortable in your room, they may try some activities. Selecting and reading a story to a child or group, listening to a child read, supervising the newsletter center, playing a game chosen from the game center with a student, supervising the puzzle table, or talking with students about their work are appropriate activities for new volunteers.

Visits by Invitation

A special invitation is sent to parents of a different child each week asking them to visit as "Parents of the Week" or VIPs, Very Important Parents. The invitation, written by the child or teacher, is accompanied by a memo from the administration that explains the objective of the visit. Have the child bring in information about brothers and sisters, favorite activities, and other interesting or important facts about the family. Place a picture of the family on the bulletin board that week. The family could include parents, grandparents, or special friends (young or old), and younger children. Parents and guests are asked to let the teacher know when they plan to visit. Trail (1971) suggested that ushers, selected from the classes, meet the parents at the principal's office and escort them to their child's classroom. An alternative plan allows the student whose parents were invited the opportunity to be the escort. Lunch might be a special treat.

You could also improve the child's self-concept by making the child "Student of the Week." Not only do the children have a chance to feel good about themselves on their special day, it helps children get to know each other better. Feedback from parents after a visit is important. A reaction sheet is given to parents with the request that they write their impressions and return it to the school. Comments range from compliments to questions about the school. This process allows two-way communication.

Breakfasts

If you have a cooperative cafeteria staff or volunteers who are willing to make a simple breakfast, you can invite parents to an early breakfast. Many parents can stop for breakfast on their way to work. Plan a breakfast meeting early in the fall to meet parents and answer questions. Breakfast meetings tend to be rushed because parents need to get to work, so hold a series of breakfasts and restrict the number of parents invited to each. In this way, real dialogue can be started. If a group is too large, the personal contact that is the prime requisite of two-way communication is prevented.

SCHOOL ATMOSPHERE AND ACCEPTANCE OF PARENTS

Schools let parents know how welcome they are. The attitude of the school personnel is reflected by the way parents are met in the principal's office, the friendly or unfriendly greetings in the hall, and the offerings in the school. School policies and services indicate whether it recognizes families as important.

Open-Door Policy

An open-door policy is more an attitude of the school than a series of activities, although periodic open houses, forums, coffee hours, and interactive seminars can add to the receptive climate of the school. Parents are welcome at any time in schools with an open-door policy. Schools that have unpleasant announcements rather than welcome on their doors and that require appointments to visit the principal, teachers, or classrooms are saying, "Come only be request or when you want to discuss a problem." Schools and parents need to avoid the problem-conference syndrome. Dialogue between parents and schools should occur before a problem develops. This can be done through coffee klatches and seminars. Parents can give suggestions and get answers; school personnel can ask questions and clarify school procedures and curriculum long before an issue might arise.

By establishing two-way communication before a problem emerges, the climate is set for parents and school to work together in behalf of, rather than suffer a confrontation over, a child.

Family Center

Parents need a place within the school where they can meet, share information, work, and relax. Ideally, parents will have a room similar to that traditional haven, the teachers' lounge, as well as a space within each classroom.

The family room can be equipped and stocked by the parents. Typical items include a sofa, comfortable chair, table, coffeepot, hot plate, telephone, typewriter, duplicator, bulletin board, storage area, supplies, and reading materials. If a room is not available, a small area shared in a workroom, an area in an unused hall, or a large closet would give minimal space. In each, both storage space and a bulletin board for notices should be available.

Teachers can help parents develop a base in each room. An extra desk, a corner, or a bulletin board can give parents the feeling they can claim a spot within their child's classroom. If the area contains information on current assignments, new curriculum ideas, activities to be used at home, taped messages from the teacher, or a display of children's work, parents will make a point to stop by. Parents of preschool, kindergarten, and elementary children can use the corner to find activities that will continue the educational experience in the home or to talk or work with individual children or small groups. Teachers can use the corner to hold a short conference with a parent.

The parents' room implies that parents are expected to be in the building. There is a place for them to stop and a base from which they can reach out in their involvement.

Parent Advisory Councils

All schools can establish parent advisory councils. Chapter I components establish two parent advisory councils, a district-wide and a local council for each involved school. The councils give input on the planning, implementation, and evaluation of the Chapter I program. Head Start and Home Start have had participatory advisory councils since the 1960s, but the public schools were not required to have such parent participation until 1974. Fifty percent of council members should be selected from among parents of students receiving Chapter I services.

The success of parent advisory councils in Head Start, Home Start, and Chapter I programs has demonstrated that parents can be involved in policy and decision making in a meaningful and constructive way. "PAC [Parent Advisory Council] members must know the program well and keep abreast of how it is operating in each project" (U.S. Department of Health, Education and Welfare, 1978, p. 26).

In establishing a parent advisory council, school districts should consider six components:

1. Preparation—districts work toward improved home-school relationships with school personnel recognizing the positive attribute of parent involvement and parents feeling comfortable in their participation.

2. Membership—parents are solicited, and their consent to run is obtained prior to an election of PAC members.

3. Training—continuous training on participation in the Chapter I program and the organization and implementation of an advisory council is provided.

4. Organization—the basic structure of the PAC is left up to the individual council.

5. Support—support of school districts includes money for supplies, transportation, and child care, as well as provision of a meeting place and availability of school officials for information about the school system.

6. Evaluation—the evaluation of success or failure of the PAC will bring out strengths and weaknesses and direct the council in the future (U.S. Department of Health, Education and Welfare, 1978).

Although other schools can implement a parent advisory council with a less formal structure, they can also learn from the Chapter I experience, which actively solicits parent participation, and gives them the information and training needed to become effective policy and decision makers.

SCHOOL ACTIVITIES AND RESOURCES

These school activities and resources encourage parent participation.

Back-to-School Nights

A time-tested school event, the back-to-school night has proven very successful. Teachers often complain that the parents who need to come to learn about the educational program are the very ones who do not come, but this type of evening program has proven successful in improving home-school relationships from pre-school through secondary schools. Parents enjoy sitting in the desk normally occupied by their child, viewing the curriculum materials, observing the displays in the room, and listening to the teacher. Parents expect the teacher to tell them about school programs. Following a presentation of the course objectives, there is usually a period for questions and answers. Back-to-school night is not a time for talking about individual children, although the teacher should identify which parents belong to which students. It is a good time to set up a special conference if you have concern about the progress of a student.

A variation on the back-to-school night is the Saturday morning session. Some working parents have difficulty attending evening programs. Offering an alternative time invites increased parental participation. The Saturday morning activity can be a workshop with parents participating in their children's normal activities, or it can be a presentation-discussion similar to the evening session. Saturday morning programs can become a meaningful educational experience for children and families by having a series of parent-child programs.

Parent Education Groups

Parent education groups are discussed in detail in Chapter 6. Meetings range from a 1-day workshop to an organized series of workshops throughout the year. Individual teachers use the parent group meetings for in-service training of volunteers in their rooms, dissemination of information to parents, or presentation of programs that answer parents' needs. Parents become real resources for the school through parent education meetings, which teach them to become effective tutors and volunteers in the school.

Parent education meetings offered by schools are viable for those with children at any age level. The parent of a young child may be interested in child development, enrichment activities, and promotion of creativity. Parents of children of all ages are concerned about drugs and alcohol. Parent education groups that allow parents to meet and discuss common concerns are a very essential part of the educational program. Interestingly, junior highs and high schools have very few parent education groups, but the parents of these students are vitally concerned about their children's futures. They need information, but, even more important, they need the support system that a parent education group offers. If parents of adolescents can discuss problems and understand that other parents have the same concerns, they are able to cope with pressures better. An advocacy group for children and parents can be formed. Responsibilities and guidelines for students, determined by parents and students in a specific community, can support parents in the rearing of their children. Schools need to offer parent education. In doing so, they strengthen parent-school-community relationships.

Parent Networks

Parent networks may naturally form out of a parent education group, but there are many parents who might join a network group of parents who might not come to parent education. Now, more than ever, parents need to cooperate with each other to handle the pressures of the social world. Drugs, alcohol, and teenage pregnancies hurt many school children. If parents form a network they can cooperate to approach the problem from two vantage points. First, they can advocate for better facilities for students. Young people need places to gather, socialize, and have fun. They need programs following school that enrich their lives and give them an opportunity to belong to a group. Second, parents can develop a code that all families can support as a guide for their children. In this way, the students will not feel that they are the only ones who have to follow rules. The community will be united in their support of children.

Summer Vacation Activities

Parents can keep students, particularly elementary-aged children, from losing academic gains during the summer. Teachers should "let parents know their help is not just incidental but vital to their child's success" (Casanova, 1987, p. 21).

Research shows that the parents who are involved by teachers become more positive about the teachers and rated the teacher higher in interpersonal skills and teaching ability. The most significant feature of parent-school involvement was providing activities for the parent to use with the child (Epstein, 1986).

Casanova (1987) suggested that teachers identify children who would be in their class the next fall and offer the parents simple suggestions such as going to the library and reading stories. This is a step toward becoming acquainted with the parents in a positive manner before the child comes into your group.

Teachers should also offer suggestions to their departing class as a farewell gift to the parents and children. Choose the activities carefully. Casanova cautioned "Remember that summer vacation provides children with a break from school routines. Try to structure activities that strengthen children's thinking skills in a natural setting" (1987, p. 21). Children might plan the meals for a week, using math to estimate costs and quantities and knowledge about nutrition to make the meals balanced.

Based on Epstein's study of parent involvement, Berliner suggested that parents of all children be involved in summer tutoring, reading to children, listening to children, playing learning games, and discussing stories. "Teachers should consider a program of parental in-volvement in at-home learning activities as a way to arrest summer drop-off of students' skill levels" (Berliner, 1987, p. 21).

School Programs and Workshops

Remember when the introduction of "modern math" made it impossible for some parents to help their children with math? Parent workshops that explained the new terminology and processes were appreciated. Schools can offer programs and workshops to the community with the same success. Parents from the community can plan and implement some of the workshops; speakers can be obtained; projects can be started.

A bookmaking project can be a great success. Although a limited number of parents can make books at one time, the workshop can be repeated. If parents make books from their own child's work, they can create remembrances to be kept for years. Simple construction paper books, as well as hardback books, can be developed. Books containing stories and poems composed by parents or children can be placed in the library and classroom for use by students.

Try to arrange alternate times to offer workshops. If you have meetings during the day, in the evening, and on Saturday, parents will be able to come to the ones that fit their schedules.

School Projects

Enlist parent help if you plan to add to the playground or build a reading loft in your classroom. Parents enjoy contributing their time for something permanent. Children will be proud that their parents helped build the jungle gym or planted the elm tree in the schoolyard. Saturday sessions give ample time to develop, plan, and build. Many fathers find this the most comfortable way to contribute to the school. It starts a relationship that brings them into a partnership with the school.

PTO or PTA

The tradition of parent-teacher associations extends back to the 1890s. Their influence on parent-school relationships has been demonstrated over the years. PTA publishes material for parents and strives for parent-school cooperation. Many parent-teacher groups (generally called Parent-Teacher Organizations—PTOs) do not join the national PTA but have similar structure and interaction with the schools. Both PTA and PTO can serve as an avenue toward greater parent-school interaction.

Fairs, Carnivals, and Suppers
Traditionally the PTO or PTA sponsors spaghetti suppers, potluck dinners, dinner theaters, or similar activities that promote a community spirit, give families a night of fun together, and usually increase the treasury. Parents and children flock to school to attend a carnival produced by parents and school staff. Money earned is generally spent on materials or equipment for the school program.

Exchanges
Children grow; toys get tiresome; books are read. Why not have an exchange? A popular exchange is one where boots, heavy jackets, and raincoats are brought to school to be traded or sold. Boots seldom wear out before they're outgrown, so a boot exchange works very well.

Toys can also be exchanged. Some schools have children bring two toys, one for exchange and one to give to another child. Children swap the toy they brought for a new one. How often have you seen toys sit for months without being used?

Children tire of some books and can exchange their old ones for books they have not read. A parent volunteer checks in the books and issues tickets to be used to buy another one. Children can look through the books until they find what they want. Then they buy the books with the tickets.

Learning Centers
Parents or volunteers from the community can be in charge of learning centers. Use the resource room to furnish ideas and supplies for parents, or have a workshop to demonstrate how they can plan and prepare a learning center. Learning centers can include (for example):

1. a place for games
2. a reading center
3. a writing-and-making books center
4. a puzzle center
5. a center for problem-solving activities
6. a science area
7. a talk-and-listen center
8. a place for music and tapes
9. a weaving center
10. an art project center

Rules and regulations for using the center should be posted.

Telephone Tutor
Take advantage of call-forwarding, which is now available in most communities. With call-forwarding, the school can set up a tutor or homework aid program via telephone calls in the evening. Volunteers or teachers could answer the telephone in the afternoon at the school. Later telephone calls may be forwarded to the homes of the volunteer or paid aide working with the children that night. In a well-coordinated program the volunteer could know what homework each teacher had assigned. If the entire district uses the telephone tutor, special numbers could be assigned for mathematics and language arts.

If call-forwarding is not available, a telephone answering machine (with names and numbers of tutors on call for that night) could direct the student to help. An excellent way to draw attention to the needs of the school district is to enlist important people in the community to serve as volunteer tutors. Their leadership will provide publicity and credibility to the volunteer program.

Resource Room

When parents see they can contribute to a project that has obvious benefits for their children, some will become actively involved. A resource room can be beneficial to both school and parents. Resource materials located in an empty room, storage closet, corner of a room, or metal cabinet can be a great help to teachers.

Use community resources. Enlist volunteers to work in the schools.

make universal game boards for reading, spelling, and math from poster card or tagboard. Felt markers are used to make lines and note directions; games are decorated with artwork, magazine cut-outs, or stickers. Game materials should be laminated or covered with clear plastic.

Recycled materials. Volunteers can collect, sort, and store materials for classroom teachers. Items such as egg cartons, wood scraps, wallpaper books, cardboard tubes, felt, fabric remnants, and plastic food holders are used for many activities. Egg cartons, for example, are used to cover a dragon, make a caterpillar, hold buttons for classification activities, and hold tempera paint for dry mixing. Milk cartons can be used for making items from simple computers to building blocks.

Science activities are enriched by a collection of machines, for example, motors, radios, computers, clocks, and typewriters. The articles can be used as they are or taken apart and rebuilt. Recycling is limited solely by the imagination.

Library

A collection can be made of magazines and books useful to parents or teachers in the development of teaching aids (e.g., games and learning activities)· or for information on how children learn. From ideas therein, a toy lending library and an activity lending library, as well as a book and magazine library, can be developed. Items can be checked out for a week or two. Checkout and return are supervised by parent volunteers.

Toy lending library. The toy lending library is developed from educational toys for young children (Nimnicht & Brown, 1972) or from a collection of toys for older children. The toys for young children can be built and collected by parents. Toys for older children can be collected from discarded toys after the toy exchange or built by parents and children.

Activity lending library. Games and activities developed by parents and children can be checked out for a week or two.

Involve parents in developing a resource center by holding a workshop to describe and discuss the concept. Brainstorm with parents and other teachers on ideas that might be significant for your school. Parents can take over after the workshop to design, stock, and run the center. Later, as assistants in the classroom, they will make use of it.

Articles on teaching. Parents and community volunteers can check old magazines related to teaching and classify useful articles according to age level and subject. These can be filed for use by teachers and aides. In searching for and classifying the articles, parents learn a great deal about teaching activities for home and school so the activity is beneficial for the parent and the school.

Games. Parents can check books, magazines, and commercial catalogues for ideas for games and adapt them to the school's needs. Volunteers can

Book and magazine library. Discarded magazines and books can be collected and used to build a comprehensive lending library. Professional magazines have many articles on child development, education, and learning activities. Booklets distributed by numerous organizations can also be loaned. Refer to the Appendix for lists of organizations that handle pertinent books. Pamphlets and articles cut from magazines can be stapled to file folders and loaned to parents. To keep track of the publications, glue a library card pocket in each book or on each folder. Make a card that states the author and title of the publication, with lines for borrowers to sign their names. As each is taken, have the borrower sign the card and leave it in the card file. When the publication is returned, the name is crossed out, and the card is returned to the pocket.

Parents as Resources

Parents should be asked early in the year if they have any talents or experiences they would like to share with classes. Parents may share their careers with children. Perhaps they have a hobby that would spark student interest or supplement learning programs. Storytelling is an art often overlooked. Invite some senior citizens to tell about their childhoods. The resources in the community are unlimited. More ideas on use of these resources will be discussed in Chapter 7.

Career Day

Plan a day or a series of days when parents and community volunteers come in and explain their careers. Rather than have parents talk to the whole class, let them work at a center. Let them explain their careers, the pros and cons, the necessary skills, and the satisfaction obtained from their work. If feasible, the parent would provide some activities the children could do related to the career. For example, a carpenter could bring in tools, demonstrate their use, and let the children make a small project, supervised by the carpenter and an aide or another parent.

Talent Sharing

Let parents tell stories, sing folk songs, lead a creative dramatics project, or share another talent. You might persuade some to perform before the class; some may wish to work with a few children at a time and let the children be involved.

Some parents may have a collection or a hobby to share. Quilting is popular and could be followed by a lesson in stitchery. Basketmaking, growing orchids, stamp collecting—all provide opportunities for enriching the classroom learning experiences. Bring those educational and fun lessons out to enjoy.

CONTACTS EARLY IN THE SCHOOL YEAR

Many teachers have found that early communication is well worth the time it takes during summer vacation. It is quite common for kindergarten teachers to invite the new kindergarten class and their parents to a spring orientation meeting. Generally, these functions have been held in the hope that the strangeness of school will diminish and that, as a result, subsequent entry into kindergarten will be more pleasant. The message to the parents that the school cares is just as important. This idea can be carried over into other levels of education with results that are just as gratifying.

Letters in August

Some teachers send letters, with pictures of themselves enclosed, to each new student coming to their classes. The student and parents learn the teacher's identity and know that the teacher cares enough to write. A good rapport between teacher and home is established before school begins.

Neighborhood Visits

Rather than waiting until the regular conference period arrives or a problem has arisen, teachers should contact each parent early in the year. Visits to the neighborhood are excellent ways to meet parents.

Block walk. Try a block walk while the weather is warm and sunny. Map the location of all your students' homes (this may be a class project) and divide the area into blocks. Schedule a series of block walks and escort the children living in each block area to their homes on a selected day. Letters or notes indicating that you will visit a particular block can be written by the students before the appointed day. Choose an alternate day in case of rain. On the appointed day, walk or ride the bus to the chosen block. Meet the parents outside and chat with them about school. You may also accumulate some curriculum materials such as leaves, sidewalk rubbings, or bits of neighborhood history to be used later by the children in the classroom. This initial contact with parents will be positive, and possibly make a second meeting even more productive. You can reinforce the positive aspect of an early meeting by making an interim telephone call to inform the parents of an activity or an interesting comment made by their child.

Bus trip and coffees. An all-school project, with teachers riding a bus to tour the school's enrollment area, allows parents and teachers to meet before the opening of school. If prior arrangements are made for coffees at parents' homes, other parents may be invited (Rich & Mattox, 1977).

Picnic

A picnic during the lunch hour or while on a field trip during the early part of the year will afford teachers the opportunity to meet some parents. Plan a field trip to the park or zoo and invite the parents to a "bring-your-own-lunch." Have another picnic after school for those who could not come at lunchtime. After the lunch or picnic, call to thank those who came. Because some parents work and will be unable to attend either picnic, you might wish to phone them for a pleasant conversation about their child.

MEETING THE NEEDS
OF YOUR SCHOOL AREA

Schools can make a special effort to help families function more effectively. Some parents travel constantly; the stay-at-home partner in those families have many of the same problems that a single parent has (see Chapter 3). A family with

a handicapped parent may need help with transportation or child care. An early survey of families will disclose what parents need and suggest ways the school can encourage participation.

Telephone Tree

A telephone tree set up by the PTO or PTA can alert parents quickly to needs in the community. One caller begins by calling four or five persons who each in turn calls four or five more. Soon the entire community is alerted.

Transportation

If the parent group is active, it can offer transportation to those who need help getting to the school or to the doctor's office. Those in need include the handicapped, a family with small children, or someone who has an ill child in the family.

Parent-to-Parent Support

Parents who do not have an extended family can find other parents with whom to team. If the parent organization organizes a file on parents that includes their needs, interests, children's ages, and location, a crossreference can be set up for parents to use. Parent education group meetings often promote friendships within the group. Parents who isolate themselves are often the ones who need the help of another parent the most. One parent may be able to manage the home efficiently, while the other needs tips and help. Some parents have never been exposed to a stable home environment and need a capable parent to use as a model. Although educators may not want to interfere in the lives of parents, they must remember that they meet and work with all parents and have the greatest access to the most parents of any community agency.

Child Care

Child care during conferences can be offered to families with young children. Older children could participate in activities in the gymnasium, while young children could be cared for in a separate room. It is difficult for some parents to arrange for child care, and a cooperative child care arrangement with parent volunteers would allow greater participation at conferences.

The teacher establishes the climate in the class-room that either encourages parents to participate or induces them to withdraw.

Crisis Nursery

A worthwhile project for a parent organization is the development of a crisis nursery. Schools would have to meet state regulations for child care to have a nursery within the school. If able to do this, schools would provide a great service as well as meet parents and children prior to school entrance. An assessment program, similar to Child Find, might alert parents and schools to developmental problems, such as a hearing loss or poor sight.

A neighborhood home can also be used as a crisis base. If a parent needs to take a child to the doctor, the crisis center can care for the other children during the parent's absence. Abusive parents can use the crisis center as a refuge for their children until they are in control of their emotions.

After-School Activities

Schools can become centers for the community. One step toward greater community involve-ment is the after-school program. With so many working parents, many children are latchkey kids, who go home to an empty house. If schools, perhaps working with other agencies, provide an after-school program for children, preschool through secondary, a great service would be done. Teachers should not be ex-pected to be involved in an after-school pro-gram. However, recreation workers, trained child care workers, and volunteers can imple-ment a program that supplements the school program. Children can be taught how to spend leisure time through participation in crafts, sports, and cultural programs.

Although it is generally recognized that young children need supervision, the needs of secondary students are ignored. Older students have 3 to 4 unsupervised hours between the time they are out of school and the time their parents arrive home. School dropouts were rarely involved in school activities. If you look at community structure, it becomes clear that schools are the major link between the family and the community.

VOLUNTEERS

Have you ever wondered why some teachers have extra help? One answer lies in the recruit-ment of volunteers and the subsequent interac-tion with them.

Parents want the best for their children; most will respond to an opportunity to volunteer if the options for working are varied and their contributions are meaningful. When both par-ents work, short-term commitments geared to their working hours will allow and encourage participation from this group. Although the world is a busy place, time spent at school can bring satisfaction and variety to a parent's life.

Volunteers: Used or User?

Volunteerism has been criticized by some as inequitable and an exploitation of "woman power." Try to choose volunteers who can afford the time, or allow busy parents to contribute in

The opportunity to volunteer can be beneficial to the volunteers as well as to the teacher.

such a way that they enjoy the time away from their other obligations. If education and training are included in your volunteer program, the participants can gain personally from the experience. For many, volunteering in school may be the first step toward a career.

If you are alert to the needs of your parents, using them as volunteers can become a means of helping their families. If you work with them over a period of time, listen and use your knowledge of community resources to support the families in solving their problems. Volunteerism should serve the volunteer as well as contribute to the school.

Who Should Ask for Volunteers?

Although all teachers can benefit from the services of volunteers, teachers should determine the extent to which they are ready to use assistance. Volunteer programs vary in their scope and design. Individual teachers may solicit volunteers from among parents; individual schools can support a volunteer program; or school districts can implement a volunteer program for the total system.

A teacher who has not used aides, assistants, or volunteers should probably start with help in one area before expanding and recruiting volunteers for each hour in the week. In preschools, the free-choice period is a natural time to have added assistance. In elementary schools assistance during art projects is often a necessity. Add to this initial use of volunteer help by securing extra tutors for reading class. In secondary schools recruitment for a special project provides an excellent initial contact.

Easing into use of volunteers may not be necessary in your school. Because most preschools and primary grades have used assistance for many years, their teachers are ready for more continuous support from volunteers. Yet involving other persons in the classroom program is an art, based on good planning and the ability to work with and to supervise others. Successful involvement of a few may lay the groundwork for greater involvement of others at a later time.

Recruitment of Volunteers by Individual Teachers

Many teachers have been successful in implementing their own volunteer programs from among the parents of their students. If you have used volunteers previously and parents in the community have heard about your program from other parents, recruitment may be easy. Early in the year, an evening program where the curriculum is explained and parents get acquainted is an effective time to recruit parents into the program. If parents have not been exposed to volunteerism, encourage them to visit the room and give them opportunities to participate in an easy activity such as reading a story to a child or playing a game with a group while they are visiting. Ask them back for an enjoyable program so that they begin to feel comfortable in the room. Sharing their hobbies with the children introduces many parents to the joys of teaching. Gradually the fear of classroom involvement will disappear, and parents may be willing to spend several hours each week with the children in the classroom.

Invitations to Visit School That Work

Suppose you have written parents notes or have published an invitation to visit school in the newsletter, but nobody comes. If this has happened to you, you need a "parent getter." Judge your activity and invitation by the following questions:

1. Does the event sound as though it is enjoyable?
2. Is there something in it for the parents?
3. Are the parents' children involved in the program?
4. Does the program have alternate times for attendance?

The first criterion should be met by the wording of the invitation. The second and third vary in importance; one or the other should be answered in each bid for parent attendance. Scheduling alternate times depends on your parents' needs.

Recently a teacher mentioned that her school had parents who just were not interested in helping. Only three had volunteered when they were asked to clean up the playyard. When asked if there were any other enticements for the parents to volunteer to help, the teacher answered, "No." "Would you have wanted to spend your Saturday morning cleaning up the playground?" she was asked. As the teacher

thought about the invitation, she recognized that she would not have participated either if she had been one of the parents. An excellent means of determining the drawing power of a program or activity is your own reaction to the project. Would you want to come? Had the Saturday cleanup project included the children, furnished refreshments, and allowed time for a get-together after the work was completed, the turnout would have been much better. Make it worth the parents' time to volunteer.

Performances

Many schools have children perform in order to get parents to turn out. The ploy works; parents attend! Some professionals discourage this method because they believe that children are being exploited to attract parents. However, it is probably the manner in which the production is conceived and readied rather than the child's involvement that is unworthy. What are your memories of your childhood performances? If the experiences were devastating, was it the programs themselves or the way they were handled that led to disappointment? If the performance is a creative, worthwhile experience for the child and does not cause embarrassment, heartache, or a sense of rejection for the child who does not perform well and if all children are included, this method of enticing parents can be valuable for both the child and parents. Experience in front of an audience can lead to poise, heightened self-concept, and pleasure for the child. Parents invited to unpolished programs enjoy the visit just as much as if they had attended refined productions. Small, simple classroom functions, held often enough so that every child has a moment in the limelight, are sure to have high parent turnouts. The more parents come to school and get involved with the activities, the better chance you have of recruiting assistance.

Field Trips

Use a field trip to talk with parents about volunteering in the classroom. Parents will often volunteer for field trips, during which teacher and parent can find time to chat. See if the parents' interests include hobbies that can be shared with the class. Be receptive to any ideas or needs that parents reveal. The informal atmosphere of a field trip encourages parents to volunteer.

Hobby Week

Miller and Wilmshurst (1975) suggested a hobby week as one successful method of involving parents. During this time, parents share their hobbies with the children. The invitation, sent to the home, has a tear-off portion at the bottom of the page on which the parents respond with hobby, agreeable time period, and space required. Each parent is scheduled into the week at a time convenient for parent and teacher. If possible, a follow-up in class of the ideas presented will make the week even more meaningful. Following the presentations, thank-you notes from the teacher with suggestions that parents might come to class again become a means of recruiting potential volunteers.

Invitations to Share

Sending home invitations with the children that ask parents if they are interested in volunteering is a direct way to recruit. Each teacher should design the invitation to fit the needs of the class. A letter that accompanies the form should stress to parents how important they are to the program. Let them know the following:

- Teachers and children need their help.
- Each parent is already experienced in working with children.
- Their child will be proud of the parents' involvement and will gain through their contributions.
- Volunteers can work in an area where they feel comfortable and productive. (Modified from Miller & Wilmshurst, 1975, p. 7)

Friendly requests along with suggestions enable parents to respond easily.

Be sure to ask parents for their ideas and contributions. You have no way of knowing what useful treasures you may find! Let parents complete a questionnaire, such as the ones in Figures 4–6 and 4–7 to indicate their interests and time schedules. Perhaps one parent cannot visit

school but is willing to make calls and coordinate the volunteer program. This parent can find substitutes when regular parent volunteers, who must be absent, call in. Others who are homebound can aid the class by sharing child care, making games and activities at home, writing newsletters, and telephoning. Parents who are able to work at school can perform both teaching and nonteaching tasks. Relate the task to the parent's interests. Nothing is as discouraging to some volunteers as to be forced to do housekeeping tasks continually with no opportunity for interaction with the children. The choice of tasks should not be difficult, however, because the opportunities are numerous and diversified as the following lists indicate:

- **Teaching tasks**
  Tutor
  Supervise learning centers
  Listen to children
  Play games with students
  Tell stories
  Play instructional games
  Work with underachievers or learning disabled students
  Help select library books for children
  Teach children to type
  Help children prepare and practice speeches
  Help children write
  Take children to resource center
  Read to children
  Help children create a play
  Supervise the making of books
  Show filmstrips
  Supervise the production of a newsletter or newspaper
  Assist in learning centers
  Share a hobby
  Speak on travel and customs around the world
  Demonstrate sewing or weaving
  Demonstrate food preparation
- **Nonteaching tasks**
  Make games
  Prepare parent bulletin board
  Repair equipment

Help Wanted
Positions Available

Tutor for Reading

Do you have an interest in children learning to read? Come tutor! We will train you in techniques to use.

Good Listener

Are you willing to listen to children share their experience and stories? Come to the listening area and let a child share with you.

Costume Designer

A class presentation will be next month. Is anyone willing to help with simple costumes?

Tour Guide

Do you have memories, slides, or tales about other states or countries? Come share.

Talent Scout

Some talented people never volunteer. We need a talent scout to help us find these people in our community.

Good-will Ambassador

Help us make everyone feel an important part of this school. Be in charge of sending get well cards or congratulatory messages.

Photographer

Anyone want to help chronicle our year? Photographer needed.

Collector

Do you hate to throw good things away? Help us in our scrounge department. Collect and organize.

Game Player

We need someone who enjoys games to spend several hours a week at the game table.

News Editor

Be a news hound. Help us develop and publish a newsletter. The children will help furnish news.

Book Designer

The class needs books, written by children, for our reading center. Turn children's work into books.

Volunteer Coordinator

The class needs volunteers, but we also need to know who, when, and how. Coordinate the volunteer time sheet.

Construction Worker

Are you good at building and putting things together? Volunteer!

SIGN UP IN YOUR CHILD'S CLASSROOM OR RETURN THIS FORM WITH YOUR INTERESTS CHECKED.

Tutor_____ Listener _____Costume Designer_____ Tour Guide_____ Talent Scout_____ Ambassador_____
Photographer_____ Collector_____ Game Player _____News Editor_____ Book Designer_____ Volunteer
Coordinator_____ Construction Worker_____ Other_____

_____   _____   _____
Name   Address   Telephone

FIGURE 4-6
One way to solicit school volunteers is through a want ad.

Please Share with the School

Dear Parents:

We need volunteers to help us with our school program. You can share your time by helping while you are at home or at school. If you want to share in any way, please let us know.

Are you interested in volunteering this year? ____ Yes ____ No

Check the ways you want to help.

____ In the classroom
____ In the resource center
____ At home

WHAT WOULD YOU LIKE TO DO?

____ Share your hobby or travel experience   ____ Tell stories
____ Help children in learning centers   ____ Check papers
____ Be a room parent   ____ Check spelling
____ Work in a resource room   ____ Help with math
____ Supervise a puppet show   ____ Read to children
____ Go on field trips   ____ Make games
____ Care for another volunteer's children   ____ Listen to children read
____ Substitute for others   ____ Play games with children
____ Develop a learning center   ____ Make books
____ Tutor reading   ____ Share your recipes

Any other suggestions? _____

_____

Comments _____

When can you come?	Monday	Tuesday	Wednesday	Thursday	Friday
	AM | PM	AM | PM	AM | PM	AM | PM	AM | PM

Name   Telephone

FIGURE 4–7
Questionnaires are another way to obtain parents' interests and time schedules.

Select and reproduce articles for resource room
Record grades
Take attendance
Collect lunch money
Plan workshop for parents
Grade and correct papers
Organize cupboards

- **Contributions from home**
Serve as telephone chairperson
Collect recycling materials
Furnish refreshments
Furnish dress-up clothes and costumes
Wash aprons
Make art aprons
Repair equipment
Make games
Care for another volunteer's children
Write newsletters
Coordinate volunteers

Teaching embraces creative ideas and methods; volunteers, responding to the challenge, can provide a vast reservoir of talent and support.

Management Techniques

Use management skill in organizing and implementing your volunteer program. A parent coordinator can be very helpful in developing effective communication between teacher and parent. Two charts, time schedules and volunteer action sheets, clarify the program and help it run more smoothly.

Time schedules. Time schedules can be adjusted if weekly charts are both posted and sent home. When parents can visualize the coverage, the class will not be inundated by help in one session and suffer from lack of help in another.

Volunteer sheet. Because volunteers are used in a variety of ways, developing an action sheet that describes each person's contribution is helpful. Figure 4–8 illustrates the scope of involvement within one classroom. With this list the parent coordinator can secure an effective substitute for someone who must be absent. If the teacher

needs games constructed, the parent coordinator can call on the parents who have volunteered for that activity. Special help at a learning center or with a student project can be found by calling one of the parents who has indicated an interest in helping in these ways. The responsibility for the volunteer program does not need to rest solely on the teacher's shoulders. Parents and teachers become partners in developing a smoothly working system.

Increasing Volunteer Usage

Although permanent volunteers are more effective in establishing continuity in a program than periodic contributions by occasional volunteers, both are needed. As the year progresses, some parents may find that they enjoy teaching immensely. These parents may extend their time obligation and, in doing so, will bring more continuity to the program. Ideally, an assistant should tutor a reading group or a child for several sessions each week rather than just one. When initiating a program, it is better to start out with easily handled time slots and enlarge the responsibilities of the parents after they become secure and familiar with the class, the objectives, and the material.

Volunteer Training

Several parents have indicated interest in becoming permanent volunteers in your classroom. What is your next step? The time spent explaining your routine, expectations, and preferences for teaching will be well worth the effort in the parents' abilities to coordinate with you in your classroom. Most teachers have specific preferences for teaching that they will want to share with the volunteers helping them. These, in addition to some general guidelines, will help prepare the volunteer. The following humanistic guidelines for working with children are appropriate for all volunteers:

1. A healthy, positive self-concept is a prerequisite to learning.
2. The act of listening to a child implies that you accept him or her as a worthwhile person.

Name	Telephone	Classroom Regularly	Classroom Substitute	Special Presen-tation	Child-care	Make Games at Home	Work in Resource Center		
							Help Students	Develop Resources	
								Type	Make games
Names of volunteers	555–5555	X								X
"	"		X	X					
"	"		X	X					
"	"	X	X	X					
"	"	X				X			
"	"				X	X	X	X	
"	"	X				X			
"	"	X							
"	"	X		X					
"	"	X					X	X	X
"	"								
"	"					X	X	X	X
"	"		X						
"	"		X			X			
"	"		X						
"	"		X			X			
"	"		X			X			
"	"			X	X				
"	"				X				
"	"			X	X		X	X	X
"	"		X		X	X			
"	"		X		X		X	X	X
"	"		X	X	X				

FIGURE 4–8
Volunteer action sheets help organize an orderly volunteer program.

3. The child will develop a better sense of self-worth if you praise specific efforts rather than deride failures.
4. Provide tasks at which the children can succeed. As they master these, move on to the next level.
5. Take time to know the student as a person. Your interest bolsters confidence in your relationship. (Adapted from DaSilva & Lucas, 1974, p. 110)

Many children who need extra help with their work also need their self-concepts strengthened. Volunteers can provide an extra touch through kindness, interest, and support.

Teacher's Responsibilities to the Volunteer

As teachers enlist the help of volunteers, certain responsibilities emerge. These are the teacher's responsibilities:

1. Make volunteers feel welcome. Smile and reassure them.
2. Explain class rules and regulations.
3. Introduce volunteers to the resources within the school.
4. Explain the routine of the class.

5. Describe your expectations for their participation.
6. Remember that volunteers are contributing and sharing time because of satisfaction received for self and/or child.
7. Give volunteers reinforcement and recognition.
8. Meet with volunteers when class is not in session to clarify, answer questions, and, if needed, give instruction and training.
9. Appreciate, respect, and encourage volunteers.

Awareness of these points will make the cooperative effort of teacher and volunteer more fulfilling for both.

Volunteer's Responsibilities to Teacher

If parents or persons from the community volunteer to help in the school, they accept certain responsibilities, which include the following:

1. Be dependable and punctual. If an emergency requires that you miss a session, obtain a substitute or contact the volunteer coordinator.
2. Keep privileged information concerning children or events confidential. Do not discuss children with persons other than school personnel.

Volunteers can help children develop a better sense of self-worth.

3. Plan responsibilities in the classroom with the teacher.
4. Cooperate with the staff. Welcome supervision.
5. Be ready to learn and grow in your work.
6. Enjoy yourself, but do not let your charges get out of control.
7. Be fair, consistent, and organized.

Volunteer aides are not helpful if they continually cancel at the last moment, disrupt the room rather than help it run smoothly, or upset the students. They are immensely helpful if they work with the teacher to strengthen and individualize the school program.

Recruitment by Schools and School Systems

Many schools and school districts assist teachers by recruiting volunteers for their classes. The first step in initiating a volunteer program for a school or school system is the development of a questionnaire to ascertain the teachers' needs. The teachers complete a form, based on the curriculum for each age level. After the forms are completed, the coordinators can determine the requirements of each room.

After teachers have indicated their needs, the coordinator begins recruitment. Many avenues are open for the recruiter. A flyer geared to the appropriate age or level of children, which requests people to share their time with the schools, can bring about the desired results. Organizations can also be contacted. The PTA or PTO, senior citizen groups, and other clubs have members who may want to be involved as volunteers in the school.

The points discussed earlier for obtaining volunteers for the individual classroom are also appropriate for volunteers who are solicited on a larger scale. The major differences are organizational. They include the following:

1. Teachers contact or reply to the volunteer coordinator's questionnaire if they want a volunteer.

2. Districts usually require that volunteers fill out an application stating background, giving references, and listing the hours they are available.

3. An extensive compilation of resource persons can be obtained by the school district. These resource persons and/or experts can share their knowledge with classes throughout the school district. Lists of topics with resource persons available to share expertise can be distributed throughout the district. Teachers request the subject and time they want a presentation. The central office handles the arrangements and obtains the volunteer presenter for the teacher (Boise School Volunteer Office, 1978; Minneapolis Public Schools, n.d.).

4. Outreach such as a community study hall can be initiated and staffed by the volunteer program. Volunteers can tutor and work with children after school hours in libraries, schools, or other public facilities (Denver Public Schools n.d.).

5. Certificates or awards distributed by the district offer a way to thank the volunteers for effort and time shared with the schools.

Individual teachers tend to use parents as aides and resource persons in the room. The district most often furnishes resource persons, drawn from the total population, in schools throughout the district. The school volunteer coordinator uses both approaches and recruits volunteers to tutor and aid in the classroom and resource persons from residents of the school's population area to enrich the curriculum.

SUMMARY

Understanding parents' feelings and concerns provides the basis for creating effective home-school relationships. Schools have character; some invite parents to participate; others suggest that they stay away. Parents have feelings about schools that range from a desire to avoid schools to such a high interest that they are overly active. Parents participate in schools as spectators, accessory volunteers, volunteer resources, paid resources, policymakers, and teachers of their children.

Schools can develop attitudes that welcome parents and conduct activities that invite them into the school. First, personnel in the school need to know what their attitudes toward parents are. Use of questionnaires helps in the recognition of feelings toward parents

Second, the schools must set up one-way communication systems. One-way communication includes newsletters, spontaneous notes, newspapers, media announcements, newspaper columns, telephone messages, and handbooks.

Third, two-way communications must be established. An open-door policy with open forums, coffees, and seminars invites comments from parents. Initial contact should be made early in the year or even during the summer before the school year begins. Suggestions for early contact include neighborhood visits, telephone calls, home visits, and breakfasts. Two-way communication continues through the year with classroom visits and participation, back-to-school nights, parent education groups, school programs, projects, workshops, PTA carnivals, exchanges, and a suggestion box.

A resource room, established and staffed by parent volunteers, makes parents significant educational resources. The resource room includes articles on teaching, games, recycled materials, and a lending library for toys, books, and games. A family center gives parents a place to stop and a base from which they can reach out to help children.

Parents today are more involved as policymakers than in former times. Parent advisory councils are part of Chapter I, and parents confer with school administrators on program planning, implementation, and evaluation.

Schools can become community centers and meet the needs of families in the area by organizing parent volunteers for parent-to-parent groups, child care centers, crisis centers, and after-school programs.

Parents and others from the community can also be included in the schools as volunteers. Teachers need to develop skills to recruit, train, and work with volunteers as part of an educational team.

SUGGESTED ACTIVITIES AND DISCUSSIONS

1. Visit a school and inquire about parent programs. Interview the principal, teachers, and counselors or social workers. Ask them about parent involvement. What are their tips for getting parents actively involved? What recommendations do they have for working with a variety of parents?

2. Make a list of suggestions in this chapter. Use it as a checklist to test your school's response to parents.

3. Contact the president of the PTA or PTO in a neighborhood school. What are their goals for parent involvement in the school? Which programs have they planned for the year? Which direction would they like the PTO or PTA to take?

4. Plan an ideal school for administrators, teachers, and parents. Which roles would each play? Which activities and programs would the school have?

5. Discuss why parents may feel intimidated by the schools and why teachers may be reluctant to have parents involved. Role play teacher and parent roles and share your feelings.

6. Describe an ideal parent-teacher relationship. List five things a teacher can do to encourage such a relationship. List five ways parents can work with the school.

7. Brainstorm for ideas that would make you want to visit school. List the ideas. Evaluate them.

8. List what makes you feel comfortable or uncomfortable when you visit a center or school.

9. Construct a values clarification questionnaire for your class. Have the members take the test. Break the class into groups and have them discuss where and how they developed their values. How much influence did their families have on the development of their values?

10. Visit a school and look at bulletin boards, notices, and family centers that might welcome parents.

11. Write guidelines for parents to use when they visit or work in the classroom. Describe the guidelines on a poster and/or handout.

12. Examine your community and develop a list of field trips and home-learning activities. Plan a packet for parents to use with their children during spring break.

13. Design a want ad or letter that invites parents to become volunteers in the classroom.

14. Search the community for resources that can be used in the school. Include specialists, materials, and places to visit.

15. Conduct a brainstorming session on tasks for parent volunteers. How many ideas are you able to list? Categorize them according to type of involvement, that is, tutoring, teaching, developing materials, housekeeping tasks, or busywork. Why is it important to allow parents to participate in meaningful work?

BIBLIOGRAPHY

Benet, J. Parents and a dream school. In D. Davies (Ed.), *Schools where parents make a difference.* Boston: Institute for Responsive Education, 1976.

Berliner, D. Parents can be great summer tutors. *Instructor,* May 1987, pp. 20, 21.

Bloom, B. S. *All our children learning.* New York: McGraw-Hill Book Company, 1981.

Boise School Volunteer Office. *Notebooks for Boise school volunteers.* Boise, Idaho: The Independent School District of Boise City, 1978.

Brofenbrenner, U. *Is early intervention effective? A report on longitudinal evaluations of preschool programs.* (U. S. Department of Health, Education and Welfare; Office of Human Development; Office of Child Development). Washington, D.C.: U. S. Government Printing Office, 1976.

Brown, P. Picture a parent conference. *Early Years,* October 1975, pp. 48–50.

Carberry, H. H. Parent-teacher conferences. *Today's Education,* January-February 1975, pp. 67–69.

Carlson, J., & Hillman, W. Facilitating parent-teacher conferences. *The School Counselor,* March 1975, pp. 128–132.

Cary, S. Forming a partnership with parents. *Day Care and Early Education,* September 1974, pp. 11–14.

Casanova, U. Parents can be great summer tutors. *Instructor,* May 1987, pp. 20, 21.

Curwin, R. L., & Fuhrmann, B. S. *Discovering your teaching self: Humanistic approaches to effective teaching.* Englewood Cliffs, N.J.: Prentice-Hall, 1975.

Daresh, J. C. Effective home-school-community relations for secondary school improvement. *The Clearing House,* 1986, pp. 312–315.

Da Silva, B., & Lucus, R. D. *Practical school volunteer and teacher-aide programs.* West Nyack, N.Y.: Parker Publishing, 1974.

Denver Public Schools. *For VIPs only. Volunteers in public schools.* Denver, Denver Public Schools, n.d.

Epstein, J. L. Parents' reactions to teacher practices of parent involvement. *The Elementary School Journal, 86,* January 1986, pp. 277–293.

Fehrmann, P. G., Keith, T. Z., & Reimers, T. M. Home influence on school learning: Direct and indirect effects of parental involvement on high school grades. *Journal of Educational Research, 80,* July/August, 1987, pp. 330–337.

Gallup, A. M. The twentieth annual Gallup Poll of the public attitudes toward the public schools. *Phi Delta Kappan,* September 1988, pp. 31–46.

Gallup, G. H. The eleventh annual Gallup Poll of the public's attitudes toward the public schools. *Phi Delta Kappan,* September 1979, pp. 33–45.

Harris, L. *The American teacher 1987. Strengthening links between home and school. The Metropolitan Life survey.* New York: Metropolitan Life Insurance Company, 1987.

Heward, W. L., & Orlansky, M. D. *Exceptional children* (3rd ed.). Columbus, Ohio: Merrill, 1988.

Hymes, J. *Effective home-school relations.* Sierra Madre: Southern California Association for the Education of Young Children, 1974.

Kroth, R. L., & Scholl, G. T. *Getting schools involved with parents.* Reston, Va.: Council for Exceptional Children, 1978.

Kroth, R. L., & Simpson, R. L. *Parent conferences as a teaching strategy.* Denver: Love Publishing, 1977.

Maslow, A. H. *Toward a psychology of being.* Princeton, N. J.: D. Von Norstrand, 1968.

Meyerhoff, M. K., & White, B. L. New parents as teachers. *Educational Leadership,* November 1986, pp. 42–46.

Miller, B. L., & Wilmshurst, A. L. *Parents and volunteers in the classroom: A handbook for teachers.* San Francisco: R. & E. Associates, 1975.

Minneapolis Public Schools. *How to initiate and administer a community resource volunteer program.* Minneapolis, Minn.: Author, n.d.

Nimnicht, G. P., & Brown, E. The toy library: Parents and children learning with toys. *Young Children,* December 1972, pp. 110–116.

Raths, L. E. *Values and teaching* (2nd ed.). Columbus, Ohio: Merrill, 1978.

Rich, D., & Mattox, B. *101 activities for building more effective school-community involvement.* Washington, D.C.: Home and School Institute, 1977.

Rogers, C. R. *Freedom to learn for the 80s.* Columbus, Ohio: Merrill, 1983.

Seefeldt, C. Parent involvement: Support or stress. *Childhood Education,* November/December, 1985, pp. 98–102.

Simon, S. B., Howe, L. W., & Kirschenbaum, H. *Values clarification.* New York: Dodd Publishing, 1985.

Trail, O. A. Are you keeping parents out of your schools? In R. C. Bradley, *Parent-teacher interviews.* Wolfe City, Tex.: University Press, 1971.

U.S. Department of Education. *What works: Research about teaching and learning.* Washington, D.C.: U.S. Government Printing Office, 1986.

———. *Schools that work: Educating disadvantaged children.* Washington, D.C.: U.S. Government Printing Office, 1987.

U.S. Department of Health, Education and Welfare. (Office of Education). *Title I ESEA: How it works: A guide for parents and parent advisory councils.* Washington, D.C.: U.S. Government Printing Office, 1978.

Williams, D. L., Jr. *Highlights from a survey of parents and educators regarding parent involvement in education.* Paper presented at the Seventh National Symposium on Building Family Strengths, Lincoln, Neb., May 1984.

5

Communication and Parent Programs

What do you have in mind when you think of effective communication? Is it the transmission of feelings, information, and signals? Is it the sending and receiving of messages? Is it a verbal exchange between people, for example, parents and teachers?

Most definitions of communication encompass more than mere interchange of information. The definitions range from the definition given in the dictionary, "giving or exchanging of information, signals, or messages by talk, gestures, writing, etc." (Guralnik, 1980, p. 287) to definitions that focus on the impact the message has on the receiver. Does the message received convey the meaning of the message that the sender meant to convey? Fotheringham notes that the reason for communication is "to help a receiver perceive a meaning similar to that in the mind of the communicator" (as cited in Fisher, 1978, p. 8). In working with parents, it is essential that the message sent and the one received is the message that is intended.

Each message is made up of at least three factors: 1) the words or verbal stimuli—what a person says, 2) the body language or physical stimuli—the gestures, and 3) the vocal characteristics or vocal stimuli—the pitch, loudness or softness, and speed (Gamble & Gamble, 1982).

The sender gives a message; it is received and interpreted by the receiver. If the intent of the message is accurately received, effective communication has occurred. To have this happen, the listener needs to be an active participant. The listener must be able to hear the message, the feeling, and the meaning of the message.

Communication includes (1) speaking, (2) listening, (3) reflection of feeling, and (4) interpretation of the meaning of the message. It is a complicated process because so many variables come into play. The voice, body language, message, the reaction of the receiver to the sender, and the expectations of the receiver on what is expected all affect the message. To be effective in communication, speakers need to understand their own reactions and the reaction of others to them, and they must listen to the meaning of the message.

Sieburg (1985) uses the term 'evoke' as descriptive of the active process between the communicators. The message evokes a response from the receiver. The meaning of the message needs to be interpreted by the receiver so that it conveys what the sender meant to produce. If the response is misinterpreted, miscommunication occurs.

Miscommunication can be overcome. The receiver may check out understanding by re-

If the intent of the message sent is accurately received by the listener, good communication has occurred.

phrasing and recycling the conversation or by further questioning within the context of the subsequent discussion.

Interpersonal communication may be pictured as messages within an ongoing circle or oval configuration. As pictured in Figure 5–1 the message (filtered through values and past experiences) goes to the receiver (where it also is filtered through values and past experiences), decoded, responded to, and sent back to begin the cycle again. Communication is a dynamic, continuous process that changes and evolves.

When talking with one another it is easy to have the impression that what one says is the most important element in the conversation. However, research shows that verbal messages (the spoken word) account for only 7% of the input; vocal and tonal messages (the way in which it is spoken) account for 38%; visual messages (body language) account for 55% (Miller, Wackman, Nunnally, & Miller 1988, p. 81). If this is the case, teachers, principals, and child care professionals need to focus on their total communication system and be aware of their body language and tone of voice, as well as their verbal messages.

COMMUNICATION IN CHILDCARE AND SCHOOLS

The goals of those who work with young children are to meet the needs of the children, to educate them, and to help them reach their potential as children and develop into productive adults. What is the challenge to parents? They have the same goals! Because parents and school personnel have the same goals in mind, it would seem that communication would be quite easy. Such is not the case. There tend to be many roadblocks to good communication between school personnel and parents.

ROADBLOCKS TO COMMUNICATION

What are some of the roadblocks that hinder effective communication between parents and school personnel? They are similar to roadblocks that affect any communication, but different concerns emerge. Some of the most common parent and school roadblocks will be described so we can work to overcome them.

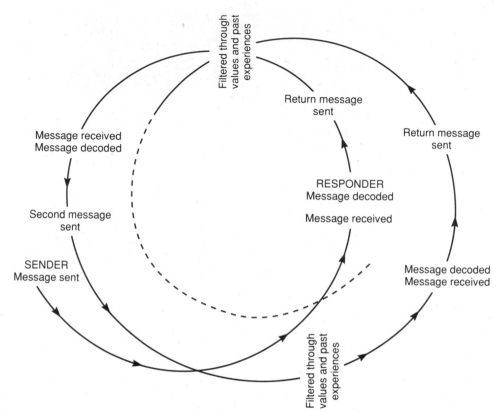

FIGURE 5–1
Messages are filtered through the receiver's value system and past experiences before they are decoded and responded to. Communication is a dynamic, continuous process.

Parent Roadblocks

Parents exhibit roles ranging from inadequacy to abrasive domineering that inhibit their ability to effectively communicate with the schools.

Protector Role Parents protect their own egos when they overprotect their children. Many parents, often unknowingly, view their children as extensions of themselves. "Criticize my child and you criticize me" seems to be their message. "Are you saying that I did not rear my children correctly?" "Is my child slow in school because I am the parent?" "Is there something that I should have done differently in my childrearing?" When a shield is put up as a defense against perceived criticism and attack, it is very difficult to communicate. When parents are hurt by a

child's inability to progress satisfactorily in school, they may withdraw from open, honest communication in an effort to protect their child and their own self-esteem.

A parent's vested interest in the child can be channeled in a positive direction. Effective communication, with positive suggestions for encouraging the child, can help the vested parent become a partner with the school.

Inadequate-Me Role Many parents do not feel comfortable talking with school personnel. These parents avoid going to civic events, including schools, because they do not feel they belong. If parents feel inadequate, they avoid coming in contact with the schools. If they do come, they find it difficult to communicate their desires or feelings to the staff. These parents can benefit from encouragement that they can contribute and be involved.

Avoidance Role The avoidance role may include self-assured parents who do not respect the school and the way it treats parents and students. It also includes parents who had a difficult time in school when they were growing up. Perhaps they dropped out of school. The school holds very bad memories for them. The schools will have to reach these parents by caring and reaching out by offering activities and services that the parents need and desire.

Indifferent-Parent Role It seems more difficult today to be a concerned, involved parent because of financial and time pressures. Although most parents want what is best for their children, some are willing to shift their parental responsibilities to others. The institution where children spend most of their working hours is the school. When children are reared by indifferent parents, their futures can be devastated. If no one cares, why should the children care? Drug abuse, teenage pregnancies, alcohol abuse, truancy, and criminal behavior are evidence that children have indifferent, dysfunctional, or too-busy parents. Early communication with parents can help reverse the trend.

Don't-Make-Waves Role Many parents are unwilling to be honest in their concerns because they do not want to have the school personnel take it out on their child. They believe that the teacher or principal might be negative toward their children if they make suggestions or express concerns. This belief represses communication.

Club-Waving-Advocate Role Sometimes parents get carried away with their devotion to their children, and they exhibit this through a power play. These advocates often become abrasive in their desire to protect their child or change school policy. These parents are the opposite of the Inadequate Me or the Don't Make Waves parents. Club-waving parents express their concerns through confrontation. Schools must ac-

knowledge these concerns, and change the situation in cases where it is sensible to do so. In addition, give the parents opportunities to be leaders in areas where they can contribute.

School Roadblocks

Many times schools install roadblocks to effective communication without realizing it. Sometimes roadblocks are established intentionally. The stress of educating and working with many children and families, pressure to accomplish many tasks, and the desire to be seen as efficient, all get in the way of unhurried, effective communication. The following roles describe some of the roadblocks that hamper effective communication between home and school.

Authority-Figure Role School personnel who act as the chief executive officer (CEO) all too often hinder communication. These teachers and administrators claim to be the authorities, ready to impart information to the parent. They neglect to set the stage for the parent to be a partner in the discussion. If the staff take all the responsibility of running the school, without considering the parents' backgrounds and knowledge, there seems to be no reason to communicate. Parents are locked out of the decision-making process. Schools that ignore parents destroy communication between parents and schools.

Sympathizing-Counselor Role School personnel who focus on the inadequacy of the child in a vain attempt to console the parent, miss a great opportunity for communication. Parents want to solve their concerns through constructive remediation or support. Parents and schools both need to focus on the achievements that can be attained through cooperation and collaboration.

Pass-the-Buck Role Communication stops when the parents and school personnel refer the concerns of the parent to another department. "Sara may need help, but we cannot schedule her for tests for 5 months." "It is too bad that Richard had such a bad experience last year. I wish I could help, but he needs special services."

Sometimes parents feel that the school is deliberately stalling while their child gets further and further behind.

Protect-the-Empire Role   A united, invincible team of staff can cause parents to feel that no one cares about their needs. School personnel need to work together and support one another, but they also need to listen to the parent and parent advocate as they formulate an educational plan for the student.

Busy-Teacher Role   Perhaps the greatest roadblock to good communication between parent and teacher is time. If you are harried, you do not have time to communicate with your students or parents. Both parents and teachers need to reduce stress and set aside time for communication. Reorganize schedules to include on-the-run conferences, telephone calls, and short personal notes to parents and children. Principals and directors might take over the classroom occasionally so teachers could make telephone calls to parents. The principals and directors would get to know the children in the classes and the importance of teacher-parent interaction would be emphasized. Roadblocks can be overcome.

EFFECTIVE COMMUNICATION WITH PARENTS

To achieve effective communication, parents and teachers need to recognize roadblocks that hinder their success. At the same time, they can increase their communication skills by practicing positive speaking, rephrasing, and attentive listening.

When teachers talk with parents they communicate in many ways—through their words, their body actions, and the manner in which they speak. Every contact communicates whether the speaker respects the other person, how they value their input, and whether they are willing to collaborate. The self-fulfilling prophecy works with parents as well as with students. If teachers treat parents as if they were incapable of being partners, the parents will fulfill that prophecy. They will not work with the teachers effectively.

Cooley's Looking-Glass-Self concept reveals that how you view yourself depends on how you perceive that others see you (1964). The Looking-Glass-Self contains three phases: *reflection* (parents looking into the mirror), *interpretation* of the reflection (how the parents interpret what they see), and *feeling of pride or mortification.* If, in the second step, the parents interpret the reflection as positive, they will, in the third step, feel pride in their being able to work with the school to the benefit of their children. If they see disregard and no respect, they will find it difficult to work as partners.

Teachers view parents either as partners or as subordinates. Teachers can help the parent feel that they are enablers, empowering them to help their child, or they can reject the parent.

Teachers can establish rapport with parents by using effective communication skills. A good partnership, however, takes two, so parents also need to work on their skills. Effective communication takes time, is honest, and is open. Good communicators listen, rephrase and check out, and avoid criticizing and acting superior. Teachers who are good communicators:

1. Give their total attention to the speaker. Establish eye contact and clearly demonstrate by body language that their interest is focused on what is being said.

2. Restate the parents' concerns. Clarify what has been said and try to discern the speaker's meaning and feeling.

3. Avoid closed responses or answering as a critic, judge, or moralist.

4. Show respect for the other person. Recognize that their concerns, opinions, and questions are significant to mutual understanding and communication.

5. Recognize the parents' feelings. How much can you discuss with the parents? Perhaps you need to establish a better parent-teacher relationship before you can completely share your concerns for the child.

Establish eye contact and show that you are interested.

6. Tailor discussions to fit the parents' ability to handle the situation. Do not touch off the fuse of a parent who might not be able to handle a child's difficulties. Don't accuse; spend more time with the parents in other communication and conferences.

7. Emphasize that concerns are no one's fault. Teacher and parents have to work on problems together to help the child. Use concerns as forums for understanding one another.

8. Remember that no one ever wins an argument. Calmly, quietly, and enthusiastically discuss the *good* points of the child before you bring up any concerns.

9. Protect the parents' egos. Don't blame or make the parents believe that they are to blame for their child's deficiencies. Focus on plans for the future. On the other hand, give parents credit for their child's achievements.

10. Focus on one issue at a time. Be specific about the child's progress or concerns.

11. Listen. Hear the feeling and meaning of the message. Rephrase and check out the message to be sure that you received it correctly.

12. Become allies with parents.

Parents become partners in the educational process when they

1. View the teacher as a source of support for their child and them.

2. Listen carefully and give total commitment to the speaker.

3. Show respect for the teacher, recognize that the teacher's concerns, opinions, and questions are significant to mutual understanding and communication.

4. Recognize that the teacher has a difficult challenge to meet the needs of all students. Help the teacher succeed.

5. Rephrase and check out understanding of messages during conversations or conferences.

6. Speak openly and honestly about the child.

7. Use concerns as forums for understanding the school and teacher.

8. Become allies with the teacher.

The following sections on Positive Speaking, Listening, Rephrasing, Reframing, and Reflective Listening elaborate upon each of these communication skills.

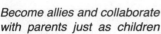

Become allies and collaborate with parents just as children cooperate at school.

POSITIVE SPEAKING

If your message is positive, the parent is more apt to want to listen. The relationship between the teacher and parent is enhanced. A positive statement needs to be accompanied by attentive behavior, good body language, and a warm tone of voice. Add clear articulation, and you have the recipe for effective communication between parent and teacher.

LISTENING

Listening is the heart of effective communication. Listening is more than hearing sounds.

Smith (1986) describes listening as the "basis for human interaction" (p. 246). It is the active process of interpreting, understanding, and evaluating the spoken and nonverbal speech into a meaningful message. Listening, not speaking, is the most used form of communication. Forty-five percent of the time spent in verbal communication is spent listening; 30% is speaking; 16% reading; and in writing, only 9% (p. 247).

In education, great attention is spent on the ability to write, yet very little training is done on listening. Greater understanding and retention of information would occur if an appropriate amount of time were spent on helping people listen effectively.

Smith (1986) recommends these steps to improve listening skills:

1. Be receptive—listeners encourage the speaker by being receptive and providing an environment where the speaker feels free to express ideas and feelings.

2. Pay attention—make a conscious effort to concentrate on what is being said.

3. Use silence—communicate that you are listening through attending behaviors while remaining silent.

4. Seek agreement—look for the broader meaning of the message rather than focusing on isolated facts.

5. Avoid ambiguity—ask questions to clarify, look for main ideas, and focus on intent as well as content.

6. Remove distractions—eliminate daydreaming, remove physical barriers, delay important messages to make the climate clear for listening.

7. Be patient—don't rush the speaker. Allow time for the message to be completed.

Teachers and parents communicate when they

- listen carefully to the other person
- have good eye contact
- encourage the speaker using body language and verbal expressions such as "yes"
- observe the speaker and have a facial expression that shows interest
- respond with attentive body language such as leaning forward and/or touching
- can rephrase the substance and meaning of the message they receive from the speaker

Poor listening is evident if the receiver

- has little eye contact
- displays a stiff appearance
- changes subjects
- looks disinterested
- is unable to rephrase or interpret the communication properly

Teachers will need to make special efforts to communicate with parents who have difficulty expressing themselves in English. For example, parents whose first language is another language may have difficulty being articulate in English. Parents who are emotionally distraught may not be able to receive the intended message. In these cases it is even of greater importance that teachers have excellent listening skills. They can recognize the miscommunication and strive for clearer understanding.

When a parent or teacher listens, they not only increase knowledge and understanding of the message, but also demonstrate a caring attitude. Listening reduces tension and stress and encourages trust (Center for Family Strengths, 1986).

REPHRASING

Rephrasing is restating the intent of the message in a condensed version. There are three steps in rephrasing. First, the listener must determine the basic message and the intent of the message. Second, the listener restates the intent of the message, and last, the listener checks out the accuracy of the rephrasing.

When a respondent seeks to check out or clarify a statement by saying, "It sounds like you feel...," or "It seems that I'm hearing you say...," the respondent is rephrasing the statement. If communicators rephrase, they can avoid misunderstanding the message by checking the accuracy. Confusion and ambiguity in communication is avoided. The interest displayed by rephrasing also shows caring and builds trust (Center for Family Strengths, 1986).

REFRAMING

Reframing in communication is illustrated by taking the "sting" out of the negative descriptors of a child. When communicating with parents, if your answer reflects your understanding of parents' concerns, the conversation will remain open, but the words you choose can bring either desirable or disastrous results.

A teacher with good intentions and great concern for a child once opened a conference by referring to a child's "problem." "I think you're obnoxious!" struck back the antagonized parent, who was already overwrought by family strain and worry over the child. The remainder of the conference time had to be devoted to rebuilding a working relationship, allowing no time for productive dialogue about the child and leaving both teacher and parent with emotional scars.

Instead of focusing on the negative aspect of the individual, start with positive comments. Then reframe the child's troublesome quality into an acceptable or even positive trait. Had the teacher started the conference with some friendly remarks and then stated, "I have some concerns about John that we should work on together," the parent might not have responded with such anger.

Examples of reframing include:

Problem	Concern
loud and boisterous	very active
gives others answers	can't help sharing
steals	takes without asking
won't follow rules	has own agenda or is innovative
stubborn	determined
shy	self-contained
talks too much	likes to share with others
does not pay attention	preoccupied

It is particularly important in parent-teacher conferences and other communication between parent and teacher that the annoying behavior be couched in terms that can be dealt with. There may be times, however, when the teacher feels that the concern has reached such proportions that it must be faced squarely and openly. After several attempts to try to communicate, it becomes obvious that the parent does not recognize that the behavior is hurting the child's progress. In those cases you may have to use more forthright terms. Just be aware. Using harsh terms may completely cut off communication.

REFLECTIVE LISTENING

Reflective listening is the ability to reflect the speaker's feelings. The listener's response identifies the basic feelings being expressed and reflects the essence of those feelings back to the speaker. Reflective or active listening is used in several parent programs such as the Parent Effectiveness Training (PET) (Gordon, 1975), Active Parenting (Popkin, 1983), and Systematic Teaching of Effective Parenting (STEP) (Dinkmeyer & McKay, 1983). These programs are described in the next section. The examples illustrate the use of active or reflective listening.

PARENT EDUCATION PROGRAMS—FOCUS ON COMMUNICATION

Many parent education programs incorporate the resources of childrearing suggestions in Parent Effectiveness Training (PET) or Systematic Training for Effective Parenting (STEP). Brief excerpts from these programs illustrate the materials and communication techniques each uses.

In reflective listening, the listener tries to better understand the speaker's feelings.

PET

In PET, Gordon discusses many topics, including active listening, "I messages," changing behavior by changing the environment, parent-child conflicts, parental power, and "no-lose" methods for resolving conflicts as well as other parent-child issues. The excerpt here relates to problem ownership and active listening.

In the parent-child relationship three situations occur that we will shortly illustrate with case histories:

1. The child has a problem because he is thwarted in satisfying a need. It is not a problem for the parent because the child's behavior in no tangible way interferes with the parent's satisfying his own needs. Therefore, *the child owns the problem.*

2. The child is satisfying his own needs (he is not thwarted) and his behavior is not interfering with the parent's own needs. Therefore, *there is no problem in the relationship.*

3. The child is satisfying his own needs (he is not thwarted). But his behavior is a problem to the parent because it is interfering in some tangible way with the parent's satisfying a need of his own. *Now the parent owns the problem.*

It is critical that parents always classify each situation that occurs in a relationship. Which of these three categories does the situation fall into? It helps to remember this diagram . . .

When a parent accepts the fact that problems are owned by the child, this in no way means he, the parent, cannot be concerned, care, or offer help. A professional counselor has real concern for, and genuinely cares about, each child he is trying to help. But, unlike most parents, he leaves the responsibility for solving the child's problem with the child. He allows the child to own the problem. He accepts the child's having the problem. He accepts the child as a person separate from himself. And he relies heavily upon and basically trusts the child's own inner resources for solving his own problem. Only because he lets the child own his problem is the professional counselor able to employ active listening.

Active listening is a powerful method for helping another person solve a problem that he owns, provided the listener can accept the other's ownership and consistently allow the person to find his own solutions. Active listening can greatly increase the effectiveness of parents as helping agents for their children, but it is a different kind of help from that which parents usually try to give.

Paradoxically, this method will increase the parent's influence on the child, but it is an influence that differs from the kind that most parents try to exert over their children. Active listening is a method of influencing children to find their own solutions to their own problems. Most parents, however, are tempted to take over ownership of their children's problems, as in the following case:

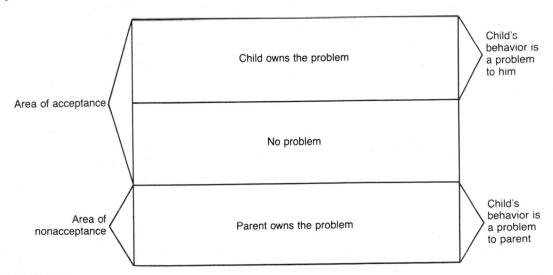

FIGURE 5–2
When the child's behavior is a problem to the parent, the parent owns the problem. (Source: T. Gordon, *P.E.T./Parent effectiveness training.* New York: Wyden, 1975, p. 64.)

JOHNNY: Tommy won't play with me today. He won't ever do what I want to do.

MOTHER: Well, why don't you offer to do what he wants to do? You've got to learn to get along with your little friends. (*advising; moralizing*)

JOHNNY: I don't like to do things he wants to do and besides I don't want to get along with that dope.

MOTHER: Well, go find someone else to play with then if you're going to be a spoilsport. (*offering a solution; name-calling*)

JOHNNY: He's the spoilsport, not me. And there isn't anyone else to play with.

MOTHER: You're just upset because you're tired. You'll feel better about this tomorrow. (*interpreting; reassuring*)

JOHNNY: I'm not tired, and I won't feel different tomorrow. You just don't understand how much I hate the little squirt.

MOTHER: Now stop talking like that! If I ever hear you talk about one of your friends like that again, you'll be sorry. (*ordering; threatening*)

JOHNNY: (walking away and sulking): I hate this neighborhood. I wish we would move.

Here is how the parent can help the same boy with active listening.

JOHNNY: Tommy won't play with me today. He won't ever do what I want to do.

MOTHER: You're kinda angry with Tommy. (*active listening*)

JOHNNY: I sure am. I never want to play with him again. I don't want him for a friend.

MOTHER: You're so angry you feel like never seeing him again. (*active listening*)

JOHNNY: That's right. But if I don't have him for a friend, I won't have anyone to play with then.

MOTHER: You would hate to be left with no one. (*active listening*)

JOHNNY: Yeah. I guess I just have to get along with him someway. But it's so hard for me to stop getting mad at him.

MOTHER: You want to get along better, but it's hard for you to keep from getting mad with Tommy. (*active listening*)

JOHNNY: I never used to—but that's when he was always willing to do what I wanted to do. He won't let me boss him anymore.

MOTHER: Tommy's not so easy to influence now. (*active listening*)

JOHNNY: He sure isn't. He's not such a baby now. He's more fun though.

MOTHER: You really like him better this way. (*active listening*)

JOHNNY: Yeah. But it's hard to stop bossing him—I'm so used to it. Maybe we wouldn't fight so much if I let him have his way once in a while. Think that would work?

MOTHER: You're thinking that if you might give in occasionally, it might help. (*active listening*)

JOHNNY: Yeah, maybe it would. I'll try it.

In the first version, the mother used eight of the "Typical Twelve" categories of responding. In the second, the mother consistently used active listening. In the first, the mother "took over the problem"; in the second, her active listening kept ownership of the problem with Johnny. In the first, Johnny resisted his mother's suggestions, his anger and frustration were never dissipated, the problem remained unresolved, and there was no growth on Johnny's part. In the second, his anger left, he initiated problem solving, and took a deeper look at himself. He arrived at his own solution and obviously grew a notch toward becoming a responsible, self-directing problem solver.*

Gordon clarifies active listening and problem ownerships through examples such as these. Parent groups follow up with a parent notebook and discussion within the group. Open discussion, led by a person knowledgeable about PET, allows parents to apply the methods to their own experiences in child rearing.

ACTIVE PARENTING

The Active Parenting program is similar to both PET and STEP in that it is also based on the theories of Alfred Adler and Rudolf Dreikurs. Goals of misbehavior, logical consequences, active communication, exploring alternatives, and family council meetings are described. A handbook and workbook supplement the group meetings and a leader's handbook gives detailed instruction on how the class should be conducted. Each session has a corresponding por-

---

*From Gordon, T. *P.E.T./Parent effectiveness training.* New York: Wyden, 1975, pp. 64 and 66–68.

tion of a video that illustrates the child and family issues under discussion.

STEP

The STEP program furnishes cassettes, a parent manual, and a leadership manual to facilitate parent meetings. Figure 5-3 is taken from the parent manual.

PARENT-TEACHER CONFERENCES

What is a parent-teacher conference? Manning defined it as an "exchange of feelings, beliefs and knowledge between parent and teacher about a particular student. This exchange should facilitate cooperation between home and school for the benefit of the student" (Manning, 1985, p. 342). To accomplish the greatest cooperation between home and school and the greatest benefit for the student, the conference needs to be the continuation of communication between the parent and school, based on agreed-upon goals for the child.

Start the school year with a positive interchange between the teacher and the parent—by an early telephone call or a block walk—to initiate the parent-school partnership. A preconference discussion can then be used to set goals and direction for the child during the school year. The goals should reflect that teacher and parent want what is best for the child. The first conference can be a progress and planning session based on those goals.

Parent-teacher conferences are personal opportunities for two-way communication between parent and teacher or three-way communication among parent, teacher, and student. Parents, as well as teachers, recognize the conference as an excellent opportunity for clarifying issues, searching for answers, deciding on goals, determining mutual strategies, and forming a team in the education of the student. Most schools schedule conferences two or three times a year. How can conferences be as productive as possible and yet nonthreatening to parents, teachers, and students?

Invitations and Schedule

The invitation to attend a conference sets the tone. If it is cordial, shows an awareness of parents' busy lives and obligations, and gives the parent time options for scheduling the conference, the teacher has shown consideration of the parents and a desire to meet with them. Most school systems have worked out procedures for scheduling conference periods. Release time is usually granted teachers. Originally, most conferences were held during afternoons. Children attended school in the mornings, and classes were dismissed at noon, with conferences between parents, usually mothers only, and school personnel held in the afternoon. With the increase in the number of working parents and single-parent families, plus the increasing number of fathers interested in their children's education, many schools are scheduling more evening conferences and retaining some afternoon conferences. Schools recognize the importance of daytime conferences and still allow release time during the day for teachers, but conference schedules now include more evening appointments.

To prepare the schedule, notes are sent to parents asking for their time preference. The formal note should be direct and specific as to time and place of the conference. A sample note is found in Figure 5-4. After the responses have been returned, staff members, including those teachers in special areas of education, meet to schedule back-to-back conferences for parents with more than one child attending school there.

A telephone call to each parent from the teacher adds a personal note. These calls, made either before or after the invitation has been sent home, may clarify questions and let the parents know they are really welcome.

Notes, with the time and date of the conference clearly indicated, should be sent home, whether the parent has been contacted or not. This ensures that both teacher and parent have the same understanding of the conference time. This confirmation note to each parent from the teacher could be personal, or a form could be

CHILD'S FAULTY BELIEF	CHILD'S GOAL*	PARENTS' FEELINGS AND REACTIONS	CHILD'S RESPONSE TO PARENTS' ATTEMPTS AT CORRECTION	ALTERNATIVES FOR PARENTS
I belong *only* when I am being noticed or served.	Attention	**Feeling:** annoyed **Reaction:** tendency to remind and coax	Temporarily stops misbehavior; later resumes same behavior or disturbs in another way	Ignore misbehavior when possible; give attention for positive behavior when child is not making a bid for it; avoid undue service; realize that reminding, punishing, rewarding, coaxing, and service are undue attention
I belong *only* when I am in control or am boss, or when I am proving no one can boss me!	Power	**Reaction:** tendency to fight or to give in **Feeling:** angry; provoked; as if one's authority is threatened	Active- or passive-aggressive misbehavior is intensified, or child submits with "defiant compliance"	Withdraw from conflict; help child see how to use power constructively by appealing for child's help and enlisting cooperation; realize that fighting or giving in only increases child's desire for power
I belong *only* by hurting others as I feel hurt. I cannot be loved.	Revenge	**Feeling:** deeply hurt **Reaction:** tendency to retaliate and get even	Seeks further revenge by intensifying misbehavior or choosing another weapon	Avoid feeling hurt; avoid punishment and retaliation; build trusting relationship; convince child that she or he is loved
I belong *only* by convincing others not to expect anything from me. I am unable; I am helpless.	Display of inadequacy	**Feeling:** despair; hopelessness; "I give up" **Reaction:** tendency to agree with child that nothing can be done	Passively responds or fails to respond to whatever is done; shows no improvement	Stop all criticism; encourage any positive attempt, no matter how small; focus on assets; above all, don't be hooked into pity, and don't give up.

*To determine your child's goal, you must check your feelings *and* the child's response to your attempts to correct him or her. Goal identification is simplified by observing:

1. Your own feelings and reaction to the child's misbehavior
2. The child's response to your attempts at correction

By considering your situation in terms of the chart, you will be able to identify the goal of the misbehavior.

FIGURE 5–3

The STEP program guides parents to relate positively with their children by checking the goals of misbehavior. (Source: Reproduced by permission of American Guidance Service from *Systematic training for effective parenting* by Don Dinkmeyer and Gary McKay, 1983.)

Dear_____ —

   We are looking forward to meeting with you and discussing _____experiences and progress at school. Will you please let us know when a conference would be most convenient for you? Please check the date and time of day you could come.

Thank you,

_____

Teacher or principal's name

Could you give a first and second choice? Please write "1" for your first preference and "2" for your second.

	Afternoon 1 to 4 PM	Evening 6 to 9 PM
Tuesday, November 12	_____	_____
Wednesday, November 13	_____	_____
Thursday, November 14	_____	_____

Please return by _____

FIGURE 5-4
Send a note home to schedule a conference.

used (see Figure 5–5). A personal note might read:

I am looking forward to meeting _____ parents. I enjoy his/her contribution to the class through his/her great interest in _____. The time and date of the conference is _____.

Private and Comfortable Meeting Place

How often have you gone into a school, walked down the halls, and seen parents and teachers trying to have a private conversation in the midst of children and other adults? To achieve open two-way communication, it is essential that the parent and teacher talk in confidence. Select a room designed for conferences or use the empty classroom, with a note attached to the door so people won't interrupt. Give the parents adult-size chairs so everyone can be comfortable and on the same level as the teacher. Place a table in front of the chairs so materials, class projects, and the student's work can be exhibited. The

parent, teacher, and student (if it is a three-way conference) can sit around the table and talk and exchange information. The room should be well ventilated and neither too warm nor too cold.

   Persons conducting interviews can set up psychological and physical barriers to maintain social distance or imply a status relationship. For example, an executive may sit behind a desk and talk with a subordinate; teachers sensitive to the "space language" that barriers imply will not put barriers between them and the parents (Chinn, Winn, & Walters, 1978).

Two-Way Communication in Conferences

"At the heart of effective parent-teacher conferences specifically and the parent-teacher relationship in general are interpersonal communication skills" (Rotter & Robinson, 1986, p. 9). Conditions necessary for effective communication during conferences include warmth—an attitude of caring—shown through attending be-

Dear _____ .

Thank you for your response to our request for a conference time about progress. Your appointment has been set for _____ (time) on (day) _____ (month and date) in room _____ .

We have set aside _____ minutes for our chance to talk together. If the above time is not convenient, please contact the office, and we can schedule another time for you.

We are looking forward to meeting with you.

Best wishes,

_____
Teacher

FIGURE 5–5
A note sent home to confirm a conference.

haviors, smiling, touching, and body language. Along with warmth is empathy, the ability to listen and respond in such a way that the parent knows you understand. Respect is a key to the success of building a collaborative connection between parent and teacher. If teachers and parents respect each other and enter the conference with a warm, caring attitude, able to listen effectively and understand the other's meanings and feelings, the stage is set for a successful conference (adapted from Rotter & Robinson, 1986).

Some school administrators and teachers make the mistake of seeing parent-school communication as the school informing the parent about the educational process, rather than as a two-way system. During the conference a teacher should speak only about one-half of the time. If teachers recognize the conference as a sharing time, half the burden has been lifted from their shoulders. They can use half the time to get to know the parent and child better.

Have you ever had a conversation with a friend who you believed was miles away in thought? During conferences communicators need to believe that what they have to say is important to the listener. Body language can reflect feelings contrary to the spoken word so the verbal message may be misunderstood or

missed altogether. It is important to be aware of what you are communicating. If you are rushed, pressured, or concerned about your own family, you will have to take a deep breath, relax, and concentrate on the conference.

Just as some physical gestures communicate distraction or disinterest, so does some body language convey your interest and attention to parents' concerns. Use appropriate attentive behavior to relay your interest.

1. *Eye contact.* Make sure you look at the person as you communicate. Failure to do so could imply evasion, deception, or lack of commitment.

2. *Forward posture.* Leaning forward creates the image of interest in what is being said. Be comfortable, but do not slouch to indicate that the whole process is boring or unimportant.

3. *Body response.* A nod in agreement, a smile, and use of the body to create an appearance of interest promote empathy. If you act aware and interested, you will probably become interested. If you do not, perhaps you are in the wrong profession.

4. *Touch.* Sometimes a touch to the arm or a clasp of the hand assures the other person that you care and understand.

Listening has been known to be an effective tool of communication since the early 1960s when Rogers made an impact on methods of psychological counseling with his concept of reflective listening. Earlier in this chapter we saw how the concept has been extended and reinterpreted in the day-to-day world of teaching parents and children. Gordon talked about the language of acceptance and the use of active listening as essential for improved parent-child relationships. Whether called "active" (Gordon, 1975), "effective" (Dinkmeyer & McKay, 1983), "responsive" (Chinn, Winn, & Walters, 1978), or "reflective" (Rogers, 1983), this kind of listening works. It helps open up the communication process.

Understandable Language   Specialized language gets in the way of communication. Although medical terminology is familiar and efficient to the doctor, it often sounds like a foreign tongue to the patient asking for an explanation of a diagnosis. Each year new terms and acronyms become common language in the schools, but they freeze communication when used with persons not familiar with the terms. Imagine a teacher explaining to a parent that the school has decided to use the SRA program this year in second grade, but the first grade is trying whole language. "I've been using behavior modification with Johnny this year, and it has been very effective, but with Janet I find TA more helpful." Jargon can create misunderstanding and stop communication.

Sometimes terms have meaning for both communicators, but the meanings are not the same. Hymes (1974) declares that lack of communication, superficial communication, and "words and vocabulary, without friendship and trust and knowledge, get in the way of understanding" (p. 33).

Look, for example, at "progressive education." Use those words and you have a fight on your hands. People get emotional and wild charges fly. Yet parents will be the first to say: "Experience is the best teacher" and there you have it! Different words but a good definition of what progressive education stands for. (Hymes, 1974, p. 33)

Practice   To achieve the ability to listen reflectively and to respond in a positive manner, practice until it becomes natural. You can practice alone, but it is more effective if you can role play the conference. Having an observer present allows both practice and feedback. Teachers can choose a typical case from among their records or invent a hypothetical one. For example,

> Andy, a precocious third grade child, spends most of the class period doodling ideas in a notebook. Although he completes his assignments, Andy takes no pride in his work and turns in messy papers. Special enrichment centers in the classroom do not attract him. Andy participates positively during recess and in physical education and music.

Each participant has basic information (real or hypothetical)—the child's sex, grade assigned, and background information. Assign one participant to act as the parent, another as the teacher. The third member of the team observes the interaction between the parent and teacher to check on

1. reflective listening
2. attentive behavior (eye contact, forward posture, etc.)
3. sensitivity to parent's feelings
4. positive language
5. cooperative decision making

Since no two teachers or parents are identical, there is no prescribed way to have a conference. The dialogue will be a constant flow, filled with emotions as well as objective analysis. You can prepare yourself, however, by practicing good reflective listening and positive communication. Look forward with pleasure to sharing together.

Preparation for the Conference

Two types of preparation will set the stage for a successful conference. The first, an optional program, involves training teachers and parents for an effective conference. The second is the essential—analyzing the child's previous records, current performance and attitude, and

Keep records, papers, and anecdotal notes to have the material needed for parent-teacher conferences.

relationship with peers, and gathering examples of work along with recent standardized test results.

Preconference Workshops and Guides

Workshops for parents, teachers, or a combination of both are fruitful. A discussion of what makes a conference a success or a calamity can bring forth an enormous number of tips for both parents and teachers. If parents and teachers form small groups, many ideas will emerge that can be recorded on the chalkboard for later discussion by the total group. Encourage parents to ask questions about their part in conferences. Clarifying objectives for conferences and what the school expects from the parents will help parents understand their responsibilities. Parents and teachers attending a workshop together can learn the art of reflective listening and communication. Role playing during conferences can elicit discussion. Many participants will see themselves in the roles portrayed and will attempt to find alternative methods of handling conference discussions. Films that illustrate common communication problems can also be used as starters for discussion.

At the close of the workshop, handouts or conference guides may be distributed to the participants. The guide should be designed with the school's objectives in mind. Parents can be told what to expect in the school's report and what the school expects from them. If your school does not schedule preconference workshops, put the handout in a newsletter and send it home to the parents before the conference.

Questions in the conference guide should be those the school would like answered and also ones the parents might be interested in knowing. Typical questions include:

1. How does your child seem to feel about school?
2. Which activities does your child talk about at home?
3. Which activities seem to stimulate his/her intellectual growth?
4. How does the student spend his/her free time?
5. Is there anything that the student dreads?
6. What are your child's interests and hobbies?

Some schools might also include questions about current concerns.

7. What concerns do you have about drugs and alcohol?
8. What kinds of support or collaboration would you like from the school to help your family?

A similar memo suggests questions that the parents might want to ask of the teacher at school:

1. How well does my child get along with other children? Who seem to be his/her best friends?
2. How does my child react to discipline? What methods do you use to promote self-discipline and cooperation?
3. Does my child select books at the proper reading level from the library?

4. Does my child use study periods effectively?
5. Are there any skills you are working on at school that I/we might reinforce at home?
6. Do you expect me to help my son or daughter with homework?
7. Are there any areas in which my child needs special help?
8. Does my child display any special interests or talents at school that we might support at home?
9. Does my child seem to be self-confident, happy, and secure? If not, what do you think the home or school can do to increase his/her feelings of self-worth?

Supplying questions before the conference is helpful in preparing parents, but it can also limit questions that develop naturally; and if these questions are strictly adhered to during conferences, they can limit the scope, direction, and outcome of the conference.

Teacher Preparation Throughout the year teachers should make a practice of accumulating anecdotal records, tests, workbooks, art projects, and papers that represent both academic and extracurricular areas. Folders created by students, an accordion file, or a file box or cabinet can store the papers until conference time. Students may then compile a notebook or folder of samples of their work to share with their parents during conferences. If the file is worked on periodically throughout the term, papers can be placed in chronologic order, thus illustrating the progress in each subject. The child's work is an essential assessment tool.

Standardized tests that reveal the child's potential compared to actual performance level are useful in tailoring an education program to fit the students. With this information, parents and teacher can discuss whether the student is performing above or below potential. Parents and teachers can use the information to plan for the future.

One word of caution on the use of standardized tests must be included. Tests are not infallible. Children may not feel well on the day of testing, some may freeze on tests. Use standardized test results as a supplement to informal assessment tools such as class papers, notebooks, class observation, and informal tests, not as a replacement for them. If standardized test results and your informal assessment are congruent and the child scores high on aptitude tests and shows moments of brilliance in class but consistently falls down on work, you can be fairly certain that the child is not working up to ability. If the child scores low but does excellent work in class, observe closely before deciding that the child is under too much pressure to achieve. In that case, the test may not indicate the child's true potential. Should the child score low on the test and also show a high level of frustration when working, you may want to make plans to gear the work closer to the child's ability. The standardized test, used as a backup to the informal assessment, can help teachers and parents plan the child's educational program.

Congruent Beliefs About the Child Have you ever had a disruptive child in a class only to discover that the child was retiring and well behaved during Scouts? Sometimes the disparity makes one wonder if it is the same child. It is difficult to discuss a child on common ground if the parents' and teachers' perceptions of the child are completely different. The Q Sort gives teachers and parents a means of comparing their perceptions of the child. It is often meaningful to have students sort their own views so the perceptions of teacher, parents, and student can be compared.

The Q Sort was developed by Stephenson (1953) as a self-referent technique to measure self-concept and was extended to be used by parents, teachers, and students in the measurement of "perceptions of behavior at home and in the classrooms" (Kroth, 1975, p. 43). Figure 5–6 is an adaptation of Kroth's tool. You can buy the Q Sort form or develop your own. You may want to check the list of items before adding your own and adapting the instrument for your use. Make sure that half the items are positive and half are negative when you develop your list.

Asks for help when needed 1	Is friendly 2	Squirms in seat 3	Excels in reading 4	Talks with other students constantly 5
Keeps busy 6	Is unhappy 7	Hands in messy work 8	Finishes work on time 9	Does poorly in academic classes 10
Excels in artwork 11	Has poor coordination 12	Enjoys music 13	Writes with poor penmanship 14	Pays attention to instruction 15
Disturbs others while they are working 16	Never finishes work 17	Walks around room without permission 18	Cooperates with students and teachers 19	Gets along well with other students 20
Excels in math 21	Pesters other children 22	Works well in group 23	Constantly gets out of seat 24	Works persistently until finished 25

FIGURE 5–6

Q sort cards, with one-half positive and one-half negative items, can be designed to evaluate any type of behavior. (Source: Modified from R. L. Kroth, *Communicating with parents of exceptional children.* Denver: Love Publishing, 1975.)

1. List 25 behaviors on small cards (Figure 5–6).

2. Make a sorting board with squares for the 25 cards (see Figure 5–7).

3. Sort the cards according to how truly descriptive they are of the student. Place only one card on each space.

4. Record the scores of each card on the recording form (Figure 5–8).

5. Record scores for both parent and teacher. If the difference between the scores is more than four, your perception of the child is significantly different than the parent's. Discuss incongruent items and clarify your views.

The Q Sort is a nonthreatening means of recognizing differences in perceptions. It forces people to make decisions of what the child is most like or most unlike. In doing this, some respondents take more time to answer a Q Sort than a questionnaire. Questionnaires can be used instead of the Q Sort and similar types of questions would be asked with the respondent able to say whether the question is like or unlike the child. Parents could answer these questions

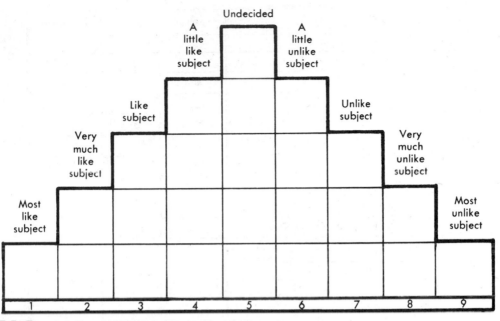

FIGURE 5–7
Enlarge this Q sort board in order to use it easily. (Source: Modified from R. L. Kroth, *Communicating with parents of exceptional children.* Denver: Love Publishing, 1975.)

while waiting for their conference time. Then the teacher's and the parent's responses could be compared.

Conference Membership

When children are taught by more than one teacher or have contact with numerous specialists (i.e., speech teacher, physical therapist), including all professionals involved with the child is appropriate and involves prior cooperative planning. Beware of the impact on the parent, however, because four professionals to one parent may be awesome and foreboding. If special care is taken to assure parents that all specialists are there to clarify and to work with the teacher and parent as a team, the cooperative discussion and planning can have worthwhile results. An alternative plan allows the parent to talk individually with each involved specialist. In some schools the homeroom teacher reports for all the specialists, but personal contact with all persons involved with the child's education is more satisfying to the parents. If time is short, the entire group could meet with the parents once in the fall and assure the parents they will be accessible whenever the parents have a concern.

Consider including the child. Who is better equipped to clarify why the child is doing well or needs extra help? Who has more at stake? Preschoolers make less sustained conference members, but as soon as the child becomes interested in assessment and evaluations and recognizes the goal of parent-teacher conferences, the teacher should consider including the child in the process. Initially, the child may attend for a short portion of the conference, but as interest and attention span increase, it is realistic to have the child present during the complete conference. If portions of the conference need to be conducted without the child present, have a supervised play area available. If older students are included as members of the team, issues can be clarified and goals set. The student is a part of the discussion and helps in setting realistic goals.

	Name *John*	Teacher	Parent	Difference
1.	Asks for help when needed	8	3	5
2.	Is friendly	2	2	0
3.	Squirms in seat	4	3	1
4.	Excels in reading	6	6	0
5.	Talks with other students constantly	7	2	5
6.	Keeps busy			
7.	Is unhappy			
8.	Hands in messy work			
9.	Finishes work on time			
10.	Does poorly in academic classes			
11.	Excels in artwork			
12.	Has poor coordination			
13.	Enjoys music			
14.	Writes with poor penmanship			
15.	Pays attention to instruction			
16.	Disturbs others while they are working			
17.	Never finishes work			
18.	Walks around room without permission			
19.	Cooperates with students and teachers			
20.	Gets along well with other students			
21.	Excels in math			
22.	Pesters other children			
23.	Works well in a group			
24.	Constantly gets out of seat			
25.	Works persistently until finished			

FIGURE 5–8
The record sheet illustrates the differences in opinions about the child's behavior.

Bjorklund and Burger (1987) describe a four-phase process for collaboration with parents. *Phase 1,* held early in the year, sets the stage with an overview of the time conferences will be held, techniques for observation of the children, and a detailed account of the curriculum, based on developmental goals. During this phase both teachers and parents are encouraged to consider the developmental goals of the program. *Phase 2* is based on the goals. Parents, teachers and administrators meet and set priorities using observation, testing, anecdotal records, and work samples. Two to four goals are given priority for each child. In *Phase 3,* observations, anecdotal records, check-lists, and rating scales are collected for review.

The final *4th phase* involves the child. The teacher sends a progress report home in which all the developmental areas are reviewed. A guide for the conference is also sent with three questions that the parents should discuss with the child prior to the meeting. These are: (1) What do you like best about school? (2) Who are some of the special friends you like to play with at school? and (3) Are there any things you would like to do more at school? "The teacher begins the progress conference by sharing examples of the child's growth through anecdotes which describe some of the child's best skills or characteristics. This leads into a discussion of the three questions with the child" (Bjorklund & Burger, 1987, p. 31). The conference promotes a good self-image for the child by emphasizing the child's positive growth.

Congruent Conferences

Conferences go more smoothly when expectations held by the teacher and parents are congruent with the performance of the child. If the child is an excellent student and both teacher and parents are pleased with the evaluation, it is easy to accept the report. If the child is handicapped and both teacher and parents recognize the handicapping condition, they can work together to plan an appropriate program for the child.

Too often the outward signs of good marks and pleasant personality and behavior fail to uncover how the child feels and whether the teacher can make the educational experience more satisfying and challenging. In working with a successful student, parents and teachers may fail to communicate about the child's potential and need to have a good self-concept. Special interests of the child, friends, reading preferences, experiences, and needs are important for the teacher to know. Bring the child into the decision-making process. Together, the parents, teacher, and child can plan activities that will encourage growth and improve self-concept. Let these parents and children communicate, too.

The Day of the Conference

The day of the conference has arrived. Review your objectives, maintain effective communication skills, discuss concrete examples of work, and plan together.

Clear Statement of Objectives Some objectives may be universal; others will be specific for the individual conference. Use the following objectives as a guide:

1. To gain a team member (the parent) in the education of the child
2. To document the child's progress for the parent
3. To explain the educational program you are using as it relates to the individual child
4. To learn about the environment in which the child lives
5. To allow the parents to express feelings, questions, and concerns
6. To get a better understanding of the expectations the parent holds for the child
7. To set up a lasting network of communication among parent, teacher, and child
8. To establish cooperative goals for the education of the child

Recognition of the Parent As Part of the Team After you have made sure that the room is comfortable, that two-way communication will be uninterrupted, and that you are ready to listen and be responsive to the parent, it is easy to recognize the parent as a part of the educational team. Parents arrive at conferences as experts on their children's history, hobbies, interests, special likes and dislikes, friends, and experiences. You, as the teacher, have a great deal of knowledge and understanding of the child to gain from the parents.

Besides being adept at reflective listening, you need to listen intuitively to determine if parents have problems within their homes or are themselves emotionally immature. Such problems make it difficult for the child to have the home support needed for educational success. When indicated, bring other professionals, such as the school social worker or principal, into the conference to support and help the family and child. You can be more understanding of the child's needs if you understand the child's home (Grissom, 1971).

Why is it that parents enter into parent-teacher conferences with apprehension? Some parents are worried because they want the best for their child but do not know how to achieve it. They are unsure of themselves in the discussion and are threatened by terminology. If parent and teacher can throw away their roles during the conference and look at it as a meeting place for the exchange of ideas and information and a chance to support each other, both can enter into the conference with anticipation and confidence.

Use the sandwich-approach when you plan a conference. (Manning, 1985). Start the conference off with pleasant and positive items. If you have negative comments or concerns to be discussed, bring them up during the middle of the conference. Always end with a positive summary, planning, and a pleasant comment about the child.

Explain to the parents that all participants in the conference are members of a team looking at the progress of the child and working together to benefit the child. How can *we* help the child who is having a difficult time? How can *we* enrich the program for the child who is accelerated? How can *we* get the child to do the tasks at hand? How can *we* promote self-esteem? These questions, when answered as a team, can be more productive than when answered by a teacher who is questioning a parent. Here are some tips that will help the parent feel a part of the team:

- Know the parent's name. Do not assume that the child's last name is the same as the parent's. Look in the record for the correct name.
- Insure the privacy of the conference.
- Know the time limitations.
- Do not use terminology that has meaning for you but not for the parent.
- Do not refer to organizations, forms, tests, materials, or ideas by their initials. Do not assume that everyone knows what the initials mean.
- Have some questions about and show interest in the child.

Encourage parents to contribute to the conference.

- Remind the parents that they may ask questions at any time and that you will be pleased to explain anything that is not clear.
- Begin on a positive note. Start by praising an accomplishment of the child or a contribution the child has made to the class.
- Review your file and know enough about the child before the parent arrives that the parent can tell you have taken a personal interest in the child's welfare.
- Keep on the subject—the child's schooling and development.
- Encourage the parents to contribute. Allow parents to talk for at least 50% of the conference.
- Show that you understand the parent by checking periodically during the conference, for example, "Would you agree with this?" or "Do you have suggestions to add about this?"
- Make a note of an idea suggested by a parent, but do not get so involved in writing that you lose the flow of the conversation.
- Maintain eye contact.
- Use attending behaviors, that is, lean forward, look interested, and nod when in agreement.
- Do not ignore a parent's question.
- Be honest, yet tactful and sensitive, to the parent's feelings.
- Base your discussion on objective observation and concrete examples of work.
- Deal in specifics more than generalities.
- Evaluate needs and select methods of remediating deficiencies.
- Evaluate strengths and select methods of enriching those strengths.
- Plan together for future educational goals.
- Clarify and summarize the discussion.
- Makes plans to continue the dialogue.

Concrete Examples of Child's Work and Behavior Both the parent and teacher are interested in the child's accomplishments. Objective observation of the child's classroom behavior, with anecdotal notes collected in a loose-leaf notebook throughout the reporting periods, documents the child's social as well as intellectual achievements. Anecdotal records of signifi-

cant behaviors are particularly valuable for conferences with parents of young children. Here papers and tests may not be available, and the anecdotal records become tools for evaluating the child's social, intellectual, and physical progress. In the case of children with behavioral problems, it is also important to be able to report specific incidents rather than vague generalizations about disturbances.

The accumulated examples of the child's work with a few words from the teacher also illustrate to parents what their child is doing. It is not necessary to state that the child has not progressed, for it will be obvious. If the child has made great progress, it will be evident from the samples collected. Consider asking the parents if they have come to the same conclusion as you when comparing early and subsequent papers.

Some teachers supplement papers and anecdotal records with videotapes of children in the room. Although time consuming, a film report is enjoyed by parents and encourages interaction between parent and teacher on the child's classroom participation.

Bringing to the conference concrete examples that illustrate the child's work eliminates a teacher-parent confrontation and allows parent and teacher to analyze the work together. Include anecdotal records and examples of the child's work in comparison to expected behavior at that age level. In preschool this may be fine motor control, large muscle activities, art, problem solving, etc. With school-age children include papers, artwork, projects, work in academic subjects, tests, notebooks, workbooks, and anecdotal records. It is also helpful to parents for the teacher to collect a set of unidentified average papers. If the parents want to compare their child's work with that of the average child, they have a basis for this comparison.

Whatever the level of the child's performance, the parent and teacher need to form a team as they evaluate the child's educational progress and work together for the good of the child. A checklist may be used for self-evaluation:

Conference Checklist

Yes	No	Did You
☐	☐	1. Prepare ahead by collecting anecdotal records, tests, papers, notebooks, workbooks, and art materials from the beginning to the end of the reporting period?
☐	☐	2. Provide book exhibits, displays, or interesting reading for parents as they wait for their conferences?
☐	☐	3. Make arrangements for coffee or tea for parents as they waited for their conferences?
☐	☐	4. Prepare your room with an attractive display of children's work?
☐	☐	5. Welcome the parents with a friendly greeting?
☐	☐	6. Start on a positive note?
☐	☐	7. Adjust your conference to the parents' needs and levels of understanding?
☐	☐	8. Have clear objectives for the conference?
☐	☐	9. Say in descriptive terms what you mean? Did you avoid educational jargon and use of initials?
☐	☐	10. Listen reflectively?
☐	☐	11. Keep the communication lines open? Were you objective and honest?
☐	☐	12. Avoid comparing students or parents? Discuss other teachers only if it was complimentary?
☐	☐	13. Check your body language? Were you alert to the parents' body language?
☐	☐	14. Plan the child's educational program together?
☐	☐	15. Summarize your decisions?
☐	☐	16. Begin and end on time? If you needed more time, did you set up another appointment?

If you are able to answer yes to these questions, you are ready to have productive parent-teacher conferences.

Dealing with Angry Parents   What do you do when a very upset and angry parent confronts you? Most professionals are confronted at one time or another by an angry parent. Margolis and Brannigan (1986) list seven steps to help you control the volatile situation and allow the parent to regain composure. By understanding anger dynamics, you can engage in reflective listening. As a result, the wrath is redirected and you can empathize with the parent. The steps include:

1. Remain calm, courteous, and maintain natural eye contact through the barrage. After the parents have expressed their anger, usually dominated by emotion, ask them to repeat their concerns so that you can understand the situation better. The second time around, the statements are usually more comprehensible and rational.

2. Use reflective listening and give reflective summaries of their statements. You can explore the content of their messages later, but during this stage attempt to establish a more relaxed and trusting atmosphere.

3. Continue with reflective listening and ask some open-ended questions that allow them to talk more and you to gain greater understanding.

4. Keep exploring until you have determined what the underlying critical issues really are. Be non-evaluative and do not be defensive.

5. After the issues have been fully explored, rephrase and summarize, including points of

agreement. Check to see if your summary of the concerns are correct. Offer to let them add to what you have summarized. By clearly defining the concerns they often seem more manageable.

6. Margolis and Brannigan point out that by this point listening has been used to build trust and defuse the anger in order to understand the problem from the parent's perspective. "When steps one through five are followed in an open, sincere, and empathetic manner, disagreements frequently dissolve and respect emerges (p. 345)." If such is not the case, go back and allow free exploration again.

7. Systematically problem-solve the issues that have not already been resolved. Steps in collaborative problem solving include a) understand each others needs and the resources available to help satisfy the needs, b) formulate a hypothesis that might solve the problem, c) brainstorm other solutions, d) combine ideas and solutions to create new solutions, e) together, develop criteria to judge the solutions, f) clarify and evaluate solutions, and g) select the most likely solution. At the end of the confrontation, the result should satisfy both educator and parent.

DEALING WITH CONCERNS THROUGHOUT THE YEAR

The following principles (Franklin, 1989) will help facilitate good home-school communication as issues emerge throughout the year.

1. Approach the parents at every meeting with the assumption that you have a common goal—a good environment for the child to learn and develop.

2. Try to facilitate the best in the parent, just as you support and try to develop the best potential in the child.

3. Avoid confrontation and defensive responses. Model working together as partners.

4. Assess your motives before giving negative feedback to parents. Why are you telling this to the parent? What do you hope will come out of the exchange? Will it help the child's learning? Do you expect a positive outcome?

5. Avoid setting yourself up as an authority figure with parents. Work towards establishing a partnership with the parents. Respect the parents' knowledge of their child and ask them to share information with you. Parents and teachers can learn from each other and provide different perspectives.

6. Try to avoid judging the parent, just as you hope they are not focused on evaluating you.

7. Give a careful and thoughtful response to parent concerns. Be available and unhurried in your interaction.

8. There are no typical responses from parents. They are as different from one another as teachers are from each other. Be an active listener and remain open to different perspectives.

Issues That May Emerge

These typical situations focus on achieving what is best for the child, based on Franklin's (1989) principles for communicating with parents. Use your own words, but express ideas in ways that will accomplish the major goal—growth and well-being of the child.

A. What are some things to keep in mind when approaching a parent for evaluation of a child for a school problem? Some parents feel threatened when they are told that their child needs evaluation for a school problem. Focus on what can be learned from the evaluation that will help the child at school. This focus is more positive and less threatening than an enumeration of the child's difficulties. Ask parents for their opinions. Let them know that their input will be helpful in the evaluation process. Explain the process in some detail. Talk about what procedures will be used and what support will be available for the child.

Parents might bring a friend, or they can have a professional attend with them. This support helps parents become working partners.

B. Mrs. Smith reports that her child does not like school this year. How can I help this? Children experience difficulty with school for many reasons. Dislike of school may result from a difficult adjustment to a new school, family issues, preoccupation with peer problems, academic frustration, and/or student-teacher conflict. Examine the issue with the parent. Perhaps this child needs additional support from the school counselor, additional evaluation, or more or less structure or individualization. Talk with the child about feelings, too. Perhaps additional structure and support are needed. Would the child enjoy a special job? Could the teacher and student prepare a short list of several things the child enjoyed at the end of each school day? Continue to talk with the child to try to determine the underlying cause of the problem. Then try to overcome the real concern.

C. How do you welcome a parent to the classroom for a visit? Classroom observations can be anxiety provoking for teachers. However, this is an appropriate activity for concerned and involved parents. Welcome the parent to the classroom. A child might even take host responsibility. A collection of photographs depicting activities and children in the room is a nice introduction into the classroom. The VIP (very important person) of the week or another child chosen to welcome the parent may describe the album to the visiting parent, or the child of the parent may want the honor. The album indicates to the parents that the teacher has an interest in the students.

A pamphlet or poster may explain the routine of the room. Many parents want to help in the classroom. A center for reading, puzzles, or games may be a place where parents can observe the class at the same time they participate.

If the teacher is occupied teaching the class, the parent may be invited to stay until a break, or an appointment may be made where the classroom can be discussed leisurely and in private. "I am busy with the class right now, but if you wait until the class goes to music, we can sit and talk." Or: "I am so glad you were able to come.

Because I have to devote myself to teaching right now, could we make a convenient appointment to talk?"

D. As a teacher, I feel Mrs. Smith is over-involved and over-protective. Whenever I give any negative feedback, she gets very defensive. A parent may be over-involved with a child for many reasons. The parent or child may have experienced some negative interactions with school staff in the past, the parent may feel guilt over the child's difficulties, or the parent may personalize feedback which is given about their child. In talking with the parent, it is important to foster a sense of working together. Ask the parent for suggestions. Give specific observations and illustrations. Focus on how things can be improved, come up with a plan which involves positive suggestions, and explain that both you and the parent will evaluate the child's progress.

E. Johnny's parents get very angry when I tell them he is not paying attention in the classroom. They demand that I discipline him and make him behave. I just want to help him. I don't think being punished each time will help. What can I do? Sometimes parents are punitive in reaction to teacher concerns. If the teacher senses this may be an issue, model alternative behaviors. Perhaps parents can observe the teacher's interaction with the child. Talk with the parents about what you plan to try with the child in the classroom and work out a plan with the parents that includes appropriate procedures at home.

F. The Smiths have given me several suggestions about how to approach their child. I feel that they are trying to tell me how to instruct my class. This makes me angry. Responding defensively to parents is usually not helpful. Instead, plan together how to address the problem. Invite parents to come to the classroom for a classroom project to make them feel more comfortable at school. Meeting together with parents and child may also be another alternative. Evaluate whether the child is presenting some unique academic or behavioral

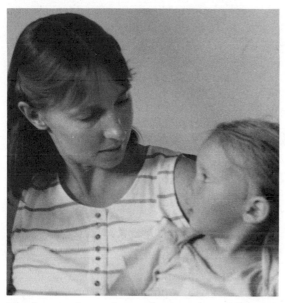

Teachers and parents can focus on how things can be improved.

issues which need to be addressed or whether the parent is unhappy with the instruction for other reasons.

G. Susy disrupts other students. When I bring this up, the parents are critical of how I manage her. What can I do? When talking about Susy's behavior with parents, try to avoid describing your interventions in terms of what is right and wrong. Sometimes it is helpful to talk about individual styles of behavior management and each person's comfort levels. Acknowledge that there can be differences between behavior at home and at school. Avoid setting up a confrontation and being critical of someone else's ideas. Model tolerance. Develop an intervention strategy with the parents that can be carried out at home and school, plan to check back with each other, and set a period of time to evaluate its effectiveness.

H. How can I involve parents of the middle/junior/senior high student in the school program? Parents of this age child are very concerned about alcohol/drug/suicide problems. Address their concerns and involve

parents in the plans—they will attend school functions. Be creative to involve them in other ways, too. Do the students have access to excellent after-school and evening programs? Could the school provide this and involve the parents? Is there a homework hotline? Is there a parent network to establish guidelines for teenagers?

Work with the adolescent to involve parents in special activities. Parents are interested in special displays or awards on the evening of conferences. Parents may also share their experiences about employment, travel, or hobbies.

I. A child in my class has leukemia. How should this be discussed in the classroom? Consult the parents about how they would like this handled. A direct, open, and supportive approach frequently increases understanding. The child, parent, and child's physician might make a classroom presentation. As the "expert" on the topic, the child could answer questions. This can be a learning experience as well as an opportunity to discuss feelings. It sets a precedent for discussing future tough issues. Educate yourself and deal with your own feelings about significant childhood illnesses.

J. A child's parent died recently. How can I help this child? Death and loss can be a learning experience for children if used appropriately to demonstrate empathy, deal directly with feelings, and provide support to a classmate. Other students need to be informed of their classmate's loss and have their feelings, fears, and questions addressed. This is an opportunity to discuss other losses children have experienced and, perhaps, to read books on the death of pets or friends. Expect the child to resume a normal routine, but anticipate that there may be immediate and delayed reactions. Ask colleagues for assistance.

K. A child's parents were recently divorced. What should I do? Divorce, like death, is a loss for children. Their family as they have known it, is changed. As in the death of a parent, the child will go through stages of grieving. They often blame themselves for the divorce. Many children will resume a normal routine, but anticipate immediate and delayed reactions just as you do for a death in the family. Give the child support and a stable environment that maintains continuity.

L. What is a *hyperactive* child? How should we evaluate this? Children seen as hyperactive may have difficulty remaining in their chairs, attending to classroom activities, and monitoring their own behavior. Impulsive, disorganized, and more active behaviors may be exhibited. Interventions are controversial. Behavior modification techniques may work. However, it is important to differentiate between whether the child is behaving in this manner because of anxiety or because of significant attentional problems that may have some other cause. A medical evaluation is essential to help understand and diagnose these symptoms. There is currently significant controversy around the use of medications for this problem. Again, this is input which can be obtained from the family physician.

M. My children always say they have no homework. Do they? How will I know? How should I handle this? Teachers and parents share a common goal—to facilitate independent functioning and responsibility. Children who cannot handle this responsibility may need a homework sheet that they bring home daily. Communicate your homework expectations in writing to parents.

N. Sherry complains that she has no friends. What can I do to help her? There are many reasons children have this difficulty. An individual child may have poor social skills, may be preoccupied with other difficulties, may be having problems containing aggressive and impulsive behaviors, or may be socially withdrawn because of problems with self-esteem or confidence. The school might have a peer group or counseling sessions at the school available for the child. Affective education and presentations of self-esteem and other issues may also be helpful to a child with these difficulties.

O. How can I increase self-esteem in the classroom? Helping each child feel that they have a unique and special place in the classroom is a challenging and effective strategy. Children may be assigned special roles and responsible jobs. The teacher can encourage and model nurturing behavior toward peers rather than setting up competitive interactions. There should be many opportunities for children to use different avenues for success. Achievements should be judged by focusing on positive evaluations. Classroom structuring which reduces comparisons and focuses more on the individual or group achievement may be helpful. Encouraging school spirit and special class activities helps children feel a part of the group and builds self-esteem. Children who are able to take risks without fear of ridicule, children whose strengths (rather than their deficiencies) are emphasized, children who feel connected to others in their play and work environment, and children who feel they are able to control their own destiny have a greater chance of having a high self-esteem than those who meet with failure. Teachers and parents are the models and reflections to help children attain a high self-concept.

SUMMARY

Effective communication between parents and schools allows parents to become partners in education. Communication includes speaking, listening, reflection of feeling, and interpretation of the meaning of the message. If the message sent is not correctly interpreted by the receiver, then miscommunication has occurred. It can be overcome by rephrasing and checking out meanings. Talking is not the most important element in communication. The way a message is spoken and body language account for 93% of the message.

Parents and schools both put up roadblocks to communication. Parent roadblocks include the following roles: protector, inadequate-me, avoidance, indifferent-parent, don't-make-waves, and club-waving advocate. Roadblocks put up by schools include the following roles: authority-figure, sympathizing-counselor, pass-the-buck, protect-the-empire, and busy-teacher.

Effective communication and trust building between parent and educator are important. The areas of communication that can be developed include positive speaking, listening, rephrasing, reframing, attentive behavior, and reflective listening. PET, STEP, and Active Parenting all include communication with an emphasis on reflective or active listening in their parent education format.

Parent-teacher conferences are the most common two-way exchange. Conferences can be effective if educators and parents prepare for them in advance. Parents need to be made to feel welcome; materials and displays should be available. Two-way conversation will build cooperation and trust. Teachers can develop expertise in conducting conferences by relating to the parents, developing trust, and learning from them about the child. A checklist is included to analyze the effectiveness of the conference.

The chapter includes suggestions for dealing with angry parents and how to deal with concerns parents may raise throughout the year.

SUGGESTED ACTIVITIES AND DISCUSSIONS

1. Practice speaking positively. Develop situations in which a child is average, learning disabled, or gifted. Role play the parent and the teacher. Make the interaction focus on positive speaking. Then reverse your approach and become negative in your analysis of the child. How did you feel during each interchange?
2. Practice listening. Divide the class into groups of three. One person is the speaker; one is the listener; and the third is the observer. Exchange roles so each person in the group gets to play each role. Have each person select a topic of interest to them, from something as simple as "My favorite hideaway" to something as serious as "Coping with death in my family." Each person tells their story; the listener listens and then repeats or rephrases the story. The observer watches for body language, attentive behavior, interest, and correct rephrasing. A checklist is an excellent way to make sure the observer watches for all elements of listening.
3. Brainstorm in the classroom for words to use in rephrasing. For example, what words could you use for a child who hands in sloppy work?
4. Role play the parent roadblocks to communication.
5. Role play the roadblocks that schools put up that block communication.
6. Write out three situations that call for a parent-teacher conference. Play the part of the parent, teacher, specialist, or child. Try your approaches using both closed and open responses and authoritarian or cooperative roles. Was there a change in the effectiveness of the conference? Discuss.
7. Conduct a parent-teacher conference utilizing your best communication techniques. Have an observer use the checklist to determine how well you conducted the conference.
8. Sit in on a staffing or a parent-teacher conference. Observe the parent and the educators' interaction.
9. Practice communicating with an angry parent. One participant plays the educator; another plays the angry parent. Go through the six or seven steps necessary to reach an agreement.
10. In the section, "Dealing with Concerns Throughout the Year," there are issues that need supportive answers. Construct positive answers to the questions parents may ask. Give answers that will help the teacher and parent work cooperatively to help the child.
    Devise some negative answers that will hinder positive communication. Why are these answers inappropriate?
    Divide into dyads or triads. Role play questions and answers. How do positive answers make you feel? How do destructive answers make you feel?
11. Compose situations that need constructive, positive answers. Make up several answers that would be appropriate for each situation.

BIBLIOGRAPHY

Bjorklund, G., & Burger, C. Making conferences work for parents, teachers, and children. *Young Children,* January 1987, pp. 26–31.

Broderick, C. B. *The therapeutic triangle.* Beverly Hills: Sage Publications, 1983.

Center for Family Strengths. *Building family strengths: A manual for facilitators.* Lincoln, Neb.: University of Nebraska-Lincoln, 1986.

Chinn, P. C., Winn, J., & Walters, R. H. *Two-way talking with parents of special children: A process of positive communication.* St. Louis: C. V. Mosby, 1978.

Cooley, H. C. *Human nature and the social order.* New York: Schoken, 1964.

DeVito, J. A. *The interpersonal communication book.* New York: Harper and Row, 1983.

Dinkmeyer, D., & McKay, G. D. *Systematic training for effective parenting: Parent's handbook.* Circle Pines, Minn.: American Guidance Service, 1983.

———. *STEP: Systematic training for effective parenting.* Circle Pines, Minn.: American Guidance Service, 1983.

Fisher, B. A. *Perspectives on human communication.* New York: Macmillan Publishing Co., Inc., 1978.

Franklin, C. J. Dealing with concerns throughout the year. Personal correspondence, Colorado Springs, Colo., May, 1989.

Gamble, T. K., & Gamble, M. *Contacts: Communicating interpersonally.* New York: Random House, 1982.

George, R. L. & Dustin, D. *Group counseling: Theory and practice.* Englewood Cliffs, N.J.: Prentice-Hall, Inc. 1988.

Gordon, T., *Parent effectiveness training.* New York: Wyden, 1975.

Grissom, C. E. Listening beyond words: Learning from parents in conferences. *Childhood Education,* December 1971, pp. 138–142.

Guralnik, D.B. (Chief Ed.) *Webster's new world dictionary of the American language.* New York: Simon & Schuster, 1980.

Hymes, J. *Effective home-school relations.* Sierra Madre: Southern California Association for the Education of Young Children, 1974.

Kroth, R. L. *Communicating with parents of exceptional children.* Denver: Love Publishing, 1975.

Manning, B. H. Conducting a worthwhile parent-teacher conference. *Education,* Summer 1985, pp. 342–348.

Margolis, H., & Brannigan, G. G. Relating to angry parents. *Academic Therapy,* 21(3); January 1986, pp. 343–346.

Miller, S., Wackman, S., Nunnally, E., & Miller, P. *Connecting with self and others.* Littleton, Co.: Interpersonal Communication Programs, Inc., 1988.

Popkin, M. H. *Active parenting.* Marietta, Ga.: Active Parenting, 1983.

Rogers, C., *Freedom to learn for the '80s.* Columbus, Ohio: Merrill, 1983.

Rotter, J. C., & Robinson, E. H. Parent-teacher conferencing: What research says to the teacher. Washington D.C.: National Education Association of the United States, 1986.

Sieburg, E. *Family communication: An integrated systems approach.* New York: Gardner Press, Inc., 1985.

Smith, V. Listening. In O. Hargie (Ed.). *A handbook of communication skills.* Washington Square, New York: New York University Press, 1986, pp. 246–265.

Stephenson, W. *The study of behavior: Q technique and its methodology.* Chicago: University of Chicago Press, 1953.

6

Leadership Training in Parent Education

ave you ever attended a relaxed meeting where everyone was accepted and encouraged to participate and still the objectives of the meeting were accomplished? Each person participated in the meeting and, in turn, developed higher self-esteem and had the opportunity to be a part of a productive group. A well-led parent group is representative of such a meeting and accomplishes its goals by educating parents and clarifying and responding to their questions and concerns.

Parent education offers the professional an exciting opportunity to work with highly motivated, interested adults. If the parents have come to parent education classes after the birth of their first child, the educator usually will find two very concerned and committed parents, ready to gain information that will help them in the first months of their baby's life. If parent educators work with parents of preschool children, they will find parents who have several years of on-the-job training with experiences that will help them build their knowledge base. In either case the parents will have concern for the well-being of their children and family. Two elements necessary for effective learning— interest and need—will be present.

Parents, as adult learners, bring with them many of the ingredients that provide a stimulat-

ing, productive learning environment. Their interest and need make it easy to develop topics that are important to the membership. The background and experience of the parents provides rich educational material, an opportunity for sharing expertise and knowledge, and an impetus for self-directed learning. Parent education groups should be carefully monitored to make sure that all levels of expertise are allowed to flourish. It is up to the leaders to provide an accepting, risk-free environment; to involve the parents in planning; to provide relevant materials and knowledge; and to devise appropriate delivery systems (such as group discussions, simulations, role playing, and experts).

WHO ARE THE LEADERS?

Leadership in parent group education may be viewed as a continuum (see Figure 6–1) that ranges from the lay leader, to the nonprofessional with little training, to a knowledgeable expert trained to expedite group processes, to the professional who lectures as an authority. As you begin a parent education program, keep in mind that groups can be organized in different fashions. A trained professional should not dominate the interaction within the group with

Parent leader with no training	Parent leader with leadership training	Parent leader with a structured curriculum	Parent leader with professional support	Professional leader with parent support	Professional teacher

FIGURE 6–1
Continuum of leaders in parent education.

specific didactic teaching, nor should the lay group be left without direction.

The use of lay leaders—parents leading their own groups—encourages parents to be actively involved. Since educational growth and positive change is what is wanted in parent education groups, active involvement is highly desired. More change will occur if the parent formulates some of the educational suggestions and acts upon the information. Parents are more able to develop their own ways of handling parent-child relationships if they develop their expertise from their own research and interact with other members of the group. This does not mean that experts in the field should not be used. At times it is necessary to have an authority give background material. After the information is received, however, parents need to discuss it and act upon it themselves. Professional leadership does not have to be overbearing and authoritarian. This concept is illustrated by the proverb credited to Lao-tze, an ancient Chinese philosopher.

> *A leader is best*
> *When people barely know that he exists*
> *Not so good when people obey and acclaim*
> *   him*
> *Worst when they despise him*
> *Fail to honor people,*
> *They fail to honor you,*
> *But of a good leader, who talks little*
> *When work is done, his aim fulfilled*
> *They will all say, "we did this ourselves."*

A professional who can support and motivate the group can accomplish the goals of the group without undermining the responsibilities of the participants. The style of the leader will be determined by the individual's training and personality as well as the makeup of the group.

Group management can be enhanced by leadership training sessions where members of the parent group can be introduced to group methods, curriculum, and resources. All parent education groups need basic understanding of group processes and communication, whether led by parent leaders or professionals.

This chapter describes various types of meetings and group processes as a guide in the development of new parent group programs. The programs discussed here range from those led by the unskilled person without curriculum guides on the left of the continuum to the authoritative meeting on the right. The center of the continuum contains the parent education group that is most appropriate for achieving parental self-determination, attitudinal change, competency, and educational gains—that of parent leadership with professional support. Descriptions of programs that illustrate each of the types include:

1. Unstructured meetings with no goals, curriculum, or trained leader
2. Meetings led by lay leaders to get feedback, solve a problem, study an issue, or become better acquainted
3. Meetings led by lay leaders who follow a curriculum devised by professionals (e.g., Parent Effectiveness Training, Systematic Training for Effective Parenting)
4. Meetings called by a parent and/or a professional that involve members and respond to their concerns with professional support
5. Meetings called and led by a professional, with participation by lay members, and
6. Meetings called, led, directed, and controlled by the professional, with members of the audience being observers only

The goal of education is to help parents become familiar with the phases of a child's growth and to become more effective parents.

Although parent education programs differ in the underlying structures—some are led by professionals, others by lay leaders—they are similar in their goal to develop decision-making abilities in parents (Auerbach, 1980; Hereford, 1963; Pickarts & Fargo, 1971; Swick, 1983; U.S. Department of Health and Human Services, 1980). Allowing parents to evaluate childrearing practices in the light of their own situations, values, and beliefs is an extension of democratic principles. Belief in the autonomy of parents inspires the promotion of their decision-making abilities and thus underscores the need for active involvement of parents in the programs.

Auerbach (1980) reinforced the need for parent involvement in her discussion of the following theories:

1. Parents can learn
2. Parents want to learn
3. Parents learn best what they are interested in learning

4. Learning is most significant when the subject matter is closely related to the parents' own immediate experiences
5. Parents can learn best when they are free to create their own response to a situation
6. Parent group education is as much an emotional experience as it is an intellectual one
7. Parents can learn from one another
8. Parent group education provides the basis for remaking experiences
9. Each parent learns in his own way

Parents, when involved in a study that interests them and one in which they are active investigators, tend to learn more and change more in attitude than parents who merely attend lectures.

With the recognition that parent education discussion groups are one of the most effective forms of parent education, organizational and planning skills, complemented by the ability to communicate with and to support parents in group discussions, become essential qualities for teachers, administrators, and parent educators.

CHANGE DUE TO PARENT EDUCATION AND PARENT INVOLVEMENT

Parent education is accomplished in a variety of ways. Just as learning continues throughout life, parent education is also a continuous process based on experience, observation of models, media coverage, as well as attendance in special classes. Parent education and parent involvement may be separated into two areas: (1) parent education to develop parenting and decision-making skills and (2) parent involvement with schools and other agencies.

The first area focuses on specially designed programs based on psychological and family life theories that encourage parents to develop and implement plans for rearing children and developing a positive family life. There are basically two types of designed parent education programs. Some are formatted programs that leaders and groups use to guide the course, for example, STEP (Dinkmeyer & McKay, 1983), PET (Gordon, 1975), Active Parenting (Popkin, 1985), and Building Family Strengths (1986). Other programs are planned and organized by the parent group and leaders to meet the needs of an individual parent group, using a variety of methods that involve parents as active learners.

The second area of parent education and involvement recognizes the educational value of parent collaboration with the school, early childhood program, and community. Parents learn by participating in the classroom, working with their children at home, and being a partner with the teacher in the school for the education of their children. They also may develop greater decision-making skills and a feeling of worth by being involved in advisory or policy boards. (See Chapters 4 and 7 for a discussion of parent involvement.)

Parent involvement improves student attitudes, student success, and retention rates. As Moles so aptly states, "Parent involvement in education is an idea whose time has come" (1987, p. 137). Children's progress has been documented where parents have been an integral part of the child's early childhood program. The benefits of early childhood programs (especially those serving low-income families) showed greater school competency during mid-

dle to adolescent years, improved attitude toward achievement in adolescence, educational attainment with less retention, and less placement in special education classes (The Consortium for Longitudinal Studies. 1983). For detailed report on literature see Chapter 1 in this book and Cataldo (1980); Clarke-Stewart (1981); Dembo, Sweitzer, and Lauritzen (1985); and Powell (1986).

Parent involvement during later childhood has also been found to be helpful. Epstein (1986) found that parents of school-aged children felt more competent when they knew what the school was doing. The parents were particularly responsive to a teacher's effort to involve them in learning activities that they could do with their children at home. Short- and long-term goals, as well as how the instructional activities fit into the educational program at the school, helped the parents. See Chapter 1 here and Gotts and Purnell (1987) for more discussion of the school-family relations and parent involvement.

Demonstrating that parenting skills improve as a result of classes in parent education is more difficult. Most research reports are based on the determination of change in the children, not

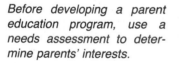

Before developing a parent education program, use a needs assessment to determine parents' interests.

the parents. A few programs have evaluated the parent outcomes of training by pre- and post-tests, but because programs are so diverse, it is not possible to generalize from one program to another.

Gordon's Parent Effectiveness Training (PET) was evaluated in 25 research projects. The research differed in scope and design, but all projects demonstrated statistically significant change: Parents showed increased confidence and self-esteem; increased acceptance, trust in, and understanding of their children; fewer problems and a reduction in anxiety (1980). Powell (1986) reviewed research including Parent Effectiveness Training, behavioral, and Adlerian programs. Although there was evidence of some change in parent attitudes, the research was not consistent and the results seemed to differ according to the assessment tool and income level of participants.

One concern about research on parent education groups has been the lack of controlled research design. The studies generally do not have comparison groups, nor do they determine whether the change reported by the parent participants has been implemented and recognized by their families. In addition, the research is usually short-term (Powell, 1986). "Somehow common sense combined with professional judgment and testimony from parents, when combined with some research evidence and the current social policy, all serve to convince participants that their efforts are worthwhile" (Cataldo, 1987, p. 15). This discussion of effectiveness of parent programs is reminiscent of the discussion of effective education in early childhood programs. The design variations did not make the difference; the environment and interaction between the participants and facilitator were significant.

NEEDS ASSESSMENTS

Before you begin a parent education program, and periodically during the program, make evaluations to determine the interests and needs of the community. First, meet with a group of parents representative of the diverse ethnic and socioeconomic levels within the community. Jot down the ideas or questions that concern and interest them. A brainstorming session is an ideal mechanism for eliciting many ideas. To facilitate the brainstorming session, duplicate and distribute a handout of the problems recognized by parents in the ninth Gallup Poll (1977) described on page 188.

Once you have developed your basic list of interests and concerns, give it to a trial group, and have them add new ideas and concerns. Next, construct a needs assessment tool listing possible choices of topics or formats for parents. Disseminate the questionnaire to adults through the school or center community. Finally, choose from the questionnaire those items that received the most requests, and develop a program to meet the needs of the community.

Be sensitive to minorities and single parents and incorporate their responses to such needs and desires into the parent program. "Among the parents who indicate greatest need for help . . . are the single parents and parents from minority races" (Yankelovich, Skelly, & White, Inc., 1977, p. 120).

The Appalachia Educational Laboratory has designed a comprehensive needs assessment to determine curriculum for a parent education course for television (Coan & Gotts, 1976). Parents of children in 186 classrooms in 26 schools located in 10 states across the United States were surveyed. From the answers of the needs assessments six factors were clustered and factored: family care, child growth and development, child management, self as parent, treating your child like a person, and baby care. This needs assessment is illustrated in Appendix A at the end of this chapter and can be used as a guide when you construct an instrument for your locality.

According to a 1989 Gallup Poll parents regarded use of drugs as the greatest problem facing the schools. Their next greatest concern was discipline. Curriculum, financial support, overcrowding, standards in the schools, and getting good teachers were also prominent concerns (Elam & Gallup, 1989, p. 52). A decade earlier, the Gallup Poll questioned parents on needs and concerns that could be addressed by parent education programs. By a four to one margin, parents favored parent education courses. In the survey, the statement, "What to do about drugs, smoking, and use of alcohol" was of greatest concern to the parents (Gallup, 1977, p. 42). The list generated by the concerns of parents of elementary school-age children is relevant for use in developing a needs assessment in the 1990s. Since these lists are used to help generate ideas and the concerns are selected on the basis of what the current group of parents indicate as their greatest needs, the final selection of interests and concerns will be based on individual needs of each group. If you are working with parents of young children, include some of the items from the Appalachia Education Laboratory needs assessment in the Appendix of this chapter when you establish your initial list. The following list from the Gallup Poll will help form a total interest listing.

Parents whose eldest child was 12 years or younger ranked the items as follows:

1. What to do about drugs, smoking, use of alcohol
2. How to help the child set high achievement goals
3. How to develop good work habits
4. How to improve the child's school behavior
5. How to improve the child's thinking and observation abilities
6. How to deal with the child's emotional problems
7. How to increase interest in school and school subjects
8. How to help the child organize his/her homework
9. How to improve parent/child relationships
10. How to help the child choose a career
11. How to use family activities to help the child do better in school
12. How to encourage reading
13. How to help the child get along with other children
14. How to reduce television viewing
15. How to deal with dating problems
16. How to improve health habits*

---

*From Gallup, G. H. The ninth annual Gallup Poll of the public's attitudes toward the public schools. *Phi Delta Kappan,* September 1977, p. 42.

Needs assessments at the individual small-group level can be less formal:

1. Brainstorm ideas for concerns and interests.
2. Collect as many ideas as your group may generate.
3. Show the group a similar list that might add to the list they have generated.
4. Form buzz groups and let the participants discuss the lists.
5. Let the members list their choices in order of importance to them.
6. Generate your programs for the year from the responses of the group.
7. If a new issue arises that concerns most of the group, find a space or add a session to cover the important topic.

Needs assessments are necessary when new programs are developed as well as when established parent groups reassess their needs. Less formal assessments are used frequently by ongoing groups.

INTEREST FINDERS

If a parent group is already established, members may use a number of informal methods to indicate their interests. These range from brainstorming among the members to soliciting suggestions in a question box.

Brainstorming   A brainstorming session can be held. Choose a recorder and encourage all members to contribute ideas for programs. A list of programs successful in former years may be distributed. Write ideas on a chalkboard or on a transparency on an overhead projector. After all the suggestions are listed, have members choose in writing three to six ideas that interest them most. Develop your program from the interests that receive the most votes (or are most frequently mentioned). If the group has difficulty thinking of items, you may be able to generate responses by having participants complete statements such as the ones in this example:

My greatest concerns are _____.
My greatest happiness comes from _____.

If I had three wishes, I would _____.
If I could eliminate one problem from my
    home, it would be _____.
Questions that concern me about my child's
    education are _____.
Questions that concern me about my child's
    development are _____.
As a parent I hope to be _____.

Annoyance Test An annoyance test is relevant for parents. The leader writes the following
on a chart or blackboard:

My children annoy me when they _____.
I annoy my children when I _____.

The parents then list points under each, and the
results are tabulated. The four or five most
popular topics may then be discussed in subsequent meetings (Denver Public Schools, n.d.).

Open-Ended Questions Soliciting requests
for a wider knowledge of the community and
suggesting ways for parents to become more
involved in schools and the community is relevant for parents' groups. The leader asks parents
to respond to such topics as:

1. What I want to know about my school
2. What I want to know about my community
3. What I would like to do about my school and/or
    community

Question-Answer Sheets Question-answer sheets,
(for example, you might develop one called *Test
Your Know-How as a Parent*), bring out differences in opinions in the group and show where
interests and room for learning occur.

Question Box Some parents are hesitant to
make suggestions in an open meeting. It is
advantageous to have a question box available in
which members can place questions and comments throughout the year.

During early planning it may also be advisable to let the members anonymously write their
ideas on a small sheet of paper. Parents may be
very concerned about drugs and alcohol, for
example, but be hesitant to mention them lest
they reveal that they have that problem in their
homes.

*What questions might the parents of these two boys
ask?*

DEVELOPMENT OF OBJECTIVES

After the group's interests have been assessed,
program development proceeds. Within most
programs at least two aspects should receive
attention: the content of the meeting and the
behavioral and attitudinal changes of the participants. Table 6–1 may be helpful in illustrating
how objectives in these two areas intertwine.
Social and emotional objectives are as important
as content objectives. Table 6–1 is merely sug-
gestive and illustrates one program's needs.

Most parents know when they want help
with parenting skills, although reticent parents
may need special encouragement. When a new
family is formed and the first baby comes home
to live, parents are intensely interested in knowing how to care for the baby. A most opportune
time for parent education is with the mother and
father prior to birth and during the first 3 years.

TABLE 6–1

Choose any or all of the content aspects of this chart. Then decide what objectives you want to accomplish related to the chosen issues. For example, in dealing with social problems the program represented in this table chose drugs/alcohol and violence as necessary topics and determined that all the behavioral objectives were relevant.

Content Aspects of the Objectives	Behavioral Aspects of the Objectives				
	Use of Facts and Materials	Familiarity of Resource Materials	Decision Making and Critical Thinking	Influence of Values on Perceptions of Daily Living	Improved Communication and Interpersonal Relations	Development of Sensitivity to Social Problems

Home and the School

1. New classroom teaching methods
2. Home-school relationships
3. Children's developmental levels
4. Parent involvement

Child Development

1. Growth
   a. Physical   X   X
   b. Mental
   c. Social
   d. Emotional
2. Behavior and misbehavior
3. Individual differences
   a. Special children (gifted or learning disabled)
   b. Diagnosis
   c. Building self-concept

4. Sexuality
   a. Sex education
   b. Bias-free education

Family Relations

1. Communication
2. Interpersonal relations
3. Sibling rivalry

Social Problems

1. Drugs/alcohol
2. Violence
3. Smoking
4. Stress
5. Living with change

Enrichment Activities of Childhood

1. Creativity/exploration, imagination, music, art
2. Experiences
3. Literature and reading
4. Influence of television

Mental and Emotional Health

1. Values
2. Self-understanding

Living in a Democracy

1. Decision making
2. Responsibilities
3. Moral values
4. Critical thinking

White (1988) emphasizes that the first 3 years are prime time for establishing positive parenting styles. The Missouri program, New Parents as Teachers, utilizes this period to help parents get off to the right start (Missouri Department of Elementary and Secondary Education, 1985).

Parents are also ready for sharing during the preschool years. Parent education and preschool programs bring the professional and the parents together to share concerns and experiences.

During the school years, parent education programs that focus on learning activities, building family strengths, and concerns specific to the group are very beneficial. And there is an increase in interest in parent education at the secondary level. Concern over drugs, alcohol, misbehavior, and suicide cause parents to look for help. At parent education meetings they may share issues, talk about common problems, become united in their efforts, and become aware of resources that are available to them. Parents want parent education when they feel the need for it. It is important at that time to offer programs which speak to their concerns and which allow them to have input into the agenda. Parents need to share, ask questions, and be a part of the decision-making process.

Swick (1983) discussed six insights that parent educators need to keep in mind as they work with parents: (1) Parents are at different levels of development in their parenting skills and they need support at their own levels. (2) Parents in different family styles may need different approaches. (3) Parents need to understand and feel comfortable with themselves. Helping them to fulfill their own needs may make it possible for them to extend themselves to fulfill needs of others—their children and spouses. (4) Parents feel more positive when they have internal and external support systems. A healthy marriage, a network of friends, and/or a child care system that furnishes positive care for their children help parents in their relationships with their families. (5) A prime time for parent education is during the first 3 years. At this time parents form behaviors that continue throughout their lives as parents. It is also a period when parents recognize the need for education. (6) Parents need to

be proactive rather than reactive. "It is essential that parents establish control and direction relative to their personal and family lives early in their parenting career" (p. 11).

Comparison of Programs

None of the structured programs that are most popular today (for example, Parent Effectiveness Training and Systematic Training for Effective Parenting), has been identified as more effective than other programs. More systematic research is needed, but the research that has been done shows parents can make positive changes through structured programs as well as unstructured discussion groups (Powell, 1986).

The curriculums in most of the structured groups are similar in scope. (See Appendix E for a list of parent education guides.) They generally contain information on behavior and misbehavior, problem ownership, communication, natural and logical consequences, developing alternatives, understanding your child and yourself, encouragement, and family councils.

The Building Family Strengths program (Center for Family Studies, 1986) includes information and activities that promote (1) positive time together; (2) communication; (3) wellness; (4) appreciation; (5) effective dealing with stress, conflict, and crisis; and (6) commitment.

These programs fit under the category of meetings with a parent leader with a structured curriculum (Figure 6–1). There is great leeway, however, in the structure of the meetings. Following the structured presentation or during the presentation, the leader may open the meeting to discussion for the whole group or may form buzz groups, thus allowing group interaction. Many parent groups have incorporated these programs into their plans for the year. For example, 12 meetings may be devoted to the STEP program, and 18 meetings may be planned to cover the other aspects of the group's objectives.

In parent education there is a combination of conditions that should be met.

1. The program should meet the needs of the parent participants.

2. The program should consider the participants' culture and experience.
3. The professional leader needs to serve as a facilitator, guiding the program and offering materials, resources, and expertise while allowing for both self-determination and active involvement by the parents.

How Parents Learn Best

Parent educators facilitate the learning experience for parents. They design the program and the environment so that the parent is an active participant in the delivery of knowledge. Parents or parent substitutes will be more apt to become involved in the learning process and thereby change their attitudes more easily if:

- A positive climate is established.
- Risk is eliminated.
- Parents are recognized as having something worthwhile to contribute.
- Parents are actively involved in their own education.
- The curriculum speaks to their concerns and needs.
- Parents discover the need for change for themselves.
- Respect and encouragement is present.
- Real situations and analogies bring the theory to life.
- Positive feedback is used.
- Different approaches (role playing, short lectures, open discussion, debates, brainstorming, workshops) allow them to learn to use a variety of techniques.
- Different approaches use a variety of sensory experiences (sight, sound, touch, taste, and smell).
- Problem solving and analysis enables the learner to continue learning beyond the personal contact.
- The topic is relevant.
- Parents are considered part of the learning-teaching team.

Group Discussions

Most meetings involve group discussion, which can range from the use of open discussion as the total meeting format to a short discussion following a formal presentation.

Informal Discussion Plan

A. Stems from interest or needs of group
   EXAMPLE: How can parents be more involved in their child's school?
B. Establishes goals and objectives
   EXAMPLE
   1. Goal—parental involvement
   2. Objectives
      a. To determine why parents do not feel comfortable coming to school
      b. To encourage parents to participate in schools
      c. To initiate a plan for getting parents involved
      d. To suggest activities in which parents can be involved
C. Provides for informal group meetings
   1. Allows parents to speak freely
   2. Emphasizes the clarification of feelings and acceptance of ideas
   3. Encourages participation
   4. Includes keeping a record of suggestions
D. Selects and analyzes relevant information that emerges during the discussion
E. Outlines plan for action, if group desires

Problem-solving Format

A. Recognition of the problem—state the hypothesis
   1. The problem should be one that is selected by the group and reflects its needs and interests.
      EXAMPLE: How can we monitor television programs for the benefit of children and families?
   2. The leader writes the question or problem for discussion on chart or chalkboard.
B. Understanding the problem—discuss the nature of problem
   EXAMPLE: Is television viewing a problem and, if so, why?
C. Data collection—gather a wide range of ideas and determine which are relevant
   1. Prior development of expertise—identify resources and read prior to meeting

2. Nonjudgmental acceptance–accept and record comments and ideas from participants

D. Analysis of the problem
1. Focus the subject so that it can be discussed thoroughly by participants
2. Establish criteria for evaluation of a solution
3. Keep participants focused on problems

E. Conclusion and summary
1. Suggest solutions
2. List possible conclusions
3. Seek an integrative conclusion that reflects the group's goals and thinking

F. Appropriate action
1. Develop a timetable
2. Determine a method of accomplishing task
3. Delegate tasks

LEADERSHIP TRAINING

Lay leaders benefit from guidelines in the development of their leadership skills. The leader's goal is to establish an environment that facilitates and guides members in achieving the objectives.

Leaders establish a model for behavior by their participation, acceptance of criticisms, non-evaluative comments, willingness to deviate from preplanned procedures, ability to listen with understanding, ability to capture and reflect feelings, by their clarifying comments and by the method of expressing their own feelings. (Gardner, 1974, p. 72)

Group members can participate more effectively if they are aware of their rights and responsibilities within the group. A handout on communication skills, given to the membership early in the school term, helps eliminate problems and encourages a relaxed, productive group (see Figure 6–2). Use the handout as a guide.

This handout, along with a description of group roles (Table 6–2) will enable the group members to grow into productive participants in group interaction. As a leader it is your responsibility to share these communication tips with the group membership.

General Qualifications   The following pointers emphasize the leader's personality, interpersonal relationships, and skill in handling group discussions:

A. Leader's personality
1. Ability to think and act quickly. The leader may need to change plans on the spur of the moment.

CRITERIA FOR GROUP COMMUNICATION

1. Come to the meeting ready to ask questions and share your ideas.
2. Once your ideas and thoughts are given to the group, do not feel compelled to defend them. Once shared, they become the group's property to discuss and consider. Clarify meaning if it would help the group proceed but don't feel responsible for the idea just because you suggested it.
3. Speak freely and communicate feelings. Listen to others with consideration and understanding for their feelings.
4. Accept others in the interchange of ideas. Allow them to have opinions that differ from yours. Do not ignore or reject members of the group.
5. Engage in friendly disagreements. Listen critically and carefully to suggestions others have to offer. Differences of opinion bring forth a variety of ideas.
6. Be sincere. Reveal your true self. Communicate in an atmosphere of mutual trust.
7. Allow and promote individual freedom. Do not manipulate, suppress, or ridicule other group members. Encourage their creativity and individuality.
8. Work hard, acknowledge contributions of others, and focus on the objectives of the group's task.

FIGURE 6–2
Criteria for group communication.

2. Ability to get along with others, to be well liked, and not have a tendency to "fly off the handle."
3. Respect for the opinions of others. The leader should be a good listener and avoid trying to "tell" others what to think.
4. Willingness to remain in the background. Instead of voicing opinions, asks questions and guides but does not dominate.
5. Freedom from prejudice.
B. Leader's knowledge and skills
   1. Knowledge of the discussion method. The leader must know the purpose and the procedure agreed upon for the meeting to be successful.
   2. Knowledge of the opinions of authorities on the subject so that conclusions may be based on evidence rather than on the leader's opinion.
   3. Skill in asking questions. The leader should present questions that bring out the opinions of others. Avoid hasty decisions or the acceptance of conclusions not based on good evidence by the use of questions. Throwing out a question to the group can help avoid expression of

personal opinions. Some examples of how to handle certain situations that arise in a discussion follow:
   a. To call attention to a point that has not been considered: "Has anyone thought about this phase of the problem—or about this possible solution?"
   b. To evaluate the strength of an argument: "What reasons do we have for accepting this statement?"
   c. To get back to causes: "Why do you suppose a child—or a parent—feels or acts this way?"
   d. To question the source of information or argument: "Who gathered these statistics that you spoke of?" or "Would you care to name the authority you are quoting?"
   e. To suggest that no new information is being added: "Can anyone add a new idea to the information already given on this point?"
   f. To register steps of agreement or disagreement: "Am I correct in assuming that all of us agree on (or disagree with) this point?"

TABLE 6–2
Role interaction. Both task and maintenance roles are necessary for effective group participation.

Task Roles	Group-building or Maintenance Roles	Dysfunctional Roles
Initiator-leader	Encourager	Dominator
Information giver	Harmonizer	Aggressor
Information seeker	Listener	Negativist
Clarifier	Follower	Playboy
Questioner	Tension breaker	Blocker
Asserter	Compromiser	Competitor
Energizer	Standard setter	Deserter
Elaborator	Observer	
Orientator	Recorder	
Opinion giver	Gatekeeper	
Opinion seeker		
Summarizer		

Source: Modified from Beal, G., Bohlen, J. M., & Raudabaugh, J. N. *Leadership and dynamic group action*, Ames, Iowa: Iowa State University, 1962, pp. 103–109; Benne, K., & Sheets, P. Functional roles of group members. *Journal of Social Issues,* 1948, 4(2), 41–49; King, C. E. *The sociology of small groups.* New York: Pageant Press,1962, pp. 108–109.

g. To bring a generalizing speaker down to earth: "Can you give us a specific example?" or "Your general idea is good, but I wonder if we can't make it more concrete. Does anyone know of a case . . .?"

h. To handle the member who has "all the answers": "Would your idea work in all cases?" or "Let's get a variety of opinions on this point."

i. To bring an individual back to the subject: "I wonder if you can relate your ideas to the subject we are discussing?"

j. To handle a question directed to the leader.

   (1) If the leader knows the answer but does not wish to be set up as an authority, the question can be redirected to the group.

   (2) The leader can quote from resource material and ask for additional opinions.

   (3) If the leader is a specialist in the area, occasional questions may be answered.

   (4) The leader can say, "I don't know. Who does? Shall we research this?"

k. To cut off a speaker who is too longwinded: "While we're on this point, let's hear from the others" or "Shall we save your next point until later?"

l. To help the members who may have difficulty expressing themselves: "I wonder if I am interpreting you correctly; were you saying . . .?" or "Can we tie in what you are saying with our subject something like this . . .?"

m. To encourage further questions: "I'm glad you raised that question. Can anyone answer?"

n. To break up a heated argument: "I'm sure all of us feel strongly about this. Would some of the rest of you care to express opinions?"

o. To be sensitive to body language of the group, watch for persons wanting to speak, and bring out their contributions.*

Napier and Gershenfeld (1981) warn against expecting leaders to always exhibit charismatic personal traits. Leaders do not have to be superhuman, charming, and physically attractive persons. Leaders initiate, plan, guide and build group norms, give support, challenge, and encourage group growth. In building the group norms, special attention should be paid to the feelings of the people in the group.

1. Each person is respected, is listened to, and recognized.
2. The meeting is a safe place to be; no one will be ridiculed or put down.
3. Feelings are important and the expression of feelings helps the group resolve problems.
4. Feelings may be discussed.
5. The participants and leader are encouraged to be objective.

Leaders who show a caring attitude are most effective. They offer protection, affection, praise, and encouragement as well as friendship. But caring is not enough. The effective leader is there to give support, explain, and clarify if needed.

ARRANGEMENTS FOR MEETINGS

In parent group meetings and PTA meetings, there are necessary procedures, regardless of the meeting format. Parents need to feel physically and emotionally comfortable at every meeting, whether formal or informal. To assure this, the person in charge of the meeting should do the following:

1. Check the meeting room to be sure the temperature is appropriate, the ventilation and

---

*Modified from Denver Public Schools. Pointers for discussion group leaders. In *Parent education and preschool department leadership handbook.* Denver: Denver Public Schools, n.d., pp. 19–21.

lighting are adequate, and the room will accommodate the group.

2. As members or guests arrive, make them feel welcome. Greet them, offer name tags, and suggest they have refreshments, look at a book display, or participate in an icebreaker activity before the meeting begins. Call members or guests by name as soon as possible.

3. Have refreshments before the meeting, during the break, or at both times. A 15-minute refreshment period before the meeting gives latecomers an opportunity to arrive before discussion commences. It also sets a relaxed tone and gives members a forum for informal interaction.

4. As participants arrive, involve them in an informal discussion through an icebreaker activity. Get-acquainted activities are important but choose an appropriate one. For meetings where very few people know one another, a signature sheet may prove beneficial, or have the entire group form pairs; each partner introduces the other one to the group.

5. In large groups where icebreakers are not appropriate, the participants can respond to group questions—where they live, what they do, how many children they have, what their interests are and so on. Responses to the questions (by a show of hands or verbal answers) help the speaker to know more about the audience to be addressed, and the audience feels that it has been recognized.

6. After the group feels comfortable, the meeting can commence. Open discussion is part of all but the most formal or informal meetings, so it is important that all group leaders are able to conduct discussion sessions. Debates, panels, audiovisual aids, buzz sessions, workshops, role playing, book reviews, dramatizations, and observations can precede open discussion. The leader should gauge the time and conclude the meeting.

7. After the presentation and discussion (or question and answer section), thank the presenters and give appropriate recognition for their contributions.

8. Announce any specific instructions necessary for the next meeting before the group disperses.

Icebreakers

To create an accepting, warm atmosphere, get-acquainted activities help people relax and become involved in the group. These icebreakers range from introductions of the person to the right to mixers during breaks.

While Members Gather

Signature sheets. Make a form before the meeting that includes statements about people. Following each statement is a signature blank. These sheets can be made specifically for the group or can be broad enough to be used in any group. The kinds of signature sheets are not limited—create original ones. As the group arrives, give one to each participant. Encourage mixing and meeting new people. By the time the period is completed, the members will have an opportunity to meet and talk with a large number of people. A typical signature sheet is shown in Figure 6–3.

Bingo card. Make a card that contains 12 to 24 squares. Ask each member to fill each blank with a signature. Signatures may not be repeated. This encourages interaction with all members.

A variation of the bingo card includes letters within each blank. Find someone with a name that begins with that letter. Check the roster ahead of time and use initials of the membership.

Who am I? Attach a piece of paper with the name of a famous person to the back of each person. Members go from person to person asking questions until they determine who they are. Questions must be phrased so that a yes or no answer is adequate. Variations include changing the famous person to an event, an animal, or an educational statement.

Scrambled name tags. Make up name tags with letters out of order, for example, Ilaehs (Sheila). Have the members try to figure out each name as

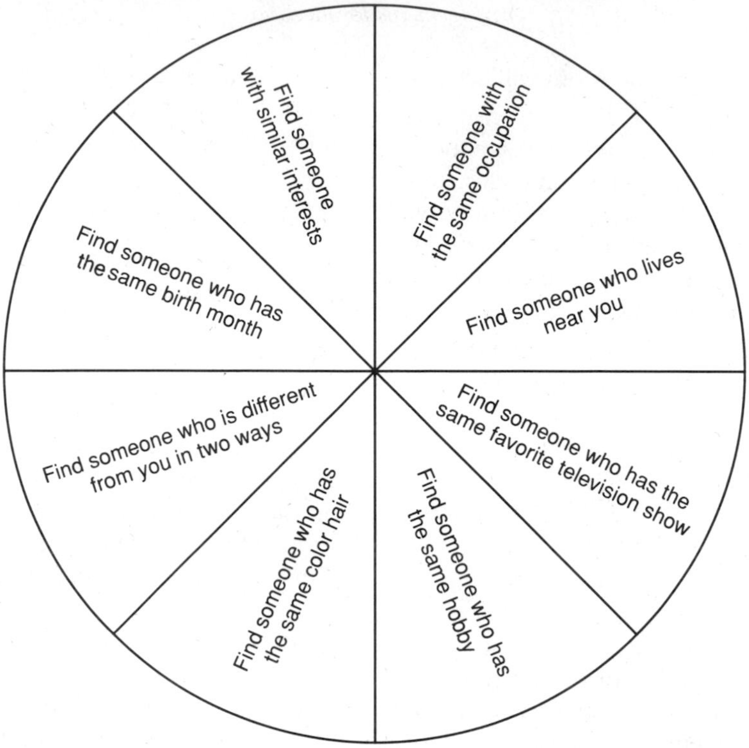

During the next few minutes you are to find someone who has the same attributes as you. Find and get as many signatures as you can. Have them write their names in the open space between the wheel spokes.

Find people who meet the qualifications listed below and have them sign their names.

1. Find someone who is wearing the same color clothes as you_____

2. Find someone who has the same color eyes as you_____

3. Find someone who has the same number of children as you_____

4 Find someone who lives in the same area as you_____

5. Find someone who has a child the same age as yours_____

6. Find someone who likes to go hiking_____

7. Find someone who plays the piano_____

8. Find someone who has the same hobby as you_____

9. Find someone who has lived in this state as long as you have_____

10. Find someone who was brought up in the same area you were _____

FIGURE 6-3
Use a get-acquainted activity such as a signature sheet or Wheel of Friendship at the beginning of meetings.

they talk with each person. Obviously, this has to be done at the first or second meeting before the group becomes acquainted.

After Members Are Seated

Dyad introductions. Have every two members talk together, with the idea that they will introduce each other. You may give specific instructions, such as ask the number of children the person has and what the member expects from parent education, or you may leave the discussion completely up to the two individuals. Following the discussion, go around the room and have members introduce their partners.

It is interesting to have the dyad discuss memory questions such as something their partner remembers that happened before the age of 5 or their happiest experience. This activity can be used later in the year as well as at the beginning.

Allow members to introduce themselves. Topics they might include are:

> My secret hiding place was _____.
>
> As a child I liked to _____ best.
>
> Summertime was _____.
>
> If I had my wish, I would be _____.
>
> What I liked best about school was _____.
>
> What I remember about walking or riding the bus home from school was _____.

I've got a secret. After people have become acquainted, each participant can write a secret on a piece of paper. (Be sure that the person does not mind having the secret revealed.) Place the pieces of paper in a bag, and as they are drawn and read, the group tries to guess who has that secret.

Activities that promote good human relations and allow members to get acquainted are limited only by the planner's imagination. The chairperson or leader may be in charge of this part of the program, or may delegate the responsibility to a number of persons charged with the task of discovering new means of interaction.

GROUP ROLES

Group members should be given descriptions of group roles to help them identify their participatory roles or roles they would like to develop (see Table 6–2). Within each group, roles emerge that are functional and task-oriented, which move the group forward; group-sustaining, which are expressive and maintain the group; and negative and dysfunctional, which reduce the effectiveness of the group.

Analysis of the interaction process illustrates the expressive (socioemotional) and task areas within a group. The center of Bales' (1950) interaction theory (Figure 6–4) includes task questions and task responses, which are both directed toward completing the task at hand as well as the socioemotional areas that involve the feelings and integration of the group (both positive and negative).

Although Bales' group interaction theory has been used primarily as a research tool to study communication and interaction in groups, it can also be used to clarify group interaction in the training of parent groups. An examination of the interaction process reveals a continuum of productive to negative interaction. The positive socioemotional reactions—for example, showing solidarity, giving help, and rewarding others—are helpful in effecting group integration. At the other end of the spectrum, showing antagonism, deflating another's status, and asserting oneself are destructive to the group's integration. In the center all the task-oriented questions and answers support the objectives of completing a task assignment. Although the answers of members are more productive than the questions, both help move the interaction process along—the first by providing direction and information while accepting another member's autonomy, the second by asking for evaluation, direction, and possible forms of action.

Roles emerge within groups and influence the interactive process. A *role,* defined as the behavior characteristic of a person occupying a particular position in the social system, influences the actions of the person and the expec-

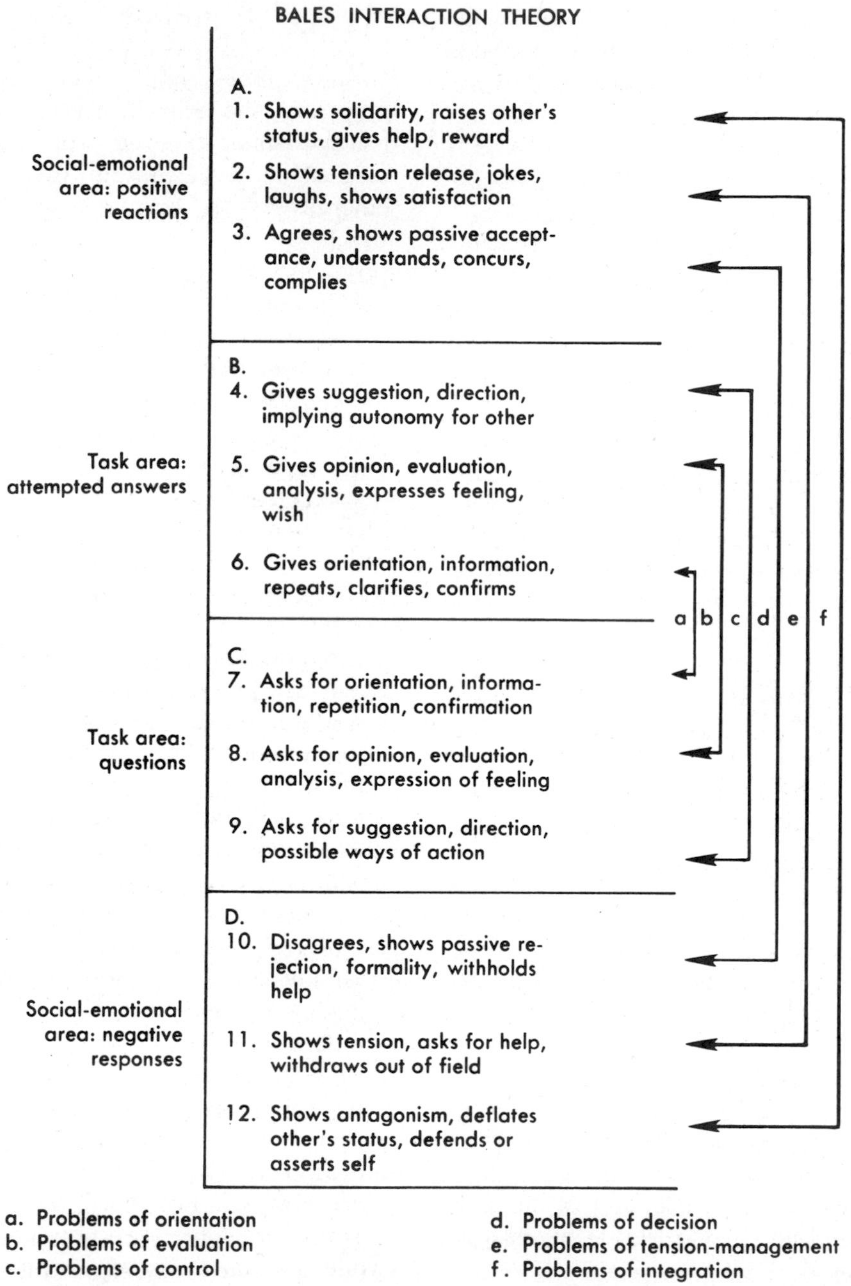

BALES INTERACTION THEORY

Social-emotional area: positive reactions	**A.**
	1. Shows solidarity, raises other's status, gives help, reward
	2. Shows tension release, jokes, laughs, shows satisfaction
	3. Agrees, shows passive acceptance, understands, concurs, complies

FIGURE 6–4

The Bales Interaction Theory illustrates social-emotional and task areas related to group interaction. Problems in each area are defined (a through f). The theory ranges from positive reactions in A to negative reactions in D. (Source: Reprinted from *Interaction process analysis: A method for study of small groups,* 1976, by Robert F. Bales by permission of The University of Chicago Press. Copyright © 1950 by the University of Chicago.)

Leaders emerge from the group if they have not been formally selected.

tations of others toward that person. Parent groups (in this text) are the "social system"; members of the group expect certain norms or standards of behavior from the perceived leader of the group. These role expectations are projected in members' role behavior toward the leader. Likewise, the leader's own interpretation of the role influences the resulting role behavior or role performance. Should members of the group hold different expectations of behavior for the leadership role from those held by the occupant of that role, inter-role conflicts may arise (Applbaum et al., 1979; Berger 1968; Biddle & Thomas, 1979.) For these reasons, it is beneficial to discuss or clarify standards and duties of roles within a group.

Role continuity is easier to obtain in parent education groups that have ongoing memberships. Parents are encouraged to participate for at least 2 years. New officers and leaders, already familiar with the standards of the group, may be elected in the spring and be ready to take over leadership in the fall. Although this system ensures greater continuity than the establishment of a new group each year, the returning members must be careful to be flexible, open to new ideas, and sensitive to the desires of new members. Early in the year a session may include a discussion of roles and group dynamics. Role playing is an excellent mechanism for clarifying

role behavior. If group members are aware of the effect roles have on the functioning of a group, they do not fall into dysfunctional roles as readily. By discussing group dynamics with the group prior to establishment of role patterns, group production is often increased (Beal et al., 1962).

A leader can deter or eliminate the problem of domination or withdrawal by group members if members are aware of roles and how each member of the group can influence the group's functioning, either positively or negatively. Most members do not want to be viewed as dysfunctional members and will, therefore, refrain from acting in ways that are detrimental to group interaction. I have used a discussion of roles in parents' groups and classes since the early 1960s and have found that a group discussion and role playing of group roles have greatly enhanced the productivity of the group.

This knowledge will encourage some members, but it can also inhibit others who worry about which role theory they are enacting. Although this is a possible negative result of a discussion of group roles, role definition is, on the other hand, a benefit to the total group in the elimination of one common problem in groups—domination of the discussion by a few participants. It is also beneficial to reticent communicators to learn that inability to express themselves does not mean that they cannot be productive group members. Asking questions, being an active listener, and being a positive member of the group are shown to be valuable contributions to a well-functioning discussion group. When balanced out, the positive aspects of discussing group roles overshadow the negative ones. One word of caution, however—do not wait until the problem has become obvious before discussing dysfunctional roles. You will embarrass and alienate the person who has been a negative contributor. It is best to handle such a problem through the leadership techniques discussed on pp. 194–96.

Dynamics of Roles Within Groups

Observation of interaction within groups shows that role behavior influences the cohesiveness and productivity of the group. Observation will be facilitated if analysis of the group is based in Bales' interaction process (Figure 6–4) or role interaction (Table 6–2), wherein behaviors within a group are divided into task, maintenance and building, and dysfunctional roles.

Task roles. The roles related to the task area in Table 6–2 are attributed to the members of the group who initiate, question, and facilitate reaching the group's goals or objectives. These tasks correspond to Bales' task areas.

Group-building and maintenance roles. The roles related to group-building or maintenance are attributed to members of the group who support and maintain the cohesiveness, solidarity, and productivity of the group. These roles include Bales' socioemotional positive reaction area and, in addition, add a maintenance aspect.

Dysfunctional or individual roles. The roles in this area are attributed to members who place their own individual needs, which are not relevant to group goals, above group needs. These individual goals are not functional or productive to group achievement, but if such members are brought into the group process, they can become contributing participants. These roles correspond to Bales' socioemotional negative reaction area.

Members of groups generally do not fit into only one role category. Members may participate in a task role and switch to a maintenance role with the next action or comment. For example, Helen is anxious about absenteeism and suggests that the group might improve attendance by organizing a car pool. May responds to the comment by suggesting a telephone network to contact members. Helen welcomes the idea, "Good thought, May. We might be able to start right away." Helen, within the space of 2 minutes, has initiated an idea, acting in a task-oriented role, and has then supported May's contribution with a group-building or maintenance statement. There may be moments when members lapse into a dysfunctional role. As long as the mix of interaction remains primarily positive and productive, the group will be effective.

The following role descriptions were based on Beal, Bohlen, and Raudabaugh (1962), Benne and Sheets (1948), and King (1962).

ROLE DESCRIPTIONS

Task

initiator-leader: Initiates the discussion, guides but does not dominate, contributes ideas or suggestions that help move the group forward

information giver: Contributes information and facts that are from authoritative sources and are relevant to the ongoing discussion

information seeker: Asks for clarification or expansion of an issue by additional relevant authoritative information

clarifier: Restates the discussion of an issue so that points are made clear to the group

questioner: Asks questions about issues, requests clarification, or offers constructive criticism

asserter: States position in a positive manner, may take a different point of view and disagree with opinions or suggestions without attacking them

energizer: Stimulates and facilitates the group to action and increased output and problem solving *elaborator:* Expands an idea or concept; brings out details, points, and alternatives that may have been overlooked

orientator: Takes a look at the group's position in relation to the objectives of the meetings and where the discussion is leading

opinion giver: States own opinion on the situation, basing the contribution on personal experiences

opinion seeker: Requests suggestions from others according to their life experiences and value orientation

summarizer: Brings out facts, ideas, and suggestions made by the group in an attempt to clarify the group's position during the meeting and at the conclusion

Group-building and Maintenance

The first six roles will emerge within the group; the last four are appointed or elected maintenance roles.

encourager: Supports, praises, and recognizes other members of the group; builds self-confidence and self-concept of others

harmonizer: Mediates misunderstandings and clarifies conflicting statements and disagreements; adds to the discussion in a calming and tension-reducing manner

listener: Is involved in the discussion through quiet attention to the group process; gives support through body language and eye contact

follower: Serves as a supportive member of the discussion by accepting the ideas and suggestions of others

tension breaker: Uses humor or clarifying statements to relieve tension within the group

compromiser: Views both sides of the questions and changes solutions or suggestions to fit into conflicting viewpoints

standard setter: Sets standards for group performance; may apply standards as an evaluative technique for the meeting

observer: Charts the group process throughout the meeting and uses the data for evaluation of group interaction

recorder: Records decisions and ideas for group use throughout the meeting

gatekeeper: Regulates time spent and membership participation during various parts

of the program; keeps the meeting on a time schedule

Dysfunctional

dominator: Monopolizes the meeting and asserts superiority by attempting to manipulate the group

aggressor: Shows aggression toward group in a variety of forms, for example, attacks ideas, criticizes others, denigrates others' contributions, and disapproves of solutions

negativist: Demonstrates pessimism and disapproval of suggestions that emerge within the group; sees the negative side of the issue and rejects new insights

playboy: Refuses to be involved in the discussion and spends time showing this indifference to the members by distracting behavior, for example, talking to others, showing cynicism, making side comments

blocker: Opposes decision making and attempts to block actions by introducing alternative plans that have already been rejected

competitor: Competes with other members of the discussion group by challenging their ideas and expressing and defending own suggestions

deserter: Leaves the group in spirit and mind but not in body; doodles, looks around room, makes a show of disinterest, and stays aloof and indifferent to the group process

Role Playing Group Roles

Early in the growth of a group, a session in which members role play task, maintenance, and dysfunctional roles while discussing an issue of high interest will illustrate to the members how role performance can support or destroy a group. It is practical to use a concentric circle, allowing the inner circle to discuss an issue in the light of the role assigned, while the outer circle observes and analyzes which roles are being demonstrated. The session will be humorous, with members enthusiastically playing dysfunctional roles but it should end with the understanding that each member is important to the effectiveness of the group process.

Observer

Analysis of group interaction reveals patterns that are not always obvious to the casual observer. A systematic observation can pinpoint problems or illustrate strengths to the members. One simple technique for analytic observation is the construction of a discussion wheel. A diagram of the participants, with names or numbers reflecting individual members, is made. If the participants are sitting in a circle, the diagram would be similar to the one in Figure 6–5.

As members speak, the observer records the interaction. A double-sided arrow indicates that the communicator is speaking to the group; a one-sided arrow represents a statement made to an individual rather than to the group (Beal, Bohlen, & Raudabaugh, 1962). A quick glance at Figure 6–5 shows that Ralph did not make a suggestion and had either withdrawn from the group or lacked its supportive encouragement. Most members contributed to the group process, rather than making side comments to individual communicators. If the observer continues

making notes throughout the meeting, cross marks on the arrows, which reflect duplication of communication, eliminate an overabundance of lines in the observation circle (Figure 6–6).

A more detailed observation sheet may be adapted from Bales' interaction process illustrated earlier in this chapter. The three task areas also provide a framework for an excellent role analysis. Beal, Bohlen, and Raudabaugh illustrated a summary sheet for recording unit–act roles; an adaptation of their form is shown in Figure 6–7.

An analysis that includes roles, speakers, and order of comments allows group leaders to study interaction within the group and emphasizes the positive areas of communication while eliminating negative aspects. Many insights may be gained by studying what actually happened during group interaction. The summary sheet illustrates that interaction.

END-OF-MEETING EVALUATIONS

Evaluations are used effectively by many groups to see if the needs of the group are being met.

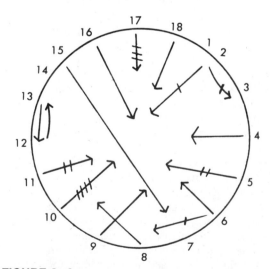

FIGURE 6–6
Group interaction anonymously recorded on an observation wheel. Each time a person speaks a mark is added to the interaction line. In this manner one can see how often and to whom each participant communicates.

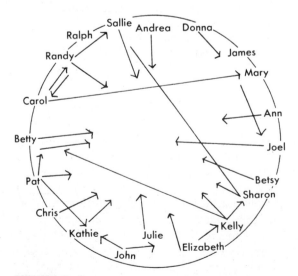

FIGURE 6–5
Group interaction recorded on an observation wheel.

Since every group is somewhat different, evaluations should be constructed to meet the needs of that group and should be based on the goals and objectives of the meeting. Sample evaluations are helpful, however, to guide the group in its development of evaluative methods that work for that particular group. The example in Figure 6–8 may be adapted to any group's needs.

TYPES OF MEETINGS

Meetings range from formal lectures to informal buzz sessions. In parent groups, informal meetings are used most often to reinforce the active involvement that proves so critical to understanding concepts and changing attitudes. The formal meeting has its place, however, if the

---

Date_____ Time_____ Meeting_____

Topic _____ Method_____

Unit–Act Roles

Task roles	Group maintenance and group–building	Dysfunctional roles
1. Initiator–leader	13. Encourager	23. Dominator
2. Information giver	14. Harmonizer	24. Aggressor
3. Information seeker	15. Listener	25. Negativist
4. Clarifier	16. Follower	26. Playboy
5. Questioner	17. Tension breaker	27. Blocker
6. Asserter	18. Compromiser	28. Competitor
7. Energizer	19. Standard setter	29. Deserter
8. Elaborator	20. Observer	
9. Orientator	21. Recorder	
10. Opinion giver	22. Gatekeeper	
11. Opinion seeker		
12. Summarizer		

Member participation record

Speaker	Spoken to	Role	Time	Comments	Speaker	Spoken to	Role	Time	Comments

FIGURE 6–7

Group observer's summary sheet for recording unit–act roles and amount and orientation of participation. (Source: Modified from Beal, G., Bohlen, J. M., & Raudabaugh, J. N. *Leadership and dynamic group action.* Ames: Iowa State University, 1962, p. 330.)

Topic _____   Date _____

Group _____

Check along the continuum

1. Was the meeting of interest to you?

Very much	Some	Very little

2. Did you receive any pertinent ideas that will be helpful to you?

Many ideas	Some	No ideas

3. Did the group participate and seem involved in the meeting?

Very involved	Some	No involvement

4. Did the meeting give you any new insights, or did you change any of your attitudes as a result of the meeting?

New insights	Some	No effect

5. Were you encouraged to contribute as much as you wanted?

Participation encouraged	Neutral	Left out

6. Did the leader respond to the needs of the group?

Good leadership	Neutral	No leadership

7. Was there adequate preparation by the members?

Excellent preparation	Some	Poor preparation

8. Was there enough time for discussion?

Too much	Just right	No time

9. Was the atmosphere conducive to freedom of expression?

Safe environment	Neutral	Felt threatened

10. Do you have any suggestions for improvement?

11. What were the strong points of the meeting?

12. Comments

You do not need to sign this sheet

FIGURE 6–8
A meeting evaluation form lets you know exactly how the participants viewed the program.

group needs a specialist to give an organized background lecture on a specific topic. Figure 6–9 illustrates types of meetings that can be used as needs, time, space, subject, and resources dictate. On the right are those meetings that are the most informal and require active involvement by the participants; in the center is the panel meeting; on the left is the most formal lecture where the only audience participation is listening to the speaker. Although all of these types of meetings have their place in parent group meetings, the informal meetings elicit

FIGURE 6-9

Types of meetings range from informal on the right to very formal on the left.

Formal	Informal
Lecture	Brainstorming
Lecture-forum	Round table
Symposium	Concentric circle
Audio	Buzz sessions
Audio-visual	Workshop
Book review	Dyad interaction and feedback
Debate	Role playing
Colloquy	Dramatization
Panel	

more participation by group members—a necessary ingredient for attitude clarification, learning, and change.

The descriptions of the types of meetings that follow are compiled from my experiences with parent education and information found in Applbaum, et al. (1979), Denver Public School (n.d.), and Kawin (1970). Resources that support the curricula are found in Appendix E.

Roundtable (Open Discussion)

Although the roundtable is not the most informal meeting available, it is a true open discussion, the mainstay of group interaction. It is used to complement most meetings, for example, panels, symposiums, role-playing sessions, or buzz sessions (see Figure 6–10).

In a roundtable discussion all members are encouraged to participate throughout the meeting. Care must be taken to promote good communication among all members of the group. To facilitate good group interaction, leaders should keep in mind the following suggestions from the Denver Public Schools:*

1. Have a clear understanding of the topic as defined by the group.
2. Obtain materials.
3. Get a general knowledge, through reading, to be able to direct and add to the contributions from the group.

---

*From Denver Public Schools. *Parent education and preschool department leadership handbook.* Denver: Denver Public Schools, n.d., pp. 12, 13.

4. Be sure to plan an introduction which will stimulate interest of the group.
5. Prepare a logical progressive list of questions to start the ball rolling and keep it moving.
6. Keep discussion on the track; keep it always directed, but let the group lay its own track to a large extent. Don't groove it narrowly yourself.
7. Be alert to adjust questions to needs of group . . . omit, change, reword.
8. Remember—the leader's opinion doesn't count in the discussion. Keep your own view out of it. Your job is to get the ideas of others out for airing.
9. If you see that some important angle is being neglected, point it out; "Bill Jones was telling me last week that he thinks. . . . What do you think of that?"
10. Keep the spirits high. Encourage ease, informality, good humor. Let everybody have a good time. Foster friendly disagreement. Listen with respect and appreciation to all ideas, but stress what is important, and turn discussion away from what is not.
11. Take time every 10 minutes or so to draw the loose ends together; "Let's see where we've been going." Be as fair and accurate in summary as possible. Close discussion with summary—your own or the secretary's.
12. Call attention to unanswered questions for future study or for your reference back to speakers. Nourish a desire in group members for continuing study and discussion through skillful closing summary.

Problems that could emerge in a roundtable meeting include domination of the discussion by one or two members, withdrawal from the group and side discussions by two or three

FIGURE 6–10
The roundtable is the basic
open discussion group.

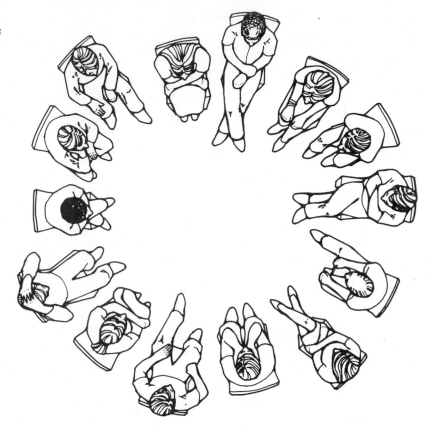

people, or lack of preparation by the membership. Good leadership makes it possible to avoid these pitfalls. If the leader is prepared for the meeting, and if the membership come to the meeting prepared, have relevant experiences, or have background expertise on the subject, the meeting can be a most effective means of changing attitudes and educating members. It allows all members to contribute and become involved in discussion, clarification of issues, and decision making.

Arrangements prior to meeting

1. Select a topic for open discussion and announce it to the membership.
2. Provide members with materials and bibliography.
   a. Duplicate and distribute background information on the topic through a distribution system or at the meeting prior to the roundtable.
   b. Select members to read relevant material prior to meeting.
   c. Come to meeting well prepared and ready to guide but not to dominate.
3. Review the Arrangements for Meetings (pp. 196–99) and make appropriate preparations.

Setup

1. Arrange chairs in a circle or semicircle or around tables in such a manner that all participants can see each other and eye contact is possible.
2. Check the room for comfort—ventilation, lighting, and heat.

Procedure

1. The leader starts the meeting with a thought-provoking question or statement of fact. Throughout the discussion, the leader tries to keep the meeting from wandering. Prior to

the meeting, the leader has prepared a list of questions or statements that may keep the discussion moving forward.

2. During the meeting the leader avoids dominating the discussion. Instead, the leadership role brings others into the discussion, helps clarify, and keeps the meeting on the topic.
3. The leader summarizes at the conclusion.
4. If the members want to take action on the conclusions, the leader should call for appropriate action, help the group make plans, and assign tasks.

Appropriate topics

1. Learning activities that work
2. Teamwork between mothers and fathers
3. What to do on a rainy day
4. Behavior and misbehavior
5. Influence of television on children
6. Rivalry between brothers and sisters

Concentric Circle

The concentric circle is a variation of the open discussion or roundtable meeting where, instead of one circle, there are two circles, one inside the other and all facing the center. The dialogue among members is similar to that of the open discussion, but only the smaller circle within the larger circle contains the communicators at first (see Figure 6–11). Divide the group so that the smaller group is from 6 to 12 people. The members within the small group discuss the issue; those in the larger group listen to the discussion. After a designated time of 5 to 10 minutes, the meeting is opened to the entire group. If you have a group of 24 to 30 persons, which contains persons who are reticent to speak out in a large group, the concentric circle will help solve the problem. Those within the inner circle form a small group with which to interact. This arrangement precipitates more discussion from them and succeeds in getting the total group interested in the discussion. Those sitting in the outer circle are required to listen, but the statements, questions, and ideas offered usually promote their interest as they listen. This method is surprisingly effective in getting

groups to discuss. By the time the discussion is opened up to the entire group, many ideas have emerged.

Arrangements prior to meeting

1. Announce the subject of the meeting to the group prior to the meeting.
2. Distribute handouts and/or reference materials suggested. (Concentric circles may also be used on the spur of the moment.)
3. Review the Arrangements for Meetings (pp. 196–99) and make appropriate preparations.

Setup

1. Arrange chairs with one large circle on the outside and a smaller circle within the larger circle. The chairs should be spaced fairly close together so the meeting is informal and all participants are able to easily hear the discussion of the inner circle.

Procedure

1. The leader of the total group may request a volunteer leader for the concentric circle, or the leader may take that role.
2. The session is started with a statement or question to promote interest and dialogue.
3. The inner circle discusses, using a small group open discussion format. The outer circle listens. At the end of a designated period, for example, 6 minutes, the discussion may be opened to all in the room. At that time the leader continues to control the meeting but not to dominate.
4. For variation, reverse the roles. Those in the outer circle now move to the inner circle and have the opportunity for more involved discussion, while those from the outer circle listen to this discussion. A separate issue or different questions concerning one issue may be used for each group in its discussion.

Appropriate topics

1. How to build self-esteem in children
2. What do you expect of 2-, 3-, 4-, or 5-year olds
3. Problem solving
4. Living with change
5. Positive uses of television

FIGURE 6–11
Concentric circles encourage those who might not participate *freely* to get *involved*.

Buzz Sessions

Buzz sessions are an excellent means of eliciting participation from all members of the group. They must be small enough to allow interaction among all participants. The smallest session consists of 2 people, and the maximum size should be 6 to 8. This makes it possible for all members to have the chance to express their opinions easily. Even in a large group, the audience can divide into smaller groups and discuss. The latter is called a 6-6 discussion, with 6 people discussing for 6 minutes. Since the session time is limited, it does not allow thorough examination of issues, but it does bring forth ideas from all involved in a very short period of time—an

Buzz groups give everyone an opportunity to talk.

objective that is not accomplished in an open discussion with a large group.

Arrangements prior to meeting

1. Buzz sessions are usually used in conjunction with other meeting formats. The buzz session itself does not need special preparation, but the leader may prepare the questions and issues in advance. The value of the session lies in optimal participation by all.
2. Review the Arrangements for Meetings (pp. 196–99) and make appropriate preparations.

Setup

1. Up to 24 people
   a. Arrange chairs in circle or semicircle.
   b. When the smaller-group session is to begin, 6 persons turn their chairs together to form their group. It is also possible for a group to remove itself in order to have a quieter meeting.
2. Large auditorium
   a. If people are sitting in rows, three people turn around and discuss with 3 people behind them.

b. Use some other technique to form groups of 6 throughout the auditorium.

Procedure

1. Buzz sessions may be at the beginning of the meeting, or they may be initiated later. The leader announces the formation of buzz groups either by proximity of chairs, a common interest in specific discussion areas, or by a mechanism to distribute the membership, such as counting off one through six and having each number for a group.
2. Each group chooses a leader and a recorder.
3. The topic is introduced to the group for discussion, and persons are encouraged to participate much as they would in any other small-group discussion.
4. The recorder keeps relevant thoughts ready to report back to the larger group. In the smaller meeting (24 persons), each group may have the time to give a short report to the total group. In an auditorium 6-6 meeting, it may not be possible to have everyone report back. Allow a specific number of groups who indicate interest in doing so to report back to the total audience.

Appropriate topics

1. Home management tips
2. Emotions and feelings about childrearing
3. Discipline
4. Moral values
5. Vacation ideas
6. Solving problems around home

Brainstorming

Brainstorming is a unique method of active interaction by all members of the group. It promotes interchange, encourages lateral thinking, and facilitates expansion of thought. In brainstorming, all contributions are accepted. Everyone is encouraged to suggest ideas and solutions. The participants may add to, combine, or modify other ideas, or they may introduce something completely new into the interchange. There are no value judgments on the quality of suggestions. Osborn (1957) suggested that the "average person can think of twice as many ideas when working with a group than when working alone" (pp. 228–229). The free and open brainstorming session provides an environment that facilitates the production of a variety of ideas from the participants. Members who have been reticent about contributing during an open discussion because they were not sure their ideas were worthy have a guaranteed-safe environment in which to contribute during brainstorming. Quantity of ideas is the object. Later, the ideas may be analyzed, judged as to quality, and reduced to selected items. The brainstorming technique, therefore, is excellent for stimulation of diversified thought and solutions to issues and problems. It also reinforces the socioemotional aspects of a group by accepting the contributions of all persons freely.

Arrangements prior to meeting

1. Because the major purpose of brainstorming is the encouragement of fresh ideas, no study program need be initiated prior to the session.
2. Review Arrangements for the Meetings (pp. 196–99) and make appropriate preparations.

Setup

1. Arrange chairs in a circle if the group has fewer than 30 members. A small group allows for more interaction.
2. Brainstorming, however, may be used in a larger group with an auditorium arrangement of chairs. In that case, the entire group has difficulty participating, but the mechanism is effective for bringing forth a quantity of ideas and thoughts.

Procedure

1. The brainstorming session requires a leader and a recorder.
   a. Appoint a recorder or request someone to volunteer.
   b. Appoint a leader or assume the leadership role.
2. The leader begins the brainstorming session by explaining the rules and emphasizing that all contributions are wanted and accepted. Even if ideas seem unusual, members should contribute. Ideas should be interjected as they occur.
3. The topic or issue is explained to the group.
4. The session is opened to contributions from the group.
5. The recorder writes on a chalkboard or piece of paper all the ideas that come from the group.
6. After a selected amount of time—4, 6, or 10 minutes, depending on the issue and the flow of ideas—the group may turn to analyzing all the suggestions and pulling out the ones that seem to answer the issue or problem best.
7. A summary of the solutions and ideas gained from brainstorming is reported by the leader.
8. If this is an action meeting, plans for action should be identified at this time.

Appropriate topics

1. Ideas to solve problems, for example, subjects for meetings, summer activities
2. How to get your child to study (eat, go to bed, etc.)
3. Creative activities
4. Exploring your environment
5. Nutrition

Workshops and Centers

Workshops are a superb means of achieving involvement by members. Most useful as a demonstration of programs and curricula, they can be used as an effective means of explaining procedures, illustrating the learning process, and developing understanding by doing. The major ingredient in a workshop is active participation by the membership, whether through making puzzles and toys, working on mathematics, painting, modeling with clay, editing a newspaper, composing music, writing poetry, or planning an action.

Although often confused with workshops, centers are different from workshops in that they do not require the participant to be actively involved in the project. Centers allow subgroups of the membership to gather simultaneously in various areas of the room, where they may see a demonstration, hear an explanation of an issue or program, or watch a media presentation. If time allows, more than one center may be visited. The variety of centers is limited only by the imagination and productivity of the planning group. The advantages of this diversified meeting are (1) it reduces group size and thus promotes more interaction and allows individual questions; (2) participants are able to select topics of interest to them; and (3) tension and anxiety of the presenters are reduced because of the informal format.

Arrangements prior to meeting

1. Review the Arrangements for Meetings (pp. 196–99) and make appropriate preparations.
2. Choose topics or areas for presentation, for example, how to make a toy, improvement of reading, editing a newspaper, or arts and crafts. If participants are going to go from workshop to workshop or center to center, designate a time limit for each center.
3. Designate persons to obtain materials and prepare and present each session.
4. Make samples of finished projects for illustration at workshop.
5. Obtain and assign space for presenters.

Setup

1. Depending on available space, workshops and centers may be held in separate rooms or in one large room with designated areas.
2. Each presenter may have different requirements. Amount of space, tables, and chairs previously requested should be set up according to those requirements.

Procedure

1. The chairperson explains the variety of workshops and/or centers available and procedures to be used.
2. Participants choose a workshop or center. These may be assigned according to several procedures: free choice, numbers on name tags, or preregistration.
3. Participants attend one or more workshops depending on time available. If plans have included a time limit for each, the groups proceed from one to the next at a signal.
4. Members may gather together for closing the meeting, or it may conclude with the final workshop.

Appropriate topics

1. Learning activities
2. Art activities
3. Making books
4. Games and toys
5. Math activities to do at home
6. Science activities to do at home
7. What to do on a rainy day

Observations and Field Trips

Although observations and field trips can be quite different in their objectives, they are similar in theory and procedure. The active viewing of a classroom, like the visit to the community, encourages the member to be involved in observing activities. The opportunity to see activities in process clarifies that process as no written or spoken word can. It is imperative, however, to discuss objectives with points to consider prior to the field trip or observation. It is also essential to analyze and discuss following the visits, in order to clarify the experience and bring it into focus. Many times the conclusion of a field trip can be the beginning of a new expanded project for the individual or group.

Arrangements prior to observations or field trips

1. Select the time and place for the observation or field trip.
   a. Plan classroom visits in advance. Specific objectives may be discussed prior to the observation.
   b. If the classroom has an observation area, observers can easily watch without disturbing the class. If there is no observation area, those going into the classroom should know the preferred procedure requested by the teacher.
   c. Field trips must be planned in advance and permission for visiting obtained.
2. Participants learn more and receive more satisfaction from field trips if background information and items to be aware of are discussed prior to the visit.
3. If the membership is going to a meeting place different from their regular meeting area, arrangements should be made for travel by car pool or bus.
4. Review the Arrangements for Meetings (pp. 196–99) and make appropriate preparations.

Procedure

1. The leader plans and conducts a previsit orientation.
2. The observation or field trip is completed.
3. Discussion of the experience clarifies the issues and focuses on the learning that has taken place. Many field trips tend to be an end in themselves, but this omits the most important follow-up where new ideas and greater understanding are generated.

Appropriate observations

1. In classroom observation, look for the following:
   a. How children learn
   b. Play—child's work
   c. Interpersonal relations

d. Aggression
e. Fine and gross motor control
f. Hand-eye coordination
g. Stages and ages

Appropriate field trips

1. Children's museum
2. Art museum
3. Park
4. Special schools
5. Newspapers
6. Hospital

Dyad or Triad Interaction and Feedback

During structured programs such as STEP and PET, interludes that allow the audience or participants to clarify, practice, and receive feedback on their interaction with others are beneficial. For example, if parents and teachers were working to improve interaction during a conference, sample statements would allow them to practice their listening and communication skills. If the topic were reflective listening, one member of the dyad or triad would share with the others an aspect or concern. The second person would answer with a reflective listening response. The third then would critique the response. Each member of the triad has an opportunity to play each role: the speaker, listener, and observer.

Arrangements prior to the meeting

1. Clarification, practice, and feedback are usually used in conjunction with a structured, planned format though they could be beneficial if the leader recognized the need for interaction at any meeting.
2. Select items in the curriculum that need to have practice, clarification, and feedback.
3. Review the Arrangements for Meetings (pp. 196–99) and make appropriate preparations.

Set up

1. Small group (up to 24)
   a. Arrange chairs in circle, semicircle, or around tables.
   b. Have participants arrange their chairs so that three can communicate with each other.

2. Large auditorium
   a. Start at the beginning of the row and have the aisle person turn and discuss with the person to the right. Dyads or triads can be formed all along each row.

Procedure

1. After a topic has been described or a video shown, stop the program and have the participants form into dyads or triads.
2. Have the dyad or triad decide who will be the speaker, the listener, and the observer.
3. Describe a situation or problem that needs to be clarified or solved. Handouts describing situations are effective at large meetings.
4. Have the participants play out their parts.
5. The observer then critiques the statement and response using positive reinforcement as well as suggestions.

Appropriate topics

1. Communication
2. Behavior and misbehavior
3. Determination of problem ownership
4. Reflective and active listening
5. Natural and logical consequences

Role Playing

Role playing is a dramatization of a situation where group members put themselves into a designated role. Role playing is a very informal type of meeting, similar to presenting a drama, so it can be adapted to a wide variety of situations. The roles that persons play can be completely initiated by the players, or there can be a set format or specific situation that players are to enact. In either situation, the persons playing the roles are to put themselves into those roles. They are to feel that they are the "role" and respond with appropriate reactions and emotions. For this reason, spontaneous role playing is advantageous over the planned drama. Figure 6–12 depicts a typical role-playing situation.

Role playing can be used to demonstrate a problem or to develop participants' sensitivities to a situation. In the first, demonstration of a situation, the group members discuss their feel-

FIGURE 6–12
Dramatizations such as role playing illustrate the dynamics of hypothetical situations.

ings and reactions and offer solutions to the role. It is an excellent means for getting many people involved in a particular situation and is easily used to illustrate parent-child interaction. In the second, development of sensitivity, role reversal is often used. An example of role reversal is when the teacher plays the role of the principal while the principal plays the role of the teacher. Not only do participants begin to understand the obligations of the other role, but through their playing of the role, they are able to demonstrate what their feelings are. This clarifies feelings for both parties. Another role reversal situation that can be used is the parent-child relationship, with one participant playing the child's role and the other playing the parent's role. The parent in the child's role develops sensitivity to the child's position.

Participants in role playing feel free to communicate their feelings and attitudes because they are not portraying themselves. This encourages greater openness and involvement. When group members begin role playing, they tend to be hesitant to get involved emotionally with the part. After using role playing for a period of time, hesitancy and reluctance to be involved disappear, and people enjoy the opportunity to participate. If the group progresses to a therapeutic enactment, professional counselors should be included and consulted.

Arrangements prior to meeting

1. Review the Arrangements for Meetings (pp. 196–99) and make appropriate preparations.
2. Prepare descriptive situations illustrating particular problems or issues prior to the meeting, if specific role assignments are planned.

Setup

1. Role playing can be used in a variety of formats: (1) the role playing is conducted within the circle of participants; the center of the circle can then be the stage; (2) when used with a larger group, participants may have the chairs formed into semicircles, with a stage in front of the group; (3) role playing may also be used in a large group meeting with an auditorium stage for the actors.
2. If the role playing is planned for participation by the entire group, allow members to meet first in a circle arrangement and to break into smaller groups after an introduction.

Procedure

1. A short discussion of the topic or situation is introduced by the leader or panel.
2. The situation that needs to be role played is introduced. This may be accomplished by (1) volunteers, (2) persons selected prior to meeting to start the initial role play, or (3) breaking up the total group into groups of four or five, who are given a topic with an outline of the role situation or are challenged to develop their own role situations.
3. The role can be played in two ways:

   a. Roles can be played in front of the entire group with the membership watching and listening to the dramatization and interaction. Following the role play, the members use the open discussion method to clarify issues, study the problem, and make decisions.

   b. If the membership is divided into smaller groups, it is beneficial to let each of the groups play its roles simultaneously within the room and have each small group discuss the feelings and attitudes that arose while they were playing their roles. Following this, the small groups may discuss alternative means, ideas, and solutions.
4. If the small groups have all met and developed specific situations, it is also meaningful to have each group perform its role playing in front of the total group. Following the performance of the groups, the larger group is allowed to discuss the role playing openly. Clarification, questions, and solutions are brought forth at this time.
5. The leader thanks those who participated in role playing.

Appropriate topics

1. Parent-teacher conferences
2. Behavioral problems
3. Building self-esteem
4. Reflective listening
5. Roles within groups

Dramatizations

Short plays, written by group members or selected from those available from commercial companies, mental health organizations, or social agencies, can be used as springboards to discussions. There is an advantage to skits composed by the membership. First, the length can be kept short and the parts easily learned. Second, the action may be specifically related to the group's needs. Third, the preparation of the skit encourages the group participants to become actively involved in the process and in the material that is presented.

A variation of the drama can be the use of puppets. Many participants are able to use puppets more freely than to perform themselves, because using puppets takes away the threat of performing.

Arrangements prior to meeting

1. Select a group to plan a drama (a play chosen or developed by group).
2. Select the cast or allow members to choose their own parts.
3. Encourage participants to study the parts and work together on the presentation.
4. Review the Arrangements for Meetings (pp. 196–99) and make appropriate preparations.

Setup

1. Depending on the number of persons at the meeting, the room can be arranged as follows:
   a. Use a circle for a small group, with the dramatization performed as a play in-the-round.
   b. If the group is small, the chairs may be formed in a semicircle with the stage at the opening. The stage may be raised or on the same level as the group members.
   c. If the group is large, an auditorium arrangement is appropriate. The dramatization can be held on a stage.

Procedure

1. The leader convenes the meeting and introduces the drama and the cast of characters.
2. The dramatization is presented.
3. Open discussion ensues, which clarifies feelings, emotions, and information presented.
4. The leader thanks the performers.

Appropriate topics

1. Family violence
2. Handling the stubborn child
3. Rivalry between children
4. Family rivalry
5. Family conferences
6. Communication among family members

Panel

A panel is an informal presentation by approximately four to six presenters who discuss an issue or idea. Panel members come prepared with background material on a selected subject and, seated behind a table or in a semicircle, discuss the subject among themselves. The presentation allows informal interaction and conversation among the members of the panel.

A chairperson, although a member of the panel, has different responsibilities from the other members. The chairperson introduces members, presents the topic, and then encourages participation by the other members. Like a leader, the chairperson can clarify, keep the panel focused on the topic, and summarize the closing.

Arrangements prior to meeting

1. Review the Arrangements for Meetings (pp. 196–99) and make appropriate arrangements. In a panel meeting with informal conversation among panel members, it is important to set the stage.
2. Choose four to six participants to discuss a specific topic.
3. The panel thoroughly researches the topic. Notes are kept for reference and introduction of ideas during the panel presentation.

Setup

1. Place a table or two tables slightly turned toward one another in front of the audience. Set chairs for the panelists behind the table, which allows members to see and converse with each other easily.
2. Seat the audience or remaining members of the group in a semicircle, with the panel facing them. If the audience is large, auditorium-style seating may be used with a panel presentation.

Procedure

1. The chairperson clarifies the panel procedure to the audience.
2. The chairperson presents the topic for discussion and the relevance of the topic to the group's concerns.
3. The chairperson introduces the panel members.
4. The chairperson starts the discussion by a question or statement, and the panelists begin

a discussion, freely interacting and conversing with one another.

5. The chairperson asks for questions from the audience. Questions are discussed among panelists.
6. The chairperson summarizes the major points and the conclusions of the panel.
7. The chairperson thanks the panel members for their contributions.

Appropriate topics

1. Child development—social, intellectual, emotional, and physical
2. New classroom teaching methods
3. Bias-free education
4. Exceptional children
5. Drugs and alcohol—influence on children
6. Discipline
7. Emotions in children
8. Managing a home with both parents working
9. Nutrition

Colloquy

The colloquy is a panel discussion by an informed or expert panel where members of the audience are encouraged by the chairperson to interject a question or comment during the presentation. This allows information specifically pertinent to the audience to be discussed during the main part of the presentation instead of waiting for the question-answer period after the presentation.

A second form of the colloquy includes two sets of panels, an expert panel and a lay panel. The lay panel uses the procedures for a panel discussion. The expert panel gives advice when called upon by the lay panel or when it feels some pertinent information is being overlooked.

Arrangements prior to meeting

1. The lay panel is selected, or if the expert and lay panel forum is being used, two panels are selected.
2. Necessary preparation of topic material is completed. The subject is researched, and notes are developed for discussion.

3. Review the Arrangements for Meetings (pp. 196–99) and make appropriate arrangements.

Setup

1. For a single panel, place chairs behind tables turned so the members of the panel can make eye contact with one another.
2. For two panels, lay and expert, seat the chairperson in the center with one panel on the left and one on the right, both slightly facing the center so that the presenters can see each other and the audience.

Procedure

1. Colloquy—single panel
   a. The leader or chairperson explains and clarifies the colloquy procedure to the audience.
   b. The topic for discussion is introduced.
   c. Panel members are introduced.
   d. The chairperson offers a stimulating comment or question to start the discussion.
   e. The chairperson encourages free interaction among panel members and takes questions and comments from the audience.
   f. An open forum follows the conclusion of the panel discussion.
   g. The leader summarizes and concludes meeting.

2. Colloquy—dual panel
   a. The chairperson explains and clarifies the two-panel colloquy to the audience.
   b. The chairperson introduces the subject for discussion.
   c. The expert and lay panels are presented to the audience.
   d. The leader starts the discussion with a stimulating remark or question.
   e. As expert advice is needed, the second panel is called upon to contribute.
   f. A question-answer period follows the presentation, with comments and questions from the audience answered and discussed by both the lay and expert panel.

g. The chairperson summarizes, thanks the participants, and concludes the colloquy.

Appropriate topics

1. Dealing with your child's fears
2. Handling stress
3. Drug addiction and alcoholism
4. Helping exceptional children
5. Nutrition

Debate

When an issue is of a pro-and-con nature, a debate is an effective means of presenting both sides. The debate team presents opposing views of a controversial issue.

Arrangements prior to meeting

1. Select two to six members for the debate team. Divide into two teams and give each group one side of the issue.
2. The debaters research the background material on the issue and develop a 2- to 4-minute speech.
3. Review the Arrangements for Meetings (pp. 196–99) and make appropriate arrangements.

Setup

1. Place enough chairs for the debate team on each side of a podium or table.
2. Place chairs in a circle for a small audience; if the group is large, use an auditorium formation.

Procedure

1. The question to be debated is announced by the chairperson, and then the issue is turned over to the speakers for each side.
2. One speaker for the affirmative begins with a 2- to 4-minute speech. The next speaker is from the opposing position. The teams alternate until each member has spoken.
3. Rebuttal following each speech is optional, or leaders of both debate teams may conclude the debate section with rebuttals.

4. The chairperson entertains questions from the audience, and the debate teams answer and discuss the issue.

Appropriate topics

1. Sex education—home or school?
2. Behavior modification vs. logical consequences
3. Open education vs. traditional education
4. Encouragement toward achievement vs. "Don't push my child"

Book Review Discussion

Book reviews by members of the group or experts provide a format that brings out stimulating new ideas or acknowledges expertise. The review may be given by one presenter or a number of members. An open discussion by the entire group follows.

Arrangements prior to meeting

1. Select the book and expert or members to give the book reviews.
2. Plan with the group how the review will be done, that is, each presenter taking one section of the book, one person doing the entire book, or a panel discussion of issues in the book.
3. Each presenter must read the book and prepare the review or a specific portion of the review.
4. The group is told about the upcoming book review and encouraged to read the book.
5. Review the Arrangements for Meetings (pp. 196–99) and make appropriate arrangements.

Setup

1. Place chairs for book reviewers behind a table in front of the group.
2. Arrange chairs for the audience in a circle or semicircle.

Procedure

1. The chairperson tells about the book to be reviewed and introduces the book reviewer or book review panel.

2. The book reviewer gives information about the author of the book.
3. The book review is given.
   a. If the book is to be reviewed by a panel discussion, the group discusses issues and ideas in a conversational format.
   b. One person may give the book review.
   c. Each of two or three persons may give a review of a portion of the book.
4. Following the review, the entire group joins in an open discussion of the book.

Appropriate topics

1. Values
2. Decision making
3. Building self-concept
4. Communication
5. Divorce
6. Role identification
7. Single parents
8. Refer to Appendix E for a list of books

Audiovisual

Visual stimuli, programmed material, and film presentations can be used as catalysts for a good open discussion. The audiovisual format is directed toward two senses, hearing and sight, whereas an audio presentation relies solely on hearing. The addition of visual stimuli is beneficial to those who learn better through sight than through sound. Charts, posters, and/or pictures accompanying any presentation help to clarify ideas. Films, filmstrips, and video presentations can present information in an interesting and succinct manner.

Techniques

1. Audio—tapes and records
2. Audiovisual
   a. Filmstrips with records or tapes
   b. Sound films
   c. Videotapes
   d. Slides with running commentary
3. Visual
   a. Charts
   b. Posters

c. Chalk drawings
d. Filmstrips with printed information
e. Opaque projector images
f. Overhead projector transparencies

Arrangements prior to meeting

1. The teacher and/or group decides on information needed by the membership through interest finders.
2. Films, slides, or tapes are reviewed and selected. (Choose only programs that are relevant, interesting, and presented well.)
3. Choose a member to give a presentation.
4. Films, video, or tapes must be reserved and equipment ordered—tape or record players, projectors, chart stands, projection carts, extension cords, outlet adapters, screen, etc.
5. Previewing of audiovisual and audio materials is necessary to be sure of quality and to develop questions and comments relevant to the presentation. Do not use audiovisual materials as fillers; use them only as relevant additions to the curriculum.
6. Review the Arrangements for Meetings (pp. 196–99) and make appropriate preparations.

Setup

1. Check and prepare equipment prior to meeting. Have film, slides, or filmstrips ready to begin and have charts and posters up.
2. Arrange chairs so membership can see the presentation.

Procedure

1. The chairperson introduces the topic and the presenter.
2. The presenter gives background information on audiovisual material and points out important aspects of the showing.
3. Following the presentation, the presenter leads an open discussion and question-answer period.

Appropriate topics

1. Foundations of reading and writing
2. Emotional growth

3. Dealing with fears
4. Exceptional children, for example, learning disabled, autistic, and gifted
5. Appendix E lists a number of films and film-strips that would make excellent starting points for a discussion

Symposium

A symposium is a formal presentation on various aspects of a topic given by several speakers. Each symposium presenter develops a specific talk of 5 to 15 minutes. The symposium is similar to a lecture, but information is given by several lecturers rather than just one. Its value, to share expert information, is the same.

Arrangements prior to meeting

1. Symposium presenters are selected.
2. A set talk, based on research of appropriate authorities and relevant articles, is prepared by each symposium member.
3. A chairperson or leader is chosen from the symposium presenters.
4. Review the Arrangements for Meetings (pp. 196–99) and make appropriate preparations.

Setup

1. Place chairs for the presenters behind a table in front of the audience.
2. Chairs for the audience may be in circle or semicircle for a small group, or auditorium arrangements can be made for a large group.

Procedure

1. The chairperson or leader introduces the symposium speakers.
2. Each presenter gives a set talk.
3. The chairperson or leader provides transitional statements between each speaker's presentation.
4. At the end of the presentations, questions directed to a specific speaker or to the entire symposium are entertained by the chairperson. A discussion of questions follows.

5. The chairperson summarizes the main points of the meeting.
6. Symposium presenters are thanked for their contributions.

Appropriate topics

1. Nonsexist education
2. Single parenthood
3. Sex-role identification
4. Multicultural understanding
5. Consumer education
6. Death and dying
7. Safety in the home (e.g., toys, poison, home arrangement)

Lecture

A lecture is a talk or speech prepared by an expert or lay presenter. During the presentation, there are no interruptions or questions allowed, but there may be a question-answer period following the address. The lecture without a forum following it results in a formal presentation with no interaction between speaker and audience. A lecture forum that includes a period for questions and answers at the end of the address permits some interaction and allows the audience an opportunity to have relevant questions answered, to clarify points, and to make comments.

Lectures are an excellent vehicle for dissemination of specific information. As a result, care must be taken to choose a speaker who not only knows the subject but who presents unbiased material.

Arrangements prior to meeting

1. Select a topic and obtain a speaker who is recognized as an unbiased authority.
2. Communicate with the speaker on group interests and needs, time limit for speech, and forum period.
3. Prepare an introduction that is based on the speaker's background and expertise.
4. Review the Arrangements for Meetings (pp. 196–99) and make appropriate preparations.

Setup

1. Place a podium or table at the center of the stage if the audience is large. Place chairs in a circle with a small table in front of the speaker if the audience is small.
2. Check the sound system if area is large.
3. Obtain a glass or pitcher of water for the speaker's use.

Procedure

1. The chairperson introduces the speaker and topic.
2. The speaker gives a talk for a specific period of time.
3. The chairperson conducts a forum for questions, with the guest speaker responding to comments and answering questions.

4. The speaker is thanked by the chairperson, and the meeting is concluded.

Appropriate topics

1. Money management
2. Specialists, for example psychiatrist, pediatrician, dentist, nutritionist, obstetrician, special educator, speech therapist, physical therapist
3. How to manage stress
4. Dealing with illness and death
5. Preventive health measures
6. Childhood diseases

Select the meeting format that fulfills your needs and is most appropriate for the topic.

SUMMARY

Parent group meetings are one of the most efficient and viable forms of parent education. Positive leadership skills are essential to facilitate productive functioning of parent groups. Included in this chapter are a description of a needs assessment and a discussion of the formation of parent groups. Leadership skills and good group interaction can be developed if groups are aware of leadership and group roles. Roles that emerge within groups have an impact on the interaction of the participants. A knowledge of task, maintenance, and dysfunctional roles improves the productiveness of group interaction through the concerted elimination of nonfunc-

tional roles. An analysis of group discussion illustrates the interaction in process.

Group meetings use a variety of meeting formats, either individually or in combination. The formats include roundtable, concentric circle, buzz session, brainstorming, workshop, field trip, role playing, dramatization, panel, colloquy, debate, book review, audiovisual, lecture, and symposium. Choice of topics for the meetings should fit the interest and needs of the groups.

Evaluations are necessary in ongoing parent groups because they provide a basis for improvement of group interaction and suggestions for the continuing program.

SUGGESTED ACTIVITIES AND DISCUSSIONS

1. Generate some innovative icebreakers. Try them out on your classmates.
2. Develop a needs assessment for your community of parents. Ask parents to complete the needs assessment. Discuss their answers.
3. Conduct an opening period of a parent meeting. Include icebreakers and interest finders.

4. Choose roles from the dysfunctional and maintenance categories. Role play these roles while the group holds an open discussion or concentric circle discussion. Let the members of the group guess which roles the others are playing. If you use a concentric circle, have each member of the inner circle role play a group role.

The outer circle can record the interaction and analyze the roles being played.

5. Make an interaction pattern on an observation wheel. Discuss the interaction pattern.

6. Obtain parent education programs such as STEP, PET, *Parents' Magazine* tapes and filmstrips, PAR (Parents as Resources) filmstrips, or other programs listed in Appendix E. Conduct meetings using the curricula from these programs.

7. Conduct a needs assessment within the total group. From the results pick one topic for each of the formats, that is, panel, debate, symposium, workshop, buzz session, etc. Let each group be responsible for a meeting using these topics and formats.

8. Attend a parent education meeting in your community. Visit with the members. Note how the meeting is conducted, the involvement of the parents, and the feelings of the members. Talk with the director about the goals and objectives of the group. Talk with the parents concerning their desires for the group.

9. Engage a group in an experiential activity such as role playing. Using the experiential stages as a guide, ask questions that carry the group forward.

10. Administer a needs assessment. From the responses, develop a curriculum plan for the semester.

11. Construct a program evaluation. Have students complete the questionnaire after a class session or a "parent" meeting. Evaluate the questionnaire. Did you get the type of feedback that you needed?

12. Develop a workshop or meeting for parents. Include the objectives of the meeting, questions to be answered, background material on the questions, and a list of additional resources.

BIBLIOGRAPHY

Applbaum, R. L., Bodaken, E. M., Sereno, K. K., & Anatol, K. W. E. *The process of group communication* (2nd ed.). Palo Alto, Calif.: Science Research Associates, 1979.

Auerbach, A. B. *Parents learn through discussion: Principles and practices of parent group education.* Melbourne, Fla.: Robert E. Krieger Publishing Co., 1980.

Bales, R. *Interaction process analysis: A method for the study of small groups.* Chicago: University of Chicago Press, 1950, reprinted 1976.

Beal, G., Bohlen, J. M., & Raudabaugh, J. N. *Leadership and dynamic group action.* Ames: Iowa State University, 1962.

Benne, K. D., & Sheets, P. Functional roles of group members. *Journal of Social Issues,* 1948,4(2), pp. 41–49.

Berger, E. H. *Mature beginning teachers: Employment, satisfaction, and role analysis.* Unpublished dissertation, University of Denver, 1968.

Biddle, B. J., & Thomas, E. J. *Role theory: Concepts and research.* Melbourne, Fla.: Robert E. Kreiger Publishing Co., 1979.

Cataldo, C. Z. The parent as the learner. *Educational Psychologist, 15*(3), 1980, pp. 172–186.

———. *Parent education for early childhood.* New York: Teachers College Press, 1987.

Center for Building Family Strengths. *Building family strengths.* Lincoln: University of Nebraska, 1986.

Clarke-Stewart, A. Parent education in the 1980s. *Educational Evaluation & Policy Analysis, 3*(6), November-December 1981, pp. 47–58.

Coan, D. L., & Gotts, E. E. *Parent education needs: A national assessment study.* Charleston, W. Va.: Appalachia Educational Laboratory, 1976. (ERIC Document Reproduction Service No. ED 132 609).

The Consortium for Longitudinal Studies. *As the twig is bent.* Hillsdale, N.J.: Lawrence Erlbaum Associates, 1983.

Dembo, M., Sweitzer, M., & Lauritzen, P. An evaluation of group parent education: Behavioral, PET, and Adlerian programs. *Review of Educational Research, 55,* 1985.

Denver Public Schools, Emily Griffith Opportunity School. *Parent education and preschool department leadership handbook.* Denver, Colo.: Denver Public Schools, n.d.

Dinkmeyer, D., & McKay; G. D. *STEP: Systematic Training for Effective Parenting.* Circle Pines, Minn.: American Guidance Service, 1983.

Elam, S. M., & Gallup, A. M. The twenty-first Gallup Poll of the public's attitudes toward the public school. *Phi Delta Kappan,* September 1989, pp. 41–54.

Epstein, J. L. Parents' reactions to teacher practices of parent involvement. *The Elementary School Journal,* January 1986, pp. 277–294.

Gallup, G. H. The ninth annual Gallup Poll of the public's attitudes toward the public schools. *Phi Delta Kappan,* September 1977, pp. 33–48.

Gardner, N. D. *Group leadership.* Washington, D.C.: National Training & Development Service Press, 1974.

Gordon, T. *P.E.T.: Parent effectiveness training.* New York: Wyden, 1975.

———. Parent Effectiveness Training: A preventive program and its effects on families. In M. J. Fine, (Ed.). *Handbook on parent education.* New York: Academic Press, 1980.

Gotts, E. E., & Purnell, R. F. (Eds.). *Education and Urban Society, 19*(2), February 1987.

Hereford, C. F. *Changing parental attitudes through group discussion.* Austin: University of Texas Press, 1963.

Kawin, E. *Parenthood in a free nation. Basic concepts for parents* (Vol. I), *Early and middle childhood* (Vol. II), *Later childhood and adolescence* (Vol. III). Lafayette, Ind.: Purdue University, 1969.

———. *A manual for group leaders and participants.* Lafayette, Ind.: Purdue University, 1970.

King, C. E. *The sociology of small groups.* New York: Pageant Press, 1962.

Missouri Department of Elementary and Secondary Education. *New Parents as Teachers Project: Executive evaluation summary.* Jefferson City: Author, 1985.

Moles, O. C. Who wants parent involvement? *Education and Urban Society, 19*(2), February 1987, pp. 137–145.

Napier, R. W., & Gershenfeld, M. K. *Groups, theory, and experience* (2nd ed.). Boston: Houghton Mifflin, 1981.

Osborn, A. F. *Applied imagination.* New York: Scribner's, 1957.

Pickarts, E., & Fargo, J. *Parent education.* Englewood Cliffs, N.J.: Prentice-Hall, 1971.

Popkin, M. H. *Active Parenting,* Active Parenting, Inc.: Marietta, GA, 1985.

Powell, D. R. Parent education and support programs, *Young Children,* March 1986, pp. 47–53.

Swick, K. J. Parent education: Focus on parents' needs and responsibilities. *Dimensions,* April 1983, pp. 9–12.

———. Critical issues in parent education. *Dimensions,* October 1985, pp. 4–7.

U.S. Department of Health and Human Services (Office of Human Development Services; Administration for Children, Youth and Families; Head Start Bureau). *A leader's guide to exploring parenting.* Washington, D.C.: U.S. Government Printing Office, 1980.

White, B. L. *Educating the infant and toddler.* Lexington, Mass.: Lexington Books, 1988.

Yankelovich, Skelly, & White, Inc. *Raising children in a changing society: The General Mills American family report, 1976–1977.* Minneapolis: General Mills, 1977.

Appendix A*: Parent Needs Assessment

Dear Parent:

Our Laboratory is preparing a new instructional series for parents. It is called "Education for Effective Parenthood."

Your local school has agreed to help us. Now we need your help. You will find a four (4) page form with this letter. The form will tell you "what to do." You can help by telling us on the form about your own needs as a parent. We hope you will talk with your husband or wife as you give your answers on the form. If you are a single parent, please let us know of your needs from this point of view.

When you finish answering, put your form in the envelope. Then seal it and return it to the school. Do not put your name on the outside of the envelope. We will not tell anyone what you said. We will use your answers to help us plan the "Education for Effective Parenthood" series.

We would like to know your answers. But you do not have to answer. Even if you do not answer, please seal your form in the envelope and return it to the school.

Soon you will hear from the school about the new instructional series. Watch for this news.

Thank you for your help.

Sincerely,

_____

*The material in this appendix is from Coan, D. L., & Gotts, E. E. *Parent education needs: A national assessment study.* Charleston, W. Va.: Appalachia Educational Laboratory, Inc., 1976, pp. 75–84. (ERIC Document Reproduction Service No. ED 132 609); *Learning to be a better parent* was developed by E. E. Gotts, D. L. Coan, & C. E. Kenoyer, 1975.

LEARNING TO BE A BETTER PARENT

Name:_____

My city and state:_____

My children's ages (in years):_____

Name of nearest grade school:_____

What to do: First, read what it says below about each thing you might learn more about. Then decide how much you feel you need or want to learn more about that. For example, if you feel you already know all or just about as much as you need or want to know about "How Children Grow and Develop," then mark the box *Nothing more at all*. However, if you feel you need or want to learn *more* about that, then you may wish to answer *A little more* or *A lot more*. Put a check mark (√) in the box under *A lot more, A little more*, or *Nothing more at all* for each question. We are interested in what you feel. You may, of course, feel that you need or want to learn more about some things, and nothing more about others. No one will judge you as a parent, whatever your answers are. If you do not want to answer a question, then leave it blank.

	A Lot More	A Little More	Nothing More at All
A. How children grow and develop			
How much do you feel you need or want to learn more about:			
1. Where you can find out about how children develop.	☐	☐	☐
2. What your child should be able to learn at his age, so as not to "push" your child too much.	☐	☐	☐
3. How children grow into special, one-of-a-kind people.	☐	☐	☐
4. How the world looks and sounds to your child, and how to help him learn about it.	☐	☐	☐
5. How your child's personality is formed.	☐	☐	☐
6. How your child learns to use his body by playing (runs, jumps).	☐	☐	☐
B. Taking better care of your baby			
How much do you feel you need or want to learn more about:			
1. What happens before the baby comes (what to eat; what drugs not to take; how long to wait before having another baby; things that can happen to the baby).	☐	☐	☐
2. How babies learn to talk (what the baby hears; what it learns from what you do and say).	☐	☐	☐
3. Helping the baby feel good (not too warm or cool; enough to eat; food that might upset the baby; giving the baby room to move around).	☐	☐	☐

	A Lot More	A Little More	Nothing More at All

C. Treating your child like a person
How much do you feel you need or want to learn more about how to:

	A Lot More	A Little More	Nothing More at All
1. Tell what children are doing by watching them.	☐	☐	☐
2. Help your child see and accept his or her own feelings.	☐	☐	☐
3. Show love and care to your child.	☐	☐	☐
4. Talk with your child about his problems and answer his questions.	☐	☐	☐
5. Help your child to behave when he starts to fight.	☐	☐	☐
6. Help your child learn to get along with family and friends.	☐	☐	☐
7. Help your child see why rules are good.	☐	☐	☐

D. Taking care of your family
How much do you feel you need or want to learn more about how to:

	A Lot More	A Little More	Nothing More at All
1. Pick things for the child's bed and for him to wear (so that they last and are easy to take care of).	☐	☐	☐
2. Find and take care of a home for your family (how to shop and pay for housing and furniture).	☐	☐	☐
3. Pick the right foods and take care of them so they will not spoil (fix meals that are good for your family's health).	☐	☐	☐

E. Teaching and training your child
How much do you feel you need or want to learn more about:

	A Lot More	A Little More	Nothing More at All
1. What ways of teaching will work best with your child (the way you teach; use of books, TV).	☐	☐	☐
2. How to control your child by using reward, praise, and correction in a loving way (how to help your child control himself).	☐	☐	☐
3. How to teach your child to be neat and clean and to show good manners.	☐	☐	☐
4. How to get your child to go to bed on time (and to rest or take naps).	☐	☐	☐
5. How to get your child to change from doing one thing to doing something else.	☐	☐	☐
6. How to plan your child's use of TV (picking TV programs; not watching too much TV).	☐	☐	☐

	A Lot More	A Little More	Nothing More at All
7. How to place your chairs, tables, and other things so that your child will have room to play and learn (and keeping some things out of sight so your child will not want them).	☐	☐	☐
8. How to feed your child; teach him to feed himself; and make eating fun for your child.	☐	☐	☐
9. How to teach your child to dress and undress.	☐	☐	☐
10. How to help your child think for himself (choose what he wants to do; make plans).	☐	☐	☐
11. How to teach your child to tell right from wrong (to be moral).	☐	☐	☐

F. Keeping your family safe and well
How much do you feel you need or want to learn more about:

	A Lot More	A Little More	Nothing More at All
1. How to keep your child from getting hurt (and how to give first aid).	☐	☐	☐
2. How to keep your child well (get shots and have the doctor check your child).	☐	☐	☐
3. How to know if something is wrong with your child (is not learning; cannot walk well; cannot see or hear well).	☐	☐	☐
4. How to know when your child is sick (has a fever or says he hurts some place).	☐	☐	☐
5. How to pick things that are safe to play with.	☐	☐	☐
6. How to tell if your child is growing right (body size, height, weight).	☐	☐	☐

G. Taking care of things at home
How much do you feel you need or want to learn more about:

	A Lot More	A Little More	Nothing More at All
1. Making good use of your time (plan your time for child care, house work, school or job, time for yourself and your friends).	☐	☐	☐
2. Getting good help with child care (day care, baby sitter, nursery school).	☐	☐	☐
3. How your child deals with the way that your family lives (people in the home, what they do together, how they get along).	☐	☐	☐
4. Finding help for people who don't take care of their children, or who hurt their children.	☐	☐	☐

	A Lot More	A Little More	Nothing More at All
H. Yourself as a parent			
How much do you feel you need or want to learn more about:			
1. Your own feelings and habits and how these help or hurt your child care (how they affect your child care).	☐	☐	☐
2. Your need to make your child mind you (how your own needs can affect how your child feels about himself, and your child's learning).	☐	☐	☐
3. Why your child will not mind you and how this bothers you (how to get over being upset).	☐	☐	☐
4. How to be sure that you are doing what is best for your child (or your worries about what other people think).	☐	☐	☐

What to do: Just as before, read what it says about each thing from which you can learn. That is, if you think you would enjoy learning about being a better parent from "reading books," then you may wish to answer *A lot* or *A little.* But if you would *not* enjoy learning from "reading books," then mark the box *Not at all.* You may, of course, think that you would like to learn from some things and not from others. Put a check mark (√) in the box under *A lot, A little* or *Not at all* for each question.

	A Lot	A Little	Not at All
I. How to learn about being a better parent			
How much would you like to learn about being a better parent from:			
1. Reading books.	☐	☐	☐
2. Talking with parents in group meetings.	☐	☐	☐
3. Watching a special TV series.	☐	☐	☐
4. Seeing movies near my home (at a school).	☐	☐	☐
5. Having a person visit my home and talk with me each week.	☐	☐	☐
6. Seeing slides and hearing a person tell about them.	☐	☐	☐
7. Reading about this in magazines or in small newspapers (4 to 8 pages long).	☐	☐	☐
8. Hearing a special radio series.	☐	☐	☐
9. Listening to records or tapes.	☐	☐	☐
10. Playing games that teach me to be a better parent.	☐	☐	☐

	A Lot	A Little	Not at All
I. How to learn about being a better parent *On TV or radio or in the movies, how much would you like to learn from:*			
1. A funny show (humor, comedy, jokes).	☐	☐	☐
2. A talk show with well-known guests and parents.	☐	☐	☐
3. Stories about real people (not humor).	☐	☐	☐
4. Special stories done by actors (not humor).	☐	☐	☐
5. An M.D. (doctor) or other expert.	☐	☐	☐
6. A show that goes into real people's homes.	☐	☐	☐

Other Ideas

What else do you think you need or want to learn more about in order to be a better parent? Print so that your ideas will be easy to read.

_____

_____

_____

_____

Appendix B—Promoting Children's Self-Esteem

Children of all ages need to feel good about themselves, to possess confidence. They need to feel that they can take risks based on their confidence in their abilities. Parents play a major role in their children's development of self-confidence.

This brief description of a parent meeting structured in a center format illustrates how parents can improve their skills.

OBJECTIVES

1. To develop ways of communication between parents and their children that helps children develop self-esteem.
2. To practice listening and communication skills that provide positive dialogue between parents and children.
3. To list activities and family practices that help develop a child's self-esteem.
4. To look for and analyze individual strengths of children that can be reinforced by the parents.

PROCEDURE

1. Prepare nametags that say "I AM SPECIAL" with a space for the parent's name on the badge.
2. Prepare an icebreaker that emphasizes self-esteem. One example is a signature sheet that allows each participant to have their best achievements listed. Each person interviews another and determines the other person's strongest asset. Have the second person sign the other person's sheet and also list their strength.
3. Gather the entire group together. Give a 10-minute general introduction to all the participants.
4. Divide the group into small groups. Number off 1 through 3 (depending on the number of centers). Another way to handle the division of participants is to have their nametags on three or four different colors of paper. Each person goes first to the center that has the same color as that on their nametag. Parents may stay together as a couple or be separated according to the desires of the parents.

WORKSHOP SET UP

1. Find a room large enough to allow the entire group to sit auditorium–style. Use this room for the 10 minute introduction to self-esteem and confidence.
2. In another room prepare three or more center areas. Set up chairs for approximately eight people at each area. Chairs may be placed in a circle or around a table. Place handouts and materials on the table.

TYPES OF CENTERS

Ideas for centers may be found in the four books listed under Resources. Other ideas include:

A. A center for practicing listening skills
   1. Prepare a handout that describes reflective listening (see chapter 5). Have dyads or triads practice reflective listening.
   2. Let the group divide into dyads. Ask one group member to describe a situation that is important to him or her. Ask another person to listen to the story and then to repeat it. Did the respondent interpret the story correctly?
   3. Encourage the group to share some activities they do at home to help their children feel confident. List things that deflate their children's ego. Then list statements and activities that might help to increase their children's self-esteem.

B. Centers to encourage self-concept

Activities may include:

   1. Family or personal shields that are designed by the participants and include their favorite activities, special abilities, families, and desires.
   2. All About Me booklets. Have the booklets already made or have instructions for constructing the booklets. Many items may be included. Each page can have a different concept. For example:

Page 1—Me (draw or write about hair color, eye color, favorite clothing)

Page 2—My family

Page 3—My home

Page 4—My pets or favorite toy

Page 5—What I like to do best

Page 6—My favorite stories

Page 7—My favorite_____

3. Paper sacks decorated on the outside with pictures of how the world sees you and on the inside with your best attributes as you see yourself.

4. A handout of favorite ideas to do with your child during weekends, holidays, or summers. Add a blank sheet with lines for participants to add their ideas. Reproduce this and send home with child at a later date.

The handout may include such things as art ideas, craft ideas, field trip opportunities, collections, drama, or music.

C. Writing and Bookmaking

1. Books created by the parents or together with the child. Ask parents to bring some snapshots of their children. Use the snapshots to illustrate the books. Write a story about the snapshots.

2. Simple cinquain poems or free verse that describes something that is exciting or beautiful about your child or family. Publish the poetry in the form of a booklet or poster.

RESOURCES

Briggs, D. C. *Your child's self-esteem.* Garden City, N.Y.: Dolphin Books, 1975.

Canfield, J., & Wells, H. C. *100 ways to enhance self-concept in the classroom.* Englewood Cliffs, N.J.: Prentice-Hall, Inc., 1976.

Frede, Ellen. *Getting involved; Workshops for parents.* Ypsilanti, Mich.: The High/Scope Press, 1984.

Rich, D. *MegaSkills.* Boston: Houghton Mifflin. 1988.

Seuss, Dr. *My book about me.* New York: Beginners Books, 1969.

Current articles and/or books can be selected for specific parent groups.

7

School-based Programs

Will the upsurge of interest in home and school cooperation work for the benefit of families and society? Both parents and schools have an extremely strong vested interest in the success of students in the schools. Parents want their children to develop into productive, intelligent, mentally healthy young adults. Schools want to provide the environment that facilitates and teaches the children as they become educated and successful, fully-functioning young adults. These desires have been expressed many times during the past decade. Scores of schools that recognized the importance of home school collaboration developed special programs which brought about a greater sense of cooperation. When the first edition of this book was published, it was difficult to find descriptions of schools that were committed to involving parents. Today, a surge toward parent involvement is expressed by many schools and described in a voluminous number of articles.

The force toward involving parents evolved from many directions. Parent involvement, however, is not new (see Chapter 2). Head Start included a parent commitment when it was first conceived in 1965. Special education programs involved parents in the development of Individualized Educational Plans after Public Law 94-142 was enacted in 1975. Hospitals and social agencies developed programs to work with schools

to provide children and families with health and diagnostic provisions. Public schools looked toward parent involvement as one method of assuring student success. The increasing number of child care facilities evoked a concern over the child and the need for child care to reinforce the family, not replace it.

As school-based programs look to this complex collaboration between home and school, issues emerge:

1. Parent-school cooperation in the education of children
2. Power
3. Advocacy
4. Parent education
5. Comprehensive programs to meet needs of total family

The first question involves the major topic of this entire text. It includes varying levels of involvement:

1. Parent as an active partner and educational leader at home and school
2. Parent as a decision maker
3. Parent actively involved with the school as a volunteer or paid employee
4. Parent as a liaison between school and home to support homework and to be aware of school activities

233

5. Parent as advocate of school through support of educational goals

The first issue, parent-school cooperation, does not always happen at all five levels. The parent who is most actively involved both at home and at school is a parent who is highly committed. The second allows a parent to be involved in the decision-making process. The third, one who volunteers or is a paid employee, also enjoys a special position with the school. In the third level, the parents make a concerted effort to know what is happening at school and see that their children do their homework. The fourth may have no apparent connection to the school, but parents can still believe that education is important and that they expect their children to do well in school.

The term, *coproduction* (Davies, 1987) adds to the concept of school-home partnership. In that partnership students and parents are essential partners with the school as coproducers of education. Education is not something doled out by the schools. The students, supported by the parents, must be actively involved in order for education to occur. "Coproduction refers to those activities, individual and collective, in school or at home, that contribute to school efforts to instruct pupils more effectively and raise pupil achievement" (Davies, 1987, p. 148).

Parents who do not seem to fit any of the five levels of parent involvement may not be empowered by the school to take an active role. Schools can build parents' abilities (Cochran & Henderson, 1986). This is accomplished by (1) positive communication at every opportunity to prevent difficulties and strengthen the parent's role, (2) informal networking among parents, (3) home activities provided by schools to reinforce the curriculum, and (4) accepting the parents as allies in education. Building parents' abilities is important. School-based programs will be more successful if parents are involved.

Are schools willing to open up to the group of parents who need help the most—low-income and minority families? Greenberg (1989) connects the self-esteem of parents with

that of the students. If the parents are not valued, the students do not feel their presence in school is valued. Why should they attempt to study and succeed in school if they are considered to be second-class citizens? She finds that schools often do not validate the parent which, in turn, hurts the child's self-esteem.

Which comes first, the parent's involvement in the child's success, or the alienation of and lack of support for the parent which results in no parental support for the school? Parents who feel good about themselves, and parents who feel validated by the school, participate. This situation is particularly true for low-income, minority parents who may be made to feel inferior by the personnel in the school, but it is also true for many middle- or upper-class parents who receive negative feedback on their involvement in the schools.

Two-parent working families and single parents may have difficulty being involved during the day activities, but they should not be "written off as unavailable" (Moles, 1987, p. 142). They may fit into the level of parents who are actively involved with their children's education at home. "Regardless of their family arrangements or characteristics, most parents care about their children's progress in school and want to know how to assist their children" (Epstein, 1987, p. 131). The benefits from parent involvement that most middle-class parents receive do not need to be closed to low-income and minority parents. "School administrators and teachers must take the initiative to reach out to 'hard to reach parents' and to devise a wide variety of ways for them to participate" (Davies, 1987, p. 157). The initiative needs to come from the school; it must reach out to the home.

The second issue, power and decision making, is seen in the use of policy committees, advisory task forces, and school boards. In research by Chavkin and Williams (1987), 93% of the superintendents and school board presidents agreed most strongly that (1) teachers should provide parents with ideas that will help children with work at home, (2) principals should provide suggestions to teachers about working with parents, and (3) teachers should consider working with parents part of their job. On the other hand, 88% strongly disagreed that parents should be involved in administrative decisions such as teacher selection or evaluation, equipment purchases, and teacher assignments. It seems that parental decision making is limited to those areas in which school officials seem comfortable.

The third issue, advocacy, has spurred the development of programs for special education students. Case advocacy, in the hands of individual parents, can give the parent the opportunity to state their case and get it resolved to their satisfaction.

The fourth, parent education, can help mothers and fathers become better informed. Research shows that families with authoritative families (rather than permissive or authoritarian) rear children who are better able to succeed in school (Dornbusch et al., 1987). The way parents raise children—combined with the knowledge of activities that increase skills and concepts needed to learn—helps those children become accomplished. For example, knowledge of the importance of language development, based in the first 4 years of life, is essential for later school success. During parent education classes it has come as a surprise to many parents, middle-class parents included, that talking and reading with their young child is important. This small amount of parent education can help make a child into a capable student.

The fifth issue, comprehensive programs, is a view to the future. With the large number of parents working, all agencies involved with the family (recreation, health, social agencies, businesses, schools, and churches) will need to collaborate to insure continuity. Employers must re-evaluate their structure to allow more part-time, shared, flexible hours, and release time for parents to visit and volunteer in the schools; as well as to collaborate with high schools to provide occupational internships. Health agencies must collaborate with schools. Social agencies can work with schools to provide support for families who are unable to provide ade-

quately for their families or who might be neglectful or abusive if they do not have needed support.

Schools can help families. Child care providers need to "work with the child as a member of a family" (Leipzig, 1987, p. 36). Bring the family together rather than cause parents to feel inadequate. In all that the teachers do, they need to ask themselves: "Will my interaction, my policies, my way of working, contribute to the growth and dignity of everyone involved?" (p. 37).

Visualize your school as the center of a wheel with the spokes stretching out to the homes in the community through programs, resources, family centers, and support systems. Figure 7–1 illustrates some of the many components possible for a school.

Head Start can be illustrated by a similar wheel, with spokes for parent involvement, dental and medical care, a nutritional program, psychological support, and community resources. Comprehensive health and educational centers also rely on a variety of components to offer families the support they need. Outreach from school-based programs takes a variety of forms, each with its own strengths. This chapter discusses many programs and ideas that reach out from the school to meet the needs of parents and children.

A WALK THROUGH A SCHOOL

Assume the role of a parent who visits a school that is committed to the involvement of parents. As you open the school door, you notice a sign that welcomes you. The office staff also greet you with smiles when you check into the office. If you want to have a cup of tea or coffee, look through the school's curricula, or read an article, you can visit the family center. There, several parents are developing curriculum material for the school's resource room. One parent is making a game for the third and fourth grade classes. Another is clipping curriculum-related articles to be filed for reference. As you sip your coffee, the

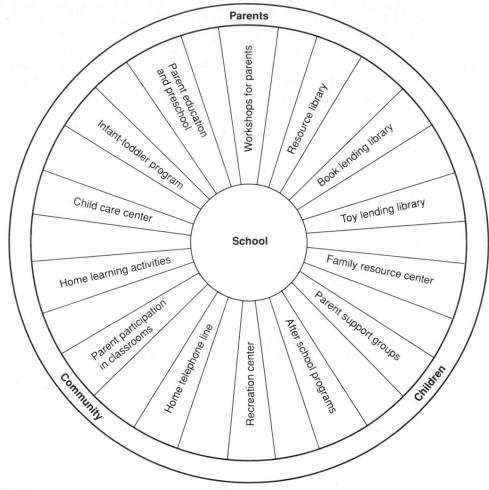

FIGURE 7–1
The spokes of the wheel radiate from the school and reveal opportunities for involvement of parents, children, and community.

sounds of young children echo down the hall from the west wing of the building. Parents and their children are arriving for their parent education and/or parent-child meetings. This school offers programs for parents of infants, toddlers, and preschool children. Both parents are invited and included in the programs. For those who cannot come during the week, a Saturday session is added.

You came to school today, however, to visit your child's classroom, so after a brief visit in the family center, you walk to your child's room.

Outside the door you pause as you read a welcome notice on the bulletin board that shows in detail what the children have been accomplishing. Here the teacher has described the happenings for the week, listed the volunteer times for parents, and has asked for contributions of plastic meat containers to be used in making tempera paint prints. Immediately aware of what is happening in the room, you promise to start collecting "scrounge materials" for recycling in the classroom. An invitation to an evening workshop reminds you that you have saved next Tuesday evening for that very event. On the space for notes to and from parents, you write a short response to the message you received from the teacher last week. Attached to the bulletin board are "Tips for Visiting." These let you know that you can become involved in a classroom activity rather than spend your time in passive observation. The teacher smiles and acknowledges your presence but, if involved with the class, continues teaching. The class greeter, a child chosen as a very important person this week, comes up and welcomes you. Later, during a center session or break, you have an opportunity to talk with the teacher and your child.

Recruitment for volunteers is underway so you are encouraged, but not forced, to contribute. Flexible hours, designated time periods, child care services, and a variety of tasks make it easy to share some time in this classroom.

Knowing that the principal holds an open forum each week at this time, you stop by and join a discussion of school policy. Parents are being encouraged to evaluate the "tote bag" home learning activities that have been sent home with children. In addition, plans are underway for an after-school recreation program. The principal will take the comments to the Parent Advisory Board meeting later this week.

After listening to others and expressing your recommendations and appreciation, you glance at your watch and realize that you must go. As you leave the school, you feel satisfied that this school responds to the needs of both you and your child.

NEW PARENTS AS TEACHERS PROJECT

Programs based primarily in the home often have their origin in the schools. The spokes from the school radiate out, helping, supporting, and caring about families in the area. One of the most isolated families in an area may be the beginning family that has recently rented or bought their first home; they begin on a real adventure after the birth of their first child.

Preschools, as well as before- and after-school programs located in the public schools, help fill a need for today's parents.

These and established couples who were having their first child were the parents selected for the New Parents as Teachers Project that was developed in four districts in Missouri. The research project reaffirmed the importance of parents in the education of their children.

First-time parents are usually very receptive to guidance. If the mother or father is not working out of the home, she or he usually has a need to visit and socialize with others as well as a desire to learn how best to raise the child. Contact and support reduces the loneliness felt by a parent who is totally responsible for an infant. In addition, new parents have no preconceived ideas gained by their experience in rearing other children that would be contrary to the research design.

Beginning in the third trimester of pregnancy and continuing until the child was 3, each family received the following:

- Information and guidance before the child was born that helped the parents prepare for the new arrival.
- Information on child development that fosters cognitive, social, motor, and language development. Clearly written handbooks describing what the parents should expect during each phase of development were published. The phases, based on White (1980), were:

    Phase 1—birth to 6 weeks

    Phase 2—6 weeks to 3½ months

    Phase 3—3½ months to 5½ months

    Phase 4—5½ months to 8 months

    Phase 5—8 months to 14 months

    Phase 6—14 months to 24 months

    Phase 7—24 months to 36 months (Ferguson-Florissant School District, 1989).

- Periodic hearing and vision checkups provided for the children in order to screen for possible problems.
- Parent resource center at the school that was available for the parent meetings.
- Individualized parent conferences each month.
- Monthly group meetings with other parents.

The research validated the parents' positive responses. It showed that children participating in the New Parents as Teachers Project scored significantly higher on all measures of verbal ability, intelligence, language ability, achievement, and auditory comprehension than did comparison children. The program proved to be so successful that it has been adopted by the Missouri Department of Elementary and Secondary Education for use throughout the state.

CHILD HEALTH SERVICES—SCHOOL COLLABORATION

The medical profession provides information, services, and health care. When this profession collaborates with the school, the chances of meeting family needs is greatly enhanced. One strong example of public school system collab-

orating with a health organization is the Brookline Early Education Project (BEEP). Brookline Public Schools and Children's Hospital Medical Center, Boston, joined to develop a coordinated plan for physical checkups and educational programs for young children, birth to kindergarten. Together, the hospital and school supplied a reassuring support system.

Based on the theory that parents are the child's most influential teachers, BEEP had three interrelated components:

1. *Parent Education and Support.* Three levels of support were provided, ranging from frequent home visits and meetings to parent-initiated support. Home visits, parent groups, and center visits were available. When children started into the child's educational program at 24 months, the parent-staff interaction was centered largely around the child's behavior in school, discussed during conferences based on guided observations. The average number of parent-program contacts during the child's first 5 years ranged from 87 to 167 (Pierson, Walker & Tivnan, 1984).

2. *Diagnostic Monitoring.* The children were periodically screened by staff at Children's Hospital Medical Center from the age of 2 weeks until entry into kindergarten. The 2-week exam was neurologic; at 3 months there was a physical and developmental exam; at 6, 11, 14, 24, 30, and 42 months there were physical, sensory, and developmental exams. During this 5-year period there were two dental screenings and one lead and anemia screening. Health history was completed at age 3 and upon entry to kindergarten (Pierson et. al, 1983).

3. *Education and Enrichment for Children.* The 2-year-old children attended weekly playgroup sessions held in the BEEP project center. For the 3- and 4-year-old children, prekindergarten classes were held in Brookline elementary schools. The classes emphasized social and mastery skills with a curriculum that was influenced by the High/Scope program. Follow-up research concludes that school-based early education is effective, especially in the area of reduction of

school-related difficulties in the elementary grades (Pierson et al. 1983, 1984).

The BEEP program, in addition to the three services just described, offered the following

- family center
- consultants
- library books and pamphlets
- films and videotapes on child development
- series of special events—workshops, films, and lectures
- transportation for parents to BEEP

Figure 7–2 illustrates the extent of the involvement of families, school, and the medical center. When schools, maternal and child health, social services, and mental health agencies work together the family benefits: "... cooperation, communication, and informal advocacy on behalf of young children can enhance prospects for improved quality of life for children" (Pierson et al., 1984, p. 454).

In Baltimore, the Sinai Hospital Department of Pediatrics, under the leadership of Dr. Barbara Howard, developed a program to meet the

FIGURE 7–2
The hospital and school work together to provide for the child's health, education, and development.

needs of high-risk children (Schorr & Schorr, 1988). Funding was obtained through lead-control and nutrition programs and Head Start. The effort aims to help through (1) a preschool program for at-risk children; (2) nutritional meals; (3) a parent program that focuses on nutrition, meal preparation, and child development advice offered by the University of Maryland Cooperative Extension Service; and (4) parent participation in preschool. The three groups, medical, Head Start, and education join to demonstrate that intervention can be economical as well as effective to reduce the dangers in at-risk families. In the second year of this new program, the children showed noticeable improvement and reduced blood-lead levels. The parents acquired skills and felt less isolated.

The King/Drew Medical Center faced issues in Los Angeles' Watts community by looking at the total environment of the children and families. One physician in the outreach program looks at it this way: "We think of health as not just providing health services. . . . That's why we are in the business of day care and prenatal care and home visits and magnet high schools" (Schorr & Schorr, 1988, p. 110). The Department of Pediatrics collaborates with the high school's program for adolescents and their babies, with a child care program, and classes on child development and parenting. Perhaps, most visionary is the magnet school on the hospital grounds, where 180 students study to become health professionals (Schorr & Schorr, 1988).

BIRMINGHAM MODEL FOR PARENT EDUCATION

The Birmingham Model, based on the premise that mothers learn from other mothers, provided new experiences and skills through modeling, role playing, discussion and self-evaluation.

The Birmingham model worked with mothers from low-income neighborhoods and public housing projects who were recruited by door-to-door canvassing. The participants were randomly assigned to either the program or a control group. Those in the program were given stipends to enable them to attend. Experienced mothers, who encouraged and trained mothers with less experience, learned in the process also. Extensive curriculum material was provided, but the primary resource was the mothers.

The Birmingham Model required participation of the infant from age 3½ months until 36 months of age. Mother and child attended sessions at the center from 9 AM to 1:30 PM, 3 days each week for 9 months. Attendance, thereafter, was increased to 5 days a week. As mothers gained experience, they took on more responsibility in the center, and with this came an increase in pay.

The program had positive results for the children in both cognitive and socioemotional areas. The use of parents as trainees and models reinforced the mother's learning. The program mothers showed a greater degree of sensitivity and responsiveness to their children than did those in the control group. The most interesting aspect of this program, from an educational viewpoint, is that mothers learned from experience and by modeling, as well as from teaching in the program. These are effective learning strategies (Lasater et al., 1975).

SCHOOL ON SATURDAY

School on Saturday? How can it work? Follow the example set by the Ferguson-Florissant School District, St. Louis, Missouri, where home and school have joined hands in partnerships that offer a LINK program, Child Development Centers, Parents as First Teachers program, and a Saturday School. The Saturday School includes two 3-hour preschool sessions on Saturday for children 4 years of age. The program has three major objectives:

- to provide an education program which will help 4-year-old children succeed in school
- to involve the parents in the education of their children
- to provide support for families

These objectives are accomplished by providing

1. Diagnostic screening at the beginning of the school year to establish appropriate goals
2. Half-day preschool held each Saturday in a public school kindergarten
3. Opportunities for participation by the parents in the preschool (Parents must participate every 4 to 6 weeks as a parent helper in the preschool)
4. Home visits, 1 hour each week, with a group of two or three children and their parents
5. Home activity guides that provide ideas for projects and other activities for the 4-year-old and younger siblings to do at home; these activities foster skills needed for success in school
6. Consultants in child development are available to consider specific concerns as well as provide parent meetings

Saturday School works! Children gain in intellectual, language, and visual motor skills. Their parents gain in ability to communicate with their children, use appropriate reinforcement techniques, and sense a child's learning readiness.

The program reaches out to fathers as well as mothers. The curriculum, dealing with motor coordination development, goes hand in hand with positive interaction between child and father (Figure 7–3).

What can other programs gain from the success of the Saturday School? These aspects seem particularly important:

1. Active participation by both parents in teaching their own children
2. Diagnostic and prescriptive activities for children with handicaps
3. Observation and participation by parents in a school setting
4. Guidance and activities that support the parents' efforts
5. Teacher visits to home, which establish a team rapport between teachers and parents

6. Opportunities for the child to experience routine school activities and an enriched curriculum each week
7. Home learning activity booklets to be used by parents of children from birth through age 3

The varied approaches of the Saturday School meet many more needs than does a program that has only one dimension (e.g., preschool without the parent component). This was recognized by the district, and although this program was initially funded with federal money, it proved its value and is now financed by the local school district and supplemented with education funds for the handicapped.

HEAD START

Head Start, a federal program with such credibility that the funding has continued since 1965, is a fine example of a program that involves parents. From its inception Head Start involved the family in its outreach, with spokes of the wheel radiating from the Head Start Center to include dental and health care, resources in the community, nutritional food for the children, and information on career opportunities.

Head Start recognizes parents as the earliest and most influential teachers of young children. Thus, the National Head Start Parent Involvement Task Force was created in 1985. The Task Force was charged with reviewing parent involvement in Head Start with the goal of strengthening that component. This included:

1. Maximizing parent participation in the decision-making process in local programs;
2. Increasing parent participation in Head Start classrooms and other activities;
3. Increasing parents' opportunities to participate in activities which they have helped to develop;
4. Insuring that parents are provided the opportunity to work with their children in cooperation with Head Start staff; and
5. Furthering the ability of parents to sustain and build upon Head Start experiences as their children move into Elementary School (Commissioner's Task Force on Parent Involvement in Head Start, 1987, p. 3).

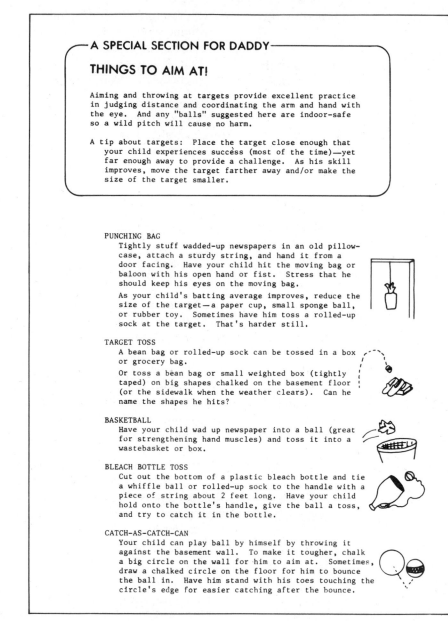

FIGURE 7–3
Fathers are an integral part of the Saturday School. Source: Reprinted with permission from the Ferguson-Florissant School District, St. Louis, Mo.

The Task Force made 21 recommendations for improving all areas of parent involvement and 17 recommendations in the areas of decision making, participation in Head Start classroom and other program activities, opportunities to participate in activities which they initiate and help to develop, opportunities to work with their children in cooperation with staff, and strengthening participation in the transition of children from Head Start to elementary school

(Commissioner's Task Force on Parent Involvement in Head Start, 1987). The thrust of the message from this Task Force is to enable parents to help themselves. Parents can do this only with more education, more options, more knowledge, greater self-esteem, and more empowerment. Although Head Start parents have had more access to parent involvement than most early childhood programs (with perhaps the exception of parent cooperatives), the Task Force encourages a more active commitment to seeing that parent involvement really happens. The minimal requirements needed to assure parent involvement are as follows:

- properly trained staff;
- comprehensive written plan for parent involvement;
- comprehensive parent interviews;
- provision of information about program prior to enrollment;
- the expectation that parents are to participate in the program to be verbalized and reinforced by staff at the time of recruitment and enrollment;
- comprehensive orientation for parents and staff, using a portfolio of information annually for consistency;
- provision of training for parents who observe or volunteer in the classrooms or any other aspects of the program;
- implementation of a buddy system, teaming up veteran parents with more years' experience with the first year parents;
- an organized and duly constituted policy group with at least 50% parents;
- training annually of policy groups, center/classroom committees, and grantee or delegate agency board members;
- ongoing training as necessary;
- opportunities for teaching staff to work with parents outside the classroom;
- posting of minutes of policy group meetings and reporting back to all parents;
- holding policy group meetings at least once monthly and more frequently as necessary;
- having ongoing component committees involving parents;
- providing more incentives and rewards for parent volunteer hours, e.g., gifts, appreciation banquets, luncheons, dinners, parent of the year awards or recognition, parents' names in newsletter, trips, etc.; and

- provision of training for parents on their children's transition to elementary school (Commissioner's Task Force on Parent Involvement in Head Start, 1987, p. 13).

The Task Force's next recommendation suggests that a policy be made that requires parents to be involved with Head Start in some way. That requirement is not viewed as punitive but, rather, as necessary in order to have maximum impact for the parents and preschool children.

Before initiating any parent program, it is wise to ask parents how they perceive their needs. Although needs will change throughout the life of any program, early assessment with periodic review will show the initial needs and the progression of later needs. A sample assessment suggests areas to investigate, as illustrated in a questionnaire directed to parents of Head Start children (Figure 7–4).

After Head Start parents complete the needs assessments, plans for parent participation can be devised with better understanding. As parents become more familiar with the program and more sophisticated in their learning, their needs and requests will vary, so provide a current assessment by continued use of questionnaires.

Decision Making

Head Start programs involve parents at two or three levels of decision making: the Head Start Center Committee, Head Start Policy Committee for the delegate agency, and/or the Head Start Policy Council (for the grantee funded by the federal government). The first is initiated by each center, which should have a committee composed of parents whose children are enrolled.

The policy committee is set up at the agency delegated to administer the Head Start program. At least 50% of the membership must be parents of children presently enrolled in Head Start. This committee is responsible for general administration, personnel, grant applications, and evaluation. The Head Start Policy Council may be this same committee if the agency responsible for running the program is also the grantee. If there are two levels involved (the grantee designates

---

HEAD START PARENT NEEDS ASSESSMENT QUESTIONNAIRE

Name: _____ Date: _____

Address: _____ Center: _____

Phone: _____ Child's Name: _____

1. In my job as a parent I have the hardest time in:

		Very difficult	Somewhat difficult	No problem
a.	Being an only parent	☐	☐	☐
b.	Teaching my child to obey	☐	☐	☐
c.	Providing proper nourishment	☐	☐	☐
d.	Making time to listen and play with my child	☐	☐	☐
e.	Disciplining my child	☐	☐	☐
f.	Having patience and understanding	☐	☐	☐
g.	Understanding my child's growth	☐	☐	☐
h.	Other (specify)_____	☐	☐	☐

2. To do my job better as a parent I would like training in:

		Very important	Somewhat important	Not important
a.	Child growth and development	☐	☐	☐
b.	Bilingual-bicultural education	☐	☐	☐
c.	Nutrition	☐	☐	☐
d.	Child behavior and discipline	☐	☐	☐
e.	First aid	☐	☐	☐
f.	Self-improvement	☐	☐	☐
g.	Home improvement	☐	☐	☐
h.	Techniques in working with the handicapped child	☐	☐	☐
i.	Other (specify)	☐	☐	☐

3. What I expect Head Start to do for my child:
   a. Learn to get along with other children _____
   b. Develop self-confidence _____
   c. Obtain medical and dental screening _____
   d. Other (specify) _____

4. What I expect Head Start to do for me as a parent:

   a. Get to know and understand my child better _____
   b. Become aware of services available for me and my family _____
   c. Develop patience with my child _____

FIGURE 7–4
Head Start Parent Needs Assessment Questionnaire (Source: Modified from R. Littlejohn & Associates. *Involving parents in Head Start: A guide for parent involvement coordinators.* Washington, D.C.: Office of Human Development, 1976.)

another agency to run the program) both levels must have policy councils, formed and run similarly. The essential feature of policy committees and/or policy councils is that both require that 50% of the membership be composed of parents. This requirement has had immense impact on increased involvement of parents in decision making, not only in the Head Start program but also in programs that followed.

d. Understand what my child is learning at school and how I can help him at home _____
e. Get acquainted with teachers and other parents _____
f. Other (specify) _____

5. As a parent, my interest in becoming involved with the Head Start Center is:

a. ☐ In the classroom working with children
b. ☐ In decision-making committees
c. ☐ In working with my child and teacher

6. As a parent my special interests are:
a. ☐ Working with young children
b. ☐ Cooking
c. ☐ Typing
d. ☐ Working on fundraising activities
e. ☐ Planning special occasion parties for the children
f. ☐ Planning parent activities
g. ☐ Music—playing piano, guitar, other

7. When would be the most convenient time for you to attend parent training and meetings:

	Morning	Afternoon	Evening
Monday	☐	☐	☐
Tuesday	☐	☐	☐
Wednesday	☐	☐	☐
Thursday	☐	☐	☐
Friday	☐	☐	☐
Weekends	☐	☐	☐

8. At home we speak mostly:
a. ☐ English
b. ☐ Spanish
c. ☐ Both English and Spanish
d. ☐ Other (specify)

9. Would you prefer parent meetings, workshops, in-service training be held in:
a. ☐ English
b. ☐ Spanish

10. Which day would be most convenient for you to volunteer to ride the bus or volunteer in the classroom:

	Morning	Afternoon
Tuesday	☐	☐
Wednesday	☐	☐
Thursday	☐	☐
Friday	☐	☐

FIGURE 7–4 continued

Parent Satisfaction and Participation

A study of 467 Head Start parents (Service Delivery Assessment study as cited in Hubbell, 1983) showed that most parents were very satisfied with the accomplishments their children made in Head Start. Another study found parents pleased with the help Head Start gave them and their children, and 97% indicated that they would send their younger children to Head Start (Abt Associates study as cited in Hubbell, 1983).

Head Start's services to families resulted in high satisfaction for parents. Parents benefitted most from their improvement of life skills, job training, employment, and satisfaction with life (Hubbell, 1983). The more involved the parents, the greater the return. Those parents felt happier, more satisfied, and more successful. It was easier to involve parents who were better educated and had higher salaries than it was to involve other parents. Those who did not participate fully felt less control over their own lives and powerless to influence their child's school (Hubbell, 1983).

Another study (Lamb-Parker as cited in Hubbell, 1983) compared the mothers' psychological well-being. Those mothers who participated most had less depression and anxiety. Their trust in others increased too. Mothers who lived in better housing and who were less depressed participated more in the Head Start program. These findings point out a problem for all parent programs. Those who are most able, participate the most; those who need the most help, do not participate as fully.

Parent coordinators can help overcome this lack of participation by making a special effort to involve the reticent parent. Show parents that you accept them and their children from the very first day:

- Provide experiences and activities which lead to enhancing the development of their skills, self-confidence, and sense of independence in fostering an environment in which their children can develop to their full potential.
- Provide experiences in child growth and development which will strengthen their role as the primary influence in their children's lives.
- Train parents in observing the growth and development of their children in the home environment and in identifying and handling special developmental needs.
- Help parents understand and use a variety of methods to foster learning and development of their children.
- Include parents in center, classroom, and home program activities.
- Include parents in program planning and curriculum development and have them serve as resource persons.
- Identify and use family and community resources to meet the basic life support needs of the family. (Littlejohn & Associates, 1976, pp. 2–6)

Head Start, initially conceived with a parent component, has integrated parents into every aspect of its program. Visualize the degree of parent involvement in the Head Start program. On a visit to a typical Head Start class, you will find a teacher and aide surrounded by 12 eager 3- and 4-year-olds, working, singing, playing, and laughing. Because the center is located in the community, parents usually bring and pick up their children each day. As they enter the school, teacher and parents exchange pleasant greetings. On some days the parents stay and help.

The teacher may be a college graduate from another neighborhood, but, just as often, the teacher is a local parent who had children enrolled in the Head Start program several years before who has earned a Child Development Associate (CDA) credential. The aide comes up and chats with the parent about something exciting the child did yesterday. The aide knows the child well; she resides in the neighborhood and has children, too. The person responsible for lunch is another community parent. Through a Head Start career ladder, many low-income parents are hired to assist in the program. After lunch the parent coordinator drops in to check on a child who has been ill. The parent coordinator was chosen by the policy committee because the parents respected and liked this neighbor. This person has not failed in establishing rapport with and support for the neighbors. Two of the most essential and greatest strengths of the Head Start philosophy are the involvement of parents and the belief that parents can achieve.

OTHER EFFECTIVE HOME-SCHOOL PROGRAMS

Programs involve parents in a variety of ways. The Richmond, Virginia, Follow Through program is "based on the active involvement of parents in the education of their children. This concept is founded on the premise that patterns of and motives for academic achievement and personal development in primary grade children (K-3) are largely the result of home study influence" (Far West Laboratory, 1983, p. B5–32). Two paraprofessional parent educators are assigned to each Follow Through class. Their time is divided between aiding in the school and visiting the homes of Follow Through children. Each week the classroom teacher demonstrates a home learning activity to the parent educator, who, in turn, teaches the activity to the parent. Ten guiding principles of the teaching-learning process support the teaching behaviors of the teacher and parent. These include using "open-ended questions, positive reinforcements, and the discovery approach to stimulate and expand the intellectual processes of the learner" (Far West Laboratory, 1983, p. B5–32).

The Mathematical Association of America and the National Council of Teachers of Mathematics recommend that parents be involved with their children in their success in and enjoyment of mathematics. They suggest that students discuss their classroom activities and what they have learned with their parents. It helps if parents take an active role and

- provide a place for the student to do homework
- participate in parent-teacher conferences
- encourage their children to persist—not to do the work for them
- engage in activities such as games and puzzles in family time
- visit mathematics classes when given the opportunity

By being aware of the following concepts, parents can complement the efforts of the school.

- mathematics is more than computation—the breadth of mathematic topics from kindergarten to Grade 12
- manipulatives as aids are important as they enable students to gain insight into problems at all grade levels
- how problem-solving is learned at home and school
- reasons for homework
- expectations of schools for their students
- process of working toward a solution rather than just obtaining the correct answer since the process is a lifetime skill
- use of calculators to computers to extend the student's mathematical power
- evaluation and interpretation of student test results
- the textbook is only one strategy in the teaching of mathematics (Mathematical Association of America and National Council of Teachers of Mathematics, 1989).

Families are being encouraged to be active in their educational pursuits through many other avenues. Family Math (EQUALS, 1986) and Family Science (Northwest EQUALS, 1988) are two programs that engage families in hands-on science or math at home. The programs support the school's program from kindergarten to eighth grade. The Family Math classes include materials and activities for parents to use while they help their children with mathematics at home. Meetings, 2 to 3 hours in length, are held one evening each week for a period of 4 to 6 weeks. Children attend the meetings with their parents.

The Family Science program is an outgrowth of Family Math. Activities that use inexpensive and available materials in the home allow parents and children to work on day-to-day science together. The programs' developers hope that minorities and females will be encouraged to develop their abilities in math and science if they learn about them in a nonthreatening environment.

The emphasis on reading is also apparent. *Becoming a Nation of Readers: What Parents Can Do* was prepared to encourage parents to read to and with their children. "Contrary to popular opinion, learning to read does not begin in school. Learning to read begins at home" (Binkley, 1988, p. 1).

The Minnesota Early Childhood Family Education Program offers support and information for parents and children, birth to kindergarten. Although there are variances in the program, the most common model is based on the St. Cloud Seton Hall validated program. Classes of 1½ to 2 hours in length are held once a week during the afternoon, morning, evening, or weekend. Some sessions are even held during lunch time at the work setting. During the first 45 minutes the parents and children are together, participating in learning activities based on a theme. Then the parents and children separate, with the parents going to a parent education session and the children to a preschool setting. The curriculum in the parent session is determined by the needs of the parents.

In addition to the sessions, the programs have resource libraries that include checkouts for toys and books. The program is available for all income levels and all ethnic populations (Kristensen & Bilman, 1987).

Chapter programs, federal programs funded under one of several titles, also illustrate innovative use of parents as partners in the educational process. Needs assessments, parent advisory councils, conferences, and home-school activities are included in typical programs. The Child Parent Center program located in Chicago, Illinois, describes its parent involvement:

CPC activity heavily emphasizes parent involvement, recognizing that the parent is the child's first teacher and that home environment and parental attitude toward school influence a child's academic success. A parent-resource teacher is provided to work solely with parents. Parents are trained to instruct their children at home and are also involved in the school program. (National Dissemination Study Group, 1989, p. I–9)

Parent involvement programs benefit infants and preschool children as well as older children.

In Huntington Beach, California, a Child Development Center identifies developmental needs of children and provides intervention before they enter school. The center is based on the belief that "the sooner educators identify young children's developmental needs and work together with parents to achieve effective intervention, the stronger the chance of children's early success in school" (Far West Laboratory, 1983, p. B5–8).

The Salt Lake City school district implemented a parent cooperative elementary school. PACE, Participating Adults and Children in Education, has parents as partners with the teachers in the classroom. Parents participate each week under the direction of the teacher. They also attend meetings where the curriculum and activities are planned, voting on programs and classroom plans. To become a part of the cooperative, families must contact the parent organization and complete an application, making sure that the children in the cooperative have parents who are able and desirous of being involved with each of their children enrolled in the program. With the added personnel, the school is able to provide many practical application activities, curriculum programs for small groups

of children, and individualized education, allowing each child to master work and move on at her or his own speed. In the process, parents learn about the educational system and their own children's abilities and strengths (Berger, 1988).

The Kate Sullivan School in Tallahassee, Florida holds a "Nooner" program that invites parents to come at lunch once a month. An exceedingly high percentage of parents, 65%, volunteer in the school, contributing more than 8,000 hours of volunteer hours each year. Parents who do not come to school receive an SOS Care visit from aides in their home (U.S. Department of Education, 1987).

In Chambers Elementary School in East Cleveland, Ohio, the community is considered to be part of an extended family. Parents are welcomed to the school. Special events at the school are attended by the parents. In addition, a club was started for students from single-parent families (U.S. Department of Education, 1987).

A Parent Training Program was started in 1985 in Memphis, Tennessee. The program has weekly parent workshops held at schools and other locations that are convenient for the parents. Parent education for parents of elementary school children has been successful (U.S. Department of Education, 1987).

Walter Kudumu, a parent, organized Education Sunday. Ministers in San Diego, California, share their pulpits with educators to encourage parents to be concerned with their children's education. Pledge cards, which mandate that parents encourage success in school for their children, are given out to parents at the church. Successful students are recognized from the pulpit. The church also offers special meetings for parents where they can learn about services such as counseling, screening, and information concerning college requirements and financial aid (U.S. Department of Education, 1987).

Developmental Play, a Title III project, uses a unique approach toward children. The program is based on a "relationship-focused activity-based intervention program for young children and a training model in child development and behavior for participating adults" (National Dissemination Study Group, 1989, p. I–9). Children and adults are paired; they get to know each other through play and expression of warmth and caring. One-half hour of one-to-one child-adult play is followed by group play during circle time and concludes with juice. The basis for this program stems from a belief in human attachment. "Children mature through an intimate or attachment relationship with specific adults. Relationship is everything. Without it, children do not mature and they certainly do not function well in a school setting" (Brody, 1976, p. 1).

These successful programs represent the best in curriculum development. Their concern for parent involvement illustrates the significance of parents in the successful education of their children.

If you want to locate other programs throughout the United States, obtain the most recent edition of *Educational Programs That Work* (National Dissemination Study Group, 1989). The 1989 edition describes 17 programs geared to young children and parent involvement. Davies (1987), Henderson (1987), and Schorr & Schorr (1988) also describe many programs that have been effective in forging home-school partnerships.

HELPING PARENTS WORK WITH THEIR CHILDREN

Warren (1963) lists many excellent ideas for parents to use in working with their children or in working with the schools. In the introduction she states:

You will notice, not one of the methods in this book involves parents taking over the job of teacher. Not one sets the parent to work doing complicated mathematics problems or actually teaching the child to read. That is the teacher's job, and unless you have been trained to teach, educators say, you may do your child more harm than good by trying. (Warren, 1963, p. x)

Warren was reflecting the beliefs of the time. The National Association of State Boards of Education (1988) reflects a change in attitude toward parent involvement. Its report focuses on two issues (1) the need for partnership between parents and schools, and (2) developmentally appropriate curriculum. The Task Force believed that programs serving preschool through grade 3 should

- promote an environment in which parents are valued as primary influences in their children's lives and are essential partners in the education of their children.
- recognize that the self-esteem of parents is integral to the development of the child and should be enhanced by the parents' positive interaction with the school.
- include parents in decisionmaking about their own child and on the overall early childhood program.
- assure opportunities and access for parents to observe and volunteer in the classrooms.
- promote exchange of information and ideas between parents and teachers which will benefit the child.
- provide a gradual and supportive transition process from home to school for those young children entering school for the first time. (National Association of State Boards of Education, 1988, p. 19)

To accomplish these objectives, both the school district and local school should have strategies for parent involvement. Parents should be involved in decisionmaking on program policy, curriculum, and evaluation. There should be communication between the parents and school. Parents should be encouraged to be teachers of their children at home and have opportunities to observe and volunteer in the classroom. The NASBE report also stressed provisions for the incremental transitions between home and school when the child first enters the public school.

The Task Force suggested in-service training concerning parent involvement for administrators and teachers. Time for teachers to plan and carry out home visits was recommended. Home activities and materials for parents to use with their children at home should be provided. Local businesses should be encouraged to provide release time for parents to enable them to attend parent-teacher conferences and volunteer in the classroom. Schools should provide leadership in developing family support services in collaboration with existing community agencies. And with this strong statement of cooperation between home and school, the Task Force supports provision of sufficient staff, training, and time to work together (National Association of State Boards of Education, 1988).

Children learn best when they are actively involved. The idea of home-school cooperation does not include viewing the parent as a taskmaster intent on forcing the child to learn. Instead, the parent is viewed as a responsive, alert facilitator. Piaget (1976) insists that learning stems from the active involvement of the person doing the inventing; once invented, the theory and/or steps are not forgotten. Piaget recommends:

The use of active methods which give broad scope to the spontaneous research of the child or adolescent and require that every new truth to be learned be rediscovered or at least reconstructed by the student and not simply imparted to him. (pp. 15, 16)

Experiential activities that afford children an opportunity to learn by discovery are facilitated best in a relaxed, natural, and rich learning environment. The setting can be either in the home or in the community. The steps to developing a home learning activity, based on Gordon's program in Florida (Gordon & Breivogel, 1976), reflect the use of the natural environment (see Chapter 8). Many of the ideas for home learning activities can be enjoyed by both parents and children. Most of the summer activities suggested by Saturday School are based on situations and opportunities that emerge or are always present if the parent just takes the time to spend a moment with the child (Figure 7–5). Most important is the attitude that learning is possible everywhere for the child.

Resources in the Home

The home is a learning center. Children learn to talk without formal instruction. They learn as they interact with others and participate in exciting events. Learning tasks at home can and should be an intriguing activity rather than difficult paperwork. A parent who reads stories to children is actually teaching reading. The development of an interest in and love of reading is the first step toward acquisition of proficient reading skills. Projects around the home can furnish experiences in math, language, art, music, science, and composition. The process of exploring an idea and carrying it to fruition requires problem solving. Ideas for activities around the home and in the community are restricted only by the imagination.

Activities at Home

Brainstorm for a moment about all the learning opportunities available in a home. Record the ideas to use with your children or to share with parents. The following ideas may lead to many more:

- *Art.* Have tempera paint, crayons, and clay available for spontaneous art projects. Try painting outdoors with water.
- *Write a family newsletter.* Write a cooperative newsletter for the neighborhood or relatives. Make a form with areas for writ-

ings by each person or descriptions of each project. Let someone fill in the information.

- *Games.* Take time to play games. The list is long; use commercial games or home-made games such as Concentration, hopscotch, jacks, jump rope, basketball, Ping-Pong, toss a ball, Lotto, Monopoly, Boggle, anagrams, and matching.
- *Garage sale.* Have a garage sale and let your child be the cashier.

Activities Away from Home

Trips around and away from home can also be adventures.

- *Take a walk.* Collect water from a stream or puddle. Examine the water through a microscope when you return home. Describe or draw the creatures found in a drop of water.
- *Visit the grocery store, post office, department or hardware stores.* Before going to a store, make out your shopping list with your child. Keep it simple. Let the child help with selection and cost of the products.
- *Explore art, natural history, historical, or specialty museums.* In museums you may find pictures or artifacts that lend themselves to artwork at home. To increase observation powers, let the child look for something specific, such as a color or materials. Talk about how the art materials were used, or which shapes were selected.
- *Visit historical buildings.* Take along your paper, pen, and crayons. Engage in art activities as you visit. Draw the shape of the building. Make a crayon rubbing of the placard that tells about the building's dedication.
- *Garage sale.* Visit garage sales and figure how many articles you could buy for $5 or $10.

Using activities that are intriguing and exciting benefits the family in two ways: (1) learning is accomplished and (2) the parent-child relationship is enhanced. Parents need to know the importance of a rich home environment; they need to be reinforced for their positive teaching behaviors. Although good times together may be reinforcement enough, schools can help support productive parent-child interaction by encouraging parents, offering workshops, and supplying home learning activities.

Workshops for Parents

A workshop is one vehicle for introducing parents to home-school learning activities. Ann Grimes, first grade teacher, invited the parents of her students to such a workshop. She greeted them, gave out nametags, and passed out a get acquainted signature sheet (see Figure 6 3). The evening went by quickly. After the signature game, during which parents enthusiastically talked with one another, the make-and-take workshop began. Mrs. Grimes explained the program, its philosophy, and what the school expected of the parents. She assured the parents that close two-way communication helps ensure that the program is meeting the needs of the child, parent, and school. If parents were interested in participating in a home-school learning project, she assured them that she would like to work with them as a member of the team.

Mrs. Grimes reminded the parents of how important it is to listen to children, to ask open ended questions, and to allow the children the opportunity to predict and problem solve. She also reminded the parents that children, like adults, work best when they have a nice, quiet, private work area and a regular time in which to work. She stressed that children are expected to enjoy and be successful at home assignments. If the child struggles with more than 20% of the projects or problems, reassessment of the activities enables the selection of appropriate activities geared to the child's level. Many home activities can be recreational and enriching to family life. As she concluded her talk, she explained the plans for the evening. Parents were asked to participate in the center activities located in different areas throughout the room. "If you will look at your nametag, you will find a number. Go to that activity first," she instructed the parents.

ME!

Home Activities

Dear Parent and Partner:

If you feel concerned about joining us as a teaching partner, relax! We consider it our pleasure to join you. After all, who knows your child better than you? Who better than you can read your child's moods and know when it's time to introduce something new, or when it's time to stop because he's had enough. And who, after all, has been his teacher for the past four years? YOU!

You have just what we look for in a teacher—experience and caring about the child. The only thing you need are ideas, and that's what this weekly Home Activity Guide is designed to supply. The activities in the guides will be divided into three sections: Explore and Discover, Listen and Understand, Apply and Express. There is a sequence to learning. First, children learn best when they use their five senses to *explore* and *discover* in a relaxed environment. Next, children need lots of opportunities to *listen* to information before they *understand* new concepts. Finally, they are ready to *apply* and *express* what they have learned by speaking, acting out, writing and drawing. You'll find we actually suggest

more ideas than we expect you to use, so you and your child's other teacher can decide which ones are best suited for your child.

Most of the activities require only "throw-away" household items which can be recycled for learning. Some require no materials at all. Sometimes just providing crayons and paper, a little how-to advice and a lot of praise is all there is to it. In fact, some of your best teaching can be done while you're doing something else. That's why we purposely will suggest some learning kinds of things to do while you're at it—while you're sorting clothes, cooking supper, riding in the car or shopping at the store.

But no matter where you are or what you are teaching, keep it fun! The game-like activities should be a pleasure for both of you. For while you are teaching your child that round things are called circles, you're also teaching him something far more important—*that learning is a joy.*

We look forward to working with you this year and sharing the pleasure of seeing your child grow.

Ferguson-Florissant School District

Apply and Express

Children need opportunities to apply their new knowledge and express it in various ways.

Create a Handbook

Ask your child to show you how many things he can do with his hands.

Cut out pictures in magazines of people using their hands in different ways. Your child can paste one picture on each page to make a book. Let him tell you what the people in the pictures are doing and write down his answer. You can do the same with feet!

Tear Your Hair

Encourage your child to draw a picture of his face. *He can then* tear tiny bits of colored paper to glue on for hair. Tearing helps develop muscles in the fingers that are used for writing.

Ears, Nose, Fingers, Toes

Talk to your child about how many body parts he has. How many eyes do you have? How many fingers do you have, etc. Touch and count them. Do you have more fingers or ears? Do you have less toes or legs? Less is a difficult skill and your child may need practice. To challenge your child further, talk about pairs of body parts. A pair means two of the same thing.

It's In the Bag

Choose different clothing worn by different members of the family and place in a large brown grocery bag. You and your child can take turns picking an item of clothing. Tell on which part or parts of the body the clothing is worn.

To make this more challenging, talk about clothing worn above or below the waist.

Bump a Pair

Play bump a pair with your child. Call out a pair of body parts and you and your child must bump those parts together. Say:

• Bump hips
• Bump hands
• Bump feet
• Bump knees
• Bump elbows
• Bump shoulders
• Bump wrists
• Bump big toes
• Bump big thumbs

Notes to Parents

Your child is special. There is no one exactly like him. He's a very unique person. He needs to know that. You'll be helping your child develop what psychologists call self-awareness by doing activities with him.

Activities that will help him:

• Appreciate more fully how amazing his body is.
• Understand his feelings and emotions.
• Learn the names of body parts.
• Gain an understanding of what each body part can do.
• Learn to listen and enjoy books.

Early Education

Listen and Understand

Remember, children need lots of opportunities to listen to information before they understand new concepts.

Look What I Can Do!

Is your child fully aware of the amazing things her body can do? Does she know the function of all her body parts? (See list).

In front of a large mirror, let your child see herself walk, run, jump, sit, bend, move her arms all about. Then, one by one, talk about each body part: what it can do and what would happen if the body part did *not* do its job. For example:

What does the *neck* do? Turn your head back and forth. See the neck move? Hold your neck stiff. Can the head turn? Look up? Down?

Note to Parents

Learning to listen is important for your child. Reading aloud develops this skill. Each week your child will pick a library book which you can read to him. Reading aloud develops a feeling of closeness between parent and child. It makes him feel special.

Research shows that reading aloud to your child is the best way to help him be a good reader later on and to develop a love of reading.

What does the *elbow* do? Eat a cookie. See the elbow bend? Hold your arm stiff. Can you get your hand to your mouth to eat?

Different Parts of the Body and Their Function:

Teach these body parts first.

Ears – hearing
Nose – smelling, breathing
Mouth, Lips, Tongue, Teeth – eating talking

Arm – reaching, holding
Hand, Fingers – picks up, holds
Legs – stand, walk, run, climb
Feet – walk, stand, run, jump
Trunk – bends twists, stretches
Skin – covers body
Head – thinks
Hair – covers head
Eyelashes – protect eyes
Eyebrows – shows expression
Chin – allows mouth to open and close
Neck – moves head
Elbow – lets arm bend
Wrist – turns hand
Knees – helps legs bend
Toes – helps us stand, walk
Ankles – helps us bend foot
Heels – helps us walk and balance

Head
Ears
Neck
Arm
Hand, Fingers

Explore and Discover

Children learn best when given an opportunity to explore.

Look At Me

Before a large mirror, have your child take a look at herself—front, side, back. Can she point to parts of her body? Which can she name? Which does she need to learn? One by one, teach her the parts she cannot name in this way:

• Touch her body part as you name it. Always have her repeat after you – "Elbow."

• Then say, "Show me *my* elbow. Show me *your* elbow."

• Touch her elbow and ask, "What is this?" Can she name it? Then with eyes closed, can she name the part you touch?

Let's Explore Movement

It's important for children to be creative problem-solvers. You can give your child some problems he can solve using different body movements.

Ask him

• How many ways can you move your hand? Foot? Ex., shake, make a fist, wave.

• How many body parts can you move up and down?

• How many parts can you bend?

Give your child time to think of ways to move. Encourage him to show you more ways.

Make A Face

Present situations to your child and ask him to show you with his face how he would feel (happy, sad).

Ask him to look into a mirror when he makes faces. Examples are:

• If Grandma gave you a present.
• If you cut your finger.
• If you went to a carnival.
• If mom or dad left you with a sitter.
• If you broke a toy.

Can he then tell you how he feels using the words "happy" or "sad?"

What's Inside of Me?

Have your child feel her own heartbeat for a while; then ask her to tap out the rhythm with her hand or foot. Have her hop around the room and then feel her heartbeat again. Is it faster or slower? Sit down quietly for a while. Is it still the same?

Show her other places where she can feel the beat of her heart (called pulses). The temple (by the eyebrows), the wrist, the right and left side of the throat. Have her feel yours, too. Do they beat at the same rhythm as yours?

Other Invisible Parts: There are invisible parts inside of your child she can't see but can feel. Have her feel some of them:

-Bones in her wrist, elbow, knee, ankle.
-Her throat as she swallows.
-Her jaws as she opens and closes her mouth. Can she hear her mouth open and close?

FIGURE 7–5
Home activities that help parents collaborate with the schools. (Source: Reprinted with permission from Ferguson-Florissant School District, St. Louis, Mo.)

The centers in the room included games and activities as well as directions on how to play them. Materials and guidelines were also available for activities that could be constructed by parents and taken home. Parents played Concentration (Figure 8–2B), and made game boards. They found that game boards could be constructed easily on cardboard, posterboard, or a file folder. Mrs. Grimes furnished stickers that the parents could place on the game boards for decoration. To protect the completed board, some parents used the laminating machine, and others spread clear, adhesive paper over their work. Each board was different, yet each was based on the same format, that is, squares on which the children placed symbols as they used a spinner or die to tell them how many spaces to go forward. Some parents wrote letters or numbers on the spaces; others developed cards that children could take as they had a turn. If the spaces were left empty, the board could be used for many skill activities by developing sets of cards for phonics, numbers, or other basic skills. Figure 7–6 illustrates a completed game board that can be used to develop many different skills. While some parents were busy with the game boards, others worked on language and math concepts, constructed books, or plied their creativity at the art center.

After a busy 2-hour session the group met again, and an animated discussion of the activities began. Two parents volunteered to make canvas tote bags for the class, and another promised to make a silk-screen print of the class emblem on each. They decided that the tote bags would be reserved for home learning adventures.

"Please be sure to evaluate the home learning activities as you use them. And, please contribute your own ideas," encouraged Mrs. Grimes. "I'll keep track of each child's activities on these record sheets. If you have any questions, be sure to write or call me."

After refreshments the parents began to leave. Some stopped by the table to sign up to volunteer in the program. Mrs. Grimes recognized that she would need help in implementing the home learning program and that she could use help in the room as well. A volunteer training session was planned for the next week; the work toward a productive home-school endeavor had just begun.

Implementation of Home Learning Activities

Home learning activities can be useful as enrichment projects, such as those described in the section Activities at Home, or they can be valuable as a sequential educational curriculum. If they are used to complement the learning that is occurring simultaneously in the school, it is necessary to monitor the child's work at home and, thereby, keep track of what is accomplished.

The process varies according to the availability of a parent coordinator. If parent coordinators are available, it will be their responsibility to keep track of the home learning activities. They can contact parents, make home visits, and report on the progress of each child. It is the teacher's responsibility to advise the parent coordinator about the child's progress in school and to recommend appropriate learning activities. If a parent coordinator is not available, a parent volunteer can help with recordkeeping and provide contact between the parents and the teacher. The following steps are appropriate for either situation:

1. Offer an orientation workshop.

2. Send learning activities home in a tote bag, deliver them personally, or give the responsibility of the delivery system to a parent coordinator.

3. Keep records of activity cards the child has taken home. Make a record card for each child with a space to indicate when each activity went home and a space for response to the activity. In this way you will know which activity the child should be given next.

4. Get feedback from parents via notes, reports, phone calls, or visits. Find out their reactions to the activities and their assessments of their child's success.

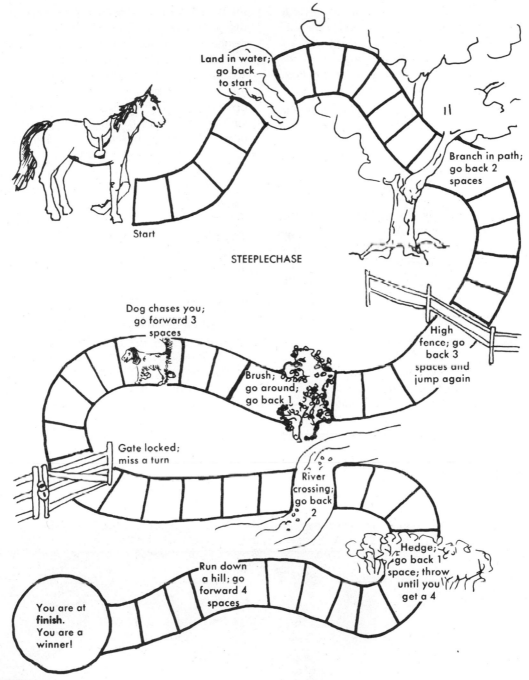

Land in water; go back to start

Branch in path; go back 2 spaces

Start

STEEPLECHASE

High fence; go back 3 spaces and jump again

Dog chases you; go forward 3 spaces

Brush; go around; go back 1

Gate locked; miss a turn

River crossing; go back 2

Hedge; go back 1 space; throw until you get a 4

Run down a hill; go forward 4 spaces

You are at **finish.** You are a winner!

FIGURE 7–6

A steeplechase sets the theme for this game board. Children can suggest their special interests, and games can be developed from their ideas.

5. Continue dialogue with parents. Include supplemental ideas and activity sheets on a skill that proved difficult for a particular student. Ask parents to reinforce skills leading up to the too-difficult level. Have them refer to previous activity cards for related projects.

6. Diversify your program to meet the needs of the parents and keep the interest level high.

7. Have an occasional meeting with parents or make home visits to support the monitoring system.

Communication is a basic ingredient in the success of home-school cooperation. Through talking with parents, you will know whether they consider home learning activities to be a joy or a threat. You will want to adapt your program according to each parent's desires.

REACHING RETICENT PARENTS

Perseverance, patience, and true interest in the parent are the three best ingredients to overcome parent reticence. Understanding, support, and interest will usually encourage the retiring parent to take that first step toward collaborating with the teacher for the good of the child. In every situation, a few parents may refuse to be involved. Some may have serious social adjust-ment problems and need professional help in that area. One difficult parent or one bad experience should not color the home visitor or teacher's commitment of working with others. Teachers should not expect to be 100% successful. Do what can be done and acknowledge possible inability to reach all parents. Do this with grace, understanding, and no recriminations. Work with the children and involve the parents who want to be involved.

If you follow the ideas presented in Chapters 4 and 5, you will probably have no difficulty in communicating with parents. Remember, a call from the teacher or home visitor should not always mean that a child is in trouble. If good communication and support has been established, that call could mean that the child is terrific.

Involving parents may be difficult because of the following reasons:

1. *Families and Parents May Be Under a Lot of Stress.* Problems can range from lack of money, illness of a loved one, unemployment, to an argument with a friend. In our high-charged society, many parents are under stress. It is possible that they cannot be actively involved at the time of hardship. They should not be made to feel guilty. Let them know you are supportive and whenever they want to be more actively involved, they may. Keep communication open through telephone calls.

Teachers enrich their school programs by collaborating with parents.

2. *Many Hard-to-reach Parents Feel Out of Their Element Whether Coming to School or Receiving Home Visitors.* They are not sure of themselves. They do not have confidence in their own ideas, or they feel that someone else will not value them. They need their self-esteem and level of trust raised. If they have the time, let them contribute in a small way. Accept their ideas. Enlist their help in an activity at which they will succeed. Build slowly; it takes time to make a change.

3. *The Parents Do Not Recognize Their Importance in the Education of Their Child.* Many parents, both those in special programs such as Home Start and Head Start and those who live in very affluent areas, do not recognize their importance as educators. Their interest and involvement are important to the child. Starting with parent-teacher conferences or home visits, the teacher needs to reflect that the parent is a true partner. The parents' knowledge about the child is important; they are the best experts on their child. Their interaction with the child is part of the child's education.

4. *"The Parent Doesn't Believe Anyone Has No Ulterior Motives"* (Honig, 1979; p. 58). According to Honig, these parents do not believe that anyone can value their ideas. Trust will build slowly. Find out parents' goals and help them accomplish them.

5. *In Working with Parents, You Need to Know Them Well.* Be able to suggest projects and activities that lend themselves to the capabilities of the parent. In one program where a home visitor was working with an abusive parent, it was suggested that the child was not using the right arm enough. At the next week's class, the home visitor found bruises up and down the child's arm. The parent, who was concerned about the teacher's comment, was "developing" the child's arm! This may seem extreme, but the response demonstrated the parent's ability to cope with everyday problems and to nurture children in appropriate ways. The parent actually wanted the child to do well. Some parents cannot work well with their children or help

with school work. They become frustrated and angry; the child responds with dejection and hurt. Rather than helping the child, the parent creates a battleground.

In working with reticent parents, develop effective strategies. Honig (1979) suggested the use of a 24-hour Crisis Center with project staff, perhaps psychiatric interns, recruited to give telephone counseling, reassurance, and referrals. A second idea was a retreat house in the countryside where families could go and, under the guidance of a staff, discuss and learn as well as have fun and food. Honig's third suggestion described a workshop where, working together, new trust could be promoted (p. 58).

It is helpful to have training sessions for parents where techniques and suggestions for working positively with the child are discussed. The STEP and PET programs give methods for communicating with children (see Chapter 6). These programs have planned programs for parents. Filmstrips and videotapes also illustrate parenting skills and parents as teachers. These resources can serve as a guide in setting up sessions on working with children. Parents also learn through modeling. Aiding in the classroom can be an effective learning experience. Methods of teaching that provide for observation, demonstration, and role playing prove useful. Parents, like children, learn best through active participation.

Prevention is far better than a cure. That is why it is important to reach reticent parents when their children are young. If parents can be involved from the start, their resistance to programs and partnerships can be reduced or eliminated.

PARENT EDUCATION FOR TEENAGERS

A powerful time for reaching new parents and parents-to-be is during adolescence. The alarming rise in the number of teenage pregnancies and the lack of parenting education directed to that age group prompted funding for development of appropriate curricula for teenage students and passage of the Adolescent Health, Services, and Pregnancy Prevention and Child Care Act of 1978. Since that time many schools have responded by offering programs for young mothers that include childcare for the children and special classes for the parents.

In 1986, out of 1 million pregnancies, 179,000 were to girls younger than 17, and 10,000 were to children 14 or younger (Children's Defense Fund, 1989). In the United States, one out of every 10 young women aged 15 to 19 becomes pregnant each year. Of these, 92% of premarital pregnancies and half of those to married girls, were unintended. In 1988 there were about 9,000 births and 14,000 abortions among females younger than 15. Among those aged 15 to 17, there were 161,000 births and 162,000 abortions. Half of these were to women who were unmarried and poor (Trussell, 1988, p. 263).

These figures point out the large number of young parents, married and unmarried, who need parent education. Lack of education makes assuming financial responsibilities more difficult for the young parent. Pregnant teenagers often receive inadequate prenatal health care, so they run a greater risk of producing infants with neurological problems, mental retardation, low birth weight or an infectious disease. Additionally, there is a higher mortality rate for baby and mother.

Over the years individual school systems have developed excellent family life programs for their students, usually in home economics and sociology classes. Schools are beginning to recognize that human development courses and child care experiences are an essential part of the curriculum. In addition, schools are mandated to allow pregnant girls to attend classes. Title IX of the Education Amendments of 1972 prohibits exclusion from any school receiving federal money on the basis of pregnancy or related conditions.

Some schools, through child care centers, allow new parents in their student bodies to bring their children to school with them. Bolstered by encouragement and understanding

and equipped with knowledge of parenting skills, the young parents are better able to care for their infants.

Teenagers without these opportunities and without positive models in their own homes face the enormous task of childrearing unprepared. Expectations by some young parents for their infant's development are often unreasonable; for example, some teenagers believe that infants should be completely toilet trained by 8 months. Understanding and knowledge of child development smooth the way for effective childrearing. Providing support and mechanisms that allow teenagers to become self-sufficient parents is essential. The problems are evident; teenage parents need special attention, skillful direction, and sensitive support.

Curriculum Development

The U.S. Department of Health, Education and Welfare funded development of an approach to parent education for teens. One program, *Exploring Childhood,* has specific curricula for junior and senior high students. The second, *Exploring Parenting,* has 20 sessions for parent education groups. The sessions range from Getting Involved in Your Child's World to Coping with Fear and Child's Play (U.S. Department of Health and Human Services, 1980). In addition, *Education for Parenthood—Curriculum and Evaluation Guide* uses the wisdom and experience of organizations that have traditionally worked with youth—that is, Boy Scouts of America, Boys' Club of America, National 4-H Club Foundation of America, Girl Scouts of USA, National Federation of Settlements and Neighborhood Centers, Salvation Army, and Save the Children Federations—to develop a resource book for use by agencies and schools in working with young parents. The third component was the establishment of a Parent/Early Childhood and Special Program center for resources and help in the development of individualized programs across the nation.

The first component, *Exploring Childhood,* divides the curricula into three modules: family and society, seeing development, and working with children. Each module has booklets, films, posters, records, cassettes, and filmstrips to support parts of the curricula. The techniques and materials are shown in Figure 7–7. By examining the titles within each module, you may see the development of a curriculum that illustrates family life, the development of children, and how to work with children.

Programs for Young Parents

In San Francisco and Lawndale, California, Teenage Pregnancy and Parenting (TAPP) programs help teen parents. TAPP coordinates agencies to provide young parents with access to education, health services, and social services. Sixty percent of those enrolled in TAPP continue in school after the birth of their children compared to only 20% of those without its services (Children's Defense Fund, 1989).

New Jersey schools provide a School-Based Youth Services Program, preventive services for youth 13 to 19 years of age. Support services help at-risk students from using drugs, dropping out of school, developing mental illness, or becoming pregnant. The program is located in or near 29 school districts and is managed by community-based agencies (Children's Defense Fund, 1989).

These types of programs are needed to help teens take control of their lives. Teen pregnancy affects all economic groups of the society. For example, two-thirds of teen births occur to nonpoor white teens who do not live in large cities. The greatest proportion of pregnancies, however, occur among poor disenfranchised youth. "There is an established relationship between poverty, limited schooling and life options, and early parenthood" (Children's Defense Fund, 1989, p. 93).

Agnes, age 15, is pregnant. Her mother is not aware of the impending birth, and Agnes, in tears, confides to her friend at school. Where should she turn? Mary, age 14 and pregnant, wants to marry her boyfriend, Tom, also 14. Tom is still in school. "If I quit," he says, "where will I get a job? Are you sure you want to have the baby?" Problems and early teenage pregnancies go hand in hand. The young teenager who lives in a city with adequate facilities and programs geared to the young mother is very fortunate. If Agnes and Mary lived in Albuquerque, they could attend the New Futures School for school-age parents, a program geared for young

Young children need parents who understand child growth and development.

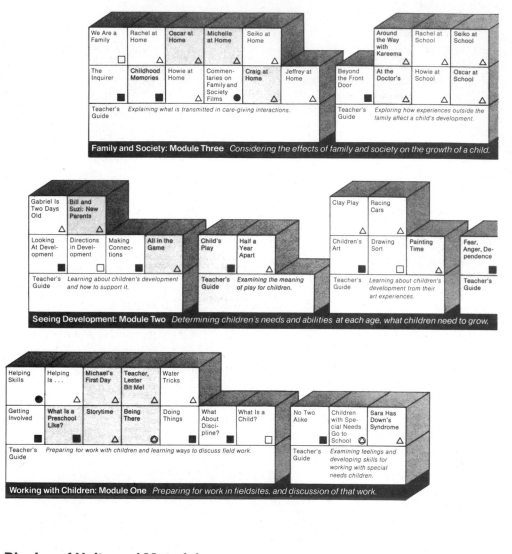

Display of Units and Materials

Key

■ Booklet	△ Film	Filmstrip
□ Poster	● Record	◓ and Record
▨ Cards	▲ Cassette	

FIGURE 7–7

The basic curriculum and material available for implementation of the Exploring Childhood program. (Source: Exploring Childhood. *Program overview and catalog of materials.* Education Development Center, Newton, Mass., 1979.)

mothers, grades 8 through 12. Child care for the children is provided while the young mothers attend classes. The program also provides health services, instruction in health care, nutrition, family living, child development, family planning, and homemaking (*Hearings Before Committee on Human Resources,* 1978).

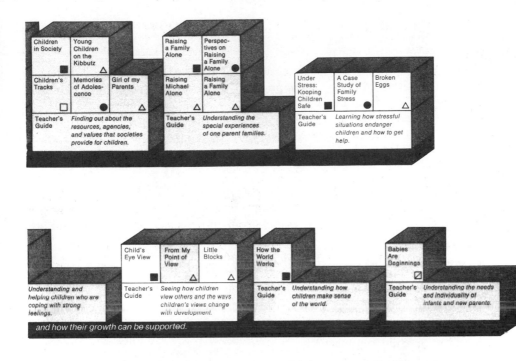

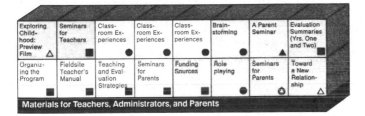

Classroom Set
(Full Year Course Selection)

Supplementary Materials

Individual items of print and media are arranged into three modules for classroom use. The white boxes represent items included in the "classroom set" as listed on page 34.

FIGURE 7–7 continued

Planned Parenthood and public health departments offer additional support systems for the young parent. Health departments are also available to schools as educational resources. Working together, these programs offer the support system needed by young parents.

Opposition to School Involvement

A major deterrent to the widespread success of parent education and family life courses is public opposition to teaching values in the schools. State legislators, concerned with the rising number of teenage pregnancies and the high divorce rate among young people, have presented bills that would require family life education. Such bills, however, have been defeated by fear of and opposition to such courses. The perennial question of responsibility emerges. Should the school step in and require programs, or are parents responsible for teaching their children about sex and family life? At which level should programs be implemented? A surprising number of elementary school students are becoming pregnant. Elective courses in family life tend to be accepted by the public; sex education for younger children faces brisk opposition. If parents are shown the material to be presented and are given the right to determine whether their child should participate, the sex education program usually wins approval.

Schools and social agencies do not oppose parent involvement in the education of the child in family life, sex education, or child rearing. Instead, they applaud such efforts. The stalemate exists, however, because many parents do not assume the responsibility or feel comfortable doing so, yet they are unwilling to let the schools assume it. The problem continues; its solution is thwarted by a vicious circle of fear, inaction, apathy, and resistance.

Perhaps in the future the crisis will be met by enlightened school districts, clubs, churches, parents, and agencies. Three outcomes, although possible, seem improbable:

1. Citizens will recognize the problems and educate themselves and their children.

2. Schools will be mandated to provide family life and sex education.

3. Schools will make family life and childrearing courses so exciting and relevant to the students' lives that the students will insist on taking them.

None of these outcomes looks as though it will be realized in the near future. Schools, however, can and are developing courses that are attracting a number of secondary students; other agencies also are responding to the challenge.

MAKING PROGRAMS HAPPEN

"How can parent programs be started?" This question can be answered from two different approaches, both related to financing. Funding can be obtained to initiate a parent program, or the individual district, school, or teacher can design a program with or without financial support.

Funding

Funding for school-related programs primarily comes from three major sources, federal and state grants, private foundations, and local school budgets. A public school's budget is based on local taxes and state distribution of funds. Private schools rely primarily on tuition and private sources to provide their budgets, although some federal grants can be obtained. Current information on funding and grant possibilities can be obtained from your regional Department of Education or Department of Health and Human Services.

The most stable funding source for public schools is the local school board. As schools begin to view the parent component as worthwhile or essential, more programs will be implemented and funded through local support. Private foundations also fund special projects for parents and children. Local businesses and foundations are probably the best source of funds and/or information on moneys available in your community.

Most grants are provided for a particular time period, usually 3 years. If the program is dependent on the extra grant funding, plans must be made for financing after the grant runs out, or the program will either deteriorate or no longer exist. The major importance of grants is the impetus they provide for developing programs, materials, and services. Many programs, now a permanent part of the community, were started on grants. Try to obtain funding and grants, but if your efforts are not rewarded, consider parent involvement as an integral part of the school program and develop your unique approach to fulfill the potential partnership. Using volunteers in a positive, useful way can help the teacher and enable the school to enrich its educational offerings. Volunteers can be an alternative to funding in making programs happen.

RESOURCES AND SOCIAL AGENCIES

Collaboration between schools and social agencies helps develop the continuity and supply the support that families need. Teachers as well as administrators can offer referrals to social services, recreation districts, libraries, and other public agencies. If the school district does not have a list, the school personnel may contact the Department of Social Services, United Way, Chamber of Commerce, or other civic agencies to obtain a list of community resources. Check to see if there is a clearinghouse in the area. The telephone book and the yellow pages of the telephone book also give listings for the types of services listed here.

Schools and Child Care Centers

Parent Teacher Association or Parent Teacher Organization programs

Parent education offered by public schools or child care

Parent education offered by hospitals and health clinics

STEP, PET, and Active Parenting classes

Adult education offered by private, nonprofit organizations, the public schools, or through the State Department of Education

Alternative education offered through public and/or private schools

Vocational education offered through public schools or Land Grant colleges or universities

Agricultural extension divisions—state specialists and county agents (through Land Grant colleges or universities)

High school equivalency granting programs

Tutoring and homework hot lines provided by schools

School social workers and psychologists

Testing and special placement for children with disabilities

National Education Association state organizations and publications

Libraries

Libraries usually offer the following:

Weekly story hours for children

Talking books, tape recorders

Bookmobiles

Seminars and discussion groups

Opportunity to check out books, paintings, filmstrips, slides, videos, recordings

Librarians who can help in selection of books and help find reference materials

Professional Organizations

There are many organizations that offer conferences, publications, and meetings. A comprehensive list may be found in Appendix E. It includes groups such as the Association for Childhood Education International, Association for Children with Learning Disabilities, International Reading Association, and the National Association for the Education of Young Children.

Community Services

Police and fire departments offer educational classes

YMCA and YWCA offer recreation and educational activities

Museums may provide a variety of education and experiences

Nonprofit Agencies

Family Resource Clearinghouse and United Way can offer references

Alcoholics Anonymous—Al-Anon and Ala-teen provide support for alcoholics and families of alcoholics

Planned Parenthood provides family planning education

Parents Anonymous is a child abuse parent group

Salvation Army provides support, food, clothing, and temporary housing

Churches have many outreach programs

Clothing Banks provide clothing for those in need

Red Cross provides training and emergency services

Health

Maternal and Child Health (look in the telephone book under state and/or national government)

Well-baby clinics, pediatric clinics, and local physicians provide examinations and prescriptions for children

Lamaze classes for pregnant women and their husbands

La Leche League helps those who want to nurse their babies

Mental health associations are organizations that refer, educate, and provide services

Visiting nurses provide service in homes

College and university diagnostic centers

Mental Health

Mental health and child guidance clinics

County mental health clinics offer services

Nonprofit emotional support and suicide prevention groups

Battered women support groups provide support and safe houses for abused and homeless women

Family therapy and Building Family Strengths programs help families

College and university offerings

Social Services

County Department of Social Services/State Department of Social Services—Food Stamps, Aid to Families of Dependent Children, Protective Services for children and adults

Family crisis center

Child abuse councils

National Center for the Prevention of Child Abuse provides education and services

Job Corps helps young people obtain training and jobs

Refugee services provide support for refugee families

If schools and community resources communicate and cooperate with one another, families and children with needs need not slip through the cracks.

SUMMARY

School-based programs that involve parents are varied. After describing a walk through a school committed to parent involvement, this chapter explores school-based programs including the Brookline Early Education Project, Birmingham Model for Parent Education, Ferguson-Florissant Saturday School, and Head Start.

Parents must be supported in home-school involvements. Teachers should share methods of

working with children, hold make-and-take workshops, and develop a home learning activity program. Teachers must work closely with parents in the development of a home-school program. They should know their parents and adapt the program to each family.

Teenage pregnancies and the need for family life education during adolescent years resulted in the development of *Exploring Childhood* and *Edu-*

cation for Parenthood to supplement traditional programs.

Ways that home-school programs can be started are discussed. Many programs are started with grants. If this monetary support is not available, schools can try to increase personnel support by soliciting volunteers.

School-based programs are diversified, but each type of involvement is essential if the needs of families are to be met.

SUGGESTED ACTIVITIES AND DISCUSSIONS

1. Visit a Chapter I program in a public school. Talk with the principal about the parent involvement specifically developed for the Chapter I program.
2. Survey three or four schools that have federal funding. How do the schools differ in their approaches to parent involvement? What are the commonalities? Are there different responses to the various types of funding, for example, Chapter I, Chapter IV-C, Chapter VII, Follow Through, or Right to Read.
3. Design a parent bulletin board that illustrates the various components of the parent program in your classroom.
4. Develop a resource file of games, articles, books, and recycled materials.
5. Hold a workshop in which you have various learning centers, for example, early reading, sorting and classifying, problem solving, creativity, self-esteem, and language development.
6. Make a universal game board and a series of cards to be used with it.
7. Develop activities that parents can use with their children at home.
8. Search the community for resources that can be used in the school. Include specialists, materials, and places to visit.

BIBLIOGRAPHY

Berger, E. H. *Participating Adults and Children in Education.* Salt Lake City, Utah: Site visit, 1988.

Binkley, M. R. *Becoming a nation of readers: What parents can do.* Lexington, Mass.: D. C. Heath and Company, 1988.

Brody, V. *Developmental play.* St. Petersburg, Fla.: All Children's Hospital, 1976.

Chavkin, N. F., & Williams, D. L., Jr. Enhancing parent involvement. *Education and Urban Society, 19* (2), February 1987, pp. 164–184.

Children's Defense Fund. *A vision for America's future.* Washington, D.C.: Author, 1989.

Cochran, M., & Henderson, C. R., Jr. Family matters: Evaluation of the parental empowerment program. In Henderson, A. (Ed.), *The evidence continues to grow.* Columbia, Md.: National Committee for Citizens in Education, 1987.

Commissioner's Task Force on Parent Involvement in Head Start. *Final report: Commissioner's task force on parent involvement in Head Start.* Washington, D.C.: U.S. Department of Health and Human Services, Office of Human Development Services, Administration for Children, Youth and Families, Head Start Bureau, 1987.

Davies, D. Parent involvement in the public schools. *Education and Urban Society, 19* (2), February 1987, pp. 147–163.

Dornbusch, S., Ritter, P., Leiderman, P. H., Roberts, D. F., & Fraleigh, M. The relation of parenting style to adolescent school performance. *Child Development, 58,* 1987, pp. 1244–1257.

Education Development Center. *Exploring Childhood, program overview and catalog of materials.* Newton, Mass.: EDC School and Society Programs, 1979.

Elkind, D. Helping parents make healthy educational choices for their children. *Educational Leadership,* November 1986, pp. 36–38.

———. Superbaby syndrome can lead to elementary school burnout. *Young Children, 42* (3), March 1987, p. 14.

Epstein, J. L. Parent involvement: What research says to administrators. *Education and Urban Society, 19*(2) February 1987, pp. 119–136.

EQUALS. *Family Math.* Berkeley: University of California, 1986.

Far West Laboratory. *Education programs that work.* San Francisco: Far West Laboratory for Educational Research and Development, 1983.

Ferguson-Florissant School District. *Parents as first teachers.* Ferguson, Mo.: Author, 1989.

_____. *Parent-child early education program.* Ferguson, Mo.: Author, 1989.

Gordon, I. J., & Breivogel, W. F. (Eds.). *Building effective home-school relationships.* Boston: Allyn & Bacon, 1976.

Gotts, E. E., & Purnell, R. F. (Eds.) *Education and Urban Society,* 19 (2), February 1987.

Greenberg, P. Parents as partners in young children's development and education: A new American fad? Why does it matter? *Young Children,* 44 (4), May 1989, pp. 61–75.

Hearings before Committee on Human Resources. Adolescent's Health Services and Pregnancy Prevention and Care Act of 1978, Washington, D.C.: U.S. Government Printing Office, 1978.

Henderson, A. T. *The evidence continues to grow.* Columbia, Md.: National Committee for Citizens in Education, 1987.

Honig, A. S. *Parent involvement in early childhood education.* Washington, D.C.: National Association for the Education of Young Children, 1979.

Hubbell, R. *A review of Head Start research since 1970.* (Administration for Children, Youth and Families, Office of Human Development Services, Department of Health and Human Services). Washington, D.C.: U.S. Government Printing Office, 1983.

Kristensen, N. & Billman, J. Supporting parents and young children. *Childhood Education,* 63 (4), April 1987, pp. 276–282.

Lasater, T. M., Briggs, J., Malone, P., Gilliam, C. F., & Weisburg, P. *The Birmingham Model for parent education.* Paper presented at the annual meeting of the Society for Research in Child Development, Denver, Colo., April 1, 1975.

Leipzig, J. Parents as partners. *Day Care and Early Education,* Winter 1987, pp. 36–37.

Littlejohn, R. & Associates. *Involving parents in Head Start: A guide for parent involvement coordinators.* Washington, D.C.: Office of Human Development, 1976.

Mathematical Association of America and National Council of Teachers of Mathematics. *Parent involvement: Essential for success in mathematics.*

Washington, D.C. and Reston, Va.: Authors, January 1989.

Moles, O. C. Who wants parent involvement? Interest, skills, and opportunities among parents and educators. *Education and Urban Society,* 19 (2), February 1987, pp. 137–145.

National Association of State Boards of Education. *Right from the start.* Alexandria, Va.: Author, 1988.

National Dissemination Study Group. *Educational programs that work.* 1140 Boston Avenue, Longmont, CO. 80501: Sopris West Inc., 1989.

Northwest EQUALS. *Family Science.* Portland: Portland State University, 1988.

Packer, A. B., Resnick, M. B., Resnick, J. L., & Wilson, J. M. An elementary school with parents and infants. *Young Children, 55,* January 1979, pp. 4–9.

Piaget, J. *To understand is to invent.* New York: Penguin Books, 1976.

Pierson, D. E., Bronson, M. B., Dromey, E., Swartz, J. P., Tivnan, T., & Walker, D. K. The impact of early education: Measured by classroom observations and teacher ratings of children in kindergarten. *Evaluation Review,* 7 (2), April 1983, pp. 191–216.

Pierson, D. E., Walker, D. K., & Tivnan, T. A school-based program from infancy to kindergarten for children and their parents. *The Personnel and Guidance Journal,* April 1984, pp. 448–455.

Population Reference Bureau. Adolescent pregnancy and childbearing—growing concerns for America. In *Population Bulletin, 31* (2). Washington, D.C.: Population Reference Bureau, 1976.

Sava, S. G. Development, not academics. *Young Children,* 42 (3), March 1987, p. 15.

Schorr, L. B., & Schorr, D. *Within our reach.* New York: Doubleday, 1988.

Seefeldt, C., & Barbour, N. Working with mandates. *Young Children,* 43 (4), May 1988, pp. 4–8.

Teen parents project. Child Development Center, Department of Pediatrics and Child Health and the Institute for Child Development and Family Life. Washington, D.C.: Howard University, 1977.

Trussell, J. Teenage pregnancy in the United States. *Family Planning Perspectives,* 20 (6), November/December 1988, pp. 263–272.

U.S. Department of Education. *What works: Schools that work: Educating disadvantaged children.* Washington, D.C.: U.S. Government Printing Office, 1987.

U.S. Department of Health and Human Services. *A leader's guide to Exploring Parenting.* Washington, D.C.: U.S. Government Printing Office, 1980.

U.S. Department of Health and Human Services, Office of Human Development Services, Administration for Children, Youth and Families, Head Start Bureau. *A guide for operating a home-based child development program.* Washington, D.C.: U.S. Government Printing Office, 1985.

Warren, V. B. *Tested ways to help your child learn.* Englewood Cliffs, N.J.: Prentice-Hall, 1963.

White, B. L. *A parent's guide to the first three years.* Englewood Cliffs, N.J.: Prentice-Hall, 1980.

8

Home-based Programs

As a concerned parent of preschool-age children, did you ever want an educational support system? Would a visit by a paraprofessional home teacher have made you feel less isolated? Perhaps you have never experienced the trials and joys of being a parent of one or more preschool children. Or if you had preschool children, you may have lived near a child development center that your children attended. Yet imagine yourself as a mother of two preschoolers living in the country at least a mile from the next home. Or pretend that you are a parent in a core-city apartment house. Some parents in urban and suburban areas have no more contact with supportive friends than those isolated by distance in the country. Both urban and rural residents, as the first teachers of their children, need the support and knowledge necessary for them to provide an enriched positive environment for their children.

HOME-BASED EDUCATION

In the 1960s several programs chose the home-based parent as their target: HOPE—Appalachia Educational Laboratory Home-Oriented Preschool Education; David Weikart's Ypsilanti High/Scope Infant Education Project, Ypsilanti, Michigan; Phyllis Levenstein's Mother-Child Home Program, New York City; Ira Gordon's Florida Parent Education Program; Susan Gray's home-based program, DARCEE, Nashville, Tennessee; and Ronald Lally's home visitor program, Children's Center, Syracuse University, New York. Some of these focused on families who lived away from the population center, for example, Gordon's home-based program and HOPE. Others worked with parents as an outreach of their center programs (High/Scope Educational Research Foundation). All recognized parents as the child's most important teacher during the formative years.

One Home-based Program

A program initiated in Yakima, Washington, acknowledged the importance of parents as their children's first teachers. This article vividly illustrates how home-based programs make a difference in families' lives.

The Winning Play at Home Base

The Rochas's home, neat and attractive, is modest by almost anyone's standards. A few fall flowers brighten the gravel walk, and a small tricycle that has seen better days lies on its side in the grass announcing the presence of at least one preschooler. From under a bush the family's gray-striped cat lifts an eyelid as a visitor approaches.

Home visitors are sometimes the only contact a parent has with anyone outside the home.

Plump, dark-haired Mrs. Rochas responds immediately to the knock, hampered only slightly by her 2½-year-old son Benjie, who manages to cling to her knee while keeping one finger in his mouth. "Hi, Jean. Come in," says Mrs. Rochas, with a smile almost as wide as the door she swings open to permit her caller to enter the small living room. As Mrs. Rochas gently eases Benjie back toward his toy collection in the corner, she tells Jean that Margaretta, her daughter who is almost 4, is still napping.

"That's fine, don't disturb her," Jean, a paraprofessional parent-educator, replies before she settles on the davenport and begins pulling some materials from her shopping bag—a stack of index cards, several old magazines, a pair of scissors, and a tube of glue.

The casual banter notwithstanding, some serious business is at hand: Mrs. Rochas is about to undergo a lesson that marks the beginning of her second "school year." She is one of 200 parents in Yakima, a central Washington community of 49,000, who are learning how to teach their own preschool children through Project Home Base, a pioneer early childhood education program. Depending on how well she learns her weekly lessons, she could have a positive and lasting effect on her child's performance in school.

Like many Home Base families, the Rochases were lured to the area from northern California during the previous fall by the promise of better wages in Yakima's fruit industry. Soon afterward they were visited by a representative from the Home Base project, who explained that all parents of children aged 8 months to 4 years in their neighborhood were being given an opportunity for special, federally sponsored training to enable them to help their preschoolers prepare for school. The Rochases were enthusiastic, but even while accepting the invitation, Mrs. Rochas had a number of doubts. Among them, her daughter (then 3 years old) did not always "take to strangers" and Benjie was still "just a baby." But as the weeks passed and the home-visitor became a familiar and friendly face, the doubts disappeared.

A half hour goes by and Margaretta awakens from her nap. Still sleepy, she enters the living room to find her mother busily engaged in a game of "Concentration." This particular exercise calls for pasting pictures of "like" objects, cut from magazines, onto cards to create a series of pairs. The cards, bearing pictures of various animals and buildings, are then shuffled and placed face down in rows. The game begins with a player picking up a card and trying to match it with a second. If no match results, both cards are returned to their original positions and a second player tries. When all the cards are matched, the player with the most pairs is the winner.

It is important, Mrs. Rochas knows from past experience, that she learns exercises like this one thoroughly before trying them with her children. Then she can become more comfortable in the unfamiliar role of "Teacher."

Before Margaretta plays the game after dinner that day and frequently during the remainder of the week, she will be encouraged to look at the cards and then talk—in complete sentences—about the pictures. As she gains a familiarity with the objects pictured and the exercise by adding more cards or, to keep the lessons fresh, change the object of the exercise to matching pairs of colors rather than pictures. It may be just fun to Margaretta, but all the while she is playing, she is acquiring some important skills, including the ability to think logically. She is thus preparing to become a better learner when she enters kindergarten the following year.

Little Benjie, meanwhile, is an important part of the action, too. Before leaving that afternoon, Jean shows Mrs. Rochas how a small hand mirror and a full-length mirror can transform him into "The Most Wonderful Thing in the World."

Examining his face in the mirror, Benjie is helped to identify his most prominent physical characteristic, such as his curly hair, bright brown eyes, and white teeth. Then he tries to figure out what makes him "special," what makes him different from everyone else in his family. He observes that one eyebrow is straighter than the other, and his ears are round. Then there are all the tricky things he can do with his face: he can squint, wrinkle his nose, and pucker his lips. He is encouraged to talk about how a smile is different than a frown. Before the full-length mirror in the bedroom, Benjie studies his posture and imitates various commonplace activities such as eating a hamburger or kicking a football. He and Margaretta look together into the mirror and discover how their appearances are different and how they are alike. The purpose? To help a child realize he or she is special and to feel good and confident about the discovery.

Although the allotted hour has flown by, Jean takes a few more minutes to discuss some new pamphlets on nutritious snacks for children she has brought along from the County Extension Office, and to confirm her appointment for next week.

The exercises for Margaretta and Benjie just described are only two drawn from more than 200 individual "tasks" for various age levels identified and developed by the Home Base staff. Each exercise has a specific goal or aim. Since most learning handicaps in the target population—preschoolers in the Yakima area—relate to language development, Home Base stresses conversations between parents and their children. There is no special significance attached to the activities' sequence. Tasks become more complex as the child's needs and intellectual capacity grow.

Parents are continually encouraged to adhere closely to a number of effective teaching techniques such as eliciting questions from the learner, asking questions that have more than one correct answer, asking questions that require more than a one-word reply, praising the learner when he or she does well, urging the child to respond according to evidence instead of guesswork, allowing the child time to think out a problem before receiving assistance, and helping him or her to become familiar with the learning situation and materials.

"As we teach parents what to expect from their children in each situation and how to respond to their child's successes or failures, we find that the parents become stronger and more confident in their teaching role," project director Carol Jackson said. "When they understand the necessity for teaching skills like problem solving, they realize the time is well spent."

Project Home Base, a National Developer/Demonstration Project, started in 1971 with funding under Title III of the Elementary and Secondary Education Act (ESEA). Currently it is funded under numerous funding sources including Chapter I, Special Education Preschool, Washington State Early Childhood Education and Assistance Program (ECEAP), and local district levy money. The project, operating on the premise that the parent is the child's first and most significant teacher, is adapted from Ira Gordon's Follow Through Parent Education Model. Home Base serves the parents of about 550 preschool children. Many reside in Yakima, the center of a major agricultural and agribusiness area with its resulting highly transient population among lower-income families. The city population is made up of about 20% ethnic minorities; the Home Base program serves 38% minorities.

Home Base employs 18 parent-educators as home visitors. Professional-technical salaried staff attend a 2-week training class in the fall and receive inservice instruction throughout the year during staff development sessions each Monday morning. The home-visitor's workday spans from 8:30 to 4, with about an hour spent at each home. It is an emotionally demanding job and requires a valid driver's license, an available vehicle, and vehicle liability insurance. Fortunately, language problems are minimized because several of the home-visitors are bilingual. Their services are constantly being used to translate tasks into Spanish and to attend meetings to serve as interpreter for Spanish-speaking parents.

A great deal of role playing is used in the training of parent-educators. They try out all of the activities scheduled. "An unusual aspect of our program is that we use few commercial learning games," Judy Popp, the district's Early Childhood Director, says. "Wood scraps from a local mill are our building-block materials. We buy flannel to make flannel boards, and we mix flour and water and salt to make dough clay. Of course we also make good use of ordinary items found in every home—coffee cans with plastic lids, measuring spoons—anything that will help to stimulate a young mind." And what Home Base doesn't have on hand, the community usually provides. As a result of more than 105,000 home visits, the community has become increasingly intimate with the project staff and has been the source of a constant stream of donated materials.

The program is comparatively economical. All the Home Base services' costs, including salaries, secretarial support, and materials, come to about $1,800 per family per year. Because of its field-centered operation only minimal office space is required. Separate collaborative funding is available for minimal preschool center space for the Special Education Preschool and the state ECEAP project. In these, preschoolers attend a group session between one to four times per week, and their parents receive the weekly home teaching visit through Home Base.

Beyond the parent and home-visitor interaction, parents also get together in small neighborhood groups (Play and Learn Groups—PLAY), and in larger sessions to hear speakers, swap information about child development, and discuss mutual concerns. These sessions are also a lot of fun. One popular gathering was called a "Small World Smorgasbord," a triumph for the cause of culinary diplomacy. Between performances of native dances, long-time Yakimans and their Japanese, Chicano, and Indian neighbors spent an evening of getting to know one another over plates full of their favorite foods.

There are always a few dropouts from the Home Base program, but the rate of attrition is much less than one might expect from a population that accepts transiency as a condition of employment. The director feels that's chiefly because of the "nonthreatening" approach the staff uses, which removes any suggestion of the remedial stigma. The program's Communication Disorder Specialist (C.D.S.) is a key figure for both parent training and staff development. A high percentage of the participating families either request or are referred to the C.D.S. for a home visit sometime during the year.

One concern early in the program was whether training parents systematically to teach developmental skills to their children during the early formative years could really be statistically measured. And how would Home Base children perform compared with children of similar economic status on school-readiness tests? To gauge the effects of the Home Base program, a realistic set of objectives was established. One goal requires mothers to teach at least 82.5% of the tasks presented to them. Another objective is for mothers to increase their use of desirable teaching behaviors when teaching their children. Both objectives continue to be met.

As a national demonstration project, Home Base has frequently been in the spotlight. During the demonstration project period alone, 54 other communities adopted the model. More recently, with increased state and national attention on the effectiveness of early intervention, Yakima has experienced a surge of training requests.

A locally developed Developmental Profile has been used for the past several years to measure parents' perceptions of their children's development from birth to age 8 in five categories—physical, self-help, social, academic, and communication. The profile provides a more complete picture of each child's progress as encouraged by home instruction.

In the Monday morning staff sessions, home-visitors discuss their problems and successes and plan new strategies for the coming week. At one such meeting, a Home Base parent-educator reported that her persistence in persuading a family to have their child's hearing checked had paid off—a 40% hearing loss had been detected. The child would be referred to the appropriate community agency for medical help. Another observed that even parents new to the program "feel reassured to discover and understand their children's needs." She added that one mother had admitted that she's experienced numerous problems with her oldest child, but, thanks to Home Base, she believes she can avoid them with the younger one. And she added that all the emphasis on language is clearly helping the younger child's speech; he has begun to speak in sentences rather than fragments, and at an appreciably younger age than his brother.

Home Base is not without benefit for the rest of the family, too. "A father told me that being involved in Home Base has made a difference in his wife," reports another of the parent-educators. "She's found out she has ability and she is using it. Her opinion of herself has been greatly improved." Keeping an otherwise isolated family in touch with the community is another valuable aspect of the Home Base program. "Instead of my feeling alone and all tied up by my problems," a woman told her visitor, "you help by just being a friend that I can talk to once a week."*

---

*From Hedrich, V., and Jackson, C. Winning Play at Home Base. *American Education,* July 1977, pp. 27–30. Revised by Judy Popp, Early Childhood Director, Project Home Base, Yakima, Washington, October 1989.

The Yakima Home Base program illustrates how schools or centers can use the home as a teaching center. The emphasis is on practices that encourage the child's educational growth: (1) learning communication skills; (2) reasoning logically; (3) developing self-concept; (4) becoming nutritionally aware; (5) using developmental activity sequences; (6) employing effective teaching techniques; (7) using easily obtained play materials; and (8) extending new expertise and knowledge about parenting to other members of the family. This program responds to the individual requirements of the community from which it evolved, but many of the techniques of effective parenting and teaching are appropriate for any home-based program.

Across the nation similar demonstration projects were initially funded by the U.S. Office of Education, Department of Health, Education and Welfare. A few of the most successful projects were duplicated by other school districts such as the Home Start programs in Waterloo, Iowa, and a Parent Education and Preschool program with Added Dimensions in Jefferson County, Colorado.

Home Start

Head Start added Home Start demonstration programs in 1972. The success of earlier home-based programs, plus the belief that parents were the "first and most important educators of their own children" (U.S. Department of Health, Education and Welfare, 1976, p. 5), resulted in the funding of 16 Home Start projects during a 3-year demonstration period from March 1972 until June 1975. Programs were founded in San Diego, California; Wichita, Kansas; Gloucester, Massachusetts; Binghamton, New York; Reno, Nevada; Huntsville, Alabama; Fairbanks, Alaska; Dardanelle, Arkansas; Fort Defiance, Arizona; Franklin, North Carolina; Laredo, Texas; Logan, Utah; Parkersburg, West Virginia; Houston, Texas; Cleveland, Ohio; and Harrogate, Tennessee. The Home Start program differed from Head Start in its location of services and its emphasis on parents as teachers in the home. Although Head Start included parents in decision making and

included home visits, Home Start's purpose was to use the home as base and, through home visitors, help parents to become teachers of their children. The diverse locations of the Home Start programs ensured the implementation of the program among different ethnic and cultural groups and varying social conditions.

ADDITIONAL FEDERAL PROGRAMS GEARED TO PARENT INVOLVEMENT

A number of comprehensive resource programs that had outreach to parents were funded approximately at the same time as Home Start. These included (1) Parent Child Development Centers (PCDC), (2) Parent and Child Centers (PCC), and (3) Child and Family Resource Programs (CFRP).

Parent Child Development Centers

Although PCDC evolved from the recognized need for parent involvement, the three programs chosen for demonstration (Birmingham, Alabama; New Orleans, Louisiana; Houston, Texas) worked with different populations and used different delivery systems. Birmingham's project was center-based, while Houston had a combination of home-based and center-based programs, and New Orleans had two models: one, home-based, and the other, center-based (Ricciuti, 1975). The projects were designed to determine the effects of intervention on the following:

1. Whether a parent intervention program would attract the attention of parents
2. What kind of programs could best help parents understand the dimensions of growth in infancy
3. How the program effects could be measured appropriately
4. What kinds of growth in children were related to what kinds of growth in parents (U.S. Department of Health, Education and Welfare, 1976, p. 19)

The Houston Model for Parent Education geared its program toward change in the mother's behavior. Working with low-income Mexican-American mothers, the home educators visited the home once a week for approximately 1½ hours and held four Saturday family workshops during the first year of the program. During the second year mothers and their 2-year-old children attended a 3-hour program at the center 4 days a week. Evening sessions were held for both parents twice a month. The model worked toward and gained greater verbal interaction between parent and child, granting more autonomy to the child, and increased warmth in parental interaction with the child (Leler et al., 1975).

Parent and Child Centers (PCC)

The 36 Parent and Child Centers were initially funded in 1967. Some models were home-based; some were center-based, and others were a combination of the two. Goals and objectives for the programs included:

1. Improving the overall developmental progress of 0- to 3 year old children
2. Increasing parents' knowledge of their roles as teachers of their own children
3. Strengthening the family and its functions through parent involvement
4. Creating community awareness in the parents of infants
5. Serving as a locus of research (U.S. Department of Health, Education and Welfare, 1976, p. 18)

Child and Family Resource Program (CFRP)

Funded in June 1973, the CFRP, as a part of Head Start, coordinated comprehensive services for families at 11 projects. The CFRP enrolled families rather than just the children and provided a child-centered family service program. By working with the total family, the program reached all children ages birth through 8 and included the children in programs related to their ages. Following were the objectives of the programs:

1. To individualize and tailor programs and services to children and their families
2. To link resources in the community so that families may choose from a variety of programs and services while relating primarily to a single resource center for all young children in the same family
3. To provide continuity of resources available to parents, enabling each family to guide the devel-

opment of its children from the prenatal period through their early school years
4. To enhance and build upon the strengths of the individual family as a childrearing system, with distinct values, culture, and aspirations; the CFRP will attempt to reinforce these strengths, treating each individual as a whole and the family as a unit (U.S. Department of Health, Education and Welfare, 1975, pp. 3 and 4)

CFRP offered the following minimum services:

1. Comprehensive individual assessment of family and child needs, based on consultation with the family
2. Preventive, treatment, and rehabilitative services as required for the individually diagnosed medical, dental, nutritional, and mental health needs of children up to 8 years of age
3. Prenatal medical care and educational services for pregnant mothers
4. Developmental services for families and children
    a. Programs to assist parents in promoting the total (emotional, cognitive, language, and physical) development of infants and toddlers through age 3
    b. Preschool comprehensive Head Start services for children from ages 3 to 5
    c. Programs designed to ensure smooth transition for children from preschool into the early elementary grades
    d. Group activities and family development programs for parents
    e. Special development programs for handicapped children
5. Family support services
    a. Individual and group counseling for children and adults
    b. Referral services for life support needs
    c. Emergency services in crises
    d. Family planning assistance and counseling
    e. Information regarding food assistance programs

The CFRP programs were expected to consider the families' cultural and ethnic backgrounds and their language patterns. Under standing of the families' needs was essential, and needs assessments were conducted prior to design of each family's program and throughout the implementation of the program.

Services for children in the family beyond the 8-year level were not unusual. Scouts were encouraged for school-age children. Tutoring was provided for school children and adults if needed. The CFRP attempted to provide a comprehensive service for participating families.

Effectiveness of Services

These three programs demonstrated that home-based education is a viable undertaking for educators and, along with Home Start, Title I, and Title IV-C programs, contributed research data and suggested procedures for implementation. The ESEA demonstration programs (Titles I, III, IV-C) and those funded through the Office of Child Development (later the Administration for Children, Youth and Families) were devel-

Outreach can touch mothers and fathers as they raise their children.

oped with the hope of disseminating and developing similar programs, wherever needed, across the nation. It was recognized that each locality would have individual needs and that individualized programs for children and their families would be both necessary and beneficial.

The variety of approaches—that is, outreach to homes as the only service, center-based operations, and home-based in combination with center programs—allowed communities that were planning to implement a home-based program many options from which to develop unique programs. The demonstration programs devised methods of implementation and developed curricula that could be modeled by schools, centers, and agencies starting home-based programs. Many Head Start agencies have added a Home Start component to their center-based program. School districts have also begun to involve parents prior to the time their children commence school. Although only a few demonstration programs still exist, their influence is felt through the implementation in Head Start and schools.

DECIDING ON A HOME-BASED PROGRAM

Before a particular home-based program is considered, the reasons for and needs of such a program must be examined. The primary goals of home-based programs include the following:

1. To enable parents to become more effective teachers of their children
2. To support the parents in the roles of caregivers and homemakers
3. To strengthen the parents' sense of autonomy and self-esteem
4. To reach the child and family early in the child's formative years
5. To respond to the family's needs and thus improve the home environment

The overriding goal of educators is the impact of the program on the child. Desirable results are the child's increased sense of well-being, a more successful educational experience in school, and the realization of the child's potential for optimum development.

Goals for programs vary according to the needs of the area. For instance, in one area, health may be an overriding concern, in another, language development, and in still another, nutrition. Although all three are probably important in varying degrees in every home-based program, the intensity of involvement may vary.

NEED FOR A PROGRAM

Although federal money is still available for existing Head Start and Chapter I programs, new funds are primarily earmarked for demonstration programs and remediation, rather than for long-term financial support. State and local funds are expected to be used to address local needs. Obtain expertise in grant writing and budgeting before seeking funds.

Schools and centers should consider parent involvement and home-based programs within the framework of their own needs. They should examine all approaches carefully and share a commitment to the child and family before embarking on a home-based program. These questions can serve as guidelines for choosing a program.

1. Are there children in current school classes who could have been helped by early intervention in the home?
2. What can the school do in a home visitation program that cannot be accomplished through other programs?
3. Could early remediation reduce the number of retentions when children go to school?
4. Are there handicapped children in the area who could be diagnosed and given service before they enter school?
5. Will the preventive program help eliminate later educational problems and thereby offset the cost to the public?
6. Will the prevention of later educational problems reduce later emotional problems and thereby offset the cost to the public?

If "yes" was the answer to a majority of these questions, the next step is to consider the feasibility of a home-based program. The following are questions that must be addressed.

1. Has there been a thorough assessment of needs to establish community interest in home-based services?
2. Are there *enough* families in the community who are definitely interested in and eligible to participate in a program that emphasizes home visits and the role of the parents?
3. Do staff members already have the skills and interests needed to work effectively with parents in their own homes? If not, does the program have, or can it obtain, the considerable training necessary to prepare staff for their new roles? Is the staff willing and interested in receiving such training? Is the staff culturally and linguistically compatible with families to be served?
4. Can transportation needs be met? In most areas, public transportation is not an efficient mode of travel, and often is not available. Home visitors need car transportation to get around quickly, to transport materials, and to take parents and children for special services needed from local resource agencies.
5. Will fathers and other family members away from home during the day be included? The answer to this usually involves meetings and home visits in the evenings and on weekends. In some ways, home-based programs require a staff selflessness and dedication that goes beyond the demands of the workload and schedules of center-based services (modified from U. S. Department of Health and Human Services, 1985, p. 8)

The next step is consideration of the following factors, which were suggested by participants at a national conference on Home Start and other programs.

1. The clientele must be identified, as to rural/urban, ethnic/cultural groups, age, income, and involvement in any existing similar programs.
2. Family and community needs must be identified. Existing census or welfare data and data from social service agencies may be used. A questionnaire may be devised, and a sample group from existing programs may be interviewed as part of this identification process.

3. Existing and needed services and resources must be identified in areas such as health (medical, dental, and mental health), education, transportation, housing, and legal services.

4. Costs of purchasing available services, providing new services, and transporting clients or staff must be considered.

5. The need for and feasibility of the program must be documented. The feasibility of going partially or completely home-based must be determined, as must the feasibility of affiliating with existing programs or agencies, and the program must be geared to family needs. (modified from U.S. Department of Health, Education and Welfare, 1976, p. 35)

Many answers will come from the identification of needs mentioned in factor two. Before a questionnaire or needs assessment is devised, data should be gathered from school files, social service agencies, city surveys, or census reports. Social services will be particularly helpful in determining services and number of children in families. School figures, questionnaires, and surveys will supplement that data so that services may be offered to all those who desire or need them. Make every effort to establish a good working relationship with the various agencies. You will need to coordinate your efforts at a later time, and initial communication and rapport are essential to later implementation of the program.

INVOLVING OTHERS IN THE PROGRAM

The four components of a Home Start program are education, social services, health services (physical and mental health, dental care, nutrition, and safety), and parent involvement. Although the project will be fully responsible for education and parent involvement, social and health services will need the support of other agencies. "Knowing what agencies are willing to handle the various family problems that will be found, and getting them involved with the program early in the planning, pay great dividends when the program swings into operation" (U.S. Department of Health, Education and Welfare, 1974, p. 12).

Social agencies may be contacted individually, or representatives may be invited to a meeting where goals, objectives, and initial plans for the programs are discussed. Elicit suggestions from the agencies as well as find out how they can contribute.

An excellent example of collaboration by social agencies is the Homebuilders, a group of therapists, social workers, and psychologists who work with families whose children may be taken from them by the courts. Working closely with schools, juvenile court, and other social agencies, the Homebuilders work with the total family, helping to overcome their difficulties through counseling, modeling, and providing any kind of support necessary to help them cope. Established in Tacoma, Washington, Homebuilders has established a most successful record of 90% of the children remaining with the families. Success has been due to (1) highly motivated families (out-of-family placement was imminent); (2) counseling and support in the family's home; (3) ample time (Homebuilders sometimes spends more than 100 hours with a family); (4) a wide variety of resources; and (5) a number of ways to help including practical help, coping with stress, therapy, assertiveness, and behavior management. The Homebuilders come to the family's crisis call at any time, day, night, or weekends. They get satisfaction from seeing the family "pull things together" (Schorr & Schorr, 1988, p. 160).

Successful programs that work with at-risk families seem to have common components. They offer comprehensive and intensive services. Staff are highly professional with an understanding of psychology and child development, and they develop a trusting relationship with their clients (Schorr & Schorr, 1988).

PARENT ADVISORY COUNCILS

Parents to be served should be actively involved in the initial planning. Many schools and preschool programs have parent advisory councils or citizen advisory councils that can give input on the needs of the community and suggest relevant questions that might be asked. If a council is not functioning in your area, it may be advisable to implement one. You can work through the existing PTO or PTA, or you can establish an entirely new council based on the parents you will serve. The formation or election of the board is advertised. Parents have an opportunity to nominate themselves or others, and an election is held to determine who will represent the community on the council. You may advertise the formation of an advisory council by sending notes home with children from school, by explaining the council at area meetings of organizations such as Boy Scouts, Camp Fire Girls, PTA, YMCA, and YWCA, and by distributing flyers throughout the community. All nominations should be accepted. If you use a democratic process, you will have to rely on the intelligence of the parents in the selection process.

Distinct advantages to using a democratic selection process rather than appointment in the formation of an advisory council are the creation of the following: (1) interest in the program, (2) a sense of self-determination and autonomy on the part of the parents, (3) a source of relevant information and feedback from those being affected, and (4) increased cooperation between school and parents.

SELECTION OF HOME VISITORS

Before selecting home visitors, the choice must be made whether to use professional parent teachers, paraprofessionals, or volunteers. Although the director, coordinator, and special services specialists will probably be professionals, many programs use paraprofessionals or volunteers for the home visit specialists. Criteria for selection will be determined by the needs of your specific program.

When recruiting paraprofessional home visitors, the available positions should be advertised widely throughout the community. Announcements must be clear and include the following:

1. Explanation of the program. Explain what your specific home-based program entails. Indicate what the goals and objectives are.

2. Job description of the position. List the duties and responsibilities, hours of work, salary range, and benefits.

3. Qualifications required. Indicate whether high school, college, and/or specific competencies are required.

4. Equal opportunity employment announcement. Make a statement of nondiscrimination.

5. Instructions for applying. Give instructions on how to apply, whom to contact, and the deadline for application.

The announcement of openings should be posted in public places, for example, libraries, schools, stores, and agencies such as Head Start. Telephone canvassing will alert many persons to the new program. To reach a large population, advertise in the newspaper and distribute flyers. Wide dissemination of information about available positions encourages individuals in the community to become involved and alerts others to the upcoming home-based program.

VISITING PARENTS AT HOME

Successful home visitors are flexible and work easily with others. These guidelines will help start home visitors on the road to success.

- Be a good listener.
- Set specific goals for each visit.
- Be flexible.
- Be prompt.
- Realize the limitations of your role.
- Help parents become more independent.
- Dress appropriately and comfortably.
- Be confident.
- Remember that small improvements lead to big ones.
- Be yourself.
- Respect cultural and ethnic values.
- Monitor your own behavior—the parent is observing you.

- Include other members of the family in the visit.
- Bring visitors only when you have the parent's permission.
- Don't socialize excessively.
- Don't impose values.
- Don't talk about families in public.
- Don't expect perfection from the parent.
- Don't ask the parent to do something you wouldn't do.
- Make the parent the focus of your visits. Help develop the parent's role as a teacher.
- Begin working with the parent and child on specific activities immediately. This sets a tone for the home visits, and parents will feel good about their abilities as they see that they can and do teach their children.
- Plan activities around daily routines.

- Make it a habit to discuss the reason for the activity before you or the parent presents it to the child. (Modified from U. S. Department of Health and Human Services, 1987, pp. 88 and 153)

Home visitors can evaluate their efforts by asking themselves the questions in Figure 8–1 after each visit.

HOME LEARNING ACTIVITIES

Each project funded by federal money has developed a unique approach to home learning activities. The Portage Project developed a systematic program for its home visitors that can be used by

---

Are YOUR Home Visits Parent-Focused?

• Do you involve the parents in the assessment of the child?	Yes	No
• Do you provide the parent with a copy of the checklist for their own use?	Yes	No
• When you arrive for the weekly home visit, do you direct your attention and greeting toward the parent?	Yes	No
• Do you discuss the previous week's visit and follow up on the weekly activities with the parent?	Yes	No
• Does the parent co-plan the activities for the home visit?	Yes	No
• Do you make sure that the child is sitting beside the parent?	Yes	No
• Does the parent demonstrate EACH new activity?	Yes	No
• Do you review each activity with the parent before presenting it?	Yes	No
• Do you hand all materials to the parent?	Yes	No
• Do you identify and reinforce the parent's teaching strengths?	Yes	No
• When the parent has difficulty, do you intervene with the parent rather than the child?	Yes	No
• Do you let the parent be the primary reinforcing agent?	Yes	No
• Do you help the parent problem solve when problems do arise instead of jumping to the rescue?	Yes	No
• Do you work on activities the parent feels are important?	Yes	No
• Do you ask the parent to provide as many materials as possible?	Yes	No
• Do you give the parent the lead, when appropriate?	Yes	No
• Do you incorporate the parent's ideas into each activity?	Yes	No
• Do you let the parent present new and exciting experiences?	Yes	No
• Do you individualize parent education activities for each parent?	Yes	No
• Do you accept the parent's values?	Yes	No
• Do you involve the parent in evaluation of the home visit?	Yes	No

FIGURE 8–1

(Source: U.S. Department of Health and Human Services Office of Human Development Services, Administration for Children, Youth and Families, Head Start Bureau. *The Head Start home visitor handbook.* Washington, D.C.: U. S. Government Printing Office, 1987, p. 6.)

others who plan programs. Levenstein's Home Child Program chose commercial games and books as the basis for verbal interaction between parent and child. Gordon's parent program in Florida devised a method of curriculum development that can be replicated in any program.

Parents and home visitors work together to develop the children's curriculum. The following tips will help.

- Choose an emerging skill that the child has shown an interest in or one in which an interest can be developed.
- Choose some skills that the parent feels are important.
- Choose a skill that the child needs to learn.
- Choose a developmentally appropriate task that is easily accommodated at home.
  (Modified from U.S. Department of Heath and Human Services, 1985, pp. 68, 69.)

In the implementation of a home-school program both teachers and parents may be supported by learning activities developed by commercial

Parents can devise curriculum ideas from everyday occurrences in the home.

companies and school districts. Appropriate learning activities can be purchased or found in the library. Refer to the references and suggested readings in Appendix E for additional developmentally appropriate activities for young children.

As the home visitor becomes involved with each family, appropriate activities to accommodate the individual strengths and needs of the family will become apparent. Some home visitors will use suggested and sequential activities for their teaching curriculum such as the Portage Program, which is discussed later in this chapter. Others will use the commercial books illustrated in Figure 8–2A or the sample from the Yakima Home Base program (Figure 8–2B). Another alternative is to develop activities related to the particular interests of the child and parent.

The Florida Parent Education Program developed by Ira Gordon and his colleagues recommends the following 5-step framework in the development of home activities.

Idea. The concept or idea emerges from the child, parent, home visitor, or special interests of the family. What does the family enjoy? Which experiences have been interesting and fun? Which collections, toys, or materials are available around the home?

Ideas are also shared among the staff—teachers, other home visitors, and curriculum specialists. When an idea occurs, a memo is jotted down to remind the home visitor of the activity.

Reason. Each idea is used for a reason. The reasons may range from learning experiences to developing self-concept. After an idea or ideas are collected, examine the skills that can be associated with each. For example, if the child picks a leaf from one of the trees in the neighborhood, start a collection of fallen leaves that can be classified according to size, color, and shape. The child can make texture and outline rubbings of them. "How many kinds of trees are represented by the variety of leaves?" you might ask the child. "Put each kind of leaf in a separate pile and count the kinds of leaves." The many learning opportunities available from collecting

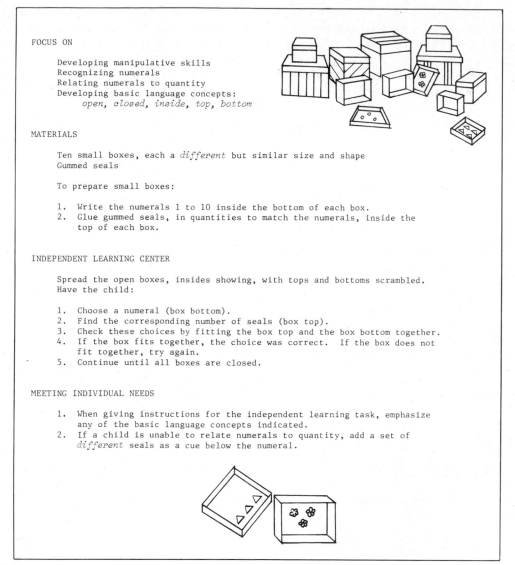

FOCUS ON

    Developing manipulative skills
    Recognizing numerals
    Relating numerals to quantity
    Developing basic language concepts:
        open, closed, inside, top, bottom

MATERIALS

    Ten small boxes, each a *different* but similar size and shape
    Gummed seals

    To prepare small boxes:

    1. Write the numerals 1 to 10 inside the bottom of each box.
    2. Glue gummed seals, in quantities to match the numerals, inside the
        top of each box.

INDEPENDENT LEARNING CENTER

    Spread the open boxes, insides showing, with tops and bottoms scrambled.
    Have the child:

    1. Choose a numeral (box bottom).
    2. Find the corresponding number of seals (box top).
    3. Check these choices by fitting the box top and the box bottom together.
    4. If the box fits together, the choice was correct. If the box does not
        fit together, try again.
    5. Continue until all boxes are closed.

MEETING INDIVIDUAL NEEDS

    1. When giving instructions for the independent learning task, emphasize
        any of the basic language concepts indicated.
    2. If a child is unable to relate numerals to quantity, add a set of
        different seals as a cue below the numeral.

FIGURE 8–2A
A sample of learning activities. (Source: J. S. McElderry & L. E. Escobedo. *Tools for learning.* Denver, Colo.: Love Publishing, 1979, p. 86.)

leaves make this a worthwhile project for as long as the child's interest continues.

Materials.   Implementing a reasonable idea requires available materials. Some experiences can be developed around materials commonly found in the home. The Utah program developed a unit on gardens and vegetables that uses

materials readily found in the home (see Figure 8–3). If the idea requires special equipment and materials, make sure they are easily available. One of the main objectives of home visits is to involve the parent as the teacher. If parents do not realize that they have readily available teaching materials or if the learning activities are not furnished for them, part of the parental auton-

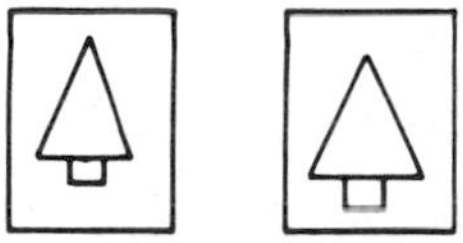

TASK SAMPLE—"CONCENTRATION"

AIM: to play a matching game with pairs of cards.

WHY: to practice visual memory, remembering the position of matching cards. To follow rules and take turns are skills used in most games.

MATERIALS: grocery sack or small cards, five pairs of matching pictures, magazines, sales pamphlets, paste, scissors.

PROCEDURE:

1. Cut pairs of like pictures (10) from magazine and paste on circles cut from paper sacks or cards.

2. Encourage child to talk about pictures and name them. Then, together, place them in pairs.

3. Collect cards, turn them face down, and mix them.

4. Place cards in rows without looking at pictures.

5. Have child pick up one card and turn it over and say what it is. (Repeat the name for child if he cannot say the name.) Then choose another card trying for a match. If no match, then both cards are turned over. Say, "That's your turn; now it's my turn."

6. The play continues until all the cards are matched. Count the "pairs" to see who is the winner.

EXTENDING THE CONCEPT:

1. Add more picture cards for pairs.

2. Play game using colors instead of pictures.

3. Use pictures of sets of objects.

FIGURE 8–2B
The game of concentration. (Source: Project Home Base, Yakima, Wash.)

omy and subsequent success of the program is lost.

Action. Follow the child's lead and let the activity develop. If the child chooses something to explore that is different from your plans for the activity, vary your plans, take a detour, and enjoy the inquiry and discovery the child is experiencing. Your ideas may be brought up later or eliminated altogether. Remember the

UTAH HOME VISITOR GUIDE
April—1st week

Unit title: Gardens and Vegetables

With the high cost of living, it's important to grow your own fresh vegetables because they are so much needed in our daily diets. Homegrown vegetables are also healthier (less chemicals, fertilizers and more nutritious). Families need information on how to store, preserve and prepare fresh vegetables. Gardening is an excellent learning and sharing experience for families.

Specific objectives:

1. To help parents realize the economical benefits gained through home gardening
2. To give parents help with methods of food preparation and preservation
3. To stress the importance of vegetables to good nutrition
4. To reinforce Basic 4

Activities

1. Discussion on growing a garden
   a. Why grow a garden
   b. How to grow a garden
   c. How to store and preserve food from the garden
   d. Handout on food storage and preserving
   e. How to involve children in gardening
   f. Children will often eat more when they grow it themselves
   g. Gardening is good exercise and teaches responsibility
   h. Handouts on planting times, spacing, what grows in this area (information from county agents)
2. Choose a garden site
3. Plan a garden
   a. What do you want to grow/like to eat?
   b. How much space, water, and time do you have?
   c. What will grow in your area?
   d. Is this to be a permanent site?
4. If no garden space, use boxes, crates, and flower beds
5. Take fruits and vegetables into home for snack/look, feel, and taste
   a. Cleanliness in handling food
6. Look at seeds and compare or match with vegetable
7. Snack tray of raw vegetables and cottage cheese dip
8. Sprout seeds
9. Plant seed in plastic bag with wet paper towel
10. Plant seed in egg carton
11. Grow plants from sweet potatoes and avocado seed in water
12. Seed collage
13. Start your own tomato plants, green pepper, and cantaloupe plants indoors in cardboard cartons
14. Count seeds
15. Pop popcorn
16. Classify vegetables and fruits—cut pictures from magazines
17. Stories and books
    a. Carrot seed
    b. Turnip seed
    c. Peter Rabbit—Mr. McGregor's Garden
    d. The Little Seed
18. Creative movement—germination and growth of seed
19. Tell parents where to get information and handouts
    a. County extension office
    b. Seed stores
20. Sprinkle grass on wet sponge
21. Print with vegetable or weed leaves
22. Talk about seeds you can eat and eat some for a snack
23. Talk about food that people and animals eat
24. Make a vegetable salad
25. Handouts on vegetables

Follow-up for positive reinforcement:

1. Show seeds—sprouted in bag or planted
2. How do you wash vegetables?
3. What did you decide about your garden?

FIGURE 8–3

The Utah Home Visitor Guide. The unit on gardens and vegetables illustrates how ordinary activities around the home can be used for education. (Source: U. S. Department of Health, Education and Welfare. *Partners with parents.* Washington, D. C.: U.S. Government Printing Office, 1978, pp. 72 and 73.)

objectives of the learning process. If they are being fulfilled, it does not matter which action brought about the learning.

Extension. Are there other activities related to this idea? If so, expand the action, follow the interest, and extend the learning (modified from Packer et al., 1976).

Toy Lending Library

A home visitor can incorporate the development of curriculum ideas along with a lending library. Toys, games, books, and patterns for making toys can be loaned for set periods of time. Other toys and books may be given to the participants. Guidelines may be obtained from the plans used by the toy lending library (Nimnicht, 1972).

Home visitors become capable of designing appropriate curriculum for young children as they learn about development and observe how children handle various tasks.

SCREENING FOR BETTER UNDERSTANDING

As home visitors and parents work with children, they informally assess the child's characteristics and skills. Informal assessments with check lists can be used while the child is playing. It is always best to view the child in a natural setting unrestricted by contrived tasks. A portfolio containing collections of art activities and projects, teacher comments, and the child's comments can aid in assessing the child's development. These kinds of assessment are essential; they provide the parent and teacher with the guidelines for developmentally appropriate activities for each child.

Parent educators also need to be able to recognize if the families under their guidance need special help. Screening for potential problems in both the developmental status of children and the children's environment—especially if they are growing up in a low socioeconomic area—will help the parent educator identify problems early and more effectively serve children and their families (Fandal, 1986).

Several instruments are available to screen the developmental progress of children. Two of the most widely used are the Denver Prescreening Developmental Questionnaire (PDQ) and the Denver Developmental Screening Test (DDST). There are also standardized methods of assessing the home environment of children, such as the Home Screening Questionnaire (HSQ) and the Home Observation for Measurement of the Environment (HOME).

Environment

Home Observation for Measurement of the Environment (HOME)
The HOME Inventory (see Figure 8–4) is used by schools, child care centers, and other social service agencies to help them determine the quality of the home environment as it relates to the child's development. "Although a child may appear to be developing at a normal rate early in life, the environment begins to either enhance or 'put a lid' on developmental progress within the first year or two" (Fandal, 1986). The HOME Inventory was developed by Caldwell and Bradley in order "to get a picture of what the child's world is like from his or her perspective—i.e., from where he or she lies or sits or stands or moves about and sees, hears, smells, feels, and tastes that world" (Caldwell & Bradley, 1984, p. 8). In addition to the standardized HOME Inventories for birth to 3- and 3- to 6-year-olds, an inventory for elementary school children is also available.

When using the program, the interviewer should

- Know the HOME Inventory well before using it
- Contact the parents and let them know that you want to visit
- Visit during a period while the child is awake and available
- Start the interview with some friendly, relaxed interaction

A suggested technique for starting the interview is described by the following statement:

You will remember that we are interested in knowing the kinds of things your baby (child) does when

HOME Inventory for Families of Infants and Toddlers

Bettye M. Caldwell and Robert H. Bradley

Family Name _____ Date _____ Visitor _____

Child's Name _____ Birthdate _____ Age _____ Sex _____

Caregiver for visit _____ Relationship to child _____

Family Composition _____
(Persons living in household, including sex and age of children)

Family   Maternal   Paternal
Ethnicity _____ Language _____ Education _____ Education _____
                   Spoken

Is Mother   Type of work   Is Father   Type of work
Employed? _____ when employed _____   Employed? _____ when employed _____

Address _____ Phone _____

Current child care arrangements _____

Summarize past
year's arrangements _____

Caregiver for visit _____ Other persons _____
                                    present

Comments _____

SUMMARY

Subscale	Score	Lowest Middle	Middle Half	Upper Fourth
I. Emotional and Verbal RESPONSIVITY of Parent		0-6	7-9	10-11
II. ACCEPTANCE of Child's Behavior		0-4	5-6	7-8
III. ORGANIZATION of Physical and Temporal Environment		0-3	4-5	6
IV. Provision of Appropriate PLAY MATERIALS		0-4	5-7	8-9
V. Parent INVOLVEMENT with Child		0-2	3-4	5-6
VI. Opportunities for VARIETY in Daily Stimulation		0-1	2-3	4-5
TOTAL SCORE		0-25	26-36	37-45

For rapid profiling of a family, place an X in the box that corresponds to the raw score on each subscale and the total score.

13

HOME Inventory*

Place a plus (+) or minus (−) in the box alongside each item if the behavior is observed during the visit or if the parent reports that the conditions or events are characteristic of the home environment. Enter the subtotal and the total on the front side of the Record Sheet.

I. Emotional and Verbal RESPONSIVITY

1. Parent spontaneously vocalized to child twice.
2. Parent responds verbally to child's verbalizations.
3. Parent tells child name of object or person during visit.
4. Parent's speech is distinct and audible.
5. Parent initiates verbal exchanges with visitor.
6. Parent converses freely and easily.
7. Parent permits child to engage in "messy" play.
8. Parent spontaneously praises child at least twice.
9. Parent's voice conveys positive feelings toward child.
10. Parent caresses or kisses child at least once.
11. Parent responds positively to praise of child offered by visitor.
   Subtotal

II. ACCEPTANCE of Child's Behavior

12. Parent does not shout at child.
13. Parent does not express annoyance with or hostility to child.
14. Parent neither slaps nor spanks child during visit.
15. No more than one instance of physical punishment during past week.
16. Parent does not scold or criticize child during visit.
17. Parent does not interfere or restrict child more than 3 times.
18. At least ten books are present and visible.
19. Family has a pet.
   Subtotal

III. ORGANIZATION of Environment

20. Substitute care is provided by one of three regular substitutes.
21. Child is taken to grocery store at least once/week.
22. Child gets out of house at least four times/week.
23. Child is taken regularly to doctor's office or clinic.
24. Child has a special place for toys and treasures.
25. Child's play environment is safe.
   Subtotal

IV. Provision of PLAY MATERIALS

26. Muscle activity toys or equipment.
27. Push or pull toy.
28. Stroller or walker, kiddie car, scooter, or tricycle.
29. Parent provides toys for child during visit.
30. Learning equipment appropriate to age—cuddly toys or role-playing toys.
31. Learning facilitators—mobile, table and chairs, high chair, play pen.
32. Simple eye-hand coordination toys.
33. Complex eye-hand coordination toys (those permitting combination).
34. Toys for literature and music.
   Subtotal

V. Parental INVOLVEMENT with Child

35. Parent keeps child in visual range, looks at often.
36. Parent talks to child while doing household work.
37. Parent consciously encourages developmental advance.
38. Parent invests maturing toys with value via personal attention.
39. Parent structures child's play periods.
40. Parent provides toys that challenge child to develop new skills.
   Subtotal

VI. Opportunities for VARIETY

41. Father provides some care daily.
42. Parent reads stories to child at least 3 times weekly.
43. Child eats at least one meal per day with mother and father.
44. Family visits relatives or receives visits once a month or so.
45. Child has 3 or more books of his/her own.
   Subtotal

TOTAL SCORE

*For complete wording of items, please refer to the Administration Manual.

14

FIGURE 8–4

Home visitors may use the Home Inventory to analyze the family's home environment. (Source: Caldwell, B. M., & Bradley, R. H. Administration manual: Home observation for measurement of the environment. Little Rock, Ark.: University of Arkansas, 1984.)

he is at home. A good way to get a picture of what his days are like is to have you think of one particular day—like yesterday—and tell me everything that happened to him as well as you can remember it. Start with the things that happened when he first woke up. It is usually easy to remember the main events once you get started. (Caldwell & Bradley, 1984, p. 3)

The administration and scoring of each of the items in the inventory is clearly described in the Administration Manuals, so the interviewer can make correct judgments on the scoring of HOME. For example, see Figure 8–4, item 4, which states, *"Parent's speech is distinct and audible."*

A positive score on this item is determined by whether the interviewer is able to understand what the parent says. This item should not be interpreted as meaning that dialect usage mandates a negative score. What is important is whether the interviewer can understand and communicate with the parent. (Caldwell & Bradley, 1984, p. 15)

Home Screening Questionnaire (HSQ)

Frankenburg and his colleagues (Coons et al., 1981) recognized the value of an earlier version of the HOME Inventory but was concerned about the length of time needed for a skilled interviewer to make a home visit, so they developed a questionnaire, the HSQ, that could be answered by parents. With the cooperation of the authors of the HOME, items were selected and reconstructed into questionnaire format as illustrated by Figure 8–5. Two questionnaires were developed that correspond to the two HOME scales (for children from birth to 3 years and from 3 to 6 years of age). They take approximately 15 minutes for a parent to complete.

The questionnaire has been validated as an effective screening tool to identify those environments that would benefit from a more intensive assessment. "The HSQ Manual gives complete instructions for scoring the questionnaires. As with all suspect screening results, questionable HSQ results should be followed with a visit by a trained home interviewer to assure that the result of the screening test is accurate and that

appropriate intervention can be planned"(Fandal, 1986).

RECRUITMENT OF FAMILIES

Many families will be identified by existing local facilities, such as Head Start, schools and social service agencies. Articles in newspapers about the new home-based program will alert other parents, and flyers can be delivered by school children. The most effective method, however, is a door-to-door canvas. Home visitors can go from house to house and chat with parents of young children and explain the program and its benefits. This personal approach seems to encourage parents to participate when a notice through the mail may not. Families new to the area or unknown to social agencies or Head Start will be contacted by a door-to-door campaign;

Curriculum and activities can be developed from outdoor experiences.

Child's Name_____ Birthdate_____ Age_____

Parent's Name_____ Phone No._____

Address_____ Date_____

HOME SCREENING QUESTIONNAIRE
Ages 3-6 Years

Please answer <u>all</u> of the following questions about how your child's time is spent and some of the activities of your family. On some questions, you may want to check more than one blank.

<table>
<tr><td>FOR OFFICE USE ONLY</td><td></td><td>FOR OFFICE USE ONLY</td><td></td></tr>
</table>

FOR OFFICE USE ONLY

1. a) Do you get any magazines in the mail?   YES   NO
   b) If yes, what kind?
      ____home and family magazines
      ____news magazines
      ____children's magazines
      ____other

2. Does your child have a toy box or other special place where he/she keeps his/her toys?   YES   NO

3. How many children's books does your family own?
   ____0 to 2
   ____3 to 9
   ____10 or more

4. How many books do you have besides children's books?
   ____0 to 9
   ____10 to 20
   ____more than 20

   Where do you keep them?
   ____in boxes (packed)
   ____on a bookcase
   ____other (explain_____)
   _____

5. How often does someone take your child into a grocery store?
   ____hardly ever; I prefer to go alone
   ____at least once a month
   ____at least twice a month
   ____at least once a week

6. About how many times in the past week did you have to spank your child? _____

7. Do you have a T.V.?   YES   NO
   About how many hours is the T.V. on each day? _____

FOR OFFICE USE ONLY

8. How often does someone get a chance to read stories to your child?
   ____hardly ever
   ____at least once a week
   ____at least 3 times a week
   ____at least 5 times a week

9. Do you ever sing to your child when he/she is nearby?   YES   NO

10. Does your child put away his/her toys by himself/herself <u>most of the time</u>?   YES   NO

11. Is your child allowed to walk or ride his tricycle by himself/herself to the house of a friend or relative?   YES   NO

12. What do you do with your child's art work?
    ____let him/her keep it
    ____put it away
    ____hang it somewhere in the house
    ____throw it away shortly after looking at it

13. In the space below write what you might say if your child said, "Look at that big truck".

14. What do you usually do when a friend is visiting you in your home and your child has nothing to do?
    ____suggest something for him/her to do
    ____offer him/her a toy
    ____give him/her a cookie or something to eat
    ____put him/her to bed for a nap
    ____play with him/her

© 1981, JFK Child Development Center

FIGURE 8-5

The HSQ is a shortened version of the HOME questionnaire. It is designed for parents to answer. (Source: C. E. Coons, E. C. Gay, A. W. Fandal, C. Ker, and W. K. Frankenburg, *Home Screening Questionnaire.* Denver, Colo.: JFK Child Development Center, 1981.)

otherwise, they might not know of the opportunity.

Articles can increase parents' interest. Curriculum and child development may be communicated through newsletters as well as personal visits. It is also a good idea to combine the two and give the parent a handout at the end of a home visit. Write your own newsletter or use a commercial one such as *Parent Talk* (Figure 8-6).

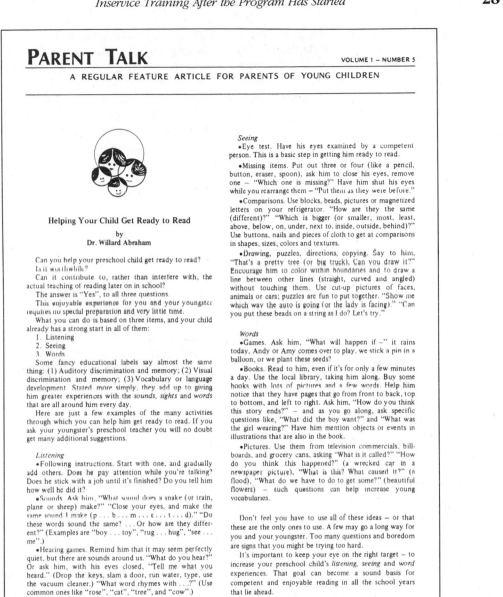

PARENT TALK

VOLUME 1 – NUMBER 5

A REGULAR FEATURE ARTICLE FOR PARENTS OF YOUNG CHILDREN

Helping Your Child Get Ready to Read

by
Dr. Willard Abraham

Can you help your preschool child get ready to read?
Is it worthwhile?
Can it contribute to, rather than interfere with, the actual teaching of reading later on in school?

The answer is "Yes", to all three questions.

This enjoyable experience for you and your youngster requires no special preparation and very little time.

What you can do is based on three items, and your child already has a strong start in all of them:

1. Listening
2. Seeing
3. Words

Some fancy educational labels say almost the same thing: (1) Auditory discrimination and memory; (2) Visual discrimination and memory; (3) Vocabulary or language development. Stated more simply, they add up to giving him greater experiences with the *sounds, sights* and *words* that are all around him every day.

Here are just a few examples of the many activities through which you can help him get ready to read. If you ask your youngster's preschool teacher you will no doubt get many additional suggestions.

Listening

• Following instructions. Start with one, and gradually add others. Does he pay attention while you're talking? Does he stick with a job until it's finished? Do you tell him how well he did it?

• Sounds. Ask him, "What sound does a snake (or train, plane or sheep) make?" "Close your eyes, and make the same sound I make (p . . . b . . . m . . . s . . . t . . . d)." "Do these words sound the same? . . . Or how are they different?" (Examples are "boy . . . toy", "rug . . . hug", "see . . . me".)

• Hearing games. Remind him that it may seem perfectly quiet, but there are sounds around us. "What do you hear?" Or ask him, with his eyes closed, "Tell me what you heard." (Drop the keys, slam a door, run water, type, use the vacuum cleaner.) "What word rhymes with . . .?" (Use common ones like "rose", "cat", "tree", and "cow").

Seeing

• Eye test. Have his eyes examined by a competent person. This is a basic step in getting him ready to read.

• Missing items. Put out three or four (like a pencil, button, eraser, spoon), ask him to close his eyes, remove one — "Which one is missing?" Have him shut his eyes while you rearrange them — "Put them as they were before."

• Comparisons. Use blocks, beads, pictures or magnetized letters on your refrigerator. "How are they the same (different)?" "Which is bigger (or smaller, most, least, above, below, on, under, next to, inside, outside, behind)?" Use buttons, nails and pieces of cloth to get at comparisons in shapes, sizes, colors and textures.

• Drawing, puzzles, directions, copying. Say to him, "That's a pretty tree (or big truck). Can you draw it?" Encourage him to color within boundaries and to draw a line between other lines (straight, curved and angled) without touching them. Use cut-up pictures of faces, animals or cars; puzzles are fun to put together. "Show me which way the auto is going (or the lady is facing)." "Can you put these beads on a string as I do? Let's try."

Words

• Games. Ask him, "What will happen if —" it rains today, Andy or Amy comes over to play, we stick a pin in a balloon, or we plant these seeds?

• Books. Read to him, even if it's for only a few minutes a day. Use the local library, taking him along. Buy some books with lots of pictures and a few words. Help him notice that they have pages that go from front to back, top to bottom, and left to right. Ask him, "How do you think this story ends?" — and as you go along, ask specific questions like, "What did the boy want?" and "What was the girl wearing?" Have him mention objects or events in illustrations that are also in the book.

• Pictures. Use them from television commercials, billboards, and grocery cans, asking "What is it called?" "How do you think this happened?" (a wrecked car in a newspaper picture), "What is this?" What caused it?" (a flood), "What do we have to do to get some?" (beautiful flowers) — such questions can help increase young vocabularies.

Don't feel you have to use all of these ideas — or that these are the only ones to use. A few may go a long way for you and your youngster. Too many questions and boredom are signs that you might be trying too hard.

It's important to keep your eye on the right target — to increase your preschool child's *listening, seeing* and *word* experiences. That goal can become a sound basis for competent and enjoyable reading in all the school years that lie ahead.

FIGURE 8–6
Parent handouts can increase the effectiveness of home visits. (Source: Abraham, W. *Parent talk.* Scottsdale, Ariz.: Sunshine Press. Reprinted with permission.)

INSERVICE TRAINING AFTER THE PROGRAM HAS STARTED

Learning by both the family and the home visitor comes to fruition during the development of the program. During this period, the home visitor responds to the individual needs, desires, and styles of the parents and children. Close contact with the program's coordinator or trainers supports the home visitor and allows administrators to keep track of what is happening in the field. Reports on each visit, filled out in duplicate with one for the home visitor and one for the program's administrators or trainers, will enable persons from both levels of the program to keep in touch with developments and needs. In doing so inservice training can be directed to enrich weak areas and clarify procedures.

Small Groups

Throughout the year questions and needs for training will arise. Small groups of home visitors, rather than all members of the program, meeting together as needs emerge encourages effective training sessions. The individualized meeting is beneficial because the session has been set up especially for the participants, and small numbers allow for a more personalized response by the trainer or coordinator.

Community Resources

Although lists of community resources are given to home visitors early in the program, more definite descriptions and procedures are useful when specific problems arise. During the year, specialists from a variety of community agencies can be invited to share their experiences and knowledge of procedures with the staff. Have them come to training meetings, meet the staff, and answer questions concerning use of their programs.

Development of a Home Activities File

The development of a home activities file depends on the objectives and philosophy of the program. Materials and experiences are based on the home environment, the children's interests, and the parents' enthusiasm. You have an excellent opportunity to involve parents in creating learning activities for their children. You may enable the parents to change through your encouragement and acceptance of their contributions.

Throughout the year home visitors involve parents in teaching their children at home. As the home visitor suggests activities for the child, additional ideas may occur to both the visitor and the parent. In addition, children themselves may elaborate on old ideas or create new activities. The home visitor should bring these ideas back to the office, where they can be classified and catalogued. Parents receive a boost if home visitors recognize their contributions. They will also continue to develop activities for children if they are reinforced. Write down their suggestions and file them for future use or include them in the program for the coming week.

EVALUATION OF PROGRAM

Ongoing evaluations of contacts made, visits completed, and services rendered are essential. Home visit reports give data that can be used to measure progress. If the home visitor systematically completes each report, the administrator will be able to evaluate progress throughout the training period.

Parent Questionnaires

Statements by parents and responses to questionnaires concerning the effect of the program on the child and family are valuable in analyzing the impact of the program. Collect these throughout the program as well as at the completion of the year. The Gloucester Parent Evaluation form is a good guide to aid in the construction of a parent questionnaire (Figure 8–7).

Evaluation is a tool to be used during the development of the program as well as a means to assess accomplishments. Include a variety of evaluations to improve the program and to demonstrate its effectiveness.

PROGRAMS THAT WORK

Numerous methods and approaches have proven effective in a variety of projects funded throughout the United States. Summaries of selected programs illustrate the scope and variety of parent involvement in the educational process. Take from them the ideas and procedures that fit into your specific situation.

Portage Project

The Portage Project is a home teaching program for parents and handicapped preschoolers, ages birth to 6 years. It serves a large rural area of 3600 square miles in south-central Wisconsin. Children who have been diagnosed as either mentally retarded, physically handicapped, hearing impaired, vision impaired, or culturally deprived and children who have speech, language, or behavioral problems are enrolled. The children chosen are referred to the project by local physicians, social workers, public schools, speech therapists, county health nurses, and local guidance teams. In addition, the project is advertised on the radio and in newspaper articles, which ask parents to refer children themselves.

Although children could not come a long distance to a center, it was feasible to have a home delivery system with professional educators going to the home on scheduled visits for 9½ months each year. A home teacher visits the home and works with the parents and child each week for 1½ hours on three behavioral goals appropriate to the child's ability level. After the home teacher demonstrates each activity and how to record the child's performance, the parent models the process. The parent continues as the teacher and records the child's performance until the next home visit. At the next home visit the teacher records the child's progress, and the parent-teacher team sets up new goals and activities for the following week.

The Portage Project staff developed materials that are valuable for use with both handicapped and nonhandicapped children. The materials include

1. A checklist of 580 developmentally sequenced behaviors divided into six areas: infant stimulation, self-help, language, cognition, motor skills, and socialization
2. A card file of 580 cards to match the checklist with suggestions for teaching the behaviors (Figure 8–8)
3. A *Manual of Instruction,* which describes how to use the Portage Guide and develop and implement curriculum goals

Because the program involves the parents in teaching their children, manuals for parents were also developed. The Portage Parent Program includes *Parent Readings and Inventories, Parental Behavior Inventory,* and an *Instructor's Manual.*

The Portage Program uses the parent as the teacher through the week. To facilitate this process, the home teacher supports the parent in the following ways:

1. Demonstrates for the parents what to do and how to do it
2. Helps parents practice teaching the skill

In many home-based programs professional educators work with children at their homes.

Directions: On the following questions put a check in the box opposite the
answer that best describes your personal opinion.

1. Since my child started Home Start, he/she
   a. has progressed greatly _____ ☐
   b. has progressed a little _____ ☐
   c. hasn't learned anything _____ ☐
2. Check one
   a. My child really likes Home Start _____ ☐
   b. My child participates because I want him/her to _____ ☐
   c. My child doesn't like Home Start _____ ☐
   d. I don't know how my child feels _____ ☐
3. In my opinion, Home Start
   a. requires too much discipline _____ ☐
   b. there is just the right amount of discipline _____ ☐
   c. there is not enough discipline _____ ☐
4. Do you feel that your child is receiving enough individual attention?
   Yes _____   No _____
5. Do you feel you are receiving enough information about your child's progress?
   Yes _____   No _____
6. Do you find it easy to talk to your Home Visitor concerning your child?
   Yes _____   No _____
7. Would you like to have more opportunity to plan with your Home Visitor
   about your child?
   Yes _____   No _____
8. Do you like the activities for your child?
   Yes _____   No _____
9. Since my child started in Home Start, I have noticed that he/she
   a. is more independent _____ ☐
   b. is less independent _____ ☐
   c. no difference _____ ☐
10. Since my child started in Home Start, I have noticed that he/she
    a. is more curious _____ ☐
    b. is less curious _____ ☐
    c. no difference _____ ☐
11. Since my child started in Home Start, I have noticed that he/she
    a. gets along better with other children _____ ☐
    b. gets along worse with other children _____ ☐
    c. no change _____ ☐
12. Since my child started in Home Start, I have noticed that he/she
    a. speaks more clearly _____ ☐
    b. speaks less clearly _____ ☐
    c. no change _____ ☐
13. Since my child started in Home Start, I have noticed that he/she
    a. follows directions more easily _____ ☐
    b. follows directions less easily _____ ☐
    c. no change _____ ☐
14. Since my child started in Home Start, I have noticed that he/she
    a. is better behaved _____ ☐
    b. behaves worse _____ ☐
    c. no change _____ ☐
15. Do you think your child will do better in public schools because of Home Start?
    Yes _____   No _____
    What did you expect your child to learn as a result of Home Start?
    a. _____
    b. _____
    c. _____

FIGURE 8–7
The Gloucester Parent Evaluation Form allows parents to analyze their child's growth. (Source: U.S.
Department of Health, Education and Welfare. *Partners with parents.* Washington, D.C.: U.S. Government
Printing Office, 1978.)

16. In your opinion, what should be done to improve the program for your child?
    a. _____
    b. _____
    c. _____
17. As a result of Home Start,
    a. I know more about my child's development _____ ☐
    b. I know a great deal more about my child's development _____ ☐
    c. I know the same about my child's development _____ ☐
18. As a result of Home Start, I have gained knowledge as the teacher of my child.
    Yes _____   No _____
19. As a result of Home Start, I know more about the services available to me in the community.
    Yes _____   No _____

PARENT ACTIVITIES EVALUATION

1. Check one
   a. I attend most of the parent activities _____ ☐
   b. I have attended at least one of the meetings _____ ☐
   c. I have not been able to attend _____ ☐
   Why? _____
2. Which statement best describes your opinion of parent activities?
   a. I find them enjoyable _____ ☐
   b. I like them a little _____ ☐
   c. I find them boring _____ ☐
   d. I haven't attended enough activities to form an opinion ____ ☐
3. As a result of the activities, I have
   a. found out a lot about Home Start _____ ☐
   b. found out a little about Home Start _____ ☐
   c. found out almost nothing _____ ☐
4. Do you feel comfortable sharing concerns and interests with other mothers at the activities?
   Yes _____   No _____
5. Have you been able at the activities to discuss the progress of your child?
   Yes _____   No _____

PROGRAM EVALUATION

1. What has Home Start meant to you?
   a. _____
   b. _____
   c. _____
2. What could be improved in Home Start?
   a. _____
   b. _____
   c. _____

FIGURE 8–7
continued

3. Encourages parents when they do well
4. Individualizes the program so it fits the needs of the parents as well as the child
5. Involves parents in planning and in taking on as much responsibility as they are able

The type of program which stimulates direct involvement of parents in teaching their children can provide parents with necessary skills and techniques to become more effective doing what they already do and being what they already are, the single most important individual in their child's life—parents and teachers. (Shearer et al., 1976, p. 40)

Mother-Child Home Program of the Verbal Interaction Project

Phyllis Levenstein's Mother-Child Home Program (MCHP) is a home-based program that

Cognitive 58

AGE 3 to 4

TITLE: Copies series of connected V strokes VVVVVVVV

WHAT TO DO:

1. Draw a series of V strokes. Encourage the child to trace over the
   letter first with his finger and later with a crayon or pencil.
   Help by guiding his hand.
2. Have him draw with you making one line at a time.
3. Make a row of connected V strokes. Then have the child draw more
   rows as you give him verbal directions "up, down, up, down."
4. Have child make a row of V strokes on paper. When he finishes,
   make it into a picture of mountains, grass, trees, etc. for him.

🏠 **PortageGuide**

Cognitive 61

AGE 3 to 4

TITLE: Names objects as same and different

WHAT TO DO:

1. Put three sets of two identical items in a box (two forks, two
   blocks, two combs). Ask child to find two things that are the
   same in the box.
2. Repeat above activity using pictures or textures.
3. Use assortment of paired items telling the child they are the same.
   Mix them up and tell the child they are different. Present pairs
   of same and different items to child and have him tell you if they
   are the same or different.
4. Help the child by giving him clues of the first sound of the word.
   Say, "These are the s-s-s." Let child finish word. ·
5. If child has difficulty, initially ask him, "Are they same or different?" Gradually fade this and just ask, "Tell me about these."

🏠 **PortageGuide**

FIGURE 8–8
Two examples from the card deck of the Portage Guide show the type of activities that parents can do with their children at home. (Source: Shearer, D., et al. *Portage guide to early education.* Portage, Wisc.: Cooperative Educational Service Agency 12, 1976.)

relies on positive verbal interaction between the young child, 2 to 4 years old, and the primary caregiver. The "mother" may be any adult who has the primary nurturing responsibilities of the child. The program is based in the child's home, and home visitors ("toy demonstrators") come twice weekly for half-hour sessions over the 2-year period (ages 2 to 4). The school year covers 7 months, two visits a week for a total of 46 visits to each home each year. The toy demonstrators use 12 books and 11 toys each year. The program progresses developmentally through the 46 visits. Guide sheets cover concepts such as colors, shapes, and sizes and cognitive skills such as matching, pretending, and differentiating. Special features of the MCHP include:

1. Guide sheets that allow the caregiver to have the curriculum in small, easily used portions
2. Training that is based on modeling rather than teaching
3. Permanent assignment of toy demonstrators over the 2 years with each demonstrator using the same 22 toys and 24 books, which ensures a stable curriculum for all participants
4. Techniques that encourage the program to be voluntary and not intrusive upon the caregiver
5. Explicit methods for 2 years that also allow for some flexibility

The goal of the program is to increase the mother's interaction with her child in a natural dialogue that enhances and enriches the child's home environment. By training toy demonstrators who are paraprofessionals with a high school education to demonstrate and model their toys without being didactic, the project facilitates relaxed verbal interaction between parent and child (Levenstein, 1988).

Levenstein recommends approaching the mothers as valuable, free, independent, and with the right to dignity. Their participation should be voluntary but with built-in incentives. The program shows respect for cultural and ethnolinguistic differences. It is easy to participate in and has reachable goals (Levenstein, 1988).

Educational Cooperative

The Home-Based early childhood education program has a varied approach of three components: home visitation, mobile classroom van, and television. During each home visitation the parent educator brings a weekly four-page *Parent Guide,* which contains a one-page discussion of child development, nutrition, or aspects of parenting plus three pages of activities to be used by the parent and child throughout the week. These activities relate to the television program and the objectives of the project. The home visitor explains and/or demonstrates the activities. Toys, books, and materials can be loaned for the week.

The second component, mobile classroom, uses a traveling van equipped as a preschool. A teacher and aide drive the van to different areas each day, and 10 to 15 children in that area attend preschool for 2 or 3 hours.

The children who participated in the Home Based programs continued to show gains after entering elementary school. Parental attitudes were also more positive than before (Far West Laboratory for Educational Research and Development, 1983).

These programs for preschool children use the home as primary centers for learning. Educational reports in the 1980s focus on home-based work for school-aged students too and emphasize the need for increased homework. Some have even called for parents to once again practice home schooling.

HOME SCHOOLING

The increasing number of home schools have forced schools and state legislators to analyze the coordination and cooperation needed between schools and parents who want to educate their children at home.

Estimates of the number of children who were schooled at home in the mid- to late 1980s range from 120,000 to more than 1 million (cited in Mayberry, 1989). Profiles of home school families suggest that they are well-educated, more likely to live in small towns or rural communities, politically conservative, and belong to small protestant denominations (Mayberry, 1989).

Home schooling is regulated by the state. The National Association of State Boards of Education offered a resource document on home schooling that recommends:

1. Children not attending public or private schools should be required to register with the local school system, county, or state.

2. A criteria for home instruction should be established which allows broad leeway in the choice of materials and curricula, but expects competencies in basic areas.

3. Reports of student progress should be required of parents who are new to home instruction.

4. Systems for evaluation need to be adopted. Alternative methods of evaluation can be used, but quarterly or yearly evaluations should be done.

5. If students are not making sufficient progress, a plan for probation and remediation should be offered (Roach, 1988).

State legislatures have been responding to parental demands, and more states are allowing home instruction. The next step to help ensure the child's success will be cooperation between the home and school. How can parents and schools accommodate each other? Suggestions include part-time attendance in school by children who are home schooled (Knowles, 1989; Mayberry, 1989). The schools can also furnish resources for the home-school families. These may include use of resource centers; enrollment in special classes such as music, art, and science; inclusion of the parents in school district programs; advisory and facilitating services; inservice workshops; and participation of the home-schooled student in extra curricular activities, summer programs, and large group or team activities (Knowles, 1989). By allowing the student to be schooled at home, but providing support and opportunity for the child to participate with other children in activities, the school helps the parents to achieve their goals of educating their children and also gives the children opportunities for social interaction with other students. If at a later time the child re-enters school, the transition is made easier.

HOMEWORK, HOMESTUDY AND/OR ENRICHMENT AT HOME

Student achievement rises significantly when teachers regularly assign homework and students conscientiously do it. (U.S. Department of Education, 1986, p. 41)

The report *What Works* emphasizes that the home and homework are essential for children to reach their full potential. However, what homework is varies according to the age of the child. First, the home environment, the interaction, and intense work with toys make up the child's learning experience; the home is the child's school and homework. As children become older, the location of school goes outside the home, and suddenly what children do at home is not considered school unless they bring home an assignment from school. But everyone knows the home is still part of the child's learning experiences, and the extra work and advice from school helps to make learning richer.

Homework takes on different dimensions at the preschool, elementary, and secondary levels. At all levels homestudy or homework can form a bridge between home and school that lets parents know what is happening at school. Homework can help form a bond between parent and child. Preschool teachers or parent educators should focus on the child's experiences at home, take advantage of what is already occurring at home, open the parent's eyes to learning opportunities, and enrich the home experience. The program or center should encourage and support parent-child interaction. Asking parents to read to their children is very positive (U.S. Department of Education, 1986). The parent-child partnership should be recognized even though it is often lost in the hustle of the business of life.

At the elementary school level, the use of assigned homework becomes more defined. The following suggestions for involving the parent with the child's schoolwork were pointed out in *What Works*:

- Some teachers ask parents to read aloud to the child, to listen to the child read, and to sign homework papers.
- Others encourage parents to drill students on math and spelling and to help with homework papers.
- Teachers also encourage parents to discuss school activities with their children and suggest ways parents can help teach their children at home. For example, a simple home activity might be alphabetizing books; a more complex one would be using kitchen supplies in an elementary science experiment.
- Teachers also send home suggestions for games or group activities related to the child's schoolwork that parent and child can play together. (U.S. Department of Education, 1986, p. 19)

If the parent is too busy or is unable to help with the home task, dissension may develop between parent and child. The use of a telephone network (see Chapter 4) to assist the child with homework can help eliminate the problem of the child not knowing how to do the assignment and the parent being embarrassed by not knowing how to do it, either.

The 1983 National Commission on Excellence in Education addressed the issue of homework and recommended that more homework be assigned to students. However, parents may not agree. The 1985 Gallup Poll questioned the public on their attitude toward homework for elementary students. The response was almost evenly divided; 40% favored and 38% opposed any homework. Parents whose children received average or below average grades were more supportive of homework than those whose children received above average marks. Nonwhites were more likely than whites to favor homework for their children; 66% to 36% at the elementary school level and 67% to 45% at the high school level (Gallup, 1985, p. 42).

Only about 6 out of 10 public school parents required their children to spend a certain amount of time on their homework. In addition, half limited television viewing. This was true regardless of socioeconomic or educational level. When public school parents did require their children to devote time to homework, the average amount was 1 hour and 25 minutes each

night (Gallup, 1985, p. 42). A slightly higher amount is reported by teachers, who say they assign about 2 hours of homework per school day. High school seniors say that they spend 4 to 5 hours a week on homework, and 10% spend no time at all (U.S. Department of Education, 1986, p. 41).

Preschool and Primary Grades

Research results do not support the use of homework for the very young (LaConte, 1981). On the other hand, research does recognize the importance of home-school involvement. A rich home environment provides homestudy; the parent is interested in and involved with the child's activities; the child does informal study at home and on visits to the store or museum. Talking and reading together foster the child's development. Selecting television programs and viewing television together, followed by discussion, fosters the child's learning and provides interaction between parent and child. Use of home computers, though not a necessity, can give even a preschool child a feeling of success when using a self-correcting activity that allows her to be in command. The time and length of involvement with computers and television must be monitored, because the most important learning takes place between people. Parents who talk, listen, and read to their children learn a lot about the children's feelings, abilities, and interests.

Elementary and Secondary Grades

Traditional homework for elementary and secondary students falls into three categories: *practice, preparation,* and *extension* (as cited in LaConte, 1981).

Practice is the most common type of homework; a skill learned at school is repeated. LaConte recommends that practice drills be limited to the classroom and homestudy be individualized. "The most effective kind of practice assignment asks the student to apply recently acquired learning in a direct and personal way"

(p. 9). The able student becomes bored with the repetition; the poor student will probably ignore the assignment. Thus, the more able students are usually given more and more homework while those who need individualized work either do not do the homework or are not assigned the work. If the teacher limits practice drill to the classroom, he can adjust assignments according to individual needs and differences. However, *What Works* reports on one study that reveals that when low-ability students do just 1 to 3 hours of homework, their grades are as high as average students who do no homework (U.S. Department of Education, 1986, p. 41).

Preparation is the assignment of material to be used to lay the groundwork for the next lesson. These assignments should be imaginative and challenging, and should include more than assigning a chapter to read. Interviews, research, gathering information, or development of an original idea could enrich the child's learning experience (LaConte, 1981). Preparation assignments are not appropriate for young children unless you involve the parents. An appropriate example would be a sound walk. Parent and child could walk around their neighborhood and the child could bring back a list of all the sounds that they heard.

Extension is an individualized approach to homestudy that takes the student beyond the traditional classroom assignment. This homework fosters a creative approach to learning and is usually reserved by schools for older children. Younger children would need their parents' help with a project or research. The young child's whole approach to learning could be labeled extension. A child has to reach and grow from the very first day of birth (and even before). The only thing that has not been required is a report on her learning.

Homework is very important in elementary and secondary schools. LaConte suggests assign-ments that are "(1) necessary and useful, (2) appropriate to the ability and maturity level of students, (3) well explained and motivated, and (4) clearly understood by both child and parent" (1981, p. 20).

Parents can help children with their homework by

- structuring time and having a place for their child to do the homework
- being available as an advisor or helper
- guiding and assisting but not taking responsibility for the homework completion
- effectively using positive and supportive ways to help their child, thereby building the child's self-esteem (Cooke & Cooke, 1988).

A report by the U.S. Department of Education also emphasizes the need for homework to be well planned. The assignments should relate to the classwork and extend the student's learning beyond the classroom. Effective homework assignments do not just supplement the classroom lesson; they also teach students to be independent learners. Homework gives students experience in following directions, making judgments and comparisons, raising additional questions for study, and developing responsibility and self-discipline (U.S. Department of Education, 1986, p. 42). Homework provides reinforcement for skills that were learned previously, practice time for developing skills, and an opportunity to "learn in one's own time and style" (Cooke & Cooke, 1988, p. 19).

Because many homes have computers connected to information services and data banks, access to cable television classes, and videotapes and videodiscs, the home is now widely recognized as a place where schoolwork can be supplemented and reinforced. Home-based education has many facets and will diversify and increase in the future. Methods may vary, but the home is still a primary educator of children.

SUMMARY

Home-based education, initiated in the 1960s, saw continued and increased use in the 1970s. The Home Start demonstration programs, Parent Child Development Centers, Child and Family Resource Programs, and ESEA Chapter I, III, and IV-C programs contributed significant research data and suggested procedures for implementation by others. In the 1980s many of the ideas developed by the Home Start demonstration programs were implemented into the Head Start programs.

If the school is interested in developing a home-based program, it should (1) show a need for the program, (2) involve others in the planning, (3) develop a parent advisory council, and (4) decide on a program format.

Home learning activities to be used by the home visitor and families can be obtained through development of individualized activities, commercial offerings, and/or activities developed by demonstration programs. Use materials that are readily available to the parents, for the parent is the primary teacher in the home-based program. The focus in a home-based program is on the parent interacting with and teaching the child after the home visitor is gone.

Screening instruments may be selected to guide teachers in their work with parents and children and to serve as a basis for referrals for more thorough evaluation.

Concern about excellence in education brought added emphasis on homework. The report *What Works* emphasized the need for homework to supplement the school curriculum. Preschool children need a rich learning environment in the home— their homework. Homework for older students includes practice, preparation, and extension.

SUGGESTED ACTIVITIES AND DISCUSSIONS

1. Discuss the type of parent-child interaction that best promotes the child's emotional and intellectual growth.
2. Brainstorm home situations that would be positive experiences for children.
3. Itemize household equipment that can be used as home learning tools. How would you use each?
4. Role play a home visit. Use attending behaviors described in Chapter 4. Practice your visit under varying conditions such as (1) a parent who is very eager to cooperate, (2) a parent who is constantly interrupted by the children, and (3) a parent who is threatened by your visit.
5. Imagine many home situations. Write role-playing opportunities based on these families.
6. Develop a home-based curriculum for a 3-, 4-, or 5-year-old.
7. Develop four home learning activities based on Gordon's five steps: idea, reason, materials, action, extension (see pp. 279–83).
8. Organize a workshop designed to introduce a parent to the learning processes of children.
9. Discuss the guidelines related to home visits.
10. Discuss value systems that may vary from your own. How can you work with parents and refrain from infringing on their beliefs? Discuss.
11. Compare the strengths and weaknesses of home-based, center-based, and home/center-based programs.

BIBLIOGRAPHY

Abraham, W. *Parent talk.* Scottsdale, Ariz.: Sunshine Press.

Appalachia Educational Laboratory. *Home visitor's handbook.* Charleston, W. Va.: Appalachia Educational Laboratory, 1972.

Bernard, D. H. Selection and recruitment of home visitors. In I. J. Gordon & W. F. Breivogel (Eds.), *Building effective home-school relationships.* Boston: Allyn & Bacon, 1976.

Brown, L., Sherbenow, R. J., & Dollar, S. J. *Test of nonverbal intelligence, a language-free measure of cognitive ability.* Austin, TX: Pro-Ed, 1982.

Caldwell, B. M., & Bradley, R. H. *Administration manual: Home observation for measurement of the environment.* Little Rock: University of Arkansas, 1984.

Cooke, G., & Cooke, S. Homework that makes a difference in children's learning. Personal communication, 1988.

Coons, C. E., Gay, E. C., Fandal, A. W., Ker, C., & Frankenburg, W. K. *Home Screening Questionnaire.* Denver: JFK Child Development Center, 1981.

Fandal, A., Personal correspondence. Denver: University of Colorado Medical Center, February 1986.

Far West Laboratory for Educational Research and Development. *Educational programs that work, 1983.* San Francisco: Author, 1983.

Frankenburg, W. K. *Denver Prescreening Developmental Questionnaire.* Denver: JFK Child Development Center, 1975.

Frankenburg, W. K., & Dodds, J. *Denver Developmental Screening Test.* Denver: University of Colorado Medical Center, n.d.

Gallup, A. M. The 17th annual Gallup Poll of the public's attitudes toward the public schools. *Phi Delta Kappan,* September 1985, *67;* pp. 35–47.

Gordon, I. J., & Breivogel, W. F., (Eds.). *Building effective home-school relationships.* Boston: Allyn & Bacon, 1976.

Gray, S. W. Home visiting programs for parents of young children. *Peabody Journal of Education,* 1971, *48,* 106–111.

Hedrich, V., & Jackson, C. Winning play at home base. *American Education,* July 1977, pp. 27–30.

Knowles, J. G. Cooperating with home school parents: A new agenda for public schools? *Urban Education,* 23 (4), January 1989, pp. 392–411.

LaConte, R. T. *Homework as a learning experience.* Washington, D.C.: National Education Association of the United States, 1981.

Leler, H., Johnson, D. L., Kahn, A. J., Hines, R. P., & Torres, M. *The Houston Model for parent education.* Paper presented at the meeting of the Society for Research in Child Development, Denver, Colo., April 13, 1975.

Levenstein, P. *Messages from home: The Mother-Child program.* Columbus: Ohio State University Press, 1988.

Mayberry, M. Home-based education in the United States: Demographics, motivations, and educational implications. *The Educational Review,* 41 (2), 1989, pp. 171–180.

McElderry, J. S., & Escobedo, L. E. *Tools for learning.* Denver, Colo.: Love Publishing, 1979.

Nimnicht, G. P., & Brown, E. The toy library: Parents and children learning with toys. *Young Children,* December 1972, pp. 110–116.

Packer, A., Hoffman, S., Bozler, B., & Bear, N. Home learning activities for children. In I. Gordon & W. F. Breivogel (Eds.), *Building effective home-school relationships.* Boston: Allyn & Bacon, 1976.

Ricciuti, H. N. *Three models for parent education: The Parent-Child Development Centers.* Paper presented at the meeting of the Society for Research in Child Development, Denver, Colo., April 15, 1975.

Roach, V. Home schooling in an era of educational reform. *School Business Affairs, LIV,* November 1988, pp. 10–14.

Schorr, L. B., & Schorr, D. *Within our reach.* New York: Doubleday, 1988.

Shearer, D., Billingsley, J., Frohman, A., Hilliard, J., Johnson, F., & Shearer, M. *Portage Project readings.* Portage, Wisc.: Portage Project, 1976.

———. *Portage guide to early education.* Portage, Wisc.: Cooperative Educational Service, Agency 12, 1976.

U.S. Department of Education. *What works: Research about teaching and learning.* Washington, D.C.: U.S. Department of Education, 1986.

U.S. Department of Health and Human Services (Office of Human Development Services, Administration for Children, Youth and Families, Head Start Bureau). *Serving handicapped children in home-based Head Start.* R. D. Boyd & J. Herwig, (Eds.), for Portage Project, Cooperative Educational Service Agency 12. Washington, D. C.: U.S. Government Printing Office, 1982.

_____. *A guide for operating a home-based child development program.* Washington, D. C.: U.S. Government Printing Office, 1985.

_____. *The Head Start home visitor handbook.* B. Wolfe & J. Herwig (Eds.), for Portage Project, Cooperative Educational Service Agency 5. Washington, D.C.: U.S. Government Printing Office, 1987.

U.S. Department of Health, Education and Welfare. (Office of Child Development.) *A guide for planning and operating home-based child development programs.* Washington, D.C.: U.S. Government Printing Office, 1974.

_____. *The child and family resource program: An overview.* Washington, D.C.: U.S. Government Printing Office, 1975.

_____. *Home Start and other programs for parents and children.* Washington, D.C.: U.S. Government Printing Office, 1976.

_____. (Office of Human Development, Administration for Children, Youth and Families, Head Start Bureau.) *Partners with parents.* Kathryn D. Hewett et al. for Abt Associates and High/Scope Educational Research Foundation. Washington, D.C.: U.S. Government Printing Office, 1978.

9

Working With Parents of the Exceptional Child

Jo Spidel

P arents are the most significant influence in an exceptional child's life. Children, raised in close proximity to parents or surrogate parents for the first 5 years of their lives, form emotional attachments and their bonding is established. When children begin school, they are shared with teachers and peer groups. As they grow older, children are also affected by the community, but parents continue to influence and shape their development.

Teachers will be wise to listen to parents to learn about the child's background and to discuss concerns. Teachers will gain respect and cooperation from parents if they are willing to share objectives and goals for the child. If teachers will allow the parents to accept some responsibility for the child's learning and will share knowledge of teaching principles and methods

of tutoring, the effectiveness of the learning experience can be doubled.

This chapter gives parents and regular classroom teachers techniques that can be used effectively with the exceptional child. There are many ways to solve problems, to communicate with parents, and to teach exceptional children. The methods presented have been proven effective. Take from them those ideas that will work for you.

DEVELOPMENT OF SPECIAL EDUCATION

Many labels have been placed on exceptional children. One need only review titles of institutions for the mentally ill, the retarded, or the inept to find such descriptions as imbecile, lunatic, crazy, and insane. Such words are indicative of people's perceptions of the problem of exceptionality. Thankfully, parents and professionals have voiced concern over and made real efforts to correct such misconceived labels, which have usually been replaced by the term *exceptional*. The word *exceptional* is used to describe those who are different in some way from the majority of whatever group to which they belong—adults, children, or youth. *Special education* refers to any special needs of or methods required to teach the exceptional child (Hallahan & Kauffman, 1988).

Jo Spidel, M.Ed., is a certified teacher of children with learning disabilities, behavioral disorders, and mental retardation, and is a qualified Director of Special Education. Her accomplishments include 15 years of pubic school teaching Special Education. She served as Curriculum Developer, Special Education Educator, and Case Manager at the Wichita Kansas Elks Training Center for the Handicapped. As the Director of Education for CPC Great Plains Hospital, she developed and implemented an in-hospital school for adolescent patients on the psychiatric and the drug and alcohol abuse treatment units. She is employed by the Wichita Public Schools as a Hospital Teacher for adolescent patients on the psychiatric and alcohol treatment units.

Parents need to accept and encourage their children.

At the middle of this century the term *special education* commonly referred to the education of the mentally retarded. It is proper and helpful that the term is becoming more recognized as open and inconclusive. The gifted, retarded, physically impaired, neurologically impaired, emotionally disturbed, socially maladjusted, speech and language impaired, hard of hearing, deaf, blind, partially seeing, learning disabled, developmentally disabled, and combinations of these are all encompassed by special education. It is significant that the condition of the child was once the labeling factor. The trend now is to label according to the educational needs of the child (Hallahan & Kauffman, 1988).

In history there are many tales of cruel and inhumane treatment of people with exceptionalities. Recalling the story of *The Hunchback of Notre Dame* quickly brings to mind these cruelties. The Spartans were known to force parents to abandon imperfect babies by exposing them to the elements (Frost, 1966; Greenleaf, 1978). There are instances, however, in very early history of persons who were more humane toward those who were different. Hippocrates (400 BC) believed that emotional problems were caused not by supernatural powers but by

natural forces. Plato (375 BC) defended the mentally disturbed as not being able to account for their deeds as normal people were. They therefore required special judgment for their criminal acts. The temples built by Alexander the Great provided asylum for the mentally ill. In 90 BC the first attempt at classification of mental illness was made by Asclepiades, who advocated humane treatment of mentally ill people. Mania and melancholia were described in 100 AD by Aretaeus. Acceptance did not arrive immediately, however, and mistreatment of those too "different" persisted.

The period of 1450 to 1700 was a difficult time for the mentally ill and people with other exceptionalities. Belief in demonology and superstition resulted in the persecution of the mentally ill, the retarded, the developmentally handicapped, and those with any other form of exceptionality (Hallahan & Kauffman, 1988). John Locke, concerned about harsh discipline, cultivated the "blank tablet" concept of the newborn's mind to overcome the popular belief that a child was born full of evil ideas. He advocated that children be given empathic understanding (Cook, Tessier, & Armbruster, 1987).

Jean Jacques Rousseau stressed the importance of beginning the child's education at birth. He believed that strong discipline and strict lessons were inappropriate conditions for optimal learning. He advocated that children should be treated with sympathy and compassion as humans in their own right (Cook, Tessier & Armbruster, 1987).

In the late 1700s Jean Marc Gaspard Itard (1775–1838) sought new methods to teach the mentally retarded. He was a physician and an authority on diseases of the ear and education of the deaf. He found a boy in the forest of Auvergne, France, naked and apparently without upbringing, whom he attempted to raise and educate to become a normal person. Influenced by the teachings of Jean Rousseau and John Locke, Itard believed that learning came through the senses and that all persons could develop the ability to learn if given adequate stimulation. He produced behavioral changes in the boy, Victor, but was unable to teach him to talk and to live independently. He felt he was a failure, but his methods were followed, which began a movement in treatment and education that had a profound effect on the development of special education. Edouard Sequin (1811–1880), Itard's student, was much impressed by Itard's work. He immigrated to the United States in 1848 and promoted the European style of residential institution (Hallahan & Kauffman, 1988; Reinert, 1987).

In the United States residential schools and asylums were built which were very much like those in Europe during the nineteenth century. The first American residential school for the deaf was established in 1817 at Hartford, Connecticut, by Thomas Hopkins Gallaudet (1787–1851). Most early schools avoided the severely or multiple handicapped and worked only with the deaf, blind, or retarded. Those more seriously handicapped were often not eligible for admission to any school. Private schools were often expensive, and the state-operated schools were often limited in their facilities (Hallahan & Kauffman, 1988). This left parents with the nearly total responsibility of caring for their handicapped children at home. I can remember driving through the countryside of the midwestern United States in the 1930s and seeing little houses that were built away from the main house. Upon inquiring what these were, I learned that they were for members of the family who were not "smart," were "off in the head," or "were not controllable."

Perkins School for the Blind, founded in Watertown, Massachusetts, was the first school for sightless people. Samuel G. Howe (1801–1876) proved that the blind could be taught when Laura Bridgemen, blind and deaf, was educated (Hallahan & Kauffman, 1988). Seeking education for his deaf and blind daughter, Arthur H. Keller, father of Helen Keller, consulted many doctors. Dr. Alexander Graham Bell advised him to write to Mr. Anagnos, director of the Perkins Institution. It was from this institution that Anne Mansfield Sullivan came to teach Helen (Keller, 1905; Van Wyck, 1956). The fame of the successful life of this handicapped person did much to persuade parents and professionals that, indeed, the handicapped could be helped.

It was not until the beginning of the twentieth century that community-based programs for exceptional children began to appear. Gallaudet College, the only college for the deaf, started a teacher-training program in the 1890s. In 1904 summer training sessions for teachers of retarded children began at the Vineland Training School in New Jersey (Hallahan & Kauffman, 1988). The community-based programs, however, often became "sunshine" rooms, in which activities such as crafts and arts were pursued but little real attempt was made to change the educational status of the children. In some cases expectations were unrealistic, and disappointment in the programs ensued. Many parents and professionals did not hold optimistic outlooks for the education of the handicapped (Hallahan & Kauffman, 1988).

The Binét-Simon Scale of Intelligence, translated and revised by Goddard, was cited in 1904 by the National Education Association to be a useful test for exceptional children, especially the mentally retarded. It was used to determine the degree of retardation and, hopefully, to guide individualized instruction. This was the beginning of an era of testing that lasted well into the 1970s.

Pearl S. Buck's frank and open discussion of her retarded child and how she learned to accept the problem reached many parents (Buck, 1950). Her urgings helped to begin the massive movement to provide educational services for handicapped people.

Educators from Europe who immigrated to the United States during World War II also made an impact on the education of the handicapped. Frostig, a psychiatric social worker and rehabilitation therapist, trained in the United States as a psychologist and worked with retarded, delinquent, and learning-disabled children (Hallahan & Kauffman, 1988). Alfred A. Strauss and Laura Lehtinen published *Psychopathology and Education of the Brain-Injured Child,* a test that influenced special education.

Others who have contributed to and influenced the special education movement include Samuel A. Kirk, known for his work on the Illinois Test of Psycholinguistic Abilities, and Barbara Bateman, who developed a linguistic approach to learning problems. N. C. Kephart (1971) presented remedial teaching techniques through a perceptual-motor concept.

The National Association for Retarded Citizens (previously the National Association for Retarded Children) was chartered in 1950 and became active in influencing state legislatures and Congress. In 1957, along with other organizations, it supported such important legislative action as the federal establishment of national programs in the field of special education and governmental support of research and leadership training in mental retardation. In 1963 support was extended to most other exceptional persons except the gifted, who did not receive support until 1979. The Bureau of Education for the Handicapped was established in 1966.

Another influence on the special education movement was the rehabilitation of World War II and Korean War veterans. Research into and efforts toward rehabilitation have carried over into the areas of working with exceptional persons. For example, with expanded programs for mobility and occupational training, it was found

that the blind or deaf did not have to be isolated and dependent upon fate. This philosophy spread to children's programs, and many schools began integrating the blind and deaf into regular classes for part of the day while separating them for the rest of their studies in a resource room with a special teacher.

The Kennedys, a powerful and influential family with a handicapped daughter, have done much to help the cause of the handicapped. They established the Joseph P. Kennedy Jr. Foundation—a multimillion dollar effort against mental retardation. The Foundation's main objectives are "the prevention of mental retardation by identifying its causes and improving means by which society deals with its mentally retarded citizens" (The Foundation Center, 1990). It supports research, special projects, consulting services, technical assistance, and conferences and seminars. Thus, parents, educators, and influential families reinforce the growing concern of all parents with handicapped children that their children should have opportunities to develop to their highest potential.

LEGISLATION FOR THE HANDICAPPED

During the 1960s parents organized effective groups that became vocal and attracted enough attention to result in legislation for their handicapped children. In 1971 the Pennsylvania Association for Retarded Children (PARC) won a landmark case against the Commonwealth of Pennsylvania. It was a decision based on the Fourteenth Amendment, which assures all children, including the handicapped, the right to a free and appropriate education. Decisions such as this one led to the passage of other important laws.

Vocational Rehabilitation Act of 1973, Section 504

The Vocational Rehabilitation Act of 1973, Section 504, which relates to nondiscrimination under Federal Grant, Public Law 93–112, required that "no otherwise qualified handicapped individual in the United States shall, solely by reason of his handicap, be excluded from the participation in, be denied the benefits of, or be subjected to discrimination under any program or activity receiving Federal financial assistance" (29 U.S.C. 794) (Sumner County Special Education Services, 1977, p. 5). These services are applicable to all handicapped children ages 3 through 21. The rights of the handicapped to equal opportunities are strongly stated in Section 504 of the Rehabilitation Act of 1973.

Family Educational Rights and Privacy Act (FERPA)—The Buckley Amendments

The Buckley Amendments, written for the rights of all citizens, had great impact on record keeping for the handicapped. They provide the following:

That all "records, files, documents and other materials which contain information directly relating to a student" and which are maintained by an educational agency such as an elementary school, an office of the school district, or university, must be available within 45 days of a request.

The most important work was the development of five principles covering data collection systems for personal data. These can effectively serve to guide school practice. They are as follows:

1. There must be no personal data record keeping systems whose very existence is secret.

2. There must be a way for an individual to find out what information about himself or herself is in a record and how it is used.

3. There must be a way for an individual to prevent information about himself/herself that was obtained for one purpose from being used or made available for other purposes without his/her consent.

4. There must be a way for an individual to correct the record of identifiable information about himself/herself.

5. Any organization creating, maintaining, using or disseminating records of identifiable personal data must assure the reliability of the data for their intended uses and must take precautions to prevent their misuse. (Sumner County Special Education Services, 1977)

This important amendment is discussed further in Chapter 11.

Education for All Handicapped Children Act of 1975

The most far-reaching and revolutionary legislation in relation to education is Public Law 94–142, the Education for All Handicapped Children Act of 1975. All persons between the ages of 3 and 18 must be provided free and appropriate education. The term *appropriate* means suited to the handicapping condition, age, maturity, and past achievements of the child and parental expectations. The education has to be given in a program that is designed to meet the child's needs in the *least restrictive* environment (Section 504). This means that the child shall be placed in the classroom that will benefit him the most. If the student will benefit more from a regular classroom, then he will be placed there. The word *mainstreaming* has become synonymous with placing exceptional children into the regular classroom. However, "least restrictive" can also refer to moving the handicapped child out of a regular classroom into a resource room or self-contained special education room. The law requires diagnosis and individualization of the educational program. This is encompassed in the Individualized Education Program (IEP) (Section 504). The teachers, special teachers, administrators, parents, and others who are concerned with the child's education are involved in the development of the IEP. If appropriate, the child is also included. Finally, the law provides for a hearing that can be initiated by the parents if they do not agree with the diagnosis of the child, the placement, and/or the IEP. This is "due process," and it is the responsibility of the school to inform the parents of their rights.

Gifted and Talented Children's Education Act of 1978

The Gifted and Talented Children's Education Act, P.L. 95–561, provided financial incentives for states and local education agencies to identify and educate gifted and talented students, to provide inservice training, and to conduct research (Heward & Orlansky, 1988).

Education of the Handicapped Act Amendments of 1983

The Education of the Handicapped Act Amendments of 1983, P.L. 98–199, extended fiscal authorization for federal aid to state and local school systems through 1987; improved reporting and information dissemination requirements; increased assistance to deaf and blind children; provided grants for transitional programs; and expanded services for children from birth through 5 years of age (Congressional Record, 1983).

Education of the Handicapped Act Amendments of 1986: Handicapped Infants and Toddlers

Public Law 99–457 establishes statewide, comprehensive, coordinated, multidisciplinary, interagency programs of early intervention services for handicapped infants and toddlers and their families (Congressional Record, 1986). This law addresses easily recognized needs of the very young handicapped.

However, there are many conditions that are not immediately recognized, so services early in life may be delayed for those with chromosomal conditions that are associated with mental retardation, congenital syndromes associated with delays in development, sensory impairments, metabolic disorders, prenatal infections (AIDS, syphillis, cytomegalic inclusion disease), and low birth weight. There are also concerns for the infants whose parents are developmentally delayed, have severe emotional disturbances, or are 15 or younger.

Parents or caretakers may find it difficult to find the necessary programs and services needed to assist them in caring for these very young children. These services are provided through the Department of Education in each state so the first contact should be through the parent or guardian's local school.

Public Law 99–457 provides for public supervision at no cost (except where federal and state laws allow), meeting the needs of handicapped infants and toddlers, family training, counseling, special instruction, physical therapy, stimulation therapy, case management, diagnosis-qualified personnel, and conformation with the Individual Family Service Plan.

The Individualized Family Service Plan or IFSP is similar to an IEP. Due to differences in the ages of the children new descriptions are being forged in the interpretation of the least restrictive environment. For example, how does one provide handicapped infants the opportunity to interact with non-handicapped peers? Solutions are being worked out in individual situations.

The Americans with Disabilities Act

A key recommendation of the National Council on the Handicapped 1986 Report, the Americans with Disabilities Act is still in legislative procedure. The Act addresses the following issues.

The Act prohibits discrimination on the basis of handicap in areas such as employment, housing, public accommodations, travel, communications, and activities of state and local governments.

The Act covers employers engaged in commerce who have 15 or more employees, housing providers covered by federal fair housing, public accommodations, transportation companies, those engaged in broadcasting or communications, and state and local governments.

The Act specifically defines discrimination, including various types of intentional and unintentional exclusions; segregation, inferior or less effective services, benefits or activities; architectural, transportation, and communication barriers; failing to make reasonable accommodations; and discriminatory qualifications and performance standards.

The Act specifies those actions that do not constitute discrimination. They include unequal treatment wholly unrelated to a disability or that which is the result of legitimate application of qualifications and performance standards necessary and substantially related to the ability to perform or participate in the essential components of a job or activity.

The Architectural and Transportation Barriers Compliance Board will issue minimum accessibility guidelines. Other regulations will be issued by the Attorney General, the U.S. Equal Opportunity Commission, The Secretary of Housing and Urban Development, The Secretary of Transportation, the Federal Communication Commission, and the Secretary of Commerce.

The Act will not repeal Sections 503 and 504 of the Vocational Rehabilitation Act of 1973 and all regulations issued under those sections will remain in full force.

Enforcement procedures include administrative remedies, a private right of action in federal court, monetary damages, injunctive relief, attorney's fees, and cutoff of federal funds. (New Jersey State Federation, 1989)

There is strong debate in both houses of Congress because of the far-reaching implications of this law. People who are handicapped are demanding fair and equal treatment. The needs addressed by this Disability Act will be accomplished.

DEVELOPMENT OF THE IEP

Each exceptional child receiving any type of special education services must have an Individualized Educational Program prepared by staff in consultation with the parents. The IEP provides the necessary information for the development and statement of a program. It takes into consideration the child's age, handicap, maturity, past achievements, and the parents' expectations. The plan is developed in a meeting of the child's teacher, other school personnel concerned with the child, the parents and, when appropriate, the child (Karnes, 1979).

The IEP shall include the following:

a. A statement of the child's present performance including where applicable, academic achievement, social adaptation, prevocational and vocational skills, sensory and motor skills, self-help skills, and speech and language skills.
b. Justification for the type of educational placement. A description of the extent to which the child will participate in regular classroom education shall be included or, where regular classroom placement is not appropriate, the extent of participation in other "less restrictive environment" activities shall be described.
c. The projected date for the initiation of the prescribed services and anticipated duration of the services.
d. A statement of annual goals which describes the educational performance anticipated in time frames of service.

e. A statement of 9- to 12-week objectives which are measurable intermediate steps between the present level of performance and the annual goals.
f. Objective criteria and evaluation procedures for determining, at least every 12 weeks, whether the short-term objectives are being achieved.*

IEPs must be reviewed at least once every 12 weeks and the child's progress reported to the parents. Each year a new IEP must be developed for the child within 30 days of the end of the school year. The child (when appropriate), parents, and staff concerned with the child are included in the yearly revision of the IEP. Federal and state statutes provide guidelines for content, procedures, and time limits. Because laws change and specific regulations are subject to frequent change, be sure to check on the current status of rules and regulations in your state (Sumner County Special Education Services, 1977).

Each school and/or special education system is required to create forms for detailing an Individualized Education Program (IEP). Forms developed by the Wichita Public Schools (1989). Examples are included here because they thoroughly cover each area of the IEP as required by P.L. 94–142 (Figures 9–1 through 9–7)*.

THE INDIVIDUALIZED FAMILY SERVICE PLAN AND FAMILY SURVEY

The format of the Individualized Family Service Plan is different from the IEP because it is designed to focus on programs for infants and preschool-age children. The intent is the same—to serve the handicapped individual. Family concerns and needs are given attention as well. The REACH Individualized Family Service Plan (Figure 9–8)* carries the same theme as the IEP.

---

*From Kearns, P. (Ed.). *Your child's right to a free public education: Parent's handbook.* Topeka, Kan.: Kansas Association for Children with Learning Disabilities, 1980, p. 9.

*Figures 9–1 through 9–7 are reprinted by permission of the Wichita Public Schools, USD #259, 217 N. Water, Wichita, KS 67202.

*Figures 9–8 and 9–9 are reprinted by permission from the REACH Preschool Developmental Center, Winfield, Kansas.

PLACEMENT STAFFING — INDIVIDUAL EDUCATIONAL PROGRAM

STUDENT'S NAME: _____ STAFFING DATE: _____

BIRTHDATE: _____ PRESENT GRADE: _____

STUDENT PHONE: _____ PRESENT TEACHERS: _____

STUDENT I.D.: _____ PRESENT SCHOOL: _____

SUGGESTED SERVICE

SERVICES PROVIDED:	REFERENCE SPECIFIC SUGGESTED GOALS	INITIATION DATE	EXPECTED DURATION	AMOUNT OF TIME IN SERVICE	PROJECTED REVIEW DATE	DATE OF REVIEW
REGULAR PROGRAM:						
SPECIAL EDUCATION:						
RELATED SERVICES:						

PLACEMENT JUSTIFICATION: _____ TOTAL LENGTH OF SCHOOL DAY: _____

TYPE OF PHYSICAL EDUCATION PROGRAM: _____
(REFERENCE SPECIFIC SENSORY/MOTOR GOALS)

RECOMMENDED PLACEMENT: _____

POSITION	SIGNATURE/DATE	POSITION (OTHERS IN ATTENDANCE)	SIGNATURE/DATE
PARENT (LAWFUL CUSTODIAN)			
STUDENT:			
TEACHER(S):			
ADMINISTRATOR:			

PERSON RESPONSIBLE FOR MAINTENANCE AND IMPLEMENTATION OF I.E.P. _____

5.1514S   First Copy — Placement Officer; Second Copy — Parent; Third Copy — Placement Officer; Fourth Copy — For Classroom Use   Phase 1-1

FIGURE 9–1
This is the master plan of the IEP.

307

INDIVIDUAL EDUCATIONAL PLAN

FOR SCHOOL YEAR _____

NAME: _____   I.D. # _____   PRESENT DATE: _____

SERVICES PROVIDED:	REFERENCE SPECIFIC SUGGESTED GOALS	INITIATION DATE	EXPECTED DURATION	AMOUNT OF TIME IN SERVICE	PROJECTED REVIEW DATE	DATE OF REVIEW
REGULAR PROGRAM:						
SPECIAL EDUCATION:						
RELATED SERVICES:						
PARENTAL RESPONSE:						

TOTAL LENGTH OF SCHOOL DAY: _____

TYPE OF PHYSICAL EDUCATION PROGRAM
(REFERENCE SPECIFIC SENSORY/MOTOR GOALS)

DATE	PARENT CONTACTS	RESPONSE

PERSON RESPONSIBLE FOR IMPLEMENTATION/DATE _____ SCHOOL _____

POSITION/DATE/NAME/ADMINISTRATIVE REPRESENTATIVE _____

POSITION/DATE/NAME/ADMINISTRATIVE REPRESENTATIVE _____

POSITION/DATE/NAME _____
I ACKNOWLEDGE THE PRESENT I.E.P. AND HAVE BEEN
GIVEN/OFFERED INPUT INTO THE PROGRAM.

PARENT/DATE _____

PARENT/DATE _____

5.1518S   First Copy — Placement Officer: Second Copy — Parent: Third Copy — Placement Officer: Fourth Copy — For Classroom Use

FIGURE 9–2

The Individual Educational Plan for the school year repeats services provided, notes the parental response, and has a place for records of parental contacts.

NAME: _____

DATE: _____

WORKSHEET

PRESENT LEVELS OF EDUCATIONAL PERFORMANCE
(ADDRESS ALL APPLICABLE AREAS)

STRENGTHS/LEARNING STYLES	WEAKNESS/NEEDS	SUGGESTED GOALS (NUMBER EACH GOAL)
A. SOCIAL ADAPTATION		A1. ___ A2. ___ A3. ___ A4. ___ A5. ___
B. ACADEMIC ACHIEVEMENT		B1. ___ B2. ___ B3. ___ B4. ___ B5. ___

NOTE: ATTACH ADDITIONAL SHEETS AS NECESSARY FOR SPACE.

5.1515S   First Copy — Placement Officer: Second Copy — Parent: Third Copy — Placement Officer: Fourth Copy — For Classroom Use

FIGURE 9–3

The areas to be addressed on this page are social adaptation and academic achievement. Note that strengths and learning styles are stated, then weaknesses, and finally the suggested goals.

PRESENT LEVELS OF EDUCATIONAL PERFORMANCE
(ADDRESS ALL APPLICABLE AREAS)

NAME: _____   DATE: _____

STRENGTHS/LEARNING STYLES	WEAKNESS/NEEDS	SUGGESTED GOALS (NUMBER EACH GOAL)
		C1.
		C2.
		C3.
		C4.
		C5.
		D1.
		D2.
		D3.
		D4.
		D5.

C. SPEECH & LANGUAGE SKILLS

D. SENSORY & MOTOR SKILLS

NOTE: ATTACH ADDITIONAL SHEETS AS NECESSARY FOR SPACE.

5.1516S   First Copy — Placement Officer: Second Copy — Parent: Third Copy — Placement Officer: Fourth Copy — For Classroom Use

Phase 1-3
Phase 2-3

FIGURE 9–4
Speech and language skills and sensory and motor skills are considered.

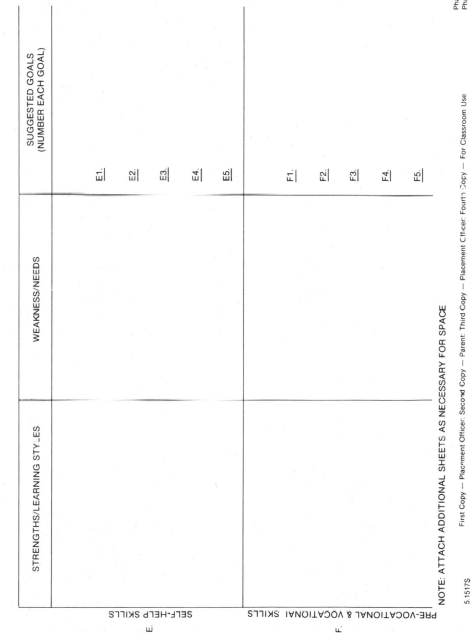

PRESENT LEVELS OF EDUCATIONAL PERFORMANCE
(ADDRESS ALL APPLICABLE AREAS)

NAME: _____   DATE: _____

STRENGTHS/LEARNING STYLES	WEAKNESS/NEEDS	SUGGESTED GOALS (NUMBER EACH GOAL)

SELF-HELP SKILLS
E.
- E1.
- E2.
- E3.
- E4.
- E5.

PRE-VOCATIONAL & VOCATIONAL SKILLS
F.
- F1.
- F2.
- F3.
- F4.
- F5.

NOTE: ATTACH ADDITIONAL SHEETS AS NECESSARY FOR SPACE

5.1517S   First Copy — Placement Officer: Second Copy — Parent: Third Copy — Placement Officer. Fourth Copy — For Classroom Use

Phase 1-4
Phase 2-4

FIGURE 9–5

Special areas to be addressed on this page are pre-vocational skills and self-help skills.

INSTRUCTIONAL AREA: _____

ANNUAL GOAL: _____

NAME: _____

DATE: _____

I.E.P. FOR YEAR _____ TO (DATE) _____

PAGE _____ OF _____

INITIATION DATE	TARGET DATE	SHORT-TERM OBJECTIVES INCLUDING EVALUATION PROCEDURE AND COMPLETION CRITERIA	SPECIAL METHODS AND MATERIALS	REVIEW DATE	COMPLETION DATE	COMMENTS

5.1519S

Phase 2-5

FIGURE 9–6

This form is a summary of the short-term objectives, evaluation procedures, and completion criteria.

I.E.P. REVIEW

NAME: _____   SCHOOL _____

I.D.# _____   PROGRAM _____

DATE OF LAST REVIEW _____   PRESENT DATE _____ GRADE _____

SUMMARY OF STUDENT'S PERFORMANCE RELATIVE TO I.E.P. _____

PARENTAL RESPONSE:

SUGGESTED FUTURE GOALS: _____

I ACKNOWLEDGE THE PRESENT I.E.P. AND HAVE BEEN
GIVEN/OFFERED INPUT INTO THE PROGRAM.

_____
PARENT/DATE

_____
TEACHER/DATE

_____
ADMINISTRATOR/DATE

5-1520S   First Copy — Placement Officer: Second Copy — Parent: Third Copy — Parent: Third Copy — Placement Officer: Fourth Copy — For Classroom Use   Phase 3-1

FIGURE 9–7
The IEP review page summarizes the student's performance relative to the IEP, the parental response, and
the suggested future goals.

CHILD: _____ PARENT SIGNATURE: _____ CASE MANAGER: _____

SKILL AREA: _____

PRESENT LEVEL OF PERFORMANCE (to include strengths & concerns): _____

Review 1	Review 2	Review 3	Review 4

SERVICE GOALS: _____

OUTCOME: _____

EVALUATION: _____

FIGURE 9–8
REACH Individualized Family Service Plan

Parents score their needs and prioritize areas for immediate attention on an extensive questionnaire (Figure 9–9).

REACH's IFSP and its Family Survey strive to cover areas that are pertinent to secure an effective plan for the infant or preschooler. The case manager works directly with the family to develop the IFSP after they have completed the Family Survey.

The foregoing describes the IEP and the IFSP from the viewpoint of the administration. The following material describes exceptional children and approaches the IEP, rights, and services available to parents from the point of informing the parents.

WHO IS THE EXCEPTIONAL CHILD?

Who meets the criterion of the exceptional student? The following descriptions of excep-tional children define and clarify those who need special programs. If a student in a class-room fits into any of the following categories, special services should be provided.

a. Specific Learning Disabilities—Children with spe-cific learning disabilities exhibit a disorder in one or more of the basic psychological processes involved in understanding or in using spoken or written language. Such disorders may be mani-fested in imperfect ability to listen, think, speak, read, write, spell, or do mathematical calcula-tions. They include conditions which have been referred to as perceptual handicaps, brain injury, minimal brain dysfunction, dyslexia, and develop-mental aphasia. They do not include learning problems which are due to primarily visual, hear-ing, or motor handicaps; mental retardation; emotional disturbances; or environmental, cul-tural, or economic disadvantage. The above defi-nition is made more operational by the delinea-tion of three concepts: intactness, discrepancy, and deviation.

FIGURE 9–9
REACH Preschool Developmental Center Family Survey

Reach Preschool Developmental Center

Family Survey

Child's name: _____ Parent's name: _____

Case manager's name: _____ Date: _____

Instructions: Please read the following and score each item on the basis of what you feel are your current needs. Please feel free to add comments or fill in sections marked "Other" with your particular concerns. Your family's Case Manager will use the results of this survey to help determine goals for your Individualized Family Service Plan.

Scoring System

Great Concern:
  This rating would be given for those items which are of immediate concern and for which you would like immediate assistance.

Some Concern:
  This rating would be given for those items which are of some interest and concern but can wait for attention until items of great concern have been taken care of.

Future Concern:
  This rating would be given for those items which may be high priority items in the future.

No Concern:
  This rating would be given for those items which are of no concern or interest.

FIGURE 9–9
continued

	Great Concern	Some Concern	Future Concern	No Concern
Please Check One Category Only for Each Item Addressed.				
I. <u>Understanding your child:</u>				
A. Interpreting and understanding diagnostic and test results				
B. Understanding your child's care needs				
C. Locating educational resources (books, journals, films, etc.) regarding your child's care				
D. Understanding child development				
E. Understanding behavior management				
F. Other:				
Comments:				
II. <u>At Home:</u>				
A. Helping siblings accept and understand your child's care				
B. Helping siblings learn to work and play with your child				
C. Helping your extended family members accept and understand child's care				
D. Coping with the public reaction to your child's condition				
E. Coping with times during the day that are particularly difficult or stressful due to your family's or child's needs				
F. Babysitting services				
G. Day care services				
H. Respite care services				
I. Transportation				
J. Health insurance				
K. Legal Aid				
L. Other:				
Comments:				

FIGURE 9–9
continued

Please Check One Category Only for Each Item Addressed.

	Great Concern	Some Concern	Future Concern	No Concern
III. Accessing Community Resources:				
A. Parent support groups				
B. Counseling agencies				
C. Local churches				
D. Planned Parenthood				
E. Professionals trained to provide services for children:				
Orthopedist				
Opthalmologist				
Genetic counselor				
Physical therapist				
Occupational therapist				
Speech pathologist				
Cleft palate team				
Dietician				
Feeding specialist				
F. Other helping agencies (Specify, i.e. A.A.)				
Comments:				
IV. Obtaining Financial Assistance:				
A. Social Security income				
B. Medical card				
C. Aid to Families with Dependent Children				
D. Food Stamps				
E. Housing				
F. Energy assistance programs				
G. WIC				
H. Day care financial assistance				
I. Kansas Crippled and Chronically Ill Children				
J. Kiwanis, Lions Club				
K. Other: (to include organizations related to the child's particular disability)				
Comments:				

FIGURE 9–9
continued

Please Check One Category Only for Each Item Addressed.	Great Concern	Some Concern	Future Concern	No Concern
V. Implementing Your Child's I.E.P.:				
A. Understanding the goals and objectives				
B. Implementing goals and objectives				
C. Time management				
D. Consistency in attending REACH sessions				
E. Following through with team recommendations for additional services				
F. Other:				
Comments:				
VI. Acquiring Employment Skills				
A. Obtaining G.E.D.				
B. Job Service Center				
C. SRS (CWEP)				
D. Mobile Job Club				
E. Carl Perkins Program				
F. Vocational Rehabilitation Services (disabled adults)				
G. Other:				
Comments:				
VII. Home Management:				
A. Nutrition				
B. Health care				
C. Personal hygiene				
D. Household safety				
E. Money management				
F. Clothing care and maintenance				
G. Care of living environment				
H. Food preparation and management				
I. Recreation				
J. Social skills/counseling				
K. Other:				
Comments:				

FIGURE 9–9
continued

Select 3 areas which are priorities for which you would like to have some immediate input or information about. These may or may not be areas listed in the preceding information.

(1) _____

_____

_____

(2) _____

_____

_____

(3) _____

_____

_____

Comments: _____

_____

Based on the above priority items, the case manager will work with you to develop an Individualized Family Service Plan which will help you as parents to be comfortable with and knowledgeable about the above priority items.

_____   _____
Parental Signature   Case Manager Signature

                 _____
                           Date

1. Learning disabled children are primarily intact children. They are not primarily visually impaired, hearing impaired, environmentally disadvantaged, mentally retarded or emotionally disturbed. In spite of the fact that these children have adequate intelligence, adequate sensory processes and adequate emotional stability, they do not learn without special assistance.

2. Learning disabled children show wide discrepancies of intra-individual differences in a profile of their development. This is often shown by marked discrepancies in one or more of the specific areas of academic learning or a serious lack of language development or language facility. These disabilities may affect his/her behavior in such areas as thinking, conceptualization, memory, language, perception, reading, writing, spelling or arithmetic.

3. The concept of deviation of the learning disabled child implies that he/she deviates so markedly from the norm of his/her group as to require specialized instruction. Such specialized instruction required for learning disabled children may be of value to other children. However, the population to be served with special education funds authorized for children does not include children with learning problems which are the result of poor instruction or economic or cultural deprivation, unless these children also have been identified as "specific learning disabled."

b. Mentally Retarded—Mental retardation is the limitation of mental ability which differs in both degree and quality to the extent that special assistance is necessary to aid the individual in the acquisition of understandings and skills for coping with environmental situations.

Each mentally retarded individual acquires a range of behaviors which he/she can use in order to perform on an independent basis in some situations, while he/she will require assistance and/or support to perform in other situations. Mental retardation occurs on a continuum range from independent performance through semi-independent, semi-dependent, dependent and totally dependent performance.

c. Gifted—Intellectually gifted individuals are those who have potential for outstanding performance by virtue of superior intellectual abilities. The intellectually gifted are those with demonstrated achievement and/or potential ability. Individuals capable of outstanding performance include both those with demonstrated achievement and those with minimal or low performance who give evidence of high potential in general intellectual ability, specific academic aptitudes, and/or creative thinking abilities.

d. Emotionally Disturbed and Socially Maladjusted—The emphasis of earlier program planning focused on the child's behavior or emotional problem. Educational thought today attempts to utilize the more positive approach of studying the child's strengths and of adjusting the program to his/her needs. The goal of programming is to enable the child to function adequately in the educational mainstream.

Personal and social adjustment problems typically manifest themselves as marked behavior excesses and deficits which persist over a period of time. Behavior excesses and deficits include the following:

1. Aggressive and/or anti-social actions which are intended to agitate and anger others or to incur punishment.
2. Inappropriate and/or uncontrollable emotional responses.
3. Persistent moods of depression or unhappiness.
4. Withdrawal from interpersonal contacts.
5. Behaviors centrally oriented to personal pleasure.

e. Visually Impaired—For educational purposes, visually impaired children and youth shall be identified as those whose limited vision interferes with their education and/or developmental progress. Two divisions for the visually impaired shall be made:

1. Partially Seeing. Those whose visual limitation constitutes an educational handicap but who are able to use print as their primary educational medium.
2. Blind. Those who must depend primarily upon tactile and auditory media for their education. The group may include individuals who have some residual vision but whose vision loss is so severe that, for educational purposes, print cannot be used as the major medium of learning.

Legal blindness is a descriptive term, applying to the blind and to certain partially seeing. It is used solely for the purpose of qualifying the State for certain amounts of federal funds for each child so identified.

f. Language, Speech and Hearing Impaired—The inclusive term, communicative disorders/deviations/needs, is used to denote the continuum of problems and needs to be found in pupils requiring language, speech, and hearing services.

1. Pupils with communicative needs include the general school population for whom organized, sequenced curricular activities should be provided to promote the development of adequate communicative skills that will be beneficial to them as part of their overall educational program.
2. Pupils with communicative deviations include those with mild developmental or nonmaturational problems in language, voice, fluence or articulation, as well as those with a hearing loss. These individuals need interventional measures in order to permit them to perform satisfactorily in the educational setting. Such measures may be programmed at different levels for those pupils with a more severe impairment.
3. Pupils with communicative disorders are those exhibiting impaired language, voice, fluency or articulation, and/or hearing to such degree that academic achievement and/or psycho-social adjustment are affected and are handicapping to the individual.

g. Multiple Handicapped/Deaf-Blind—Those with two or more conditions requiring special educational services designed to ameliorate the effects of the combined impairments are identified in this category. The multiple handicapped hearing and/or visually impaired refers to a child having significant physical, emotional, mental or specific learning disabilities in addition to or concurrent with a hearing and/or visual impairment. When communicative disorders/deviations/needs are present, the provision of language, speech, and/or hearing services is considered essential.

h. Physically Impaired—Physically impaired individuals are those with physically impairing conditions so severe as to require special education and/or supportive services. These conditions include, but are not limited to, cerebral palsy, spina bifida, convulsive disorders, musculoskeletal conditions, congenital malformation and other crippling or health conditions.

If our school district is unable to provide services, that district may negotiate a contract for those services with an approved public or private educational agency.

The instructional program offered by an approved contracted agency must be of a quality at least equal to that offered by an approved public school program. Certification of such private programs and approval for contracts are made by the State Board of Education after investigation by the State Department of Education reasonably assures such quality.

It is the responsibility of the local district or special district of residence to have available a complete file of appropriate records for each student enrolled in a contractual program.*

RIGHTS AND SERVICES AVAILABLE TO PARENTS

Many parents of exceptional children are unaware of the rights and services available to them. They have the right to refer their child for an assessment. The evaluations must relate to the child's suspected handicap and be conducted by a qualified interdisciplinary team. The testing will be completed in the child's primary language and must not be racially or culturally discriminating. Teachers can share the following rights and procedures with them.

Notification Of and Permission From Parents

Parents have rights as well as responsibilities in the implementation of Public Law 94–142. They must be notified and permission obtained from them in the following situations:

1. Before the child is tested to determine the extent of the child's handicap and educational needs
2. Before the child is placed in, transferred out, or refused a special education program
3. Before the child is transferred or excluded from a regular classroom "on the grounds that he/she is an exceptional child and cannot materially benefit from education in a regular classroom" (Kearns, 1980, p. 9).

If parents disagree with the placement of the child and wish to request a hearing, they should follow this procedure:

1. The parents request the local school board of education for a hearing. (Check your area for time limitations.)

2. A hearing must be held within 15 to 30 days after the parents make the request.

3. An impartial hearing officer conducts the meeting.

4. Parents and their counsel have access to school reports, records, and files related to the case.

5. Parents may have counsels and witnesses to support their position.

6. The burden of proof is on the local education agency.

7. The meeting is closed unless an open meeting is requested.

8. The meeting is recorded.

9. A decision should be given to the parents by registered mail from the hearing officer within 7 days.

*From Kearns, P. (Ed.). *Your child's right to a free public education: Parent's handbook*. Topeka, Kan.: Kansas Association for Children with Learning Disabilities, 1980, pp. 18–23. Reprinted by permission.

10. If a satisfactory solution is not reached in the hearing, the parents may appeal to the State Board of Education.

Review by State Board of Education

1. A written appeal to the Commission of Education must be made within 10 days. (Check the time limitation within your state.)

2. The appeal requires that the State Board of Education will examine the record of the meeting and determine if the hearing procedure was in accordance with due process.

3. Oral and/or written arguments will be requested at the discretion of the State Board.

4. The Board will give their decision within 5 days after completion of the review.

5. A written notice will be sent to the parent and the local board of education.

6. Should the decision be unacceptable to the parents, it can be appealed to district court. If it is acceptable, it must be upheld by the school and parents. (Modified from Kearns, 1980, pp. 9–11)

Although hearings tend to sound threatening, their purpose is not to create an adversary approach to parent-teacher interaction. They are a safeguard for the child. Parents and school personnel are the child's advocates. Both want what is best for the child.

How to File a Complaint of Discrimination

No one enjoys being being a complainer. Most of us do not enjoy confrontations. But every U.S. law was written because someone cared enough to speak up and worked to get the law passed. Then the legislature built in procedures for citizens to protect their rights. If parents and friends of the handicapped do not stand up for these rights, those rights will be lost. Whenever discrimination occurs, it hurts not just the people involved, but our nation as well. Figure

9–10* explains how to file a complaint of discrimination with the U.S. Department of Education. Figure 9–11 is the discrimination complaint form for the Office for Civil Rights, Region VIII, Denver, Colorado, 1989.

PARENT INVOLVEMENT IN EDUCATION

In addition to an advocacy role, parents should also take an active role in the education of their children. Parent involvement in the regular classroom is an asset that is often overlooked or mismanaged. The parent is involved in planning the IEP and has the right of input and due process. Although parents are aware of these rights, many probably do not feel self-assured enough to fully capitalize on them. They rely on the teacher, the administrator, the psychologist, or whomever they are in contact with to keep them informed of what they, as parents, should be doing. Many parents feel that the teacher or person in the authority role knows what is best and that it is up to that person to decide if the parent can be of assistance. The counterpart is the teacher who is fearful of parent involvement, perhaps from misconceptions or a bad experience. Thus there is a lack of communication or overt action that prevents the use of an influential work force, the parents, for the education of the exceptional student.

Because implementation of Public Law 94–142 mandates that exceptional children be given a free and equal education, new programs have been installed in schools; certification programs have been quickly developed, and teachers and students have undergone many changes in a short time. From the passage of Public Law 94–142, which ensures that every child shall have a free education, to the recent emphasis on mainstreaming, the teacher has been buffeted with rules, new demands, and concerns. When

---

*Figures 9–10 and 9–11 are reprinted by permission from Region VIII Office for Civil Rights, Denver, Colorado.

Anyone who believes there has been an act of discrimination on the basis of race, color, national origin, sex, or handicap, against any person or group, in a program or activity which receives U.S. Department of Education financial assistance, may file a complaint of discrimination with the Office for Civil Rights. Complaints may be filed under Title VI of the Civil Rights Act of 1964, which prohibits discrimination on the basis of race, color, or national origin; Title IX of the Education Amendments of 1972, which prohibit discrimination of the basis of sex; and Section 504 of the Rehabilitation Act of 1973, which prohibits discrimination on the basis of handicap.

The person or organization filing the complaint need not be a victim of the alleged discrimination but may complain on behalf of another person or group. A complaint should be sent to the OCR Regional VIII which serves North Dakota, South Dakota, Montana, Wyoming, Utah, and Colorado. (see address below).

A complaint must be filed within 180 days of the date of the alleged discrimination. Time for filing a complaint can be extended for a good cause by the Regional Civil Rights Director.

Letters of Complaint should explain who was discriminated against; in what way; by whom or by what institution or agency; when the discrimination took place; who was harmed; who can be contacted for further information; as well as the name, address, and the telephone number of the complainant and the recipient. The complaint should include as much background information as possible about the alleged discriminatory act.

> United States Department of Education
> Office for Civil Rights, Region VIII
> 1961 Stout Street
> Denver, COLORADO, 80294

FIGURE 9-10
How to file a complaint of discrimination with the U.S. Department of Education, Office for Civil Rights.

mainstreaming was first implemented, Wheeler made these observations:

In general, the regular classroom teachers indicated a lack of support for mainstreaming. Their responses tended to be slightly negative. Special education teachers, as a group, tended to respond more favorably toward mainstreaming. Regular classroom teachers were less willing to accept an educably mentally retarded student into their classrooms because they believed that they, as teachers, had inadequate knowledge and skills to be able to teach the student effectively. (Wheeler, 1978, p. 54)

Both parents and teachers are uncertain as to how to go about helping the exceptional student fulfill his educational potential. "The law clearly states that the local school district must provide appropriate special education services. The responsibility for assuring that your child's rights are protected may fall upon you, the parents" (Kearns, p. 13). This responsibility is

achieved more easily if the school provides sufficient educational alternatives to meet the varying degrees and different kinds of handicaps. Kearns (1980) describes a service continuum that provides several placement options for exceptional students. They may include the following:

1. Provide a continuous series of service levels as needed on a progressive scale from least to most intensive.
2. Provide for moving learners from one level to another in accordance with the least restrictive environment principle. This principle states that:
   a. Learners are placed where they benefit most at the least distance away from mainstream society.
   b. Exceptional learners are moved toward more intensive service levels only as far as necessary.
   c. All exceptional learners are moved toward the mainstream as soon as possible. (p. 13)

FIGURE 9–11
Office for Civil Rights, Discrimination Complaint Form

Note: If you have any questions regarding this form, please call Charles E. Taylor, Staff Director, Program Review and Management Support, at 303 844–4957.

Part I

1. Name of person filing complaint:

Last	First	Middle

Address

City	State	Zip Code

Area Code   Home Phone   Area Code   Work Phone

2. Complete this portion *only* if the aggrieved party of the alleged discriminatory act(s) is *not* the complainant listed above:

Last Name	First	Middle

Address

City	State	Zip Code

Area Code   Home Phone   Area Code   Work Phone

Is the aggrieved party older than 18 years of age?   Yes _____   No _____
Has the person listed in #2 given you permission to file on his/her behalf?   Yes _____   No _____
   If yes, please attach the enclosed *Delegation of Representative* sheet to this form.

3. Person and/or institution you allege has discriminated:

Last Name	First	Title

Institution

City	State	Zip Code

Area Code   Phone Number

FIGURE 9–11
continued

Part II

Please provide a brief statement indicating the alleged act(s) of discrimination, the date(s), and the basis or bases (e.g. race, color, national origin, handicap, etc.) of the alleged discrimination.

Attach additional sheets of paper, if necessary.

Statement:

_____

_____

_____

_____

_____

_____

_____

_____

_____

_____

_____

_____

_____

_____

_____

_____

_____

_____

_____

_____

_____

_____

_____

_____

Signature   Date

FIGURE 9–11
continued
Part III

1. Have you filed this complaint with any other agency?
   Yes ____   No ____
   If yes, please provide:

_____

Name of Agency   Date Filed

_____

Address of Agency   City   State   Zip

_____

Agency (Area Code)   Phone Number

If filed with more than one agency, please provide, on an attached sheet, the same information for each agency. If filed in court, please provide the docket number and trial date:

_____

Docket Number   Trial Date

2. Please provide the name, address, and phone number(s) of a person whom we may contact if this Office is unable to locate you:

_____

Name

_____

Address   City   State   Zip

_____

Area Code   Phone Number

I wish OCR to investigate this complaint:

_____

                              Signature   Date

_____

The levels shown in Box 9–1, starting from an entry level that does not require a comprehensive evaluation, continue on to reach the most severely disabled and those who are temporarily incapacitated.

The challenge lies in three areas. First, a positive match between child and program is essential. In addition, the professional who works with exceptional children must be able to work with both the children and their parents. Third, parents must learn to exercise their right to understand their child's diagnosis and the reasons for special treatment or educational placement. They must be actively involved in the development of the IEP.

THE IMPORTANCE OF NUTRITION

Nutrition and the role it plays in regard to the handicapped is just beginning to be recognized. At present, the thrust has been toward the relationship of foods and learning disabilities. Recently more interest has begun to focus on the

BOX 9–1
Progressive Service Levels

Entry Level Services Plan

Some learners require only special instructional materials or equipment for progress in the education mainstream. For example, a visually impaired student may need nothing more than large print reading materials. This is a minimal special education service. Periodic monitoring of pupil progress is necessary to ensure that the degree of support is sufficient.

The first two models, Special Instructional Materials and/or Equipment, and Consultant Teacher Plan are the level of least intensive special education services and are identified as entry level. Such services can be distinguished as "indirect" rather than "direct" services to children. These services may be initiated after an appropriate educational assessment and without completion of a comprehensive evaluation.

In addition, entry level services may include speech services provided after a diagnostic evaluation by an approved speech clinician and without completion of a comprehensive evaluation, if the child shows no accompanying academic problems.

No child shall be maintained on entry level services if the assistance given does not produce a satisfactory educational adjustment. Referral for a comprehensive evaluation shall be made whenever lack of progress in entry level services indicates the child may need more intensive special education.

Consulting Teacher Plan

The consulting teacher is a certified special education teacher whose role is to facilitate the maintenance of exceptional children in the educational setting most nearly approximating that of their normal peers. The consulting teacher functions as an instructional specialist who may work in several areas of exceptionality. The main thrust of this program is to assist classroom teachers in making their own educational diagnosis, prescriptive decision, and delivery of treatment. Direct service to children is limited to short-term instruction carried out with individual children in their classrooms for the purpose of demonstrating special skills to their teacher. No more than one-third of the consulting teacher's time is devoted to direct child instruction.

Itinerant Teacher Plan

The itinerant teacher provides direct service to learners enrolled in the regular classroom. The major role of the itinerant teacher is to provide specialized tutoring and small group instruction, although some time is devoted to consulting with regular teachers. Whenever possible, instruction should be done in the classroom setting in order to facilitate communication between the specialist and the regular teacher. Adequate facilities should also be available for instructional activities which cannot be appropriately carried out in the classroom.

Resource Room Plan

In the resource room program, the exceptional learner is enrolled in a regular classroom, but goes to a specially equipped room to receive part of his instruction from a special teacher. The resource room teacher is responsible not only for his/her own classroom, but also for maintaining communication with the student's regular classroom teachers.

BOX 9–1 *continued*

Like the itinerant teacher, he/she provides both instructional and consultative services. This implies that scheduling must allow for work with other teachers. The amount of time spent by students in the resource room depends upon individual needs. However, the intent of the plan, which is to provide supportive assistance to exceptional learners in the educational mainstream, is violated if children spend most of their time in the resource room.

Integrated Special Classroom

In the integrated special classroom program, exceptional children are assigned to a special class, but receive most academic instruction in regular classes. The extent of integration is determined by the learner's individual capabilities. The special education teacher is responsible for monitoring the progress of his/her students in regular classes and providing appropriate support. The major different between this program and the resource room plan is that in the resource room the pupil is enrolled in a regular education program.

Self-contained Special Class

Students requiring a specialized curriculum are served in this program. They are enrolled in a special class and receive most academic instruction from a special education teacher. Like regular students, they engage in total school activities (such as school clubs, assemblies, and sports) and, whenever possible, participate in general education classes.

Special Day Schools

Special day schools are generally designed to provide specialized curricula; modified facilities and equipment; and/or interdisciplinary, ancillary, medical, psychiatric and social services for exceptional children. Day care centers, work activity centers or sheltered workshops are common types of special day schools.

School districts may contract with accredited special day schools for services to children or youth for whom the program is appropriate. School districts may also employ a teacher to work in the special day school setting.

Inasmuch as exceptional children enrolled in special day schools are segregated from their normal peers, this alternative should be used only when the unique needs of a learner cannot be met within the public school system. It is the responsibility of the district to monitor student progress and to facilitate reentry into the public schools whenever possible.

---

relationship of food and the problems of memory loss, mental retardation, and senility. The following review of information in this area, (Box 9–2) written upon request by a research scientist, will be of interest to parents and teachers alike.

MASLOW'S HIERARCHY OF NEEDS

When schools become involved with parents, it is wise to list the basic needs that must be satisfied before parents can effectively assist in the education of their exceptional children. Co-

Residential Schools

A few handicapped children profit most from intensive and comprehensive services provided by residential or boarding school facilities. The total residential treatment program should include educational experiences which optimize the learner's ability to cope with his environment. The ultimate goal should be to return learners to the community and the public schools. Cooperative agreements between residential centers and school districts can increase the program variations available to children and youth. Some learners may not require residential placement, but may benefit from the residential educational program. Others, who reside at the center, may be able to function successfully in the public school setting.

Hospital Instruction

In this program students confined to hospitals or convalescent homes for psychiatric or medical treatment receive individual or group instruction from a special education teacher. Training requirements for the certified teacher utilized will depend upon the nature of the population served. This teacher serves both children with chronic disorders and those recovering from accidents or illness who are hospitalized for short periods of time. Satisfactory programming requires a team approach involving the physician, other hospital personnel, and the school to which the student will return when he has sufficiently recovered.

Homebound Instruction

Homebound instruction is appropriate for children and youth whose health problems are so serious that school attendance is impossible, or for those temporarily disabled by an illness, operation or accident. In some cases, students with severe and/or unusual handicapping conditions may receive short-term homebound instruction as a temporary measure until more appropriate arrangements can be made. Instruction in the home is provided either by an itinerant special teacher or after school hours by the student's regular teacher. Frequent reevaluation of pupils in a homebound program is necessary. Inasmuch as this is the most segregated of all special education plans, discretion in its use is necessary.*

---

*From Kearns, P. (Ed.). *Your child's right to a free public education. Parent's handbook.* Topeka: Kan.: Kansas Association for Children with Learning Disabilities, 1980, pp. 14–18. Reprinted by permission.

letta (1977) elaborates on Maslow's hierarchy of needs in *Working Together: A Guide to Parent Involvement.*

How does Maslow's hierarchy apply to exceptional children? When teachers or administrators work with parents, it is helpful if they understand the parents' feelings, motivations, and concerns. Maslow's hierarchy of needs serves as a guide to this understanding. Parents who are poor and struggling to provide the necessities of life have a different view of their problems than urban affluent parents. That is,

BOX 9–2
Nutrition and Learning Disabilities

By M. M. Tinterow, M.D., Ph.D.
Olive W. Garvey Center for the Improvement of Human Functioning, Inc.

Today we are learning more about the relationship between nutrition and learning disabilities. The currently calculated recommended allowance by the Food and Nutrition Board of the National Research Council is really less than that needed for good nutrition. The RDA for Vitamin C is 60 mg. a day, and yet many individuals when tested do not have that level of plasma Vitamin C.

Every vitamin, amino acid, and trace mineral has a part to play in our everyday nutritional needs. Physicians believed that you could get all the vitamins that you needed when you went to the grocery store and bought a basket of food. Our everyday nutritional needs are gotten from our foods; however, it is necessary to find out the nutritional content of fresh foods, such as fresh fruit, fresh vegetables, fish, chicken, and turkey.

There are some vitamin deficiencies that have an effect on learning disabilities, and traditional medicine does not recommend nutrient supplementation. It is impossible to eat a diet that provides all your nutritional needs. Many environmental hazards place additional nutritional needs on the body, as do illness and disease.

The relationship of nutrition to learning disabilities has long been a subject of discussion. Niacin plays an important part in the maintenance of the circulatory system, but it is also recognized in having profound applications in the treatment of learning disabilities. Mental and learning impairment is probably due to the Vitamin B3 (niacin) impact on essential fatty-acid metabolism and prostaglandin balance. Both hyperactivity and the mental infirmation of age respond to niacin therapy. Hyperactive children with learning disorders have a subpellagra condition which responds to niacin therapy.

Phenylketonuria, an inborn error of phenylalanine metabolism, is a serious health problem and the most prevalent form of amino aciduria (excess amino acid secretion in the

physiological needs such as food and shelter must be satisfied before individuals can attend to higher order needs such as success and fulfillment. All parents' love and concern for their children will be the same. Therefore, all parents—regardless of economic standing—must be treated with dignity and respect.

The various levels of Maslow's hierarchy are discussed here:

Physical needs. The needs for sustaining life, nourishment, protection from the elements, and sexual activity are physical. There must be pro-

tection from the cold, wind, and rain, which usually means a shelter, such as a house, and clothing. There must be food, and to be effective, it must be nourishing. There is a need for companionship and sexual activity.

Psychologic needs. One needs to feel secure in oneself. It is important to know that one will awake to have a job. It is difficult to handle change, conflict, and uncertainty. It is important to reduce these frustrations. Much emphasis is placed on norms and rules, which results in little flexibility at this level.

urine). It accounts for about 0.5 of presently institutionalized retarded individuals. Learning disabilities should be one of the signs of amino acid elevations in the body.

In humans, brain cell multiplication continues for a time after birth. After the cells stop multiplying, development, maturation, and growth in the bulk of brain cells continue. In those whose brain development was hampered by inadequate or unbalanced nutrition, excellent and fully adequate nutrition during the entire growing period of about 20 years is recommended. Early stages of brain development are crucial, and nothing can be done to overcome the setback completely if early development is retarded. If nutrition is to be related to intelligence, we must be concerned with the nutrition of the cerebral cortex. Williams (1977) has shown that if children are given the opportunity to use their heads, the result will be a substantial increase in the size of the head and an increase in intelligence. If educational opportunities are given, but the individual child is not adequately furnished with raw materials necessary for building up the cerebral cortex, underdevelopment still results just as it does when no learning opportunities are provided. A child needs continuously two things: food for thought and food for building the cerebral cortex.

Because of the role as an essential building block in so many biochemical processes, folic acid has been found to be important as a component of general supplemental therapy in a wide range of disorders. When taken in sufficient quantities, folic acid appears to be effective in treating the subtle problem of learning disorders and anxiety. There is still much to be learned in relation to the part nutrition plays in learning disabilities in children.

Bibliography

Braverman, E. R., & Pfeiffer, C. C. The healing nutrients within. New Canaan, Conn.: Keats Publishing Co., 1987.

Pfeiffer, C. C. Mental and elemental nutrients. New Canaan, Conn.: Keats Publishing Co., 1975.

Williams, R. J. The wonderful world within you. Wichita, Kan.: Bio-Communication Press, 1977.

Emotional love and belonging. At this level there is a need to feel a part of a group where one is accepted, wanted, loved, and respected. When these needs are met or satisfied, then there can be love, respect for others, and consideration or helpfulness for others. When these needs are not being met, there may be self-defeating, attention-getting behaviors such as suspicion and aggression.

Self-esteem. It is wise to remember that basic needs must be met before one can satisfy the need for self-esteem. When one is regarded as valuable and competent by others, one has self-esteem. Growth in awareness of self-worth leads to less dependence upon another's judgment of one's worth. The key is for the professional to find ways to help parents see themselves as worthwhile contributors to their children's education.

Fulfillment. This is referred to as self-actualization and is achieved after all four of the previous levels have been reached. The person strives for self-development, directs energies for self-established goals, and takes risks willingly.

This hierarchy of needs is applicable to children, teachers, and administrators as well as parents. It is wise to mentally note where we are in the hierarchy as well as where the people are we would like to help. If there is an understanding of needs, then our expectations and suggestions for helping may be more valid.

PARENTS SHARE THEIR FEELINGS

Many parents of special children are willing to share their experiences. Mullins (1987) chose 60 books written by parents of special children and analyzed them for issues and concerns that were prominent in their lives. Parents of children with handicaps paint a picture of parenthood as one with "exceptional parenting, with its attendant special problems, pain, and pleasure" (Mullins, 1987, p. 31).

Although the authors of the books presented their concerns in a variety of ways and used different approaches, the same four themes were repeated: (1) realistic appraisal of disability, (2) extraordinary demands on families, (3) extraordinary emotional stress, and (4) resolution.

1. The parents who wrote the books were realistic about the handicapping condition. Many shared their manner of coping and information about their child's disability. Mullins pointed out Jablow's (1982) book about her Down Syndrome child, Park's (1982) discussion on the autistic child, and the Turnbulls' (1985) book, *Parents Speak Out.*

2. Rearing a child with a disability affects the whole family, and in much greater depth than one who has not had a disabled child can imagine. Some siblings worry about becoming parents themselves. They also have to share a greater amount of their parents' time and may feel the obligation of having to help care for the exceptional child is overwhelming. Parents have greater difficulty deciding on the best way to handle the special child and many marriages fail to survive. The books show that parents use creative ways to handle the challenge, but having

a disabled child places "extraordinary demands on the physical and financial resources of the family" (Mullins, 1987, p. 31).

Concerns included inaccurate or ambiguous diagnosis in which families have had to search for the answers to their concerns. A great deal of insensitivity to the parents was exhibited by some professionals who worked with them. Some parents had to work for years to get their children placed in appropriate schools. On the other hand, parents were forever grateful for professionals who were helpful and caring.

3. Parents express emotional ambivalence and grieve for the ideal child they did not have. Children may also wish what could have been. Sometimes parents blame themselves for their child's handicap. Parents who live with a child who has a degenerative condition are under constant stress about the future. These intense emotional concerns, joined with the physical and financial stress on the family, make for an extraordinary impact on family life.

4. After gaining insights and living with their special child, most parents feel that their lives were "enriched and made more meaningful" (p. 32) by their child.

SPECIAL PROBLEMS OF PARENTS OF EXCEPTIONAL CHILDREN

Parents react differently and sometimes unpredictably to the birth or the diagnosis of a child with a handicap. Reactions are a result of feelings; parents may experience frustration, hurt, fear, guilt, disappointment, ambivalence, or despair. In order for the professional to work effectively with parents of the handicapped, there must be an ability to recognize these feelings and a willingness to honor them (Chinn, Winn, & Walters, 1978; Chinn, 1984).

It is usually easier for the professional to view the handicapped child objectively than it is for the parents. The professional deals with the child on a day-to-day basis or only occasionally, whereas the parents deal with the child before and after school and on weekends. Parents of severely handicapped children may be faced with a lifetime of care. There is a need to offer parents relief from the constant care that is often required. Foster parents, substitute grandparents, and knowledgeable volunteers are becoming more available to give these parents helpful breaks (Chinn, Winn, & Walters, 1978; Chinn, 1984).

PARENTAL REACTIONS

Parents usually go through definite steps in dealing with the problem of a child with a handicap. First, they become aware of and recognize the basic problem. They then become occupied with trying to discover a cause and later begin to look for a cure. Acceptance is the last stage (Chinn, Winn, & Walters, 1978; Chinn, 1984).

Denial. Parents who deny the existence of a child's handicap feel threatened. Their security is unsure, and they are defending their egos or self-concepts. This is a difficult reaction for the professional to deal with. Time, patience, and support will help these parents to see that much can be gained through helping children with handicaps realize their potentials.

Projection of blame. A common reaction is to project blame for the situation on something or someone else. It may be the psychologist, the teacher, or the doctor. They may or may not be the basis for criticism. Often parents' statements begin with "If only...." Again, patience, willingness to listen to the parent, and tact will help the professional deal with a potentially hostile situation.

Fear. The parents may not be acquainted with the cause of the characteristics of the handicapping condition. They may have misfounded suspicions or erroneous information, which causes anxiety or fear. Information, in an amount that the parent can handle, is the best remedy for fear

of the unknown. A positive communication process helps the professional to judge the time for additional information to be added.

Guilt. Feeling guilty, that perhaps if they had done something differently or that the handicapping condition is in retribution for a misdeed, is a reaction that is difficult to deal with. The professional will help by encouraging guilt-stricken parents to channel their energies into more productive activities after genuine communication has been established and continues throughout the relationship.

Mourning or grief. Grief is a natural reaction to a situation that brings extreme pain and disappointment. Parents who have not been able to accept their child as a child with a handicap but look upon the child as handicapped may become grief stricken. In this case it is necessary to allow the parents to go through a healing process before they can learn about their child and how the child can develop.

Withdrawal. Being able to withdraw and collect oneself is a healthy, necessary action. It is when one begins to shun others, avoid situations, and maintain isolation that it becomes potentially damaging.

Rejection. There are many reasons for rejection and many ways of exhibiting rejection. It may be subtle, feigning acceptance, or it may be open and hostile. Some forms of rejection are failing to recognize positive attributes, setting unrealistic goals, escape by desertion, or presenting a favorable impression to others while inwardly rejecting the child.

Acceptance. Finally, the reaction of parents may be one of acceptance, acceptance that the child has a handicap, acceptance of the child and of themselves. This is the goal and realization of maturity. The parents and the child can grow and develop into stronger, wiser, and more compassionate human beings (Chinn, Winn, & Walters, 1978; Chinn, 1984).

REACHING THE PARENT OF THE YOUNG EXCEPTIONAL CHILD

When parents are confronted with the task of rearing an exceptional child, they need both emotional support and specific information. One program for fathers of exceptional infants illustrates an innovative way to reach out to parents. Sam W. Delaney conducts classes for fathers and their special infants at Seattle Community College and the Model Preschool Center for Handicapped Children at the University of Washington. "What we need is a method for fostering and facilitating the awareness that a father can be spontaneous in his feelings of tenderness and love toward his infant son or daughter" (Delaney, 1980, p. 1). Early joyful interaction between parent and child facilitates the emotional bond. "The researchers suggest that early and sustained contact with the infant releases the father's potential for involvement with the child" (Delaney, 1980, p. 1). The model, therefore, is based on two concepts. The first is the establishment of attachment between father and infant. The second is the development of parenting qualities in the father. This ability is acquired when the father is able to read cues and understand the baby's behavior. The cues and behavior patterns of a handicapped child may not be the same as those exhibited by a normal infant. If misinterpreted by the parents, the behavior may cause parents to become confused, frustrated, and to eventually withdraw from meaningful relationships, "thereby impairing the attachment process and leaving the child at risk for a secondary handicap" (Delaney as cited in Delaney, Meyer, & Ward, 1980, p. 8).

The class for fathers and infants offers a support group, provides time for father-child interaction, shares appropriate childrearing information, and fosters awareness of community resources (Delaney, 1980). The class meets each Saturday and follows this schedule.

Sharing, 10:00 to 10:15. During the sharing period fathers discuss their observations of their children. "Fathers are able to develop a sense of community in which common concerns are made known, and each develops a sense of going through an experience similar to that of other fathers" (Delaney, Meyer, & Ward, 1980, p. 9). This period may also be used to bring up questions about the topic of the day.

Music and exercise, 10:15 to 10:45. Fathers join in song and rhythm exercises with their infants. Songs that greet are followed by songs pertaining to parts of the body, action songs, recorded music for dancing, and relaxing songs (lullabies and tender music) to bring the period to a pleasant ending.

Zingers, 10:45 to 11:00. Zingers are distributed at the previous class so that fathers can discuss them during the week and can come to class ready for a lively discussion. Many zingers are controversial; others are thought provoking. Examples include:

The average American middle-class father spends 39 seconds per day with his children (as cited in Delaney, Meyer, & Ward, 1980, p. 11).

Parents should respond to a baby every time he or she cries (as cited in Delaney, Meyer, & Ward, 1980, p. 11).

Snack, 11:00 to 11:15. Two fathers volunteer to bring snacks for the group each Saturday. Snacks must be nutritionally sound and appropriate for infants.

Guest speaker: child/family development, 11:15 to 11:55. In an informal presentation a professional who is able to relate to the fathers shares expertise and knowledge about a variety of subjects, for example, physical therapy, health, nutrition, special education, and group care.

Preview, 11:55. The last five minutes focus on the issues to be covered the next week.

Those fathers who must, leave, while others stay and socialize for a time. Delaney cautions that although there is a schedule, the class is not tied to a rigid plan. Mothers who are interested in a particular topic can join the group. Field trips, swimming, or a picnic can be substituted for the routine (Delaney, Meyer, & Ward, 1980).

This program illustrates how a small amount of time spent with parents of exceptional children can bring understanding and support. Although it is not meant to be a substitute for counselors and professionals in the health field, it serves as a model for reaching fathers (or mothers) with exceptional children.

EXCEPTIONAL CHILDREN IN HEAD START

In 1974, with the passage of the Community Services Act (Public Law 96–644), Head Start received a mandate from Congress that 10 percent of the total enrollment of its children were to be handicapped. Handicapped children are defined as "mentally retarded, hard of hearing, deaf, speech-impaired, visually handicapped, seriously emotionally disturbed, physically handicapped, crippled, and other health impaired children or children with specific learning disabilities who by reason thereof require a special education and related services" (Riley, 1976, p. 9). Head Start procedures and policies were developed to respond to the needs of these exceptional children with individualized and appropriate education.

CHILD FIND PROJECT

Concern over reaching parents and their exceptional children resulted in the federal funding of the Child Find Project. Child Find is designated to locate handicapped children through using any feasible methods available such as door-to-door surveys, media campaigns, dissemination of information from the schools, and home visits by staff and/or volunteers (Lerner, Mardell-Czudnowski, & Goldenberg, 1987).

In recent years other logos such as Count Your Kid In and Make a Difference have been used to designate this program. In many cases this program is funded by both federal and state governments. Preschool screenings have been very successful in finding children in need and communicating to parents the help that is available.

ADVOCACY IN SPECIAL EDUCATION

Advocacy, pleading for the cause of another, is growing year by year. The need for informed advocates for the handicapped is great. Each state department of education will be able to inform you of their sponsored programs and of independent organizations' programs such as the Association of Retarded Children & Adults (ARC) or the Association for Children and Adults with Learning Disabilities (ACLD). The addresses and phone numbers may be found in local telephone directories and the *Encyclopedia of Associations,* which is available in public libraries.

INVOLVING PARENTS OF VERY YOUNG HANDICAPPED CHILDREN

Precise Early Education for Children with Handicaps (PEECH) involves parents through offering conferences, group meetings, home visits, classroom observations, and a lending library, as well as through being receptive to their questions and suggestions. This program integrates handicapped children in a classroom with children who have no special education needs. The children, age 3 to 6, attend the program half a day, 5 days a week (Far West Laboratory, 1983).

Merle Karnes, director of the project, emphasizes the importance of family involvement and the necessity of skillful staff interaction with parents. She finds that parents are interested in their handicapped children and want to become knowledgeable and skilled in working with them. To ensure success in your work with parents, give specific directions and objective feedback on their contributions. Respect them as individuals and be flexible in responding to their needs and value systems. If parents are included in decision making, if the program makes sense to them, if their goals and values are compatible with those of the school, if they are approached as individuals and are convinced that you, the professional, are interested in helping them, they will join with you in developing their abilities and contributing their time.

Parents can work effectively in the classroom, and they will extend their newfound understandings to other members of the family. They may become so knowledgeable and skillful that they can reach out to help parents of other handicapped children (Karnes, 1989).

TYPICAL DEVELOPMENT FOR PRESCHOOLERS

A few typical developmental expectations for very young children are listed here. If young children cannot perform most of the activities by the end of the year of their age level, professional help should be sought for further screening.

Age two. Children can run well; build a tower of six or seven blocks; walk up and down stairs alone; use three-word sentences; use *I, me,* and *you* correctly. They know their name, and know approximately 270 words.

Age three. They can put on shoes and button buttons, use four-word sentences and give commands, stand on one foot for a moment, jump from a bottom stair, and build a tower with 10 blocks. They know and use about 900 words, speak rather fluently, feed themselves without too many spills, identify drawings, and know their own sex.

Age four. Now the children can skip on one foot and walk down the stairs one foot at a time. They know front and back of clothes, wash themselves and dress with help, count to three, recognize colors, brush teeth, build a house with blocks, and stand on one foot for several seconds.

Age five. Children can skip, draw human figures, count to 12 or more, use fingers to show how old they are, dress and undress without help, name four or more colors, and stand on one foot 8 to 10 seconds.

PLAY IS IMPORTANT

How do you play with an exceptional baby or small child? Play is especially important to the

deaf and/or blind. These handicaps do not interfere with the natural phenomenon of learning about the world around oneself and growing and developing while doing so. Activities that are appropriate for normal babies are appropriate for the exceptional, too. Clapping hands, cooing, playing peek-a-boo, and cuddling are necessary and helpful. Provide the baby or small child with objects to grasp. Firm cushions may be used for crawling babies. Rock children back and forth or play with them on a swing, so they will have the experiences needed to develop. Of course, infants should never be left unsupervised. Babies and small children must have the opportunity to think, to experiment, to investigate, and to learn about their environment.

A SHARED CONCERN

Suzanne Crane is the mother of a handicapped child. She has shared her feelings and thoughts about this so that others may benefit from her experiences.

Having a handicapped child was not what we expected. I remember the feelings likened to having run into a brick wall, the heartbreak of having a broken doll and no one able to fix her. The uncertainties were even more of a struggle due to fragmented medical care and follow-up on her development. We were told of the absolute and immediate necessity of finding special help for her and then sent home with no guidance as to who and where we could turn to for this help. However, through community support and the efforts of other parents we were able to secure services for our child. I do not believe our daughter would be walking or talking now if we hadn't persevered in this. She presently is 7 years old and being served by special education in the public school system. However, I will always crusade for the infants, toddlers, and preschoolers with special needs and their families who are faced with the overwhelming situation of no help available.

I feel that we are more like other families than set apart. I have seen other children accept her with open arms, bridging the gap. Our daughter's celebrative spirit, her love for music, her essence has affected us, her parents, and our second child in positive ways. She has shaped our perspective on the world and life. She has taught us to be happy. We hope that her future will enhance her internal spirit and allow her to be accepted by others. (Crane, 1986)

For Friends of the Handicapped

Blessed are you who take the time
To listen to difficult speech
For you help me to know that
If I persevere, I can be understood.

Blessed are you who never bid me to "hurry
*   up"*
Or take my tasks from me and do them for me,
For I often need time rather than help.

Blessed are you who stand beside me
As I enter new and untried ventures,
For my failures will be outweighed
By the times I surprise myself and you.

Blessed are you who asked for my help
For my greatest need is to be needed.

Blessed are you who understand that
It is difficult for me to put my thoughts into
*   words.*

Blessed are you who never remind me
That today I asked the same question twice.

Blessed are you who respect me
And love me just as I am.

(Reprinted by Permission from Ann Landers, Author Unknown; News America Syndicate)

BURNOUT

Burnout is a term applied to the loss of concern and emotional feeling for those people you work with or live with (Maslach, 1982). Both teachers and parents experience burnout. It is felt most when what you are trying to do seems unproductive, or you may feel you have few alternatives that would change or improve the course of events. This is a frustrating situation, and it leads to a feeling of being trapped. It can happen to any teacher and any parent. The obligations of teaching and parenting are similar. The teacher or the parent is in the authoritarian role and is responsible for setting up the program. Balancing the student's needs with time constraints, the mechanical constraints of run-

ning a classroom or a home, and the constraints of the personal needs of the authoritarian figure is a role for a magician. Indeed, when parents and teachers are successful, the result does seem to be magical. No teacher or parent will agree that it is magical. They know it is hard work, good planning, cooperation, and perseverance.

Those who set high standards and aim for perfection are sometimes more likely to experience burnout. Also, those who feel a need to be in control may experience burnout. Feelings of anger, guilt, depression, self-doubt, and irritability are symptoms of burnout. When these occur, take a hard look at what is really going on and what needs to be going on. Are you neglecting yourself? Are the things you want to do essential? Do some things need to be changed? Learn to accept the fact that change can occur. Be willing to give yourself and others credit when credit is due. Build in rewards so that you and others feel good about what you are doing. Always have some goals that are short term and accessible. There is nothing that feels better than having success. This is one of the best methods to combat burnout. Remember, burnout is reversible.

Depression and Suicide

People who parent or work with exceptional children need to know that these children are in a high risk group for depression and suicide. Learning disabled children are particularly at risk because of the frustration they often encounter in trying to learn. Gifted children often find it difficult to feel comfortable in the environment.

It is important to know the symptoms of depression and impending suicide and be willing to take appropriate action. Generally the child will be depressed or irritable, lacking enjoyment in normally pleasurable activities. Changes in weight, appetite, or eating habits may be signals. Sleeplessness, hyperactivity, loss of energy, or being fatigued are also flags that something is wrong. Loss of self-esteem and feelings of inadequacy or decreased ability to concentrate should alert teachers and parents to a very real need for help. Thoughts of death or suicide should not be taken lightly. Recognize these as very serious symptoms and get professional help. Mental health centers and public schools have programs for crisis intervention and can give guidance and help in a time of need.

COMMUNICATING WITH PARENTS OF EXCEPTIONAL CHILDREN

Parents are receptive to open and direct communication. The message should be clear and in language the parents can understand. It is necessary to realize that the teacher or professional will deal with a wide variance of language efficiency. Professionals should acquaint themselves with the parents' backgrounds and be receptive to clues from the parents to determine if the message being communicated is indeed being received and accommodated. Ask a leading question to let the parents express what they understand about the topic being discussed. It may be a surprise to find that the interpretations are different.

It takes skill, tact, and ingenuity for a professional to communicate with all types of people who have different kinds of needs. Mistakes to avoid include "talking down" to the parents, assuming an understanding exists where in fact none may, and using jargon or technical language.

The professional should include the support and consultation of the medical and theological professions if the parents exhibit a need for these services. Be aware of the agencies and organizations that assist parents and professional workers in the local community as well as national organizations.

I recommend *Two-way Talking with Parents of Special Children, A Process of Positive Communication* (Chinn, Winn, & Walters, 1978) as a resource for learning more about communicating with parents. This book discusses in depth communication, semantics, transactional analysis, stroking, family interactions, and transactions.

Although two-way communication is essential, important tips and information can be relayed to parents through newsletters, personal letters, or charts. These can be used in conjunction with the conference, or they can be separate forms of communication.

Newsletter

Use a newsletter to offer tips for parents. There are things that all parents can do to help their children in school that are important to parents of both handicapped and typical children. Select from the following tips.

Healthy environment. First of all, it is important to provide an environment that will promote the good health of your child. Adequate housing, clothing, and food affect the development of every child. The low-income child is handicapped, indeed, when these basic needs are not available.

Communicate with children. It is important to talk with your children. This is the way children learn their language, and they must be given opportunities to practice using their skill. Talk naturally so the child can understand and be able to develop language. When your child talks, listen. How do you feel when you talk to someone who will not listen to what you are saying? Most adults don't waste time talking to people who do not listen to them. Children don't either. If you want your children to express themselves, then let them initiate conversations and respond by giving them your attention.

Praise, praise, praise. Praise reinforces learning and behaviors. Let children know when you are pleased with what they are doing. We all work for rewards, and praise is one of the most important rewards you can give. Be patient with your children. It takes many trials and errors to learn skills. Adults forget over the years how it was. If the situation gets out of hand and you become impatient or angry, leave the situation, do something else, and come back to it when you are in control of yourself.

No comparisons. Don't compare your children. Allow for individuality. Every child is different with special characteristics that make up his personality and no one else's.

Good work habits. When it comes time for school, set the stage for good homework habits. A well-lighted place to study that is quiet with room for books, pencils, and papers helps. Schedule home study on a regular basis.

Sufficient rest. Set a bedtime and stick to it. Children need a lot of rest to be able to do good mental work. Rest is necessary for proper growth.

Regular school attendance. Do your part to see that your child attends school regularly and on time. Visit with teachers to learn how your child is getting along in school and listen to what they have to tell you about your child.

Enrichment activities. Help increase your children's knowledge by taking them places such as zoos, libraries, or airports. Use television as a learning tool by selecting appropriate programs and discussing the program after it is viewed. Another learning experience that is often overlooked is the family mealtime. Sharing experiences, talking about interesting subjects, and improving conversational skills can happen around the dining table.

Read and talk together. Read to your children, have them read to you, and listen to them read. Let them tell you about what they have been reading. Magazines, newspapers, comics, and books can all be used to increase a child's knowledge and reading ability.

Letters

Letters are often effective means of communicating an idea or message to parents. Letters need to state the concern, then present a method or suggestions for dealing with or changing the situation, include any guidelines or datelines that are pertinent, and finally, end with a conclusion and an offer for assistance if needed.

There are as many ways to write the message you wish to convey as there are teachers. Each will need to adapt the contents to the concerns of the situation.

Charts

Charts are a valuable tool to communicate progress. They are a graphic picture for easy reference and serve as a record of day-to-day or week-to-week events. There is as much variety in graphs and charts as there are situations, so it is important to learn to use the one that will complement your needs. It should clearly indicate the child's work so parents can immediately recognize their child's progress.

HOW PARENTS CAN HELP AT HOME

As a teacher or a parent the goal is to have all students or children perform to their full potential.

It may become necessary to give exceptional students extra help at home in order for them to be able to keep up their schoolwork. Special tutoring by someone outside the family may be needed, and it can be very effective. If the parents are planning to work with their child, the following suggestions should help guide them in their endeavor.

Visit with the teacher. Explain that you want to help your child at home with schoolwork. Ask the teacher to explain the material the class will be covering and how assignments should be done. Try to get a time schedule for assignments if your student doesn't have one.

Set a definite time. Set a definite time to work with your child. Go over the day's experiences and listen to how your student felt about them. Discuss how the assignments can be completed and turned in on time.

Monitor progress. Keep a record of the assignments handed in and the scores received. In this way you can tell how the student is doing. If the grades are low or you do not understand them, visit with the teacher so you will know exactly what the teacher expects.

Flashcards. Flashcards can be bought for times tables, word recognition, fractions, and many other skills. It is not hard to use tagboard to make cards that fit your child's specific needs. Use them in a consistent manner and review learned skills periodically to help establish skills that must be available for instant recall.

How to promote success. Your child will be more likely to succeed in the home-school program if you do the following:

1. Use a pleasant, firm approach, one that says, "Yes, this must be done, and we'll do it as quickly and pleasantly as we can."

2. Set up a reward system. None of us will work at a job we do not receive satisfaction from or get paid for. Our praise and approval is the students' pay for doing a job well. If they get scolded all of the time, they are unlikely to want to work for another scolding.

3. Work, play, and rest. There has to be some work, play, and rest in everyone's life. If we do too much of one, the other two will suffer. Parents are the best persons to determine how to keep this balance.

Charting

Keeping track of daily grades, attendance, and projects is a big task for student or parent. A converted 9-weeks attendance chart works very well (Figure 9–12). Place the grade earned in the line for the first 9 weeks. The attendance can

be placed on the second 9-weeks line. Behavior or special projects can be placed on the next two lines. Encouraging children or students to keep track of their scores helps to build organizational skills. It also gives the parent a natural time for children or students to relate the day's events and discuss problems that may have come up. The chart gives a record of progress that can be used handily for a reward system.

To ensure success we should use every available aid, method, or technique that is appropriate and effective. Many times the proper technique, the mechanical aid, or different method is not used because there is the fear of being different. Sometimes it is because of lack of familiarity. Whatever the reason, it must be put aside, and that which will help students learn to their potential must be pursued with determination and compassion.

RULES OF LEARNING

When a teacher or parent is working with exceptional children, the rules of learning are the same as those for nonexceptional children. All learning takes place in the same pattern, but there are differences in the ways individuals handle learning. Two approaches will be presented to give broader coverage and more adaptability to different levels.

Conceptual Levels

Readiness. The readiness level represents the knowledge that already exists before one begins

Name					Class			Sex			Birth									Days on roll	Days taught	Days present	Days absent
	First week		Second week		Third week		Fourth week		Fifth week		Sixth week		Seventh week		Eighth week		Ninth week						
	M T W T F	M T W T F	M T W T F	M T W T F	M T W T F	M T W T F	M T W T F	M T W T F	M T W T F															
1st 9 wks																								
2nd 9 wks																								
3rd 9 wks																								
4th 9 wks																								
		Parent						Address								Total								

FIGURE 9–12

A converted 9-weeks attendance chart can be used as follows: first 9 weeks for grades; second 9 weeks for attendance; third 9 weeks for behavior in class; and fourth 9 weeks for projects or extra work.

to teach. Therefore, all teaching should begin at the readiness level.

Motivation. Motivation is the level of stimulating a desire or need on the part of the student to learn what is being taught.

Awareness. Awareness is the actual teaching phase. According to scientific reference, something is learned when it is repeated once.

Assimilation. Assimilation refers to the actual acceptance of the information by students. They now have the information for reference.

Accommodation. Accommodation becomes a fact when students use the information they have learned in new circumstances.

With the learning accommodated, the student is using the information in new situations, yet the learning is still considered dependent. It is not until the learned information becomes automatic, without conscious thought, that it is called independent (Cochran, 1974).

PQ4R: A Reading Approach

PQ4R means

Preview	or set the stage for learning
Questions	arouse curiosity
Read	present your lesson
Reflect	discuss your lesson
Recite	give feedback— immediate response
Review	revisit and test

Both the PQ4R and the conceptual method are effective. It is easy to see the similarities of the two approaches. Either can be adapted to any learning situation. They do produce results (Thomas & Robinson, 1981).

A FEW THINGS TO REMEMBER

When teaching exceptional children, teachers and parents should follow these suggestions:

1. Encourage correct responses—wrong responses have to be relearned.

2. Use tests as learning instruments. More learning takes place when tests are answered and corrected soon after being given.

3. Learning occurs more effectively when more channels of learning are involved. If you involve the visual and hearing channels, it is more effective than involving just vision or just hearing.

4. Putting what has been learned into action through verbal or physical reaction increases the learning experience.

5. Learning is reinforced by repetition, that is, reviewing often at first and then again at varying intervals.

6. Begin with concrete items and move gradually to teaching abstract items.

7. When teaching motor skills, always begin with large muscle activities and gradually approach fine muscle activities.

HOW PARENTS CAN TUTOR AT HOME

Tutoring is one of the most effective and necessary tools in education. It is a skill that can be learned and developed. For some it seems to come easily, but for others it is difficult. It requires understanding another's rate of learning and being responsive to feelings and moods.

The cassette recorder is one of the most valuable instruments available in helping the student learn at home or at school. With a recorder, parents (in this case, the tutors) can put exactly what they want in a lesson and determine its format. This means that parents are able to adapt the lesson to the student's level and are able to develop it in a way that will be most beneficial to the student. A set of headphones further enhances the learning situation. A carrel made from plywood or a cardboard box produces a one-to-one tutoring situation. This allows parents to go on with other duties.

What can the cassette recorder be used for? It is excellent for recording spelling words and for having children take spelling tests as they would in a classroom. If the children can read the words, then they should put the words on the tape and take them as in a spelling lesson. When the students listen to the words, they automatically monitor the sound of the word, the inflection, and the phrasing. Corrections are made unconsciously as the mind corrects errors that the ear hears.

The cassette recorder is valuable for taping messages to family members. It is particularly useful for giving directions to be followed. Directions for setting a table, making pudding, or making a bed can be put on tape to give a child valuable experience in learning to follow directions.

Another important use is letting the child put a reading lesson on the tape and then having the child correct errors. A chart of the time, number of words read, and errors made can be kept to show progress.

Suggestions for Putting Lessons on Cassettes

1. Limit the time of the lesson to 5 minutes less than the period you want the lesson to last. This allows a little flexibility for handling interruptions.

2. Arrange the tasks in sequential order. Check the order by doing the lesson once yourself.

3. Speak slowly, more slowly than your normal rate of conversation. Children with learning problems do not process words and thoughts as quickly as most people do. Check to see if the child knows what the tape is saying by asking him to repeat what he hears. Be careful not to ask if the child understands it. The student may think he does, but on your testing you may find out the child doesn't.

4. Include a set of questions at the end of the taped lesson for an immediate review of the material. This also is helpful for the teacher who has students who have missed reading lessons or lectures.

WHAT THE PARENT EXPECTS OF THE PROFESSIONAL

As a professional working with exceptional children, it is important for you to remember what the parent looks for in a teacher. The parent will be on the lookout for the specialist who:

1. Understands his child's assets as well as his deficiencies.
2. Appreciates his child's accomplishments whenever and however they appear.
3. Helps the parent live without guilt or blame, both on the part of the child or himself.
4. Tells his child how it really is. The truth about himself may be difficult for a learning-disabled child, but not as difficult as the bewilderments and heartaches he experiences from half-truths and evasions. (Kratoville, 1977, p. 231)

LEARNING IS HARD

For a period of years the popular philosophy has been that we could best motivate young people in pleasing and attractive settings. The lesson would stimulate interest, be fun, and be relevant to the learner; because one enjoyed doing it, one would be willing to learn. This is an excellent theory, and there is no quarrel with its premise. However, we have produced some youth who did not meet their potential because, in real life, work is not always pleasing.

Work involves diligence, tenacity, endurance, sacrifice, discipline, and repetition. It requires deep concentration and dedication. Work is *not* always fun. It is often boring! Most of us spend our lives doing work. We are willing to make this sacrifice not only for the extrinsic values of status, income, and fringe benefits but also for the intrinsic values of self-worth, dignity, and contribution to society. Our children have become confused because we gave them the impression that life should be fun and games. It is not, and we need to set them straight. Work is work.

The exceptional child works harder and longer to accomplish what other peers do easily and quickly. It is not easy always for them to accept this. It is hard for parents not to expect the school, the teacher, to lighten the load, to not expect too much because the child is handicapped. This deprives the child of the feeling of accomplishment, of striving for and reaching his/her potential. The Individualized Education Program provides for the appropriate level of accommodation. Use this effective tool to see that every exceptional child is given the opportunity to reach his/her goals.

KEEPERS OF THE FLAME

Parents are the keepers of the flame. Sometimes the flame flickers and almost goes out, and those are the hard days when clear heads, resolve, quick wits, and optimism must be pulled from reserve. Other times the flame burns brightly and steadily, a welcome and needed respite. But at all times the flame must be watched, with extra fuel and nourishment applied when indicated. It is not a thankless charge. That particular flame kindles a glow and warmth unlike any other and, if carefully tended, will one day burst into its special radiance. (Kratoville, 1977, p. 231)

Just as the parent feels warmth and joy with the development of a child with a handicap so, also, will you as a professional when your help and guidance has led to better family relations, improved schoolwork, and an ability to participate in life more fully for the child with a handicap. It is a worthy and mighty undertaking.

SUMMARY

Parents, teachers, and other professionals are effective forces in influencing the life of the exceptional child. It is important that each be able and willing to work together for the benefit of the exceptional child. Special educational terms, once crude, have been replaced with more inclusive, educational terms.

During the twentieth century the special education movement grew, and in 1971 the Pennsylvania Association for Retarded Children (PARC) won a case against the Commonwealth of Pennsylvania. This court decision assured the right of all children to a free and appropriate education. This includes the handicapped or exceptional child. The Vocational Rehabilitation Act of 1973, the Buckley Amendments, the Education of All Handicapped Children Act of 1975 (Public Law 94–142), and the Education of the Handicapped Act Amendments of 1983 (Public Law 98–199) are some of the far-reaching legislation passed in the third quarter of the century.

From the Education of All Handicapped Children Act of 1975 came the Individualized Education Program (IEP). It is a plan that involves the parents, child, teachers, administrators, special teachers, psychologists, and any who are involved with the child's education. The plan assures a continuum of services, appropriate to age, maturity, handicapping condition, past achievements, and parental expectations. The exceptional child or student includes the learning disabled; mentally retarded; emotionally disturbed; socially maladjusted; visually impaired; language, speech, and hearing impaired; multiple handicapped/deaf-blind, and physically impaired. This law also provides for due process, the right of a hearing if parents do not agree with the educational placement.

Parents have been effective forces in securing this legislation. Parents should and do have an important role in the life and education of their exceptional children. The parent's role begins as one of nurturing in the home but can become an effective force in the school as the parent supports the teacher at home as a tutor or at school as a volunteer.

SUGGESTED ACTIVITIES AND DISCUSSIONS

1. Write a brief review of the development of special education.
2. List the five principles covering data collection systems for personal data. Which legislation provided these guidelines?
3. Describe in your own words exactly what "least restrictive" means?
4. Which "rights and services" are available to parents?
5. List and describe briefly the eight categories of exceptional students.
6. A staffing refers to the meeting that is held when an exceptional student's IEP is developed or changed. Who is included in such a meeting? What do they decide?
7. "Mainstreaming" is a misunderstood term. Read carefully about mainstreaming and write in your own words what you think mainstreaming means.
8. Using Maslow's hierarchy of needs, assess yourself and five other acquaintances. Try to select those from different professions. Use this as background material for a general class discussion to increase awareness of these needs.
9. Discuss the IEP, listing the six criteria each IEP must include. Conclude with a statement of your own opinion of the IEP. Is there more that should be added? Is there too much? If so, what?
10. Choose one of the problems a parent of exceptional children may encounter and describe how you as a professional would try to help that parent.
11. Develop lesson plans for teaching a specific skill using one set of the "Rules of Learning."

BIBLIOGRAPHY

Buck, P. S. *The child who never grew.* New York: John Day, 1950.

Chinn, P. C. (Ed.). *Education of culturally and linguistically exceptional children.* Reston, Va.: Council for Exceptional Children, 1984.

Chinn, P. C., Winn, J., & Walters, R. H. *Two-way talking with parents of special children: A process of positive communications.* St. Louis: C. V. Mosby, 1978.

Cochran, C. E. Class lecture. Assistant Professor of Educational Psychology, Mental Retardation Program, Wichita State University, Wichita, Kan., 1974.

Coletta, A. J. *Working together: A guide to parent involvement.* Atlanta, Ga.: Humanics Limited, 1977.

Congressional Record. 98th Congress, Vol. 129, pt. 24: 33310–33329, 1983, 98–199.

Congressional Record. 99th Congress, Vol. 132, pt. 125: H7908–H7912, 1986, 457.

Cook, R. E., Tessier, A., & Armbruster, V. B., *Adapting early childhood curricula for children with special needs,* (2nd ed.). Columbus, Ohio: Merrill, 1987.

Crane, S. Personal communication, 1986.

Delaney, S. W. Fathers and infants class: A model program. *Exceptional Teacher,* March 1980, pp. 12–16.

Delaney, S. W., Meyer, D. J., & Ward, M. J. *Fathers and infants class: A model for facilitating attachment between fathers and their infants.* Seattle, Wash.: Experimental Education Unit, Child Development and Mental Retardation Center, University of Washington, 1980.

Far West Laboratory. *Educational programs that work, 1983.* San Francisco: Far West Laboratory for Educational Research and Development, 1983.

The Foundation Center. *The foundation directory.* New York: Author, 1990.

Frost, S. E., Jr. *Historical and philosophical foundations of Western education.* Columbus, Ohio: Merrill, 1966.

Gearheart, B. R., & Gearheart. *Learning disabilities: Educational strategies* (5th ed.). Columbus, Ohio: Merrill, 1989.

Greenleaf, B. *Children through the ages: History of childhood.* New York, NY: McGraw–Hill, 1978.

Hallahan, D. P., & Kauffman, J. M. *Exceptional children: Introduction to special education.* Englewood Cliffs, N.J.: Prentice-Hall, 1988.

Heward, W. L., & Orlansky, M. D. *Exceptional children: An introductory survey of special education* (3rd ed.). Columbus, Ohio: Merrill, 1988.

Jablow, M. M. *Cara: Growing with a retarded child.* Philadelphia: Temple University Press, 1982.

Karnes, M. B. RAPYHT—Retrieval and Acceleration of Promising Young Handicapped and Talented. *Journal for the Education of the Gifted, 1979, 2*(3), 157–172.

_____. *Basic assumptions underlying the family involvement program.* (PEECH Project Institute for Child Behavior and Development). Urbana, Il.: University of Illinois, 1989.

Kearns, P. (Ed.). *Your child's right to a free public education: Parent's handbook.* Topeka, Kan.: Kansas Association for Children with Learning Disabilities, 1980.

Keller, H. *The story of my life.* New York: Grosset & Dunlap, 1905.

Kephart, N. C. *The slow learner in the classroom.* Columbus, Ohio: Merrill, 1971.

Kirk, S. A. *Educating exceptional children* (5th ed.). Boston: Houghton Mifflin, 1989.

Kratoville, B. L. Dealing with public schools. *Academic Therapy,* 1977, *3*(2), 225–232.

Kroth, R. L. *Communicating with parents of exceptional children.* Denver, Colo.: Love Publishing, 1985.

Landers, A. For friends of the handicapped. (Ann Lander's column, author unknown, News America Syndicate.) In *Special Educational Instructional Paraprofessional Facilitator Program.* Topeka, Kan.: Kansas State Department of Education, 1986.

Lerner, J., Mardell-Czudnowski, C., & Goldenberg, D. *Special education for the early childhood years.* Englewood Cliffs, N.J.: Prentice-Hall, 1987.

Maslach, C. *Burnout: The cost of caring.* Englewood Cliffs, N.J.: Prentice-Hall, 1982.

Mullins, J. B. Authentic voices from parents of exceptional children. *Family Relations, 36*(1), January 1987, pp. 30–33.

New Jersey State Federation, Council for Exceptional Children. New Brunswick, N.J.: *CEC Newsletter,* May 1989.

Park, C. C. *The seige: The first eight years of an autistic child with an epilogue, fifteen years after.* Boston: Little, Brown, 1982.

P.L. 94–142, Part B of the Education of All Handicapped Children Act, Title 20 of the United States Code, Sections 1400–1420. Regulations, Title 34 of the Code of Federal Regulations, Sections 300.1–300.754 and Appendix C, IEP Notice of Interpretation.

Rehabilitation Act of 1973, Section 504, 34CFD Chapter, Pt. 104. *Nondiscrimination on basis of handicapped in program and activities receiving or benefiting from federal financial assistance.* November 1, 1989.

Reinert, H. R. *Children in conflict: Educational strategies for the emotionally disturbed and behaviorally disordered* (3rd ed.). Columbus, Ohio: Merrill, 1987.

Riley, M. T. *Project LATON: The parent book.* Lubbock, Tex.: Texas Tech Press, 1976.

Rust, P. D. REACH Preschool Developmental Center, R.R. #1, Box 123, Winfield, KS 67156.

Section 504 Regulations, Title 34 of the Federal Regulations, Sections 104.1–104.61 and Appendix A: Analysis of Final Regulations (29 U.S.C. 794) Title 29 of the United States Code, Section 794.

Sumner County Special Education Services. *Commentary regarding the Individual Educational Plan (IEP).* Wellington, Kan.: Author, 1977.

Spidel, J. *Exceptional students in the regular classroom, how we help them learn.* (Unpublished.) Presentation Showcase Kansas, Wichita State University, Wichita, Kan., March 15, 1980.

Thomas, E. L., & Robinson, A. H. *Improving reading in every class.* Boston: Allyn & Bacon, 1981.

Tintcrow, M. M., M.D. Olive W. Garvey Center for the Improvement of Human Functioning, Inc., 3100 N. Hillside, Wichita, KS 67219.

Turnbull, A. P., & Turnbull, H. R. III. *Parents speak out: Then and now* (2nd ed.). Columbus, Ohio: Merrill, 1985.

Van Wyck, B. *Helen Keller.* New York: E. P. Dutton, 1956.

Wallace, G., & Kaufman, J. M. *Teaching students with learning and behavior problems.* (3rd ed.). Columbus, Ohio: Merrill, 1986.

Wheeler, J. *Attitudes toward mainstreaming.* Unpublished thesis, College of Emporia, Emporia, Kan., 1978.

Wichita Public Schools, USD #259, James A. Gates, Special Education Services, 217 N. Water, Wichita, KS 67202, 1990.

10

The Abused Child

What is child abuse? According to U.S. law (Child Abuse Prevention and Treatment Act of 1974, 1977):

The physical or mental injury, sexual abuse, negligent treatment or maltreatment of a child under the age of 18 by a person who is responsible for the child's welfare under circumstances which indicate that the child's health or welfare is harmed or threatened thereby. (p. 1826)

An aspect of parent-school involvement that requires an approach different from other parent-school relationships is the issue of child abuse and neglect. What are the obligations of the teacher and school (or child care center) to the child and family with abusive parents?

The responsibilities are great, and an affirmative response by schools is vital to the well-being of thousands of children throughout the United States. Because of required school attendance and an increase in the use of child care centers, caregivers and teachers have an expanded opportunity for contact with families and children. The professionals work closely with children and families over extended periods of time. In so doing, they are also the agencies most able to detect and prevent abuse and neglect. Schools have not always been recognized as an important agency in the detection of child abuse.

Earlier it was believed that most cases of child abuse concerned battered infants. When infants are abused, they are vulnerable to serious injury or death, but it is now recognized that older children are also victims. More than 70% of the children who are abused or neglected may have contact with schools or child care centers. Through Home Start, Head Start, and private and public preschool programs, the detection of abuse of 2- to 6-year-olds has become easier to achieve. Increasingly, the detection and prevention of child abuse and neglect is recognized as a concern and responsibility of the schools.

Abuse and neglect include many degrees and varieties of neglect, physical abuse, emotional abuse, and sexual abuse. The impact on the child differs by age and development, degree of intensity, duration, the relationship between abused and abuser (Steele, 1986) and the intervention that the child receives.

Physical abuse that causes permanent damage to a child is generally easy to recognize and easily evokes outrage. The damage to the child's psychological development is much more difficult to recognize and assess. The unpredictable parental behavior gives the child a "sense of insecurity and difficulty trusting other human beings" (Steele, 1986, p. 285). Parents who lack appropriate parenting behavior exhibit inconsis-

346

tent caregiving; they most often learned to parent from their own neglected or abused early years.

Schools should serve as a defense against child abuse: first, as an educational institution offering parent education to adults and students; second, as a referral agency to child protection agencies; and third, as a support system for families.

BACKGROUND

Child abuse and neglect have been social phenomena for centuries. Childhood was described by DeMause (1988) as a history of child abuse. The child was considered property of the father to be worked, sold, loved, or killed as the father willed it. The child had no rights (Gelles & Lancaster, 1987; Helfer & Kempe, 1987; Nagi, 1977). "The notion that parents have the right to rear children as they see fit, in the privacy of their home, is a deeply-rooted tradition in American history" (Vondra & Toth, 1989). Actions that would be called child abuse today were overlooked or considered to be the parent's right to discipline.

In the 1800s it was common for children to work 12 hours a day under the threat of beatings. Children were cheap and useful laborers. It was not until 1874 in New York City that the first case of abuse was reported. In involved a 9-year-old girl, Mary Ellen, who was beaten daily by her parents and was severely undernourished when found by church workers. The only organization to which the workers could turn was the American Society for the Prevention of Cruelty to Animals. One year later the New York Society for the Prevention of Cruelty to Children was organized (Fontana & Besharov, 1979). There were other early evidences of growing concern for children. A paper published in 1888 discussed acute periosteal swelling in infants (Nagi, 1977). National groups such as the Child Study Association of America and the National Congress of Parents and Teachers were formed. Mounting concern over working conditions and care of children culminated in the First White House Conference on Children, held in 1909, which resulted in the 1912 legislation that established the Children's Bureau.

During recent years, wide concern over and protective action for the child at risk has become a mandate to schools, and medical care agencies have recognized the prevalence of children who are abused. This relatively recent overwhelming concern over the tragedy of child abuse resulted in the nearly unanimous passage of the federal Child Abuse Prevention and Treatment Act of 1974 by a vote of 247 to 57 in the Senate and 354 to 36 in the House of Representatives (Besharov, 1977; Mondale, 1977). What transpired between 1913 and recent decades to focus attention on the child at risk?

Dr. John Caffey began collecting data that indicated child abuse in the early 1920s, but he was not supported in his beliefs by his associates. Thus, it was not until after World War II that he published the first of several studies relating to fractures in young children (American Humane Association, 1978; Elmer, 1982). Caffey's first medical paper, written in 1946, reported the histories of six traumatized infants and questioned the cause of their injuries. In it he reported that fractures of the long bones and subdural hematomas occurring concurrently were not caused by disease (pp. 163–173).

Dr. Frederick Silverman, a former student of Caffey's, followed in 1953 with an article that indicated that skeletal trauma in infants could be the result of abuse (American Humane Association, 1978; Elmer, 1982). Reports began appearing more frequently (Altman & Smith, 1960; Bakwin, 1956; Fisher, 1958; Silver & Kempe, 1959; Wooley & Evans, 1955), but it was an article by Kempe et al., "The Battered-Child Syndrome" (1962), that brought national attention to the abused child. They began their article with the following charge to physicians:

The battered-child syndrome, a clinical condition in young children who have received serious physical abuse, is a frequent cause of permanent injury or death. The syndrome should be considered in any child exhibiting evidence of fracture of any bone, subdural hematoma, failure to thrive, soft tissue swellings or skin bruising, in any child who dies suddenly, or where the degree and type of injury is at variance with the history given regarding the occurrence of the trauma. Psychiatric factors are probably of prime importance in the pathogenesis of the disorder, but knowledge of these factors is limited. Physicians have a duty and responsibility to the child to require a full evaluation of the problem and to guarantee that no expected repetition of trauma will be permitted to occur. (Kempe et al., 1962, p. 17)

The article went on to describe the status of child abuse in the nation and to point out the effectiveness of X-ray examinations in determining abuse. The term *battered* came from the description of bruises, lacerations, bites, brain injury, deep body injury, pulled joints, burns and scalds, fractures of arms, legs, skull, ribs, and other injuries that resulted from beating, whipping, throwing the child about, or slamming the child against something. Fontana (1973) described battering by parents as follows:

Parents bash, lash, beat, flay, stomp, suffocate, strangle, gut-punch, choke with rags or hot pepper, poison, crack heads open, slice, rip, steam, fry, boil, dismember. They use fists, belt buckles, straps, hairbrushes, lamp cords, sticks, baseball bats, rulers, shoes and boots, lead or iron pipes, bottles, brick walls, bicycle chains, pokers, knives, scissors, chemicals, lighted cigarettes, boiling water, steaming radiators, and open gas flames. (pp. 16–17)

The term *battered* and the picture it evoked aroused the nation. By 1967 all 50 states had mandated legislation to facilitate the reporting of incidences of child abuse. There was, however, no provision for the coordination of procedures, nor was there a standard definition of abuse and neglect. Other conditions that precluded standard reporting included the inconsistent ages of children covered by law, hesitation of professional and private citizens to report cases, different systems of official record keeping, and varied criteria on which to judge abuse.

In 1987, 2,178,000 cases of child abuse and neglect were reported (American Humane Association, 1989). Of these, 686,000 cases were substantiated and the true number may be as high as 835,000 (American Association for Protecting Children, 1989). More than 1,100 children died of the abuse (Green, 1988). Most experts disagree on the exact number of child abuse cases in the United States each year, but most do agree that it affects at least 1 million children each year and the number may be three or four times that high (Gelles & Lancaster, 1987).

Fontana, a pediatrician who works with abused children, believes that one or two children are killed and thousands are permanently injured by their parents each day. He stated that "In New York City two children per week die at the hands of their care providers" (as cited in Green, 1988, p. 10). Although others may believe that the incidence of abuse is exaggerated, doctors who view children each day feel that child abuse occurs more often than data indicate and that what statistics reveal is merely the tip of an iceberg (Fontana, 1973; Gelles & Lancaster, 1987; Green, 1988).

Gelles (1980) defined and operationalized *violence* in an effort to determine the extent of abuse in the United States. Violence was stated as "an act carried out with the intention of, or perceived intention of, physically injuring another person" (p. 875). The research included 2,143 participants who had at least one child, 3 to 17 years of age, living at home. The survey revealed that 3.8% of the children in the United States, aged 3 to 17, were abused each year. When this percentage is projected to the 46 million children in the United States, it means that between 1.5 and 2 million children are abused by their parents each year (Gelles, 1980).

Other statistics vary in their numbers, but the story is clear; there is a great amount of child abuse and neglect in our society. For many, violence has become an accepted mode of behavior. Television often depicts violence and force as the normal way of life. Physical punishment has long been condoned and is sanctioned by the schools in many states as an alternative to other forms of discipline. The long acceptance of physical abuse makes its detection and control more difficult.

Zigler noted that "the widespread acceptance of physical abuse as an appropriate disciplinary technique implicitly condones the physical abuse of children" (as cited in Green, 1988, p. 10). Although we have made considerable progress since the 1700s and 1800s when child labor was rampant, our cultural values, socialization patterns, and resultant discipline still support the use of physical force with children.

The National Committee for Prevention of Child Abuse accepted the following policy statement in 1983:

Since corporal punishment in schools and custodial settings contradicts our national policy dedicated to the eradication of child abuse from our society, and since appropriate disciplinary alternatives can be made available, we will work towards the elimination of corporal punishment in the schools and toward the adoption of alternatives to corporal punishment (as cited in Green, 1988, pp. 9, 10).

Twenty-seven national organizations have policies that oppose corporal punishment in the schools. Included in this list are the American Medical Association, American Bar Association, National Education Association, American Psychological Association, National Congress of Parents and Teachers, American Public Health Association, and the Association for Childhood Education International.

Nineteen nations have abolished corporal punishment including Germany, Switzerland, Britain, Italy, France, Russia, Norway, Rumania, Portugal, Sweden, Denmark, Spain, Ireland, Holland, Belgium, Austria, Finland, and Turkey. Poland abolished corporal punishment in the schools in 1783 while Britain is the most recent having abolished it in 1986.

In the United States more than 80% of the states permit hitting children (End Violence Against the Next Generation, Inc., n.d.). Thus, schools model and perpetuate the use of force to discipline children. In addition, schools who use ridicule, fear, and ostracism to discipline children may cause emotional abuse in the classroom (Krugman & Krugman, 1984). Schools have been alarmingly slow to join the national

movement to reduce abuse—a movement that began in the 1960s and continued into the 90s.

In 1974 the federal Child Abuse Act established the National Center on Child Abuse and Neglect in Washington, D.C. Subsequently, regional centers on child abuse were funded. Their purpose was to conduct research to determine the cause of child abuse and neglect, its identification and prevention, and the amount of child abuse in the nation.

Working first with the Children's Bureau and then with the National Center, the American Humane Association (now with a division called the American Association for Protecting Children), an organization that has focused on child protection since it was founded more than 100 years ago, established a national clearinghouse in 1973 for reporting child abuse and neglect and analyzing reported data. Previously, in 1962, the American Humane Association completed one of the first surveys on child abuse by analyzing newspaper reports. It found 662 cases reported in 48 states and the District of Columbia. In 1987 the same organization disclosed 2,178,000 reports of child abuse (American Association for Protecting Children, 1989). From 1976 to 1987, reported child abuse cases increased 128% (see Figure 10–1). Reports of sexual abuse increased 54% between 1983 and 1984. The growth in reported cases reflects both better reporting and increase in abuse.

ABUSE AND NEGLECT

The *physically abused* child shows signs of injury—welts, cuts, bruises, burns, fractures, and/or lacerations. Educators should be aware of repeated injuries, untreated injuries, multiple injuries, and new injuries added to old.

It is more difficult to identify *emotional neglect and abuse,* a situation in which the caretaker provides less of the warm, sensitive, nurturing environment than is required for the child's healthy growth and development (Steele, 1977). The parents are usually overly harsh and critical. They withhold love and acceptance and

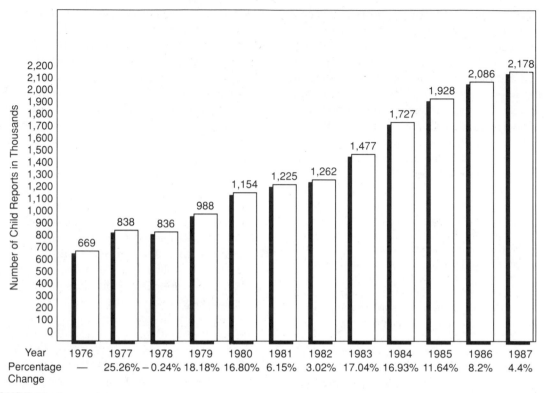

FIGURE 10-1

National estimates of child abuse and neglect reports. Source: American Association for Protecting Children. *Highlights of official child neglect and abuse reporting, 1987.* Denver, Colo.: American Humane Association, 1989, p. 5.

do not give the child either physical or verbal encouragement and praise. Although they expect performance, they do not support the child's endeavors.

Physical neglect refers to the parents' failure to provide the necessities—adequate shelter, care and supervision, food, clothing, and protection. The child shows signs of malnutrition, is usually irritable, and may be in need of medical attention. The child often goes hungry and needs supervision after school hours. The parents are either unable or unwilling to give proper care.

Medical neglect and *educational neglect* result in the child's inability to develop fully. Parents may not be indifferent; they may not recognize the importance of medical care or a developmental environment, or they may be incapable of furnishing them. Abandonment represents renunciation and total rejection of the child by the parent.

Multiple maltreatment often occurs in a child who suffers abuse or neglect. While emotional maltreatment can be isolated, incidences of physical abuse or neglect usually are accompanied by emotional abuse.

Identification of Physical Abuse

What are the evidences of physical abuse? Although many bruises and abrasions are accidental, others give cause for the teacher to believe that they were intentionally inflicted. Bruises are the most common symptoms of physical abuse. Other symptoms include welts, lumps, or ridges on the body, usually caused by a blow; burns, shown by redness, blistering, or peeling of the skin; fractured bones; scars; lacerations or torn cuts; abrasions or scraped skin.

Head Start personnel are given guidelines that give four criteria for identification of child abuse in the preschool child. These guidelines are useful for detection of abuse in any age child. The first is location of the injury. Bruises found on the knees, elbows, shins, and, for the preschool child, the forehead, are considered normal in most circumstances. "If these bruises were found on the back, genital area, thighs, buttocks, face or back of legs, one should be suspicious" (U.S. Department of Health, Education and Welfare, 1977, p. 67). (See Figure 10–2.)

The second criterion is evidence of repetition of injury. A significantly large number of bruises or cuts and injuries that are at various stages of healing should be suspect. There are instances, however, when repetition could be accidental—the child could be accident prone, so criterion four needs to be kept in mind.

The third criterion is the appearance of the injury. If it is obvious that the bruise, cut, or burn was inflicted by an object such as a belt, stick, or

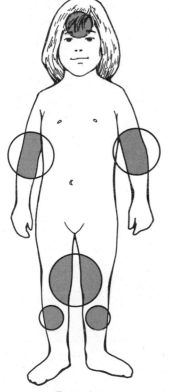

Front view

Normal bruising areas

Front and back views

Suspicious bruising areas

FIGURE 10–2

Comparison of typical and suspicious bruising areas. The bruises children receive in play are depicted on the left. The bruises on the right would not normally happen in everyday play. Source: Head Start Bureau and Children's Bureau, U.S. Department of Health, Education and Welfare. *Child abuse and neglect: A self-instructional text for Head Start personnel.* Washington, D.C.: U.S. Government Printing Office, 1977.

cigarette, the teacher or caregiver should suspect abuse.

The fourth criterion is the correlation between the injury and the explanation given by the child or the parent. The accident as described should be able to produce the resultant injury. For example, could round burns shaped like cigarettes be caused by the child playing too near the stove?

In ascertaining the extent of suspected physical abuse, the teacher should not remove any of the child's clothing. Only personnel, such as a nurse or doctor, who would undress a child as part of their professional responsibilities should do so.

After reviewing the four criteria and checking school policy—the suspicious placement of injury, the severity and repetition of injuries, evidence of infliction by an object, and inconsistent explanation (or consistent if the child reports the abuse)—the educator must report the injury to the appropriate authorities.

Identification of Sexual Abuse

Sexual abuse is when any person, adult or child, forces, coerces, or threatens a child to have any form of sexual contact or to engage in any type of sexual activity at his or her direction. Keep in mind that while the child might be forced to cooperate, he or she is (by legal definitions) not capable of giving consent (Hagans & Case, 1988, p. 21).

Categories of sexual abuse include:

1. Incest—physical sexual activity between members of the extended family
2. Pedophilia—sexual preference by an adult for prepubertal children
3. Exhibitionism—exposure of genitals by a male to boys, girls, and women
4. Molestation—fondling, touching, engaging in masturbation; kissing child especially in breast and genital areas
5. Sexual intercourse (statutory rape)—includes penile-vaginal intercourse, fellatio (oral-genital contact), and sodomy (anal-genital contact)
6. Rape—sexual intercourse or attempted sexual intercourse without consent of the child

7. Sexual sadism—infliction of bodily harm
8. Child pornography—photographs, videos, or films showing sexual acts including children. There are an estimated 300,000 children involved in child pornography.
9. Child prostitution—children in sex acts for profit (Kempe & Kempe, 1984)

Sexual abuse is very difficult to identify. Most of the offenders, approximately 80%, are known to the family or are family members. The victims are primarily girls, ranging from infants to adolescents.

Although historically most societies have had taboos against such behavior, sexual abuse and incest have always existed. But generally sexual abuse has been concealed, mythicized, or ignored. Not until the late 1970s and 1980s did its existence become realistically recognized, and even then, most persons gathering information on the problem felt that only the "tip of the iceberg" had been revealed. Sexual abuse appears to be increasing. According to the American Humane Association, sexual abuse reports increased by 54% from 1983 until 1984.

Incest and other sexual abuse occur in all socioeconomic groups, and therefore, teachers in all schools or child care settings should be aware of the indicators since they have a legal and moral obligation to report suspected sexual abuse. Teachers and caregivers who report in good faith are immune from legal liability.

Signs for identifying sexual abuse include the following physical and behavioral characteristics (Riggs, 1982; Krugman, 1986):

Physical signs
- bruises or bleeding in external genitalia, vaginal, or anal area
- uncomfortable while sitting
- difficulty in walking
- pregnancy in young child
- torn, bloody, or stained underclothing
- sexually transmitted disease in young child

Behavioral signs
- appetite disorders
- phobias
- guilt

- temper tantrums
- neurotic and conduct disorders
- truancy
- suicide attempts
- confides with teacher or nurse that she/he has been sexually mistreated
- reports by other children that their friend is being sexually mistreated
- displays precocious sexual behavior and/or knowledge
- unwilling to change for gym
- withdrawn, engages in fantasy
- depressed, sad, and weepy
- confused about own identity
- frequent absences justified by male caregiver or parent
- acts out in a seductive manner
- reluctance to go home
- young child regresses to earlier behavior by thumbsucking, bed wetting, difficulty in eating, sleeping, and being afraid of the dark
- older child turns to drugs, tries to run away, and has difficulty accomplishing school work

Concern about sexual abuse has steadily risen not only because of the reported increase in incidence but also because of the deleterious effects that sexual abuse can have on the child and, later, the adult (Krugman, 1986). There are probably 250,000 to 300,000 cases of sexual abuse occurring each year. One-sixth of all males and one-third of all females will experience some form of sexual abuse before they are adults (Krugman, 1986). Psychological and emotional reactions are common. Children feel trapped, confused, betrayed, and disgraced. They may have fear, phobias, somatic complaints, mood changes, anxieties, hysterical seizures, multiple personalities, and nightmares. They may become prostitutes, self-mutilating, or suicidal. At school they may show developmental lags, communication problems, and apparent learning deficiencies (Finkelhor, 1986; Ryan, 1989; Wodarski & Johnson, 1988).

Children who are caught in sexual abuse often go through five phases: (1) secrecy; (2) helplessness; (3) entrapment and accommodation; (4) delayed, conflicted, and unconvinc-

ing disclosure; and (5) retraction (Summit, 1983, p. 181). To understand the child's predicament, you have to understand the helplessness that the child feels in responding to the adult who is both more physically powerful and supposedly more knowledgeable. The adult first approaches the child with the need for secrecy: "Everything will be all right if you do not tell. No one else will understand our secret. Your mother will hate you. If you tell, it will break up the family. If you tell, I'll kill your pet. If you tell, I'll spank you." Whatever the secrets, the child is in a no-win position. The child fears being hurt if she/he tells the secret. When the child does tell, the reaction is often one of disbelief. "Unless the victim can find some permission and power to share the secret and unless there is the possibility of an engaging, non-punitive response" the child may spend a life of "self-imposed exile from intimacy, trust and self-validation" (Summit, 1983, p. 182). In a study by Cupoli and Sewell (1988), 28% of the known perpetrators were family members; 58% were known others including the mothers' boyfriends; and nearly 14% were strangers. In this study of 1,059 children, 86% of the sexual abuse was done at the hands of someone the child knew. Incest was committed by 28% of the perpetrators. Fathers committed 12% of the incest; stepfathers committed 8%. Most sexual abuse was committed by someone who continued to be near the child, placing the child at high risk for repeat attacks.

An alarming finding is the number of sexual abusers who are adolescents—20%. Victims tend to become victimizers. Ryan (1988) cites studies which show that as many as 70% to 80% of adult sexual abusers were abused themselves as children.

The teacher or child caregiver who suspects sexual abuse must report his suspicions to proper authorities—social service and child protection agencies are established in every state.

The teacher's role is a supportive one. Continue to have normal expectations for the child, keep a stable environment for the child, and do not make the child feel ostracized or different. Treat the child with understanding, be sensitive to the child's needs, and help build the child's self-esteem. Several programs have been developed to help the child develop defenses against personal abuse (see Appendix).

TALKING WITH FAMILIES

Just as there are varieties and levels of abuse and neglect, so also are there variations in your interaction with the parents. Child care workers and school personnel who want to help an abused child must exercise good judgment. Their first response may be to want to call the parent to determine how the injury occurred. In the case of violent abuse, the child may be in danger of being permanently damaged or killed. Calling the family to discuss the problem not only fails to help the family but may also precipitate more abuse. In addition, the family may become alarmed and move to another area; the child may be abused for many more months before the new school or center identifies the problem. *With serious abuse do not call the parents or try to handle the situation by yourself. Contact the appropriate authorities immediately.*

When neglect rather than abuse is the problem, and a child comes to school hungry or inappropriately dressed, a supportive visit or call to the family is in order. The school can provide not only emotional support but clothing and food as well. Working *with* parents shows them they are not alone with their overwhelming problems. If providing services is beyond the capability of the school, or if the family needs professional help, social services should be called.

DEVELOPMENT OF POLICIES

School districts and child care centers need to develop the policies and training programs vital to successful child abuse intervention. If there is no policy, the teacher should see the school nurse, psychologist, director, counselor, social worker, or principal, depending on the staffing of the school. Even in the school district with a policy statement, each school or child care center staff should have one person who is responsible for receiving reports of child abuse. Making

one person responsible results in greater awareness of the problem of abuse and facilitates the reporting process. It is also helpful to establish a committee to view evidence and support the conclusions of the original observer.

Suspected child abuse must be reported in all states. Evidence of violent physical abuse must be reported immediately. If school officials refuse to act, one can call social services, a law enforcement agency, or a family crisis center. The reporter should have the right to remain anonymous. When reporting in good faith, the person reporting is protected by immunity described in state legislation. Colorado law specifically states: "Any person participating in good faith in the making of a report or in a judicial proceeding held pursuant to this title shall be immune from any liability, civil or criminal, that otherwise might result by reason of such reporting" (Denver Public Schools, 1985).

Needs Assessment

Schools and child care centers first have to determine the prevention and protection delivery systems that are already available in the community. They should consider social service departments, child protection teams, child welfare agencies, law enforcement, juvenile court system, Head Start, child care centers, hospitals, clinics, public health nurses, mental health programs, public and private service groups, fundraising agencies such as United Way, and service organizations that might be unique to their community. Questions to ask include:

1. Which functions are being served by each agency?
   a. Identification
   b. Investigation
   c. Treatment planning
   d. Remediation
   e. Referral
2. Which preventive services are available in the community?
   a. Child development classes
   b. Prenatal counseling
   c. Self-help groups such as Parents Anonymous

3. Which groups are available for outreach?
4. Which training activities are available?
5. Are there crisis hot lines where help can be reached at all hours?
6. Which services are available for parents in the community?
   a. Lay therapists
   b. Parent aides
   c. Counseling
7. Which services are available for children?
   a. Crisis nurseries
   b. Therapeutic child care
   c. Residential and foster home care
   d. Play therapy

Following assessment of the community, the school and child care centers have to determine their role in an integrated approach to abuse and neglect. Communication lines must be kept open at all times. A representative of the schools should serve on the child protection team. One role that is mandated is identification of abuse and neglect. Other roles will be individualized according to the needs of the community, the resources in the schools and child care centers, and the commitment of the personnel.

Policy

Child abuse is found in all socioeconomic groups in the United States, so all school districts must be prepared to work with interdisciplinary agencies in the detection and prevention of this national social problem.

Policies should be written in compliance with the requirements of each state's reporting statute, details of which may be learned by consulting the state's attorney general. Because reporting is required in all states, the policy should include a clear statement of reporting requirements. The policy should also inform the school personnel of their immunity and legal obligations. (See Denver Public Schools' *Child Abuse Bulletin* in Appendix C.) Dissemination of the policy should include the community as well as all school employees. Not only is it important that the community realize the obligation of the school or child care center to report suspected abuse or neglect, it is vital that the community becomes aware of the extent of the problem.

Teacher's Role in Carrying Out Policy

Child Abuse and Neglect, Vol. 2, The Roles and Responsibilities of Professionals (U.S. Department of Health, Education and Welfare, 1975) includes a special charge to teachers:

You should be aware of the official policy and specific reporting procedures of your school system, and should know your legal obligations and the protections from civil and criminal liability specified in your state's reporting law. (All states provide immunity for mandated, good-faith reports.)

Although you should be familiar with your state's legal definition of abuse and neglect, you are not required to make legal distinctions in order to report. Definitions should serve as guides. If you suspect that a child is abused or neglected, you should report it. The teacher's value lies in noticing conditions that indicate that a child's welfare may be in jeopardy.

Be concerned about the rights of the child—the rights to life, food, shelter, clothing, and security. But also be aware of the parents' rights—particularly their rights to be treated with respect and to be given needed help and support.

Bear in mind that reporting does not stigmatize a parent as "evil." The report is the start of a rehabilitative process that seeks to protect the child and help the family as a whole.

A report signifies only the suspicion of abuse or neglect. Teachers' reports are seldom unfounded. At the very least, they tend to indicate a need for help and support to the family.

If you report a borderline case in good faith, do not feel guilty or upset if it is dismissed as unfounded upon investigation. Some marginal cases are found to be valid.

Don't put off making a report until the end of the school year. Teachers sometimes live with their suspicions until they suddenly fear for the child's safety during the summer months. A delayed report may mean a delay in needed help for the child and the family. Moreover, by reporting late in the school year, you remove yourself as a continued support to both the child protection agency and the reporting family.

If you remove yourself from a case of suspected abuse or neglect by passing it on to a superior, you deprive child protective services of one of their most competent sources of information. For example, a teacher who tells a CPS worker that the child is especially upset on Mondays directs the worker to investigate conditions in the homes on weekends. Few persons other than teachers are able to provide this kind of information. Your guidelines should be to resolve any question in favor of the child. When in doubt, report. Even if you, as a teacher, have no immunity from liability and prosecution under state law, the fact that your report is made in good faith will free you from liability and prosecution. (p. 71)

After a case is reported to the child protection agency, there should be a follow-up. If the agency does not provide feedback, the teacher should inquire about the disposition of the case. If the agency refuses to give information because of confidentiality, the teacher can still be supportive of the family and particularly sensitive to the child's needs. The teacher can give the child additional attention, talk with her, be warm and loving, and assure the child that someone cares. The pressure that the child is dealing with at home might make it necessary to individualize schoolwork. "Lower your academic expectations and make few demands on the child's performance" (U.S. Department of Health, Education and Welfare, *Child Abuse and Neglect, Vol. 2,* 1975, p. 2).

Over time, the child protection agency in your district and the schools should be able to develop an excellent working relationship. This can be facilitated by joint meetings of school representatives and social workers. Each agency needs to understand the procedures and obligations of the other. Child abuse protection requires good communication and cooperative working relationships among all agencies involved in the child's welfare.

WHAT PRECIPITATES CHILD ABUSE?

Three factors must be present for child abuse to occur. The first is parents or caregivers who have the potential for abusing. The second, most obviously, is the child, but not just any child. This child is one who is seen by the parents as being different. The third factor is a stress situation that brings on a crisis.

According to Helfer and Kempe (1987), abusive parents or caregivers have acquired the potential to abuse over the years. These parents usually had deprived childhoods. They lacked a consistent, loving, nurturing environment when they were young. They have a poor self-image, and their mates are passive and do not or are not able to give their spouses the emotional support that they need. It is probable that the family has isolated itself. The parents have no support system from neighbors or community. Since few of them understand child development, they have unrealistic expectations of their children.

Such parents are most likely to abuse children whom they see as being different. Child abuse also occurs against a child who actually is different from the norm: the disabled, hyperactive, or mentally retarded child.

Before the abusive act occurs, there is a precipitating event—one that does not directly cause the specific act against the child, but a minor or major crisis that sets the stage for the parent to lose control and abuse the child. This crisis may be physical (e.g., a broken washing machine) or personal (e.g., spouse desertion, death in the family). With these three factors the stage is set. The parent or caregiver loses control and abuses the child (Helfer, 1975).

WHO ARE THE ABUSED AND THE ABUSERS?

The abusive person is generally the natural parent; 81.5% of major physical injury is caused by the natural parent (see Table 10–1). Neglect cases are the result of the parent's inability to supply necessary care in 90% of those reported. The case is different for sexual maltreatment. Natural parents are responsible for 58.9% of sexual abuse, but more than 30% can be attributed to adoptive, step, or foster parents, and 3% is caused by other relatives. From these data it is clear that incest is the largest cause of sexual

TABLE 10–1

Type of maltreatment and child relationship to perpetrator—caretakers (N = 85,039 children). The natural parent is most often responsible for maltreatment of the child.

Child-Perpetrator Relationship	Major or Major with Minor Physical Injury (N = 1,356)	Minor or Unspecified Physical Injury (N = 15,339)	Sexual Maltreatment (N = 3,683)	Deprivation of Necessities (N = 44,591)	Emotional Maltreatment (N = 6,311)	Other Maltreatment[1] (N = 1,424)	Multiple Maltreatment (N = 12,335)	Percent of All Relationships
Natural parent	81.5%	76.1%	58.9%	90.7%	80.0%	91.5%	80.8%	84.3%
Other parent[2]	9.1%	13.5%	30.8%	1.2%	6.7%	2.4%	5.8%	5.9%
Natural and other parent	4.7%	5.7%	4.4%	4.8%	10.0%	4.8%	8.9%	5.9%
Other relative	1.8%	2.3%	3.0%	2.1%	2.1%	0.9%	2.1%	2.1%
Nonrelative	1.6%	1.4%	2.3%	0.1%	0.5%	0.1%	0.4%	0.5%
Other perpetrator combinations	1.2%	1.1%	0.7%	1.1%	0.7%	0.3%	2.1%	1.2%
Total	100%	100%	100%	100%	100%	100%	100%	100%

[1] Refers to relationships in which a child has more than one type of maltreatment indicated and "Major or Major with Minor Physical Injury" or "Minor or Unspecified Physical Injury" does not apply.

[2] "Other parent" refers to adoptive, step and foster parents.

Source: American Association for Protecting Children. *Highlights of Official Child Neglect and Abuse Reporting, 1983.* Denver, Colo.: American Humane Association, 1985, p. 13.

abuse; people outside of the family caused only 3% of the sexual abuse cases.

Neglect of children is reported more often than any other form of abuse. Both boys and girls are equally involved in reports. Forty percent of the reported families are headed by single mothers, most of whom are in difficult financial conditions. Insufficient income is cited as the greatest cause of neglect. Deprivation of necessities is the most frequently cited type of neglect (58.4%) with minor physical injury represented by 18.5%. Major physical injury was indicated 3.2% of the time and sexual maltreatment, 8.5% (see Figure 10–3).

Young children from infancy through age 5 are the victims of the greatest number of major physical injuries. Child care centers need to be particularly alert for signs of physical damage. Table 10–2 shows that while the young children represent 34.5% of all children, they are over-represented in all forms of abuse except sexual and emotional maltreatments. They account for 64.1% of major physical injury and 48.6% of deprivation of necessities. Children 6 years of age and older accounted for 75% of sexual maltreatment.

WHO REPORTS MALTREATMENT CASES?

Cases of child maltreatment are reported by more nonprofessionals than professionals. The largest reporting group is friends, neighbors, relatives, and the abusers themselves, with 39.2% coming from that group. As Figure 10–4 illustrates, more than 11% of the reporters are anonymous and probably contain some of the same group. The professional group is evenly divided among medical, school, law, and social services. Child care providers report only 1.9% of the cases.

BEHAVIORS AND ATTITUDES OF PARENTS AND CHILDREN THAT MAY INDICATE CHILD ABUSE

Specialists working with child abuse (Fontana, 1973; Kempe & Helfer, 1987) have developed some guidelines to help educators determine the existence of child abuse. The following are modified from publications from Head Start, the U.S. Department of Health and Human Services, and the American Humane Association.

The Child of Preschool Age

1. Does the child seem to fear his or her parents?

2. Does the child miss preschool or the child care center often?

3. Does the child bear evidence of physical abuse? Are there signs of battering such as bruises or welts, belt or buckle marks, lacerations, or burns?

4. Does the child exhibit extreme behavior changes? Is the child very aggressive at times and then fearful, withdrawn, and/or depressed?

5. Does the child have sores, bruises, or cuts that are not adequately cared for?

6. Does the child come to school inadequately dressed? Does the child look uncared for?

7. Does the child take over the parent role and try to "mother" the parent?

8. Does the child seem to be hungry for affection?

The Child of Elementary School Age

1. Does the child exhibit behavior that deviates from the norm? Is the child aggressive, destructive, and disruptive or passive and withdrawn? The first may be a child who is shouting for help, demanding attention and striking out; whereas the second may be out of touch with reality, remote, submissive, and subdued, but crying for help in another way.

2. Does the child miss classes or is the child often late or tardy? Does the child come to school too early and stay around after school is over? In the first instance, the child's behavior suggests problems at home. In the second, the child may be pushed out in the morning and have nowhere to go after school.

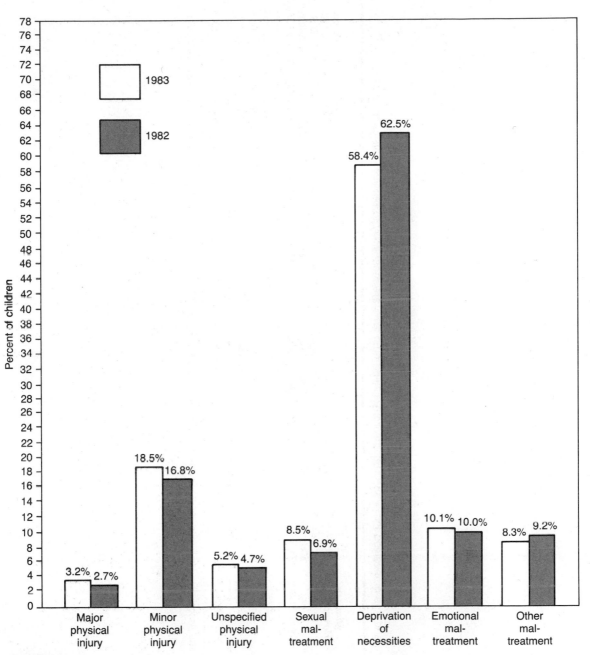

FIGURE 10–3

Type of maltreatment. Neglect, as shown through deprivation of necessities, is the most frequently reported form of abuse and neglect. Source: American Association for Protecting Children. *Highlights of official child neglect and abuse reporting, 1983.* Denver, Colo.: American Humane Association, 1985, p. 11.

TABLE 10-2

Type of maltreatment and age of involved (N = 381,168 children). Children under 5 are most likely to receive physical injuries.

Age	Major or Major with Minor Physical Injury (N = 8,800)	Minor or Unspecified Physical Injury (N = 71,884)	Sexual Maltreatment (N = 27,714)	Deprivation of Necessities (N = 192,223)	Emotional Maltreatment (N = 24,808)	Other Maltreatment (N = 15,917)	Multiple Maltreatment (N = 39,822)	Percent of All Involved Children (N = 717,315)	Percent of All U.S. Children (N = 62,580,000)
0–5	64.1%	37.3%	24.8%	48.6%	34.0%	47.0%	41.5%	43.3%	34.5%
6–11	19.8%	32.6%	34.3%	33.2%	34.2%	26.8%	31.7%	32.5%	30.7%
12–17	15.9%	30.0%	40.6%	18.2%	31.9%	26.2%	27.0%	24.1%	34.7%
Total	100%	100%	100%	100%	100%	100%	100%	100%	100%

Source: American Humane Association. *Highlights of Official Child Neglect and Abuse Reporting, 1983. Denver, Colo.: American Humane Association, 1985, p. 16.*

360

FIGURE 10–4
Most cases of child abuse and neglect are reported by nonprofessionals—friends, neighbors, relatives, or sometimes the perpetrators or victims themselves.
Source: American Association for Protecting Children. *Highlights of official child neglect and abuse reporting, 1983.* Denver, Colo.: American Humane Association, 1985, p. 7.

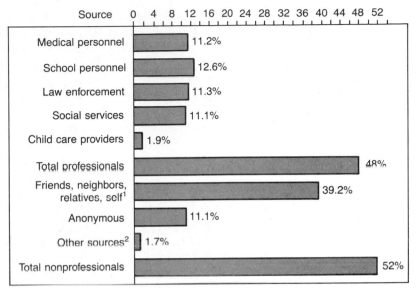

Source   0 4 8 12 16 20 24 28 32 36 40 44 48 52

Medical personnel	11.2%
School personnel	12.6%
Law enforcement	11.3%
Social services	11.1%
Child care providers	1.9%
Total professionals	48%
Friends, neighbors, relatives, self[1]	39.2%
Anonymous	11.1%
Other sources[2]	1.7%
Total nonprofessionals	52%

[1] "Self" includes both victims and perpetrators and accounts for about three percent of all reports.

[2] "Other Sources" includes, as examples, landlords and religious personnel, individuals not readily categorized by the other standard categories.

3. Does the child bear evidence of physical abuse? Are there obvious signs of battering: bruises, belt or buckle marks, welts, lacerations, or burns?

4. Does the child lack social skills? Is the child unable to approach children and play with them?

5. Does the child have learning problems that cannot be diagnosed? Does the child underperform? If intelligence tests show average academic ability and the child is not able to do the work, there may be problems at home.

6. Does the child show great sensitivity to others' feelings? Does the child get upset when another person is criticized? Abused children often have to "mother" their abusive parents, and some are overly sensitive to the feelings of others.

7. Does the child come to school inadequately dressed? Is the child unwashed and uncared for? This may be a signal of neglect.

8. Does the child feel tired and fall asleep in class?

9. Does the child seem to be undernourished? Does the child attempt to save food? Is there real poverty in the home, or are there just parents who do not care?

10. Does the child seem to be afraid of his or her parents?

The Secondary Level Student

Most of the traits just mentioned are relevant to detection of abuse in the junior and senior high child, but there are additional signs to watch for in the upper levels. In addition to evidence of physical abuse, neglect, truancy, and tardiness, the older student may experience the following:

1. Does the student have to assume too much responsibility at home?
2. Does the parent expect unrealistic and overly strict behavior?

3. Does the student have difficulty conforming to school regulations and policies?
4. Does the student have problems communicating with his or her parents?
5. Does the student have a history of running away from home and refusing to go home?
6. Does the student act out sexually?
7. Does the student lack freedom and friends?

Behavior and Psychologic Characteristics of the Child in School

The largest group of children who chronically act out in the classroom are not psychotic or cognitively impaired, but are behaviorally disordered children. Hochstedler (in Sandberg, 1987) categorizes three disorders: attention deficit disorder, conduct disorder, and adjustment disorder. While overlapping occurs, each disorder needs an individualized analysis of the appropriate intervention plan. *In each case, however, it is harmful to punish and make the child feel even more inadequate*. In conduct disorders the "alarming process is fueled by punishment approaches, when what is needed is to hold the child responsible for his/her destructive behavior without branding the child 'bad' " (Sandberg, 1987, p. 11). Acting out is a coping mechanism used by children who do not have an appropriate response repertoire.

Children with attention deficit disorders (ADD) appear in almost every classroom. These children do not seem to be able to stay on task, to concentrate, and to get the assignment completed. Children who are hyperactive probably have attention deficit disorder, but it is not necessary to be hyperkinetic or hyperactive to be unable to concentrate and sit still. Every teacher has experienced the child who disrupts the room, fails to progress, and is constantly distracted, going from the assigned task to watch another child, flitting from one task to another and, thus, failing to progress in the academic program. Some of these children may have too much energy, or they may be hyperactive. ADD is distinguished by poorly organized, haphazard, and non-goal-directed activities. It is 10 times more likely to happen to a boy than to a girl.

In addition, without early intervention, ADD is a precursor to more intense problems. Hochstedler observed that "the pattern we see over and over with ADD children in the early years is their inability to pay attention and behave properly, followed by parents and teachers viewing the child as bad or unacceptable" (in Sandberg, 1987, p. 10). This hurts the child's self-esteem and leads to a worsening of the condition rather than an improvement. If these patterns continue, the child may become conduct disordered, a child who breaks rules and is "calloused toward the needs and rights of others" (Sandberg, 1987, p. 10). Conduct-disordered children are at risk to develop adult personality disorders. A comprehensive intervention plan that limits the acting out behavior needs to be developed. Multiple factors may affect the child. Some of these factors are child abuse, family violence, adoption, divorce, and harsh discipline. The child may live in a family with an antisocial lifestyle or the parents may be engaged in criminal activity. The factors related to each child need to be addressed by the therapist (Sandberg, 1987).

Adjustment disorder is connected either to a single or multiple traumatic events that affect the child. The treatment and prognosis for success varies with the social-emotional condition of the child. Children who do not have persistent psychiatric and social impairment may be helped by therapy and by talking through the critical event to help them understand and resolve their pain.

"A significant body of child abuse research suggests that child abuse precipitates disorders in children" (Sandberg, 1987, p. 12). What does this mean for teachers? Teachers should not assume child abuse just because the child has attention deficiencies. However, the school must be "involved with identifying and remediating assorted problems, including child abuse, that severely jeopardize a child's opportunity to learn" (Sandberg, 1987, p. xvi). It is important for teachers to help the child learn appropriate behaviors at an early age. They should use disciplinary methods that help the child learn self-control rather than discipline that is actually punishment. Classrooms should give support and continuity to children. They should provide special help for children with learning deficiencies, use special education services to help social-emotional deficient children get the help they need, and above all else, make sure the child does not feel inadequate. How can teachers accomplish all of this? Teachers need parent volunteers or aids in the classroom plus a support system in order to meet the needs of each child and to make sure that each child has more successes than failures.

Halperin (1979) cites some practical guidelines for teachers to follow in identifying the child who needs attention. He cautions against jumping to conclusions concerning maltreatment. Marks on a body may come from many circumstances. "Only when school personnel have gathered substantial information on the family and its internal functioning are they in a position to assess if a child is being maltreated at home" (p. 67).

If educators bear in mind that children are unique and may respond to the same treatment in opposite ways and that children display a wide range of behaviors, they will be cautious in labeling a child.

When educators recognize Halperin's clues for children who need attention, whether or not there is any suspicion of maltreatment, they will be doing a great service to all the children in their classrooms. Individualization of academic program as well as individualization for emotional needs will result in a well-rounded educational program for the child. As the teacher gets to know the child better and responds to the child with needed praise or reinforcement, as well as with an individualized curriculum, the results will be improved education. The following descriptions are modified from Halperin.

Aggressive child
Typical characteristics
Defiant

Domineering

Blames others

Possible reasons for actions
Little self-esteem

Cannot control impulses

Unhappy

Little self-discipline

Show-off
Typical characteristics
Extremely extroverted

Answers questions without knowing the answer

May appear hyperactive

Wants to be center of attention

Possible reasons for actions
Masks insecurity

Little attention at home

Shows off to compete for praise and love

Disobedient child
Typical characteristics
Purposely breaks rules

Impolite and insolent

Struggles against authority

Possible reasons for actions
Unhappy

Disobeys to get attention

Models parental attitude toward authority

Inconsistent discipline at home

Prefers punishment to indifference

Has internalized feelings of worthlessness

Child who lies, cheats, and steals
Typical characteristics
Lies

Cheats

Steals

Possible reasons for actions
Lies to escape punishment

Wants to get away with action without being caught

Gains attention

Little supervision at home

Actions of dishonesty are condoned at home

Child nobody likes

Typical characteristics

Sullen

Depressed

Jealous

Blames others for acts

Absent a lot

Possible reasons for actions

Little warmth from parents

Unable to establish healthy relationship with others

Lives an isolated life

Not fond of self

Poor self-concept

Unkempt child

Typical characteristics

Soiled clothes

Unkempt hair and body

General lack of care in work

Possible reasons for actions

Lack of adult supervision and concern

Poor self-image

Listless child

Typical characteristics

Unable to concentrate

Little energy

Daydreams

Slouches

Seldom volunteers

Possible reasons for actions

May be physically neglected at home

Nutritional neglect

Medical neglect

Cannot meet expectations of parents and teachers

May be bored

Leaves tasks incomplete to minimize parental rebukes

Careless child

Typical characteristics

Messy papers

Many errors in work

Personal appearance in disarray

Possible reasons for actions

Lack of structure at home

Too-great expectations at home so child gives up trying to satisfy

Accident-prone child

Typical characteristics

Hurts self

Poor coordination

Possible reasons for actions

Organic dysfunction

Wants attention

Feigns injuries as excuse

Low self-esteem

Self-destructive

Fearful child

Typical characteristics

Anxious

Uneasy

Emotionally unstable

Possible reasons for actions

Neurotic family life

Harsh punishment from caregivers

Unpredictable home environment

Shy child

Typical characteristics

Fearful in contacts with others

Sits quietly with lowered head

Seldom defends self

Seldom expresses self

Possible reasons for actions

Lacks encouragement and acceptance at school

Excessively critical parents

Fears failure

May share same timid characteristics as parents

Withdrawn child

Typical characteristics

Isolates self

Appears tense, nervous, and unhappy

Easily discouraged and frustrated

Abandons tasks if they prove difficult

Possible reasons for actions

Unsatisfactory experiences in past

Unsatisfactory experiences at school

Excessive demands from parents

Frequently lacks love, affection, and praise

Parents may be unpredictable and unable to establish relationships

Emotionally unstable child

Typical characteristics

Volatile and unpredictable

Attitude toward life is negative

Appears agitated, worried, or preoccupied

Possible reasons for actions

Little attention or affection

Inadequate supervision or psychologic support at home

Under tremendous pressure

Low-achieving child

Typical characteristics

Short attention span

Withdrawn from classroom activities

Disobedient and disruptive

Rarely completes assignments

Possible reasons for actions

Brain damage

Physically neglected

Medical problems

Educational neglect

If these characteristics and causes are kept in mind when working with children, along with the realization that typical factors may not affect a particular child, the educator can adapt the educational program to the needs of the child. The opportunity to raise a child's self-esteem will often improve the child's behavior. It is a safe beginning.

The Abusing Parent

School personnel and child care workers will attempt to make contact with parents of the suspected abused child. The following behavioral characteristics can help the professional to determine the possibility of abuse or neglect:

1. Do the parents fail to show up for appointments? Do they stay away from school? When they come to school, are they uncooperative and unresponsive?

2. Do the parents have unrealistically high expectations for themselves and the child? Do the parents describe the child as "different" or "bad"?

3. Do the parents have expectations for the child that are inconsistent and inappropriate for the child's age?

4. Do the parents become aggressive or abusive when school personnel want to talk about the child's problems?

5. Do the parents lose control or express fear of losing control?

6. Do the parents feel that beating the child is the correct way in which to discipline? Do the parents rationalize the punishment by saying it is necessary to keep the child in line?

7. Do the parents avoid others? Are they isolated? Do they know other parents in the school? Are they known by other parents?

8. Do they lack knowledge of child development and the child's physical and psychologic needs?

9. Do the parents report that they were abused or neglected as children?

10. Do the parents refuse to participate in school events?

11. Do the parents ignore the child and avoid touching?

12. Do the parents show little interest in the child's activities or concern for the child's well-being?

Characteristics and Risk Factors of Abusive Parents

Three approaches for understanding abusive parents have been investigated: the psychological model, the sociological model, and parent-child interaction model. In the psychological model, lack of empathy distinguishes the abusive parent. In the sociological model, cultural attitudes toward violence, social stress, family size, and social isolation are factors that relate to child abuse. Prevention and treatment based on the sociological model focus on the impact the community and society have on the family. In the interactional model, the parents lack skill in interacting with their children, handling discipline, and teaching their children appropriate behavior (Wiehe, 1989).

Children learn parenting patterns from their parents. Only rarely are there abusive parents who did not have some form of maltreatment when young (Steele, 1986). These parents did not have a childhood that allowed them to become independent, productive, functioning adults. Generally they had to disregard their own needs and desires for the wishes of an authority figure. They were unable to develop inner controls and looked to outside figures for direction. Such parents also exhibit dependence on others in their search for love and affection. They are still affected by maternal deprivation. Their parents were their only models. "Learned patterns of abusive parenting are transmitted from parent to child and are replicated by the child upon becoming a parent in his/her own right" (Bavolek, 1989, p. 99). These practices include:

1. *Inappropriate expectations.* Abusive parents often perceive the child's abilities to be greater than they are. Parents expect children to take on responsibilities that are not appropriate for their ages. These parents may have expectations such as toilet training the child at 6 to 12 months, talking by age 2, and taking on housekeeping chores at an early age. Young or inexperienced parents, who do not know child development, may interpret an infant or toddler's appropriate behavior as stubbornness and rebellion. Combine this with a belief that physical punishment will help the child behave, and you have the conditions for abuse. Children in these families develop a low self-concept, and feel incapable, unacceptable, and worthless (Hamilton, 1989; Bavolek, 1989).

2. *Lack of empathy.* Abusive parents did not experience loving care when they were growing up, so they do not have a model to follow. They cannot change their own personality traits until they receive the support and love they need. These parents usually have dependency needs and are unable to empathize with their children. The child's basic needs are ignored. Such parents may justify cruel and abusive behaviors under the guise of teaching and guiding their children. Mothers who were brought up by uncaring, unattentive mothers mother in the same way. Their own children grow up with a low sense of self-esteem and inadequate identity (Bavolek, 1989; Hamilton, 1989; Steele, 1977, 1986.)

3. *Belief in physical punishment.* Abusive parents often believe that physical punishment is necessary to rear their children without spoiling them. Although this is a common fear in childrearing practices in the United States, abusive parents go to extremes and believe that babies and children should not be allowed to get away with anything. They punish to correct perceived misbehavior or inadequacy on the part of their child. The child does not live up to expectations and is considered bad. The parents think they have the moral duty to correct their child's behavior in any way they choose.

4. *Parent-child role reversal.* In these abusive families, children are looked upon by the parents as providing the love and support that the parent needs. The parent is like a needy child, so the child must play the role of the adult. If the child is able to take on some of the parental roles, abuse may be avoided, but only at the expense of the child's normal development. This is destructive to children; they do not go through normal developmental stages, do not develop their own identities, and see themselves as existing to meet the needs of their parents (Bavolek, 1989; Hamilton, 1989).

5. *Social isolation.* Social isolation is recognized by most child abuse researchers as one of the factors that perpetuates neglect and abuse. Either the absence of social support or inability to use any support has the same effect. The abusive family isolates itself, attempts to solve its problems by itself, and avoids contact with others. Isolation is a defense against being hurt and rejected. Although abusive parents may act self-sufficient and sure of themselves, they are dependent, frightened, and immature. Cross-cultural research indicates that child maltreatment occurs less often in cultures with multiple caregivers including extended families (Hamilton, 1989).

6. *Difficulty in experiencing pleasure.* In other abusing families, the parents do not enjoy life. Their social relationships are minimal and unrewarding. They do not feel competent, have difficulty planning for the future, and do not trust their own performances. Children in these families exhibit similar behaviors.

7. *Intergenerational ties.* Although the history of maltreatment and lack of parenting skills are conditions that set the scene for more neglect and abuse, the "majority of maltreated children do not maltreat their own children" (Hamilton, 1989, p. 38). The data indicates that one-third of the maltreated are abusive to their children (Vondra & Toth, 1989, p. 13). If abuse and neglect is viewed in a broad sense, however, an alarming number of parents did not receive adequate parenting, did not develop a positive attachment to their parents and other loved ones, and thus have a difficult time providing the kind of environment that nourishes and cares for a child adequately (Steele, 1986).

The American Association for Protecting Children, a division of The American Humane Association, has developed a flyer that briefly describes parental attitudes, the child's behavior, and the child's appearance. This flyer succinctly focuses on the highlights of the foregoing discussion. Schools may purchase this flyer from the American Humane Association for a nominal fee and distribute it to staff and teachers. The flyer is illustrated in Box 10–1.

HOW TO TALK WITH CHILDREN AND PARENTS

Care must be taken in talking with or interviewing children or parents. The conversation should take place in a private, relaxed, and comfortable atmosphere. Children should not feel threatened, nor should they be pressed for information or details they do not want to reveal. Parents should be aware of the school's legal obligation to report suspected neglect and abuse. If they feel that the school is supportive of the family, the interaction between parents and school will be more positive. Some guidelines (U.S. Department of Health and Human Services, 1984) to follow include:

When talking with the child
DO:

Make sure the interviewer is someone the child trusts

Conduct the interview in private

Sit next to the child, not across a table or desk

Tell the child that the interview is confidential

Conduct the interview in a language the child understands

Ask the child to clarify words/terms which are not understood

BOX 10–1
Indicators of a Child's Potential Need for Protection*

	Physical Indicators	*Behavioral Indicators*
Physical Abuse	• unexplained bruises (in various stages of healing), welts, human bite marks, bald spots • unexplained burns, especially cigarette burns or immersion burns (glove like) • unexplained fractures, lacerations or abrasions	• self destructive • withdrawn and aggressive — behavioral extremes • uncomfortable with physical contact • arrives at school early or stays late as if afraid to be at home • chronic runaway (adolescents) • complains of soreness or moves uncomfortably • wears clothing inappropriate to weather, to cover body
Physical Neglect	• abandonment • unattended medical needs • consistent lack of supervision • consistent hunger, inappropriate dress, poor hygiene • lice, distended stomach, emaciated	• regularly displays fatigue or listlessness, falls asleep in class • steals food, begs from classmates • reports that no caretaker is at home • frequently absent or tardy • self destructive • school dropout (adolescents)
Sexual Abuse	• torn, stained or bloody underclothing • pain or itching in genital area	• withdrawal, chronic depression • excessive seductiveness • role reversal, overly concerned for siblings

Tell the child if any future action will be required

DON'T:

Allow the child to feel "in trouble" or "at fault"

Disparage or criticize the child's choice of words or language

Suggest answers to the child

Probe or press for answers the child is unwilling to give

Display horror, shock, or disapproval of parents, child, or the situation

Force the child to remove clothing

Conduct the interview with a group of interviewers

Leave the child alone with a stranger (e.g., a CPS worker)

	Physical Indicators	*Behavioral Indicators*
Sexual Abuse cont.	• difficulty walking or sitting • bruises or bleeding in external genitalia • venereal disease • frequent urinary or yeast infections	• poor self esteem, self devaluation, lack of confidence • peer problems, lack of involvement • massive weight change • suicide attempts (especially adolescents) • hysteria, lack of emotional control • sudden school difficulties • inappropriate sex play or premature understanding of sex • threatened by physical contact, closeness
Emotional Maltreatment	• speech disorders • delayed physical development • substance abuse • ulcers, asthma, severe allergies	• habit disorders (sucking, rocking) • antisocial, destructive • neurotic traits (sleep disorders, inhibition of play) • passive and aggressive—behavioral extremes • delinquent behavior (especially adolescents) • developmentally delayed

Source: American Association for Protecting Children, Inc. *Guidelines for schools.* Denver, Colo.: The American Humane Association, n.d.

*Adapted in part from Broadhurst, D. D.; Edmunds, M.; MacDicken, R. A., *Early Childhood Programs and the Prevention and Treatment of Child Abuse and Neglect.* The User Manual Series. Washington, D.C.: U.S. Department of Health, Education and Welfare, 1979.

When talking with the parents
DO:
Select interviewer(s) appropriate to the situation

Conduct the interview in private

Tell the parent(s) why the interview is taking place

Be direct, honest, and professional

Tell the parent(s) the interview is confidential

Reassure the parents of the support of the school

Tell the parents if a report has been made or will be made

Advise the parent(s) of the school's legal responsibilities to report

DON'T:

Try to "prove" abuse or neglect by accusations or demands

Display horror, anger, or disapproval of parent(s), child, or situation

Pry into family matters unrelated to the specific situation

Place blame or make judgements about the parent(s) or child

BREAKING THE ABUSE CYCLE

Prevention and/or intervention in child abuse and neglect is a many-faceted undertaking. Prevention works best and is most successful before families establish destructive family patterns. The birth of the first baby is an excellent time to offer parent education through classes and modeling support. New parents, whose own parents were neglectful and uncaring, have only their parent's modeling to use in their own childrearing, so one of the first efforts at prevention is parent education and caring for new parents.

A second facet in intervening in child abuse occurs when families are identified as abusive. Intervention may include social services, school counselors, social workers, mental health centers, self-help groups such as Parents Anonymous, family therapy, psychiatrists, pediatricians, and psychologists, as well as parent education. It is much more difficult to change existing patterns than to remediate those patterns before they become habit.

Examples of the levels of prevention and intervention include the following programs.

Programs Prior to Abuse

Parent Education. Parent education can be delivered in high school, provided by hospitals when parents have their first child, offered through adult education, or provided by social services. The STEP, Parent Effectiveness Training, and Active Parenting courses have been effective. Building Family Strengths programs reinforce the positive aspects of a family. Specially-designed programs are also appropriate.

Caring Programs. The Community Caring Project, a joint project of the Center and the Junior League of Denver (C. Henry Kempe National Center for the Prevention and Treatment of Child Abuse and Neglect, n.d.) is based on the concept of intervention. It was developed to provide support and parenting skills to new mothers. These mothers, selected from four hospitals in the Denver area, are matched with a community volunteer who offers assistance, modeling, and education to new mothers.

The Caring program is an offshoot of programs developed by researchers at the University of Colorado Medical School. Mothers who were at high risk for abnormal parental practices (following observations made during and after labor and delivery) are offered special programs. When identified as high risk, the family received a pediatric follow-up by a physician, lay health visitor, and/or public health nurse. The study is a positive indicator that early intervention significantly decreases abnormal parent reactions and reduces subsequent physical injury to the child (Gray et al., 1976; Kempe, 1977).

Support Offered by Schools. The position statement by the American School Counselor Association supports programs to help eliminate child abuse. They hope to provide children with coping skills; help teachers understand abuse; provide continuing counseling to the child and the family; and offer workshops for parents that focus on handling anger, parent skills, and methods of discipline other than corporal punishment (American School Counselor Association, 1988).

Programs After Abuse Is Recognized

Professionals who work with the abusive parent must first understand themselves and their values so that they can come to peace with their feelings toward abuse and neglect of children. To help the family, professionals should not have a punitive attitude toward the parents. It helps to remember that the parents are probably rearing their child in the same way in which they were reared. It is a lifelong pattern that must be broken (Bavolek, 1989; Steele, 1977; Vondra & Toth, 1989).

Although the parents may be resistant to intrusion or suggestion, they desperately need help in feeling good about themselves. They need support, comfort, and someone they can trust and lean on. They need someone who will come when they have needs. Instead of criticism, they need help and assurance that they are worthwhile. Because they are unable to cope with their children, someone must help them understand their children without shaming them. Parents need to feel valuable and adequate.

Parents Anonymous. Parents Anonymous (PA) is a self-help parent program that gives parents the chance to share their feelings with others who have had similar experiences (1985). Parents can use Parents Anonymous and the crisis-intervention hot lines without fear of public disclosure. The members help each other avoid abuse by providing the opportunity to talk out problems. Groups are generally co-led by a chairperson and a sponsor. The chairperson is chosen from the parent group. The sponsor, not an abuser, is often a mental health worker who facilitates the group's growth. PA believes that abuse comes about because parents have unresolved issues about their own childhood, stressful current problems and unmet needs, and a precipitating crisis that brings about the abuse. The goal of Parents Anonymous is to prevent abuse (Post-Kammer, 1988). Positive ways of behaving and relating to others are learned as they work through their pain and anger of the past (Holmes, 1982).

Community Help. Help from social services or nonprofit organizations may include treatment that is offered by parent-aides, homemakers, and health visitors (Hamilton, 1989). The helper may serve as an advocate for the family to get the extra assistance it needs. This can include family therapy (Pardeck, 1989), assertiveness training, and Building Family Strengths programs. These programs try to bolster the positive elements in the family and eliminate the destructive elements. "Treatment may require in-depth, long-term, therapy and a lot of permanent social support systems" (Hamilton 1989, p. 41).

Many abusive parents want help. When they reveal their desires, they indicate that they want another parent to help them develop childrearing skills through modeling and friendship. Professionals can give them psychiatric help and other support, but because these parents may have missed a childhood with nurturing parents, their greatest need is the opportunity to have an active experience with a nurturing model. The importance of bonding and of a close relationship between parent and infant has been recognized as necessary for the child's emotional and physical growth. Severe deprivation can result in failure to thrive and marasmus (Skeels & Dye, 1939; Spitz, 1945). Lack of development of close and trusting bonds as infants and children results later in parents who need special help in their ability to relate to their own child. These parents are still looking for someone to mother them. The supportive help of another parent can function as a nurturing model for both parent and child.

Preschool Settings. Young children who have been abused adapt in two ways, according to Pearl (1988): The children either internalize and overcontrol their behavior or they externalize and undercontrol their actions. Children who fit the first category will be easy to overlook; their behavior is often fearful, withdrawn, depressed, and shy. The externalized child will demand attention, be aggressive, and act out (Pearl, 1988; Steele, 1986). Both types of children have low self-esteem. Aggressive, externalized children see themselves as unlovable and bad. The withdrawn child tries to please but feels little pleasure. Abused children will often scan their environment, avert their eyes, and stare in order to avoid eye contact. Preschool teachers can help both types of children if they

1. Use a quiet clear voice
2. Have good eye contact
3. Stand near the child when giving directions
4. Have body language that says the same thing as the oral message
5. Give directions that tell the child the appropriate behavior using specific instructions
6. Set limits and have expectations for behavior
7. Accept all feelings, but be consistent with behavioral expectations (adapted from Pearl, 1988)

Intervening in Sexual Abuse

Programs that help children say "No" to sexual abuse have been developed throughout the nation. Some of these programs are excellent (see Appendix E). Teachers and social services personnel who use the methods suggested in these programs need to be careful to insure that the child does not become fearful, however (Binder & McNiel, 1987).

Another concern of sexually abused children is the need these children have for concerned intervention. The intervention needs to address the issue and help the child overcome the feelings of unworthiness. The high rate of victims becoming victimizers also makes it necessary to work with children who have been sexually abused so they will not victimize another (Ryan, 1989).

SUPPORT SYSTEMS FOR THE CHILD, PARENTS, AND PROFESSIONALS

Working with the family after identification of abuse requires persons with exceptional sensitivity to others. Although the schools can provide help in parent education classes and other prevention and remediation programs and support, after the case has been reported to social ser-

vices or a family crisis center, a case worker will be assigned to the family. It might be well for the teacher to be aware of the characteristics needed by these workers, for most of these characteristics are also needed by teachers.

Workers must be able to accept hostility and rejection without being devastated by it or needing to retaliate; they must be able to feel at ease with parents' criticisms, yet not be critical of the parents' behavior; share themselves, without sharing their problems; befriend while being aware of their helping role; think first of the parents' needs, rather than their own; avoid using the parents to increase their own feelings of self-worth; and have a sense of personal worth and achievement that will sustain them through demanding work that offers few immediate rewards. (U.S. Department of Health, Education and Welfare, 1975, pp. 5–6)

The responsibilities and demands are enormous, and case workers need reliable supportive services from other agencies as well as their own. Some communities have developed child protection teams where professionals can recommend procedures and give support. (In Colorado any county with 50 or more incidents annually must establish a child protection team.) The makeup of the team may vary, but a typical team would include a physician; representatives of each of the following: the juvenile court, local law enforcement agency, county social services department, mental health clinic, public health department, and public school district; as well as an attorney, and one or more members of the lay community. The case worker reviews the case with the team and indicates the treatment plan; the team advises the worker of resources available and comments on problems and strengths that it sees in the treatment plan.

Other supportive services aid the main case worker. There are medical and psychiatric services available for the abusive parent. In some areas there are crisis nurseries where the parent needing immediate assistance can take a child. Another emergency service for the parent is the crisis-intervention hot line, where assistance is as close as the telephone. Public health nurse visits are often well-received by the parents, as are homemaking services. In some cases the children are taken from the parents for a short period and placed in foster homes or detention centers until the parents are in control of themselves. The availability of temporary foster homes or therapeutic child care centers helps the child as well as the family. Parent education is often a part of the therapeutic child care center; here the parents can learn to understand themselves and their children. These professionals, who are available to help the case worker in handling a family in need, are joined by a new group of lay persons who contribute yet another dimension (Kempe & Helfer, 1987).

Response by Schools and Child Care Centers

Schools must do more than give lip service to the letter of the law. Even in the face of mushrooming curricula and increased parental demands, personnel need to become so actively involved in the prevention of child abuse and neglect that their efforts have great impact. The children, after all, are the persons at stake.

Standards that are applicable to the role of the educator include the following:

1. The State Department of Education should develop and implement child abuse and neglect reporting policies and procedures.

2. The State Department of Education and the Local Education Agency should ensure that the rights of all school personnel, students, and families are respected and protected.

3. The State Department of Education should participate on the State Child Protection Coordinating Committee, and the Local Education Agency should participate on the Community Child Protection Coordinating Council.

4. The Local Education Agency should offer programs to students and adults on parenting and child rearing.

5. The Local Education Agency, in cooperation with community organizations, should ensure the provision of child care services for school-age parents.

6. The Local Education Agency, in cooperation with community organizations, should ensure that child care services for children and families at risk are available.

7. The Local Education Agency, in cooperation with community organizations, should encourage the establishment of programs to identify and serve adolescents at risk.

8. All school personnel should know the indicators of child abuse and neglect and the effect that abuse and neglect may have on the child's performance and behavior in school.

9. The Local Education Agency should participate on the community's multi-disciplinary case consultation team.

10. The Local Education Agency should provide annual in-service training for all school personnel on identifying and reporting suspected child abuse and neglect.

11. The State Department of Education and the Local Education Agency should conduct annual evaluations of their child abuse and neglect efforts.

12. The State Department of Education and the Local Education Agency, in cooperation with the State Child Protection Coordinating Committee and the Community Child Protection Coordinating Council, should develop, implement, and support public and professional education programs on child abuse and neglect. (U.S. Department of Health and Human Services, 1984, pp. A-1 and A-2)

In addition to the active involvement of the school in the formation and implementation of child abuse programs, individual schools should respond to the needs of the families in their district. Supportive services, counseling programs, individual educational plans, and warm, understanding teachers can make the future brighter for the abused or neglected child. Financial support in the form of lunch programs, field trips, and extracurricular activities, provided free or at a reduced cost, may enable the child to participate more fully. Schools can also provide or work with agencies that provide glasses, hearing aids, and other equipment needed by the child.

Checklist for Schools and Centers

- Does the school have a policy statement for reporting child abuse and neglect?
- Did the school do a needs assessment that shows the resources in your area and the status

of child abuse and neglect in the school district?

- Does the school or center coordinate activities and resources with other social agencies?
- Does the school or center hold periodic meetings for improved communication and coordination among agencies?
- Does someone in the school district serve on the child protection team?
- Does the school or center have a training program?
- Do parents feel welcome in the school?
- Does the school or center have a parent education program for parents of preschoolers?
- Does the school or center have a parent education program for parents of infants and toddlers?
- Is the PTA or other parent group involved with the school or center in a meaningful way for parents?
- Is there a parent resource room in the school?
- Do parents feel welcome to visit the school?
- Is there regular contact with parents, the teacher, and school or center? Do the teachers have frequent communication with parents when there is something good to report?

UNITED NATIONS DECLARATION OF THE RIGHTS OF THE CHILD

In the International Year of the Child, 1979, the United Nations published the rights of children. These are appropriate for children of all nations, regardless of socioeconomic level, parentage, or status, and are particularly relevant to the abused child.

Every child has the right to:

Affection, love, and understanding

Adequate nutrition and medical care

Free education

Full opportunity for play and recreation

A name and nationality

Special care, if handicapped

Be among the first to receive relief in times of disaster

Learn to be a useful member of society and to develop individual abilities

Be brought up in a spirit of peace and universal brotherhood

Enjoy these rights, regardless of race, color, sex, religion, nationality, or social origin

SUMMARY

The rash of child abuse cases reveals a phenomenon that is not new. Child abuse has been with society since very early times, but it was not recognized as a problem until the second half of the twentieth century, and no concerted effort was made to stem the crisis until the 1960s.

Legislation mandated that schools report cases of abuse and neglect. Schools work with children more than any other agency so they need to be in the foreground in preventing child abuse.

The chapter includes characteristics of families who tend to be abusive, ways to identify the abused or neglected child, and psychologic characteristics of abusive parents and abused children.

Training has been developed by the U.S. Department of Health and Human Services based to a large degree on the work done by the National Center for the Treatment and Prevention of Child Abuse. Examples of training materials are given.

School district policy and responsibility are described and illustrated by a typical policy statement. Points useful for interviewing the child and/or parents are given, and suggestions that enable the school to be supportive of potentially abusive parents are discussed. Recognition of and response to the problem by financial support from the school, parent education groups, school curricula, resource rooms, crisis nurseries, and/or parent-to-parent support groups are necessary.

SUGGESTED ACTIVITIES AND DISCUSSIONS

1. Attend a Child Protection Council meeting. What is the composition of the council, for example, doctors, educators, social workers, or a judge? How does the wide spectrum of specialists show the need for cooperation among agencies working with families?
2. Discuss the signs that teachers may observe in suspected child abuse and neglect cases.
3. What are the steps a teacher should take if child abuse or neglect is suspected?
4. Contact a school in your district and obtain a copy of its policy on child abuse and neglect.
5. Invite a social worker who is involved with child abuse cases to share experiences with the class. Investigate the policies, difficulties, and successes of child abuse programs.
6. Develop a policy for dealing with child abuse and neglect in a hypothetical school.
7. Visit with teachers and discuss how they feel about reporting child abuse. Which policies do they follow in reporting suspected child abuse or neglect cases?
8. Interview teachers, principals, and social workers in the schools. Find out if there has been an increase in the number of children who have behavior disorders. How are they helping these children?
9. Research material on bonding (see Chapter 1). Discuss the problems inherent in removing children from their homes.
10. Investigate the manner in which the courts handle child abuse and neglect cases. How do they manage out of home placements? Which rights are guaranteed the parents?
11. Obtain *A Curriculum on Child Abuse and Neglect.* Use the case studies for discussion.
12. Make a list of guidelines for identifying mal treated children. Base your discussion on Halperin's descriptions of these children. What are some of the ways that a teacher can give support to maltreated children?

BIBLIOGRAPHY

Altman, D. H., & Smith, R. L. Unrecognized trauma in infants and children. *Journal of Bone and Joint Surgery,* 1960, *42A,* pp. 407–413.

American Association for Protecting Children. *Guidelines for schools to help protect abused and neglected children.* Denver, Colo.: American Humane Association, n.d.

———. *Highlights of official child neglect and abuse reporting 1983.* Denver, Colo.: Author, 1985.

———. *Highlights of official aggregate child neglect and abuse reporting 1987.* Denver, Colo.: Author, 1989.

American Humane Association. *National analysis of official child neglect and abuse reporting.* Denver, Colo.: Author, 1978.

American School Counselor Association. The school counselor and child abuse/neglect prevention. *Elementary School Guidance & Counseling, 22,* April 1988, pp. 261–263.

Bakwin, H. Multiple skeletal lesions in young children due to trauma. *Journal of Pediatrics, 49,* 1956, pp. 7–15.

Bavolek, S. J. Assessing and treating high-risk parenting attitudes. *Early Child Development and Care, 42,* 1989, pp. 99–111.

Besharov, D. The status of child abuse and neglect prevention and treatment. In *Proceedings of the First National Conference on Child Abuse and Neglect.* U.S. Department of Health, Education and Welfare. (The National Center on Child Abuse and Neglect, Children's Bureau, Office of Child Development, Office of Human Development.) Washington, D.C.: U.S. Government Printing Office, 1977.

Binder, R. L., & McNiel, D. E. Evaluation of a school-based sexual abuse prevention program: Cognitive and emotional effects. *Child Abuse and Neglect, 11,*(4), 1987, pp. 497–506.

Caffey, J. Multiple fractures in long bones of infants suffering from chronic subdural hematoma. *Amer-*

ican Journal of Roentgenology, 56, 1946, pp. 163–173.

C. Henry Kempe National Center for the Prevention and Treatment of Child Abuse and Neglect. *Kempe Center Programs.* Denver: Author, n.d.

Child Abuse Prevention and Treatment Act of 1974. *United States Code, 1976, The Public Health and Welfare,* Section 5101, vol. 10. Washington, D.C.: U.S. Government Printing Office, 1977.

Cupoli, J. M., & Sewell, P. M. One thousand fifty-nine children with a chief complaint of sexual abuse. *Child Abuse and Neglect, 12*(2), 1988, pp. 151–161.

DeMause, L. *The history of childhood: The untold story of child abuse.* New York: Harper & Row, 1988.

————. Our forebearers made childhood a nightmare. *Psychology Today,* April 1975, pp. 85–88.

Denver Public Schools. *Child Abuse Bulletin,* Denver, Colo.: Author, 1985.

Eisenberg, S., & O'Dell, F. Teaching children to trust in a nontrusting world. *Elementary School Guidance & Counseling, 22,* April 1988, pp. 264–267.

Elmer, E. Abused young children seen in hospitals. In Antler, S. (Ed.). *Child abuse and child protection: Policy and practice.* Silver Spring, Md.: National Association of Social Workers, 1982.

End Violence Against the Next Generation, Inc. *Child abuse in schools: A national disgrace.* Berkeley, Calif.: Author, n.d.

Finkelhor, D. *A sourcebook on child sexual abuse.* Beverly Hills, Calif.: Sage Publications, 1986.

Fisher, S. H. Skeletal manifestations of parent-induced trauma in infants and children. *Southern Medical Journal,* August 1958, pp. 956–960.

Fontana, V. The diagnosis of the maltreatment syndrome in children. *Pediatrics, 51,* 1973, pp. 780–782.

————. *Somewhere a child is crying.* New York: Macmillan, 1973.

————. *Maltreated child.* Springfield, Ill.: Charles C. Thomas, 1979.

Fontana, V. J., & Besharov, D. J. *The maltreated child: The maltreatment syndrome in children.* Springfield, Ill.: Charles C. Thomas, 1979.

Gelles, R. *Violence towards children in the United States.* Paper presented at the meeting of the American Association for the Advancement of Science, Denver, Colo., February 25, 1977.

————. Violence in the family: A review of research in the seventies. *Journal of Marriage and Family, 42,* November 1980, pp. 873–885.

Gelles, R. J., & Lancaster, J. B. (Eds.). *Child abuse and neglect: Biosocial dimensions.* New York: Aldine de Gruyter, 1987.

Gray, J. D., Cutler, C. A., Dean, J. C., & Kempe, C. H. *Prediction and prevention of child abuse and neglect.* Denver, Colo.: National Center for the Prevention and Treatment of Child Abuse and Neglect, 1976.

Green, F. Corporal punishment and child abuse. *The Humanist, 48*(6), November 1, 1988, pp. 9, 10, & 32.

Hagans, K. B., & Case, J. *When your child has been molested: A parent's guide to healing and recovery.* Lexington, Mass.: Lexington Books, 1988.

Halperin, M. *Helping maltreated children: School and community involvement.* St. Louis: C. V. Mosby, 1979.

Hamilton, L. R. Child maltreatment: Prevention and treatment. *Early Child Development and Care, 42,* 1989, pp. 31–56.

Helfer, R. E. *The diagnostic process and treatment programs.* U.S. Department of Health, Education and Welfare. (Office of Human Development, Office of Child Development, Children's Bureau, National Center for Child Abuse and Neglect.) Washington, D.C.: U.S. Government Printing Office, 1975.

Helfer, R. E., & Kempe, R. S. (Eds.). *The battered child* (4th ed.). Chicago: The University of Chicago Press, 1987.

Holmes, S. Parents Anonymous: A treatment method for child abuse. In S. Antler (Ed.), *Child abuse and child protection.* Silver Spring, Md.: National Association of Social Workers, 1982.

Kempe, C. H. Predicting and preventing child abuse: Establishing children's rights in assuring access to health care through the health visitor concept. In *Proceedings of the First National Conference on Child Abuse and Neglect.* U.S. Department of Health, Education and Welfare. (The National Center on Child Abuse and Neglect, Children's Bureau, Office of Child Development.) Washington, D.C.: U.S. Government Printing Office, 1977.

Kempe, C. H., & Kempe, R. *The common secret: Sexual abuse of children and adults.* San Francisco, Calif.: W. H. Freeman, 1984.

Kempe, C. H., Silverman, F. N., Steele, B. F., Droegemueller, W., & Silver, H. The battered-child syndrome. *Journal of the American Medical Association, 181,* 1962, pp. 17–24.

Krugman, R. D. Recognition of sexual abuse in children. *Pediatrics in Review 8*(1), July 1986, pp. 25–30.

Krugman, R. D., & Krugman, M. K. Emotional abuse in the classroom. *American Journal of Diseases of Children, 138,* March 1984, pp. 284–286.

Metzner, J. L. The adolescent sex offender: An overview. *Interchange,* Denver, Colo.: The C. Henry Kempe National Center for Prevention and Treatment of Child Abuse and Neglect, 1988.

Mondale, W. F. Symposium on prevention: Helping parents parent. In *Proceedings of the First National Conference on Child Abuse and Neglect.* U.S. Department of Health, Education and Welfare. (The National Center on Child Abuse and Neglect, Children's Bureau, Office of Child Development, Office of Human Development.) Washington, D.C.: U.S. Government Printing Office, 1977.

Mowles, C. Educational barriers. In Sandberg, D. *Chronic acting-out students and child abuse: A handbook for intervention.* Lexington, Mass.: Lexington Books, 1987.

Nagi, S. Z. *Child maltreatment in the United States.* New York: Columbia University Press, 1977.

Pardeck, J. T. Family therapy as a treatment approach to child maltreatment. *Early Child Development and Care, 42,* 1989, pp. 151–157.

Parents Anonymous. *The program development manual.* Los Angeles: Parents Anonymous, 1985.

Pearl, P. Working with preschool-aged child abuse victims in group settings. *Child and Youth Care Quarterly, 17*(3), Fall 1988, pp. 185–194.

Post Kammer, P. Does Parents Anonymous reduce child abuse? *Education Digest, 54*(3), November 1, 1988, pp. 33–39.

Riggs, R. C. Incest: The school's role. *The Journal of School Health, 52,* August 1982, pp. 365–370.

Ryan, G. Victim to victimizer: Re-thinking victim treatment. *Journal of Interpersonal Violence, 4*(3), September 1989, pp. 325–341.

Sandberg, D. N. *Chronic acting-out students and child abuse: A handbook for intervention.* Lexington, Mass.: Lexington Books, 1987.

Shanas, B. Child abuse: A killer teachers can help control. *Phi Delta Kappan, 61,* 1975, pp. 479–482.

Silver, H. K., & Kempe, C. H. Problems of parental criminal neglect and severe physical abuse of children. *American Journal of Diseases of Children,* 1959.

Silverman, F. Roentgen manifestations of unrecognized skeletal trauma in infants. *American Journal of Roentgenology, 69,* 1953, pp. 413–427.

Skeels, H. M., & Dye, H. B. A study of the effects of differential stimulation on mentally retarded children. *Proceedings and Addresses of the American Association on Mental Deficiency, 44,* 1939, pp. 114–136.

Spitz, R. A. Hospitalism: An inquiry into the genesis of psychiatric conditions in early childhood. In A. Freud et al., (Eds.). *The Psychoanalytic Study of the Child* (Vol. 2). New York: International Universities Press, 1945.

Spungen, C. A., Jensen, S. E., Finelstein, N. W., & Stinsky, F. A. Child personal safety: Model program for prevention of child sexual abuse. *Social Work,* March 1989, pp. 127–131.

Steele, B. F. *Working with abusive parents from a psychiatric point of view.* U.S. Department of Health, Education and Welfare. Washington, D.C.: U.S. Government Printing Office, 1977.

_____. Notes on the lasting effects of early child abuse throughout the life cycle. *Child Abuse and Neglect, 10,* 1986, pp. 283–291.

_____. C. Henry Kempe memorial lecture. *Child Abuse and Neglect, 11,* 1987, pp. 313–318.

Summit, R. C. The child sexual abuse accommodation syndrome. *Child Abuse and Neglect, 7,* 1983, pp. 177–193.

United Nations International Children's Emergency Fund. Declaration of the rights of the child. New York: Author, 1979.

U.S. Department of Health, Education and Welfare. (Office of Human Development, Office of Child Development, Children's Bureau, National Center for Child Abuse and Neglect.) *Child abuse and neglect: The diagnostic process and treatment programs.* Washington, D.C.: U.S. Government Printing Office, 1975.

_____. *Child abuse and neglect (Vol. 1): An overview of the problem. The problem and its management.* Washington, D.C.: U.S. Government Printing Office, 1975.

_____. *Child abuse and neglect (Vol. 2): The roles and responsibilities of professionals. The problem and its management.* Washington, D.C.: U.S. Government Printing Office, 1975.

_____. *Child abuse and neglect (Vol. 3): The community team. An approach to case management and prevention. The problem and its management.* Washington, D.C.: U.S. Government Printing Office, 1975.

_____. (National Center on Child Abuse and Neglect, Children's Bureau, Office of Child Development, Office of Human Development.) *Planning and implementing child abuse and neglect service programs: The experience of eleven demonstration projects.* (Publication No. 30093). Washington, D.C.: U.S. Government Printing Office, 1976.

———. (Head Start Bureau, Children's Bureau, Administration for Children, Youth and Families, Office of Human Development.) *Child abuse and neglect: A self-instructional text for Head Start personnel.* Publication No. OHDS 8-31103. Washington, D.C.: U.S. Government Printing Office, 1977.

———. *A curriculum on child abuse and neglect. Resource materials.* Washington, D.C.: U.S. Government Printing Office, 1979.

———. *Child abuse and neglect. The user manual series. The educator's role in the prevention and treatment of child abuse and neglect.* Washington, D.C.: U.S. Government Printing Office, 1984.

Vondra, J. I., and Toth, S. L. Child maltreatment research and intervention. *Early Child Development and Care, 42,* 1989, pp. 11–24.

Wertham, F. *A sign for Cain.* New York: Macmillan, 1966.

Wiehe, V. R. Child abuse: An ecological perspective. *Early Child Development and Care, 42,* 1989, pp. 141–148.

Wodarski, J. S., & Johnson, S. R. Child sexual abuse: Contributing factors, effects and relevant practice issues. *Family Therapy, XV(2),* 1988, pp. 157–173.

Woolley, P. V., Jr., & Evans, W. A. Significance of skeletal lesions in infants resembling those of traumatic origin. *Journal of American Medical Association,* June 1955, pp. 539–543.

Appendix C

DENVER PUBLIC SCHOOLS
Department of Health and Social Services
*Child Abuse Bulletin**
August 1985
To all principals, nurses, social workers,
psychologists and concerned personnel

Synopsis:
Updated Procedures (supersedes August 1980 Child Abuse Bulletin HE-47) for reporting child abuse and neglect:

I. *Background Information*

With each passing year, the importance and magnitude of the problem of child abuse and neglect becomes progressively more apparent. Child abuse is now being viewed as a major psychosocial and health problem by those concerned about the welfare of children. The scope of the problem is now being recognized to extend beyond "nonaccidental trauma" to physical and emotional deprivation, sexual abuse, and pervasive negative parental attitudes about children. The consequences of unremitting abuse are serious: disability, social deviance, death, and in virtually all cases, a lasting corrosion of self-esteem that both perpetuates child abuse from generation to generation and robs an individual of the opportunity to maximize his/her innate potentials.

The schools have become a major resource in the early identification of child abuse and neglect. During the 1984–1985 school year, 2967 reports of child abuse/neglect were investigated by the Denver Department of Social Services. Of these, 837 (28%) were initiated by Denver Public Schools personnel. The first year the present laws went into effect there were 161 cases referred by school district personnel.

This trend of better recognition and reporting of child abuse and neglect will not only help hundreds of children within the Denver Public Schools now, but untold numbers of future children will also be saved the personal misery and suffering that is associated with the ongoing perpetuation of abuse and neglect within families.

*Reprinted with permission from John M. Lampe, M.D.

II. *Legal Responsibilities re: Child Abuse and Neglect*
In accord with Colorado statutes, Denver Public Schools has responsibilities in the area of child abuse. Both statutes and procedures have been revised several times since they were instituted in 1963. To clarify the roles and responsibilities of the school district and its personnel, the following sections of the law are stated:
Article 10 of Title 19, Colorado Revised Statutes 1973 as *Repealed and reenacted, with amendments,* in 1980.

A. *Definitions of Abuse and Neglect* (19–10–103)
   (1) (a) "Abuse" or "child abuse or neglect" means *an act or omission* in one of the following categories *which threatens the health or welfare of a child:*
   (I) Any case in which a child exhibits evidence of skin bruising, bleeding, malnutrition, failure to thrive, burns, fracture of any bone, subdural hematoma, soft tissue swelling, or death, and such condition or death is not justifiably explained, or where the history given concerning such condition or death, or circumstances indicate that such condition or death may not be the product of an accidental occurrence;
   (II) Any case in which a child is subjected to sexual assault or molestation, sexual exploitation, or prostitution;
   (III) Any case in which the child's parents, legal guardians, or custodians fail to take the same actions to provide adequate food, clothing, shelter, or supervision that a prudent parent would take.

B. *Persons Required to Report Child Abuse or Neglect* (19–10–104)
   (I) Any person specified in subsection (2) of this section who has reasonable cause to know or suspect that a child has been subjected to abuse or neglect or who has observed the child being subjected to circumstances or conditions which would reasonably result in abuse or neglect, shall immediately report or cause a report to be made of such fact to the county department or local law enforcement agency.
   (2) Persons required to report such abuse or neglect or circumstances or conditions shall include any:

   (a) Physician or surgeon, including a physician in training;
   . . .
   (i) Registered nurse or licensed practical nurse;
   . . .
   (1) School official or employee;
   (m) Social worker, or worker in a family care home or child care center, as defined in Section 26–6–102, C.R.S. 1973.

In addition, *any* citizen may report what he or she suspects to be child abuse or neglect by calling the Family Crisis Center at 893–6111. Anonymous as well as identified callers can be assured the complaint will be investigated.

C. *Penalty for Failure to Report* (19–10–104, subsection 4)
Any person who willfully violates the provisions of subsection (1) of this section:
   (a) Commits a class 3 misdemeanor and, upon conviction thereof, shall be punished by a fine of $750.00 or 6 months in jail.
   (b) Shall be liable for damages proximately caused thereby.

D. *Role of Department of Social Services*
By the revision of 1975, the implementation of this law, as of January 1976, becomes the responsibility of the Division of Services for Families, Children and Youth of the Denver Department of Social Services (DDSS-FCY) with the cooperation of reporting agencies. The initial investigation of all abuse reports is the responsibility of a division within DDSS-FCY, i.e., the *Family Crisis Center.*

E. *Protection for Persons Reporting*
The law specifically states (19–10–110) "Any person participating in good faith in the making of a report or in a judicial proceeding held pursuant to this title . . . shall be immune from any liability, civil or criminal, that otherwise might result by reason of such reporting."
Ernest L. Boyer, U.S. Commissioner of Education stated that, "We agree that reporting of such incidents (child abuse, neglect) made in good faith, will not violate FERPA (Family Educational Rights and Privacy Act)."

F. *Required Teacher In-Service*
During the 1983–1984 session, the Colorado General Assembly passed a law reading as follows:

Board of Education—specific duties.

To provide for a periodic in-service program for all district teachers which shall provide information about the "Child Protection Act of 1975," article 10 of title 19, C.R.S., instruction designed to assist teachers in recognizing child abuse or neglect, and instruction designed to provide teachers with information on how to report suspected incidents of child abuse or neglect and how to assist the child-victim and his family.

III. *Denver Public Schools Procedures for Reporting Child Abuse*

To fulfill our obligations to pupils, in conformity with the law of the State, the following procedures have been developed for Denver Public Schools personnel:

A. *Telephone Reporting*

Family Crisis Center—phone 893–6111

When there is good reason to suspect that a child has been abused, the suspecting person should consult with the principal or his designee, social worker and nurse, if available. At this time, the decision will be made as to who will call to make the report. Please note that no one within the school district shall have the authority to "veto" the reporting of any suspected case of child abuse. Any *SUSPICION* of abuse *MUST* be reported to the Family Crisis Center.

The incident should be reported as soon as possible after discovery. This will help to facilitate additional investigations within the confines of the school day. Do not wait if the nurse, social worker, or principal is not available; rather, the suspecting person or designee of the principal should make the call. In emergencies, the social worker and nurse may be contacted at their other schools of assignment. Time is of the essence!

Reporting a case to the Family Crisis Center does not mean you have labeled the family as perpetrators, as neglectful, or as abusers. It does mean that you are aware of injuries, maltreatment, or inadequate caring that has occurred to a child. Child Welfare and the court system determine if abuse or neglect has occurred. Remember that under the law, all suspected abuse must be reported!

1. *Steps in Telephone Reporting*

The caller should:
- contact the Family Crisis Center—893–6111 (call as soon as possible. A call early in the school day will allow for adequate time for the Crisis Center worker to arrive at school and initiate the evaluation before school is dismissed.)
- identify self
- give location and telephone number of school
- provide identifying data pertaining to child
- provide information regarding suspected abuse
- note the name of the person who accepts the report and the time that the report was made
- ascertain at time of initial phone call whether Crisis Center worker will be coming before school is out for the day and if not, what course of action the worker recommends.

If the Family Crisis Center worker has not arrived by the time school is dismissed for the day, school personnel should:
- call the police if the child is afraid to go home, refusing to go home, or is felt to be in imminent danger
- send the child home if the abuse is minor and the child does not appear to be in imminent danger
- remain at school with the child to assist in the investigation if the police and/or Crisis Center worker indicate they will be coming to school the day of the call.

2. *Reporting Of Abuse Inflicted By School Personnel*

Unfortunately, there have been a few instances where school personnel in their over-zealous use of discipline have bruised or physically injured students. Since the schools are functioning in loco parentis (in place of parents), abuse inflicted by school personnel must be reported to the Crisis Center. Follow the same reporting procedure outline in Section III–A–1, . . . except that the school administrator must immediately be made aware of any abusive situation involving school personnel.

B. *Written Reporting*

After reporting any abuse or neglect situation by telephone to the Family Crisis Center, the principal or his designee or reporting person *must* also write a Child Abuse Report using Form CAR 983 (available from Nursing Service, 837–1000, ext. 2615). The written Child Abuse Report should be completed and mailed as soon as possible, but in any event, no later than 24 hours after the telephone reporting. One original and three copies should be made.

1. Original (to be mailed within 24 hours of telephone reporting):
   Denver Department of Social Services
   Division of Services for Families, Children and Youth
   2200 W. Alameda
   Denver 80223
   (Do *not* hand the report to the worker responding to the crisis.)

2. Copy one—give to the nurse for inclusion in the student's Health Record

3. Copy two—give to the nurse for inclusion with her monthly report to Nursing Service

4. Copy three—give to the social worker for inclusion in the local social work record.

C. *Reporting to the Denver Public Schools Social Work Office*

The social worker (or in his/her absence, the nurse or reporting person) should call the Denver Public Schools Social Work Office to give information regarding the report so that it will be available to the person representing Denver Public Schools on the Child Protection Team. This is *very important* in order to assist the representative in clarifying and presenting any concerns of school personnel about specific cases. The Social Work Office should be called (837–1000, ext. 2611) to report the incident *before* the next weekly meeting of the Child Protection Team. (Usually on Thursday)

IV. *The Family Crisis Center Investigation*

A social worker will respond in person or by phone from the Family Crisis Center. It is the responsibility of the social worker from the Family Crisis Center, using whatever information school personnel can supply, to make an immediate judgement as to disposition.

A. THE FAMILY CRISIS CENTER ALTERNATIVES ARE:

1. to leave the child in school

2. to request the assistance of the police to
   (a) take the child to Denver General Hospital for medical examination, or
   (b) take the child into custody if it is felt that the child cannot safely return home at that time.

3. to obtain a verbal court order to arrange for care

4. There will be instances where the Crisis Center worker will accept the case but will decide that it is safe for the child to return to his home. It is important to determine if the Family Crisis Center worker or school personnel will notify the parents.

5. There may be other instances where the Crisis Center worker may decide to take no action. If this happens, each situation must be viewed individually to determine if parents should be notified.

B. *Facilitating Cooperation with Family Crisis Center*

1. *Family Crisis Center Investigation On School Grounds*

   Our Denver Public Schools Office of Social Work Services is one of seven agencies serving on the Interagency Child Protection Team. The team meets weekly to review all cases of reported child abuse and neglect and makes recommendations for follow-up. It is critical that agencies work cooperatively in dealing with these cases.

   The Denver City Attorney assigned to the Family Crisis Center points out that their social workers are required by law to interview or observe a child reported as having been abused or neglected, and occasionally these interviews cannot be conducted in the home for various reasons. As a result, a Family Crisis Center worker may request school authorities to allow a child abuse investigation (i.e., observation and/or interview) to take place on school grounds. This may occur even when the initial report came from outside the school district. It is important that the interview or observation be permitted at school when requested. However, it is suggested that the principal or his designee, usually the school social worker or nurse, sit in on the interview.

DENVER PUBLIC SCHOOLS
Notification Card

To_____

(Parent, Parents, or Guardian)

Address_____

Telephone Number_____

   We have tried and were unable to notify you regarding your son_____

daughter _____ , _____
                                           (Name)

who was taken into custody by the following officer (or officers) of the Police Department at approximately

_____A.M./P.M. for_____

(Name and Division, Department or Bureau of Officer)	(Badge Number)
(Name and Division, Department or Bureau of Officer)	(Badge Number)

   Please call the following number of the Police Department to secure information relative to your

child _____

(Signature of Officer taking custody)	(Signature of principal, or other school employee presently in charge of building)
(Date)	(School)
	(Date)

In such instances, the following procedures are recommended:

(a) The Child Welfare representative should produce identification.

(b) The principal or the principal's designee is to be present during any interview of a student.

(c) Notify the Child Welfare representative that the pupil's parent will be notified of the visit unless specifically requested by the representative not to do this.

(d) Unless specifically requested not to notify the parent, notify the parent of the details of the visit.

(e) Document the visit on your records. The Child Welfare workers also will conduct interviews with the parents of these children where there is suspected abuse.

2. *Requests for Nurse Examinations*
Nurses may be requested and should comply with the request by Family Crisis Center to examine a child for signs of physical abuse. This should be done even if the report in question was not initiated by the Denver Public Schools. Generally, these examinations should take place on a day when the nurse is assigned to the building where the child is in attendance. Special arrangements may be made in case of emergencies.

V. *Additional Guidelines*
A. *Child in Imminent Danger*
1. *When To Notify Police:*
If a Family Crisis Center worker has not arrived at school to do the school investigation by dismissal time and the child is considered to be in *imminent danger,* the police should be called.
The law makes provision that if the child is considered in imminent danger, the police may be called immediately—575–2011 or 911. Except in rare instances, we would not consider a child in the custody of school officials to be in imminent danger and hence this provision will be seldom used. If a uniformed officer responds, his alternatives would be:
a. to leave the child in the school
b. to remove the child for medical examination or further investigation
c. to place the child in a receiving center. In any event, once the officer considers the child to be physically safe, he will turn the investigation over to the Denver Department of Social Services, Services for Families, Children and Youth.
2. *When A Child Is Taken Into Police Custody:*
When it is necessary to place the child in the custody of the police, the following policy applies and must be strictly observed.
Denver Public Schools Policy
1206C
PUPILS, DISMISSAL OF DURING SCHOOL SESSION. Sections D and E
"D. *Custody requested by a Police Officer.* Whenever a police officer desires to take a child into temporary custody, the principal shall ascertain from the officer the reasons

for the officer's action. The principal shall release the child to the police officer and shall immediately notify the child's parents of the action by telephone. If it is not possible to reach the parents by telephone, the principal shall prepare the notification memorandum (see attached form #01–1500–06). One copy shall be maintained in the school file, one copy taken to the child's home that day, and a third copy sent to the office of the appropriate Assistant Superintendent.
E. The principal will make every effort possible to insure that the taking of custody will be made in privacy, preferably in the principal's office."
Important: The notification memorandum (see attached form) shall be enclosed in a sealed envelope and the envelope properly addressed to the parent or guardian of the pupil involved. The envelope may be slipped under the door of the residence or otherwise put in a conspicuous place. It shall not be placed in the mailbox. (The placing of anything other than U.S. Mail in residence mailboxes is contrary to regulations of the Post Office Department.) If a telephone exists in the home, but no contact has been made, the principal shall follow up at intervals until the parent has been advised. In case of uncertainties or situations which appear beyond the scope of this policy, principals shall request additional instructions from their supervisor or from the Department of Health and Social Services.
B. *Handling Nonemergent Problems—Neglect*
Many children are found in long-term neglectful situations which do not pose immediate danger, but will be to their detriment if not corrected. School social workers and/or nurses should counsel with parents. If after concerted effort, the situation has not been sufficiently improved or corrected, it may be reported. It is often helpful to discuss these situations with the social work supervisor or nursing coordinator before making the report. Nurses and social workers should use the CAR 983 form. Social workers should also use the Social Work Summary referral form (used for agency referrals) and send it to the Social Work Office for typing and forwarding. (Form

CAR 983 available from Nursing Service, 837–1000, ext. 2615).

C. *Unsupervised Children*

1. *Children Under 12 Years of Age*

The Colorado Child Labor Law requires that children must be at least 12 years old in order to act as babysitters. It follows that children under 12 years should not be left alone. When children less than 12 years of age are left alone, the Family Crisis Center considers them unsupervised and neglected.

We know of the danger that children may be exposed to when left unsupervised, i.e., fire or harmful strangers. Parents are not always aware of the dangers and the existence of the law, and therefore many situations may be remediated by counseling with them. However, if this situation is not corrected, or young children are discovered alone, the situation should be reported. Judgement needs to be used in de-

termining the action to take. When consultation is needed, contact the offices of Health (837–1000, ext. 2615) or Social Work Services (837–1000, ext. 2611).

To report these cases, call the Family Crisis Center at 893–6111, utilizing the same procedures as in Section III–A–1. Written report must also be made, as per Section III–B. . . .

2. *Handicapped Children*

Children with certain handicaps may need ongoing, direct supervision, regardless of their age and physical maturity level. When school personnel become aware of any handicapped student who appears to lack appropriate supervision, the same guidelines as above should be followed even though the child may be 12 years of age or older. If the child is over 18 the situation should be referred to the Adult Protection Unit of the Denver Department of Social Services (936–3666).

11

Rights, Responsibilities, and Advocacy

G. R. Berger
Eugenia Hepworth Berger

Parents and students as well as professional educators have rights and responsibilities as members of the school community. Could mutual recognition of privileges and obligations provide guidelines for productive dialogue between schools and families? Today the school and the family, two of our most important social institutions, face a challenge to provide what is best for the child.

ORIGIN OF PARENTS' AND CHILDREN'S RIGHTS

Parents have long been recognized as having guardianship rights over their biological children. Parents of adopted children are guaranteed those same rights, which can be terminated only by court action or voluntary relinquishment. At the same time parents have responsibility toward their children. They have the right and responsibility to socialize their children; choose and provide health services for them; discipline and rear them; choose whether they will be educated in private or public schools; and give them care, shelter, and nourishment. It is only when they ignore or misuse these responsibilities that authorities have the right to interfere.

The rights and responsibilities of parents are derived from custom, legislation, and opinions of state and federal courts. The basis for these rights in the United States are the Bill of Rights and the Fourteenth Amendment of the Constitution (see Appendix D). The First Amendment of the Constitution states that

Congress shall make no law respecting an establishment of religion, or prohibiting the free exercise thereof; or abridging the freedom of speech, or of the press; or the right of the people peaceably to assemble, and to petition the Government for a redress of grievances.

Thus, all citizens, including parents and their children, are guaranteed freedom of religion, freedom of speech, the right to assemble peacefully, a free press, and the right to petition for redress of grievances.

Constitutional Law

The Constitution forms the framework that guides the federal government. Each state also has its own constitution. Rights are prescribed by the federal Constitution and by individual state constitutions. The federal Constitution and the Supreme Court hold precedent over lower courts and states. Some powers, however, are

Children and their parents have responsibilities as well as rights.

delegated completely to the states. According to Amendment X of the Constitution,

The powers not delegated to the United States by the Constitution, not prohibited by it to the States, are reserved to the States respectively, or to the people.

Education was not included as a responsibility of the federal government and was designated as an obligation and right of the individual states. The federal Constitution provides basic rights that are common throughout the United States, but since regulations and laws vary in each state, persons concerned about their rights should check their state constitution.

Statute Law

The legislative branch of the government passes enactments on statutes that affect individual rights. These laws extend from the United States Congress to state legislatures, down to county or city governments. These laws may be reviewed by the courts to determine their constitutionality.

The state constitution usually provides for the establishment of the public school system.

The structure and operation of the school system are provided, revised, and supplemented by legislative enactment of education statutes (Valente, 1987).

Court Law

Court decisions handed down by judges at the federal, state, or local level are called court law, common law, or case law. The Supreme Court is the highest court in the land and its decisions are binding on all lower courts. Other court decisions are binding only within their own jurisdiction.

Administrative Law

Regulations and rules within federal and state agencies also affect the rights of parents and families. The Federal Register publishes the regulations of federal administrative agencies. Check in your state for specific regulations guiding your rights as a parent or teacher.

You can see that rights vary, depending on the rights and authority of the courts and administrative agencies. The Supreme Court has jurisdiction over the nation. But because federal courts, state courts, and local courts have jurisdiction over their own areas, check with the attorney general's office or ask your legal counsel to find out the laws and regulations in your own state.

PARENTS' RIGHT TO SELECT THEIR CHILD'S EDUCATION

The fact that parents have the right to choose and guide their child's education is substantiated by several court decisions. In 1923 the *Meyer v. Nebraska* decision found that parents had the right to teach their own children. In 1925 it was found that parents had the right to choose parochial rather than public schools to teach their children. The Supreme Court in *Pierce v. Society of Sisters of the Holy Name* found that an Oregon law requiring children to attend public school was unconstitutional. The requirement for an educated citizenry could be met by acceptable private, parochial or secular, as well as public schools.

All states have compulsory attendance laws. Children usually must start school at the age of 5 or 6 and attend until they are 16 or 17. Parents have the responsibility to see that their children attend school. All states have free public schools. Children must attend them or their parents must provide acceptable and approved schooling at home or in a private school.

A few exceptions have been approved by the courts. In *Wisconsin v. Yoder* (1972), the Supreme Court decision found in favor of the parents of Amish children. Messrs. Yoder, Miller, and Yutzy, Amish living in Green County, Wisconsin, refused to send their children to school after they completed 8th grade. The Amish religion emphasizes a life separate from worldly influences. The parents did not object to their children learning basic reading, writing, and mathematics. Basic education is necessary for them to be able to read the Bible and work on the communal farms. They objected to their children attending school until they were 16 years of age. In high school, values are learned that

conflict with Amish religious beliefs. Secondary schools are based on competitiveness, self-achievement, and success, quite different than the cooperative, simple life of the Amish. The adolescent years were viewed as formative years that could influence the young adults and take them away from the ways of the church. Amish children did not need to learn modern science, claimed the parents; their work on their farms could be taught at home in their own shops under the supervision of the Amish.

Chief Justice Burger delivered the majority report. The court held that Wisconsin's compulsory attendance laws were invalid for the Amish. The decision was based primarily on the First Amendment that states: "Congress shall make no law respecting an establishment of religion, or prohibiting the free exercise thereof."

Justice Douglas wrote a dissenting opinion in the *Wisconsin v. Yoder* case. If a child "is harnessed to the Amish way of life by those in authority over him or if his education is truncated, his entire life may be stunted and deformed." A mature child "may well be able to override the parents' religiously motivated objections."

Two concerns are at issue: the First Amendment of free exercise of religious beliefs and the need and rights for states to have an educated citizenry. If both of these issues are resolved, the Courts may find in favor of the parents as they did in the Yoder case. In 1980, an Ohio case, *Nagle v. Olin,* the Yoder provision prevailed. In this case the father wanted to send his daughter to Kopperts' Korner, an Amish school that did not meet state standards. The school was the only one close enough to the family's home that met the family's religious beliefs. Although the father was not Amish, the Court found in favor of him because the school met his religious needs (Lines, 1982).

Other cases have not met the Yoder test. In *State v. Faith Baptist Church* (1981) the Nebraska high court rejected a request for exemption from compulsory education. In *State v. Shaver* (1980) a North Dakota court found that, though the religious beliefs were sincere, the attendance at public school did not contradict free exercise of those beliefs. In North Carolina, Peter Duro refused to send his children to school because he believed his children's religious beliefs would be undermined. The Duros were not members of an established self-sufficient community as the Amish were, nor had the children attended school for 8 years like the Amish children, so the courts did not find in favor of Duro. In questions such as these, both concerns must be filled: the need for an educated citizenry, and established religious tenets undermined by the school (Schimmel & Fischer, 1987).

At the same time there is a growing movement to educate children at home. Although parents have no constitutional right to educate their children at home, state law can determine the regulations for home education or refuse to allow home education. The majority of states permit parents to teach their own children. Four states permit parents to teach at home and have no statutory provision for home education (IL, KY, MI, NH). Ten states either refuse to accept home instruction or they have difficult provisions (AR, KS, MN, NC, ND, NE, NM, TN, TX, WY). The states have varied requirements. Alabama and California allow instruction at home if there is a private tutor (Lines, 1982). To obtain current restrictions or permissions, contact the Department of Education in each state.

Student Records—Open Record Policy

In 1974 Congress passed the Family Educational Rights and Privacy Act (Buckley Amendment) which gives parents of students under the age of 18 and students 18 and older the right to see and control their school records, except for information placed in the file prior to January 1, 1975. These records, including health files, grades, school records, and other documents concerning the person and kept by the school, must be available within 45 days.

Directory information is given to newspapers and others who request it unless the parents or person over 18 years old request that their name or the child's name be removed from the directory information list. Directory informa-

tion includes the student's name, address, telephone number, place and date of birth, dates of attendance, degrees and awards, participation in recognized activities of the school, height and weight of members of athletic teams, and the most recent previously attended educational agency. Some parents do not want their child's address and telephone number to be known. They should request that the school take their child's name off the list so that it will not be issued for news reports or similar reporting.

Privacy procedures
1. Schools must permit eligible students or parents to inspect student records.
   a. The teacher's gradebook is to be shared only with a substitute teacher. It is exempt from inspection.
   b. Parents or students may ask for explanations of the records. Explanation must be provided.
   c. Records may be destroyed prior to a request, but once a request has been made, the records may not be destroyed until the parent or eligible student has seen them.
   d. Psychiatric or treatment records may be available only to a medical doctor who can review them for the parent or eligible student.
   e. If parents are unable to come to school, the school should send the records to them. The school may charge a reasonable amount for the copying, but not for the time spent preparing and obtaining the records.
2. Schools must let parents or eligible students correct misleading or false information.
   a. If the school administrator agrees with the parents' or student's request, the official may remove the data that is questionable.
   b. If the official refuses to change or remove the questionable information, a hearing may be requested. This hearing must be held within a reasonable time period, although no specific time period is required by law. Parents and students

may bring a lawyer or friend to present evidence for them. Both sides may present evidence at a meeting presided over by an impartial hearing officer. If the decision is against the parents, they may insert a written statement about why they disagree with the information.

3. Schools must inform eligible students and parents of their rights of record disclosure and privacy.
4. Schools must obtain written permission from parents or eligible students before giving information to others, with the following exceptions:
   a. School officials and teachers with a legitimate educational interest.
   b. Federal and state officials for use in an audit or evaluation of state or federal-supported programs.
   c. Accreditation associations doing accreditation work.
   d. Financial aid officials seeking information for processing financial aid requests.
   e. Administrators of another school district to which the student is transferring. Parents and eligible students have the right to review the file before it is processed.
   f. Persons doing research may use the material if the individuals are not identified.
   g. Emergencies where the information is necessary to protect the health of the individual.
5. No information on a student may be kept in secret.

If these requirements are met, eligible students and their parents can ensure that student records are accurate and that the records are not used for any purpose other than those stated above without their approval (Berger & Berger, 1985).

RIGHTS AND RESPONSIBILITIES OF STUDENTS

Students and their parents have rights and responsibilities while the child is attending school. This section includes a discussion of these rights

and responsibilities. Because laws change and vary, you should check the most recent law in your state if a specific incident occurs within your district.

Free Speech and Expression

The First Amendment provides that "Congress shall make no law ... abridging the freedom of speech or of the press; or the right of the people peaceably to assemble...." Students have the right, therefore, to express themselves, verbally or symbolically (armbands, symbols on clothing, and salutes), even if their position is in disfavor. They have the responsibility, however, not to slander another or disrupt the operation of the school. Misconduct in the guise of free expression does not need to be tolerated. Student rallies may have prescribed times and places that they may be held. Students do not have the right to commandeer the school and intrude on the rights of others (Valente, 1987).

Freedom of Expression

The landmark decision on freedom of expression came in 1969 during the Vietnam War. In *Tinker v. Des Moines Independent Community School District* (1969) the Supreme Court ruled that students had the right to expression while they were at school: "It can hardly be argued that either students or teachers shed their constitutional rights to freedom of speech or expression at the school house gate."

The case involved a protest against the Vietnam War. The petitioners, John F. Tinker, Christopher Eckhardt, and Mary Beth Tinker were among a group of adults and students who held a meeting at the Eckhardt home. They determined that they would wear black armbands during the holiday season commencing December 16, 1965, in order to protest against the war in Vietnam (Schimmel & Fischer, 1987). The parents, who were Quakers, supported their children's actions. The school administrator heard of the plan and passed a rule that those who wore black armbands would be asked to remove them and, if they refused, would be suspended. The students refused to remove their armbands and were subsequently suspended. After the students were suspended the parents protested the action and took the case to court. Both the Federal District Court and the Eighth Circuit Court of Appeals found in favor of the schools, stating that their action prevented disturbance. When the Supreme Court wrote their decision they emphasized that schools must have the right "to prescribe and control conduct in the schools," but in order to prohibit an expression of opinion, the school must show that it substantially interfered with "appropriate discipline in the operation of the school" (393, U.S. 503, 1969). The passive use of arm bands was not disruptive in this situation. The principal had put the suspension policy in place because he opposed the action by the students; it was not because he feared a disturbance.

The threat of a disturbance influences court decisions. In *Guzick v. Drebus* (1971), Guzick, a high school student in Shaw High School, East Cleveland, Ohio, wore a button which was a symbol against the Vietnam War. Shaw High School, with a student ratio 70% black and 30% white students, had a long-standing rule against wearing symbols and buttons. Wearing of symbols had promoted racial disturbances. The court ruled against Guzick in this case, because wearing of symbols could start a racial disturbance in the school.

Freedom of Press

A recent Supreme Court case, *Hazelwood School District v. Kuhlmeier* (1988) has affected the supervisory capacity that schools have over publications. Up until that time the governing theory was that the schools could regulate grammar and technical quality of a newspaper produced in connection with a high school journalism class, but that they could not remove articles because they might be controversial or unpopular. The Hazelwood case involved a Journalism II class that had traditionally had a review by the principal. In 1983, he rejected one story on pregnancy because the students were identifiable and another on divorce because he saw the article as invasion of privacy for the students interviewed. The trial court upheld the principal's action stating that his deletions were "legit-

imate and reasonable" based on invasion of privacy. The federal appeals court reversed that decision because it held that a journalism newspaper is a public form for students and not just an academic project and therefore deserved the protection of the First Amendment (Schimmel & Fischer, 1987). The decision by the Supreme Court placed the newspaper as a curriculum project. Justice White wrote the majority opinion. "A school need not tolerate speech that is inconsistent with its basic education mission, even though the government could not censor similar speech outside the school."

Suspension and Due Process

The Fourteenth Amendment guarantees the right to due process for all citizens—"nor shall any State deprive any person of life, liberty, or property without due process of law." When students are suspended the act impacts the parent's rights as well as the child's. An early case concerning due process, *Dixon v. Alabama State Board of Education* (1961), involved college students who were expelled or placed on probation after they had a sit-in at a lunch counter. The students had not been given a hearing or notice of the charges against them. The court established the right to notice and to a hearing prior to suspension or expulsion.

A landmark case, *Goss v. Lopez* (1975), resulted from a disturbance at a school lunchroom during the winter of 1971. Seventy-five students were suspended including Dwight Lopez and eight others. In Ohio, a principal could suspend students for up to 10 days if parents were notified within 24 hours and told the reason for the suspension. In order to get a hearing, the parents or students had to appeal. Nine students filed a suit in Federal District Court citing the lack of due process. The Supreme Court found in favor of the students, holding that students are entitled to a public education and the right could only be taken away from them after due process.

Students who are suspended for a short period of time (up to 10 days) must be given (1) notice of the charges, (2) an explanation of the charge and reasons for the suspension, and

(3) an opportunity to explain their side of the situation. In writing the opinion of the *Goss v. Lopez* case, the Court recognized that formal adversarial proceedings would take too much of the school's time, but "effective notice and informal hearing permitting the student to give his version of the events will provide a meaningful hedge against erroneous action" (Schimmel & Fischer, 1987, p. 251). Students who are presenting a danger to the school can be removed immediately. In the decision, the court addressed short suspensions, stating that longer suspension or expulsions may require more formal hearings. The procedures for longer suspensions have not been addressed by the Supreme Court but notice, the right to counsel, presentation of evidence, and cross-examination of witnesses should be a part of any such hearing. The student and parents should also have a statement of findings, conclusions, recommendations, and the right to appeal (Schimmel & Fischer, 1987).

Valente (1987) points out that brief in-school sanctions do not require prepunishment hearings. Nor did *Goss v. Lopez* apply in corporal punishment cases (*Ingraham v. Wright,* 1977) because the corporal punishment did not require the student to miss school. "The student's right to demand an *open hearing* is not settled" (Valente, 1987, p. 307).

Flag Salute and Pledge of Allegiance

Students do not have to salute the flag or say the Pledge of Allegiance if it violates their religious beliefs. In *West Virginia State Board of Education v. Barnette* (1943), Jehovah's Witnesses parents objected to their children being required by state law to salute the flag. The U.S. Supreme Court found in their favor. Children did not have to salute the flag if the salute violated their beliefs or values. Although students had the right to refuse to salute the flag, they also had responsibilities. They had to stand and remain silent and could not disrupt the salute by others. The decision that students do not have to salute the flag has since been extended to cases in which a

person objects as a matter of conscience. In a Coral Gables high school, a student objected to having to stand during the Pledge of Allegiance. The Florida court found in favor of the student: "standing is an integral portion of the pledge ceremony and is no less a gesture of acceptance and respect than is the salute or the utterance of the words of allegiance" (as cited in Schimmel & Fischer, 1987, p. 57). The student objected to standing as a matter of conscience and his objection was upheld.

Racial Discrimination

The *Brown v. Topeka Board of Education* decision on racial discrimination in 1954 set the stage for a process to implement racial equality in the schools. The court stated:

Today, education is perhaps the most important function of state and local governments. Compulsory school attendance laws and the great expenditures for education both demonstrate our recognition of the importance of education to our democratic society. It is required in the performance of our most basic public responsibilities, even service in the armed forces. It is the very foundation of good citizenship. (p. 493)

Congress enacted the Civil Rights Act of 1964 as an instrument to eliminate continued discrimination. Recipients of federal funds, including schools, have to meet its guidelines in order to receive government support. Title VI of the Act states:

that no person in the United States shall; on the grounds of race, color, or national origin, be excluded from participation in, be denied the benefits of, or be otherwise subjected to discrimination under any program or activity receiving Federal financial assistance from the Department of Education. (Sec. 601, Civil Rights Act of 1964)

A "recipient under any program to which this part applies may not, directly or through contractual or other arrangements, on the basis of race, color, or national origin" engage in the following discrimination practices (*Federal Register,* 1980, p. 30918). Because most schools

Since the Civil Rights Act of 1964, the children in this extended family have more opportunities for educational pursuits.

receive federal financial support and are therefore recipients, they must abide these regulations:

1. Deny an individual any service, financial aid or other benefit provided under the program;
2. Provide any service, financial aid or other benefit to an individual which is different or is provided in a different manner from that provided to others under the program;
3. Subject an individual to segregation or separate treatment in any matter related to his receipt of any service, financial aid or other benefit under the program;
4. Restrict an individual in any way in the enjoyment of any advantage or privilege enjoyed by others

receiving any service, financial aid or other benefit under the program;

5. Treat an individual differently from others in determining whether he satisfies any admission, enrollment, quota, eligibility, membership or other requirement or condition which individuals must meet in order to be provided any service, financial aid or other benefit provided under the program.
6. Deny an individual an opportunity to participate in the program through the provision of services or otherwise afford him an opportunity to do so which is different from that afforded others under the program. . . .
7. Deny a person the opportunity to participate as a member of a planning or advisory body which is an integral part of the program.

8. ... Utilize criteria or methods of administration which have the effect of subjecting individuals to discrimination because of their race, color, or national origin, or have the effect of defeating or substantially impairing accomplishment of the objectives of the program as respect individuals of a particular race, color, or national origin (*Federal Register,* 1980, pp. 30918, 30919).

Schools must not, therefore, separate students based on race, use methods to determine services for the students which are in effect discriminatory against that person, or in any way discriminate against students based on race, color, or national origin.

Sex Discrimination

Title IX of Educational Amendments of 1972 provides: No person in the United States shall, on the basis of sex, be excluded from participation in, be denied the benefits of, or be subjected to discrimination under any program or activity receiving Federal financial assistance.... (U.S. Department of Education, n.d.)

The Office for Civil Rights based in the Department of Education enforces the laws that apply to elementary, secondary, and postsecondary schools. In 1975, a federal regulation required schools to examine their programs to see if discriminatory policies were in effect. Military schools, religious organizations where the regulations are at variance with the religious beliefs, and single-sex colleges are exempt. Other than these, educational institutions receiving federal funds cannot "assign students to separate classrooms or activities, or prevent them from enrolling in courses of their choice, on the basis of sex. This includes health, physical education, industrial arts, business, vocational, technical, home economics, music and adult education courses" (U.S. Department of Education, n.d., p. 1).

Educational institutions receiving federal funds cannot do the following:

1. Exclude students of one sex from participation in any academic, extracurricular, research, occupational training or other educational program or activity.

2. Subject any student to separate or different rules of discipline, sanctions or other treatment.

3. Apply different rules of appearance to males and females (for example, requiring males to wear their hair shorter than females).

4. Aid or perpetuate discrimination against any person by providing significant assistance to any agency, organization or person which discriminates on the basis of sex in providing any aid, benefit or service to students.

5. Assign pregnant students to separate classes or activities, although schools may require the student to obtain a physician's certificate as to her ability to participate in the normal educational program or activity so long as such a certificate is required of all students for other physical or emotional conditions requiring the attention of a physician.

6. Refuse to excuse any absence because of pregnancy or refuse to allow the student to return to the same grade level which she held when she left school because of pregnancy.

7. Discriminate against any person on the basis of sex in the counseling or guidance of students or the use of different tests or materials for counseling unless such different materials cover the same occupation and interest areas and the use of such different materials is shown to be essential to eliminate sex bias.

Exceptions include

1. In music classes, schools may have requirements based on vocal range or quality, which may result in all-male or all-female choruses.

2. In elementary and secondary schools, portions of classes that deal exclusively with human sexuality may be conducted in separate sessions for boys and girls.

3. In physical education classes or activities, students may be separated by sex when participating in sports where the major purpose or activity involves bodily contact (for example, wrestling, boxing, rugby, ice hockey, football and basketball).

4. Students may be grouped in physical education classes by ability if objective standards of individual performances are applied. This may result in all-male or all-female ability groups.

5. If the use of a single standard to measure skill or progress in a physical education class has an

Girls can participate in all noncontact sports if those activities are offered by the school.

adverse effect on members of one sex, schools must use appropriate standards that do not have such an effect. For example, if the ability to lift a certain weight is used as a standard for assignment to a swimming class, application of this standard may exclude some girls. The school would have to use other, appropriate standards to make the selection for that class. (U.S. Department of Education, n.d., pp. 1, 2)

Handicapped and Special Education Students

Section 504 of the Rehabilitation Act of 1973 provides that "no qualified handicapped individual shall, on the basis of handicap, be excluded from participation in, be denied the benefits of, or otherwise be subjected to discrimination under any program or activity receiving Federal financial assistance" (U.S. Department of Education, 1980, pp. 30937, 30938). Public Law 94–142, The Education for All Handicapped Children Act of 1975, ensures that handicapped children have an appropriate public education. Public Law 94–457 extended the concept to preschool children. The child is to be educated in the least restrictive environment—one that fits the child's needs. An Individualized Education Program or Individualized Family Service Plan, developed by professionals and parents, protects the child's interest. Refer to Chapter 9 for more complete information.

Corporal Punishment

Although parents may object to corporal punishment, schools do not always honor their request. Punishment must not be harsh and excessive. If it is, teachers and administrators may be subject to civil and criminal liability. In 33 states, however, corporal punishment was still allowed in 1989 (National PTA, 1989). The court decision of *Ingraham v. Wright* (1977) upheld corporal punishment as a means of control in public schools so schools in most states and cities have the right to use corporal punishment on children without the necessity of due process.

Rights for Non-English Speaking Students

In 1965, the Elementary and Secondary Act supported bilingual education for non-English speaking students. This was followed in 1974 by a Supreme Court decision in *Lau v. Nichols* that found that children who could not speak English did not have equal educational opportunity if they did not receive education in their own language. In this case, 1,800 Chinese-origin children in San Francisco attended classes conducted in English. The parents contended that the children were discriminated against because no classes were provided that would benefit them. The Supreme Court agreed and stated that schools must take affirmative action and provide classes for non-English speaking students by providing bilingual education or English as a Second Language programs. The court did not offer regulations concerning language programs and left the decision of provisions up to the states.

Selection of Texts

In general, schools choose text materials to achieve their educational objectives and goals. When parents object to the use of particular books, the courts make decisions based on each individual circumstance and how the book relates to the school's objectives. Courts determine the constitutionality of a position; legislatures may set curriculum requirements to be achieved by public schools. Private schools and early childhood centers that are not connected to the public school system have autonomy in text selection. However, it is wise for both public and private schools to include parents in book selection to prevent later disagreements.

Obscenity is not protected by the First Amendment, but the Supreme Court has not defined the term definitively. When the issue over a book or other media becomes so heated that it ends up in court, the court will judge whether it lacks serious literary, artistic, political, or scientific value and if it is obscene because it appeals to the prurient interest of minors (*Miller v. California,* 1973). Whether it is obscene will be judged by contemporary local community standards.

DEVELOPING CRITERIA TOGETHER

Only when parents and teachers work together does the opportunity for optimum education exist. A delineation of three levels of involvement for home and school will clarify and help establish procedures that support positive home-school interaction:

1. Development and periodic review of a code of rights and responsibilities for each class, school, or local school district
2. Election of and active involvement with a parent or citizen advisory council
3. Implementation of the educational program in a classroom community

The first two levels can be accomplished by administrators and parents working together; however, individual classrooms can develop

codes and advisory councils as well. The third level of teacher-parent involvement is that essential area where the benefits of positive relationships most make a difference—the classroom. The teacher-child-parent relationship nourishes the opportunity for learning. The clarification of issues and development of codes, a two-way communication system, and advisory councils are but means of supporting direct involvement with the classroom and its most important member, the child.

Development of a Code

An opportunity for participating in a democratic decision-making process exists in the formation of a school or classroom code. If parents and students join school staff in developing a code for their class or school, both rights and responsibilities are learned through a democratic process. *The Rights and Responsibilities of Students: A Handbook for the School Community* (1979) suggests a model code and a procedure for implementing a code. Recommended steps include:

1. *Identification of the level of interest.* Determine the interest in and awareness of codes with a questionnaire or informal survey of the school community. Include the teachers, administrators, students, parents, and interested community residents. If there is a lack of understanding of the purpose of a code, you must launch an awareness campaign to explain the code, its benefits, and why it is needed.

2. *Research.* Background information on the current rules and regulations should be gathered before writing a code. Samples of codes from other schools or states, legal groups, professional associations, and civil liberty organizations are helpful in the process. Key issues that need to be addressed in your individual area should be identified.

3. *Formulation of a draft code.* The actual writing of the code needs to be accomplished by a committee of parents, teachers, students, and administrators. Include the regulations that are

This child is too young to be involved in developing a code, but his parents can help the schools develop a code that will protect him.

important for your school and community. If guidance is needed, base your draft on the samples obtained.

4. *Feedback.* After the code is drafted, distribute copies or publish the document in the newsletter. Hold an open forum or ask for written comments on the code. The responses will reveal questions and areas of confusion or vagueness, which will enable the committee to revise the draft in final form.

5. *Approval and implementation.* The code should be approved by the student body as well as by the school staff. If the code is being developed for the entire district, the school board should review and approve the code. Their support is essential for implementation. At the preschool level the students will not need to approve the code, but their parents should be involved, and discussion of rules and regulations with the children is appropriate.

6. *Review.* Each year, the student body or governing committee should review the code. If needed, items may be revised. The review makes the code relevant to the current student body and is a learning as well as a decision-making process.

The three levels of involvement—the code, the parent advisory council, and the classroom—strengthen a school-home partnership. The parent advisory council is discussed in more detail in Chapter 4; good classroom relations are discussed in Chapters 4, 5, and 7. The code can be developed on a formal level in the entire school district, or individual teachers may modify it and use it in an informal way in their classrooms.

A SLEEPING GIANT: THE CHILD ADVOCATE

Children do not have the skills or power to advocate for themselves. It rests with parents and teachers to recognize their needs and advocate for them. The issues of the 90s vividly illustrate why children need to have advocates. The increase in incest, child abuse, homelessness, poverty, and demand for child care shout to the public. These social problems need great action to help overcome the obstacles that children face. But children also need advocates at a personal level. Many children who come to child care centers or schools lack self-esteem. They need advocates—individual teachers who may be able to help such children feel important and wanted. Advocacy is needed at all levels; both teachers and parents must stand up for the children. If they do not, who will?

The Child Advocate

The advocate is a person, parent, teacher, or citizen, alone or in a group, who speaks or acts on behalf of the child's welfare. The advocate must grasp the need of the child, the resources available within the school system, and the alternative resources outside the school system. Ad-

Parents are the prime advocates for their children from early childhood to young adulthood.

vocates may be involved in three areas of advocacy:

1. Personal advocacy
   • advocate on a personal level for an individual child or group of children
2. Private advocacy
   • advocate for a cause in the private sector
3. Public advocacy
   • advocate in a group—one of many advocating for political change or legislation
   • advocate for a child through the courts
   • advocate for a cause

Child advocacy varies by country. A look at other systems provides insight into the strategies that are employed in the U.S.

Advocacy for Children Around the World

Norway, Sweden, Israel, and Finland have set up ombudsmen systems for children. In Norway, the system was created by national legislation. In Sweden, the set-up was established through Raada Barnen (Save the Children), a large private organization. In Finland the ombudsman is the legal aspect of the Mannerheim League for

Child Welfare, a private advocacy group, and in Israel the ombudsman is under the direction of the Jerusalem Children's Council (Rauche-Elnekave, 1989). In each of the countries in addition to working on behalf of individual children, the ombudsmen work toward betterment for groups of children and answer general complaints.

Norway and Sweden have a highly developed system of ombudsmanship—a comprehensive child advocacy office. Norway's involvement with families reaches back several centuries. In 1621 a Norwegian law required that parents find a useful occupation for their children. If the children were found idle, public guardians would take over the responsibility of the parents. Now Norway has one of the first national ombudsman for children (Flekkoy, 1989).

In Sweden, the Ombudsman for Children works outside the government system. The ombudsmen are employed by Radda Barnen— Swedish Save the Children—a organization of more than 200,000 Swedes who are members, donors, and sponsors (Ronstrom, 1989). Five staff members—professionals with backgrounds in sociology, social work, psychology, and law—respond to challenges. They strengthen children's legal security, work toward legislation, and offer public education about children's rights and needs. The goals of Radda Barnen are to (1) mold public opinion and influence the government and Parliament; (2) spread information about children's needs and rights to decision makers; (3) conduct research and invite professionals to present their papers concerning children; (4) undertake projects to change public opinion and work out model programs; (5) organize seminars and inservice training for professionals including information on child abuse and sexual abuse, and (6) offer telephone advisory service for professionals and the public. The most typical questions asked through the telephone service deal with child abuse and neglect, children in care, and conflicts over custody.

Sweden is concerned about the children who come from homes where the children are at risk. The debate continues: Should children be separated from biological parents or stay with them and live in a home detrimental to the child? Concern is shown for children whose parents are severe drug addicts, alcoholics, mentally ill, or mentally retarded. The question remains: "Shall we sacrifice them in order to satisfy grown-ups' need to have children? Have children no human rights of their own?" (Ronstrom, 1989, p. 127).

In Finland and Israel the ombudsman works alone, dealing with complaints and problems that individual children have. In Israel, the organization Working Group on Children's Rights, includes all faiths (Jewish, Arab, ultra-orthodox, and Christian) and works for all children, including preschool and children of prisoners (Rauche-Elnekave, 1989; Utriainen, 1989).

The United States has a social service system, but the emphasis is not ombudsmanship for the children. An ombudsman who has no connection with the public social services could provide helpful and anonymous service for children in need. At present, however, groups and individuals must carry the responsibility for this role.

Working as an Advocate on a Personal Level

The most common kind of advocacy is one that many teachers and parents do without calling it advocacy. If parents and teachers look upon positive intervention to help a child live a full and meaningful life as advocacy, and if they recognize that children cannot advocate for themselves, they will accept the responsibility and challenge of advocacy as a necessary role for them. Individual advocates who work for children in their own child care programs or classroom can make a huge impact on children's lives. There is no excuse for anyone not to be an advocate, either as a parent, a classroom teacher, friend, or child care worker. If everyone who works or lives with children considers that they are important advocates for the children they touch, the lives of children would be changed for the better. That would indeed be a giant step toward providing children with the childhood they deserve and need.

Child care is also affected by personal advocacy. About one-third of children in the U.S. are cared for in their own homes or in the homes of others (see Table 3-2: 17.8% in their own home; 14.4% in another person's home). More than one-half of all children are cared for at school; many are latch key children before and after school and in the summer.

If working parents have the opportunity to use grandparents, neighbors, friends, and other relatives, it is important that the community offer parent support, education, enrichment, and recreation to help these caregivers provide an excellent environment which will benefit the children. This can be addressed at the grass roots level. Private agencies can help, as can churches, recreation districts, and schools. They may provide crisis child care, parent education, and drop-in child care. Parents who provide their own care could also benefit from this community support, as could child care centers. Children are the responsibility of country and community as well as parents.

Parents and teachers can advocate on a personal level in roles such as these:

- provide a stimulating, appropriate environment so the child can play and work productively
- advocate for a child in a classroom or for your own child
- spend time with children, listening to what concerns or interests them
- see that children are in educationally and socially appropriate classes
- seek out interesting excursions and activities that will benefit the child
- determine the best facilities for a child who needs special help
- take time to give proper care to your children
- report physical and sexual abuse
- become an ombudsman and share resources or develop resources for a parent who is neglectful because of lack of resources
- share information about good childrearing practices
- communicate with the teacher if you are a parent, and with the parents if you are a teacher
- attend meetings and speak out on issues (e.g. school board, child care, PTA, League of Women Voters)
- become active in professional organizations (e.g., local affiliate of the Association for the Education of Young Children, National Association for the Education of Young Children, National Council on Family Relations)
- write and contact your legislator about upcoming legislation

Qualifications for Personal Advocates

Qualifications for advocates are few. Essentially what qualifies a person to be a good child advocate is the intrinsic quality of being truly motivated to help children. The help must be systematic, knowledgeable, and thorough. The advocate is committed to finding out all the needs of the child or children being helped. Although it is time-consuming and difficult work, advocacy, when supported by the best available data, is helpful to community, parents, and schools.

It must be remembered that each situation is different. The strategies that work vary, and the decision as to which strategy is most appropriate ultimately rests on two factors: (1) that the strategy accomplishes its objectives and (2) that it paves the way for long-range continuation of the practice of supplying the needed resources (Kappelman & Ackerman, 1977).

Procedure

To achieve their objectives, advocates must systematically study and proceed with a sound foundation. They first list the needs of the child and justify these needs by making certain they have been professionally determined. They read the literature and speak to experts in the field so that they are supported by reputable observations. Good advocates make sure that their positions are based not just on their own beliefs but on the true needs of the child, the group of children, and the society at large. Their positions are strengthened if the advocates are associated with a group. In fact, greater educational change and progress comes from advocacy groups than from the dedicated, but individual, parent or citizen. Proficient advocates set out to pursue all resources available (Kappelman & Ackerman, 1977).

An effective child advocate is a person who works very hard at discovering the full story behind children's needs, the total picture of the available resources, and the most appropriate method of blending the two. If a child advocate works well, he changes the system—for the better. (Kappelman & Ackerman, 1977, p. 329)

The following guidelines describe the steps to take when working on an individual advocacy case.

1. *Know your facts.* Be sure they are correct. Find out: Who? What? Where? When? and Why?

2. *Know the rights* of the child, the parent, or other parties in the case. Contact an advocacy organization or lawyer if you have any questions.

3. *Know the policy* and/or procedures that relate to the problem. Get it in writing, don't just accept a verbal version.

4. *Keep accurate notes.* Document as much evidence as possible. Date everything.

5. *Discuss various options* with the child or parents you are assisting. Do not tell the young person or parent what to do. Rather let the person (child or parent) *choose* the option and course of action that is wisest and that he/she is willing to live with.

6. *Never go alone* (except in unusual circumstances) to a meeting with officials. Take the young person, the parent, or other concerned person with you.

7. In meeting with officials, *keep to the point,* be firm but not antagonistic, keep focused on the problem and the need for a resolution of the problem. Try to steer clear of personalities.

8. *Follow channels.* Don't go over a person's head until you have seen him/her about the problem. It is wise to let that person know you are dissatisfied with the result of your meeting and that you intend to go to the next person in authority.

9. If appropriate, send a letter to indicate your understanding of what took place at a meeting with officials or administrators. (Fernandez, 1980, p. 83. Reprinted by permission.)

Case or Class Action

Advocates may work with individual cases or in class actions. The individual or case advocate works on behalf of a specific child. The class or social advocate works for a whole group of children who need special or basic services (e.g., Children's Defense Fund works for child rights; The Pennsylvania Association for Retarded Children began the advocacy for the rights of retarded). Lay advocates must obtain the necessary services and help. When legal issues and court cases are involved, legal counsel from a lawyer, a professional advocate, is needed.

Administrative or Legislative Levels

Advocates can make change at administrative and legislative levels. The advocate may work toward change in regulations and guidelines at the administrative level, or toward change in the laws through legislative advocacy (Goffin & Lombardi, 1988).

Advocacy on the Public Level

Individuals work together and separately to advocate on the public level. Most successful advocacy requires a broad-based approach, whether it is achieved through many individuals responding, by professional organizations advocating, or by the powerful lobbying of political action committees. The issue of child care affects many people—parents, children, grandparents, employers, schools, and the entire society. Children who do not have satisfactory childhoods are adults who are unable to hold a job, who look to drugs or alcohol to cover the pain, or who end up serving time in prison. In the long term, adequate and fulfilling child care is very cost effective.

The Alliance for Better Child Care, an example of advocacy and collaboration, is a group of more than 130 national organizations including these: American Academy of Pediatrics, American Association of University Women, Camp Fire Inc., Child Welfare League of America, Children's Defense Fund, National Association of Elementary School Principals, National Congress of Parents and Teachers, National Council of Catholic Women, and National Association of School Psychologists. This collaboration supported the Act for Better Child Care which was brought before the Senate and House of Representatives. Legislators must be made to realize the importance of an issue and the feelings of their constituents if funding is to be gained from the federal government. The Act responds to the need for

- assistance for affordable child care. (Families with lower incomes would receive greater assistance.)
- increasing the availability of child care through grants and loan programs, recruitment of family day care providers, and referral systems. Utilizing the Head Start and Chapter I programs would also assist in meeting the needs of full-time working parents.

In order to successfully advocate on the public level, coalitions of groups must be formed, individuals must become active, and both must establish good public relations. First, facts must be collected. The Children's Defense Fund (1987; 1988; 1989) has been fulfilling a great need for up-to-date figures and analysis of legislation for professionals and the general public. The Ad Hoc Day Care Coalition (1985) published material about the crisis in infant and toddler care. Groups such as these make it easy for the advocate to obtain facts and figures that will grip even the most jaundiced of legislatures. Use them to keep current on the facts about children and child care.

Facts on Children and Families

Many sources are available to help advocates obtain the facts they need. In addition to the Children's Defense Fund and the National Association for the Education of Young Children, look for government publications, professional journals, books, and literature from private advocacy groups. Organizations are listed in the Appendix at the end of this text under the title, Advocacy. The following facts may be supplemented by that list and the information in Chapter 3.

- The proportion of children living in poverty grew by 23% between 1979 and 1988. One in every 5 children live in poverty in the United States. If the trend toward poverty continues, 1 in every 4 children will live in poverty by 2000 (Children's Defense Fund, 1990, p. 26).
- 32.5 million Americans are poor; of these, 12.4 million are children. In 1987, 23% of children younger than 6 lived in poverty (Children's Defense Fund, 1989, p. 71). Children make up the largest group of poor in the United States.
- Most poor people are white. The chances of being poor are 1 in 7 for whites, 4 in 9 for African Americans, and 3 in 8 for Hispanics.
- In 1987, 34.3% of families headed by women were poor (Children's Defense Fund, 1989, p. 17). The chances of being poor for female-headed families are 1 in 2 (Children's Defense Fund, 1990, p. 28).

- The chances of being poor, if families are headed by parents younger than 25, are 1 in 2 (Children's Defense Fund, 1989, xlvi).
- More than half of preschool children have mothers in the work force (Children's Defense Fund, 1989, p. xiv). It is projected that 7 out of 10 mothers of preschool children will work outside the home by 2000 (Children's Defense Fund, 1990, p. 27).
- In 1986 there were 179,000 births to children younger than 17 and 10,000 of these were to children 14 and younger (Children's Defense Fund, 1989, p. 90). Thirty-seven million Americans lack health insurance (Children's Defense Fund, 1990, p. 27). Nearly one-fourth of the women in United States do not receive early prenatal care, and 555,000 women who give birth do not have health insurance (p. 108).
- Of mothers awarded child support, only one-half received the designated amount, one-fourth received partial payment, and the remaining quarter did not receive any help (Children's Defense Fund, 1989, p. 20).
- Skyrocketing rents and higher housing costs have caused homelessness for many poor Americans. Being homeless, which is devastating for families, is especially hard on children. "Homeless families resemble poor families with stable homes in many respects: educational achievement, work history, family structure, drug use, and psychiatric history" (Children's Defense Fund, 1989, p. 31). Research suggests, however, that the homeless lack a support network—families and friends—that could help them through a crisis. Becoming homeless also takes them away from whatever network they may have established with former neighbors, friends, churches, or communities (p. 31).
- The U.S. ranked 18th in the world in infant mortality, with 10.6 deaths per thousand infants born each year (Children's Defense Fund, 1989 p. 4).
- In 1985, the Physician Task Force on Hunger reported that malnutrition affects 500,000 chil-

dren in the United States (Children's Defense Fund, 1989, p. 38).

- One in four poor children drops out of school (Children's Defense Fund, 1989, p. 70).
- 2.5 million children are eligible for Head Start, but only 18% are served (Children's Defense Fund, 1989, p. 62).
- Only 28 states provide Aid to Families of Dependent Children if there are two parents in the family (Shapiro & Greenstein, 1988).
- In 32 states the AFDC cash benefit for a family of three is less than 50% of the poverty line (Shapiro & Greenstein, 1988).
- In every state except Alaska, the AFDC and food stamps combined do not reach poverty level (Shapiro & Greenstein, 1988).

PREPARING FOR ADVOCACY

To be a successful advocate, one needs to be knowledgeable about the case at hand. The Child Care Employee Project has developed a curriculum to be used with students to help them develop their advocacy skills. These are some of the areas discussed: Advocates are better prepared for long-term advocacy if they

- know about the past history of child care, child abuse, and rights of children
- recognize the process of social change—how change is accomplished and the past history of change in the nation
- recognize the impact that social and economic conditions and organization of society have on themselves and other families and children.
- are aware of the impact that technology, power, class, and race have on families in a given society
- view children as a protected class, with children of all races and class having needs. See them as the future of the society.
- view child care in a positive light, a profession with ethical guidelines and practices
- identify and use resources in the community, state, and nation (modified from Whitebook & Ginsburg, 1984, p. 2).

Steps to Take for Public Advocacy

In advocating for the Act for Better Child Care, many organizations joined together to show their commitment for children. They advocated for legislation at the national level to effect change in the United States. Many other issues are handled at the state level, such as licensing and teacher certification. These are the basic steps involved in public advocacy at this level:

1. Write federal legislators. Individual letters written by constituents are more effective than form letters with many signatures. If you want help to write the letter, use the suggested form letter as a guide, but make it reflect your feelings. Send letters about national issues and legislation to:

President of the United States—The White House, Washington, DC 20500

Representatives—The Honorable (*name*), U.S. House of Representatives, Washington, DC 20515

Senators—The Honorable (*name*), U.S. Senate, Washington, DC 20510

For representatives' telephone numbers, call the Capitol switchboard, 202-224-3121.

2. Talk with and write to state legislators. On the state level, write or call

Your State representative

· Your State senators

Work with your representative before the assembly or legislature meets if you or your group have a bill that you want to have introduced.

3. Get involved before elections. Campaign for legislators that agree with your position on child care, families, and children.

4. After the election, invite elected officials to speak with your organization.

5. Join professional organizations in your region; for example, National Association for the Education of Young Children, Council for Excep-

tional Children, National Association for Children with Learning Disabilities, your local Association for the Education of Young Children, and the National Council on Family Relations. (Addresses are in the Appendix).

6. Visit child care centers, homeless shelters, schools, and other facilities so that you have first-hand experience about your concerns.

Developing an Advocacy Approach in Your Community School

If you have decided to change the local environment to help children, it is necessary to involve others. Each community has its own special needs and background, so each program should be geared to the individual problems. A two-pronged approach is one way to get started. First, begin a series of seminars, workshops, and presentations that inform the total community. Second, simultaneously find out how the community, including adults and children, views the crisis.

Determine Needs.
In order to respond to the problems of a community, you first need to know what the needs are. To set up a needs assessment, gather representatives from groups interested in children's rights and needs, brainstorm about the problems in their areas, list these concerns, and construct a questionnaire for use with a larger population. Tabulate responses and select a target issue.

Organize the Parent Community.
In some communities parents are very aware of problems and want to get involved in solutions. In other communities they avoid issues, hoping the problems will go away. Under both circumstances it is better to have an informed community, and a series of community meetings, school seminars, and articles in the newspapers will start the education process. Once the community is informed, it is easier to get involvement and cooperation.

Informing the community takes time. Many communities spend a great deal of time and effort in establishing community seminars and outreach to the schools before they feel the groundwork is established for developing alternatives and programs in the community. Working through PTA, PTO, parent education groups, and community task forces, many communities have educated their citizens with seminars given by authorities in the field.

Hold Student/Parent Rap Sessions.
Students are generally better informed on children's problems than their parents are. Opportunities for students to talk about the problems in their lives can be very helpful to them and very informative to those who are able to listen to them. A very effective method of communication is school exchanges. Students rap while parents from another school listen and join in the discussion. Parents learn what is happening in young peoples' lives. Students get an opportunity to share and explore. No value judgments are made, but parents go home much wiser and students have had an opportunity to express their frustrations and desires. Later, in an open and nonblaming atmosphere parents may be able to rap with students from their own school area. This exchange is an opportunity for parents to become more aware of the social world their children face.

Sponsor Parent Peer Groups.
A movement that is helpful for parents and, subsequently, their children is parent peer involvement. Parents need to be able to express their concerns and talk with others who have similar concerns. Communicating with parents lets them know that they are not alone in the challenges of rearing children.

Parent peer groups may evolve from different needs and reasons. Parents may get involved in a peer group just for the opportunity of knowing the parents of some of their own children's friends. Others get involved because they have been exposed to the increased use of drugs by their own or neighborhood children.

Peer groups may be established by the PTO, PTA, or parent education groups, or they may evolve from a concern by a single parent in a neighborhood. When a single parent attempts to organize a parent peer group, that parent may get mixed reactions from the parents contacted. This barrier is sometimes very difficult to break. If great care is taken to establish a nonblaming campaign to inform parents of problems, many parents may accept the true situation. Establishment of a parent group to establish common guidelines for their young children gives parents an opportunity to get acquainted before serious issues such as delinquency or drug use enter into the discussions.

Parent peer groups vary according to their needs. They may serve as support groups, as well as action groups. Develop them according to the needs of your specific community.

Organize Student Groups.

Involving older students is a necessary step. Nothing can be accomplished to solve most problems without their cooperation and support. In order to promote student involvement, do the following:

1. If students do not initiate a student group on their own, select a representative group and try to include those who are involved and interested. Students who volunteer are more likely to be committed to the problem. Initiating a student group may be accomplished by one of the following:
   a. Ask for volunteers via bulletin boards or school newspapers.
   b. Request that the student council solicit and appoint a committee.
   c. Work with teachers of social studies or family life education and use their classes as a forum for discussion of the issues.
   d. Request that counselors or administrators appoint a committee.
2. At an initial meeting encourage the students to brainstorm on the following issues:
   a. Problems
   b. Reasons why students experience such problems
   c. Information and activities that make the community, school, and parents

more aware and responsive to student needs
   d. Alternatives that would be welcomed by them
3. At a subsequent meeting encourage the students to evaluate the ideas discussed at the initial meeting and to develop a questionnaire for other students to complete.
4. Test the questionnaire on a few students. Rework it if the questions or statements are not clear. Add to it if new ideas are important and relevant.
5. Ask teachers of required classes at each level to allow their students to answer the questionnaires.
6. Tabulate the answers to the questionnaires. Share the information with the school, task force, and other students.
7. Make plans to implement requested changes. Share student plans and desires with the parent group and school.

Form Parent-School Teams.

Parent-school teams, formed in each school, keep parents informed. The groups can reflect the needs of each school. Students serve on each team, allowing the team to have an ongoing awareness of student needs from elementary through junior and senior high school.

Establish Alternative Programs.

The most crucial part of solving community problems is the development of alternatives—a change in the environment. As students, parents, and community work together, the needs of the students are addressed. Older students take the lead with support and backing from the parents and community.

Perhaps a new code is developed. (A suggested format for the development of a behavior code was discussed earlier in this chapter.) Rules and plans for social get togethers are established and followed. Instead of focusing on past negative behavior, a positive approach should be used. "We are serving cider, apples, and cookies. If you wish alcohol tonight, come back another time."

It is important to increase opportunities for students to develop meaningful relationships, to feel competent, and to have a chance to contribute in a significant way. Review the needs assessment completed by the students. What do they say that their needs are?

First, what facilities in the community provide a wholesome environment for young people? Does the community reflect a recognition of the needs of the population?

Second, how can schools, recreational districts, and parents help provide alternatives the children would enjoy? Is there an active after-school program? Are tutors available to help students who have difficulty in school? Are there rap times available for students during the school day? Are there activities such as crafts, auto mechanics, and art that fit the needs of all? *Advocate for the children's needs!*

Think of all the good that can come from recognizing and attacking problems. Families may start communicating more. Schools and parents will start working together to solve the problems. The whole community can become involved. You will live where people care about each other and where they are willing to advocate for needed change.

SUMMARY

Rights and responsibilities of parents, students, and professional educators are explored in this chapter. Criticisms of schools make cooperation between home and schools even more essential than in previous periods.

Rights and responsibilities of parents and students are expressed on the following topics: suspension and expulsion, speech and expression, flag salute and Pledge of Allegiance, racial discrimination, sex discrimination, handicapped and special education students, corporal punishment, and the Buckley Amendment on open record policy.

Three levels of involvement between home and school help clarify and delineate procedures that support positive home-school relationships. These include: (1) development and periodic review of a code of rights and responsibilities for each class, school, or local school district; (2) election of and active involvement with a parent or citizen advisory council; and (3) implementation of the educational program in a classroom community. Development of a code involves identification of interests, research and gathering of background material, formulation of a draft code, feedback, approval, implementation, and review.

The child advocate, a sleeping giant, has begun to have an effect on children's rights. Working as both case advocates and class advocates, individuals and groups are being heard. Parents and teachers must advocate for children's rights. This can be accomplished by organizing, planning, and advocating for a more caring and healthy environment. Parents and schools working together can provide a wholesome, intellectually stimulating, and challenging environment for families and children.

SUGGESTED ACTIVITIES AND DISCUSSIONS

1. Develop a code of conduct for students in a hypothetical school. What would the differences be between an elementary school code and a secondary school code?

2. Who should be involved in the development of a conduct code? Discuss.

3. Discuss the changes in sex stereotyping. Go to the library and skim textbooks of the 1960s and the 1980s. Can you find a difference in the subliminal messages about sex roles? Devise a test about sex roles. Have the class test their own beliefs about the roles of each sex.

4. What is free speech? How are the boundaries defined? Discuss.
5. Which rights do parents and students have to see school records?
6. Discuss the concept that rights are also accompanied by responsibilities.
7. How have schools responded to the need to eliminate racial discrimination? Investigate the changes that have occurred in schools in your area as a result of affirmative action.
8. Which changes were needed in schools to accommodate handicapped children? Visit a school and note which changes were instituted for the handicapped child. Discuss.
9. Contact a school in your area and find out what alternative programs exist.
10. Follow the legislative action in your state, choose a bill that you strongly support, and advocate for its passage.
11. Brainstorm and come up with a list of needs that should be addressed by an advocate or advocacy groups.

BIBLIOGRAPHY

Ad Hoc Day Care Coalition. *The crisis in infant and toddler child care.* Washington, D.C.: Author, 1985.

Berger, E. H., & Berger, G. R. Parents and law: Rights and responsibilities. In L. Sametz & C. S. McLoughlin (Eds.), *Educators, children and the law.* Springfield, Ill.: Charles C. Thomas, 1985.

Brown v. Topeka Board of Education, 347, U.S. 483 (1954).

Child Care Action Campaign Media Kit. New York: Child Care Action Committee, n.d.

Children's Defense Fund. *Child care: The time is now.* Washington, D.C.: Author, 1987.

_____. *A children's defense budget: FY 1989. An analysis of our nation's investment in children.* Washington, D.C.: Author, 1988.

_____. *A vision for America's future.* Washington, D.C.: Author, 1989.

_____. *The nation's investment in children.* Washington, D.C.: Author, 1989.

_____. *Children 1990: A report card, briefing book, and action primer.* Washington, D.C.: Author, 1990.

Citizens for Parental Rights v. San Mateo County Board of Education, 124 Cal. Reptr. 68 (1975).

Civil Rights Act of 1964. Sec. 601; 78 Stat. 252; 42 U.S.C. 2000d. Cited in the *Federal Register, 45*(92).

Dixon v. Alabama State Board of Education, 368 U.S. 930 (1961).

Federal Register. *Part II Department of Education, 45* (92), May 9, 1980, pp. 30919–30965.

Fernandez, H. C. *The child advocacy handbook.* New York: The Pilgrim Press, 1980.

Fischer, L., & Schimmel, D. *The rights of students and teachers.* New York: Harper & Row, 1982.

Flekkoy, M. G. Child advocacy in Norway: The ombudsman. *Child Welfare, 68* (2), March-April 1989, pp. 113–122.

Goffin, S. G., & Lombardi, J. *Speaking out: Early childhood advocacy.* Washington, D.C.: National Association for the Education of Young Children, 1988.

Goss v. Lopez, 419 U.S. 565 (1975).

Guzick v. Drebus, 401 U.S. 948 (1971).

Hazelwood School District v. Kuhlmeier, 484 U.S. 592 (1988).

Ingraham v. Wright, 430 U.S. 651 (1977).

Kappelman, M., & Ackerman, P. *Between parent and school.* New York: Dial Press, 1977.

Lau v. Nichols, 424 U.S. 563 (1974).

Lines, P. M. *Compulsory education laws and their impact on public and private education.* Denver, Colo.: Education Commission of the States, 1982.

_____. *Private education alternatives and state regulations.* Denver, Colo.: Education Commission of the States, 1982.

Lombardi, J. Now more than ever . . . It is time to become an advocate for better child care. *Young Children, 43* (5), July 1988, pp. 41–43.

Macchiarola, F. J., & Gartner, A. (Eds.). *A caring for America's children.* New York: The Academy of Political Science, 1989.

Meyer v. Nebraska, 262 U.S. 390, 399 (1923).

Miller v. California, 413 U.S. 15 (1973).

Nagle v. Olin, 415 N.E. 2d, 179 (Ohio, 1980).

National PTA. Putting Away the Paddle—Corporal Punishment in the Schools. *Nuts & Bolts #8.* Chicago: Author, 1989.

Pennsylvania Association for Retarded Children v. Commonwealth of Pennsylvania 343 F. Supp. E.D. Penn. (1972).

Pierce v. Society of Sisters of the Holy Name, 268 U.S. 510 (1925).

Public Policy Report. Questions and answers about the Act for Better Child Care. *Young Children, 43* (4), May 1988, pp. 32–38.

Rauche-Elnekave, H. Advocacy and ombudswork for children: Implications of the Israeli experience. *Child Welfare, 68* (2), March-April 1989, pp. 101–112.

Ronstrom, A. Sweden's children's ombudsman: A spokesperson for children. *Child Welfare, 68* (2), March-April, 1989, pp. 123–128.

Saxe, R. W. *School-community relations in transition.* Berkeley, Calif.: McCutchan Publishing, 1984.

Schimmel, D., & Fischer, L. *Parents, schools and the law.* Columbia, Md.: National Committee for Citizens in Education, 1987.

Shapiro, I., & Greenstein, R. *Holes in the safety net.* Washington, D.C.: Center on Budget and Policy Priorities, 1988.

State v. Faith Baptist Church, 107, Neb. 802, N.W. 2nd 571 (1981).

State v. Shaver, 294 N.W. 2d 883 (N.D. 1980).

Tinker v. Des Moines Independent Community School District, 393 U.S. 503 (1969).

U.S. Department of Education. Establishment of Title 34, Section 504, Rehabilitation Act of 1973, Rules and Regulations. *Federal Register 45*(92), Friday May 9, 1980, pp. 30937–30938.

U.S. Department of Education, Office for Civil Rights. *Student assignment in elementary and secondary schools and Title IX.* Washington, D.C.: Author, n.d.

U.S. Department of Health, Education and Welfare. (Office of Human Development Services, Administration for Children, Youth and Families. Youth Development Bureau.) *The rights and responsibilities of students: A handbook for the school community.* Washington, D.C.: U.S. Government Printing Office, 1979.

United States Supreme Court Reports: Lawyer Edition, 98 L Ed. 2nd, U.S. 484, Court Rules, p. 597.

Utriainen, S. Child welfare service in Finland. *Child Welfare, 68*(2), 1989, pp. 129–130.

Valente, W. D. *Law in the schools (2nd ed.).* Columbus, Ohio: Merrill, 1987.

West Virginia State Board of Education v. Barnette, 319 U.S. 624, (1943).

Whitebook, M., & Ginsburg G. (Eds.). *Beyond "just working with kids": Preparing early childhood teachers to advocate for themselves and others.* Berkeley, Calif.: Child Care Employee Project, 1984.

Wisconsin v. Yoder, 406 U.S. 205, 233 (1972).

Appendix D:
Constitutional Amendments

Amendment I Congress shall make no law respecting an establishment of religion, or prohibiting the free exercise thereof; or abridging the freedom of speech, or of the press; or the right of the people peaceably to assemble, and to petition the government for a redress of grievances.

Amendment IV The right of the people to be secure in their persons, houses, papers, and effects, against unreasonable searches and seizures, shall not be violated, and no warrants shall issue, but upon probable cause, supported by oath or affirmation, and particularly describing the place to be searched, and the persons or things to be seized.

Amendment V No person shall be held to answer for a capital, or otherwise infamous crime, unless on a presentment or indictment of a grand jury, except in cases arising in the land or naval forces, or in the militia, when in actual service in time of war or public danger; nor shall any person be subject for the same offense to be twice put in jeopardy of life or limb; nor shall be compelled in any criminal case to be a witness against himself, nor be deprived of life, liberty, or property, without due process of law; nor shall private property be taken for public use, without just compensation.

Amendment IX The enumeration in the Constitution of certain rights shall not be construed to deny or disparage others retained by the people.

Amendment X The powers not delegated to the United States by the Constitution, nor prohibited by it to the States, are reserved to the States respectively, or to the people.

Amendment XIV All persons born or naturalized in the United States, and subject to the jurisdiction thereof, are citizens of the United States and of the State wherein they reside. No State shall make or enforce any law which shall abridge the privileges or immunities of citizens of the United States; nor shall any State deprive any person of life, liberty, or property, without due process of law, nor deny to any person within its jurisdiction the equal protection of the laws.

APPENDIX
Resources for Home and School Programs

A resource center or library is necessary for effective school-based and home-based programs. Compile references that discuss the issues of communication, child development, health, and other topics concerning parents. Collect books, pamphlets, magazines, and media materials that cover the many aspects of working with parents. This appendix lists resources for a basic parent education program.

Books form a basis for reference in a resource center, but pamphlets and short articles are very practical for parent groups. Refer to the section on organizations that furnish free or inexpensive pamphlets to obtain materials that can be loaned on a wide scale. The size of a handout or pamphlet is less intimidating than a large book to parents who are very busy. In addition, books are expensive; you cannot have copies for everyone. Buy books for a basic library but supplement them with pamphlets and copies of articles (abide by copyright regulations). Government publications can generally be duplicated freely. Permission to make copies of articles from professional magazines can usually be obtained by writing the publisher. After copies of articles are duplicated, staple each into a file folder or back each with a piece of construction paper. Mark the folder with the name of the resource center. Classify and file the articles for easy retrieval and subsequent loan. With reference books, pamphlets, and articles you can plan and develop many diverse parent meetings.

For current information about the availability of materials, write to the National Maternal and Child Health Clearinghouse, the Southwest Educational Development Laboratory, and the Superintendent of Documents. Look under publication sources in this appendix for addresses. For a complete listing of new books available, check *Books in Print* under subject titles, such as child development. This reference may be found in your public library. It lists books that are currently available, but you will have to determine whether the books are appropriate.

PROGRAMS HELPFUL IN DEVELOPING PARENTING SKILLS

Numerous formats have been developed to help parent educators teach parenting skills. These range from books to sound or video cassettes. The following selections illustrate the types of programs available.

Abidin, R. R. *Parenting skills: Workbook and trainer's manual.* (2nd ed.) New York: Human Sciences Press, 1982.

A trainer's manual accompanies the workbook. The text guides parents in their behavior with children, emphasizing that the parent has an impact on the child's development. The author includes parent-child relationships and a discussion on feelings. The book is based on behavior modification principles.

Bavolek, S., & Comstock, C. M. *The Nurturing Program for Parents and Children.* 219 East Madison Street, Eau Claire, WI 54703: Family Development Resources, Inc., 1985.

A training program designed to promote and build nurturing skills in families. Focuses on self-esteem and positive approaches to behavior management.

The innovative plans for this playground reflect the creative ideas that can help all children grow into productive and happy adults.

Boyd, R. D., Stauber, K. A., & Bluma, S. M. *Portage parent program.* Portage, Wisc.: Cooperative Educational Services Agency, 1977.

The Portage Parent Program has 20 filmstrips and tape cassettes to be used in training. They include: (1) managing behavior, (2) what to teach, (3) how to teach, and (4) generalization and maintenance.

Portage also offers a Portage *Guide to Early Education* which includes 580 developmentally sequenced behaviors packaged in a kit with a manual and card file. The Portage project was originated to design programs and serve preschoolers who were at risk developmentally. It has been expanded to use these offerings for all parents. Books they distribute include *Portage Home Teaching Handbook, A Parent's Guide to Early Education,* and *Get a Jump on Kindergarten.*

Bradshaw, J. *The family: A revolutionary way of self discovery.* Deerfield Beach, Fla.: Health Communications, Inc., 1988.

This book is an expansion of the television program on the family. It could be used along with the TV program or as a separate text. Its emphasis is on family emotional health and social interaction.

Dinkmeyer, D., & McKay, G. D. *STEP (Systematic Training for Effective Parenting).* Circle Pines, Minn.: American Guidance Service, 1982.

This very usable set, which includes a trainer's manual, parent's manual, 10 charts, 9 posters, and 5 cassettes, can be used as a training program for parents. The authors emphasize reflective listening, problem ownership, logical and natural consequences, and "I" messages in the solving of parent-child communication difficulties. (See Chapter 5.)

American Guidance Service also has these sets:
STEP/Teen—Systematic Training for Effective Parenting of Teens
TIME—Training in Marriage Enrichment
Responsive Parenting
Strengthening Stepfamilies
PREP for Effective Family Living—Prepurenting materials for students in marriage and family living classes.

Dinkmeyer, D., McKay, D., & McKay, J. L. *New Beginnings: Skills for Single Parents and Stepfamily Parents.* Champaign, Ill.: Research Press, 1987.

New Beginnings helps single parents and stepfamilies develop their families' self-esteem. Included in the book are discussions of relationships, communication, decision-making, discipline, and new parenting methods, as well as practical suggestions for activities that will enhance the family.

Faber, A., & Mazlish, E. *How to talk so kids will listen and listen so kids will talk.* New York: Avon, 1982.

Workshops are developed around sessions on (1) helping children deal with their feelings, (2) engaging cooperation, (3) alternatives to punishment, (4) encouraging autonomy, (5) praise, (6) freeing children from playing roles, and (7) final review. The kit includes a chairperson's guide, participant's workbook, and reading material.

———. *Siblings without rivalry.* Chicago: Nightingale-Conant, 1988.

Workshop material incudes this book, a chairperson's guide, and a participant's workbook. Sessions are (1) helping siblings deal with their feelings about each other, (2) keeping children separate and unequal, (3) siblings in roles, (4) when the kids fight, (5) problem solving, and (6) a final review.

Ferguson-Florissant (Mo.) School District. *Parents as Teachers Project (NPAT).* Author, 1985.

This project developed excellent curriculum materials for children aged birth through age 3. Described in Chapter 8, the project has been evaluated and found to be effective in increasing the very young child's aptitude. It includes guides for parents to use with their children at home.

The books may be ordered from Early Childhood Education Section, Missouri Department of Elementary and Secondary Education, Box 480, Jefferson City, MO 65102.

Frede, E. *Getting involved: Workshops for parents.* Ypsilanti, Mich.: The High/Scope Press, 1984.

Frede developed workshops to be used by leaders in parent education programs. There is a wide range of programs, based on attitudes toward learning, play, language, reading, writing, math, science, TV, and problem solving. The book was developed through a federal grant so workshops can be reproduced.

Gordon, T. *PET: Parent Effectiveness Training.* New York: New American Library, 1975.

Gordon uses active listening, "I-messages," and a "no-lose" method in his program for parents. The program has been helpful for many parents in the development of communication with children (see Chapter 5).

———. *Leader Effectiveness Training.* New York: Bantam, 1984. Gordon stresses leadership development.

Guerney, L. F. *Parenting: A skills training manual.* State College, Penn.: Institute for the Development of Emotional and Life Skills, Inc., 1980.

Guerney has written an easily read book that focuses on the concerns and issues of childrearing. It includes structuring, communication, rules, limits, consequences, and putting it all together. Practice sections help the reader develop the skills.

Lerman, S. *Parent awareness training.* New York: A & W Publishers, 1980.

Lerman led parent awareness groups from which he selected questions that came up at meetings. These are included in his book with a discussion of each response.

Patterson, G. R. *Living with children.* Champaign, Ill.: Research Press, 1976.

Based on social learning theory, this text was written using a programmed format to help parents develop parenting skills.

Popkin, M. H. *Active Parenting.* Atlanta, Ga.: Active Parenting, Inc., 1985.

This parent education format contains videotapes for six sessions: (1) The Active Parent, (2) Understanding Your Child, (3) Instilling Courage, (4) Developing Responsibility, (5) Winning Cooperation, and (6) The Democratic Family in Action. There are also a *Parents' Handbook* and *Action Guide* that accompany the tapes.

———. *The Active Parenting mini-series program.* Atlanta, Ga.: Active Parenting, Inc., 1987.

The mini-series presents the Active Parenting sessions in six half-hour videos. These videos may be used without a leader, at home, or in a large group presentation. The sessions are the same as those listed above. Popkin's book, *Active Parenting,* can be used with the mini-series.

Popkin continues to add programs. An Active Parenting audiocassette system is now available, as well as two books, *Quality Parenting* written with Linda Albert, and *So . . . Why aren't you perfect yet?*

Ryley, H. *You've got to be kid-ding.* Boulder, Colo.: American Training Center, Inc., 1987.

Ryley developed video discussions that include Virginia Satir, Joel Macht, Bill Page, Ed Frierson, and Stephen Glenn as the featured speakers. These are accompanied by training handbooks. It is directed toward parents of elementary school children.

Stratton, C. *Parent and children series.* Carrboro, N.C.: Health Sciences Consortium, 1985.

A series of 10 videotapes to teach parents. *Play:* (1) How to play with a child, (2) Helping Children

Learn; *Praise and Reward:* (1) The Art of Effective Praising, (2) Tangible Rewards; *Effective Limit Setting:* (1) How to Set Limits, (2) Helping Children Learn to Accept Limits, (3) Dealing with Noncompliance; *Handling Misbehavior:* (1) Avoiding and Ignoring Misbehavior, (2) Time Out and Other Penalties, (3) Preventive Approaches. This may be ordered from the Health Sciences Consortium, 103 Laurel Avenue, Carrboro, NC 27510.

Wagonseller, B. R., Burnett, M., Salzberg, B., & Burnett, J. *The art of parenting.* Champaign, Ill.: Research Press, 1977.

This kit contains five color filmstrips, audiocassettes, parents' review manuals, and a leader's guide. It includes communication, assertion training, and behavior management (motivation, methods, and discipline).

PARENT-SCHOOL RELATIONSHIPS

Bell, T. H. *Active parent concern: A new home guide to help your child in school.* Englewood Cliffs, N.J.: Prentice-Hall, 1976.

Bell gives tips to strengthen families and to educate children at home and at school.

Bradley, R. C. *Parent-teacher interviews.* Wolfe City, Tex.: University Press, 1971.

This comprehensive book on parent teacher conference includes a series of short articles by experts on conferring with parents as well as a systematic plan for preparing for parent-teacher interviews.

Brandt, R. S. *Partners: Parents and schools.* Alexandria, Va.: Association for Supervision and Curriculum Development, 1979.

This booklet is a compilation of articles on parent-school relationships.

Brigham Young University Press, (Ed.). *How to involve parents in early childhood education.* Salt Lake City, Utah: Author, 1982.

Brigham Young publishes quite a number of books on early childhood, parenting, and parent involvement. They offer good material on parent education.

Brim, O. G., Jr. *Education for child rearing.* New York: Free Press, 1965.

Brim wrote this classic on parent education for the Russell Sage Foundation in the 1950's. The material is still quite relevant for professionals concerned with parent education. The appendix includes the history of education for childrearing. The main body of the book discusses the nature and aims of parent education, influence of parent on child, causes of parent behavior, and methods for education programs.

Canady, R. L., & Seyfarth, J. T. *How parent-teacher conferences build partnerships.* Bloomington, Ind.: Phi Delta Kappa, 1979.

This is a short book on parent-teacher conferences and their use to develop working partnerships with parents.

Cataldo, C. Z. *Parent education for early childhood.* New York: Teachers College Press, 1987.

Cataldo's comprehensive book on parent education in the schools emphasizes early childhood and families.

Chinn, P. C., Winn, J., & Walters, R. H. *Two-way talking with parents of special children: A process of positive communication.* St. Louis: C. V. Mosby, 1978.

This book contains an excellent discussion of the communication process and its importance in education.

Croft, D. J. *Parents and teachers: A resource book for home, school, and community relations.* Belmont, Calif.: Wadsworth, 1979.

This book fills the need for a practical guide for the early childhood education professional. It contains program ideas and information and suggestions for improving communication with parents of young children.

Curran, D. *In the beginning there were the parents. Discussion guide.* Minneapolis: Winston Press, 1980.

Curran offers an inexpensive guide to discussion of parenting.

Gestwicki, C. *Home, school and community relations: A guide to working with parents.* Albany, N.Y.: Delmar, 1987.

Gestwicki's parent-home book emphasizes communication and working with parents of preschool children.

Honig, A. *Parent involvement in early childhood education.* Washington, D. C.: National Association for the Education of Young Children, 1979.

Honig discusses parent involvement and parent education based on research projects and demonstration programs that involve parents in the education of their young children.

Hymes, J. L. *Effective home-school relations.* Sierra Madre, Calif.: Southern California Association for the Education of Young Children, 1974.

This easily read book discusses elementary school parents and the schools.

Kawin, E. *Basic concepts for parents: Parenthood in a free nation.* W. Lafayette, Ind.: Purdue University, 1969.

Kawin's series of books includes the *Basic Concepts for Parents, Early & Middle Childhood* and *Later Childhood & Adolescence.* All are designed for parent education courses. These well-written guides stress the responsibilities of raising children in a democracy.

Kroth, R. L. *Communicating with parents of exceptional children.* Denver, Colo.: Love Publishing, 1985.

The title depicts the theme of the book, but many of the ideas can be used with parents of most other children as well.

Larrick, N. *A parent's guide to children's reading* (5th ed.). New York: Westminster Press, 1983.

This is an inexpensive paperback that teachers and administrators can give parents to guide them in home activities. Written first in 1958, this classic book is as good as when it was first written.

Lombana, J. H. *Home-school partnerships.* New York: Grune & Stratton, 1983.

Lombana's book gives strategies and guidelines for educators. It is particularly helpful in the area of communication.

Miller, M. S., & Baker, S. S. *Straight talk to parents: How to help your child get the best out of school.* Chelsea, Mich.: Scarborough House, 1977.

This book provides guidance to parents in their relationship with schools.

Rich, D. *Megaskills: How families help children succeed in school and beyond.* Boston: Houghton Mifflin, 1988.

Rich's book is also listed under activities for the young child, because it not only discusses how to help children succeed in school, it also includes many activities that can be done at home to help the child feel successful. The megaskills include confidence, motivation, effort, responsibility, initiative, perseverance, caring, teamwork, common sense, and problem solving.

Robbins, P., & Smith, A. *Involving parents: A handbook for participation in schools.* Ypsilanti, Mich.: The High/Scope Press, 1984.

The authors did a study on parent involvement and federal programs. From this, they chose ideas and findings on project governance, instruction, noninstructional support, community-school relations, and parent education. They discuss activities, forms, and information based on the various programs.

Stone, J. G. *Teacher-parent relationships.* Washington, D.C.: National Association for the Education of Young Children, 1987.

This 40-page booklet focuses on teacher-parent relationships in child care programs and preschools.

Swick, K. *Inviting parents into the young child's world.* Champaign, Ill.: Stipes, 1984.

Swick clearly discusses children's need to have continuity and support from all those around them. Swick relates his discussion to the realities of today's society and the child's world.

Turnbull, A. P., & Turnbull, H. R. (Eds.). *Parents speak out: Then and now* (2nd ed.). Columbus, Ohio: Merrill, 1985.

Parents, who are also professionals, write of their experiences with their mentally retarded, autistic, or otherwise handicapped children. The stories are very moving.

CHILDREARING

Beaty, J. J. *Observing development of the young child* (2nd ed.). Columbus, Ohio: Merrill, 1990.

The author includes child skills checklists in the study of child development. Written in an informal conversational style, this child development book may be used by parents as well as teachers.

Bettelheim, B. *Dialogues with mothers.* New York: Avon, 1971.

Bettelheim reflects psychoanalytic theories in his answers to parents.

Bigner, J. J. *Parent-child relations.* New York: Macmillan, 1985.

Bigner's attractively illustrated book explores the process of interaction between parents and children during the childrearing period.

Brazelton, T. B. *Infants and mothers.* New York: Dell, 1983.

Brazelton describes three infants—quiet, active, and average—as they interact with their parents. The book is written in a descriptive style that enables inexperienced parents to gain a feeling for the newborn and the variations that occur in childrearing.

_____. *Toddlers and parents.* New York: Doubleday, 1989.

Brazelton includes a discussion of working parents, single parents, and the problems of coping with demanding, hyperactive, and withdrawn toddlers. Written in an easily read style, it allows parents of toddlers to identify with the situations.

_____. *What every baby knows.* New York: Ballantine, 1988.

What Every Baby Knows is based on the Lifetime Cablevision series that follows five families through life situations. Brazelton guides the questioning and gives insightful answers to concerns about childhood problems.

_____. *Working and caring* Reading, Mass.: Addison-Wesley, 1985.

Brazelton recognizes the difficult task of caring for children while working outside the home. Case studies are used to consider the issues of juggling both child care and work.

Briggs, D. C. *Your child's self-esteem.* New York: Doubleday, 1975.

This book supports parents in their approach to childrearing and illustrates how they can build self-esteem and self-respect in their children. It has proved to be a very supportive and excellent book for helping parents develop a positive self-image in their children.

Chess, S., & Thomas, A. *Know your child: An authoritative guide for today's parents.* New York: Basic Books, Inc., 1989.

The authors focus on the child and on approaches parents can take to help their children grow into healthy adults.

Comer, J. P., & Poussaint, A. F. *Black child care, how to bring up a healthy black child in America: A guide to psychological and emotional development.* New York: Simon & Schuster, 1975.

The title of the book describes the intent and content of the book—a practical book on childrearing for black parents. The format uses questions and answers to cover the material. The book is good for parents and professionals of all ethnic backgrounds.

Dodson, F. *How to parent.* New York: Signet Books, 1973.

The book, based on psychological theories, discusses childrearing and gives practical advice to parents on parenting practices.

_____. *How to single parent.* New York: Harper & Row, 1987.

With the increasing number of single parents, Dodson has responded to that need and written a book especially for the single parent.

Dodson, F., & Alexander, A. *Your child: Pregnancy through preschool.* New York: Simon & Schuster, 1986.

Dodson has written several effective books on parenting. This one, written with Alexander, focuses on the early years.

Dodson, F., & Reuben, P. *How to grandparent.* New York: New American Library, 1982.

Dodson and Reuben wrote this book to help grandparents fulfill their supportive roles in the rearing of their grandchildren.

Faber, A., & Mazlish, E. *How to talk so kids will listen and listen so kids will talk.* New York: Avon, 1982.

Two mothers who studied with Haim Ginott continue his emphasis on effective communication.

Fisher, J. J. *Johnson & Johnson. From baby to toddler.* New York: Putnam, 1988.

The young child's development is described month by month. Discipline, safety, separation anxiety, development of individuality, and sleep problems are discussed.

Fraiberg, S. H. *The magic years: Understanding and handling problems of early childhood.* New York: Scribner's, 1984.

This book concentrates on infancy through 6 years of age. Emotional issues that arise during this period are discussed in an easily read and understandable manner. Issues include imagination, reality, sex education, and development of a conscience. Fraiberg's book is an excellent classic book to recommend to parents.

Gerber Library. *500 questions new parents ask.* New York: Dell, 1982.

As the title states, the book covers typical questions that parents will ask.

Ginott, H. G. *Between parent and child.* New York: Avon, 1976.

Ginott emphasizes reflective listening and open communication lines as necessary ingredients to productive child-parent relationships. Ginott's message is still clear, years after his death: learn to listen to your child, and respond accordingly.

_____. *Between parent and teen-ager.* New York: Avon, 1982.

The author writes in a style that promotes understanding on the part of parent and teenager. Communication that is open establishes an understanding that allows parent and teenager to develop a process of cooperation and/or coping behavior.

_____. *Teacher & child.* New York: Avon, 1976.

Ginott's excellent book helps teachers effect positive student teacher relationships.

Gordon, I. J. *Baby learning through baby play.* New York: St. Martin's Press, 1970.

This book is restricted to infancy through toddlerhood. Games and activities for parents to use with their infants are described. The author recommends that the activities be enjoyed by both parents and child. Gordon also has a similar book on toddlers.

Kelly, J. *Solving your child's behavior problems.* Boston: Little, Brown, 1983.

Kelly advises parents on techniques for reducing unacceptable behavior in young children. Praise and encouragement are suggested with easy-to-follow directions that help parents implement behavior modification.

Leach, P. *The child care encyclopedia: A parents' guide to the physical and emotional well-being of children from birth to adolescence.* New York: Knopf, 1984.

Leach covers the entire span of the child's life, from birth to adolescence, and discusses the emotional as well as the physical well-being of the child.

_____. *The first six months: Getting together with your baby.* New York: Knopf, 1987.

New parents have so many questions about their first child. This book helps answer those questions and supports the new and experienced parent.

_____. *Your baby and child.* New York: Knopf, 1978.

The book discusses the stages of development in young children, birth to 5 years of age. She gives very clear and specific guidance about questions related to children. It has proved to be a most helpful and popular book for new parents.

Metzger, M., & Whittaker, C. P. *Childproofing checklist: A parents guide to accident prevention.* New York: Doubleday, 1988.

If you use this book, you will be aware of the pitfalls that await your child.

Neifert, M. E. *Dr. Mom.* New York: New American Library, 1987.

Dr. Mom is a practical, comprehensive book written by an M.D. on day-to-day child rearing. A section on childhood illnesses is included.

Pearce, J. C. *Magical child.* New York: Bantam, 1981.

The author looks at the child's life from the child's point of view, beginning with the birthing process. He examines the child's rights and needs and discusses how a child feels and reacts to life's experiences.

Salk, L. *Preparing for parenthood.* New York: Bantam Books, 1980.

Salk's book for new parents clarifies feelings about pregnancy, childbirth, and new babies.

_____. *The complete Dr. Salk: An A–Z guide to raising your child.* New York: New American Library, 1985.

Dr. Salk's titles describe his intent. This book covers the points that he feels are essential in raising a healthy child.

_____. *What every child would like his parent to know to help him with emotional problems of everyday life.* New York: Simon & Schuster, 1984.

This title sets the tone for this readable book in which Salk discusses how parents can help their children develop emotional health.

Schmitt, B. D. *Your child's health: A pediatric guide for parents.* New York: Bantam, 1987.

Dr. Schmitt concentrates on the child's health including emergencies, trauma, behavior problems, medicines, immunization, and common illnesses of the newborn.

Spock, B. *Dr. Spock on parenting.* New York: Pocket Books, 1988.

Dr. Spock discusses the anxieties of parenthood—the new baby, being a father, discipline, stages of childhood, and difficult relationships.

_____. *Dr. Spock talks with mothers.* Westport, Conn.: Greenwood Press, 1982.

There is material in this book that is easily understood and relevant to questions parents ask. This type of book helps parent groups in the search for answers to specific problems. It can be used as a discussion starter.

_____. *Problems of parents.* Westport, Conn.: Greenwood, 1979.

Another book by Spock addresses itself to problems of childrearing.

_____. *Raising children in a difficult time* (rev. ed.). New York: W. W. Norton, 1985.

Spock responded to the troubled times of the 1960s and 1970s with a book that helps parents with difficult decisions. Included are control of children, adolescence and rebellion, sex education, drugs, divorce, and discussion of families and family values.

Spock, B., & Rothenberg, M. B. *Baby and child care.* New York: Pocket Books, 1985.

Spock's classic on childrearing covers everything from health to discipline. It became a best seller because it is an excellent book to answer parents questions about health as well as child care.

Swick, K., & Duff, R. E. *Involving children in parenting-caring experiences.* Dubuque, Iowa: Kendall/Hunt Publishing Co., 1982.

Swick and Duff's pleasant book brings out the importance of a caring and sharing relationship.

Turecki, S., & Tonner, L. *The difficult child.* New York: Bantam, 1985.

Turecki and Tonner focus on understanding the child's behavior. Even though Turecki is a child psychiatrist, he experienced the problems of raising a difficult child, so the book is based on both professional training and life experiences. Brazelton endorses the book as a real contribution to parents.

U.S. Department of Health and Human Services. Washington, D.C.: U.S. Government Printing Office.

Send for the most recent publication list from the government and order a series of booklets on childrearing. Include these in your resource library for parents. The booklets are written in a clear and concise style.

> *Infant care/elcuidado el su bebe*
> *Prenatal care*
> *Your child from 1 to 6*
> *Your child from 1 to 3*
> *Your child from 6 to 12*
> *Your child from 3 to 4*

Wessel, M. A. *Parents book for raising a healthy child.* New York: Ballantine Books, 1987.

This is a comprehensive book on early parenting with a strong emphasis on health and illnesses.

White, B. L. *The first three years of life.* Englewood Cliffs, N.J.: Prentice-Hall, 1985.

White divides the first 36 months into seven developmental stages. Within each stage he gives a comprehensive discussion of intellectual, emotional, and physical development. The book also includes advice on childrearing based on social learning theory and appropriate toys and materials that enrich the child's world.

Zimbardo, P., and Radl, S. *The shy child.* New York: McGraw-Hill, 1981.

The authors discuss the parenting style that encourages self-confidence in a child. Based on the causes of shyness, the book provides methods to help build the child's self-esteem and reduce shyness.

FAMILY—RAISING CHILDREN IN THE UNITED STATES

Ashery, R., & Basen, M. *Guide for parents with careers.* Washington, D.C.: Acropolis Books, 1986.

The author gives a guide, advice, and worksheets to help parents manage the concerns of handling a job and taking care of their family at the same time.

Bradshaw, J. *Bradshaw on the family.* Deerfield Beach, Fla.: Health Communications, Inc. 1988.

Based on a television series by the same title, Bradshaw describes in more depth the concepts he presents in the series. He discusses the family as a rule-bound system, identifies dysfunctions within the family, and suggests ways to improve the functioning of the family.

Brazelton, T. B. *Working and caring.* Reading, Mass.: Addison-Wesley Publishing Company, Inc., 1987.

Dr. Brazelton, a pediatrician, used case studies to develop the issues of working and still caring for children. The juggling of work and child care is difficult, but Brazelton tries to help parents with the problems of doing both.

Building Family Strengths Project. *Building Family Strengths.* Lincoln: University of Nebraska, 1986.

The University of Nebraska Building Family Strengths Project developed a program based on family research that focuses on strengths instead of weaknesses. A trainer's manual, a facilitator's manual, and activity cards are available for use in training sessions. A series of books, compiled from conferences of the same name, are also available.

Children's Defense Fund. *A vision for America's future.* Washington, D.C.: Author, 1989.

This is but one of numerous publications put out by the Children's Defense Fund that analyzes the position of children and their families in the United States. The information is updated regularly, and the source is valuable for those working in and advocating for children's services.

Curran, D. *Stress and the healthy family.* Minneapolis: Winston Press, 1985.

Curran followed her book on traits of a healthy family with one that concerns stress. In healthy families, couples try to find solutions; in "less communicative couples" blame is placed on someone else. She suggests ways that families can live together, working toward relating and relaxing rather than driving for economic success. "More marriages suffer from disagreement on how to spend money than on insufficient money, from loss of communication than loss of health, and from overscheduled calendars than an extramarital affair."

_____. *Traits of a healthy family.* Minneapolis: Winston Press, 1983.

This book has become a best seller. It focuses on the strengths of the family, listing and discussing 15 traits that healthy families have. Parent groups enjoy discussing this material.

Galinsky, E. *The six stages of parenthood.* Reading, Mass.: Addison-Wesley, 1987.

Galinsky divides parenthood into six stages commencing prior to the birth of a child through departure of the child from the home. Parenthood has stages just as children have stages of development. They are (1) image-making stage, when images are formed and preparations made before the birth; (2) nurturing, the period of infancy and attachment; (3) authority; (4) interpretive, preschool to adolescence; (5) interdependent, teen years; and (6) departure.

Macchiarola, F. J., & Gartner, A. *Caring for America's children.* New York: The Academy of Political Science, 1989.

Emerging concerns about the welfare of the children in our society are addressed by the contributors in this book. Public policy, schools, and the future of children in our society are discussed.

Schorr, L. B., & Schorr, D. *Within our reach: Breaking the cycle of disadvantage and despair.* New York: Doubleday, 1988.

The Schorrs' interesting book is filled with examples of at-risk children who have been touched by programs that can help. Their thesis is that the children can achieve and become productive adults when given help to break the bondage of poverty and disadvantage.

Swick, K. *Involving children in parenting/caring experiences.* Dubuque, Iowa: Kendall/Hunt Publishing Company, 1982.

Swick has written a number of books that relate to children, families, and society. Check for his other books as well as this. He writes with an easy style and the book could be used with parent groups.

THE STEPPARENT

Burns, C. *Stepmotherhood: How to survive without feeling frustrated, left out, or wicked.* New York: Harper & Row, 1985.

This book recognizes the concerns of the stepmother and points out ways to cope with adapting to a new family.

Gardner, R. A. *The boys and girls book about stepfamilies.* Cresskill, N.J.: Creative Therapeutics, 1985.

Moving into a stepfamily is a difficult transition for children. This book deals with their concerns.

Visher, E. B., & Visher, J. S. *How to win as a stepfamily.* Chicago: Contemporary Books, 1983.

The Vishers, recognized authorities on stepparenting, write about positive methods to use to have a winning stepfamily.

_____. *Old loyalties, new ties: Therapeutic strategies with stepfamilies.* New York: Brunner/Mazel, 1988.

Written for both therapists and stepfamilies, the Vishers' book presents an overview of stepfamily research and intervention methods, followed by chapters focused on the difficulties stepfamilies have in integrating and establishing their identity.

DISCIPLINE—BEHAVIOR OR MISBEHAVIOR

Association for Childhood Education International. *Toward self-discipline: A guide for parents and educators.* Wheaton, Md.: Author, 1981.

This 49-page booklet gives the pointers on effective discipline.

Bettleheim, B. *A good enough parent: A book on childrearing.* New York: Knopf, 1987.

Bettleheim, a psychoanalytical theorist, wrote this book based on the emotional needs of the child.

Brenner, B. *Love and discipline.* New York: Ballantine Books, 1983.

Brenner looks at discipline as an opportunity for children to acquire self-discipline. She looks at the environment that affects the child—parenting styles of parents, the child, and the development of boundaries.

Cherry, C. *Please don't sit on the kids: Alternatives to punitive discipline.* Belmont, Calif.: Pitman Learning, 1982.

Cherry, author of many excellent children's books, talks about discipline. She offers workable alternatives to punitive discipline.

Dodson, F. *How to discipline with love.* New York: New American Library, 1987.

This was recommended by parents who felt it was very helpful to them.

Dreikurs, R. *Discipline without tears.* New York: Dutton, 1974.

Dreikurs uses a system of consequences based on Adlerian psychology with the result that children become responsible for their actions. Logical and natural consequences related to children's behavior form a basis for discipline and guidance.

Dreikurs, R., & Soltz, V. *Children: The challenge.* New York: Dutton, 1987.

The four goals of misbehavior, attention, power, revenge, and inadequacy are discussed, as are the use of consequences. His book supports parents in their development of guidelines for children's behavior.

Krumboltz, J. D., & Krumboltz, H. B. *Changing children's behavior.* Englewood Cliffs, N.J.: Prentice-Hall, 1972.

Guides parents and teachers in the process of changing the child's behavior. Many examples of behavior and misbehavior are used as illustrations.

Nelsen, J. *Positive Discipline.* New York: Ballantine Books, 1987.

Nelsen's step-by-step approach, for both parents and teachers, combines the best of Adler, Dreikurs, and other knowledge about how to promote children's long-term development. She focuses on self-discipline, responsibility, and cooperation. Her recommendations are both sensible and sensitive, and she raises many thought-provoking questions.

Samalin, N., & Jablow, M. M. *Loving your child is not enough: Positive discipline that works.* New York: Penguin Books, 1987.

This is an easily read book that starts with suggestions on how to avoid battles and goes on to discuss positive and consistent guidelines to deal with discipline issues.

Simon, S. B., & Olds, S. W. *Helping your child learn right from wrong: A guide to values clarification.* New York: McGraw-Hill, 1977.

Values clarification and understanding one's own motives and attitudes helps in the development of responsibility. Children learn to examine problem solving and develop their own system of values.

Wyckoff, J., & Unell, B. C. *Discipline without shouting or spanking.* Deerhaven, Minn.: Meadowbrook, 1984.

This small book gives specific responses to common behavior problems during the preschool years.

FATHERS

Dodson, F. *How to father.* New York: Signet Books, 1975.

Dodson, who wrote *How to Parent* in 1970, added this publication in order to cover the father's role more adequately. Practical material on fathering and information on older children are included in this book.

Greenberg, M. *The birth of a father.* New York: Continuum, 1985.

Greenberg based his book on his own experience at fatherhood as well as studies on parenthood. He encourages fathers to get involved with their children.

Lamb, M. E. (Ed.) *The father's role.* Hillsdale, New Jersey: Lawrence Erlbaum Associates, 1987.

Contributors to this book looked at the history of fatherhood, and encouraged that fathers should take more responsibility for parenthood.

_____. (Ed.). *The role of the father in child development* (2nd ed.). New York: Wiley, 1981.

Based on research and studies on children, articles were selected from many authorities in the field. They conclude that fathers are important to the psychological development of children.

Pruett, K. D. *The nurturing father.* New York: Warner Books, 1987.

As the title suggests, Pruett looks at the nurturing role that a father can develop as a parent. Fathers can play an important part in their children's development.

DIVORCE AND THE SINGLE PARENT

Arnold, W. V., Baird, D. M., Langan, J. T., & Vaughn, E. G. *Divorce: Prevention or survival.* New York: Westminster, 1977.

This small book discusses ways to thoroughly examine options before divorce. Suggestions are also offered for those who are divorced.

Atkin, E., & Rubin, E. *Part-time father.* New York: Vanguard, 1977.

The book discusses the uprootings and upheavals involved in divorce from the father's perspective. Included are sections on the basics of divorce, new lives and remarriage, and fathers with their sons and daughters.

Atlas, S. L. *Single parenting.* Englewood Cliffs, N.J.: Prentice-Hall, 1981.

This book was written by a father who was first noncustodial parent and later a custodial parent of his children. Through the help of Parents Without Partners he was able to obtain information from other single parents. With this and his background, he wrote a book that shows that single-parent families can be healthy.

Baruth, L. G. *A single parent's survival guide: How to raise the children.* Dubuque, Iowa: Kendall-Hunt Publishing Co., 1979.

The title tells the story. Baruth gives tips on surviving a divorce and rearing children.

Bienefeld, F. *Helping your child succeed after divorce.* Claremont, Calif.: Hunter House Inc., 1987.

Bienefeld focuses on the problems children suffer as the result of a divorce. She points out concerns and ways in which parents can be supportive.

Cherlin, A. J. *Marriage, divorce, remarriage.* Cambridge, Mass.: Harvard University Press, 1981.

This book does not solve all the problems of divorce, but it analyzes the trends of families in the United States by discussing social change and social thought.

DeFrain, J. *On our own: A single parent's survival guide.* Lexington, Mass.: D. C. Heath and Company, 1987.

DeFrain, a family specialist, wrote this book to help the single parent cope.

Francke, L. B. *Growing up divorced.* New York: Fawcett Crest, 1983.

The author discusses the issues of growing up in a divorced family. She analyzes how divorce affects babies and toddlers; preschoolers, the age of guilt; 6 to 8, the age of sadness; 9 to 12, the age of anger; and teenagers, the age of false maturity.

Greif, C. L. *Single fathers.* Lexington, Mass.: Lexington Books, 1985.

Greif includes case studies and family profiles to describe the life of the single father, the family before the divorce, the divorce, custody, balancing work and childrearing, and relationships.

Greywolf, E. *The single mother's handbook.* New York: Quill, 1984.

Greywolf gives practical advice on handling all the issues of being a single parent—work, childrearing, time, and money.

Grollman, E. *Talking about divorce and separation.* Iowa City, Iowa: Beacon Press, 1976.

This book has an illustrated story that is to be read with the children. Written in an interesting style, it encourages dialogue between parent and child, and helps them share feelings about divorce.

Spilke, F. *What about the children?* New York: Crown Publishers, 1980.

Spilke wrote three books. This one is a divorced parent's handbook. The other two are for the children. *The Family that Changed* is a primer for the very young; *What About Me?* is a guide for young people.

Weiss, R. S. *Going it alone.* New York: Basic Books, 1979.

Weiss examines the social situation of the woman or man who is the custodial parent. He discusses how custodial parents can establish a new life in the community and also develop a satisfactory personal life for themselves and their children.

HEALTH AND NUTRITION

American Academy of Pediatrics, Committee on Nutrition. *Pediatric Nutrition Handbook.* Evanston, Ill.: Author, 1985.

American Academy of Pediatrics, Committee on School Health Staff. *School health: A guide for health professionals.* Evanston, Ill.: Author, 1987.

These references were produced by the academy and contain the knowledge and approved practices of that prestigious organization.

Baker, A., & Henry R. R. *Parent's guide to nutrition: Healthy eating from birth through adolescence.* Reading, Mass.: Addison-Wesley, 1986.

Designed for parents, this book relates social pressures on food selection, essential nutrients, and issues surrounding nutrition.

Boston Hospital Staff. *The new child health encyclopedia.* New York: Dell Books, 1987.

This encyclopedia is a comprehensive book that answers many of parents' common questions about illness, childhood diseases, and preventive health care.

Castle, S. *The complete guide to preparing baby foods at home.* Toronto: Bantam, 1983.

Parents may use this reference to help in preparation of food for infants.

———. *Nutrition for your child's most important years: Birth to age three.* New York: Simon & Schuster, 1984.

Castle has written an additional book on preparation and nutrition for the infant and toddler.

Davis, A. *Let's have healthy children* (rev. ed.). New York: New American Library, 1981.

Another book about nutrition by Adele Davis, but this one is written especially for children.

Endres, J. B., & Rockwell, R. E. *Food, nutrition, and the young child* (3rd ed.). Columbus, Ohio: Merrill, 1990.

This practical book examines nutrition and dietary guides and standards. It focuses on the role of nutrition in early childhood programs and provides basic concepts about food and nutrition, suggestions for menus, methods of interrelating curriculum, basic nutrient concepts, and suggestions for working with parents.

Feingold, B. F. *Why your child is hyperactive.* New York: Random House, 1985.

Although parent groups must keep in mind the controversies surrounding Feingold's theories, they might also like to discuss his ideas about food and hyperactivity.

Green, M. I. *A sigh of relief: First aid handbook for childhood emergencies* (rev. ed.). New York: Bantam Books, 1984.

This handbook gives needed information on first aid; good for everyday care and emergencies.

Reuben, D. *Everything you always wanted to know about nutrition.* New York: Avon Books, 1979.

In a question-answer format, Reuben discusses many of the controversial concerns about nutrition—vitamins, fats, carbohydrates, proteins, minerals, and sugar.

Salk, L. *Dear Dr. Salk: Answers to your questions about your family.* New York: Warner Books, 1980.

Dr. Salk uses a question-answer format to inform parents about their children's health and development needs.

Samuels, M., & Samuels, N. *The well child book.* New York: Summit Books, 1982.

———. *The well pregnancy book.* New York: Summit Books, 1985.

The Well Child Book, a popular book on health and staying well, was followed by *The Well Pregnancy Book.*

Smith, L. *Feed your kids right.* New York: Dell Books, 1981.

Smith, a pediatrician, writes for parents about nutrition and preventive diets. He includes the nutrient connection, allergies, metabolism, and energy in his easily read discussions.

U.S. Department of Health and Human Services and U.S. Department of Education furnish many booklets concerning health and nutrition. Write to the Consumer Information Center, Pueblo, CO 81009 for a copy of the Consumer Information Catalog. Educators, libraries, consumers, and other nonprofit groups who wish to receive 25 copies of their quarterly catalog on consumer information may get on the mailing list. Articles and booklets cover information from 30 agencies of the federal government. More than half of these articles are free. The following reference is typical of the offerings.

Nutritive value of food. Pueblo, Colo.: Consumer Information Center, 1985.

A guide to better diet with information about the nutritive value of 900 foods, calories, and nutritional information.

CHILD ABUSE

Sexual Abuse

Adams, C., & Fay, J. *No more secrets: Protecting your child from sexual assault.* San Luis Obispo, Calif.: Impact Publishers, 1981.

Parents have found this to be a valuable book because it offers an approach to use in the prevention of the sexual abuse of their children.

Committee for Children. *Prevention of child abuse. A trainer's manual.* Seattle: Committee for Children, 1984.

Committee for Children is a nonprofit organization designed to provide training and information that will help reduce violence against children. It has developed training material that gives a complete list of available resources, in-service training, preventive education, identification, and reporting. Two curricula, *Talking about Touching* and *Talking about Touching with Preschoolers,* use laminated photographs and accompanying lessons to teach children how to handle situations. Information may be obtained by writing Committee for Children, 172 20th Avenue, Seattle, WA 98122.

Finkelhor, D. *A sourcebook on child sexual abuse.* Beverly Hills, Calif.: Sage Publications, 1986.

This is a thorough and well-documented book on sexual abuse of children.

Hagans, K. B., & Case, J. *When your child has been molested: A parent's guide to healing and recovery.* Lexington, Mass.: Lexington Books, 1988.

The title tells the intent of this book. Children who have been abused need help to recover.

Herman, J. L. *Father-daughter incest.* Cambridge, Mass.: Harvard University Press, 1981.

This book analyzes the sexual abuse problem based on clinical experience with incest victims.

Kempe, C. H., & Kempe, R. *The common secret: Sexual abuse of children and adolescents.* New York: W. H. Freeman, 1984.

This book, by the Kempes, is written in an easy to read style utilizing case studies. It includes definitions, legal aspects, evaluation, and treatment of incest and extrafamilial abuse. Its appendix gives data collection forms and descriptions to use in working with child sexual abuse.

Kent, C. *Child sexual abuse prevention project: An educational program for children.* Minneapolis: Sexual Assault Services, n.d.

A program entitled *Child Sexual Abuse Prevention Project: An Educational Program for Children* was tested on 800 children in the Minneapolis public schools. The training manual is available from Sexual Assault Services, Hennepin County Attorney's Office, C-2100 Government Center, Minneapolis, MN 55487.

Kraizer, S. K. *The safe child book.* New York: Health Education Systems, 1985.

The author has developed a training program, *Children Need to Know,* that has been presented to thousands of children and was featured in the television program, *Saying No to Strangers.* This program can be obtained by writing P.O. Box 1235, New York, NY 10116.

May, G. *Understanding sexual child abuse.* Chicago: National Committee for Prevention of Child Abuse, 1979.

This book describes the offender and the victim. It also describes the various types of abuse that may be perpetrated against a child.

U.S. Department of Health and Human Services (Office of Human Development Services, Administration for

Children, Youth and Families, Children's Bureau, Clearinghouse on Child Abuse and Neglect). *Child sexual abuse: Incest, assault and sexual exploitation.* Washington, D.C.: U.S. Government Printing Office, 1981.

This government publication provides an overview of techniques for prevention and treatment of sexual abuse on children.

Physical Abuse and Neglect Resources

American Humane Association. *National analysis of official child neglect and abuse reporting.* Denver, Colo.: American Humane Association, 1989.

Each year the American Humane Association publishes a report of the incidence of reported child abuse cases in the United States.

Antler, S. (Ed.). *Child abuse and child protection; Policy and practice.* Silver Spring, Md.: National Association of Social Workers, 1982.

This book, published by social workers, contains a series of articles pertaining to child abuse, ranging from the definition of the problem to strategies for dealing with the violence. It discusses treating the abused and the abuser as well as protecting the child protective worker.

Ebeling, N. B., & Hill, D. A. (Eds.). *Child abuse and neglect.* Littleton, Mass.: John Write PSG, 1983.

This book is intended for social workers and those who give service to families. Written by professionals from the Boston area and the British Isles, it covers a wide range of information from home visits to assessment and treatment. It includes case studies, treatment of the child, and integration of individual and family therapy.

Fontana, V. J. *Somewhere a child is crying: Maltreatment—causes and prevention.* New York: New American Library, 1976.

Fontana has written several excellent books on the subject of child abuse. They give good background information.

Green, M. R. (Ed.). *Violence and the family.* Boulder, Colo.: Westview Press, 1981.

The American Association for the Advancement of Science held a symposium on which this book was based. It includes material that is not found in other texts such as television viewing, family style, and cultural differences.

Kempe, C. H., & Helfer, R. E. (Eds.). *The battered child* (3rd rev. enlarged ed.). Chicago: University of Chicago Press, 1982.

Kempe and Helfer were early pioneers in the field of child abuse. Their books are excellent references.

Newberger, E. H. (Ed.). *Child abuse*. Boston: Little, Brown, 1982.

Newberger selected 14 professionals to write chapters for this book on child abuse. The information ranges from the social context of child abuse to principles and ethics of practice. Information based on medical expertise is included.

U.S. Department of Health and Human Services (Office of Human Development Services, Administration for Children, Youth and Families, Children's Bureau, Clearinghouse on Child Abuse and Neglect). *A curriculum on child abuse and neglect.*

Leader's manual. Washington, D.C.: U.S. Government Printing Office, 1979.

The U.S. Government Printing Office has published an enormous amount of excellent materials on child abuse and neglect. This leader's manual is a comprehensive text on teaching others about child abuse and neglect.

U.S. Department of Health and Human Services (Office of Human Development Services, Administration for Children, Youth and Families, Head Start Bureau). *Child abuse and neglect: A self-instructional text for Head Start personnel.* Washington, D.C.: U.S. Government Printing Office, 1980.

This self-instructional text is excellent to use with anyone who works in a child care center or school. It is easily used, self-correcting, and easily read.

Centers and Associations Concerned with Child Abuse

American Humane Association
9725 East Hampden Avenue
Denver, CO 80231

C. Henry Kempe National Center for Prevention and Treatment of Child Abuse and Neglect
1205 Oneida
Denver, CO 80220

Clearinghouse on Child Abuse and Neglect
Children's Bureau, ACYF
Department of Health and Human Services
P.O. Box 1182
Washington, DC 20013

National Coalition Against Domestic Violence
1500 Massachusetts Avenue, N.W. #35
Washington, DC 20005

National Committee for Prevention of Child Abuse
332 South Michigan Avenue, Suite 1250
Chicago, IL 60604

NCCAN Child Abuse Clearinghouse
Aspen Systems
1600 Research Boulevard
Rockville, MD 20850

Parents Anonymous
7120 Franklin Avenue
Los Angeles, CA 90046

PUBLICATION SOURCES FROM ORGANIZATIONS AND AGENCIES ON CHILDREARING AND PARENT EDUCATION

The following organizations and governmental agencies publish periodicals, pamphlets, and booklets that can be used for a parent resource center. Articles range from prenatal care to adolescent motherhood. Write to them for current publications lists. The addresses listed here were current at the time of publication. For changes in addresses check the Encyclopedia of Associations found in the public library.

Alexander Graham Bell Association for the Deaf
3417 Volta Place
Washington, DC 20007

American Academy of Child Psychiatry
3615 Wisconsin Avenue, N.W.
Washington, DC 20016

American Academy of Pediatrics
P.O. Box 927
141 Northwest Point Road
Elk Grove Village, IL 60007

American Alliance for Health, Physical Education, Recreation, and Dance
1900 Association Drive
Reston, VA 22091

American Association for Adult and Continuing Education
1112 16th St. N.W., Suite 420
Washington, DC 20036

American Association of Psychiatric Services for Children
1133 15th St. N.W., Suite 1000
Washington, DC 20005

American Foundation for the Blind
15 West Sixteenth Street
New York, NY 10011

American Home Economics Association
2010 Massachusetts Avenue, N.W.
Washington, DC 20036

American Humane Association
9725 East Hampden Avenue
Denver, CO 80231

American Library Association
50 East Huron Street
Chicago, IL 60611

American Montessori Society
175 Fifth Ave.
New York, NY 10010

American Society for Deaf Children
814 Thayer Avenue
Silver Spring, MD 20910

American Speech-Language-Hearing Association
10801 Rockville Place
Rockville, MD 20852

Appalachia Educational Laboratory, Inc.
P.O. Box 1348
Charleston, WV 25325

Association for Childhood Education International
11141 Georgia Avenue, Suite 200
Wheaton, MD 20902

Association for Children and Adults with Learning Disabilities
4156 Library Road
Pittsburgh, PA 15234

Association for Retarded Citizens
P.O. Box 6109
Arlington, TX 76011

C. Henry Kempe National Center for Prevention and Treatment of Child Abuse and Neglect
1205 Oneida
Denver, CO 80220

Child Welfare League of America
440 First Street, N.W.
Washington, DC 20001

Children's Defense Fund
122 C Street, N.W.
Washington, DC 20001

Clearinghouse on Child Abuse and Neglect Information
P.O. Box 1182
Washington, DC 20013

Closer Look
P.O. Box 1492
Washington, DC 20036

Council for Basic Education
725 Fifteenth Street, N.W.
Washington, DC 20005

Council for Exceptional Children
1920 Association Drive
Reston, VA 22091

Council on Interracial Books for Children
1841 Broadway Room 500
New York, NY 10023

Department of Education
400 Maryland Avenue, S.W.
Washington, DC 20202

Education Commission of the States
300 Lincoln Tower Bldg.
1860 Lincoln Street
Denver, CO 80295

Educational Resources Information Center/Elementary and Early Childhood Education (ERIC/EECE)
805 W. Pennsylvania Avenue
Urbana, IL 61801-4897

EPIE Institute
P.O. Box 839
Water Mill, NY 11976

Families in Action Drug Information Center
3845 North Druid Hills Road, Suite 300
Decatur, Georgia 30033

Family Resource Coalition
230 North Michigan Avenue, Room 1625
Chicago, IL 60601

Family Service Association of America
44 East Twenty-third Street
New York, NY 10010

High/Scope Educational Research Foundation
600 North River Street
Ypsilanti, MI 48197

Home and School Institute
1201 Sixteenth Street, N.W.
Washington, DC 20036

Institute for Responsive Education
605 Commonwealth Avenue
Boston, MA 02215

International Reading Association
P.O. Box 8139
800 Barksdale Road
Newark, DE 19714

La Leche League International
9616 Minneapolis Avenue
Franklin Park, IL 60131

Mental Health Materials Center
Nine Willow Circle
Bronxville, NY 10708

National Association for Hearing and Speech Action
10801 Rockville Place
Rockville, MD 20852

National Association for Mental Health
1800 North Kent Street
Arlington, VA 22209

National Association for the Education of Young Children
1834 Connecticut Avenue, N.W.
Washington, DC 20009-5786

National Black Child Development Institute
1463 Rhode Island Avenue, N.W.
Washington, DC 20005

National Committee for Citizens in Education (NCCE)
10840 Little Patuxent Parkway, Suite 301
Columbia, MD 21044

National Committee for Prevention of Child Abuse
332 South Michigan Avenue, Suite 950
Chicago, IL 60604

National Congress of Parents and Teachers
700 North Rush Street
Chicago, IL 60611

National Council on Family Relations
3989 Central Avenue N.E., Suite 550
Minneapolis, MN 55421

National Education Association
1201 16th Street, N.W.
Washington, DC 20036

National Institute of Mental Health
5600 Fishers Lane
Rockville, MD 20857

National Institute on Drug Abuse
5600 Fishers Lane
Rockville, MD 20857

National Institutes of Health
9000 Rockville Pike
Bethesda, MD 20205

National Maternal and Child Health Clearinghouse
38th and R Streets, N.W.
Washington, DC 20057

National Mental Health Association
1021 Prince Street
Arlington, VA 22314

National School Boards Association
1680 Duke Street
Alexandria, VA 22314

National School Volunteer Program
16 Arlington Street
Boston, MA 02116

Pacer Center Inc. (handicapped child's education)
Parent Advocacy Coalition for Educational Rights
4826 Chicago Avenue South
Minneapolis, MN 55417

Public Affairs Committee
381 Park Avenue South
New York, NY 10016-8884

Science Research Associates
259 East Erie Street
Chicago, IL 60611

Southwest Educational Development Laboratory
211 East Seventh Street
Austin, TX 78701

Stepfamily Association of America
602 East Joppa Road
Baltimore, MD 21204

Stepfamily Foundation
333 West End Avenue
New York, NY 10023

Superintendent of Documents
U.S. Government Printing Office
Washington, DC 20402

Check the Children's Bureau, Administration for Children, Youth and Families, Department of Health and Human Services, and the Department of Education for publication lists pertaining to children and families.

Sample Materials from Publication Sources

The American Humane Association
9725 Hampden Avenue
Denver, CO 80231

Guidelines for schools. This leaflet is available for schools and agencies to use in the identification of child abuse. Indicators include the child's behaviors, child's appearance, and parental attitudes. (L-5)

Neglecting parents. A study of psychosocial characteristics of neglecting parents by M. Cohen, R. Mulford, and E. Philbrick identifies problem characteristics. (No. 37)

American Library Association
50 East Huron Street
Chicago, IL 60611

Information on everyday survival: What you need and where to get it (1976). A book crammed full of information compiled by P. Gotsick, S. Moore, S. Cotner, and J. Flanery, Appalachian Adult Education Center; it is included here because it gives much information that would be helpful to a parent education program.

Association for Childhood Education International
11141 Georgia Avenue, Suite 200
Wheaton, MD 20902

Bibliography of books for children (1983). Titles of books arranged by subject and age level; annotated; excellent reference.

Children and stress: Helping children cope (1982). Articles by psychologists that discuss the internal and external factors that cause stress. Edited by A. S. McNamee.

Children and TV two: Mediating the medium (1982). Recommends the use of TV for education purposes. Written by M. P. Winick and J. S. Wehrenberg.

Children's Defense Fund
122 C Street, N.W.
Washington, DC 20001

The health of America's children: Maternal and child health data book (1989). This book reviews the health of all children in the United States. Prenatal care, infant mortality, and low birthweights are examined by race and state data.

The health of America's black children (1988). Many factors influence the health of black children. Infant and maternal mortality, immunization, prenatal care, low birthweight, and other concerns are examined.

State child care fact book (1988). The Children's Defense Fund publishes state-by-state child care surveys that show the funding levels and offerings in each state.

Public Affairs Committee
381 Park Avenue South
New York, NY 10016-8884

Children and drugs (1980). Jules Sugarman describes the characteristics of marijuana, angel dust, acid, amphetamines, cocaine, and narcotics and identifies their effects.

Schools and parents (1980). Sol Gordon describes a sex education program for schools. He emphasizes that parent involvement is necessary for an effective program.

National Association for Mental Health
1800 North Kent Street
Arlington, VA 22209

Child alone in need of help. This pamphlet describes the mentally ill child, the kind of help available, and where to find it.

Depression: Dark night of the soul. This 20-page booklet describes depression, its origin, its symptoms, and its treatment.

How to deal with your tensions. This pamphlet, part of the *Learning to Cope* film package, suggests 11 ways to deal with tension. It helps people recognize when life situations have assumed crisis proportion and gives guidance on how to obtain professional help.

National Association for the Education of Young Children
1834 Connecticut Avenue, N.W.
Washington, DC 20009-5786

Families and early childhood programs (1989). D.R. Powell gives a review of the rationale for home-school involvement.

Emerging literacy: Young children learn to read and write (1989). D. S. Strickland & L. M. Morrow (Eds.) present information on how children learn to read and write; an International Reading Association offering.

Developmentally appropriate practice in early childhood programs serving children from birth through age 8 (1987). S. Bredekamp (Ed.) gives NAEYC's position on appropriate educational practices for young children.

How to choose a good early childhood program (1986). Outlines the basics to look for in selecting a program.

National Council on Family Relations
3989 Central Avenue, N.E., Suite 550
Minneapolis, MN 55421

A journal published by NCFR, *Family Relations* has published issues on stepfamilies, remarriage, stepchildren, stepgrandparents, and AIDS and the family.

MAGAZINES AND JOURNALS

Magazines and journals are important because they contain relevant and up-to-date information. Most of the following journals and magazines can be found in public libraries. Some are journals published by professional organizations; others are published by companies. They may be delivered to your home by subscribing or by belonging to the professional organization that publishes them.

Black Child Advocate
National Black Child Development Institute
1463 Rhode Island Avenue, N.W.
Washington, DC 20005

Concerned primarily with issues of public policy related to black children, this monthly magazine also includes articles on curriculum and other subjects related to the development of the black child.

Building Blocks
Box 31
Dundee, IL 60118

Building Blocks is a newspaper for parents and their young children. It is filled with activities for them to do together.

Child Care Information Exchange
P.O. Box 2890
Redmond, WA 98073

This magazine focuses on the concerns and issues that affect directors of child care centers.

Child Care: The Management Magazine
Cara Communications Ltd.
100 Court Avenue, Suite 312
Des Moines, IA 50309

A new magazine designed to keep early childhood educators abreast of the latest developments in the field.

Child Care Quarterly
Behavioral Publications
72 Fifth Avenue
New York, NY 10011

Published four times a year, this publication discusses issues concerned with providing good child care.

Child Development
Society for Research in Child Development
University of Chicago Press
5801 Ellis Avenue
Chicago, IL 60637

This professional journal is concerned with research related to various topics in child development.

Childhood Education
Association for Childhood Education International
11141 Georgia Avenue, Suite 200
Wheaton, MD 20902

Assorted articles containing information on education of young children, materials, and activities that encourage optimal development in children are included. Many of the articles contain theory and educational philosophy.

Children Today
Children's Bureau
Administration for Children, Youth and Families
Office of Human Development
Superintendent of Documents
U.S. Government Printing Office
Washington, DC 20402

This government magazine includes a wide selection of articles on children, birth through adolescence. The articles range from mental health, education, child care, health, and handicapped to social services and crime prevention.

Child Welfare
Child Welfare League of America
440 First Street, N.W.
Washington, DC 20001

Contains both research and applied articles related to children and examines social services and policies as well as practical implementation of programs for children.

CIBC Bulletin
Council on Interracial Books for Children
1841 Broadway
New York, NY 10023

The *CIBC Bulletin* is concerned with abolishing sexism, racism, and other forms of discrimination in reading and learning materials.

Day Care & Early Education
Human Sciences Press, Inc.
72 Fifth Avenue
New York, NY 10011-8004

This magazine is designed especially for child care workers, preschool teachers, and others who work with young children. It includes articles, research reviews, and activities for young children.

Early Childhood Research Quarterly
Ablex Publishing Corporation
355 Chestnut Street
Norwood, NJ 07648

A joint venture between ERIC/EECE, NAEYC, and Ablex, this new research journal publishes recent research in early childhood education.

Exceptional Children
Council for Exceptional Children
1920 Association Drive
Reston, VA 22091

The journal for the Council for Exceptional Children contains articles related to special education and exceptional children. It provides information on materials, books, films, and legislation.

First Teacher
955 Connecticut Street
Bridgeport, CT 06607

First Teacher is printed in newspaper style. Each issue develops a theme and gives many practical suggestions for activities that parents can do with their young children.

Gifted Child Quarterly
National Association for Gifted Children
4175 Lovell Road, Suite 140
Box 30
Circle Pines, MN 55014

This is the journal for the National Association for Gifted Children. It is published quarterly, and focuses on various issues and research concerning gifted children and education.

High/Scope Resources
The High/Scope Press
600 North River Street
Ypsilanti, MI 48198

The High/Scope Educational Research Foundation publishes a newspaper that describes the most recent publications put out by High/Scope. It also includes articles and discussion of early childhood from a High/Scope position.

Journal of Research in Childhood Education
Association for Childhood Education International
11141 Georgia Avenue, Suite 200
Wheaton, MD 20902

A scholarly journal published twice a year to advance knowledge and theory of the education of children, infancy through early adolescence.

Learning: The Magazine for Creative Teaching
Education Today Company
530 University Avenue
Palo Alto, CA 94301

Learning includes many suggestions for implementing a creative learning environment in the school or home. It features a swap shop, ideas for learning centers, articles on innovations and strategies, and a potpourri of suggestions, concepts, and creative activities.

Lollipops
Good Apple, Inc.
P. O. Box 299
1204 Buchanan Street
Carthage, IL 62321-0299

Published five times a year, *Lollipops* includes ideas for the classroom or the home. Tear out units are included.

Pro-Education
5000 Park Street North
St. Petersburg, FL 33709

Pro-Education is a magazine about partnerships with education. It discusses issues concerning parents, schools, and organizations concerned with education. Articles cover a wide range of interests and contributors include the Education Commission of the States and the National Education Association.

The Single Parent
Parents Without Partners
7910 Woodmont Avenue, Suite 1000
Bethesda, MD 20812

Parents Without Partners publishes a journal concerned with special problems and issues confronting the single parent.

Teacher
Macmillan Professional Magazines
262 Mason Street
Greenwich, CT 06830

Teacher includes articles for all age groups and many features that are adaptable for all ages. Special departments include a creative calendar, book bonanza, television talk, early education workshop, and the creative classroom.

Young Children
National Association for the Education of Young Children
1834 Connecticut Avenue, N.W.
Washington, DC 20009-5786

In keeping with the organization's goals, NAEYC publishes *Young Children,* geared to teachers and parents of children from birth to 8 years. It includes a wide selection of articles related to childrearing, professional objectives, and education.

Children's Magazines

There are many magazines written for children as well as magazines that both children and adults enjoy. Barbara Hatcher annotated a comprehensive list of these magazines in the June 1987 issue of *Childhood Education,* pp. 393–404.

The Mailbox
The Education Center, Inc.
Box 9753
Greensboro, NC 27429

The Mailbox is a magazine with an edition for early childhood as well as one for elementary. Filled with practical ideas for teaching, it contains curriculum ideas, reproducible worksheets, bulletin board ideas, and games.

Pre-K Today
Scholastic Inc.
P.O. Box 513
Dalton, MA 01227-0513

Pre-K is a magazine about young children. Scholastic also publishes educational materials for students.

The Preschool Papers
T.S. Denison & Co., Inc.
9601 Newton Avenue, South
Minneapolis, MN 55431

The Preschool Papers is published 10 times a year. It includes a story, fine motor and art activities, gross motor, music, language, learning games, finger plays, and reproducible activity sheets.

LEARNING ACTIVITES FOR HOME AND SCHOOL

Adcock, D., & Segal, M. *Play together, grow together.* White Plains, NY: Mailman Family Press, 1983.

Anderson, S. S., & Honess, C. M. *Getting ready for school.* Glenview, Ill.: Scott, Foresman & Company, 1988.

_____. *Mathematics their way.* Menlo Park, Calif.: Addison-Wesley, 1989.

Baratta-Lorton, M. *Workjobs.* Menlo Park, Calif.: Addison-Wesley, 1988.

_____. *Workjobs for parents.* Menlo Park, Calif.: Addison-Wesley, 1987.

Baratta-Lorton, B., & Baratta-Lorton, M. *Baratta-Lorton Reading Program (Dekodiphukan).* Menlo Park, Calif.: Addison-Wesley, 1985.

Burtt, K. G., & Kalstein, K. *Smart toys.* New York: Harper & Row, 1981.

Canfield, J., & Wells, H. C. *100 ways to enhance self concepts in the classroom.* Englewood Cliffs, N. J.: Prentice-Hall, 1976.

Children's Television Workshop. *Parents' guide to raising kids who love to learn.* New York: Prentice-Hall, 1989.

Cole, A., Hass, C., Bushness, F., & Weinberger, B. *I saw a purple cow and 100 other recipes for learning.* Boston: Little, Brown, 1972.

Croft, D., & Hess, R. D. *An activities handbook for teachers of young children* (4th ed.). New York: Houghton Mifflin, 1984.

Derman-Sparks, L., and the A.B.C. Task Force. *Antibias curriculum: Tools for empowering young children.* Washington, D.C.: National Association for the Education of Young Children, 1989.

Feingold, I. R. *Teaching gems.* Kansas City, Missouri: Corporate Press, 1982.

Ferguson-Florissant School District. *Parents as first teachers.* Ferguson, Mo.: Author, 1985.

Fleming, B. M., Hamilton, D. S., & Hicks, J. D. *Resources for creative teaching in early childhood education.* New York: Harcourt Brace Jovanovich, 1977.

Forgan, H. S. *The reading corner.* Glenview, Ill.: Scott, Foresman, 1977.

Gordon, I. *Baby learning through baby play: A parent's guide for the first two years.* New York: St. Martin's Press, 1970.

Hendrick, J. *The whole child.* Columbus, Ohio: Merrill, 1988.

Honig, A. *Playtime learning games for young children.* Syracuse, N.Y.: Syracuse University Press, 1982.

Jenkins, P. D. *Art for the fun of it.* Englewood Cliffs, N.J.: Prentice-Hall, 1980.

Karnes, M. B. *Learning mathematical concepts at home.* Reston, Va.: Council for Exceptional Children, 1980.

_____. *Creative art for learning.* Reston, Va.: Council for Exceptional Children, 1979.

_____. *You and your small wonder: Book 1* and *Book 2.* New York: Random House, 1984.

Larrick, N. *A parents' guide to children's reading* (5th rev. ed.). Louisville, Ky.: Westminster John Knox, 1983.

Levy, J. *Baby exercise book: The first fifteen months.* New York: Pantheon, 1974.

Marzollo, J., & Lloyd, J. *Learning through play.* New York: Harper & Row, 1974.

Marzollo, J. *Supertot.* New York: Harper & Row, 1979.

Miller, K. *Things to do with toddlers and twos.* Marshfield, Mass.: Tellshare Publishing, 1984.

Orlick, T. *The cooperative sports and games book.* New York: Pantheon, 1975.

Parent-Child Early Education. *Parent-child home activities for threes, some fours. A curriculum on cards for kindergarten. Learning activities for fours and fives. Skill and concept activities for threes and fours.* Ferguson, Mo.: Ferguson-Florissant School District.

Rich, D. *Megaskills. How families help children succeed in school and beyond.* Boston: Houghton Mifflin, 1988.

Schminke, C. W. *Math activities for child involvement* (4th ed.). Austin, Tex.: Pro-Ed, 1985.

U.S. Department of Health and Human Services. Office of Human Development Services, Administration for Children, Youth and Families, Head Start Bureau. *Getting involved.* Washington, D.C.: U.S. Government Printing Office, 1981.

Wilmes, D., & Wilmes, L. *Circle time book* (1982), *Everyday circle times* (1983), *Felt board fun* (1984), *Parachute play* (1985). Elgin, Ill.: Building Blocks.

New Materials

There has been a wealth of new pamphlets and books developed in the last few years. These are distributed by publishers and distribution centers.

Good Apple
P.O. Box 299
1204 Buchanan St.
Carthage, IL 62321-0299

Good Apple has something for parents or teachers, preschool through junior high.

Gryphon House
3706 Otis Street, P.O. Box 275
Mt. Rainier, MD 20712

Gryphon House sends a resource catalog that lists the new books they distribute. There are home learning ideas galore!

Toys 'n Things Press
450 North Syndicate Avenue, Suite 5
St. Paul, MN 55104

Toys 'n Things Press, a division of Resources for Child Caring, supplies a catalog with learning activities books.

FILMS ON CHILD DEVELOPMENT AND PARENTING

Films are valuable sources of information and can serve as catalysts of discussion and questions. Many films are now available on videotape. Check on availability before ordering.

Modern Talking Picture Films

During the 1960s many films were developed for use by Head Start. These films were distributed on a free-loan basis through the libraries of the Modern Talking Picture Services to schools, child care centers, colleges, and other groups working with children. Some of these films may still be available for distribution, but MTP has stopped issuing them. At present MTP has the following films available. Write Modern Talking Picture Services or call 202-293-1222 for information on these films and a list of MTP distributors.

Becoming a Family
(Color, 25 minutes, MTP No. 16419)

This film portrays the way it feels for a couple to become parents for the first time. Through interviews with first-time parents the film probes the changes in lifestyle that occur after the birth of the first child.

Newborn
(Color, 28 minutes, MTP No. 20156)

The infant's world during the first 3 months of life is viewed through the eyes of the child. The film shows a first-time mother and father as they nurture their newborn.

The Special Journey
(Color, 22 minutes, MTP No. 16713)

Six women are portrayed. Their approaches to infant feeding, nutrition, and mother-child relationships illustrate their choices in making informed decisions regarding the rearing of their children.

Parents and Schools

Parent: Advocate or Adversary?
(Color, 55 minutes, Individual & Family Development Services, Inc.)

This video shows parents of five children who had a variety of special needs. It shows the "approach-avoidance dilemma" most parents face in their dealing with schools and their special children. IFDS also has two other videos on families and schools.

How Children Learn

Child's Play
(Color, 20 minutes, CRM Films)

This lovely film of multiethnic children involved in play explains the importance of play in a young child's life. It is narrated by Goldenson and Croft.

Development of the Child: Cognition
(Color, 30 minutes, Harper & Row)

Research into the way a child develops intellectually and the differences between the young child's cognitive development are shown.

Developmentally Appropriate Practice: Birth through Age 5
(Color, 27 minutes, National Association for the Education of Young Children)

This videotape points out both appropriate and inappropriate practices in early childhood.

Both the National Association for the Education of Young Children and the Association for Childhood Education International have videotapes of speakers at conferences as well as a variety of other videotapes.

Foundations of Reading and Writing
(Color, 26 minutes, Campus Films)

This beautiful film is an excellent means of illustrating to parents, teachers, and students that learning occurs while young children are involved in activities and play. Use it for parent meetings early in the school year to explain the early childhood curriculum. The film focuses on painting, building with blocks, clay modeling, and other activities that form a basis for reading and writing, eye-hand coordination, perceptional development, and coordination.

Good Talking with You
(Color, 30 minutes each, Educational Productions)

Five video tapes for adults who work with children to help them acquire language. Tapes cover language stimulation, conversation, child to child conversation, and environmental factors.

What Do You Think?
(Color, 32 minutes, Parents Magazine Films)

Dr. David Elkind explores the way children think with six children who reveal their concepts of the physical, moral, and religious world. This film clarifies and illustrates Piaget's three stages of cognitive development, for ages 4 to 11 years.

Parent-Child Relationships

Adapting to Parenthood
(Color, 20 minutes, Polymorph Films)

Focused on the new parent, this film can be used to bring forth discussions of parents' feelings.

Day One: A Positive Beginning for Parents and Their Infants
(Color, 30 minutes, New Horizons for Learning)

The video focuses on what babies can do and how they learn through all their senses. It offers parents ways to help their child develop.

Footsteps
(Color, 30 minutes, National Audio Visual Center)

The films and study guides (University Park Press, 233 East Redmond Street, Baltimore, MD 21202) were produced for public television. Footsteps is a complete curriculum on parenting. Five families were illustrated in the 20 films that discuss all aspects of family living, including identity, discipline, attachment, TV parenting styles, and 16 other topics.

Growing into Parenthood
(Color, 29 1/2 minutes, VIDA Health Communications)

This film shows four couples before the birth of their children. It addresses such issues as newborn behavior and the adaptation to new roles.

New Relations
(Color, 34 minutes, Fanlight Productions)

New Relations is about fathers and sons. It explores three generations of men and the issues of integrating parental responsibility, marital obligations, and career.

Nicholas and the Baby
(Color, 23 minutes, Centre Productions)

Nicholas is a 4-year-old boy whose mother is going to have a baby. The film follows the child and family through pregnancy, labor, birth, and the baby coming home.

On Being an Effective Parent
(Color, 45 minutes, American Personnel and Guidance Association)

If you are using Parent Effectiveness Training, you are aware of the program developed by Dr. Thomas Gordon. This film demonstrates Gordon's method of active listening and communication between parent and child.

Parent-Child Interaction: Child's Game
(Color, 24 minutes, Health Sciences Consortium)

Parents work on three basic skills: describing, praising, and ignoring. The first two reinforce good behavior and the third is used to diminish bad behavior. The film shows vignettes that illustrate the three skills. Health Sciences Consortium also has a follow-up film.

Parental Roles: Don and Mae
(Color, 25 minutes, Encyclopaedia Britannica Films)

The film was taken inside a home where a family is shown unable to communicate with one another. The parents are not able to reach their sons. After family counseling, the family's problems are left unresolved, ready for the audience's interpretations.

Parenting: Growing with Children
(Color, 22 minutes, Film Fair Communications)

The film describes four families: a young couple, a large family, working parents, and a single mother. It focuses on the responsibilities, rewards, and realities of parenting.

Step Parenting: New Families, Old Ties
(Color, 25 minutes, Polymorph Films)

This film is directed toward a large part of the population—the divorced and remarried. It deals with the problems and satisfactions of developing new relationships.

The Terrific Twos
(Color, 15 minutes, Professional Research)

Reassures parents about the need for children to become independent and suggests ways to handle the toddler without crushing the child's self-esteem.

2 AM Feedings
(Color, 24 minutes, New Day Films)

This film is for parents of infants. A diverse group of new parents relate their experiences with nursing, crying, colic, fathering, and returning to work.

What Every Baby Knows
(Color, Family Home Entertainment)

Four videotapes based on Brazelton's television series are available: (1) Most Common Questions about Newborns, Infants and Toddlers; (2) The Working Parent: Day Care, Separation and Your Child's Development; (3) A Guide to Pregnancy and Childbirth; and (4) On Being a Father.

Child Development

Cambridge Home Economics publishes a catalogue of videos and other media that are appropriate for parent education classes. Topics include child development, pregnancy, the newborn, and health concerns. Write for the publication at One Players Club Drive, Dept. HE3 Charleston, WV 25311.

The Child: Part I, The First Two Months
(Color, 29 minutes, CRM Films)
The Child: Part II, 2–14 Months
(Color, 28 minutes, CRM Films)
The Child: Part III, 12–24 Months
(Color, 29 minutes, CRM Films)
The Child: Part IV, Three Year Olds
(Color, 28 minutes, CRM Films)
The Child: Part V, Four to Six Years Old
(Color, 30 minutes, CRM Films)

These films are from the National Film Board of Canada series and are documentary style with emphasis on filming normal children and family action without elaborate narrative. Each film focuses on a time period within the life of the infant through the 6-year-old.

Development of the Child: Language
(Color, 24 minutes, Harper & Row)

This film explains the development of language in the child.

Development of Feelings in Children
(Color, 50 minutes, Parents Magazine Films)

The film examines the child's emotional makeup and illustrates how to cope with fear, love, joy, sadness, and anger as you interact with the child.

Emotional Development: Aggression
(Color, 19 minutes, CRM Films)

Aggression is studied from a social-learning viewpoint, learned primarily in a social context. It discusses the manner in which aggression is learned and how it can be changed.

In the Beginning
(Color, 15 minutes, Davidson Films)

This film examines early infant development and the stages of growth. It is narrated by Bettye Caldwell.

Individual Differences
(Color, 18 minutes, CRM Films)

The film examines individual differences and the wide variety of normal characteristics. Included is a discussion of the Denver Developmental Screening Test and the Gesell Infant test.

Infancy
(Color, 19 minutes, CRM Films)

An infant's abilities, innate and learned, are examined. As the child develops socialization skills, language, cognition, and motor abilities, independent functioning of the child becomes possible.

Infant Development in the Kibbutz
(Color, 27 minutes, Campus Films)

The film visually explores a kibbutz and the infant's development in an infant house. Care of children by the metapelet and the parents' involvement with their children are depicted. The children interact with each other, the metapelets, and the parents in a positive manner, reflecting excellent motor, social, and cognitive development.

Nurturing
(Color, 15 minutes, Davidson Films)

Nurturing describes the role of the caregiver in the development of the young child. The commentator is Bettye Caldwell.

On Their Own/With Our Help
(Color, 14 minutes, Bradley Wright Films)

Film showing examples of selective intervention.

Our Prime Time
(Color, Bradley Wright Films)

This is an important film for parents because it shows how ordinary events of each day can be prime time for learning and developing human attachment.

Personality: Early Childhood
(Color, 20 minutes, CRM Films)

Dr. Paul Mussen explains emotional and instrumental dependency, and Dr. Robert Liebert discusses identification and modeling. Aggressive behavior tied to television violence and family aggression illustrate aggressive modeling.

Prenatal Development
(Color, 23 minutes, CRM Films)

This well-produced film examines the biologic and psychologic impact on the fetus during pregnancy. The film shows the developing fetus and explains the prenatal development by interviewing researchers and doctors. Nutrition, drugs, maternal emotional influence, and developmental processes are examined.

Rock-a-Bye Baby
(Color, 30 minutes, Ambrose)

This beautiful film shows the importance of human attachment through examination of research on premature babies, institutionalized children, and monkeys.

The Sleeping Feel Good Movie
(Color, 6 minutes, Churchill Films)

A short movie that shows children getting out of bed and then going to school. Those who had enough sleep are rested; others are not. The film is good for illustrating the importance of rest for the child.

The Way We See Them
(Color, 17 minutes, Bradley Wright Films)

Learning to observe infants is depicted.

Child Development Training Films

These films were developed for use with the program, Exploring Childhood, and may be obtained from the Education Development Center. They vary in quality from excellent to fair.

Module One: Working with Children

Michael's First Day (Black and white, 6 minutes)

Water Tricks (Color, 13 minutes)

Storytime (Color, 5 minutes)

Teacher, Lester Bit Me (Color, 9 minutes)

Helping Is . . . (Color, 12 minutes)

Sara Has Down's Syndrome (Color, 16 minutes)

Module Two: Seeing Development

Half a Year Apart (Color, 12 minutes)

Gabriel is Two Days Old (Black and white, 15 minutes)

Bill and Suzi: New Parents (Black and white, 13 minutes)

From My Point of View (Color, 13 minutes)

Little Blocks (Color, 8 minutes)

Painting Time (Color, 7 minutes)

Racing Cars (Color, 7 minutes)

Clay Play (Color, 8 minutes)

All in the Game (Color, 22 minutes)

Module Three: Family and Society

Craig at Home (Black and white, 13 minutes)

Jeffrey at Home (Black and white, 11 minutes)

Howie at Home (Black and white, 13 minutes)

Rachel at Home (Black and white, 11 minutes)

Oscar at Home (Black and white, 10 minutes)

Michelle at Home (Hi, Daddy!) (Color, 10 minutes)

Seiko at Home (Color, 12 minutes)

Howie at School (Black and white, 7 minutes)

Rachel at School (Black and white, 11 minutes)

Oscar at School (Black and white, 6 minutes)

Seiko at School (Color, 7 minutes)

At the Doctor's (Black and white, 10 minutes)

Around the Way with Kareema (Color, 18 minutes)

Girl of my Parents (Color, 8 minutes)

Young Children on the Kibbutz (Black and white, 25 minutes)

Broken Eggs (Color, 10 minutes)

Raising Michael Alone (Color, 17 minutes)

Raising a Family Alone (Daniel) (Black and white, 9 minutes)

Families Revisited: Jenny Is Four: Rachel Is Seven (18 minutes)

Issues that Affect Family Life

The AIDS Movie
(Color, 26 minutes, New Day Films)

Features three people with AIDS who describe what it is like to live with the disease. The film has received a number of awards for excellence.

Crime of Innocence
(Color, 27 minutes, Paulist Productions)

The issue of mentally retarded persons moving into community neighborhoods is explored in this film. Peter and his "family" of eight mentally retarded children move into a middle-class area.

The film shows reactions from homeowners who fear for their property values and their safety. The film explores these feelings and illustrates the plight of the mentally retarded.

The Fall of Freddie the Leaf
(Color, 16 minutes, AIMS Media)

A Leo Buscaglia story that traces the life and death of a single leaf. The film can be followed by a discussion on death.

I Don't Have to Hide
(Color, 28 minutes, Fanlight Productions)

This film by Anne Fischef looks at her own childhood when she had anorexia nervosa and searches for clues to that health problem. She also discusses bulimia with Cope, a 30-year-old who had suffered from a 9-year bout of being bulimic.

Innocent Addicts
(Color, 27 minutes, Pyramid Films)

The film shows how drugs and alcohol affect the fetus by telling the stories of 12 women who used drugs (alcohol, tobacco, PCP, cocaine, heroin, and pills) during their pregnancies.

John Baker's Last Race
(Color, 33 minutes, Brigham Young University)

This is the heart-rending story of an athlete, John Baker, who had great hopes for running the mile in the Olympics when he found that he had cancer. He continued working with children, helping them to do their best in spite of the odds. His remaining life was spent working with children at Aspen Elementary School, handicapped children, and a group of girls known as the Duke City Dashers. The children do their best for John Baker.

Joint Custody: A New Kind of Family
(Color, 3 parts: 32 minutes, 18 minutes, and 33 minutes; New Day Films)

This is a documentary about custody. Each part examines a different type of custody. The first explores alternate week co-parenting; the second focuses on joint custody, and the third looks at a complicated family system of double joint custody.

Kevin's Story
(Color, 19 minutes, New Day Films)

Kevin was convicted of drunk driving and the resulting manslaughter of an 18-year-old girl. His sentence required him to speak to high school students, parents, and teachers for one year. This is an account of his story.

Married Lives Today
(Color, 19 minutes, BFA Educational Media)

Three couples work at their marriages in different ways. One couple works together operating a business and considers themselves equal partners; a second couple has a traditional relationship; and a third, separated, couple shares the responsibilities for their child.

No Place to Call Home
(Color, 59 minutes, WCBS-TV)

This undercover investigation examines the lives of children growing up in welfare hotels in New York.

Peege
(Color, 28 minutes, Phoenix)

This is a sensitive film about a senile grandmother in a nursing home who is visited by her family at Christmas. After the rest of the family leaves, Peege stays with his grandmother and talks with her about old times and his memories of times with her. After he leaves, she manages to smile.

Walk Me to the Water
(Black and white, 28 minutes, Walk Me to the Water)

Three terminally ill cancer patients and those close to them tell their stories of preparing for death. This film received several awards for excellence.

When a Child Enters the Hospital
(Color, 16 minutes, Polymorph Films)

This film discusses the issue of hospitalization of children. The child's fears and how parents and hospital staff can lessen these anxieties are discussed.

Teenagers

And Baby Makes Two: A Look at Teenage Single Parents
(Color, 25 minutes, NEWIST/CESA)

This video shows teenagers who have infants. It looks at possible solutions to the problems.

How Can I Tell if I'm Really in Love
(Color, 51 minutes, Paramount Home Video)

The film answers questions about love and sex. Its focus is on questions most often asked by teenagers.

Sex: A Topic for Conversation
(Color, 25 minutes each, Media Projects, Inc.)

Three video programs explore the topic of sex education with Dr. Sol Gordon. The first video is for parents of young children, the second is for parents of teenagers, and the third is for the teenagers.

The Teen Years: War or Peace
(Color, 40 minutes, Media Projects, Inc.)

Through animation, a parent discussion group, and a clinical psychologist, Dr. Ken Magid, this video explores the concerns that parents and teenagers have during their adolescence.

Special Children

A Matter of Expectations
(Color, 23 minutes, Cinecare International)

This film accompanies *What Was I Supposed to Do?* and focuses on practical issues of raising the handicapped child. Included are suggestions for using the latest knowledge and techniques in working with the handicapped child.

Early Intervention
(Color, 30 minutes, Cinecare International)

Early Intervention stresses the importance of working with the young child. It recommends effective programs that should be implemented as early in the infant's life as feasible.

Hidden Handicaps
(Color, 23 minutes, McGraw-Hill Video)

Early programs that meet the needs of young children can benefit the special child who is yet unrecognized. Parents, teachers, and counselors have roles in preparing curricula that meet the needs of children with learning disabilities.

It's Cool to Be Smart
(Color, 23 minutes, McGraw-Hill Video)

This film examines a variety of programs for the gifted child. It focuses on the child's feelings and the teacher's role.

Nicky: One of My Best Friends
(Color, 15 minutes, McGraw-Hill Video)

The mainstreaming of Nicky, a blind, cerebral palsied 10-year-old is illustrated. McGraw-Hill has issued a number of films to help with mainstreaming. These include *Fulfillment of Human Potential; Mainstreaming Techniques: Life Science and Art; First Steps; Token Economy: Behaviorism Applied;* and *Special Education Techniques: Lab Science and Art.*

What Was I Supposed to Do?
(Color, 28 minutes, Cinecare International)

This documentary film illustrates the emotional impact on families who have handicapped children and points out the problems and the support systems.

Child Abuse

Physical Abuse

Barb: Breaking the Cycle of Child Abuse
(Color, 28 minutes, MTI Film & Video)

This film shows a case history of child abuse, including the police investigator who comes to the home and the mother's treatment in group sessions.

Child Abuse and the Law
(Color, 22 minutes, Perennial Education)

This film familiarizes teachers and others working with children with the signals of child abuse and their responsibility according to the law.

Child Abuse: Cradle of Violence
(Color, 20 minutes, MTI Film & Video)

This film discusses the causes of abuse and what can be done to reduce it. Actual child abusers discuss the problems of abuse.

Children in Peril
(Color, 22 minutes, Learning International)

Dr. C. Henry Kempe discusses the causes of abuse. Women in therapy also reveal their feelings toward themselves and to the abuse they had forced on their children.

Cipher in the Snow
(Color, 24 minutes, Brigham Young University)

This is a story about a young boy who is ignored until his death in the snow makes those who knew him examine their feelings toward him. The film brings about the point that every child has the need for a nurturing relationship.

War of Eggs
(Color, 27 minutes, Paulist Productions)

A drama that points out that we can only love others if we love ourselves.

Sexual Abuse

A Touchy Subject
(Color, 27 minutes, ODN Productions)

Parents are taught to teach their children that "this is my body." It serves as a resource to help parents learn how to protect their children from sexual abuse.

Better Safe than Sorry
(Color, 16 1/2 minutes, Vitascope)

The film deals with sexual abuse by persons known to the child. By using dramatized situations, the audience can identify the problems and discuss methods of problem solving.

Child Sexual Abuse Prevention: Socio-Cultural & Community Issues
(Color, 30 minutes, Committee for Children)

The video presents basic facts concerning child abuse. It discusses the issue of cultural relevance and differences.

Choices (grades 7–12)
(Color, 53 minutes, Committee for Children)

At 15, Laurie runs from exploitation at home to the streets, where she painfully develops decision-making skill and learns to make choices.

Identifying, Reporting, and Handling Disclosure of the Sexually Abused Child
(Color, 25 minutes, Committee for Children)

Helps professionals identify sexual abuse by showing examples of common behavioral indicators.

Incest: The victim nobody believes
(Color, 23 minutes, MTI Film & Video)

Incest is a taboo that has not been openly discussed, but in this film three women discuss their experiences as incest victims.

No more secrets
(Color, 13 minutes, ODN Productions)

This is a film to help prevent sexual abuse. It encourages no more secrets and teaches children to believe in themselves and their own reactions to good or bad touching.

Strong Kids, Safe Kids
(Color, 42 minutes, Paramount Home Video)

This video features Henry Winkler. Cartoon characters show children how to handle improper advances from adults. Child development specialists and television personalities show parents how to answer difficult questions and how to identify abuse.

Why God? Why Me?
(Color, 27 minutes, Varied Directions Inc.)

The video focuses on the nature and repercussions of child sexual abuse. Sexual abuse is brought out in the open so young people realize they can do something about it.

Yes You Can Say No (grades 2–6)
(Color, 19 minutes, Committee for Children)

David is being sexually exploited. The film shows how David learns effective, assertive responses. (This video has won nine awards.)

FILM DISTRIBUTORS

AIMS Media
6901 Woodley Avenue
Van Nuys, CA 91406-4878

Ambrose Video Publishing (formerly Time-Life)
1271 Avenue of the Americas
New York, NY 10020

American Personnel and Guidance
5999 Stevenson Avenue
Alexandria, VA 22304

Association for Childhood Education International
11141 Georgia Avenue, Suite 200
Wheaton, MD 20902

BFA Educational Media
Division of Phoenix Films
468 Park Avenue
New York, NY 10016

Bradley Wright Films
234 Ninth Street
San Francisco, CA 94103

Brigham Young University
Audio Visual Services
Provo, UT 84602

Campus Films
24 Depot Square
Tuckahoe, NY 10707

Carousel Films
241 East 34th, Room 304
New York, NY 10016

Centre Productions
1800 30th Street
Boulder, CO 80302

Churchill Films
662 North Robertson Boulevard
Los Angeles, CA 90069

Cinecare International
(formerly Stanfield)
1044 N. 19th
Suite 1
Santa Monica, CA 90403

Committee for Children
172 20th Avenue
Seattle, WA 98122

CRM Films (McGraw-Hill)
Box 641
Via de la Vall
Del Mar, CA 92014

Davidson Films
231 "E" St.
Davis, CA 95616

Education Development Center
Distribution Center
55 Chapel Street
Newton, MA 02160

Educational Productions
4925 S.W. Humphrey Park Crest
Portland, OR 94221

Encyclopaedia Britannica Films
425 North Michigan Avenue
Chicago, IL 60611

Family Home Entertainment
15400 Sherman Way
P.O. Box 10124
Van Nuys, CA 91410-0124

Fanlight Productions
47 Halifax Street
Boston, MA 02130

Film Fair Communication
10900 Ventura Boulevard
P.O. Box 1728
Studio City, CA 91604

Harper & Row
10 East 53rd Street
New York, NY 10022

Health Sciences Consortium
201 Silver Creek Court
Chapel Hill, NC 27514

High/Scope Educational Research Foundation
600 North River Street
Ypsilanti, MI 48197

Individual & Family Development Services, Inc.
1201 South Queen Street
York, PA 17403

International Film Bureau
332 South Michigan Avenue
Chicago, IL 60604

Learning Corporation of America
16 West 61st Street
New York, NY 10023

Learning International
Box 10211
Stamford, CT 06904
(formerly Xerox)

McGraw-Hill Video
11 W. 19th St.
New York, NY 10011

Media Projects, Inc.
5415 Homer
Dallas, TX 75206

Modern Talking Picture Services
1901 L Street N.W.
Washington, DC 20036

MTI Film & Video
108 Wilmot Road
Deerfield, IL 60015

National Association for the Education of Young
Children
1834 Connecticut Avenue, N.W.
Washington, DC 20009-5786

National Audio Visual Center
National Archives and Records Service
General Services Administration Reference Section
Washington, DC 20409

New Day Films
22 Riverview Drive
Wayne, NJ 07417

New Horizons for Learning
P.O. Box 51140
Seattle, WA 98115-1140

NEWIST/CESA #7
c/o Media Center
1110 Instructional Services Building
University of Wisconsin
Green Bay Campus
Green Bay, WI 54301

ODN Productions
74 Varick Street, Suite 304
New York, NY 10013

Paramount Home Video
Paramount Pictures Corp.
5555 Melrose Avenue
Hollywood, CA 90038

Parents Magazine Film
Box 5000
9050 Bedford Road
Communications Park
Mount Kisco, NY 10549

Paulist Productions
17575 Pacific Coast Highway
Box 1057
Pacific Palisades, CA 90272

Perennial Education
930 Pitner Avenue
Evanston, IL 60202

Phoenix
468 Park Avenue South
New York, NY 10016

Polymorph Films
118 South Street
Boston, MA 02111

Professional Research, Inc.
930 Pitner
Evanston, IL 60202

Pyramid Films
Box 1048
Santa Monica, CA 90406

Roche Laboratories/Association Films
600 Grand Avenue
Ridgefield, NJ 07657

Sunburst Communication
39 Washington Avenue
Pleasantville, NY 10570

Third Eye Films
12 Arrow Street
Cambridge, MA 02138

Varied Directions Inc.
69 Elm Street
Camden, ME 04856

VIDA Health Communications
335 Huron Avenue
Cambridge, MA 02138

Vitascope
8532 Dacosta
Downey, CA 90240

Walk Me to the Water
Box 258
Mountain Road
New Lebanon, NY 12125

WCBS-TV
524 West 57th Street
New York, NY 10019

REFERENCES TO BE USED IN THE DEVELOPMENT OF A HOME-BASED PROGRAM

If you plan to develop a home-based educational program for children, use some of the following resources. They describe programs that were developed and tested. Some of these are no longer being published and will have to be found in a library, but the material is still relevant and helpful.

Day, M. C., & Parker, R. K. *The preschool in action: Exploring early childhood programs.* Boston: Allyn & Bacon, 1977.

- An entire section of this text is devoted to home-based programs for preschoolers and infants. These include chapters by Merle Karnes and R. Reid Zehrbach, Glen Nimnicht, Phyllis Levenstein, Earl Schaeffer, Alice S. Honig, and J. Ronald Lally.

Gordon, I. E., & Breivogel, W. F. (Eds.). *Building effective home-school relationships.* Boston: Allyn & Bacon, 1977.

- Ira Gordon and William Breivogel edited this text which illustrates a successful home-based program in Florida. It includes chapters that describe the roles and duties of teachers, administrators, home visitors, and parents.

Gotts, E. E. (Ed.). *The home visitor's kit: Training and practitioner materials for paraprofessionals in family settings.* New York: Human Sciences Press, 1977.

- This kit, developed by the Appalachia Educational Laboratory, includes a Home Visitor's Notebook, Parents Notes, and resource materials for use in training paraprofessionals to work in home-based programs.

Grogan, M., et al. *The homesbook: What home-based programs can do with children and families.* Cambridge: Abt Associates, 1976.

- Abt Associates developed a book that demonstrates activities and curriculum that can be used in home-based programs.

Hewett, K. D., Jerome, C. M., Grogan, M., Nauta, M., Rubin, A. D., & Stein, M. *Partners with parents: The Home Start experience with preschoolers and their families.* U.S. Department of Health, Education and Welfare (Office of Human Development Services, Administration for Children, Youth and Families, Head Start Bureau). Washington, D.C.: U.S. Government Printing Office, 1978.

- This book describes many of the Home Start programs that were funded during the 1970s. It includes suggested training plans and reports that can be used by persons interested in starting a home-based program.

Lambie, D. Z., Bond, J. T., & Weikart, D. *Home teaching with mothers and infants.* Ypsilanti, Mich.: High/Scope Educational Research Foundation, 1981.

- Developed by the Ypsilanti-Carnegie Infant Education Project, this book summarizes the curriculum used with mothers and infants in the program.

Massoglio, E. T. *Early childhood education in the home.* Albany, N.Y.: Delmar Publishers, 1977.

- This is a textbook that describes the steps for implementing a home-based program.

Portage Project. *The Portage guide to early education.* Portage, Wis.: The Portage Project, 1976.

- This book contains the complete developmental curriculum used in the Portage Project. The curriculum has three components: (1) Checklist of Behaviors, (2) Card File, and (3) Manual of Instruction.

U.S. Department of Health, Education and Welfare (Office of Human Development, Office of Child Development, Home Start). *A guide for planning and operating home-based child development programs.* Washington, D.C.: U.S. Government Printing Office, 1974.

- This guide was developed to be used in assisting in the implementation of a home-based program. It draws from the experience of 16 funded Home Start demonstration projects and gives information, methods, and procedures for setting up a home-based program.

U.S. Department of Health and Human Services (Office of Human Development Services, Administration for Children, Youth and Families, Head Start Bureau). *A guide for operating a home-based child development program.* Washington, D.C.: U.S. Government Printing Office, 1985.

_____. *The Head Start home visitor handbook.* B. Wolfe & J. Herwig (Eds.) for Portage Project, Cooperative Educational Service Agency #5. Washington, D.C.: U.S. Government Printing Office, 1987.

_____. *Serving handicapped children in home-based Head Start.* R. D. Boyd & J. Herwig, (Eds.) for Portage Project, Cooperative Educational Service Agency #12. Washington, D.C.: U.S. Government Printing Office, 1982.

These three books represent an update of government publications on Home Start. They contain good information, charts, directions, and guidance.

ADVOCACY

The following organizations form a base from which to obtain information on legal rights, responsibilities, and advocacy. Because addresses and telephone numbers change with regularity, some will be outdated. Check with your library for the yearly update on associations and organizations in the United States if you find an address has changed.

Children's Defense Fund

122 C Street, N.W.
Washington, DC 20001

- Long-range advocacy of children was the goal of the Children's Defense Fund when founded in 1973. Since that time, it has monitored areas of education, child care, health, and juvenile justice. The agency works with individuals, agencies, or community groups.

Child Welfare League of America

440 First Street N.W.
Washington, DC 20001

- The League, a privately supported organization with 376 affiliate groups, works for the benefit of dependent and neglected children and their families. They have also published a *Parenting Curriculum* by Grace C. Cooper for adolescent mothers.

Institute for Responsive Education

605 Commonwealth Avenue
Boston, MA 02215

- Founded in 1973 to assist citizen involvement in educational decision making, the Institute believes that parents and community, in collaboration with school officials and teachers, can make a difference. To foster parent and community involvement in the schools, the Institute publishes a quarterly journal, *Citizen Action in Education.*

National Coalition of ESEA Title I/Chapter I Parents

1314 14th Street N.W., Suite 6
Washington, DC 20005

- The federal Title I program has made great strides in involving parents in the education of their chil-

dren. Its findings and suggestions are appropriate for parents and schools in any economic area. Currently called Chapter I, the Coalition supports Chapter I parents as well as others. The organization established the National Parent Center.

National Congress of Parents and Teachers

700 North Rush Street
Chicago, IL 60611

- The PTA is the oldest organization devoted to improving relations between home and school on behalf of children. Founded in 1897, this organization has fluctuated in the acceptance of its role as the spokesperson for parents and teachers but has consistently furnished educational information through the following publications: *PTA Today, PTA Communique,* and pamphlets on parent education, juvenile protection, safety, parent-teacher relationships, and improvement of the quality of education in schools.

National School Boards Association

1680 Duke Street
Alexandria, VA 22314

- This association, founded in 1940, furnishes information on curriculum development and legislation that affects education and school administration. Members of school boards are familiar with their publications, *Insider's Report,* a weekly newsletter, and the *American School Board Journal,* a monthly journal. These publications are also informative for parents concerned about schools.

National School Volunteer Program

701 North Fairfax Street, Suite 320
Alexandria, VA 22314

- Volunteers have made great strides in opening schools to parent involvement. They have state groups, some of which give six training sessions to volunteers. Housewives, professionals, and young people are typical volunteers.

National Committee for Citizens in Education (NCCE)

10840 Little Patuxent Parkway, Suite 301
Columbia, MD 21044

- NCCE has established a Parents' Network and has developed a series of pamphlets to help parents advocate for their children.

INDEX